Plumes of Smoke

The Destruction of Montecassino 1944

Derek James

Helion & Company

Helion & Company Limited
Unit 8 Amherst Business Centre
Budbrooke Road
Warwick
CV34 5WE
England
Tel. 01926 499 619
Email: info@helion.co.uk
Website: www.helion.co.uk
X (formerly Twitter): @helionbooks
Visit our blog at https://helionbooks.wordpress.com/

Published by Helion & Company Ltd 2024
Designed and typeset by Mach 3 Solutions (www.mach3solutions.co.uk)
Cover designed by Paul Hewitt, Battlefield Design (www.battlefield-design.co.uk)

Text © Derek James 2024
Images © as individually credited
Maps drawn by Paul Hewitt, Battlefield Design (www.battlefield-design.co.uk)
© Helion & Company Ltd 2024

ISBN 978-1-804515-36-5

British Library Cataloguing-in-Publication Data.
A catalogue record for this book is available from the British Library.

For details of other military history titles published by Helion & Company Limited
contact the above address or visit our website: http://www.helion.co.uk.

We always welcome receipt of book proposals from prospective authors.

Contents

List of Photographs   iv
List of Maps   xi
Preface   xii
Introduction   xvi

1   Decisions for a Secondary Theatre: 1943-44   23
2   Mud and Mountains: The Winter Campaign   43
3   Across the Rapido: The First Battle of Cassino   60
4   Fates Entwined: Anzio and Cassino   76
5   The Forgotten Fighters: Allied Morale in Italy   84
6   The Poor Bloody Infantry Above Cassino   93
7   The Abbey: A Story of Europe   105
8   A New Broom   117
9   The Red Eagles: Cast at Some Awful Fortress   126
10   Who is Responsible To Whom, For What?   146
11   What is the Price of Our History?   175
12   The Law of War and Military Necessity   203
13   What is the Right Thing to be Done?   223
14   Our Eyes and Ears: Do They Deceive Us?   235
15   Making the Decision   260
16   The Making of an Air Force   275
17   The Most Powerful Force   296
18   The Flight of General Eaker   318
19   Sledgehammer to Crack a Nut?   329
20   Bombs and Bombing   349
21   Una Giornata da B-17   372
22   The Results   385
23   What did the Spooks Say?   393
24   Irrefutable Evidence   402
25   Mandarins   413
26   Aftermath   431
Conclusions   451

Bibliography   463
Index   489

List of Photographs

The new basilica of Montecassino. The destruction of 15 February has been fully restored, but one never forgets that this is not the Abbey that existed before the bombing but is merely a beautiful facsimile. The destruction can never really be reversed (Author)   xv

A photographic reconnaissance image of the Abbey following the bombing. The extent of the damage can be clearly seen (UK TNA)   xvii

The Combined Chiefs of Staff meeting in Cairo at the SEXTANT Conference in November 1943. (NARA RG342-FH-000817)   25

The 'Big Three' meet at the EUREKA Conference in Teheran in November 1943. Stalin, backing the US strategy demoted operations in Italy. Behind can be seen Admiral William Leahy, General Sir Alan Brooke, General Henry Arnold, Admiral Ernest King, General George Marshall and Field Marshal Sir John Dill. (NARA RG342-FH-000696)   31

Prime Minister Churchill's military advisor, Major General Sir Hastings Ismay, British First Sea Lord, Admiral of the Fleet Sir Dudley Pound and the Chief of the Imperial General Staff, General Sir Alan Brooke on 22 May 1943 at the TRIDENT Conference in Washington DC. Two days later Brooke's strategic frustrations emerged in his famous diary. (NARA RG80-G-042152)   32

The C-in-C Allied Force, General Eisenhower and the 'committee' of Mediterranean commanders, a system he loathed. From l-r, Air Marshal Sir Arthur Tedder, General Sir Harold Alexander and Admiral Sir Andrew Cunningham. Eisenhower, the Operational-level commander relied on these officers for planning operations in the Mediterranean and Italy. (NARA RG342-FH-001016)   35

The German Operational level Commander, *Luftwaffe Generalfeldmarschal* Albert Kesselring. Unlike the allies, Germany had no separate land commander. Seated next to Kesselring is Commander German Tenth Army, *Generaloberst* Heinrich von Vietinghoff. (Bundesarchiv Bild 101I-304-0624-05A/Fotograf: Luthge)   45

The Liri Valley, taken from the village of Rocco d'Evandro. The road to Rome, Route 6, runs through the Valley to Frosinone. The only flat terrain, the valley is dominated by high ground on both sides throughout its length. (Author)   51

Monte Trocchio, the Abbey and the entrance to the Liri Valley. (Author)   51

General der Panzertruppen Fridolin Senger und Etterlin, the Commander of XIV Panzer Corps, defender of Cassino and lay member of the Benedictine Order. He is pictured following the bombing of the Abbey at his HQ at Castelmassimo with Abbot Gregory Diamare and his secretary Dom Martino Matronola. (Bundesarchiv Bild 101I-310-0892-06/Fotograf: Schmidt)   53

Generals Eisenhower, Clark and Gruenther visit Major General Walker of the US 36th (Texans) Infantry Division in December 1943. (NARA RG111-SC-443420)   55

The Commanding General of US II Corps at Cassino, Major General Geoffrey Keyes, standing second left, next to his mentor, Lieutenant General George Patton. (NARA RG18-JC0002)   57

The commander of 90th *Panzer-Grenadier* Division, *Generalmajor* Ernst-Gunther Baade. An
    inspirational leader, his troops were close to the Abbey when it was destroyed. He was
    one of four officers to receive the Knight's Cross with Oak Leaves and Swords at Cassino.
    (Bundesarchiv Bild 101I-315-1110-06/Fotograf: Luthge)   68
The architects of the Rapido disaster. General Mark Clark and his two principal subordinates at
    US Fifth Army. On the left is Major General Alfred Gruenther, his Chief of Staff, and in
    the centre, Brigadier General Donald Brann, Chief of Operations. (Library of Congress)   71
There can be no doubt of the psychological impact of the Abbey on fighting soldiers. This view
    from the Rapido Valley shows how much the building dominated the area. Soldiers of the
    34th 'Red Bulls' and 36th 'Texans' Infantry divisions were constantly under its gaze in
    January 1944. (Author)   73
One of the most popular reasons for the bombing of the Abbey was its utility for observation.
    As can be seen from this image from German-held territory near Terrelle, there were many
    better positions from where Allied activity could be observed by the defenders. (Author)   74
Commanding General of US VI Corps at Anzio, Major General John Lucas speaks with
    the commander of the Special Service Force, Brigadier General Robert Frederick.
    (NARA RG111-SC-212642_001)   79
B-26 Marauders from 42nd Bombardment Wing. The Wing was based at the southern Sardinian
    airfield at Decimommanu and operated extensively in support of the Anzio defence.
    (NARA RG342-FH-000913)   83
Perhaps the most celebrated war correspondent, Ernie Pyle, who shared the deprivations of US
    soldiers. His book *Brave Men* vividly described the hardships of the soldier in an Italian
    winter. (NARA RG111-SC-191705)   86
The Abbey held all in its shadow. In a sense, it became the visible representation of the enemy. Its
    destruction was therefore partly to improve the morale of Allied soldiers that fought below
    it. (Author)   89
Monte Castellone and the Monte Cassino massif, leading to the Abbey viewed from the excellent
    observation positions around Belvedere, the objective of Juin's French corps. (Author)   95
From a window on the northern wall of the Abbey, this modern view shows Snakeshead Ridge.
    German positions were located on the rocky bluff directly above the valley (Point 569) and
    the summit to its right is Point 593. Monte Cairo, with its observation looms over all these
    positions. The small building is the "Doctor's House". (Author)   99
Major Rudolph Kratzert, the Austrian officer who received the Knight's Cross for his defence
    of the critical point in the German line, Point 593. (Bundesarchiv Bild 146-2006-0083/
    Fotograf: o.Ang)   100
Oberst Sebastian Ludwig Heilmann and *Generalmajor* Richard Heidrich of the 1st *Fallschirmjager*
    Division. Both officers were awarded the Knight's Cross with Oak Leaves and Swords for
    their defence at Cassino. (Bundesarchiv Bild 101I-577-1920-31/Fotograf Zscheile)   101
Statue of perhaps Montecassino's greatest Abbot, Desiderius, who became Pope Victor III and
    adopted the Abbey as his papal seat. (Author)   108
The reconstructed basilica of the Abbey of Montecassino. The central doors of the basilica date
    back to 1066 and were built in Constantinople. (Author)   110
The Abbey viewed from Point 593. The point, a little higher than the Abbey, was the key terrain
    in the German defences. In bitter fighting in the first days of February 1944 it changed
    hands numerous times, finally being secured by the German paratroopers. It was not
    bombarded from the air to any great extent. (Author)   111
Taken in March 1944 at a conference between senior officers of the US 1st Armoured Division
    and the provisional New Zealand Corps. From left to right the New Zealanders were Major
    General Parkinson, GOC 2nd NZ Division, Brigadier Ray Queree, Brigadier General Staff,
    NZ Corps and Lt Gen Bernard Freyberg VC wearing the B-3 flying jacket given to him by
    General Clark. (NARA RG 111-SC-189378)   118

The General Officer Commanding-in-Chief, 15th Army Group, General Sir Harold Alexander
      chats with the crew of his personal C-47 'Stardust.' Alexander moved Eighth Army
      divisions from the Adriatic sector to exploit any breakthrough by Clark at Cassino.
      (NARA RG342-FH000065)   119
General Clark with his key officers following the capture of Rome. From l-r, US II Corps, Major
      General Keyes, General Clark, US VI Corps, Major General Truscott, FEC, General Juin
      and Fifth Army Chief of Staff, Major General Gruenther. (NARA RG80-G-252537)   121
Mediterranean Allied Air Forces Deputy Commander, Air Marshal Sir John Slessor awards
      the Commander of the Order of the British Empire to the MAAF Chief of Staff, Major
      General Idwal Edwards. (NARA RG342-FH-002217)   123
The Mediterranean air commanders. Lieutenant General Ira Eaker, Major General John Cannon
      and Major General Nathan Twining. (NARA RG342-FH-000582)   139
'Not a house left standing for miles.' The results of the New Zealand Corps, Operations
      AVENGER and DICKENS in February and March 1944. Despite the destruction, the
      Allies still did not hold the town, nor the Abbey and could not advance up the Liri Valley.
      (Library of Congress)   144
British Prime Minister, Sir Winston Churchill with the British Chief of the Imperial General
      Staff, General Sir Alan Brooke. Both Churchill and Brooke favoured operations in the
      Mediterranean. Brooke often had to prevent Churchill's interference in military matters.
      (NARA RG111-SC-190284)   147
Below: The commanders. From left to right: Vice Admiral H Kent Hewitt, Lieutenant General
      Ira Eaker, Air Marshal Sir John Slessor, General Sir Harold Alexander, Major General
      John Cannon, General Sir Henry Maitland-Wilson and Admiral Sir John Cunningham.
      (NARA RG342-FH-002215)   147
Up until the end of 1943, the Operational level commander for operations in Italy
      was General Eisenhower. His title was Commander-in-Chief Allied Force, not
      Supreme Commander Mediterranean, a position established after his departure.
      (NARA RG319-AP6406-SC444392)   149
The forgotten American. Following Eisenhower's departure, all American forces in the
      Mediterranean came under the Command of Lieutenant General Jacob Devers. Devers was
      also Deputy Commander of the Allied Force and then Deputy Supreme Commander in the
      Mediterranean Theatre. (NARA RG208-N-S-1938)   149
Lieutenant General Carl Spaatz (on right with glasses) with General Sir Harold Alexander.
      Spaatz was the Operational Level commander of all US heavy bombers in Europe.
      (NARA RG342-FH-000197)   152
Devers and Eisenhower were both protégés of General Marshall but had completely different
      personalities. The two men were never close, and Eisenhower's fame may have added to
      Devers' future obscurity. (NARA RG319-AP-6406-SC232833)   153
Overall land commander in Italy, General Sir Harold Alexander examines some
      photographic reconnaissance photographs with President Roosevelt's son, Elliot.
      (NARA RG342-FH-000408)   157
Clark in a typically posed publicity photograph aboard USS Ancon on 12 September 1943, a day
      before crisis struck his Army at Salerno. Clark liked his photographs to be of his better left
      visage. (NARA RG80-G-087335)   162
Nicknamed the 'American Eagle' by Churchill, Clark retained this name as his codename in
      correspondence with Eisenhower. (Library of Congress)   163
Despite their long relationship, Eisenhower rated Clark behind Patton and Bradley and made no
      efforts to take him to Normandy. (NARA RG342-FH000405)   164
General Clark delivering his Press Conference to journalists on 5 June 1944 in Rome. Clark
      constantly annoyed the pressmen with his publicity stunts. (NARA RG80-G252537)   169

Oberstleutnant Julius Schlegel, credited with saving Montecassino's treasures in October 1943, although his efforts may not have been entirely altruistic. He is pictured here with an officer from the Hermann Göring Panzer Division and *General* Kurt Malzer, Commandant of Rome. (Bundesarchiv Bild 101I-729-0004-18/Fotograf:Linke)   177

Archbishop Francis Spellman, Archbishop of New York and to the US Armed Forces often represented President Roosevelt around the world. Spellman assisted in an abortive attempt to save the Abbey. (NARA RG111-SC-192047)   180

Brigadier-General Charles Born (centre), the Chief of Operations at Fifteenth Air Force, warned aircrews about damaging Italian cities. It was Born who would have approved the target selections for the B-17 bombers on 15 February 1944. (NARA RG342-FH-0000   182

Pope Pius XII meets Allied soldiers following the capture of Rome in June 1944. Pius was highly critical of Allied bombing, less so of German atrocities (NARA RG80-G-059409)   187

German ambassador to the Vatican, Baron Ernst von Weizsäcker. Weizsäcker was never a keen Nazi and was possibly a participant in efforts to rid Germany of Hitler. He had no reason to offer the Nazis the propaganda victory destroying the Abbey would provide. (NARA RG306-NT-222A-7)   188

B-26 Marauders from the 42nd Bombardment Wing bomb rail facilities in Florence in March 1944. The bombing of Florence was of deep concern to Mediterranean Allied Air Forces Deputy Commander, Air Marshal Sir John Slessor. (NARA RG342-FH-000408)   199

British Chief of the Air Staff and agent for strategic bombing on the Combined Chiefs of Staff, Air Chief Marshal Sir Charles Portal. Although an area bombing advocate, Portal warned Eaker regarding excessive civilian casualties outside Germany. (NARA RG80-G-042146)   212

Italian civilians in Cassino. Several hundred, mostly women, children and the elderly were in the Abbey on the day it was bombed. It is likely that several hundred were killed in the attack, although the exact figure is unknown. These are the survivors. (Bundesarchiv Bild 101I-310-0889-30A/Fotograf: Schmidt)   224

A high-oblique image of the destroyed Abbey. Photographic Reconnaissance missions such as this were called 'dicing' sorties as the pilots considered them more dangerous than high level sorties. (NCAP)   246

A high-level stereo-pair image of the destroyed Abbey, possibly taken by Lieutenant Hersey on the afternoon of 15 February 1944. (NARA RG342-FH-000157)   246

At the beginning of 1944, command of the Mediterranean Allied Photographic Reconnaissance Wing passed from Colonel Roosevelt to Colonel Karl Polifka. (NARA RG342-FH-002302)   249

Photo Interpreters work on prints at the Mediterranean Allied Photographic Reconnaissance Wing. (NARA RG342-FH-000205)   251

Two Royal Air Force technicians prepare to fit a reconnaissance camera to a Spitfire aircraft. (NARA RG342-FH-000142)   251

Decisionmakers. Major General John Cannon, Lieutenant General Carl Spaatz, Lieutenant General Mark Clark and General Henry Arnold. (NARA RG342-FH-000584)   264

Forward Air Controllers in light aircraft assisted fighter-bombers in target location. This L-5 aircraft is accompanied by P-40 Kitty bombers. (NARA RG342-FH-000588)   264

A pre-attack reconnaissance image of the Abbey. This is probably taken shortly before the attack as damage to the Basilica can be clearly seen on the image. Note that there are no bomb craters around the Abbey. (NARA RG342-FH-000143)   265

A post-war picture of Alexander with his former Deputy Chief of Staff, General Lyman Lemnitzer. Lemnitzer claims to have had a part in the planning for the bombing of the Abbey with General Lauris Norstad. (NARA RG73-2355)   269

Commanding General of the Mediterranean Allied Strategic Air Forces, Major General Nathan Twining delivers briefing to General Maitland-Wilson on bombing targets in Italy. Wilson could not routinely task Twining's heavy bombers. (NARA RG342-FH-000474)   273

General Henry 'Hap' Arnold, Commanding General of the USAAF. Arnold could be called the 'father of the modern air force.' He drove his staff hard. (NARA RG342-FH-000373)   277

Pilot, engineer and airpower commentator, Alexander de Seversky. De Seversky was a major critic of Arnold's management of US airpower, especially upon his failure to deliver a balanced force. (NARA RG58-753-01)   279

The Top Table. Arnold on the CCS at Casablanca. Also visible at the top are Generals Marshall and Brooke and opposite Air Chief Marshall Portal, Field Marshal Dill and Admiral Pound. Dill was quite critical of Arnold's staff work. (NARA RG342-FH-000812)   282

Kindred spirits. Arnold and Eaker pose with the daughter of Air Chief Marshal Sir Arthur 'Bomber' Harris. The longstanding relationship between the two men became strained in late 1943 as Arnold failed to deliver the resources and Eaker failed to deliver the results. (NARA RG342-FH-000039)   282

Slightly xenophobic, Arnold tried to blame the RAF for his bomber force's failure in late 1943. When presented with the facts by Portal he turned his ire on Eaker instead. (NARA RG342-000562)   284

By the end of 1943, the doctrine of unescorted high-level daylight precision bombing had become untenable. Results were poor and losses unsustainable. This formation bears the markings of the 5th Bombardment Wing of the Fifteenth Air Force. (NARA RG342-FH-000907)   284

Major General Laurence Kuter (centre). Kuter was the architect of the USAAF doctrine, Field Manual FM 100-20. This was essentially the air's declaration of independence from the ground forces. It meant that targeting decisions were made by airmen rather than soldiers. (NARA RG342-000451)   286

With Air Chief Marshal Sir Arthur Harris are Lieutenant General Frank Andrews, then in Command of all Americans in Britain and Ira Eaker. The case for air force independence relied on its bombing doctrine. The US did not want to join the RAF night area campaign. (NARA RG342-FH-000591)   291

Key Eaker staff officer Colonel Harris Hull chats with veteran journalist William Shirer. The USAAF had a long history of enhancing its reputation through what could be described as 'publicity stunts'. (NARA RG342-FH-000794)   293

Commanding General of the Twelfth Air Force's Air Support Command, Brigadier General Gordon Saville and his boss Lieutenant General Ira Eaker visit Major General Lucian Truscott in the Anzio beachhead. Saville did not see eye-to-eye with Eaker over air support. (NARA RG342-FH-002344)   301

B-25 Mitchell medium bombers of 57th Bombardment Wing of the Tactical Bomber Force. The TBF was disbanded in March 1944. (NARA RG342-FH-000192)   304

Eaker and Twining talk to Colonel Herbert Rice. Rice commanded the 2nd Bombardment Group that led the attack on the Abbey on 15 February 1944. (NARA RG342-FH-000442)   311

Marshall and Arnold with Brigadier-General Lauris Norstad. As one of Arnold's first Advisory Council members, he was given great latitude to do Arnold's thinking for him. Did he continue this role in Italy when Eaker was absent? (NARA RG18-2772a)   317

Arnold took a ride in an L-4 Cub artillery spotting aircraft in December 1943. It is likely that he saw the Abbey during this trip. (NARA RG342-FH-000588)   317

Devers and Eaker stated that they flew over the Abbey in a spotter aircraft on 14 February 1944. Neither man was in Italy at the time and neither corrected their story before their deaths. (NARA RG342-FH-000571)   319

On the day of the bombing, Eaker's diary shows that whilst his aircraft destroyed the Abbey he was having lunch with Ralph Royce followed by a trip to the bazaar and the Pyramids. (AFHRA)   322

Personal message from the RAF's Air Officer Commanding Middle East, Air Marshal Sir Keith
   Park to Air Marshal Sir John Slessor, dated 13 February 1944, confirming that Lieutenant
   General Eaker had arrived in Cairo. (UK TNA)   322
This picture of General Eaker was taken at Cassino on 15 March 1944 when the town was
   bombed. It proves he was in Cassino for the town bombing. He was not in Italy on 15
   February. (NARA RG342-FH-000472)   326
Commander in Chief of the Mediterranean Air Command until the end of 1943, Air Chief
   Marshal Sir Arthur Tedder and his Chief of Staff, Brigadier General Patrick Timberlake
   visit the photo interpreters at the Mediterranean Allied Photographic Reconnaissance
   Wing. (NARA RG342-FH-002386)   333
The Bombing Problem. The Norden bombsight was designed to solve the complex task of
   placing a bomber in the exact spot in the sky from where, given the aircraft's speed, altitude
   and environmental conditions, a bomb would strike accurately a target on the ground.
   (Bombardier Information File)   350
Although the USAAF had bombs of different sizes, these were mostly General Purpose.
   Unlike the RAF they had developed few specialist weapons for different target types.
   (NARA RG342-FH-000903)   350
B-26 Marauder from the 42nd Bombardment Wing of the Mediterranean Allied Tactical Air
   Forces releasing 4 x 1000lb General Purpose bombs, the same as delivered against the
   Abbey. (NARA RG342-FH-001110)   351
The ultimate 'Blockbuster.' This 12,000lb weapon could only be carried by RAF Lancasters
   of 617 Squadron. Its thin casing and high charge to weight ratio of explosive
   ensured a large blast effect. This effect is what is required to knock down buildings.
   (NARA RG342-FH-000919)   353
The Norden M-Type bombsight. The promise of 'pickle barrel' accuracy was pivotal to America's
   high-level daylight precision bombing doctrine. Unfortunately, the accuracy of the testbed
   did not always transfer to operational use. (Bombardier Information File)   354
This post-attack image of the Abbey shows the inefficiency of pattern bombing. While clearly
   the Abbey has been hit and badly damaged, there are many craters around the building that
   have made no contribution to the damage. (NARA RG342-FH-000151)   360
Whilst a useful tactic for large industrial complexes, or when mutual self-defence is a necessity,
   the bomber box ensured that for pinpoint targets such as the Abbey, most bombs would fall
   astray. (NARA RG342-FH-001688)   363
The first aircraft over the target would generally be the most accurate. The dust and obscurants
   thrown up reduce the accuracy of succeeding waves. (NARA RG342-FH-000147)   364
The intervalometer. This equipment allowed the Bombardier to drop all the bombs at once – the salvo
   setting, or to space them out to increase the chances of a hit. (Bombardier Information File)   369
Truce on Castellone. On 14 February, the 36th US Infantry Division and the 90th *Panzer-*
   Grenadier Division agreed a truce to remove their dead from Monte Castellone. The same
   day the leaflet was dropped on the Abbey. No truce was offered to allow the brothers and
   civilians to leave. (NARA-RG111-SC-421528_001)   375
Commanding Officer of 96th Bomb Squadron and leader of the Monte Cassino attack, Major
   Bradford Evans lands his B-17 with one engine on fire at the end of his 46th mission. He
   eventually completed 53 missions. (NARA RG342-FH-000663)   379
Post-attack image of the Abbey. Cursory analysis of the building shows damage,
   but not destruction. The black line shows the frontline on 15 February 1944.
   (NARA RG342-FH-000155)   387
B-25 Mitchell from 57th Bombardment Wing of the Mediterranean Allied Tactical
   Air Force pictured bombing in the vicinity of Cassino on 15 March 1944.
   (NARA RG342-FH-000166)   388

The mediums. Four x 1000lb bombs head towards the Abbey. The shadow suggests that
    this is mid-afternoon, so probably the attack of the 42nd Bombardment Wing's B-26s
    (NARA RG342-FH-000145)   392
General Alexander receives a briefing on photographic reconnaissance from an RAF Flight
    Lieutenant of MAPRW. (NARA RG342-FH-000090)   394
Inaccurate bombing. An image taken by an aircraft from the 2nd Bombardment Group shows
    that the Abbey has taken several direct hits, but also shows several explosions a great
    distance from the building. (NARA RG342-FH-000130)   396
Occupation of this building at Albaneta (Point 468), about a mile from the Abbey was cited by
    Wilson's staff as 'irrefutable evidence' that the Abbey was occupied by Germans. (Author)   407
This is roughly the position from where a battalion commander from the 133rd Infantry claims
    to have seen a telescope in a window on the Abbey's eastern face. Even with powerful
    binoculars, this seems highly unlikely. (Author)   410
Message from Observation Posts on Monte Trocchio following the attack on the Abbey. – '50 to
    100 enemy coming out of S end of Monastery – taking them under fire' (NARA RG407)   411
This is the view of the Abbey from the top of Monte Trocchio, some three miles distant.
    Observation Post Wisdom reported soldiers fleeing after the attack, but from the distance it
    would be impossible to distinguish soldiers from civilians (Author)   412
General Eisenhower in conversation with British Foreign Secretary Sir Anthony Eden.
    Eisenhower placed the Abbey on a protected list. Eden and his civil servants hushed up the
    lack of evidence for its destruction. (NARA)   420

List of Maps

1	German Lines.	49
2	The First Battle.	62
3	Cassino.	94
4	The Massif.	140
5	The Route.	378

Preface

For, as the valley from its sleep awoke,
I saw the iron horses of the steam
Toss to the morning air their plumes of smoke,
And woke, as one awaketh from a dream.

'Monte Cassino'
Henry Wadsworth Longfellow

I first visited the *Abbazia di Montecassino*[1] during the cold November of 2002. For most of the visit, the great Abbey was shrouded in late autumnal cloud, similar to how it was in early February 1944. The visit was part of the preparation for a proposed staff ride for both Royal Air Force (RAF) and British Army students to the battlefield the next Spring. There were three of us; a British infantry officer, a New Zealand artillery officer and me, a RAF officer specialising in intelligence and targeting. Not surprisingly, we had markedly different views on the necessity for the bombing of the Abbey. My infantry colleague would have been totally in accord with the infantry units tasked to take the Cassino massif and the associated high points and assistance from the air would have been demanded as the highest priority. Any damage was justified to save the soldiers from being casualties. My New Zealand colleague mostly agreed with this view, with the addition that Generals Freyberg and Kippenberger are national heroes. Whilst I agreed that air power should provide utmost support to ground forces, I was not convinced that the bombing of the Abbey was at all necessary and I held the view that air forces were more effectively employed elsewhere. We had a vigorous debate over pasta and tiramisu.

The next day, we decided to take a proper look at the ground. In the days before Google Earth and smartphones, we had no detailed maps of the area, so we scoured shops in Cassino. As luck would have it, we found a small shop with a few black and white photocopied maps in the window. Inside the shop was a man of around 70-years' old who spoke reasonable English. His name was Federico Lamberti and he had lived in Cassino all his life. He was eight years old during the battle. In addition to selling us some maps Federico offered to show us around some key points on the battlefield. Perhaps the most important of these was not the Abbey, but Monte

---

1   The *Abbazia di Montecassino* will be referred to as the Abbey or Montecassino throughout. It was also widely referred by Allied reporting as the monastery but will only be referred to as such in direct quotations. The hill upon which the Abbey is built is referred to as Montecassino, Monte Cassino, Monastery Hill or Point 516. I will use Monte Cassino to refer to the hill upon which the Abbey stands unless otherwise quoted directly. Cassino refers to the town or area and will be suffixed accordingly.

Calvario, the infamous Point 593, about two-thirds of a mile away from, and slightly higher than, the Abbey. You could not then get to Point 593, with its Polish memorial, without getting a key to the gate next to the Polish Cemetery. Federico got the key from the monks in the Abbey and we wound our way up to the top along a narrow track. As we approached the end of the track, we had to walk the last fifty yards or so up some steps to the memorial, the clouds drew in and it began gently snowing. Although winter had not yet set-in in November, this scene gave us some idea of the conditions under which the fighting took place nearly 59-years earlier. On that day, standing in the old fort where the memorial now stands and which was stoutly defended by German troops throughout the battles, the Abbey was hardly visible through the misty gloom. In places, visibility was around 100-yards, decreasing when the occasional snow flurries increased in their intensity. It was not a good place to observe what was going on in the valley below, nor would the view from the Abbey have been any better.

After several visits over the next couple of years, my opinion remained that the attack on the Abbey could not be justified by Military Necessity. I therefore approached this project with a perspective biased in favour of that position. I am not a professional historian, but I have tried to include all the differing perspectives of this controversial act, including those of many of the professional historians who have covered it since. I am, however, a professional military staff officer and I possess some skills and experiences that many historians may not. I found all the available accounts unsatisfactory in varying degrees. This is an investigation rather than a history; that has been told often enough. I did not want to be constrained in my opinions by having to definitively prove every point. I have tried to use as much contemporaneous material as possible, but I have always found, ever since I started looking at the primary sources, that much of the material has been lost. This is especially true of the air records. I have trawled through thousands of pages of archives, both from the UK National Archives and from the US Air Force Historical Research Agency but have been unsuccessful in finding any official orders to carry out this attack. On several occasions, promising leads peter out just before the crucial time. Considering the breadth of records on the Italian air campaign that have been retained, it seems unlikely that these records never existed, and the attack could not have occurred through word of mouth alone. This attack was an embarrassing mistake, one that if admitted post-war could have led to litigation against the Allies for the damages caused. The British opted to bury the controversy, choosing to remain silent about the incident. Could the Americans, who carried out the attack, have similarly chosen to hide their guilty consciences by deliberately expunging the records? Many of the biographies or memoirs of those involved are equally unenlightening. The problem with biographies is often that for authors to get close to their subject or gain access through their families to personal papers or recollections, the results end up being quite sympathetic. Similarly, memoirs are rarely self-critical, and memories fade over time. The resulting books, whilst interesting in a general sense often fail to objectively examine the decisions made or the tensions of personal differences that always occur in such relationships. I have been unable to positively identify who ordered the attack that day, but the list of possibilities is short. The flight of the most senior US officer in Italy and his air commander over the Abbey the day before the attack has become lore to those convinced of the rightness of the attack. This flight, and the consequent observations of the participants, that are used in many histories, including by Official Historians, never happened. Memory is a poor arbiter of truth over the expanse of time.

My interest piqued, my next visit to the Abbey of Monte Cassino was in the fine spring weather of the next year. We took our group of trainee officers on the visit to the Italian battlefield so that they could learn the realities of the military profession. I was again struck by the majesty of the Abbey and its dominating position above the town and the Liri Valley below, now easily viewed in the bright spring sunshine. I could understand the perception of threat that it held for those surrounding it in that cold winter of 1944. But the mild and sunny weather failed to offer the perspective given to the three of us the previous November. For the last six years of my regular RAF career, I was responsible for training personnel for the British military responsible for planning air targeting, those who compile the evidence and make the case for military attacks. My job was to teach those people the tools to guide and advise senior military officers who would be asked to make the same difficult decisions of life and death in the twenty-first century that General Mark Clark and others made in February 1944. Would we have come to different conclusions; would a contemporary targeteer advise the destruction of a protected and valuable religious building? Would our senior decision-makers act in the same way as those in 1944? I sincerely believe that they would not. I have been very aware that second-guessing decisions that were made in the crucible of war, when those officers asked to make such difficult decisions were under enormous pressure, is problematic especially as I sit comfortably in an office with no-one trying to kill me. Nevertheless, shying away from a critical examination of decisions made, simply due to the circumstances in which they were made, is equally unsatisfactory. Officers make bad decisions all the time, this does not make them bad officers or callous murderers. It makes them human but denying that mistakes are made or excusing them due to the conditions in which they were made makes repetition of these mistakes far more likely. Therefore, an honest and sometimes critical judgement from afar is justified and indeed vital to learning lessons from these events.

Looking at the Abbey again in 2022 I thought how magnificent it appeared, a marvel of architecture. Yet upon reflection, it was not the real Abbey of Montecassino; it was a facsimile of the building that was destroyed in 1944. The frescoes in the basilica are only copies of those painted over the centuries. However accurate the rebuilding was, the destruction cannot be undone, and the decision to destroy it cannot be unmade. The opinion of the Vatican Secretary of State at the time, Cardinal Luigi Maglione, is patently true, 'Even if Monte Cassino is rebuilt in gold and precious stones, it will no longer be the same.'[2]

This decision, however, can be understood. Too many accounts contain excuses or mere apathy at the destruction. Whilst accounts continue to be dishonest for national pride or protection of personal reputation, the risks that such an event could happen again remain. We have seen recently in Ukraine how easy it is for warfare to descend into atrocity. Almost all the accounts of the battles of Cassino are told from the perspective of the ground soldier; usually it is historians of land forces that tell the story. Yet it was the air forces that destroyed the Abbey of Montecassino, an environment that the soldier storytellers sometimes don't fully understand. I have tried to add much more of the airman's perspective to this story of who, when and why the heavy air weapon was used to destroy the greatest monastery in Europe. War is a nasty business, people die, and buildings are destroyed. But it is also a much-studied business, where lessons can be learned and adopted. That is the reason why I decided to write this book in the hope that those who take on my former profession in the future can learn lessons from the past.

---

2   Eusebio Grossetti and Martino Matronola (Faustino Avagliano ed.), *Monte Cassino Under Fire – War Diaries From The Abbey* (Cassino IT: Abbazia Di Montecassino, 2017), p.234.

The new basilica of Montecassino. The destruction of 15 February has been fully restored, but one never forgets that this is not the Abbey that existed before the bombing but is merely a beautiful facsimile. The destruction can never really be reversed (Author)

Introduction

Cultural treasures like Monte Cassino are the people's patrimony – humanity's inheritance to which all are entitled, for which all are responsible, and for which all must be held accountable.

Dr Kriston R. Rennie
Dean, Faculty of Indigenous Studies, Social Sciences and Humanities
at the University of Northern British Columbia
Author of *The Destruction and Recovery of Monte Cassino, 529-1964*[1]

In 1973, the historian and Montecassino scholar Herbert Bloch wrote an account of the bombing of the Abbey at Montecassino. One of the first things he quoted was a statement by Gaetano De Sanctis, the president of the Pontifica Accademia Romana d'Archeologia at the time of the bombing, when it was convened just nine days after the Abbey's destruction. De Sanctis observed:

> To remain silent in the face of such horrible manifestations of the fury of war … would be tantamount to being culpable of indifference, or worse, of cowardly acquiescence not only in the eyes of our contemporaries, but also in the eyes of future generations. It is not our task to fix the specific responsibility for such a mass of ruins, but this must be said: to have caused it will remain an everlasting shame to our age and to our civilisation.[2]

In the intervening years scholars and commentators have certainly not remained silent over the matter, but many of those that have written about this event do seem keen to excuse what De Sanctis called the 'horrible manifestations of war.' Many writers have glossed over the facts that led up to the destruction of one of the treasures of western civilisation; many blamed the Germans or mitigated the action as a necessary consequence of Total War. They said that war is not a game played by gentlemen, but that military leaders have a duty to do whatever is necessary to win, regardless of the consequences. Victory is the only arbiter of right or wrong; only the losers end up in war crimes tribunals. In a way they are right. War is not a game; it was and remains a nasty brutal business where people die and where innocent people often get in the way. Sometimes there is justifiable necessity for them to die too. Millions of them have over the centuries, and still today despite all our intelligence and our precision weapons and our checks

---

1   Kriston Rennie, *The Destruction and Recovery of Monte Cassino, 529-1964* (Amsterdam: Amsterdam University Press, 2021), p.171.
2   Herbert Bloch, *The Bombardment of Monte Cassino* (Cassino: Montecassino, 1979), p.9.

A photographic reconnaissance image of the Abbey following the bombing. The extent of the damage can be clearly seen (UK TNA)

and balances they continue to die. In a more important way those that unquestioningly support the justification of 'Military Necessity' for the destruction of the Abbey are very wrong. War does have rules; it has always had rules, from medieval chivalry to the Geneva Conventions. To be without them leads us down the path of horrors, to where the Nazis went, to Srebrenica and to Rwanda. As I write, we see on the television every day in Ukraine the results of a flagrant disregard of the rules and the unwillingness to act of those who could stop it if they had more courage to uphold the standards that they have set. It is only boundaries that keep us from committing the errors that were made in Cassino. It is ridiculous to think, as many senior officers on the Allied side patently did, that this thing called Military Necessity was the only thing that counted. That the conduct of war is the pursuit of political aims was as correct in Clausewitz's day as it was in the Second World War. All actions in war not only have consequences for those fighting, but for diplomacy, economics, and society. As soon as anything can be justified, everything will be justified. What is war, and what separates it from mere violence? The answer to this question is complicated, but essentially boils down to two things. Wars are fought by armed forces controlled by the political forces of States. These States agree to a set of rules to regulate and limit their actions. Perhaps naively I believe that when a democracy commits its armed forces to war it does so in part to uphold the values of that society and that if we undertake activities that undermine those values, we begin to undermine the very foundations of civilisation. The ends never justify unlimited means.

The nub of the problem facing me is whether the destruction of the Abbey of Montecassino was a necessary act? In a way it is an easy question to answer if we strip away the detail and look at the facts as they were in the winter of 1944. Everywhere, the Allies were masters of the seas and skies. Germany was on the back foot in every theatre. It had lost the Battle of the Atlantic and the power of the United States flowed virtually unchallenged across the ocean with ever increasing vigour to reinforce its armies massing in Europe. All, apart from the most ardent Nazis, knew that the game was up, that defeat was only a matter of time. The *Luftwaffe* had lost any notion of being able to strike back as the Allied Combined Bomber Offensive battered German cities and industries around the clock. Within weeks, Allied air forces would effectively defeat Germany in the air and operate over the Reich more freely. In the East, the *Wehrmacht* was in terminal decline following its defeat at Kursk in summer 1943. It would never challenge the power of the Red Army again. Italy was a pivotal, yet secondary theatre of operations. Its value had been in galvanising the embryonic Anglo-American war machine as it prepared to conduct decisive operations in Normandy. That task was complete. Despite some British protestations, the Mediterranean did not hold the path to victory. Its strategic purpose was achieved by mid-1944; the Allies were prepared to launch their invasion and Italy continued to fix some capable German divisions. Beyond 6 June 1944, the Italian Campaign's purpose gradually diminished. This would remain the case whether the Allies advanced in Italy or not but the presence of powerful Allied armies fed German dictator Adolf Hitler's obsession with defending every inch. He would not, could not, allow a voluntary retreat. By February 1944, the French beaches that would be attacked that summer would not be defended by the highly experienced combat divisions that faced the Fifth Army in Italy, but by the sick, the old, the very young and often foreign conscripts, including such diversity as Russians, Poles and even Mongolians who fought from fear, with no loyalty to the Reich.

With this grand strategic background in mind, Rome was a military irrelevance. It held no real operational level value to the Allies, except as a vanity bauble dangling in front of generals and politicians alike, and its loss would be a psychological blow to the Axis. In November 1943, the Allied Commander in the Mediterranean, General Dwight D Eisenhower, in a letter to the US Joint Chiefs of Staff (JCS), was clear that, 'I do not regard Rome as valuable to enemy as a fortress.'[3] British Prime Minister Winston Churchill's claim that whoever held Rome held the 'title deeds to Italy' proved to be wrong as the Germans fiercely fought on after it fell.[4] The Combined Chiefs of Staff (CCS) had not included Rome as a military objective of the Italian Campaign, although all knew Churchill's desire for it. All roads may lead to Rome, but the city was a strategic *cul de sac*. Even the defeat of the German armies facing the Allies in Italy was not strategically vital. Merely holding them in place was sufficient. This was ultimately the purpose

3   Alfred D Chandler, Stephen E Ambrose, Joseph P Hobbs, Edwin A Thompson and Elizabeth F Smith, *The Papers of Dwight David Eisenhower: The War Years, Volume III* (Baltimore MD: The Johns Hopkins Press, 1971), p.1554.
4   Maurice Matloff, *Strategic Planning for Coalition Warfare 1943-1944* (Washington DC: Center of Military History, 1994 (Kindle Edition)), Kindle location, 8406.

of the Italian campaign as the growing strength of the US made it the senior partner in the Anglo-American alliance. It could, therefore, dictate the path to victory and this path would lead through France, both north and south, not through Italy. So, the answer to the Military Necessity question for the Abbey is easy. If the capture of Rome was not necessary to achieve victory, the battles around Cassino were also not necessary. Therefore, there can be no necessity to destroy the Abbey. Simple. Of course, it is not simple. Very little that I have said was clearly evident. To those fighting and those directing, victory was far from certain. It was not universally accepted that Italy was a secondary theatre. Some politicians and generals, Churchill amongst them, continued to believe that winning in Italy offered a route to the Balkans and a peace less dominated by the Russians. Rome was an enemy capital city; that fact alone justified fighting for it. It was also a prize, justifying the hardships of the troops that fought in Italy and satisfying the egos of those who commanded them.

There was never any chance that those generals commanding the armies in Italy were going to accept a holding role. Generals have a habit for being competitive, for having big reputations to protect and even bigger egos. They also have the morale of their troops to consider. Those in Italy were no exception. Battlefield success held the key to their future careers and their legacies. Being upstaged by the Allied invasion on northwest Europe was probably foremost in their minds and they were determined not to let that happen. Most of them probably realised that the fact that they were not chosen for the Normandy 'big push' placed them in the second tier. They were often under extreme pressure, from above and self-imposed, to see the job done. Looking beyond the strategic necessity, what could justify the destruction of an ancient cultural artefact such as the Abbey of Montecassino to these men? What were the rules that constrained them? Were these rules ignored in the heat of battle? If so, how and why? That is what this volume will attempt to answer.

In his account, Major Bradford Evans, the pilot who commanded the heavy bombers on the Monte Cassino mission, afterwards questioned the basis upon which he was ordered to carry it out. Evans was a highly experienced and respected officer within the US 2nd Bombardment Group and the Commanding Officer of the 96th Bombardment Squadron with 49 operational missions to his name. He was selected not only to lead the Abbey attack, but he had already participated in operations against Pantelleria, Sicily, Eboli and led the first air support mission against German supply lines near Anzio, where his group had scored direct hits on rail yards and other targets. He was also selected to lead the attack to flatten Cassino town. Evans subsequently completed 53-missions, finishing his tour on 22 March 1944. In an interview with Italian media in 1995, Evans considered that the attack on the Abbey was a mistake and despite admitting prior knowledge of civilians in the Abbey, he said that when he learnt that there were no Germans, it was 'a very unpleasant discovery.' He asked in his account of the Abbey bombing, 'On what military intelligence estimates did Generals Tucker[sic] and Freyberg base their requests for the bombing?'[5] This is also a question that this volume will attempt to answer.

It was the Americans and British who decided the fate of the Abbey and following the end of the war they set-up the Nuremburg International Military Tribunal to punish those who committed war crimes and to deter those who may commit them in the future. Although some criticise the tribunal for bringing 'victor's justice', it claimed to provide a universality of

5   Bradford Evans, *The Bombing of Monte Cassino* (Cassino: Pubblicazioni Cassinesi, 1988), p.25.

behaviour for the future. It feels appropriate to recount the opening words of the US chief pros-
ecution counsel to the tribunal, Justice Robert Jackson:

> If certain acts of violations of treaties are crimes, they are crimes whether the United States
> does them or whether Germany does them, and we are not prepared to lay down a rule of
> criminal conduct against others which we would not be willing to have invoked against
> us…We must never forget that the record on which we judge these defendants is the record
> on which history will judge us tomorrow.[6]

Churchill made it clear that the British would not be judged for their actions. There was therefore, and despite Jackson's statement, no accountability for those who were responsible for the
destruction of the Abbey of Montecassino and the deaths of hundreds of innocent civilians. It
is for you to judge whether there should have been?

To help come to a conclusion, this volume is divided into a number of parts. The first part
will deal with the strategic, operational and tactical events that brought the Allies to Monte
Cassino. The strategic background needs examination to place the decision to attack the Abbey
into context. What were Allied strategic aims and how did these influence events in Italy?
Decisions made by Allied commanders in the Mediterranean were all made in this context.
Every compromise that led to the attack on the Abbey began with political and strategic decisions made by leaders outside the Mediterranean. Had these decisions been different or had they
had greater resources or more time, would the result have been different?

Following success at Salerno, the capture of Naples and the strategically important airfield
complex around Foggia, the Allied armies slowly made their way northwards against determined German defenders. As autumn closed-in and the weather worsened their tempo slowed.
Casualties grew and the armies became tired and demoralised. Eventually, by the beginning
of 1944 after months of struggle and thousands of casualties, they reached the *Gustav* Line at
Cassino. I will then describe the events at Cassino in January 1944, as the Americans tried and
failed to breakthrough. The Abbey at Montecassino was now visible to all who fought nearby; it
became an unreachable goal and it was often perceived as the enemy. This part culminates with
the actions of the US Fifth Army at Cassino prior to mid-February 1944 when the provisional
New Zealand Corps occupied American positions near the Abbey. Prior to this point, there
had been no apparent necessity to destroy the Abbey and, apart from in newspaper articles, no
requests to attack it.

The second part will take us through the difficulties making the decision. It will begin with
a chapter on one of the most important and most complicated parts of military operations,
that of command and control. Who could actually make the decision to bomb the Abbey of
Montecassino? Those that can make these decisions need to take into account many factors.
The first of these is policy advice on what protections should be given to cultural property.
What was the Law of War that the commander had to take into account before ordering an
attack? Despite post-attack assertions that German occupation of the Abbey was not necessary
to meet the Military Necessity criteria, it is clear that proof of occupation was a requirement

---

6   Mark Selden 'A Forgotten Holocaust: US Bombing Strategy, The Destruction Of Japanese Cities,
     and the American Way of War from the Pacific War to Iraq' in Yuki Tanaka and Marilyn B Young
     (eds.), *Bombing Civilians: A Twentieth Century History* (New York: The New Press, 2009), p.92.

in law and was a major factor in the decision-making process. The law is intimately connected with the moral and ethical decisions, especially when considering the lives of innocent civilians embroiled in the battlefield. The principle of Military Necessity requires a commander to have sufficient confidence in the military nature of his target and the advantage to be gained by attacking it. On what bases were decisions made; how did the key leaders decide? This is usually heavily influenced by the intelligence that the commander possesses, and the next chapter will discuss the intelligence available to those decision-makers and the use they put to it. What sources of information were available to determine whether the Germans were using the Abbey for military purposes? A chapter describes the wide array of intelligence sources available to US Fifth Army, and to the 15th Army Group.[7] There were striking differences in the conclusions that different commanders made regarding the necessity to attack the Abbey. The final chapter in this part is on the circumstances leading up to the attack. When was it decided to attack the building and why? Were any alternatives considered? As has been stated, the decision to bomb the Abbey was made largely by British officers with American contrary views seemingly overruled or ignored. This chapter discusses the Allied decision-making process and the differing views of Allies towards the question of Military Necessity.

The third part of this volume is dedicated to the air forces. One of the key judgements is that the bombing of the Abbey of Montecassino with heavy bombers was a decision taken entirely by the air forces, as was the doctrine at the time. The first chapter in this part will look at the development of the United States Army Air Force (USAAF) and especially the development of doctrine that led up to the attack and set the conditions for its ultimate independence from the US Army. One man dominates this struggle, Chief of Air Corps, General Henry 'Hap' Arnold, and his influence will be discussed at length. The next chapter places Arnold's creation into the Italian campaign. How were air forces organised and commanded? What were their principal roles and priorities? One of the key events used to justify the bombing of the Abbey by historians was a flight by the Mediterranean air commander, Lieutenant General Ira Eaker, over the Abbey the day before, where he claims to have observed Germans in the building. This flight could not have happened and Eaker was not in Italy on the day in question. Effective use of airpower in the land battle takes practices and procedures that are well-integrated and understood by each service. The next chapter looks at the development of air-land integration in Italy and takes a detailed look at how heavy bombers, under different command arrangements and with little experience with this sort of work, were integrated into the attack. The next chapter is technical, discussing the methodology and weaknesses of high-altitude precision bombing. Precision is a relative term; the majority of bombs did not hit the Abbey. The next two chapters will deal with the events on the day itself and the results of the attack.

The fourth part of this volume examines the aftermath of the attack. Having information does not always result in good use of it. The first chapter in this section examines the evidence available to commanders at the time and assesses whether the intelligence justified the decision. It is now beyond reasonable doubt that the Germans were not and never had used the Abbey. Yet much of the evidence supporting this conclusion only became apparent after the bombing.

---

7   The 15th Army Group became Allied Central Mediterranean Force (ACMF) and then Allied Armies in Italy (AAI) during 1944, reverting to 15th Army Group by early 1945. For clarity, the organisation in command of British Eighth and US Fifth Armies will be called 15th Army Group throughout.

Some post-war historians have continued to couch their arguments with the word 'probably', muddying the waters with doubt where none exists. In assessing the evidence, it is important to bear hindsight in mind. Although it is certain that no Germans occupied the Abbey, was that information available to Allied decision-makers at the time? I will use only the evidence available prior to 15 February 1944 to draw final conclusions.

The next two chapters conclude that the intelligence prior to the decision to destroy the Abbey was sufficiently detailed to allow a reasonable degree of certainty as to whether the attack met the Rules of War for Military Necessity.[8] The attack on the Abbey cannot be judged as a failure of intelligence, but rather a failure of the application of intelligence. If there were no Germans present, why did it happen? How was it justified when the German propaganda machine inevitably focused on the event, and when complaints from the Vatican arrived in Allied capitals? The responses from Allied Force Headquarters (AFHQ) and especially from the British Foreign Office unambiguously expose as untrue later Allied and scholarly assertions that occupation was not the principal justifying factor. The sparseness and unreliability of the occupation evidence and the unwillingness of the Supreme Allied Commander in the Mediterranean, General Sir Henry Maitland-Wilson, to release his evidence to the Vatican is illuminating.

The final part of this volume examines the years following the fighting. It was one of the most controversial acts of the Second World War and in the intervening 80-years it continues to generate books and opinions, including this one. Many histories have been mired in bias and national perspectives. A few, more recent, and generally non-military accounts, have questioned the earlier works and the Official Histories, yet the inertia of those works stubbornly persists. The narrative of the 'bad' Germans and the 'good' Allies is understandable but has clouded the judgement of many a writer. As I write this final part of this introduction, mid-way through 2022, the long thought unthinkable is happening, a full-scale war in Europe. Despite the advances in International Humanitarian Law since 1945, when one sees the abuses of civilians and the wanton destruction of civilian property, one wonders whether the world has learnt anything at all from the events eight decades ago?

8   *British Manual of Military Law*, Chapter XIV (1940).

1

Decisions for a Secondary Theatre: 1943-44

By knocking Italy out of the war, gaining control of the Italian Fleet, acquiring air bases in Italy, and occupying Sardinia and Sicily, the United States and United Kingdom had already achieved their basic strategic objectives in the Mediterranean and had achieved them earlier than anticipated.

Maurice Matloff[1]

Britain and America largely agreed on what needed to be done, but not on the method. The difference in approach permeated down to the foot soldiers. Correspondent Frank Gervasi identified that British Tommies were fighting for a better life afterwards, whereas the Americans were fighting to win and go home.[2] Perhaps one of the clearest examples of the difference was the declaration of 'Unconditional Surrender,' delivered after the Casablanca Conference (SYMBOL) in January 1943. Whilst this policy suffered no public disagreement by the British, it was essentially the President's idea, and was not an agenda item. Cyrus Sulzberger, in conversation with the President's personal Vatican envoy, Myron Taylor, discovered that Churchill hated the idea, and had only agreed to it in exchange for a free hand in the Eastern Mediterranean.[3] The idea of Unconditional Surrender was entirely in accord with US Army military philosophy for the use of its military to destroy an enemy armed force. 'It represented not only the American war aim in the Second World War but also a basic American attitude towards the enemy, towards international politics, and towards warfare.'[4]

The British philosophy had always been different. Throughout the era of the British Empire, the use of military force had usually been a last resort, a useful tool to assist in striking a reasonable bargain. The British liked to act in a more coercive manner, threatening violence or delivering limited violence to persuade rather than destroy. The Unconditional Surrender declaration offered no room for negotiation. The aim of war should not merely be the military defeat of the enemy but an acceptable peace. By 1944, Germany was clearly going to be defeated and Britain

---

1   Matloff, Kindle loc, 6326.
2   Frank Gervasi. *The Violent Decade: A Foreign Correspondent in Europe and the Middle East 1935*-1945 (New York: W.W. Norton, 1989), p.513.
3   Cyrus L Sulzberger, *A Long Row of Candles* (Toronto: The Macmillan Company, 1969), p.391.
4   Anne Armstrong, *Unconditional Surrender: The Impact of the Casablanca Policy upon World War II* (Westport CT: Greenwood Press, 1961), p. ix.

became greatly concerned by the intentions of Soviet Premier, Joseph Stalin and the Soviet Union, hence Churchill's concern with so-called peripheral areas such as Poland, Greece and the other Balkan states. His concern and frustration with the synthesis of military and political is best summed up by the title of the final volume in his memoirs, *Triumph and Tragedy*.

The US fought its war according to different priorities. Despite their great friendship and a common culture, the British and Americans had very different views as to how the war should be fought. Even this simplifies the issue. There were divisions within both the British and American Chiefs as to what strategy to follow. Both desired victory, but the US thought in terms of the quickest way to achieve a decisive military victory. The rest could be sorted out later, and it was not interested in restoring the Imperial possessions of Europe, including those of its principal ally. The US Army Chief of Staff, General George Marshall, strongly favoured the most direct approach, attacking Germany decisively through Northern France at the earliest opportunity using brute force born from their immense industrial and manpower potential.

He wanted this in 1942 (Operation SLEDGEHAMMER) as a contingency plan for emergencies, was keen for 1943 (Operation ROUNDUP), but had to settle for spring 1944 (Operation OVERLORD). Often, blame for this compromise has been laid at the feet of the British, notably their better staff organisation at Casablanca, but the US Chiefs were not united in supporting Marshall's position. The US Navy, and the President, were ambivalent over a 1943 invasion date. The British, although mostly supportive of a cross-channel attack at some time in the future feared German land strength and favoured a broader strategy to weaken Germany peripherally, with campaigns in Italy and the Balkans before delivering the decisive blow across the Channel.[5] This strategy was typical of the British and was 'deeply embedded in England's military tradition.'[6] Following a Mediterranean strategy at all for the Americans was down to Roosevelt who vetoed his Service chiefs. The one military supporter of TORCH, landing US and British forces in French North Africa in November 1942, who had known Roosevelt since 1913 and was more than just an adviser, was Admiral William Leahy. He saw the capture of North Africa as the effective encirclement of Germany.[7] Conflation of his support of TORCH with support of a Mediterranean strategy, however, would be wrong. Leahy, and the President, wanted the strategy that would result in the quickest defeat of the Axis with the fewest American casualties – going to Italy was not part of Leahy's calculation. The British strategic theory, on the other hand, involved using all the military, informational and political levers of power. Speed, movement and surprise had effects out of proportion to the ferocity and extent of the fighting. Similarly, the British became masters of unconventional war. The US adopted some of these methods, especially early on, but they never had the enthusiasm or effort of the British. Even at their first meeting in mid-1941, it was clear that the Americans' ideas were to throw big armies and air forces at the heart of Germany. Britain wanted to use cunning, subversion, strategic bombing to affect morale and propaganda to whittle away at Germany. They viewed the proper line of attack to be via the

5   Winston S Churchill, *The Second World War Volume V: Closing the Ring* (London: The Reprint Society, 1952), p.78; Arthur Bryant, *The Turn of the Tide 1939-1943* (London: Grafton Books, 1986), p.700.
6   Leo J Meyer, 'The Decision To Invade North Africa (TORCH)' in Kent Roberts Greenfield (ed.), *Command Decisions* (Washington DC: Center of Military History, Department of the Army, 2000), p.175.
7   Philips Payson O'Brien, *The Second Most Powerful Man In The World: The Life of Admiral William D Leahy, Roosevelt's Chief of Staff* (New York NY: Dutton, 2019), p.191.

weaker Axis partner through the Mediterranean and Italy.[8]

Although geographically adjacent, the campaigns in Sicily and Italy served different purposes and were planned separately and iteratively; 'much more off the cuff' in the words of one staff officer.[9] A holistic Mediterranean planning process may have resulted in a direct landing on the toe or shin of Italy, isolating Axis forces on Sicily, rather than fighting them. The incremental approach could never achieve this, but the conservative Eisenhower would not take such risks. He did, however, in a conversation with his assistant, Commander Harry Butcher, consider the decision not to directly attack on either side of the Messina Strait as one of his biggest mistakes whilst Allied Commander-in-Chief (C-in-C).[10] That Sicily was a mistake was also the view of one of Eisenhower's opponents, soon to be Italian Prime Minister Pietro Badoglio, who thought Sardinia was the better option, calling Sicily a

The Combined Chiefs of Staff meeting in Cairo at the SEXTANT Conference in November 1943. (NARA RG342-FH-000817)

'strategic error.'[11] The Germans expected the Allies to seize the strait and the fortunate escape of German forces across it, virtually undamaged and unopposed was to haunt the Allies. The failure of Allied air forces to interdict the vulnerable ferries crossing the strait should have warned them of the weakness of their air weapon where accuracy of bombing was required. It seemed not to have done so.

The Sicily operation was more an extension of the North African campaign; its objectives were final victory in Africa and the opening of the Mediterranean to shipping. Use of the Suez Canal and the Mediterranean to allow access to the Middle East and to connect India with its imperial homeland was much shorter and quicker than the route around the Cape of Good

8   Matloff, Kindle loc, 367.
9   David Hunt, *A Don At War* (London: Frank Cass, 1990), p.202.
10   Alfred D. Chandler, Stephen E Ambrose, Joseph P Hobbs, Edwin A Thompson and Elizabeth F Smith, *The Papers of Dwight David Eisenhower: The War Years, Volume II* (Baltimore MD: The Johns Hopkins Press, 1971), p.1321.
11   Mario Canciani, *Il Fronte di Cassino* (Formia: Stabalimento Graficart, 2003), p.12.

Hope that had been used for most of the previous three years. The Mediterranean route would offer a saving of 200-ships per month.[12] This was less important to the Americans, who relied on self-produced oil and oil from Venezuela and of course they had no Empire. The British Chief of the Imperial General Staff (CIGS), General Sir Alan Brooke, considered it a strategic necessity to free-up sufficient shipping to allow cross-channel operations to succeed. Although Britain managed most of the fledgling Middle East oil exploitation, she too received much of her wartime supplies for use in Europe from across the Atlantic. Middle Eastern oil production was generally reserved for military operations in the Middle and Far Eastern theatres.[13] Victory in Sicily on 17 August 1943 saw this strategic aim fulfilled.[14] The continuance of Allied operations into Italy had broader, yet less defined aims and the decision came only after disagreements between American and British leaders. Animosities plagued operations in Italy at all levels, affecting both operational decisions and personal relationships. The US Chiefs were determined that there were to be no more delays, no more sideshows and no more British prevarications. The British dominated the earlier meetings up until and including Casablanca. British planners had conducted estimates on potential future operations and had determined the 'art of the possible'. The Americans didn't initially consider all contingencies and thereby argued from a position of weakness in future strategy discussions. Wedemeyer said, 'they swarmed down upon us like locusts.'[15] The US learned quickly and by the QUADRANT Conference in Quebec the Americans had their act together and were properly prepared. The British knew the US line on Mediterranean operations and a note dated 10 August 1943 from the British Chiefs of Staff (CoS) representatives in Washington, prior to the conference, revealed that:

> The United States Chiefs of Staff have no intention of allowing themselves to be committed to an operation of unknown magnitude in Italy which might well prejudice 'Overlord' and other operations agreed upon at 'Trident'.[16]

Whether pursuing the Italian campaign after Sicily was worthwhile has long been argued, suggesting that there was little to offer the Americans or the Russians in Italy, and that the Mediterranean served the British national interests. This was mostly true; the British retained critical interests in the Middle East, India and the Far East that relied on unrestricted transit through the Mediterranean and the Suez Canal. To the British this was possibly more important than defeating a weakened Hitler through France, savaged as he was by Russia. Hitler too, was sensitive to his southern flank. The Mediterranean mattered, sending forces to assist the Italian Duce, Benito Mussolini, in North Africa and Greece thereby indicated that Hitler saw value in significant southern investment. After Mussolini's fall, he continued to spend German blood and treasure in this region. Oil, bauxite and other war critical resources were available to Germany only from southern Europe.

---

12   Matloff, Kindle loc 481.
13   Air Force Historical Research Agency (AFHRA) Reel A1372, Memorandum for the Executive Committee, Army-Navy Petroleum Board dated 21 October 1943.
14   Harold Alexander, *Supplement to the London Gazette: The Allied Armies in Italy from 3 September 1943 to 12 December 1944* (London, HMSO, 1950), p.2879.
15   Albert Wedemeyer, *Wedemeyer Reports!* (New York: Henry Holt and Company, 1959), 192.
16   The National Archives (TNA) CAB 80/74/513, COS (43) 513 Part A, QUADRANT Record of Plenary Meetings and the Proceedings of the Combined Chiefs of Staff, Quebec, August 1943, dated 11 September 1943. COS Q 7th Meeting Minutes Annex dated 11 August 1943.

The military theorist J F C Fuller referred to the Italian Campaign as a 'campaign which for lack of strategic sense and tactical imagination is unique in military history,' and to the destruction of the Benedictine Abbey as 'not so much a piece of vandalism, as an act of sheer tactical stupidity.'[17] Fuller was wrong in the strategic sense, but right about the tactics employed by Allied commanders. The invasion of mainland Italy was not a foregone conclusion following the capture of Sicily. AFHQ in the Mediterranean had been developing several courses of action including operations in southern France, the Balkans and Italy. All these options had advantages and disadvantages, as did doing nothing. At their first meeting at the TRIDENT Conference in May 1943, Churchill and Roosevelt had different views, although both considered that knocking Italy out of the war was desirable. The British Prime Minister was not only keen to force Italy out of the war but to capture Rome, whereas the US President, advised mainly by Admiral Leahy, was reluctant to commit large forces to a major campaign that could compete with the Cross-Channel plans. The Allied CCS considered the matter. Their conclusions largely mirrored those of their political leadership, with Marshall being the least interested in a Mediterranean strategy. The American view was that operations against Italy should be restricted to air attacks only. Hitler clearly disagreed, promptly cancelling the Kursk offensive in Russia in response to the Allies landing in Sicily. That Italy could be forced to surrender from air attack only, was considered and supported by UK Joint Intelligence Sub-Committee (JIC) assessments.[18] On the day that Sicily was conquered, 17 August 1943, Hitler received signals intelligence that Italy was in surrender negotiations with the Allies.[19]

It was not only strategic outlook that separated the allies, but also war philosophy. In the *American Way of War*, Russell Weigley examined what German military historian Hans Delbruck called the two types of war strategy, Annihilation and Attrition.[20] He described the US Army philosophy as favouring a war of annihilation, whereas Britain, with more limited resources adopted a different philosophy, that of attrition. Churchill, a fierce proponent of the peripheral strategy wanted greater emphasis on the Mediterranean Theatre. His memoir of this time was aptly entitled *Closing The Ring*. The strategic theory of this approach was summed up by Basil Liddell-Hart:

> A strategy of limited aim is that of awaiting a change in the balance of force – a change often sought and achieved by draining the enemy's force, weakening him by pricks instead of risking blows. The essential condition of such a strategy is that the drain on him should be disproportionately greater than on oneself…by causing an excessively wide distribution of his force; and, not least, by exhausting his moral and physical energy.[21]

The US Army had since the mid-nineteenth century adopted the philosophy of the Swiss military theorist Baron Antoine de Jomini. Jomini's theory, boiled to its simplest terms in his 1838 book *The Art of War*, was that it was a necessity to bring the maximum available force to bear

17   J.F.C. Fuller, *The Second World War* (London: Eyre and Spottiswoode, 1962), p.272.
18   F.H. Hinsley, E E Thomas, C F G Ransom and R C Knight, *British Intelligence in the Second World War Volume 3 Part 1* (London: HMSO, 1984), p.5.
19   Air Historical Branch Translation No VII/97. The Campaign in Italy Chapter VII – General von Vietinghoff, December 1947, Translated by Air Ministry, AHB6, June 1950.
20   Russel F Weigley, *The American Way of War* (Bloomington IN: Indiana University Press, 1973), p. xxii.
21   Basil Liddell-Hart, *Strategy* (London: Faber and Faber Ltd, 1991), p.321.

against the enemy's decisive point.[22] The more well-known Clausewitz was less important and was not translated into English until 1873, and not published in America until 1943.[23] It was Jomini's theories on the Napoleonic wars that became the standard syllabus at West Point, although the German theorist greatly influenced one of the War Department's principal planners, General Albert Wedemeyer, whose staff training was conducted by the *Wehrmacht* in the late 1930s. In its Training Regulation 10-5, issued in 1921, the Army published its Principles of War. The first three principles illustrated the direction of US strategic thought:

1.   The Principle of the Objective.
2.   The Principle of the Offensive.
3.   The Principle of Mass.[24]

The principal aim of US Army doctrine manuals of 1939 remained, 'the destruction of the enemy's armed forces in battle.'[25] War College instructor in the 1920s, Colonel W K Naylor stated:

> An army strong enough to choose the strategy of annihilation should always choose it, because the most certain and probably the most rapid route to victory lay through the destruction of the enemy's armed forces.[26]

By early 1944, the US Army was strengthening, but the British were weakening as they had gradually used up their resources in over four years of battle. The US JCS, the key decision-making military body had two naval officers as well as two army officers, who looked upon war strategy differently. The Commander-in-Chief, Roosevelt, as a former Assistant Secretary of the Navy often found the naval view of strategy more persuasive. Despite American strength, politically a mass land army butting its head against Germany and Japan as in the previous war was not attractive as this generated the greatest number of casualties. Leahy, Roosevelt's closest military adviser, saw no reason to invade the mainland of Europe in northwest France until victory was assured through air and sea power. The British did not have the mass for a large continental army, able to execute the Jominian theory, but effectively levelled the playing field in other ways. The British operated deception plans to maintain German forces in the Mediterranean. A go-no go criterion for OVERLORD was that no more than 12-German divisions could be in France and the Low Countries and that they would be unable to deploy more than 15-divisions by D+60. In the Mediterranean the aim was to create the impression that Allied forces were stronger than they were, to force Germany to station more forces in this region. To the British a head-on battle was a failure of strategy; to Marshall at least, its creation was its essence. In late 1943 operations in the Mediterranean, both real and imagined, contributed to the cover plan for OVERLORD.

22   Weigley, p.83.
23   Weigley, pp.82, 210.
24   Weigley, p.213.
25   Weigley, p.221.
26   Quoted by Weigley, p.313.

Sound strategy to US chiefs was opting for the course of action that would destroy the enemy's armed forces most quickly. Whilst the British agreed that destruction of the German Armed Forces was a priority, they would have chosen a more indirect method, waiting until the opportune time, avoiding prolonged battle and attacking when the enemy was sufficiently weakened. Britain wished to cross the Channel when the right conditions existed; Marshall wanted to work to a strict timetable. The disadvantages of the British method were that the Russians may have taken more of Europe and that the war in the Pacific may have been prolonged, atomic attacks notwithstanding. In short, many influential Americans considered Operation OVERLORD to be the entire banquet; Churchill, the British Chiefs and perhaps the President as well, considered it as just the pudding.

In many ways, Roosevelt's and Leahy's outlook favoured the delay if it assisted in reducing American casualties. Both, however, considered 1944 to be the optimum year. One of the chief planners of the US Army and OVERLORD apostle, Wedemeyer, considered that the British were so opposed to the Normandy landings that the US needed the entire 'weight of national policy' behind it.[27] There is little to commend this extreme view. Marshall stated that each diversion from the main plot 'acts as a suction pump.'[28] On 16 October 1943, the British military representative to Washington, Field Marshal Sir John Dill wrote to Brooke stating: 'Our difficulties with the Americans are going to increase rather than diminish with their growing strength and a Presidential Election approaching.'[29] In the beginning, the British policies held sway; they had fought Hitler for over two years and had earned the greater say. Even so, just before Churchill left for Cairo and Teheran, he continued to scheme, charging his CoS to look for opportunities that would undermine the timing and perhaps even the necessity for OVERLORD:

> Pray let this enquiry be conducted in a most secret manner and on the assumption that commitments into which we have already entered with the Americans particularly as regards OVERLORD could be modified by agreement to meet the exigencies of a changing situation.[30]

The extent of British policy and the response to Churchill's request can be seen in a minute from the British CoS on 11 November 1943; a minute to which he appended the comment. 'I cordially agree.' The CoS memo is worth quoting at length:

> For some time past it has been clear to us, and doubtless also to the US Chiefs of Staff, that disagreement exists between us as to what we should do now in the Mediterranean, with particular reference to the effect of future action on OVERLORD. The point at issue is how far what might be termed the 'sanctity of OVERLORD' is to be preserved in its entirety, irrespective of developments in the Mediterranean theatre. This issue is clouding the whole of our future strategic outlook and must be resolved at SEXTANT.

27   Matloff, Kindle loc, 2769.
28   Matloff, Kindle loc, 625.
29   David Fraser *Alanbrooke*, (London: Harper Collins, 1997), p.346.
30   TNA CAB 80/75/639: COS (43) 639 (0), RELATION OF OVERLORD TO MEDITERRANEAN Minute by the Prime Minister (D178/3), dated 19 October 1943.

At the outset we must point out that, since the decisions taken at QUADRANT, there have been major developments in the situation. The Russian campaign has succeeded beyond all hope or expectations and their victorious advance continues. Italy has been knocked out of the war; and it is certainly not beyond the bounds of possibility that Turkey will come in on our side before the New Year. In these changed conditions, we feel that consideration of adjustments of, if not actual departures from, the decisions taken at TRIDENT and QUADRANT are not only fully justified but positively essential …

…With the Germans in their present plight the surest way to win the war in the shortest time is to attack them remorselessly and continuously in any and every area where we can do so with superiority. The number of places at which we can thus attack them depends mainly on the extent to which they are stretched. Our policy is therefore clear; we should stretch the German forces to the utmost by threatening as many of their vital interests and areas as possible and, holding them thus, we should attack wherever we can do so in superior force.

If we pursue the above policy we firmly believe that OVERLORD (perhaps in the form of RANKIN) will take place next summer. We do not, however, attach vital importance to any particular date or to any particular number of divisions in the assault and follow-up, though naturally the latter should be made as large as possible consistent with the policy stated above. It is, of course, valuable to have a target date to which all may work, but we are firmly opposed to allowing this date to become our master, and to prevent us from taking full advantage of all opportunities that occur to us to follow what we believe to be the correct strategy.[31]

This policy was the epitome of the British way of warfare. In it, there is an underlying weakness as Britain's military chiefs only wished to fight where they had 'superior force'; Britain's relatively small army may not be superior in France. As 1943 progressed, American military power overtook the British and they demanded and imposed greater influence on strategic decisions. The fulcrum of change tipped towards the American Chiefs' point of view in the latter half of 1943, and Britain's lesser role was confirmed at the EUREKA Conference in Teheran in November 1943.

The pressure to defeat Germany quickly and get on with the Pacific was constant, and the switch to a Pacific-first strategy became a greater subliminal threat at each of the Allied conferences. The British, with half an eye on the Balkans, wanted a much greater offensive commitment to Italy to break the Axis. The arguments between the Allies' principal commanders became so intense that junior officers were sometimes asked to leave to allow the seniors to argue without restraint or have 'a heart to heart' as CIGS described them.[32] The clashing priorities can be summed up by quoting directly from one of Brooke's previous diary entries of 24 May 1943:

King thinks the war can only be won by action in the Pacific at the expense of all other fronts.

31   TNA CAB 80/76/708: COS (43) 708 (0), OVERLORD AND THE MEDITERRANEAN –
      Draft Aide Memoire dated 11th November 1943.
32   Alex Danchev and Daniel Todman, *War Diaries 1939-1945: Field Marshal Lord Alanbrooke* (London: Wiedenfeld and Nicholson, 2001), p.406.

The 'Big Three' meet at the EUREKA Conference in Teheran in November 1943. Stalin, backing the US strategy demoted operations in Italy. Behind can be seen Admiral William Leahy, General Sir Alan Brooke, General Henry Arnold, Admiral Ernest King, General George Marshall and Field Marshal Sir John Dill. (NARA RG342-FH-000696)

Marshall considers that our solution lies in a cross-Channel operation, with some 20 to 30 divisions, irrespective of the situation on the Russian front, with which he proposes to clear Europe and win the war.

Portal considers that success lies in accumulating the largest air force possible in England and that then, and then only, success lies assured through the bombing of Europe.

Dudley Pound on the other hand is obsessed with the anti-U-boat warfare and considers that success can only be secured by the defeat of this menace.

Brooke considers that success can only be secured by pressing operations in the Mediterranean to force a dispersal of German forces, help Russia and thus eventually produce a situation where cross Channel operations are possible.

And Winston??? Thinks one thing at one moment and another at another moment…But more often than all he wants to carry out ALL operations simultaneously irrespective of shortages of shipping![33]

It is hardly surprising that such divided opinions at the very highest levels of Allied military decision-making resulted in the thing often lethal to effective military plans, the compromise, that allowed operations to proceed but without an optimum solution. The decision to conduct operations in Italy is one such result. This emphasis left the Mediterranean under-resourced to

33   Danchev and Todman, pp.409-10.

Prime Minister Churchill's military advisor, Major General Sir Hastings Ismay, British First Sea Lord, Admiral of the Fleet Sir Dudley Pound and the Chief of the Imperial General Staff, General Sir Alan Brooke on 22 May 1943 at the TRIDENT Conference in Washington DC. Two days later Brooke's strategic frustrations emerged in his famous diary. (NARA RG80-G-042152)

achieve British strategic ideas. The seesaw from British to US hegemony in their partnership had not entirely swung to the Americans in the first months of 1944. The American Chiefs, despite their convictions over the decisive blow still had to consider British sensitivities. Later in 1943, Brooke's diary gave an indication of his frustration at the British position with their principal ally:

> It is becoming more and more evident that our operations in Italy are coming to a standstill … Our build up in Italy is much slower than the German and far slower than I had expected. We shall have an almighty row with the Americans who have put us in this position with their insistence to abandon the Mediterranean operations for the very problematical cross Channel operations. We are now beginning to see the full beauty of the Marshall strategy!! It is quite heart-breaking when we see what we might have done this year if our strategy had not been distorted by the Americans.[34]

Brooke often used his personal diary as a release valve for the enormous pressure he was under. Nevertheless, the comments showed how different strategic philosophies were affecting strategy implementation by the end of 1943.[35] Despite his usual subservience to the arch anti-Italian campaign leader, Marshall, Eisenhower wrote the following to the CCS justifying the campaign:

34   Danchev and Todman, pp.462-3.
35   Michael Howard, *The Mediterranean Strategy in the Second World War* (London: Weidenfeld and Nicolson, 1968), p.47.

My principal commanders and I are in complete agreement that it is essential for us to retain the initiative until the time approaches for mounting OVERLORD, otherwise the enemy will himself seize the initiative and may force us on the defensive prematurely, thus enabling him to withdraw divisions from our front in time to oppose OVERLORD. If we can keep him on his heels until Spring then the more divisions he uses in a counteroffensive against us the better it will be for OVERLORD, and it then makes little difference what happens to us if OVERLORD is a success.[36]

This is subtly different reasoning than Brooke's, but no less emphatic. It also shows the paradox of the Italian campaign in that a quick win would not benefit the overall strategy. To Britain, operations in the Mediterranean offered strategic options. Italy, Greece, the Balkans or the South of France all had to be guarded by the Axis, thereby diluting their combat power. Invading Italy, however, would impose a huge burden on the Allied occupying force as they would have to govern, feed and repair the Italian state, all whilst fighting the Germans.

Putting every effort towards north-west France would have been obvious to Berlin as it was an all or nothing strategy with fewer dilemmas. It was not that Britain opposed the cross-channel invasion. If it became necessary it was supported, but their thoughts on war strategy were not fixed to a date, time and place when conditions would undoubtedly have changed. Despite this argument, the Mediterranean remained of little interest to the Americans and Stalin clearly preferred to dominate Eastern Europe free of British interference, even suggesting the suspension of operations in Italy to allow simultaneous invasions of Northern and Southern France.[37] With the benefit of hindsight, this was a ploy to keep the Allies out of south-eastern Europe. The death knell for major operations in Italy was sealed at Teheran in November 1943 with the following declaration:

'Overlord' and 'Anvil' are the supreme operations for 1944. They must be carried out during May 1944. Nothing must be undertaken in any other part of the world which hazards the success of these two operations.[38]

The compromises accepted by the Allies allowed Italian operations to proceed, but they were to become increasingly secondary as preparations for OVERLORD developed in early 1944. The CCS stated on 19 August 1943 at Quebec that the cross-Channel operation was the main effort with a target date of 1 May 1944; other operations would only receive resources if they did not interfere with it.[39] This decision disappointed the British, and the acerbic Brooke wrote in his diary, 'We have not really arrived at the best strategy, but I suppose that when working with allies, compromises, with all their evils, become inevitable.'[40] Italian strategy was to provide support to OVERLORD by occupying the maximum number of German divisions and preventing their redeployment. As Lieutenant Colonel David Hunt, one of the intelli-

---

36   Chandler et al, *Eisenhower Papers Vol III*, p.1529.
37   Richard M. Leighton 'OVERLORD Versus the Mediterranean at the Cairo-Teheran Conferences', in Kent Roberts Greenfield (ed.), *Command Decisions* (Washington DC: Center of Military History, Department of the Army, 2000), p.272.
38   Hinsley et al, p.17.
39   Churchill, p.79.
40   Bryant, *'Turn of the Tide'* p.715.

gence officers of General Officer Commanding-in-Chief, 15th Army Group, General Sir Harold Alexander, and a principal author of his war despatches, wrote, 'its aim was to draw German strength away from the Channel coast.'[41] There was no geographical objective, beyond securing airfields for the bomber offensive. Rome was a tertiary political objective, although the capture of a major enemy capital city was always going to have a seductive attraction, as proved to be the case.[42] Objectives such as Rome tended to be favoured over German fighting formations or less tangible military benefits. That this was so demonstrated by Clark's actions when he chose, against his orders, to capture Rome rather than trap and destroy the German Tenth *Armeeoberkommando* (AOK). One US officer, the Commanding General of the XII Air Support Command (ASC), Brigadier-General Gordon Saville, recognised the importance of the German army over Rome when he said: 'As an air commander, I wasn't particularly interested in Rome. What I was interested in was getting rid of that goddamn German Army.'[43]

Like their Chiefs, it took US combat commanders and units time to be fully prepared to take on the might of the *Wehrmacht*. Roosevelt was right before TORCH when he thought that his commanders must learn on the job. Leahy always preferred 1944 for the invasion year and ensured prioritisation of war production so that the Army would not be sufficiently ready to launch Marshall's preferred 1943 operation.[44] The risks of going early in the decisive theatre were just too great. The US Army had to suffer the taste of battle before it could tackle the very great trials of an invasion of northwest Europe. Like Britain who selected its winning generals in North Africa, the Americans had to conduct their ultimate job interviews in battle. Just like Wavell, Ritchie and Cunningham on the British side, American army generals Dawley and Fredendall were found wanting, making way for winners such as Bradley and Patton who would sweep the field in France. Only in the Mediterranean could this selection test be accomplished. It could not be achieved through attendance at a staff college or by studying a map. The Mediterranean was a secondary theatre; the war was not going to be lost there. Therefore, experimentation was possible, and mistakes were not strategically fatal. That a cross-channel invasion success was possible in 1942 or 1943 was a naïve thought. They would only get one shot and it had to happen when the Allies were absolutely prepared. At this time the Battle of the Atlantic and the campaign to seize air superiority over Germany had yet to be won. Even Hitler in his Directive of 28 January recognised that operations in the Mediterranean gave the Allies invaluable experience. It was not true, as many believed, that the British did not want a cross-channel invasion or that they were haunted by 'shadows of Passchendaele and Dunkerque' as US Secretary of War Henry L Stimson claimed.[45] The British knew from bitter experience in both wars the fighting qualities of the Germans and what it would take to defeat them.

The planning of complex military operations firstly needs the assigned commander to conduct a mission analysis. Eisenhower, universally known as 'Ike,' was the Allied Commander-in-Chief in the Mediterranean until January 1944. His rise through the ranks was meteoric. In summer 1943, he remained a substantive lieutenant colonel. Due to Marshall's largesse and confidence and the skill he had shown during North African operations, he was promoted three

41   David Hunt, *A Don At War* (London: Frank Cass, 1990), p.203.
42   TNA WO 70/55: AFHQ Appreciation of the Situation in Italy on 7 Feb 44.
43   AFHRA Iris NO 1103217, Interview with Major General Gordon Saville, San Antonio, Texas, dated 9 February 1970, p.51.
44   O'Brien, p.207.
45   Leighton, p.262.

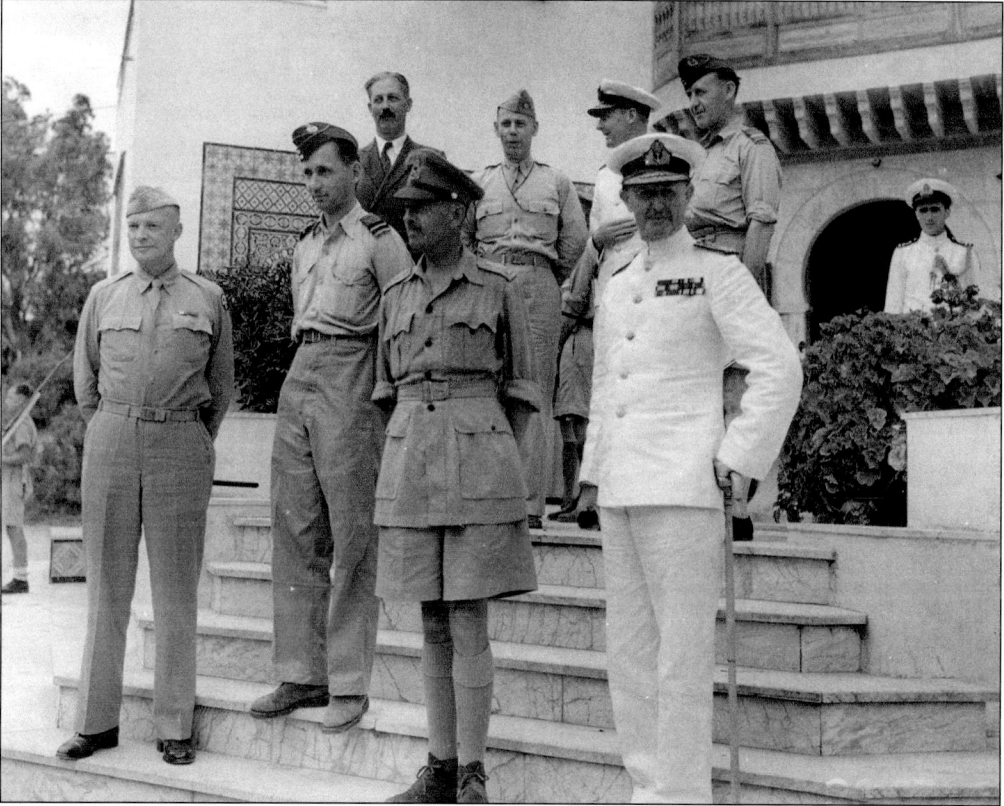

The C-in-C Allied Force, General Eisenhower and the 'committee' of Mediterranean commanders, a system he loathed. From l-r, Air Marshal Sir Arthur Tedder, General Sir Harold Alexander and Admiral Sir Andrew Cunningham. Eisenhower, the Operational-level commander relied on these officers for planning operations in the Mediterranean and Italy. (NARA RG342-FH-001016)

regular ranks on 30 August 1943 becoming a substantive major general. During his time in the Mediterranean, he had been responsible for the planning and execution of Operation TORCH, culminating in the Axis defeat at Cape Bon in Tunisia in May 1943. Although since November 1942 he had personally favoured an operation against Sardinia, he commanded the invasion of Sicily in July 1943 and the subsequent landings in mainland Italy, Operations BAYTOWN and AVALANCHE. Brooke in his diary, suggests that the British agreed to Eisenhower's command so that he could deal with the politicians whilst British generals managed the actual fighting.[46] He was a strategic general, good with people, able to bring fractious allies together, although he struggled with the British at first, calling early talks with them 'wearisome' and their methods of warfare 'dilatory.'[47] His decisions in the Mediterranean were often driven by the views of Marshall, with whom he had very regular contact.

---

46   Danchev and Todman, p.365.
47   Robert Ferrell, *The Eisenhower Diaries* (New York: W.W Norton, 1981), p.40.

He was keen on bold tactical actions, but at the operational level he could be somewhat conservative. He had been made aware early of the importance of cultural property in Italy and had placed the Abbey at Montecassino and the Papal estate at Castelgandolfo on protected target lists on 4 November 1943.[48] The secondary nature of the task and knowledge of his future role resulted in drift in the Italian campaign and he 'changed his mind too often' in the last three months of his command.[49] The result was a slow advance, putting excessive time pressure to capture Rome on those who succeeded him and whom he left behind. He remained under the spell of Marshall throughout the war, always referring to him as 'General' even after they became equivalent ranks. Eisenhower rose to the five-star rank of General of the Army and went on to lead the Allies to victory in Europe in May 1945.

His mission started with the strategy. In military terms this is usually articulated as the relationship between ends, ways and means. The art of the general officer is to plan operations within his means that achieve the ends. Strategy depends for success, first and most, on a sound *calculation and co-ordination of the ends and the means.* The ends must be proportioned to the total means.[50] The ends tell the commander the desired outcome, the ways, at the operational level of war, are the plans that describe the methods of how this should be achieved, and the means are the resources required to achieve the task. It is crucial, but often ignored, that the ways are appropriate to meet the ends. Equally important is that the means are sufficient to meet the ends. Most important is the unambiguous articulation of the ends. It does not matter how good the commander is, or how brilliant the operational plans are, if the ends are unattainable or vague, or the means insufficient to reach them. In the case of carrying the war to Italy, the ends statement was provided to Eisenhower on 20 May 1943. It read that he 'was to plan such operations…as are best calculated to eliminate Italy from the war and to contain the maximum number of German forces.'[51]

This guidance from the CCS appears clear. However, several problems can be deduced that added to his difficulties. Eliminating Italy from the war was not only a military problem and had to be coordinated at the political and diplomatic levels. It was also achieved early in the process, before Eisenhower had launched his main attack when Italy surrendered on the eve of the Salerno landings on 8 September 1943. The second task is more problematic, its wording highly ambiguous and open-ended. What does the term 'maximum number' mean? Intelligence available in late summer 1943 supported the conventional wisdom which expected the Germans to withdraw at least north of Rome, probably to the Pisa-Rimini Line and possibly to the Po Valley. Therefore, the Allies would contain no German divisions in Southern Italy. Could Eisenhower have claimed mission success if the Germans withdrew and sent their divisions to France or Russia? German Commander-in-Chief South, *Generalfeldmarschal* Albert Kesselring's persuasiveness with Hitler to defend Italy south of Rome was unexpected but allowed Allied strategy in Italy to be fulfilled. The problem with this strategy once this happened was that the strategic ends and the operational ways were incompatible, and the tactical means were insufficient.

48   TNA WO 214/38: Msg 0-1478 dated 4 November 1943, 15th Army Group to Fifth and Eighth Armies.
49   Dominick Graham and Shelford Bidwell, *Tug of War: The Battle For Italy 1943-45* (Barnsley: Pen and Sword Military Classics, 2004, pp.124-6.
50   Liddell-Hart, *Strategy*, p.322.
51   Ralph Bennett, *ULTRA and Mediterranean Strategy 1941-1945* (London: Hamish Hamilton Ltd, 1989), p.239.

To develop a plan of action, commanders go through a planning process. The first thing is to gain a thorough understanding of the current situation. For Italian plans this meant an understanding of the political situation between Germany and Italy, and the possible changes following the fall of Mussolini. The situation in late July was somewhat different to that encountered in early September 1943 and vastly different to February 1944. The enemy military situation also had to be considered. When planning began for the move into Italy, the Allies expected to face poor quality Italian divisions and Germans battered in Sicily, not high-quality units from Germany. Other factors are geography and climate and how they affect or constrain the planning. The second step is for commanders to analyse the mission, conducting an in-depth study on what immediate superiors and their superiors wish you to do. This must have been incredibly difficult for Eisenhower and for all his subordinate commanders. His immediate superior was the CCS, who all had different ideas on how the war strategy should be executed. Importantly, each ultimately controlled parts of the resources that Eisenhower would need. Above them were the political leaders, Churchill and Roosevelt. Brooke was clear that Churchill did not give clear strategic guidance, thereby adding to Eisenhower's planning difficulties, especially as the Prime Minister often tried to intervene directly, something Ike fought hard to resist.

The next part of the commander's appreciation as part of mission analysis is to work out what tasks have been given and, more intuitively, what tasks can be implied, but that are not specifically demanded. In the case of Italy air superiority was an implied task. Therefore, Eisenhower's operation to land a force on mainland Italy could not be further north than Naples, sacrificing an element of surprise in space if not time. This leads into an analysis of his freedoms and constraints. What had he been allowed to do and what could he not do to fulfil his superiors' strategic intent? In the case of Italy, this again caused some difficulties as the principal allies disagreed on the extent of Mediterranean operations and the resources that be given to Eisenhower. Planning is an ongoing process and the final step demanded that the commander considered changes. In Italy, changes to the plan, and therefore the resources required to accomplish it came along frequently. The first major change was of course the surrender of Italy, followed swiftly by the German decision to defend Italy in the south. These two critical events should have led to a reassessment of Allied planning. The resources required for invading and occupying a defeated Italy were different to those needed to overcome stubborn German defences. The predictable geography and the less predictable, but still inhospitable, climate of Italy should have pointed the Allies towards greater use of amphibious assaults along both Italian coasts. Not only were the resources for this not available due to OVERLORD, but any greater commitment to Italy was philosophically an anathema to the US Joint Chiefs.

Before being tasked at the TRIDENT Conference, Eisenhower tried to glean Marshall's intent for further operations in a letter on 19 April 1943. Eisenhower favoured Sardinia and Corsica if operations on Sicily went as planned.[52] Marshall advised him to plan for these operations, but almost ruled out Italy as it would prevent other operations elsewhere. Marshall did not favour any further Mediterranean strategy at all at this point. Following this advice, several courses of action would be developed by the AFHQ staff for consideration.

---

52   Chandler et al, *Eisenhower Papers, Vol II*, p.1097.

On 20 May 1943, after an off the record 'heart to heart' meeting the day before,[53] the CCS gave Eisenhower his assigned task.[54] This open-ended direction was largely an abdication of responsibility due to the disagreements between the British and American Chiefs as well as a *quid pro quo* for the British agreeing to 1 May 1944 as a target date for OVERLORD. The main protagonists met in Algiers immediately after the Washington DC Conference ended, but this resulted in only a minor shift in the American position. Eisenhower had set-up his planning staff by 25 May 1943.[55] Now that both sides agreed that victory lay across the Channel rather than through the Mediterranean, and as a conciliation to the British, the US Joint Chiefs stopped resisting continued Mediterranean operations as long as they did not impinge on OVERLORD.[56] Eisenhower refined his courses of action and developed two likely possibilities for Italy by 29 June 1943 for the toe and heel of Italy and for Corsica and Sardinia.

Eisenhower presented these thoughts at the end of June 1943, with the proviso that no firm decisions would be made until Sicily's success could be judged.[57] At this stage there was little consideration of Salerno. By mid-July 1943, Marshall and the CCS were warming to the idea of an amphibious operation in southern Italy and approved the venture on 16 July 1943.[58] Churchill was very pleased; he was given an inch by Marshall, and he intended to take a mile.[59] The next day Eisenhower cancelled plans to attack Sardinia and Corsica in expectation that any successful Italian mainland operation would see an Axis evacuation as they would be logistically unsustainable. On 18 July, in a note to CCS, Eisenhower reported that planning on an attack near Naples had been restarted, although it remained just one of several options.[60] An attack on the toe and instep of the Italian boot were preferred by 20 July. The thought to place a landing force around Naples itself was discounted due to air cover limitations from Sicilian airfields, but Salerno now offered some attraction, being just within fighter range and having a convenient airfield at Montecorvino. On 22 July, Brooke referred to Salerno as 'a gamble, but probably one worth taking.'[61]

The option was then presented by AFHQ on 24 July. The CCS would have preferred a landing further north, but they did not interfere at the operational level. On 26 July, the day after the fall of Mussolini, the CCS instructed Eisenhower to plan the landing in Salerno Bay, named Operation AVALANCHE, to be 'mounted at the earliest possible date.'[62] He tasked Lieutenant General Mark Clark's US Fifth Army to carry out the operation.

Clark would follow the same planning process to determine how his Army could meet the intent of firstly Alexander, the Army Group Commander, and then Eisenhower. By 9 August Eisenhower informed his subordinate commanders of the planned date of between 7 and 9 September 1943. On 16 August it was decided that elements of the British Eighth Army would

53   Danchev and Todman, pp.406-7.
54   Bennett, p.239.
55   Joseph P. Hobbs, *Dear General: Eisenhower's Wartime Letters to Marshall* (Baltimore MD: Johns Hopkins University Press, 1999), p.114.
56   Matloff, Kindle loc, 3306.
57   Chandler et al, *Eisenhower Papers, Vol II*, p.1224.
58   Trumbell Higgins, *Soft Underbelly: The Anglo-American Controversy over the Italian Campaign 1939-1945* (New York: Macmillan, 1968), p.85.
59   Matloff, Kindle loc, 3884.
60   Chandler et al, *Eisenhower Papers, Vol II*, p.1261.
61   Fraser, p.328.
62   AAFRH-15, p.31.

jump the Strait of Messina on 3 September in a supporting operation named BAYTOWN. The final decision to carry the war onto mainland Italy was taken by Eisenhower on 23 August 1943.[63] The Calabrian preliminary operation, however, gave the Germans a clue that the main event probably would not be very far north, narrowing the options to Salerno or Gaeta. Eisenhower's decision was approved by Allied leaders at the QUADRANT conference held in Quebec.[64] Despite this approval, it was made clear that no extra US reinforcements would be sent to the Mediterranean at the expense of the Normandy operation and that Eisenhower was to lose seven divisions from November 1943:

> As between Operation 'Overlord' and operations in the Mediterranean, where there is a shortage of resources, available resources will be distributed and employed with the main object of ensuring the success of 'Overlord'. Operations in the Mediterranean Theatre will be carried out with the forces allotted at 'Trident', except in so far as these may be varied by decision of the Combined Chiefs of Staff.[65]

Did the Italian campaign aid Normandy? On 6 June 1944, British, Canadian and American forces successfully overcame Rommel's Atlantic Wall. Facing them that fateful day were four poor quality infantry divisions. Rommel, Hitler's youngest *Generalfeldmarschal,* only had three *Panzer* Divisions, two of which were deployed close to the Pas de Calais with only one in the immediate assault area. The 709th and 716th Infantry Divisions were static divisions, relegated to coastal defence and manned with low quality troops, often Poles or ex-Soviet POWs and led by lower-quality German NCOs and officers. In the first ten days of the landing these divisions were virtually destroyed. Only the 352nd Infantry Division was of sufficient quality to effectively resist. This division defended the landing area of Pointe du Hoc and Omaha Beach. Despite being the best infantry division defending the Normandy coast, it was not top notch and contained worn-out soldiers from the Eastern Front. The assault on Omaha beach was a close-run thing and the US Army suffered significant casualties. 'Had there been a single manoeuvre element present near the beach, or even a handful of tanks as at Salerno, the battle for Omaha would almost certainly have ended in disaster for the Americans.'[66]

In Italy, there were 27 *Wehrmacht* divisions, seven of them were first-class manoeuvre divisions. Some have argued that Italy tied down more Allied soldiers than it did Germans. This is true, but it was not about the quantity, but about the quality. Despite all the complex assertions of historians, perhaps the point is best argued by a private soldier, a D-Day Dodger who fought in Italy:

> One indisputable fact was that the Germans, in the Parachute Division, sent their finest soldiers in the defence of the mountain stronghold. They fought with unsurpassed gallantry,

63 Martin Blumenson, *Salerno to Cassino* (Washington DC: Center of Military History, United States Army, 1993), p.24.
64 Arthur Bryant, *The Turn of the Tide 1939-1943* (London: Grafton Books, 1986), p.706.
65 TNA CAB 80/74/513: COS (43) 513 Part A, QUADRANT Record of Plenary Meetings and the Proceedings of the Combined Chiefs of Staff, Quebec, August 1943, dated 11 September 1943. Final Report to the President and Prime Minister.
66 Robert M Citino, *The Wehrmacht's Last Stand: The German Campaigns of 1944-1945* (Lawrence KS: University Press of Kansas, 2017), p.136.

and proved a very formidable foe, eliciting no small praise from the Allies whose job it was to attack the Cassino fortifications.[67]

Britain and America could afford to have their forces in Italy and Normandy, Germany could not. It had at most 30-divisions to fight in France; many of these were second- or third-rate outfits. The important question is: Why did the Allies face such poor opposition in an area that was considered at least a strong possibility as a landing ground for an expected invasion of mainland Europe, the defeat of which was strategically vital, and possibly decisive, for Hitler? The Allied strategic deception effort kept many of Hitler's best forces in the west in the Pas de Calais region, and the eastern front occupied the vast bulk of the German Army. Italy held several of the very best German defenders. Concerned with his southern flank, Hitler also held a considerable force in Yugoslavia and Greece, an invasion of which the Germans considered Italy to be a launch pad. This was two full AOKs out of 15 in the German order of battle, or around 40-divisions, 20 per cent of German ground forces.[68] They retained that fierce determination to hold-up the Allies through all the Cassino battles and continued to do so until nearly the last day of the war. Imagine the scene in Normandy had the beaches been defended by the 15th *Panzer-Grenadiers*, defenders on the Rapido, the 90th *Panzer-Grenadiers* or the 1st *Fallschirmjager* Division, defenders of Cassino? These German divisions inflicted extremely heavy damage on the 'D-Day Dodgers' of the armies in Italy. This is not idle speculation. At the beginning of 1944, the Germans had recognised their weakness in France and considered moving at least some mechanised units. The 3rd, 29th and 90th *Panzer-Grenadiers*, the 26th *Panzer* and the 1st *Fallschirmjager* divisions were all considered.[69] Two German divisions, one *Panzer* and one *Panzer-Grenadier* would have been moved from Italy to France in January 1944. At various times over 20-German divisions opposed the Allies at Cassino and Anzio, with another 14 in the Balkans. Almost all these were of higher quality than those that opposed the D-Day landings. It seems reasonable to surmise that without the Italian Campaign, the OVERLORD landings would have required much greater force to be successful or they could have failed. A short analysis of the speed with which German formations could deploy from all over occupied Europe in response to the Allied landing at Anzio reveals that a movement of these high-quality divisions from Italy to France would have been entirely possible. Most German soldiers, from general to private knew the war was lost by early 1944, yet they continued to resist fiercely, whether a supporter of the Nazi Party or not. They had taken an oath. Their country and their family expected them not to let Germany down. The same could not be said of a Pole or Ukrainian forced to fight on the Atlantic Wall with a German NCO's bayonet at his back.

The Italian campaign also gave the Allies vital experience in several areas that assisted this success. The US Army in early 1943 suffered a dramatic, but minor, setback in Tunisia at the Kasserine Pass. Although the operation in North Africa was ultimately successful, British commanders such as Alexander and General Sir Bernard Montgomery, had little confidence

---

67   J.M. Lee Harvey, *D-Day Dodger* (London: William Kimber, 1979), p.122.
68   Westphal, p.167.
69   Air Historical Branch Translation No VII/98. The Campaign in Italy Chapter VII – The Army Group's Version by General Westphal. Written for US Historical Division – December 1947, Translated by Air Ministry AHB6 – August 1950, p.10.

in US ability, assigning them a secondary role in Sicily. During early 1943, Alexander wrote to Brooke expressing serious concerns about US fighting ability. 'They simply do not know their job as soldiers,' he said.[70] Their performance remained patchy during the Salerno landings in September 1943, when the US VI Corps came perilously close to being forced off the beaches by smaller, but more experienced, German opposition. These doubts persisted even after the Anzio landings as evidenced by a report to Churchill from Alexander in February 1944, 'all the American higher commanders lack the years of practical battle experience we have had, and this is an undoubted weakness when it comes to fighting difficult battles against veterans.'[71] The Americans gained a lot of valuable practical battle experience between autumn 1943 and early summer 1944. Had their performance at Salerno been translated to D-Day as it would have been without the subsequent Italian campaign, the risks of failure would have been far greater, especially had the enemy been able to reinforce with better quality units.

In addition to experience, operations in Italy welded the British and Americans into a fighting team that engendered mutual trust despite the strategic disagreements and doubts over performance. Amphibious operations against defended coastlines are complex and hazardous undertakings. Getting them wrong results in disaster as at Dieppe in 1942. By June 1944, the Allies had a well-practiced team that had sharpened their skills in the Mediterranean theatre. Landings in North Africa in November 1942 and in Sicily in July 1943 taught the Allies much, but these were largely unopposed or opposed by limited enemy forces. The landings at Salerno and later at Anzio were both close-run things, where the desired ends were greater than the means available to achieve them. Despite this, both had succeeded in landing a force on an enemy shore and remaining there.

Allied air forces and armies were well-practised in supporting each other. Procedures developed by the British RAF and the British Army in the Western Desert had been improved and strengthened by the arrival of the USAAF during 1943 and early 1944. The USAAF arrived, however, as a subordinate to the Ground Forces, employed in a supporting role for ground operations. It took time for the American fliers in Italy to absorb lessons from the RAF and develop them to their own culture and practice. The skies over Italy allowed these air forces to integrate with the operations of land forces, developing air support request systems that proved so lethal in France. It also took time for the USAAF to adapt to the weather of the European theatre.

These command-and-control procedures in the Mediterranean were transferred to northwest Europe where they overwhelmed German land forces. That they could do this without effective interference from the *Luftwaffe* can be traced back to the campaigns in Africa, Sicily and Italy. During these campaigns Hitler committed thousands of combat aircraft, most of which were destroyed between November 1942 and June 1944. He could muster barely 200-sorties on D-Day compared with the Allied 14,000.

One key factor that prevented a swift Italian campaign was the availability of amphibious forces. Italy is mountainous, but it was not easy for the Germans to defend if the Allies had decided to use amphibious forces to threaten their rear areas. This may have forced Hitler to abandon its defence. The resultant redeployment of over 20-German divisions to other theatres could have been decisive, especially if they had gone to France. This is not what the Allies, especially the Americans, desired. On the other hand, an attack up the boot of Italy, which

70   Fraser, p.287.
71   TNA WO214/14: Alexander to Churchill MA1091 dated 11 February 1944.

was highly conducive to defence, would fix the Germans and keep them from reinforcing more decisive regions. The priority of OVERLORD denied this amphibious leap-frogging option to Allied commanders in Italy and Allied forces never received sufficient resources to achieve commanders' ambitions via the seaborne flanks and the only attempt nearly ended in disaster at Anzio. This was a factor that Allied senior commanders were aware of. In October 1943, Commander-in-Chief Mediterranean Air Command, Air Chief Marshal Tedder, had learned that Alexander, because of the terrain, his lack of options and the quality of defence 'saw no reason why we should ever get to Rome.'[72] The land campaign of attrition suited Allied grand strategy, but it came at a cost at the campaign or operational level and ultimately determined the type of operations that could be carried out. If obstacles such as the *Gustav* Line could not be circumvented, they must be tackled head-on with the consequences in casualties and damage to towns, cities and monasteries that this method could not avoid. The strategic decision to occupy Italy and the operational decisions made by Eisenhower and his staff to start at Salerno and work northwards made the clash at Cassino inevitable.

72   John Ellis, *Cassino: The Hollow Victory* (London: Andre Deutsch, 1984), p.25.

2

Mud and Mountains: The Winter Campaign

Germany is now on the defensive on all fronts. She has no decisive offensive capabilities. Her
military resources are inadequate to meet all of her defensive requirements.

United States Chiefs of Staff
Estimate of Enemy Situation – 1944 – Europe
as of 1 November 1943[1]

The US Army was concentrating on preparing the cross-Channel invasion. It did not want to leave considerable resources in the Mediterranean and had left insufficient combat units to raise a wholly American Army. The Fifth Army was landed in Salerno Bay with a single US Corps (VI Corps) and a British Corps (X Corps) along with US and British Ranger and Commando units. The US Fifth Army at Salerno had a greater proportion of British soldiers than American.

In September 1943, there existed the potential for an effective Axis resistance to the Salerno landings had the Italians not capitulated, and had German reinforcements been despatched sooner. Allied intelligence did not expect Hitler to defend southern Italy. This opinion was given in an Intelligence Report from the AFHQ JIC in Algiers on 7 August 1943 and signed off by Eisenhower's British intelligence chief, Brigadier Kenneth Strong.[2] Hitler had three strategic courses of action to consider. Germany could defend all of Italy and Greece, it could surrender all of Italy or it could defend part of Italy securing the agricultural and industrial north. In order of priority, AFHQ Intelligence judged that Germany would most likely make its stand on the Pisa-Rimini Line, with the next most likely a stand on the Po and then finally South of Rome. Their analysis pointed towards a steady withdrawal to a line between Pisa and Rimini and then to the Po Valley.

This viewpoint was also repeated by the JIC in London, who previously considered in April 1943 that the Germans would not risk disaster to defend a collapsing Italy.[3] Much of this intelligence was still assumed to be their intentions through ULTRA, although it had not been

---

1   Combined Chiefs of Staff Memorandum CCS 300/3 dated 18 November 1943.
2   AFHRA Reel A6024, AFHQ JIC (Algiers)/17/43 dated 7 August 1943 – German Strategy In Italy
     In The Event Of An Italian Collapse. Frame 0831.
3   Hinsley et al, p.5.

confirmed when the US Fifth Army executed Operation AVALANCHE on 9 September.[4] German intentions were confirmed through ULTRA intercepts the next day. This intelligence was the basis of the Allied Italian strategy decided upon at the QUADRANT conference. This strategy was split into three distinct phases:

> *First Phase.* The elimination of Italy as a belligerent and establishment of air bases in the Rome area and, if feasible, further north.
> *Second Phase.* Seizure of Sardinia and Corsica.
> *Third Phase.* The maintenance of unremitting pressure on the German forces in north Italy.[5]

The above *ways* to meet the strategy is based upon the assumption of a German withdrawal at least to the north of Rome. The subsequent stubborn defence by the German Tenth AOK in the Salerno area was therefore a surprise. The strong showing put doubts into Hitler's mind as to whether he needed to abandon Italy after all. Two senior German commanders, and fierce rivals, attempted to gain the upper hand. Kesselring was convinced that a defence of southern Italy was possible, whereas Rommel advocated a withdrawal to the Po. To achieve this defence, Kesselring had, under Tenth AOK, the LXXVI *Panzerkorps* in the east and the XIV *Panzerkorps* in the west. Upon reaching the mountains a third Corps was added, the LI *Gebirgskorps*.

A *Luftwaffe* officer, Kesselring commanded or controlled all German forces in Italy in February 1944. In *Hitler's Generals*, Richard Brett-Smith reserves the term 'great' for just two German generals. These are von Manstein and Kesselring.[6] Brett-Smith's view on Kesselring would be echoed by his British biographer, Kenneth Macksey, who compared him with the great von Scharnhorst. However, the chronicler of the *Luftwaffe*, Williamson Murray is less laudatory, considering him ineffective as the Chief of the Air Staff.[7] His tactics in Italy and especially as a *Luftwaffe* officer, the surrender of the Foggia airfields without a fight, are highly questionable.

Kesselring was Bavarian, born to an ancient aristocratic family but with more humble roots and without von in his name.[8] He had been commissioned into the Bavarian Artillery in 1906. In the First World War he served as an artillery officer on both the Western and Eastern fronts and became interested in aviation whilst in Metz in 1914.[9] He remained in the military joining the *Reichswehr Truppenamt* in 1922. Following promotion to *Oberst*, he was officially forced to leave the Army in 1933, being sent to the Reich Commissariat for Aviation. The Versailles Treaty barred Germany from having military aviation, so this organisation had a civilian façade. Responsible for the secret development of the *Luftwaffe*, Kesselring learned to fly at the age of 48. By 1936 he was a *Generalleutnant* and Chief of Staff of the *Luftwaffe*, which had come into the open as part of Hitler's defiance of Germany's treaty responsibilities. Germany debated

4   Hinsley et al, pp.107-8.
5   TNA CAB 80/74/513: COS (43) 513 Part A, QUADRANT Record of Plenary Meetings and the Proceedings of the Combined Chiefs of Staff, Quebec, August 1943, dated 11 September 1943, Implementation of Assumed Basic Undertakings and Specific Operations for the Conduct of the War 1943-44.
6   Richard Brett-Smith, *Hitler's Generals* (London: Osprey Publishing, 1976), p.221.
7   Williamson Murray, *Luftwaffe: Strategy for Defeat 1933–45* (London: Grafton Books, 1988), p.32.
8   Kenneth Macksey, *Kesselring: The Making of the Luftwaffe* (London: Batsford Books, 1978), p.16.
9   Macksey, p.21.

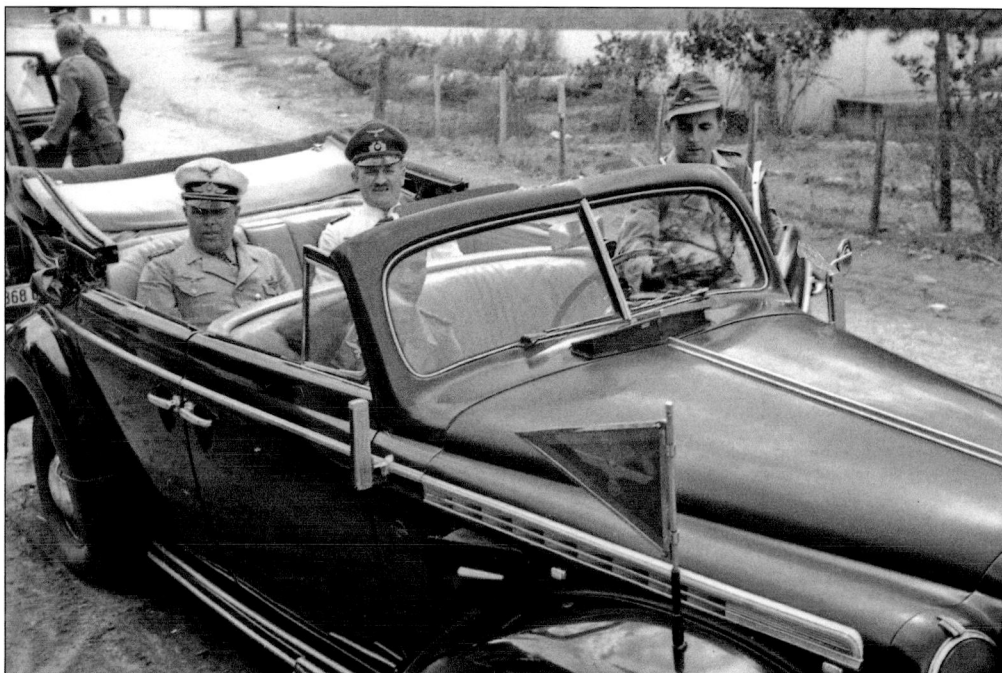

The German Operational level Commander, *Luftwaffe Generalfeldmarschal* Albert Kesselring. Unlike the allies, Germany had no separate land commander. Seated next to Kesselring is Commander German Tenth Army, *Generaloberst* Heinrich von Vietinghoff. (Bundesarchiv Bild 101I-304-0624-05A/Fotograf: Luthge)

whether to follow the British with its independent air force and long-range bombing or whether it should follow a route where support to ground forces dominated. Kesselring's predecessor, Walter Wever, favoured the former. He was killed in an air crash in 1936 and Kesselring, who favoured the latter, took over. From this point the *Luftwaffe* became the tool to deliver *bewegungskreig* but not strategic bombing, with all the repercussions that this decision realised in the war. Kesselring cancelled the heavy bombers that Wever may have brought into service.[10] The resource implications and technical difficulties of developing a four-engine bomber force were considerable and may not have been tenable whoever was in charge. The programme was cancelled in 1937.[11] His effective cooperation and some would say subservient attitude towards the land army was a double-edged sword. When things were going well, his use of German airpower was extremely effective. When on the back foot, the lack of a strategic long-range weapon to strike at Allied production or to interdict strategic communication nodes was a war losing deficiency.

He constantly clashed with his boss, Secretary of State for Aviation, *Generaloberst* Erhard Milch over command chains. This did not significantly affect his career. He was promoted to full *General der Flieger* and eventually sent to command *Luftflotte1* in Berlin. Kesselring was at the helm of operations throughout the first years of the war leading against Poland, Belgium and

10   Brett-Smith, p.236.
11   Pier Paolo Battistelli, *Albert Kesselring* (Oxford: Osprey Publishing, 2012), p.31.

Holland, France and in the Battle of Britain and subsequent Blitz, including command of para-troopers, gliders and air-landing forces. He was promoted to *Generalfeldmarschal* in July 1940 and played a key role in the Germans' cardinal error of switching attacks from the RAF to London.[12] In May 1941, his *Luftflotte* was transferred to Poland to support *Heersgruppenkommando* Centre, the principal thrust against the Soviet Union. His air fleet destroyed at least 2,500 Soviet aircraft and quickly achieved air supremacy. That November, he was appointed to the Mediterranean as Commander-in-Chief South, a joint command. This made him a rarity, in that only very few air force officers from any nation have commanded jointly at such a high level in wartime. This command was known as a *wehrmachtfeuhrung* and was the only one of its kind. It didn't last as jealousies and politics resulted in the *Luftwaffe* re-imposing direct command of air operations in October 1943, followed thereafter by the *Kriegsmarine*. This still made Kesselring a *primus inter pares* amongst German commanders, but he practised a supported/supporting control rela-tionship rather than overall command.[13] Kesselring found Rommel increasingly difficult, disa-greeing with him over whether to attack in Egypt or against Malta. Hitler sided with Rommel and the disastrous Egypt campaign resulted in his defeat at El Alamein in November 1942. Following Rommel's defeat and TORCH, Kesselring was on the defensive and despite numer-ical and qualitative weaknesses he showed his qualities by holding the Allies in North Africa for several months. Nevertheless, according to his Chief of Staff, his defeat in Tunisia left him 'out of favour' with Hitler.[14]

Kesselring anticipated the Sicily invasion and after a visit knew that he could only offer a delaying action. He thought that he could hold-up any rapid Allied advance in the difficult terrain south of Rome. In this plan he faced opposition from Rommel who was actively plotting against him and even from his own air commander, *General der Flieger* Wolfram von Richthofen.[15] Hitler had been concerned about the loyalty of his Axis partner for some time. From May 1943, he had made plans in case of Italian defection, although he had not trusted Kesselring with these due to his optimistic and pro-Italian outlook, initially planning his replacement once the Allied invasion started. As well as Rommel, he was opposed by the powerful OKW Chief of Staff, *Generaloberst* Alfred Jodl, and by the OKW, an organisation dominated by Army officers.[16] In August, Jodl and Rommel connived to have meetings with the Italians without Kesselring or his staff being present. This resulted in him offering his resignation on 14 August 1943; Hitler refused it.[17] A few days later Hitler received intelligence that the Italians were talking to the Allies. Many senior officers are often only optimistic with their superiors to enhance their career prospects. This was not the case with Kesselring. His optimistic outlook, according to his subor-dinate, the Commander of the German XIV *Panzerkorps*, *General der Panzertruppen* Fridolin

12   Murray, p.90.
13   Air Historical Branch Translation No. VII/98. The Campaign in Italy Chapter VII – The Army Group's Version by General Westphal. Written for US Historical Division – December 1947, Translated by Air Ministry AHB6 – August 1950, p.7.
14   Air Historical Branch Translation No. VII/98. The Campaign in Italy Chapter VII – The Army Group's Version by General Westphal. Written for US Historical Division – December 1947. Translated by Air Ministry AHB6 – August 1950, p.7.
15   Macksey, p.163.
16   Macksey, pp.162-3.
17   Ralph S Mavrogordato, 'Hitler's Decision on the Defence of Italy' in Kent Roberts Greenfield (ed.), *Command Decisions* (Washington DC: Center of Military History, Department of the Army, 2000), p.311.

von Senger und Etterlin, was down to deep convictions.[18] He also held beliefs, gained through experience, that Allied generals lacked creativity and that they demurred when faced with risks. This was a view that was proven to be correct again and again. When the Italians capitulated, followed immediately by the Allied operation at Salerno, the solid performance of the German defences and the slowness of the Allied advance started to convince OKW and Hitler that holding them south of Rome was indeed possible. The Allies initially became aware of this shift through ULTRA on 2 October 1943.[19] The key question was not whether southern Italy could be defended, but whether this was strategically beneficial?

Another area in which his record was deficient was intelligence. The Allies always achieved surprise at the tactical level. Kesselring possessed the agility of thought and action to be able to respond more quickly than his opponents. Throughout late 1943 and 1944, he was ably assisted by perhaps the best Chief of Staff (COS) in the German Army, *Generalleutnant* Siegfried Westphal. Westphal, young for his rank, was also at times COS to Rommel and von Rundstedt, and was, according to Senger, 'one of the best horses in the stable.'[20] As a reward for his Italian defence, Kesselring was awarded the Knight's Cross with Oak Leaves, Swords and Diamonds in July 1944, one of only 27-officers to be awarded this honour. Although he proved himself to be one of the most accomplished German military leaders, he also had a darker side. He was loyal to the Nazi Party, and carried out its bidding, including the exportation of Italian Jews to the death camps and the authorising of reprisals and atrocities against Italians.[21] Following defeat in May 1945, Kesselring was incarcerated and tried in 1947 by a British court in Italy for war crimes, specifically the killing of 335-Italian civilians in the Ardeatine Cave massacre in March 1944. He was found guilty and sentenced to execution; this was commuted to life imprisonment by an old adversary from the 15th Army Group, Lieutenant General Sir John Harding, possibly after interventions by Churchill and Alexander. In 1952 he was released on the grounds of 'ill health'. In retrospect, Kesselring was a better joint operational commander than he was a tactical commander and he performed better in the defence than he did in the attack. His key aptitude was his ability to influence those whom he needed to influence which included, unlike most German generals, the ability to occasionally persuade Hitler to change his mind.

German intelligence believed that Allied strategy was to use Italy for further operations in the Balkans.[22] This belief stemmed from concerns over Germany's southern European allies, Hungary and Rumania, and fears for the security of their principal oil supplies from Ploeşti. German intelligence was not aware of the disagreements between the Allies and the disinterest in the Balkans shown by the Americans. The German assessment remained the case by 15 September 1943 when Kesselring informed OKW that he expected an Allied attack on the Balkans once the Foggia airfields had been captured.[23]

Kesselring thought he could contain the Allies south of the Apennines for between six and nine months. German strategy wavered until around 4 October 1943, when ULTRA confirmed that the German Tenth AOK was to retire sparingly to a final defence line, the *winterstellung*

---

18   Frido von Senger Und Etterlin, *Neither Fear Nor Hope* (Novato, CA: Presidio Press, 1989), p.180.
19   Hinsley et al, p.14.
20   Brett-Smith, p.180.
21   Lamb, Richard, *War In Italy: 1943-1945 A Brutal Story* (Abingdon: John Murray Publishers, 1993 (2019 Kindle Edition), Kindle location 193.
22   Mavrogordato, *Command Decisions*, p.309.
23   Mavrogordato, *Command Decisions*, p.317.

south of Rome.[24] The intent to hold a line south of Rome was confirmed through a *Luftwaffe* intercept on 8 October.[25] Even then, Hitler had not made a final decision. In a message on 7 October to the Japanese Ambassador to Berlin, Hitler, perhaps somewhat boastfully, hoped to switch to the offensive in southern Italy. These fears remained throughout October, at least at the JIC in Algiers, and resulted in the abandonment of the Rome by November plan.[26]

One Allied operational level decision, questioned by a group of German senior officers, including Kesselring and von Vietinghoff, when interviewed after the war, was the decision to make the Italian west coast the Allied main effort, rather than the eastern route. Despite fierce battles, the terrain was far more favourable to the Allies than the fearsome route to Rome in the west. This decision, which appears never to have been seriously discussed by Eisenhower, was set following the Volturno crossings. The seduction of Rome, undoubtedly played its part. But as the German officers remarked, had the Allied armies broken out into the flatter terrain after Pescara, German formations in Rome and all western Italy would have been either forced to withdraw or risk being trapped as the Allies advanced through very little opposition to the Po Valley. Another advantage was that any German resupply and reinforcement down the Adriatic coast was extremely vulnerable as the rail line and the single highway, were adjacent to the coastline and within easy reach of naval gunfire. Once Eighth Army had seized the Foggia complex its operations in the east became secondary to Mark Clark's slow advance. The Germans, rightly as it transpired, assumed that the Allies wanted Rome. Switching their main defensive effort from west to east would have been an extremely challenging and slow task, especially when Allied air supremacy is accounted for. An Adriatic advance was more supportable from the sea than the west, with several ports already in Allied hands and substantial ports along the route of advance. An east coast amphibious assault, had it become necessary, would have been much more supportable than that at Anzio.[27]

The first main defence line, the *Bernhardt* or Winter Line, reached by Tenth AOK around 4 November, contained a switch line known as the *Gustav* Line that ran through the town of Cassino, and then headed south along the Rapido, Gari and Garigliano rivers to the Tyrrhenian Sea near Minturno. The infamous crossing of the Rapido by 36th US Infantry Division was actually a crossing of the Gari. The Gari flows towards the sea until it joins with the Liri River around Sant' Ambrogio, from whence it is known as the Garigliano. The position was decided by Kesselring when he visited Cassino on 19 September 1943. He was accompanied by the Japanese Military Attaché, Colonel Moraki Shimirz, who recalled the Italian General Staff exercise to defend the head of the Liri Valley.[28] The Tenth AOK began work on strengthening the position.[29] On 23 December 1943, Hitler declared Cassino to be of 'fortress strength'; it was declared by Jodl, in a sycophantic *volte face,* that the Cassino position 'must on no account be lost.'[30] From

24   Bennett 250, Hinsley et al, p.173.
25   Hinsley et al, p.173.
26   Hinsley et al, p.174.
27   German Version of the History of the Italian Campaign, 7 September 1949.
28   Canciani, p.40.
29   Ralph S Mavrogordato, *XIV Panzer Corps Defensive Operations Along The Garigliano, Gari and Rapido Rivers, 17–31 January 1944* (Washington DC: Foreign Studies Branch, Office of the Chief of Military History, 1955), p.4.
30   C.J.C. Molony, *The Mediterranean and Middle East, Volume V, Part II, The Campaign in Sicily 1943 and the Campaign in Italy 3rd September 1943 to 31st March 1944* (Uckfield: The Naval & Military Press Ltd, 2004), pp.694-5.

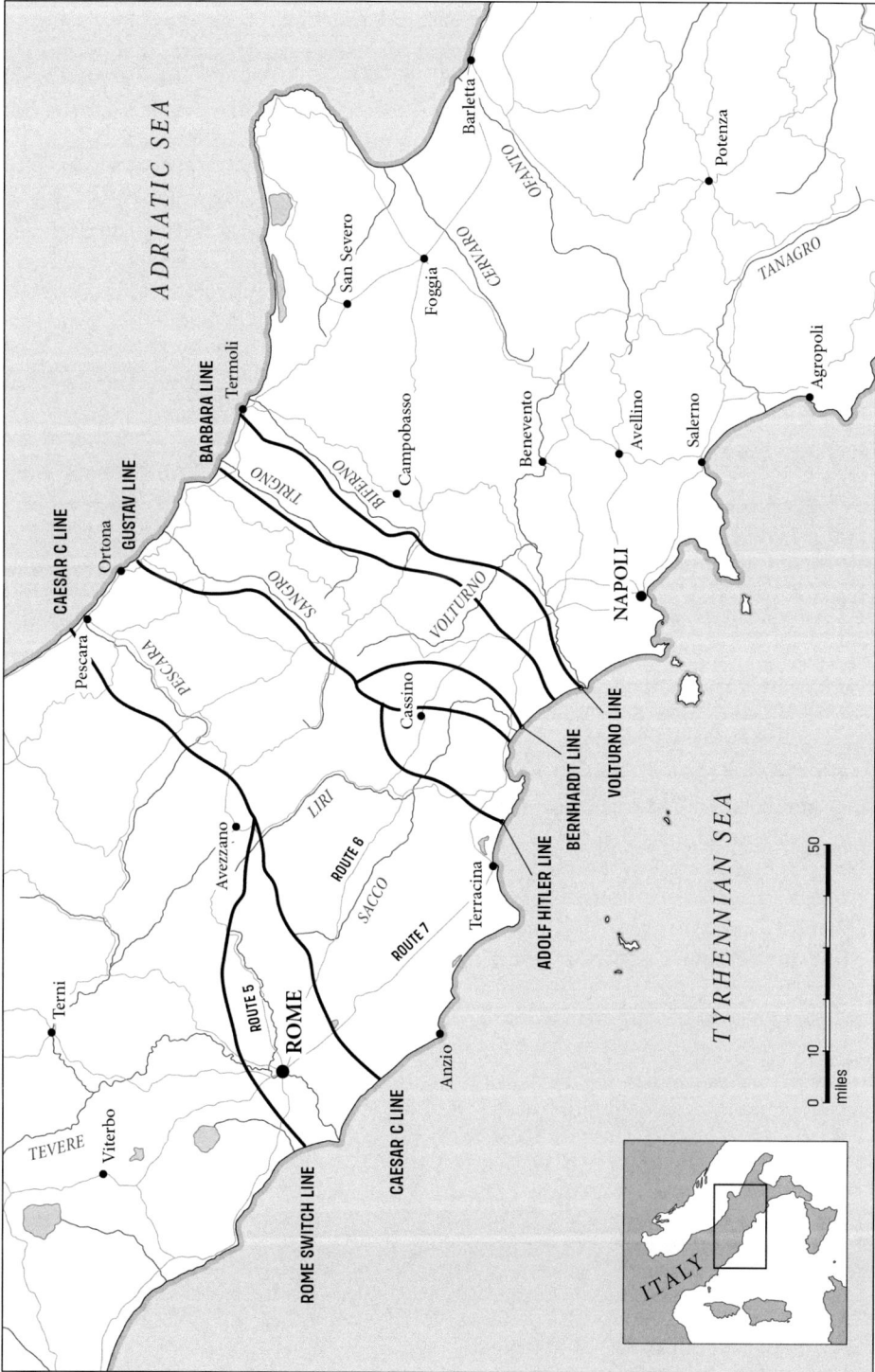

Map 1 German Lines.

a German perspective, Cassino was the obvious, indeed perhaps the only, place to make their stand, and by 7 January 1944, the *Gustav* Line was considered by the commander of the German Tenth AOK, *Generaloberst* Heinrich von Vietinghoff gennant Scheel, to be 'good' north and south of Cassino, but it 'needed improvement' in the Cassino area.[31] Beyond it stood the 10-mile wide Liri Valley, the only flat ground for miles pointing like an arrow towards Rome.

Despite the saying, only one road led to Rome for the Allies – Highway SS6, the Roman *Via Casalina*. The gap into the valley had to be defended if the Germans were to remain south of the Italian capital. Looking at it from the Allied point of view, the Fifth Army had to attack the gap if it didn't want a slog through the mountains. The high ground, therefore, was key terrain to both sides. The German defence was not placed at Cassino because of the Abbey, but because the high ground upon which it sat was the best terrain for a sound defence of the gap.

Because it was the obvious place to attack, it was also obvious that it would have the strongest defences. Senger stated in his War Diary that all were agreed in the higher German chain of command that an Allied advance through the mountains was 'inconceivable.'[32]

Hitler's change of heart was ironic. He perhaps foolishly chose to follow Kesselring's optimistic strategy, rather than taking Rommel's advice that the peninsula was indefensible. Hitler misread the Allied strategic intent, believing that a successful defence in Italy would discourage offensives elsewhere. This was a strategic blunder. Defending a secondary theatre made no strategic sense, except that an Allied occupation of Italy would open the Balkans and a possible link-up with the Red Army in south-eastern Europe, quickly depriving Germany of its main oil supplies. The defence of Italy did nothing positive to alter Germany's chances of winning the war. Jodl's deputy in OKW, *General der Artillerie* Walter Warlimont, commented after the war that, 'Hitler's Mediterranean strategy threw a far greater strain upon the German war potential than the military situation justified.'[33] In their pre-SEXTANT evaluation, the Allies made the assessment that by November 1943, the Germans had exhausted their manpower reserves. The only way to maintain their fighting numbers was to recruit the young, the old and to coerce foreigners and Nazi fellow travellers.[34] By deciding to defend south of Rome, Hitler played straight into Allied hands. Stephen Ambrose correctly pointed out that Eisenhower, by October 1943, had already fulfilled his strategic tasks of defeating Italy and tying down German divisions, 24 of which were then deployed in Italy.[35] By January this number had reduced to 21½. Of these, the front-line divisions were mostly around 50 per cent or less effective strength and those in the north were mostly inexperienced or untrained. The threat of Italy's defection had resulted in a threefold increase in German divisions in the Balkans between January and July 1943.[36] Even so, pressure needed to be maintained to keep them away from Normandy. Should the Allies have gone over to the defensive in Italy at this point? This would have allowed them to re-distribute forces to more important theatres, but it would also have allowed the Germans

---

31   Mavrogordato, *XIV Panzer Corps*, p.6.
32   Frido von Senger und Etterlin, *MS C095b – War Diary of the Italian Campaign* (Foreign Military Studies, Historical Division, US Army HQ in Europe, 1953), p.16.
33   Howard, p.44.
34   Combined Chiefs of Staff Memorandum CCS 300/3 dated 18 November 1943, Appendix.
35   Stephen E. Ambrose, *The Supreme Commander: The War Years of Dwight D Eisenhower* (Jackson, MS: University Press of Mississippi, 1999), p.283.
36   Mavrogordato, *Command Decisions*, p.310.

The Liri Valley, taken from the village of Rocco d'Evandro. The road to Rome, Route 6, runs through the Valley to Frosinone. The only flat terrain, the valley is dominated by high ground on both sides throughout its length. (Author)

Monte Trocchio, the Abbey and the entrance to the Liri Valley. (Author)

to do the same and the release of pressure may have allowed a recovery of sorts. Only a continued offensive strategy could contain the Germans and continue to eat away at their manpower and machinery.

Rommel was correct that Italy was indefensible from the sea, but the Allies had not bargained on the Germans defending lower Italy, expecting to be in Rome by late autumn.[37] There was insufficient shipping to execute the amphibious hop strategy as had happened in Sicily, only leaving the alternative of battling the difficult terrain and appalling winter weather head-on; a battle of attrition culminating at Cassino. Hitler, despite his no withdrawal rhetoric, understood Kesselring's battle in Italy was never to end in victory, but it could delay and frustrate the Allies and he was sometimes successful in getting permission to withdraw at least to Cassino.[38] These tactics forced the Germans from time to time, especially at Anzio, to pour forces into Italy which sucked up resources in line with Allied strategy to keep as many Germans as possible in Italy.

The ordeal of the US Fifth Army started in mid-September 1943 with a skilful withdrawal by the Germans to the north of Naples, where they were ordered to hold the Volturno River crossings, known as 'Position A,' until at least 15 October 1943 whilst preparing the defences further north.[39] The next defensive line, only briefly held was the *Barbara* Line that ran from the River Trigno on Italy's east coast across the country to the Tyrennhian coast. Kesselring had planned this scheme of withdrawal only days after the landings and kept to it with little change.[40] Hitler eventually stopped vacillating, deciding to defend Italy south of Rome on 21 November 1943, appointing Kesselring as *OB SUEDWEST* and Commander of *Heersgruppenkommando* C.[41] Prior to taking command, at his headquarters at Monte Sorrate, on 6 November, OKW gave him the following mission:

1.   Defence of Central Italy along the line Gaeta – Ortona.
2.   Defence of the coastline against possible invasion attempts with particular emphasis on the Genoa area and the coast along the Tyrennhian Sea in general.
3.   Pacification of partisan infested areas.
4.   Preparation of plans for an offensive in Apulia if and when Allied moves to mount an attack against the Balkans from Southern Italy should become apparent.[42]

This mission, known through ULTRA, made inevitable the battles at Cassino.[43] Shortly afterwards, Kesselring gained a valuable ally, one that slowed his opponents more than his grenadiers. At the end of November, it started to rain. It rained and rained, and the mud got deeper and deeper.

Senger, the new commander of XIV *Panzerkorps* and the principal architect of the Cassino defence began to plan his withdrawal to the *Gustav* Line in mid-November following the

37   Ambrose, p.282.
38   Macksey, p.215.
39   Blumenson, 'Salerno to Cassino', pp.191-2. Albert Kesselring, *The Memoirs of Field Marshal Kesselring* (London: Greenhill Books, 2007), p.187.
40   Kesselring, pp.186-7.
41   Kesselring, p.191. Blumenson, 'Salerno to Cassino', p.245. m, *XIV Panzer Corps*, p.8.
42   Mavrogordato, *XIV Panzer Corps*, p.9.
43   Hinsley, et al, p.179.

capture of the Mignano Gap. He was a Catholic petty noble from southern Germany and became a Rhodes Scholar at St John's College at the University of Oxford in 1912 where he became fluent in both French and English. He was cultured and intellectual, not presenting the typical Prussian officer profile. His education was cut short by war in 1914 and he returned home, accepting a commission in the cavalry. He remained in the *Reichswehr* gaining the rank of *Oberst* by 1938. His first combat upon the outbreak of war was in the Battle of France in 1940 where his cavalry brigade captured Cherbourg and Le Havre. He was promoted in 1942 to command the 17th *Panzer* Division in Russia where he took part in the attempted relief of Stalingrad as part of Fourth *Panzer* Army. He failed, and from that point he knew the war was lost. He was sent to the Mediterranean as a liaison officer to the Italian Army on Sicily and commanded German forces on Sardinia and Corsica.

General der Panzertruppen Fridolin Senger und Etterlin, the Commander of XIV Panzer Corps, defender of Cassino and lay member of the Benedictine Order. He is pictured following the bombing of the Abbey at his HQ at Castelmassimo with Abbot Gregory Diamare and his secretary Dom Martino Matronola. (Bundesarchiv Bild 101I-310-0892-06/Fotograf: Schmidt)

A month after the Allied landing in Salerno Bay, Senger was appointed as commander of the XIV *Panzerkorps*. He conducted a skilful defence and withdrawal over the winter, settling into the *Gustav* Line by mid-January 1944. His defence, in the face of overwhelming Allied superiority, was perhaps one of the finest examples of the military art in the entire war, but the costs were high. He was known as a competent and fair commander, whose political leanings were anti-Nazi. Nevertheless, his Corps did not always live up to these standards, for which he bears responsibility. Most notably, on 27 December 1943 in Cardito dei Collelungo, north-east of Cassino, soldiers of the 15th *Panzer-Grenadier* Division summarily executed 42-Italian civilians, including ten children. It does not appear that Senger knew about or condoned this behaviour, but under the rules of war as the commander he bore responsibility for his troops' actions.

He surrounded himself with like-minded staff officers including some closely acquainted with the attempted July coup of 1944. Stauffenberg had once been a junior cavalry officer under Senger's command. However much he hated Nazism, he remained true to his oath as a German officer and did not become involved. As an anti-Nazi who was aware of the plot, he admitted that his life was saved when Kesselring, who probably also knew of the plot as did Westphal, interceded on his behalf.[44] His task was to carry out his orders, although he understood that the war was a lost cause and he said that 'Evil, is having to continue to fight and fight, knowing from the beginning that we have lost this war.'[45] His war diary claims that, apart from the guard posted to ensure Germans did not enter the Abbey, he was the only German to do so between the evacuation in October 1943 and the destruction in February 1944 when as a lay member of the Benedictine Order he attended the Abbey for Christmas Mass. The Monks' diary tells a different tale. They record Dom Eusebio Grossetti, one of the monks, showed numerous German officers around the cloister.[46] Senger was also a friend to the Abbot Primate of the Benedictine Order, Baron Fidelis von Stotzingen. He was not motivated whatsoever to desire the destruction of the seat of his own monastic Order, but the irony is that Senger by his tenacious defence must take a portion of the responsibility for the Abbey's destruction.[47] He was an inspirational leader, known for his loping gait in the Italian mountains whilst visiting his forward units. His personality was very different to that of Clark, his principal opponent. He was self-effacing and considered climbing the hills to meet his men face-to-face a duty, although Clark was also not short of personal bravery. He would talk, eat and learn from his soldiers. His career was the last thing on his mind. Following the Cassino battles, he continued to withdraw his corps slowly north of Rome until the end of April 1945 when he negotiated the surrender to the US Fifth Army.

By the end of November 1943, the German defences on the *Bernhardt* Line, also known as 'Position B' around Venafro were beginning to buckle, although Senger still held the key positions of Monte Camino and Monte Sammucro. By 10 December both these bastions had been lost. The next allied objective was the village of San Pietro Infine, the battle for which was immortalized by John Huston's 1945 film, '*The Battle of San Pietro*', and the heights of Monte Lungo. San Pietro was eventually captured on 16 December by the US 36th 'Texans' Infantry Division. This small village cost the division 1,200 casualties; a month later the same division would attempt to cross the Rapido at Cassino with lots of green troops and disastrous results. The efforts against fierce defences, harsh terrain and miserable weather had taken their toll. Alan Moorehead reported their suffering before Christmas 1943:

> There comes a time when the mind will react no more to cold and danger. Those who had been exposed up there for two days and nights slept waist deep in water. In utter weariness they lost all sense of time and place and even perhaps a sense of hope. Only the sense of pain remained, constantly reiterated pain that invaded sleep and waited for the end of sleep to increase. For these soldiers the risk of war had passed out of consciousness and was replaced by the misery and discomfort of war, which in the end is worse than anything.[48]

The equally bitter battle that British X Corps fought on Monte Camino may also have influenced future thoughts on the German occupation of Montecassino. The correspondent for the

44   Macksey, p.217.
45   Guiseppe Trulli, *Von Senger: Un uomo, un generale* (Italia Storica E-Book), Kindle location 603.
46   David Hapgood and David Richardson, *Monte Cassino: The Story of the Most Controversial Battle of World War II* (New York: Da Capo Press, 2002), p.102.
47   Ellis, *Hollow Victory*, p. xvi.
48   Ellis, *Hollow Victory*, p.31.

Generals Eisenhower, Clark and Gruenther visit Major General Walker of the US 36th (Texans) Infantry Division in December 1943. (NARA RG111-SC-443420)

British *Daily Telegraph,* Christopher Buckley, reported that German soldiers made a last stand in a monastery close to the summit.[49] In mid-December, Brooke visited Italy and he concluded that the conditions and the enemy would not allow the current operations to succeed and that more landings were necessary. On the summit of Monte Camino, he could see Monte Cassino in the near distance whilst discussing the *Gustav* Line plan with Alexander.[50] Did the two Irish Protestant generals discuss the fate of the Roman Catholic Abbey? There were months more of winter, many more peaks and mountains and they had not yet faced the toughest defences. These were yet to come and there would be little respite for the hard-pressed Allied divisions playing second fiddle to Normandy from now on. On 12 January, Alexander stressed that the Germans must not be allowed respite.[51] Unfortunately, that meant no rest for his soldiers either, but this generated surprise for the Allied armies as the Germans expected them to undertake a recuperation period before attempting Cassino.

In early 1944, Vietinghoff had prepared the area around Cassino or 'Position C', with great care. He bore overall responsibility for the defence against both the British Eighth and US Fifth

---

49   Christopher Buckley, *The Road To Rome* (London: Hodder and Stoughton, 1945), p.246.
50   Danchev and Todman, p.501.
51   Ellis, *Hollow Victory*, p.37.

Armies from his headquarters near Avezzano. His army had a ration strength of over 270,000 men, but only 88,000 were effective. He was born in Mainz and was the son of a general.[52] Lying about his age, he joined the German Army at 15-years old and served on both the western and eastern Fronts in the First World War. Remaining in the *Reichswehr* he had risen to *Generaleutnant* by 1938 and saw active service in Spain. He was commanding the 5th *Panzer* Division in the invasion of Poland. Again promoted, he commanded XIII *Armeecorps* in the invasion of the west in 1940 and XXXXVI *Armeecorps* in the invasion of Yugoslavia in April 1941 and in *Heersgruppenkommando* Centre during Operation *BARBAROSSA*. Promoted again in December 1941, he was posted to command the Ninth AOK in Russia and then the Fifteenth AOK in France where he remained until he was retired due to ill health. Recalled to active duty he was posted to command the Tenth AOK in Italy in August 1943, becoming Kesselring's tactician for developing the German defences in southern Italy. During his retreat northwards in late 1943, after a particularly difficult time for his army he asked Kesselring to be sent on sick leave, although he had returned to duty before the Cassino battles began. After a brief period in command in East Prussia in January 1945, he returned to Italy to replace Kesselring in March as commander of *Heersgruppenkommando* C. He negotiated an independent surrender with the Allies in late April 1945. Vietinghoff was detained by the British until 1947 when he was released.

The Allies slowly advanced, and by February 1944, the Eighth Army had advanced as far as the River Sangro and remained to the east of the Abruzzi. The Fifth Army had reached the River Garigliano in the west. Clark's army at the beginning of February was even more heterogeneous than it had been at Salerno and had expanded to four corps. He retained the US VI Corps, although this was now a multinational corps comprising a British division, as well as its US units. It landed at Anzio on 22 January 1944. On the main *Gustav* Line, Clark still possessed the British X Corps, but had also gained the US II Corps and the French Expeditionary Corps (FEC). US II Corps comprised two US infantry divisions (34th and 36th) and a Combat Command (Brigade sized) of the US 1st Armoured Division. It was commanded by Major General Geoffrey Keyes.

He was a career cavalry officer, and his soldiers had the closest contact with the Abbey as they battled on the Cassino massif in late January and early February. He graduated from West Point in 1913 and fought in the Pancho Villa punitive expedition but did not serve on the western Front. By 1940, after various staff and command positions, he was a Colonel serving as Patton's COS in the 2nd Armoured Division. He rated him very highly, and he was promoted to Brigadier-General in December 1941, commanding Combat Command B in the 3rd Armoured Division. In July 1942 he was again promoted to establish the 9th Armoured Division. His first combat was again under Patton in Sicily, where he was given the responsibility of capturing the western half of the island for which he commanded a provisional corps of three divisions. Although his achievement was impressive, he had not yet been tested against quality German units. His chance was to come when he was appointed to command US II Corps in September 1943, deploying it into the Italian battlefield in November. A career armour officer, it was his subordinate divisional commander, General Fred Walker's opinion that he was out of place in infantry battles, although his tactical views on the inadvisability of Clark's Rapido plan were sound, although the poor prospects for the 36th Infantry Division and the exploiting armoured

---

52   Jeffery Plowman and Perry Rowe, *The Battles of Monte Cassino Then and Now* (Old Harlow: Battle of Britain Publishing, 2011), p.18.

The Commanding General of US II Corps at Cassino, Major General Geoffrey Keyes, standing second left, next to his mentor, Lieutenant General George Patton. (NARA RG18-JC0002)

combat command at the Rapido were obvious. Keyes was a devout Roman Catholic, which may have influenced his absolute opposition to the bombing of the Abbey. He remained in command of his corps throughout the Italy campaign, and after the war was promoted to lieutenant general eventually inheriting the US Third and Seventh Armies – Patton's commands.

The FEC under General Alphonse Juin, comprised 65,000 North African troops with French officers. His two divisions were the *2nd Division d'Infanterie Marocaine*, commanded by *General de division* Andre-Marie Dody and the *3rd Division d'Infanterie Algerienne* commanded by the 'Gascon Gentleman', *General de division* Joseph de Monsabert.[53] A potentially delicate issue was quickly resolved by the pragmatic attitude of Juin. He had commanded all French troops in North Africa and was a full *General d'Armee*, one rank senior to Clark. Juin decided to revert to the rank of *General de Corps d'Armee*, the US equivalent of Lieutenant General.[54] Juin was a mountain warfare expert having fought in the Rif in the 1930s, but when Clark and Juin first met, the Frenchman sensed some embarrassment in his younger American commander. He felt that Clark had no confidence in the French and that his intention was to use them only as auxiliary forces.[55]

53   Alphonse Juin, *Campagne d'Italie* (Paris: Editions Guy Victor, 1962), p.27.
54   Anthony Clayton, *Three Marshals of France* (London: Brassey's, 1992), p.79.
55   Juin, p.40.

On 15 January 1944, soldiers from two regiments of the US 34th (Red Bull) Infantry Division, commanded by Major General Charles 'Doc' Ryder, clambered to the summit of Monte Trocchio, the last peak before the *Gustav* Line. It had been abandoned, the Germans having retired into their main defensive positions.[56] The German XIV *Panzerkorps*, defending the *Gustav* Line from the Abruzzi Mountains north of Cassino to the Tyhrennian coast withdrew its divisions gradually giving the weakest divisions, the Austrian 44th (*Hoch und Deutschmeister*) Infantry and 5th *Gebirgs* Division, more time to establish their defensive positions whilst using the more accomplished 29th *Panzer-Grenadier* Division as the rear guard. These too were forced back after the capture of the village of Cervaro opened the way to Trocchio and the neighbouring Monte Porchia.

By 17 January 1944 Senger's Corps had an effective strength of just over 27,000 men, approximately half its assigned strength.[57] That the Abbey was likely to be damaged was accepted by the German defenders, but Senger and the German Tenth AOK commander faced a different dilemma. They needed Monte Cassino as part of the defence, but they knew that to defend it could result in damage. They assumed, probably rightly, that the Allies would not respect Monte Cassino as neutral ground. Vietinghoff gave orders that the Germans were to refrain from occupying the Abbey, but only the Abbey – 'only the building alone is to be spared.'

The campaign had been expensive, with 37,773 casualties in Fifth Army.[58] It was to cost many more lives in the next months. It had taken the Allied armies four months to reach the *Gustav* Line; it would take them five more and four bloody battles to break through the stubborn defences to Rome, only 80-miles to the north-west. The plan to breach it was assessed by one of the generals as, 'a worse plan it would be difficult to conceive.'[59] The question of the strategic value of the Cassino battles when compared to their costs is one that has been argued for the last 80-years. Whatever the value, getting north of Rome was important for the success of Allied strategy agreed with Stalin. Rome should have fallen by January 1944 to allow the concurrent operations in north-western and southern France to proceed as planned.[60] This had not happened and therefore the commanders in the Mediterranean came under ever increasing pressure from their grand strategic masters. In planning for Anzio on Christmas Day 1943, Churchill wrote the following to his CoS:

> I am in agreement with your general line of argument, but facts are as follows: we cannot leave the Rome situation to stagnate and fester for the three months without crippling preparation of 'Anvil' and thus hampering 'Overlord'. We cannot go to the other task and leave this unfinished job behind us.[61]

The strategic consequences of the failure of the first two battles at Cassino, including the destruction of the Abbey, are contained in a paragraph sent by Wilson to the British CoS on 22 February 1944:

56   John Breit, *Phase VIII 135th Infantry Regiment History* <http://www.34infdiv.org/ history/135inf/135inf_jb4312.pdf > (accessed 4 June 2010).
57   Mavrogordato, *XIV Panzer Corps*, p.19.
58   Fifth Army History Part IV – Cassino and Anzio, p.188.
59   Lucian Truscott, *Command Missions* (New Orleans, LA: Quid Pro Books, 2012), p.289.
60   John Ehrman, *Grand Strategy Volume V, August 1943-September 1944* (London: HMSO, 1956), p.207.
61   Ehrman, p.217.

I recommend that 'Anvil' be cancelled and that I be given a fresh directive to conduct operations with the object of containing the maximum number of German troops in Southern Europe with the forces now earmarked to be placed at my disposal including an assault lift for one division plus.[62]

The price of failure was not the cancellation of ANVIL, but it could no longer be launched concurrently with Normandy, thereby breaking a promise made to Stalin. The final plenary meeting in Teheran had made it clear that both OVERLORD and ANVIL could not be compromised. Failure to crack Cassino, and failure to get to Rome in February 1944 meant that they were.

62   Ehrman, p.231.

3

Across the Rapido: The First Battle of Cassino

From a military standpoint it was an impossible thing to attempt.

Feldmarschall Albert Kesselring[1]

The Commander in Chief of the 15th Army Group and the overall land commander was Alexander. His plan to overcome the defences south of Rome was his favourite 'double-punch' laid out in Operations Instruction No.32 of 2 January 1944.[2]

1. Fifth Army will prepare an amphibious operation of two divisions plus to carry out an assault landing on the beaches in the vicinity of Rome with the object of cutting the enemy lines of communication and threatening the rear of the German 14 Corps. The operation will take place between 20 January and 31 January 44, but the target date should be as near 20 January as possible to allow a few days should bad weather cause a postponement.

2. The main forces for the operation will consist of:
   Commander – Maj General J P Lucas commanding VI US Corps
   Hq VI Corps (US)
   An armoured element (US)
   Ranger Battalion (US)
   1 RCT 82 Airborne Division (US)
   1 Division (British)
   An armoured element (British)
   Two commandos (British)

3. Eighth Army will release 1 Division for the amphibious operation as soon as possible followed by 5 Division to reinforce 10 Corps. It is of the utmost importance that the move of these divisions is kept secret from the enemy. Eighth Army will maintain

---

1   Rick Atkinson, *The Day of Battle: The War in Sicily and Italy, 1943-1944* (New York: Henry Holt and Company, 2007), p.349.
2   Headquarters 15th Army Group, Operations Instruction Number 32, 2 January 1944. Appendix E

sufficient pressure and take all deceptive measures to prevent the Germans from transferring divisions from the northern sector of the front to that opposing Fifth Army. Cover plans and deceptive measures will be coordinated by this Headquarters. If Eighth Army, in spite of its reduction in strength can reach the PESCARA line and develop a threat toward ROME through POPOLI by 20 January this would have a great bearing on the success of the whole operation. Reserve formations such as Headquarters Canadian Corps and 4 Indian Division will be moved forward to make show of strength on Eighth Army front.

4. Fifth Army will make as strong a thrust as possible toward CASSINO and FROSINONE shortly prior to the assault to draw in enemy reserves which might be employed against the landing forces and then to create a breach in his front through which every opportunity will be taken to link up rapidly with the seaborne operation.

The aim was the destruction of German forces on the *Gustav* Line by cutting their communications and attacking them in the rear. The plan to go to the Alban Hills came later and the Fifth Army Outline Plan for Anzio on 12 January 1944 has the Alban Hills as its mission once the beachhead was seized and secured. The initial punch was to be delivered at Cassino, where the Fifth Army faced four German divisions plus two additional regiments and a *Panzer* division in reserve.[3] Clark's seven and a half divisions was insufficient to breakthrough on a wide frontage as he planned. He should have created a doctrinal three to one advantage by concentrating his force against an enemy vulnerability, but instead his plan was to attack in four separate places. None of these attacks on their own had much chance of overcoming the German defences, especially as they were not well synchronised.

The division was the basic combat unit for both sides, but German divisions were smaller than those of the Allies. In Italy, they had an average effective strength of around 60 per cent – all divisions manning the *Gustav* Line were between 4,500-5,000 men effective strength by 20 January. The German *infanteriedivision* generally comprised three infantry regiments, one artillery regiment, a reconnaissance battalion, an anti-tank battalion, an engineering battalion, and a signals battalion. An infantry regiment had an effective strength of around 1,000 and the strength of battalions was 5-600 men. There were also motorised, or *Panzer-Grenadier* divisions which unlike the infantry divisions, had two or three motorised regiments and a tank battalion. On 17 January these were the 5th *Gebirgs* Division, the 44th Infantry Division, the 15th *Panzer-Grenadier* Division and the 94th Infantry Division. The 211th Infantry Regiment from the 71st Infantry Division and the 8th *Panzer-Grenadier* Regiment from the 3rd *Panzer-Grenadier* Division were also in the line and the Hermann Göring *Panzer* Division was in army reserve. This 'private' *Luftwaffe Panzer* Division had been in Italy since its reformation in June 1943 and comprised a full *panzer* regiment and nominally two *panzer-grenadier* regiments; it had been short of infantry since before Salerno, only possessing two battalions in December 1943. It was due to be replaced by the 71st Infantry Division from Trieste. All these units had been destroyed either at Stalingrad or Tunisia and had been reformed in the latter part of 1943.[4] In its SHINGLE Intelligence Summary, dated 16 January 1944, Fifth Army G-2 suggested

3   Mavrogordato, *XIV Panzer Corps*, p.18.
4   German Order of Battle, February 1944.

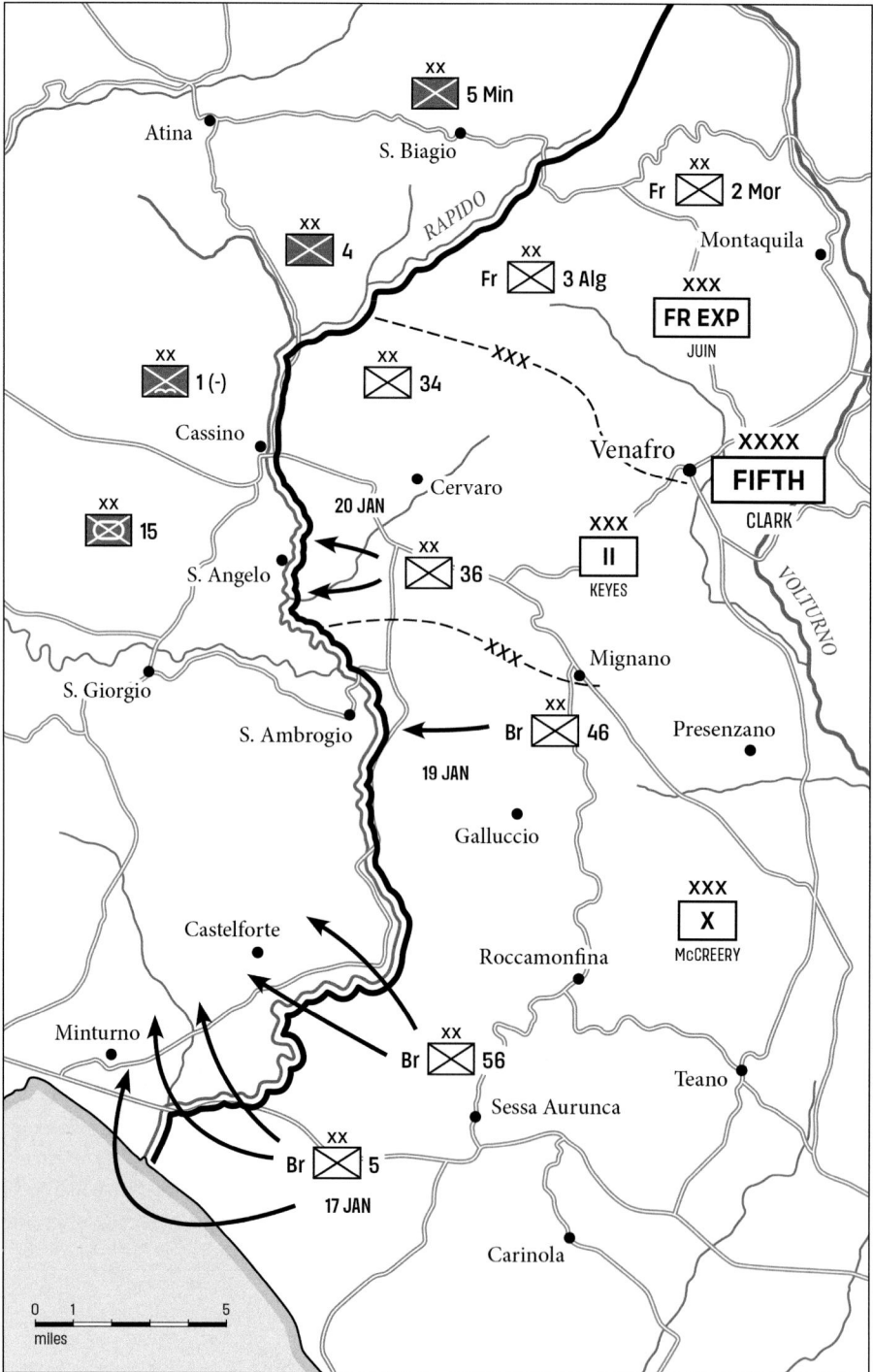

Map 2 The First Battle.

that the German strength was 'ebbing due to casualties, exhaustion and possibly lowering of morale.'[5] This assessment would turn out to be wishful thinking.

Despite the hardships, Clark's exhausted corps were to attack immediately between Cassino and the sea in separate and sequential attacks. German intelligence felt their presence on 13 January. The newly arrived FEC was to attack through the high ground north of Cassino against the weak 5th *Gebirgs* Division, swinging south, bisecting the Liri valley behind the *Gustav* Line and cutting-off Cassino. Senger considered the French to be superior to his mountain division and was concerned that their attack towards the village of Atina could unlock the entire position.[6] He had reinforced the mountain soldiers with mixed units from the 3rd *Panzer-Grenadier* Division, the 15th *Panzer-Grenadier* Division and the 305th Infantry Division facing the Moroccans and the 44th Infantry Division facing the Algerians. The French Corps began its attempt to outflank Cassino on 12 January with the Moroccans heading for the village of San Biagio and the Algerians heading for Sant Elia. According to Juin, Clark gave him freedom of action in this task. This was unusual, as Clark did not permit such freedoms with his other corps commanders. Perhaps he now fully trusted the Frenchman in the mountains, or possibly he accepted that this advance was secondary to his plan and he viewed the outcome as unimportant? The French had reached the upper Rapido by 15 January, delivering a hard knock to the opposing German mountain troops, who that night retreated into the *Gustav* Line west of the Rapido. Sant Elia had fallen to the French by 16 January, where Juin paused until 21 January. Near San Biagio, the Moroccans faced a mountain bastion on the road to Atina, the 3-mile-long ridge of L'Arena Hill and the peaks of Monte Carella, Monte Bianco and Monte Cifalco, the last of these a key position within Senger's defences.

The German engineers who surveyed the terrain for the planned defensives were not mountain troop engineers and they underestimated the abilities of trained mountain soldiers to scale steep slopes. Juin observed in his diary:

> With an extra division, perhaps it could have been possible on the evening of 15 January to penetrate deeper towards Atina, a strategic point on which we could develop a wide flanking movement into the Liri Valley. But behind my two exhausted divisions I have nothing left.[7]

That he didn't get the extra division he attributed to Clark, saying in his memoir, 'I only had two divisions and was quite out of breath. Nothing was coming behind them because the Anglo-Saxon war leadership was lacking a logical and clearly defined army manoeuvre.'[8] Juin renewed his offensive on 21 January with the Algerians aiming to capture Monte Bianco and the Moroccans La Manna Hill.[9] The Moroccans began badly, forcing a day of reorganisation on 22 January. The next day saw success for the Moroccans and the Algerians captured Monte Carella, but the attacking regiment suffered 75 per cent casualties. That day, Juin was told by Clark

5   HQ Fifth Army, SHINGLE intelligence Summary No. 9 dated 16 January 1944 in V Army Outline Plan for Operation SHINGLE (Military Library Research Service).
6   Senger, *War Diary*, p.45.
7   Angelos Mansolas, *Monte Cassino January–May 1944: The Legend of the Green Devils* (Fonthill, PA: Fonthill Media, 2017), p.32.
8   Juin, p.58.
9   Fifth Army History Part IV, p.49.

that he was to support the northern flank of the 34th Infantry Division around the Belvedere and Monte Abate and his push to Atina ended. He was aware of the lack of forces for such a formidable task and had been so since he arrived in Italy. The failure of the principal Allies to adequately support its offensive prompted a prescient letter to his superior, *General* Henri Giraud in December 1943 stating that the Allies were short of at least ten divisions.[10]

This remained the case a month later and fortunately for Senger and unfortunately for the Abbey, the extra division never came. Clark had little confidence in the French ability and could not rely on them because of poor performance in the war thus far and therefore he did not exploit their success, although the 5th *Gebirgs* Division was shattered, had fewer than 200-effective soldiers, and poor morale.[11] Juin was highly critical of British and American failure to exploit his success. Had they done so, it is arguable that the Abbey would have been spared.

Alexander hoped that these initial moves would force Kesselring to commit his reserves, easing the path for a two-division amphibious assault at the seaside resort town of Anzio, 35-miles south of Rome on 22 January 1944. These were the British 1st Infantry Division and the US 3rd Infantry Division. The Intelligence Summary from Fifth Army thought the same:

> In view of the weakening of enemy strength on the front as indicated above, it would appear doubtful if the enemy can hold the organised defensive line through CASSINO against a coordinated Army attack. Since this coordinated attack is to be launched before Operation SHINGLE, it is considered likely that the additional threat created by SHINGLE Operation will cause him to withdraw from his defensive position after he has appreciated the magnitude of that operation.[12]

Time was of the essence as the assault shipping in the Mediterranean was needed for OVERLORD. It was therefore impossible for Alexander to allow Fifth Army sufficient rest and reorganization if he was to take advantage of Churchill's efforts to retain the assault shipping.[13]

Unfortunately, the Fifth Army attack would lack coordination, allowing Senger to adopt a moveable defence. With the FEC attacking north of Cassino, the British X Corps, commanded by Lieutenant General Sir Richard McCreery began its assault, Operation PANTHER, on the lower Garigliano on the evening of 17 January against the German 94th Infantry Division.[14] This division had not yet been seriously engaged, and it had a very long frontage of around 30-miles.[15] In response on 20 January, Hitler issued a typical order to his troops:

> The enemy in Southern Italy has apparently commenced his offensive on the XIV Army Corps sector, with the capture of Rome as his objective, by attacking the 94th Infantry Division. No position is shorter, more favourable as regards terrain, and more economical as regards troops, than that we have taken up at present. I therefore order that this position

10   Ellis, *Hollow Victory*, p.51.
11   Gooderson, Ian, *A Hard Way to Fight a War: The Allied Campaign in Italy in the Second World War* (London: Conway Books, 2008), p.263; Ellis, *Hollow Victory*, pp.61-2.
12   HQ Fifth Army, SHINGLE intelligence Summary No.9 dated 16 January 1944.
13   Churchill, 335-342. Atkinson, p 330.
14   Fifth Army History Part IV, p.30. British X Corps.
15   HQ Fifth Army, SHINGLE intelligence Summary No.9 dated 16 January 1944.

be held and that all reserves be used in a decisive battle for it. A defensive victory may have extensive political effects and will disorganise enemy invasion plans …[16]

The Germans had been aware of the build-up on the Garigliano since 13 January, but von Vietinghoff in a conversation with Kesselring expressed the opinion that the British would not choose a moonless night for their assault. He was surprised when they did. They were also unaware that the 5th British Infantry Division had joined X Corps. McCreery had been under Clark's command since Salerno and had no high opinion of his military ability. The relationship had been strained since both set foot on the beach at Salerno; he challenged his orders at the Volturno and the poor relationship was exacerbated by the advance on the Winter Line and the animosity continued at Cassino. Author Rick Atkinson's quotation from McCreery about Clark perhaps sums up best the Britisher's view: 'the Man of Destiny I somehow imagined he always wanted to be.'[17] Conscious of Britain's limited and reducing manpower pool McCreery considered Clark's insistence on attacking weakly on a broad front to be wasteful.[18] An illustration of his personnel problems could be seen by the January 1944 manpower requirement for X Corps. He required 4,686 replacements; he received 219.[19] His divisions were extremely tired after months in the front line and this was a task that McCreery felt unlikely to succeed. He was not going to waste resources on a fool's errand, especially as he knew they were unlikely to be replaced. Clark had attacked with meagre resources at Salerno, along the Volturno and was now to do it again at the *Gustav* Line. The Garigliano attack by the British 5th and 56th (London) Infantry Divisions caught the Germans by surprise, with only three battalions defending the initial attack sector.[20] It threatened to roll-up their line from the south.[21] The German defences had been weakened due to a fear of amphibious assault. The 94th Division was spread thin, covering the coastline as far north as Terracina. After a slow and chaotic start, by the 18 January McCreery's divisions were moving up the Ausente Valley and were threatening the towns of Minturno and Castelforte. This prompted Senger to commit his few local reserves, including *Kampfgruppe* Corvin of the Hermann Göring *Panzer* Division and elements of the 44th Infantry Division. At first both Senger and von Vietinghoff considered Operation PANTHER to be a diversionary attack. Whilst assessing the worsening situation from the 94th's headquarters he was prompted to request the release of the *Heersgruppenkommando* reserve on 18 January. His request had already been anticipated by Kesselring, who did not share the view of the attack's diversionary intent.[22] At 9.40am on the 18 January he expressed the view, 'I am convinced that we are now faced with the greatest crisis yet encountered in the Italian Campaign.'

In an interview in 1955 Senger stated that had he been in Kesselring's position he would not have approved the request.[23] Later, the Germans realised that the activity on the Garigliano was

16   Air Historical Branch Translation No VII/82, High Level Reports and Directives Dealing with the Italian Campaign in 1944. Translated by Air Ministry, AHB6, 29 November 1948.
17   Atkinson, p.337.
18   Richard Mead, *The Last Great Cavalryman: The Life of General Sir Richard McCreery* (Barnsley: Pen & Sword, 2012), p 124.
19   Molony, p 603.
20   Mavrogordato, *XIV Panzer Corps*, p.27.
21   Senger, *Neither Fear Nor Hope*, pp.189-90.
22   Senger, *Neither Fear Nor Hope*; Molony, p.614; Hinsley et al, p.510. These were the 90th and 29th Panzer-Grenadier divisions
23   Blumenson, *Salerno to Cassino*, p.319.

only a large-scale diversion for the amphibious landing. Westphal wrote in his memoirs that moving the reserves 'was clearly a mistake,' but he did not express this opinion at the time.[24] Despite their clear military skill, on this occasion both were wrong and Kesselring made the right decision to commit his reserve.

To determine why, we need to look at the concept of the centre of gravity. As the operational level commander, Kesselring had a single objective. This was to keep the Allies bogged down south of Rome for as long as possible. To achieve this, his appreciation of the situation and his assessment of the Allied capabilities would have told him that there were two likely courses of action for the Allies. The first of these was to keep battering away at the *Gustav* Line and the second was to also conduct an amphibious landing, probably on the west coast of Italy near Rome. He therefore had two operational tasks to complete; maintain the defence on the *Gustav* Line and have sufficient reserves to repel any amphibious assault. At the time of the Garigliano crisis, Kesselring had some intelligence that the Allies were preparing an amphibious assault, but he assumed, and was correct to do so, that they would wait until the Fifth Army had moved forward to a supportable distance, the most likely locations for which were, he thought, Anzio and Civitavecchia. Tides, the moon and the weather all pointed to a mid-February timeframe. January was by far the worst month in Italy for weather; it made little military sense to launch any assault during this month. Kesselring, with his usual poor intelligence, knew nothing of the Allied landing ship situation or of the great desire of some to snatch Rome, that trumped military sense. He also had to judge where the greatest risk lay, the collapse of the *Gustav* Line or an amphibious assault. He chose the former based upon what he knew and what he could surmise. What was the centre of gravity of his defence?

The definition of a Centre of Gravity Level in NATO military doctrine is:

> A centre of gravity is the primary source of power that provides an actor its strength, freedom of action or will to fight. It is always a physical entity.[25]

What was Kesselring's Centre of Gravity? What, if defeated, would deny him the ability to meet his operational objective? Which thing provided him with his power to defend Italy south of Rome? Where is the greatest threat to this? He would have concluded by January 1944 that the main effort of the Allied land forces was in the Fifth Army; he was content to denude the Adriatic to reinforce either Rome or the Garigliano. The greatest threat was against the *Gustav* Line. It was his defences here that were the primary source of power and therefore Senger's XIV *Panzerkorps* was Kesselring's operational level centre of gravity. Had the town of Castelforte fallen, the route through the Ausente Valley would have allowed entry to the Liri Valley in the rear of the defenders on the Rapido (Gari), thus fatally piercing the *Gustav* Line. The centre of gravity can change with the situation, but in mid-January 1944 there was no Anzio and no indication to Kesselring that an assault was imminent. Kesselring was not to know, as his subordinates did not know, that the British X Corps assault on the Garigliano was not Clark's main effort. He was correct in prioritising the integrity of his centre of gravity over the defence from another possible contingency. Whether threatened at Anzio or on the Garigliano, Kesselring's

---

24 Westphal, p.158.
25 *NATO Allied Joint Publication 5 – Allied Joint Doctrine for the Planning of Operations*, Annex B dated June 2019.

centre of gravity remained the XIV *Panzerkorps* and therefore prior to the landing on 22 January he must take all measures to defend it.

Although German reconnaissance had detected activity in Naples that could indicate an imminent amphibious assault, Kesselring thought he could afford to send his reserve. He had been assured by the chief of the *Abwehr*, Admiral Wilhelm Canaris, only the previous day that no such Allied operation was planned and in his judgement no landing would occur until mid-February.

The reserve divisions had been held back by Kesselring to respond to any Allied amphibious attack, the threat of which he was constantly aware. The 29th *Panzer-Grenadiers* arrived in strength on 19/20 January deploying into the area between the 15th *Panzer-Grenadiers* and the 94th Division. The 90th *Panzer-Grenadiers* were released to join them the day after. The committal of the 90th *Panzer-Grenadier* Division offered a bonus to the Allies as the Division was to leave the Italian theatre by the end of February 1944.[26] This high-quality division along with the Hermann Göring *Panzer* Division, were both earmarked for France. Instead, they stayed in Italy until after OVERLORD. Elements of other front-line divisions were quickly moved to shore up the 94th Infantry Division and to reinforce the 15th *Panzer-Grenadiers* who were expecting an assault across the Gari. By 19 January, German commanders were concerned that the 94th Division was nearing exhaustion and could only last another 48-hours. Minturno was lost that afternoon.

The 90th *Panzer-Grenadier* Division, known as *Kampfgruppe* Baade and comprising the 200th and 361st *Panzer-Grenadier* Regiments was not fully prepared and was at much-reduced strength with less than 1,000 soldiers available on 21 January.[27] It was still recovering from action against the Canadians on the Adriatic front and was being moved into the rear near Rome.[28] At the end of December, it was joined near Rome by the remnants of the 200th Regiment which had been fighting on the Adriatic front.[29] The redeployment was not complete by the turning of the year. Its armour and artillery remained in the east of Italy until April 1944.[30] This division was slower to deploy as it was short of fuel and under air attack at Priverno, some 30-miles to the north-west of the lower Garigliano. It started to arrive in the Minturno area on 21 January.[31] Following this, the division was used as a 'fire brigade', when it was next deployed to the Cassino massif to shore up the faltering defences of 44th Infantry Division in early February. Its strength had been increased to over 8,000.[32] *Generalmajor* Ernst-Gunther Baade commanded the 90th *Panzer-Grenadier* Division in February 1944.

Baade's troops, as well as others attached to his division, were the closest to the Abbey when it was destroyed. Baade had joined the German Army in 1914 fighting in the First World War. He left in 1920 but re-joined in 1924 as a cavalry officer. When war broke out, he was under Senger's command.[33] His own opportunity for command arose in April 1942 when he was

26   Molony, p.586 fn.2.
27   Mavrogordato, *XIV Panzer Corps*, p.70.
28   Gooderson, *A Hard Way to Fight a War*, p.261.
29   Sandri, p.22.
30   Sandri, p.24.
31   Molony, p.616.
32   Molony, p.700, fn.2.
33   Brett-Smith, p.179.

The commander of 90th *Panzer-Grenadier* Division, *Generalmajor* Ernst-Gunther Baade.
An inspirational leader, his troops were close to the Abbey when it was destroyed.
He was one of four officers to receive the Knight's Cross with Oak Leaves and Swords at Cassino.
(Bundesarchiv Bild 101I-315-1110-06/Fotograf: Luthge)

given the 115th Rifle Regt in North Africa, for which he was awarded the Knight's Cross.[34] He was wounded at the first battle of El-Alamein and remained out of action until April 1943. Posted to Italy, he facilitated the evacuation of Sicily through a skilful air defence of the Strait of Messina and was rewarded with the command of the 90th *Panzer-Grenadier* Division, the old 90th Light Division of the *Afrika Korps,* on 14 December 1943. Baade was an eccentric officer who sometimes wore a kilt on the battlefield. There were also stories that he had freed a British POW after he helped him through an Allied minefield. Senger received a call asking whether it was true that Baade had asked British officers to his mess for Christmas dinner. Although Senger debunked the story, he discovered that Baade had sent New Year greetings to the Allies in English, which he spoke well.[35] He was very popular, making regular trips to the front line and his defensive skill at Cassino earned him the Oak Leaves to his Knight's Cross on 22 February 1944.[36]

Senger, who went to Baade at his Division HQ to observe the Abbey being bombed wrote of him:

34   Franz Kurowski, *Battleground Italy 1943-1945* (Winnipeg: JJ Fedorowicz Publishing Inc, 2003), p.73.
35   Brett-Smith, p.179.
36   Kurowski, *Battleground Italy*, p.73.

Through his personality alone he manages in a few days of fighting to restore his half-defeated divisions, breathing new life into them, putting them into better shape, enhancing their powers of resistance by the very fact that he commands them. The magic stream of confidence begins to flow.

In these severe battles we saw him in his hole in the ground with shells exploding all about him, sitting there with a clear view of the fighting around the monastery hill. Logs are burning in a crater, giving off a steady heat. The water boils in the battered little tea-kettle – indispensable in many a campaign and battle.[37]

It was no coincidence that his division had the highest German morale on the *Gustav* Line. He remained in command until December 1944, also gaining the Swords to the Knight's Cross, the third highest award in the Third Reich. This was bestowed to only 143 men in the war, 38 fewer times than the Victoria Cross. Four of these were at Cassino. Baade was appointed to a Corps command position in March 1945, but was wounded in action following an RAF fighter-bomber attack in northern Germany. He died of his wounds on VE-Day, 8 May 1945.

The other reserve division, the 29th *Panzer-Grenadiers*, had been in the front line in Sicily and had faced almost constant action since. The division was in reserve around Velletri on 15 January, where it was responsible for 62-miles of coastline. A worn-out battalion of this division recuperating in the rear was all that opposed the Allied landing at Anzio. The 29th's deployment to the Garigliano sector slowed X Corps' progress, through the innovative meshing of units, but also opened the door to Rome through Anzio. Minturno was lost, but by the evening of 19 January the Allies had failed to capture Castelforte as reinforcements strengthened the German line. All that was left to Kesselring in reserve was two Regiments of the 3rd *Panzer-Grenadier* Division, a division with large numbers of foreign German or *Volksdeutsche* soldiers that Senger assessed as having poor morale. He was in the process of reorganising his reserves, replacing the 3rd *Panzer-Grenadiers* with the 90th *Panzer-Grenadiers* when the crisis struck. The Germans began counterattacking on 21 January but were forced to abandon it when the Anzio landings occurred the next day. The X Corps assault over the Garigliano was only partially successful, and the front had stabilised by 23 January.

The second element of this assault, by the 128th Brigade of Major General John Hawkesworth's 46th (Midland) Infantry Division was carried out overnight on 19/20 January. The attack aimed to secure high ground to the south of the upcoming US 36th Infantry Division assault on the Rapido, to prevent the Americans from being attacked in the flank. It failed completely. A few days before the 46th Division's assault, in preparing for the Anzio landings, the US 3rd Infantry Division lost vital DUKW amphibious vehicles. These were not available to the British to whom they had been allocated, and this was to cost them dearly. Hawkesworth had no success in crossing the fast-flowing Upper Garigliano at San Ambrogio, abandoning the attempt early on 20 January, and the high ground remained in German hands, again attracting the ire of the Army Commander towards the British. On this occasion, Clark may have been justified in his criticism. He said of the attack in his diary: 'I was fearful that General Hawkesworth had a mental reservation as to the possibilities of success of his operation.'[38]

---

37   Senger, *Neither Fear Nor Hope*, pp.208-9.
38   Blumenson, *Salerno to Cassino*, p.320.

Following the flanking attacks, Clark's plan was to attack in the centre to open the River Liri valley for exploitation by Major General Ernest Harmon's 1st US Armoured Division. This initial attack across the Rapido was carried out by Walker's US 36th Infantry Division, with a Regimental Combat Team (RCT) attacking each side of the village of Sant Angelo in Theodice, 3-miles south of Cassino. An effective and well dug-in German 15th *Panzer-Grenadier* Division, with five battalions in the front-line from the 104th and 129th *Grenadier* Regiments defended the eastern bank. The village had been virtually destroyed to create stronger defensive positions. The Rapido was around 50-feet wide, flowing at around 8-miles per hour with banks 3-4 feet high. It had rained incessantly for days prior to the crossing attempt, further swelling the river. A US Army RCT was commanded by a Colonel, with approximately 4,000 men.[39] In Italy, each US division was also generally overmanned by about 750-soldiers and 50-junior officers so that battle casualties could be replaced without diminishing combat effectiveness.[40] Each US Infantry Division contained three Infantry Regiments (RCTs), with a total manpower of around 15,000 men. A British Division was somewhat larger at full establishment with just over 18,000 men. The 36th Division had been battered over the preceding months and was short of men and low of morale. The crossing was expected by Kesselring and US II Corps was identified in the Sant Angelo area by German intelligence as early as the 19 January.[41] Aggressive German patrolling on the Allied side of the Rapido identified the engineer activity to remove minefields, a clear indicator of a planned crossing. McCreery of British X Corps had always been unhappy with Clark's scheme of manoeuvre. He considered that it broke one of the accepted principles of war, that of 'concentration of force.' He was not the only one. Juin thought that Clark's plan was to 'entail many useless sacrifices throughout the winter.'[42] Initially, McCreery's opinion was supported by Keyes.[43] He had originally wanted to support the British in a two-corps attack through the Aurunci Mountains, the so-called Big Cassino plan, and the eventual key to the door of the *Gustav* Line. Clark, however, persuaded him that the terrain was too difficult, and McCreery was less than keen because his forces were not mountain troops, and he had few mules at his disposal for resupply. The post-war view of the German defenders was that had the force been concentrated at this point, the *Gustav* Line would have been breached in January 1944 and the battles at Cassino avoided.

McCreery told the Fifth Army COS, Major General Alfred Gruenther, to expect a disaster.[44] This occurred a few days later. The success achieved on the lower Garigliano was wasted with no available force to exploit it and it bogged down.

Hawkesworth's failure to get across the fast-flowing river should also have given Clark second thoughts, but it did not. His orders had been issued and he was not going to change them. Clark fully recognised the difficulties Walker would face. On 19 January, he wrote:

39   See Martin Blumenson, *Bloody River: The Real Tragedy of the Rapido* (College Station TX: Texas A&M University Press, 1998), pp.139-140.
40   A Military Encyclopaedia Based on Operations in the Italian Campaigns 1943-1945. Prepared by G-3 Section, Headquarters Fifteenth Army Group, Italy, Chapter 1 – Personnel 3. Military History Network, <http://www.milhist.net/docs/milencyc/MilEncyc.02G2.pdf> (accessed 27 February 2019).
41   Mavrogordato, *XIV Panzer Corps*, p.30.
42   Juin, p.50.
43   Mead, p.143.
44   Mead, p.144.

The architects of the Rapido disaster. General Mark Clark and his two principal subordinates at US Fifth Army. On the left is Major General Alfred Gruenther, his Chief of Staff, and in the centre, Brigadier General Donald Brann, Chief of Operations. (Library of Congress)

I sent General Gruenther by plane to see McCreery, who feels that the attack of the 36th Division has little chance of success on account of the heavy defensive position of the enemy west of the Rapido. I maintain that it is essential that I make that attack fully expecting heavy losses in order to hold all the troops on my front and draw more to it, thereby clearing the way for SHINGLE.[45]

The German defences were more than capable of dealing a mortal blow to the tired and understrength Texans who launched only two of their three regiments across the Rapido in what could be described as a forlorn hope. Major General Lucian Truscott, Commanding General of the US 3rd Infantry Division, told Clark that his plan was 'unsound'. Juin considered Clark to be 'impetuous' and that he had a 'false notion of distances,' referring to the distance between the *Gustav* Line and Anzio.[46] Launched on the night of 20 January, the assault was a disaster, resulting in 1,681 casualties.[47] Even before the operation to cross the Rapido, 36th Infantry

45   Blumenson, *Salerno to Cassino,* pp.320-1.
46   Juin, pp.48-9.
47   Blumenson, *Bloody River*, p.110; Casualties from 20-22 Jan 44.

Division was at barely 50 per cent strength. The unused 142nd Infantry was estimated to have around only 20 per cent effective strength. The entire Division was in desperate need of rest and replenishment.[48] About 400-soldiers from the 141st Infantry made it across the river under cover of darkness. By dawn they were pinned down and stranded. To the south of Sant Angelo, a battalion of 143rd Infantry made it across, but the same fate awaited them when light came, and they could be observed from the observation positions on high ground. Walker thought that both Clark and Keyes had misjudged the enemy; 'I also felt that neither of them fully realised that the Germans had ceased their delaying tactics and were going to defend the Gustav Line indefinitely.'

This attack caused no concern for the German commanders and was not even recognised as a serious divisional level effort to break into the Liri Valley. Vietinghoff described the attempt as 'a reconnaissance in force.'[49] Not even local German reserves were required. The ironic thing about this attack was that the German reserves had already been pulled to the *Gustav* Line by McCreery's attack. Senger, in his War Diary, considered this attack to be 'unwarranted and too costly.' He could not understand why the Allies continued to try and breakthrough the *Gustav* Line in small packets in different places instead of bolstering the partially successful British X Corps assault.[50] Reporting from the Rapido, *New York Times* correspondent Cyrus Sulzberger was appalled at the losses, stating later, 'for the first time in my experience I heard American GIs muttering to each other of mutiny.'[51] *Collier's* reporter Frank Gervasi heard the same when he visited the division on 29 January.[52]

The Allies knew that the Germans were sensitive to McCreery's assault; their ULTRA decrypts quickly revealed the despatch of Kesselring's reserves. Looking at the battle through the advantage of hindsight, had Clark used the US II Corps to exploit the successes of X Corps, the battles around Cassino may never have occurred. From a psychological perspective the assault of 36th Division was the first action fully visible from the Abbey; there was a general assumption that observers were responsible for the accuracy of the enemy's artillery.[53] Although assumed by the rank and file that it was being used as an observation post, as Senger rightly stated such an obvious position made no tactical sense. There was no advantage placing soldiers in the Abbey, most of the time the valley was obscured by cloud or mist. The doomed assault did not come as a surprise to the defenders and their artillery was already zeroed to likely crossing points and assembly areas. Observation from the Abbey was unnecessary. Nevertheless, one journalist, Hal Boyle, commented 'Sooner or later, somebody's going to have to blow that place all to hell.'[54] The official US Army historian, Martin Blumenson, suggested, the commanding heights, 'crushed the troops psychologically and made them feel helpless.'[55]

48   Eric Morris, *Circles of Hell* (London: Hutchinson Publishing, 1993), p.229.
49   Mavrogordato, *XIV Panzer Corps*, p.30.
50   Senger, *War Diary*, p.7.
51   Quoting Sulzberger in Steven Casey, *The War Beat, Europe: The American Media at War Against Nazi Germany* (Oxford: Oxford Scholarship Online, 2017), p.3.
52   Gervasi, p.542.
53   Harold L Bond, *Return to Cassino* (London: J M Dent & Sons Ltd, 1964), p.39.
54   Atkinson, p.350, Gervasi, p.546.
55   Blumenson, *Bloody River*, p.72.

There can be no doubt of the psychological impact of the Abbey on fighting soldiers. This view from the Rapido Valley shows how much the building dominated the area. Soldiers of the 34th 'Red Bulls' and 36th 'Texans' Infantry divisions were constantly under its gaze in January 1944. (Author)

One of the most popular reasons for the bombing of the Abbey was its utility for observation. As can be seen from this image from German-held territory near Terrelle, there were many better positions from where Allied activity could be observed by the defenders. (Author)

The monks in 'that place' could see little due to heavy fog, but they felt the battle, 'the noise was terrible and the whole monastery shook.'[56] Even divisional engineers laying safe lanes to the river got lost in the heavy fog with visibility less than 50-yards.[57] It also did not occur to Allied officers who dreamed up this reason for bombing the Abbey that whether intact or not it could still be used as an observation post. W M Gould of the British Air Historical Branch (AHB) in his RAF Narrative of the Italian Campaign points out that 'The Abbey was by no means the only point of vantage, nor even the most important, but its value as an observation post cannot be questioned.'[58] Destroying the Abbey did not change or impede the observer's vision from the summit. There was no advantage to be had by destroying it. Senger considered it against German doctrine to site positions where they would receive the most attention. Because of the convex shape of Monte Cassino, most of Cassino town could not be observed. Senger ordered

56   Grossetti and Matronola, p.81.
57   Fifth Army History, Part IV, pp.44-6.
58   G.260700/VFW/2/50, RAF Narrative – The Italian Campaign 1943-1945, Volume 1 – Planning and Invasion to the Fall of Rome, British Air Historical Branch, p.272.

that observation posts should be placed halfway down a hill where there would be little back-drop and where they can be effectively camouflaged.[59]

The attack could have been avoided. Choosing to attack in strength on either flank would have bypassed the Cassino bastion entirely and would probably have had greater chances of success. Both attacks had made considerable progress, and it was on the flanks where the German commanders were most concerned as the Allies appeared on several occasions to be on the verge of success. Instead, the offensives were diluted by pursuing doomed and unsupported attacks that could not be exploited. The flanks were occupied by French and British troops, not American. The papers at home wanted success for 'Mark Clark's *US* Fifth Army,' and so did Clark.

As the second phase of the fighting for the *Gustav* Line beckoned, Hitler issued his Directive No 52 on 28 January. He was aware of the secondary nature of the Italian battle, and knew that the Allies' strategy was to keep German divisions away from France. Hitler saw the fight in Italy and in France as part of the same battle to prevent German and European 'annihilation.' If he could halt the Allies in Italy, he could dissuade them from launching a Cross-Channel attack. Hitler, perhaps read the British well, but he failed to understand the more direct strategy of the US:

> Within the next few days the 'Battle for Rome' will begin. It will be decisive for the defence of Central Italy and for fate of 10th Army.
>
> But the significance of this struggle goes even beyond that, because the landing at Nettuno marked the opening of the invasion of Europe planned for 1944.
>
> The purpose of the enemy is to hold down large German forces as far away as possible from the bases in England where the main invasion forces are still standing ready, to wear down the German forces, and to gain experience for future operations …
>
> … The enemy must be forced to recognise, as he did in the fighting in Sicily, on the Rapido river, and at Ortona, that the fighting strength of Germany is unbroken, and that the great invasion of 1944 is a hazardous enterprise which will be drowned in the blood of Anglo-Saxon soldiers.[60]

---

59   Senger *War Diary*, p.78.
60   Hugh Trevor-Roper, *Hitler's War Directives 1939-1945* (London: Pan Books Ltd, 1966), pp.233-4.

4

Fates Entwined: Anzio and Cassino

A bum operation from the very beginning – it was poorly conceived, poorly executed and tactically unsound.

Brigadier-General Gordon P Saville USAAF
Acting Commanding General XII Air Support Command
Italy 1944[1]

The progress of US Fifth Army, crawling up the western side of the Italian peninsula was going to get slower as the terrain, weather and German defences increasingly restricted movement. Discussions to land a force in the enemy's rear began as early as September 1943. In a letter to Marshall on 24 September, Eisenhower doubted whether he had sufficient force for a landing either at Gaeta or near Rome.[2] Clark established a team to look at potential amphibious operations as early as October 1943 that identified the port and beaches at Anzio as a potential landing site, but which initially considered it too far away from the main front to survive the inevitable German reaction. Allied intelligence was aware that the German units in the Rome area and those conducting coastal defence were either worn-out after time at the front or incomplete. In the final months of 1943, *Generaloberst* Eberhard von Mackensen's new German Fourteenth AOK, became a feeder army for the meat grinder further south. The original outline Fifth Army plan, dated 19 October 1943, was communicated to the CCS by Eisenhower on 4 November 1943 and was further articulated in 15th Army Group's Operational Instruction No 31, dated 8 November 1943, to place a force south of Rome.[3] It depended upon Fifth Army's success in breaking through the *Gustav* Line and reaching Frosinone.[4] Gruenther gave the task to G-3 Operations chief, Brigadier-General Donald Brann to plan a landing of a single reinforced division of 23,000 men by 20 December.[5] The plan had two phases; first, to establish a beachhead

---

1   AFHRA Iris NO 1103217, Interview with Major General Gordon Saville, San Antonio, Texas, dated 9 February 1970, p.51.
2   Chandler et al, *Eisenhower Papers Vol III*, p.1452.
3   Chandler et al, *Eisenhower Papers Vol III*, p.1549.
4   Major Glenn L King, *From Salerno To Rome: General Mark Clark and The Challenges Of Coalition Warfare* (Potomac, MD: Pickle Partners Publishing, 2014), Kindle Location 819.
5   Fifth Army History, Part IV, p.12.

and second to attack in the direction of the Alban Hills.[6] Rome is not mentioned and it was evident that the securing of a beachhead was a prerequisite to further advancing even in this early plan. Eisenhower, worried about the stagnation on the main front, requested that the theatre's landing ships be retained in the Mediterranean on 4 November and again on 22 November 1943.[7] This force was to be the US 3rd Infantry, and it was to have only 7-days of supply, as this was the expectation for relief from the Fifth Army. The operation's commander, Truscott, had no confidence in the plan, telling Clark, 'if we undertake it you are going to destroy the best damned division in the US Army, for there will be no survivors.'[8] Only a day after Instruction No31, Alexander and Eisenhower exchanged letters sharing serious reservations about whether an opportunity for the assault would arise.[9] The weather in southern Italy had been awful, and during December and January, only two days a week of good weather was expected. Nevertheless, Clark approved Brann's plan on 25 November.[10] Eisenhower thought that if a line near Frosinone could be reached before mid-December, relief was possible, but this had not happened, and Clark reassessed the earliest date to reach this line to be around 10 January. The original Operation SHINGLE was shelved on Clark's advice on 18 December.[11] It was resurrected at Churchill's initiative on a larger scale and delinked from the Fifth Army's progress. He consulted several senior British officers to resurrect the operation.[12] On 19 December the British CoS replied to his accusation that the 'stagnation of the whole campaign is becoming scandalous'. Therefore:

> We are in full agreement with you that the present stagnation cannot be allowed to continue. For every reason it is essential that something should be done to speed things up. The solution, as you say, clearly lies in making use of our amphibious power to strike round the enemy's flank and open up the way for a rapid advance on Rome.[13]

The revival of Anzio can be traced to Churchill's illness after the Cairo conference; otherwise, he would have departed the Mediterranean and been occupied with other matters at home. At a conference on 25 December 1943 in Carthage, he finalised the revised plan, which retained the name Operation SHINGLE. Americans were invited this time but Clark, the army commander, was not there. He was informed the same day by Alexander.[14] Churchill was keen to ensure Rome was in Allied hands before the landings in France, but at this pace, he was not going to succeed. Clark also suggested, probably rightly, that the Anzio landing served another purpose for Churchill. Aware that an amphibious failure could not be tolerated prior to OVERLORD, Anzio would need to retain forces in the Mediterranean that may otherwise have been redeployed and he wanted Mediterranean operations to maintain their tempo.[15] It was agreed that

6   HQ Fifth Army, Outline Plan Operation SHINGLE dated 19 October 1943.
7   Chandler et al, *Eisenhower Papers, Vol III*, 1548 and Combined Chiefs of Staff Memorandum CCS 379/7 dated 27 November 1943.
8   Truscott, p.291.
9   Chandler et al, *Eisenhower Papers, Vol III*, p.1555.
10   Fifth Army History, Part IV, p.13.
11   W G F Jackson, *The Battle for Italy* (London: BT Batsford Ltd, 1967), p.166.
12   Blumenson, *Salerno to Cassino*, p.297.
13   Molony, p.588.
14   Blumenson, *Salerno to Cassino*, p.298.
15   Mark Clark, *Calculated Risk* (New York: Enigma Books, 2007), p.206.

the operation was to be launched with at least two assault divisions at Anzio and Nettuno. There was considerable doubt from intelligence and logistics whether the operation was feasible.[16] The larger force would still have only eight days of supply and could not be supported without the further retention of the landing ships required in England. On 2 January, Clark reported to Alexander that he did not foresee VI Corps making a junction with Fifth Army until at least 6 February.[17] The attendees at a conference in North Africa on 7 January were however, 'Churchilled' and the operation persisted with the specialist advice being brushed aside. Alexander pressed for, and Churchill fixed, the further retention of 24-landing ships, giving the operation 35-days of supply.[18] The logistics of the operation was to present Clark's Chief G-4 Supply Officer, Brigadier-General Ralph Tate, with enormous difficulties. The initial lift plan on 14 January required 84-Landing Ship Tanks (LST), 84-Landing Craft Infantry (LCI) and 57-Landing Craft Tank (LCT). After this, it was calculated that 14-LSTs were required every 3-days to keep the force supplied. Not only did the British and Americans have separate equipment, but separate supply organisations, rations and casualty evacuation procedures. Tate could also not rely on the use of Anzio port and his plan assumed that supplies would come across the beaches. For that he required 30-LCTs to remain at Anzio for unloading.[19]

As the force grew, and went onto the offensive, which is voracious of stores, so did his problems in supplying them. There was no discussion of the ends that this operation was supposed to attain. It was apparently more important for Churchill that it go ahead than that it achieves anything substantive. By 8 January it was a definite go as he made the final decision whilst recuperating in Marrakech.

The rejuvenated plan was issued on 12 January 1944. The mission's two phases from the October plan remained the same. The new plan was to place an initial 36,000 men and over 3,000 vehicles, rising to 74,660 Allied personnel and nearly 13,000 vehicles onto the Anzio beaches.[20] On 18 January, Fifth Army G-2 issued its intelligence assessment, again as with that a couple of days earlier, an overoptimistic view of the operation's prospects.[21]

This assessment showed that the Allied forces intended to push inland to seize the Alban hills and ultimately threaten Rome, at the same time cutting the German Tenth AOK lines of communication. The size of the landing force should have been calculated to fulfil that mission, yet it was mostly determined by the amount of amphibious assault available. These were not the same and SHINGLE was another example of where Allied ends were supported by insufficient means. One general said, 'You can get ashore, but you can't get off the beachhead.'[22] Anzio's intent should have been to persuade Kesselring to face the threat in XIV *Panzerkorps* rear, fear for Rome and be forced to withdraw from the *Gustav* Line. Its power was more psychological than physical; the dilemma of being trapped should have coerced Kesselring into taking actions advantageous to the Allies. By 8 January, a D-Day of 22 January was decided. Seizure of the Alban Hills would have allowed the Allies to sever communications in the Velletri and

16   Blumenson, *Salerno to Cassino*, p.300.
17   Fifth Army History, Part IV, p.17.
18   Fifth Army History, Part IV, p.20.
19   Outline Plan for Operation SHINGLE – G-4 Annex dated 5 January 1944.
20   HQ Fifth Army, Outline Plan for Operation SHINGLE – Annex 2 dated 12 January 1944.
21   HQ Fifth Army, Outline Plan for Operation SHINGLE – Intelligence Annex dated 18 January 1944.
22   Atkinson, p.327.

Commanding General of US VI Corps at Anzio, Major General John Lucas speaks with the commander
of the Special Service Force, Brigadier General Robert Frederick. (NARA RG111-SC-212642_001)

Valmontone areas, and once achieved, the Germans would have an Allied force to their rear and
would be forced from the *Gustav* Line. The assault in the early hours of 22 January achieved
complete tactical surprise. There was, however, insufficient force to secure the beachhead and
to make the thrust northwards without grave risk to the landing force. The choice was to stay at
Anzio and achieve nothing or to drive rapidly northwards and likely lose the landing force as the
Germans reinforced from the north as they undoubtedly would do. For a few precious hours the
road to Rome was open; Kesselring thought they could be in Rome by the morning of 23 January.
On the morning of the landing US Army engineer, Lieutenant John Cummings and his driver
set off along the *Via Appia* to conduct a planned reconnaissance. They crossed the Alban Hills
and nearly reached the outskirts of Rome at Frattocchie before any Germans were spotted.[23]

Lucas, was given deliberately vague orders.[24] Should he gamble or play it safe? Either way,
if it went wrong, he was a readily available scapegoat. He was aware that he was the potential

---

23   Robert Katz, *The Battle for Rome: The Germans, The Allies. The Partisans and The Pope* (New York: Simon
     and Schuster, 2003), p.151 and Canciani, p.104.
24   Martin Blumenson, 'General Lucas at Anzio' in Kent Roberts Greenfield (ed.), *Command Decisions*
     (Washington DC: Center of Military History, Department of the Army, 2000), p.323.

fall-guy for Clark and Alexander: 'They will end up by putting me ashore with inadequate forces and get me in a serious jam. Then, who will take the blame?'[25]

Another reason to break the deadlock at Cassino was that the force at Anzio was in trouble by early February. Allied commanders committed what Liddell-Hart called a 'fundamental error … giving your opponent freedom and time to concentrate to meet your concentration.'[26] Although achieving tactical surprise, at the operational level Kesselring was ready. In December 1943, the *Wehrmacht* allocated units to reinforce Italy in the event of an amphibious assault under Operation *MARDER*. Kesselring had five contingency plans: the most likely, *RICHARD* in Rome. He quickly initiated Plan *RICHARD*, to isolate and destroy the beachhead with reinforcements from northern Italy and elsewhere.[27] Allied intelligence thought that Kesselring would have two regiments and 20-30 tanks in the area on D-Day, a total of 14,300 men. By D+3 they expected this to have grown to 31,000 men to initially oppose the landing in mixed units and that two more divisions could be expected from northern Italy by D+16, giving a maximum of 61,300 men. He did much better than that. Despite tactical surprise, Westphal was woken at 3:00am, just a couple of hours after the assault. The initial shock, where German staff officers thought the Allies would be in Rome in less than 24-hours soon dissipated and by the end of the first day German intelligence had a mostly accurate assessment of the Allied order of battle in the beachhead. Kesselring did not panic or withdraw his forces from the *Gustav* Line to defend Rome.

In reality, he had no need, because VI Corps made no moves from the beach to threaten Tenth AOK's rear areas. Despite 2-million leaflets being dropped over German lines, making them aware that the Allies were in their rear, there was no aggressive move from the beachhead. Kesselring sensed this lack of aggression and therefore did not feel his force to be unbalanced with peril to its rear. This decided his course of action by the first evening.[28] He began to implement his plan on the morning of the landing when he ordered 1st *Fallschirmjager* Corps to command the defence, which it did by that evening, and ordered the 3rd *Panzer-Grenadier* Division and 71st Infantry Division from *Heersgruppenkommando* reserve and the Hermann Göring Panzer Division from Tenth AOK reserve to the beachhead. From the Adriatic sector, he moved parts of 1st *Fallschirmjager* Division and the 26th *Panzer* Division. He also ordered *Luftwaffe General der Flieger* Maximilian Ritter von Pohl, responsible for the air defences of Rome, to move his 88mm guns to the beachhead in an anti-tank role.[29] Kesselring also rightly assumed that the Allied immediate objective would be the Alban Hills. He therefore sent all his initial reinforcements to the north of Anzio to prevent the expected Allied advance. He could do little else without withdrawing units from Tenth AOK. Allied inaction convinced Kesselring by 24 January that he could mount a counterattack that would push them back into the sea. One of the unfortunate ironies of the Anzio landings was that the Allied plan effectively made-up Kesselring's mind for him and allowed him to concentrate his force. It was the only thing that he could effectively defend against without operational-level cost; any other plan would have resulted in the Tenth AOK either being cut-off and destroyed or forced to

---

25   Blumenson, *Command Decisions*, p.335.
26   Liddell-Hart, *Strategy*, p.334.
27   Westphal, pp.156-158.
28   Blumenson, *Command Decisions*, p.339.
29   Jackson, p.183.

withdraw. Little was sent to the south or east of the landing area in the first few days, exposing the rear of XIV *Panzerkorps* to any Allied moves in this direction. All his major reinforcements came from the north. He gambled that the Allies were going for Rome, rather than to encircle XIV *Panzerkorps*; his gamble paid off. The only elements moved from Cassino to Anzio were a Regiment from the 15th *Panzer-Grenadier* Division and a handful of artillery battalions.[30]

The large force of fighter and medium bombers were unable to interdict Kesselring's Anzio reinforcement through the destruction of lines of communication, mostly due to poor weather and the proximity to Rome. Kesselring's poor intelligence did not connect the increase in air interdiction north of Rome with planning for a landing. The Fifteenth Air Force and the Tactical Bomber Force (TBF) interdicted the Italian rail system by bombing infrastructure in central Italy.[31] This could not contain the Germans fully.

By the end of January, the beachhead was contained. Kesselring's chief opponent was new to the theatre and the land commander displayed a light touch that allowed Clark and Lucas too much latitude in interpreting the mission. Clark with his 'Salerno Complex' and Lucas, a competent but cautious commander, chose to build the beachhead rather than risk everything for Rome. Lucas, who had been in action since the autumn was both physically and mentally tired and was never a keen advocate of the operation. In his diary prior to the operation, he wrote:

> Unless we can get what we want, the operation becomes such a desperate undertaking that it should not, in my opinion, be attempted…a crack on the chin is certain…these 'Battles of the Little Big Horn' aren't much fun and a failure now would ruin Clark, probably kill me and certainly prolong the war…the whole affair has a strong odor of Gallipoli and apparently the same amateur was still on the coach's bench.[32]

The window of opportunity to drive towards Rome was narrow and was not taken, although according to the Office of Strategic Services (OSS) Chief of Operations, there were no more than 1,500 Germans in the city.[33] This figure was reached through the OSS agent 'Cervo', a Rome police Lieutenant named Maurizio Giglio who had access to accurate statistics in the Rome Questura. They knew where they were and where they lived and the figures, sent to Caserta, were accurate to the 19 January.[34] Two days of inactivity followed. Nothing was done beyond building the beachhead and allowing Kesselring time to prepare his defence and develop a counterattack. The Anzio operation had become a hostage to fortune. It now needed rescue, and this could only come from the main front. There was no time to waste. Radio Vittoria, the allied clandestine radio run by Cervo warned on 29 January of an impending German counterattack.[35] An air attack on 1st *Fallschirmjager* Corps HQ delayed the attack, but by 3 February Kesselring had sufficient force to launch his counterattack. Lucas, by contrast, thought that just by remaining at Anzio that he was achieving 'something of a victory.'[36] The force had drawn

30   Mavrogordato, *XIV Panzer Corps*, p.49.
31   Fifth Army History, Part IV, p.60.
32   Blumenson, *Command Decisions*, p.333-4.
33   Adleman and Walton, p.163.
34   Peter Tompkins, *Spion in Rome* (Utrecht NL: Prisma Boeken, 1966), p.50.
35   Katz, p.166.
36   Blumenson, *Command Decisions*, p.346.

considerable German force to it, but its purpose other than that had become opaque. It was not threatening Rome and it was not assisting the main front to break through the *Gustav* Line. Anzio itself was a poor choice for the assault because, although it had all the features desired for a landing, it was too far from the Fifth Army.

Rome was an obsession for Churchill and later for Clark, but it was unreachable with Lucas' VI Corps alone, and the Fifth Army was nowhere near breaking through. Alexander's orders on 2 January tasked Clark with cutting the communications and threatening the rear of the German XIV *Panzerkorps*. A thrust towards the Alban Hills and Rome was unnecessary to achieve this. There is no mention in this mission, or in the overall mission of Rome as an objective, although the Alban Hills are given as an objective by Alexander in his Operational Instruction on 12 January.[37] The direction Clark planned to take VI Corps in his outline plan was away from the main Fifth Army, making a link-up of the two forces more difficult. The British Official History considered this distance acceptable stating: 'Anzio and its hinterland were only some seventy miles distant from 5th Army's main front, a distance which was not too great to rule out the main body of 5th Army advancing to join hands with the force at Anzio within a short period.'[38] This statement, published in 1973, demonstrates that hindsight isn't always infallible. It had taken the main front two months to move ten miles. The chances of it rapidly moving 70-miles through the German main defensive line were vanishingly small.

In a note to the British CoS on 9 February Churchill called the situation 'organized insanity.'[39] SHINGLE was large enough to secure a beachhead or advance to the Alban Hills. It could not do both within acceptable risk. Von Mackensen's Fourteenth AOK, replacing 1st *Fallschirmjager* Corps in command, had made preliminary preparations to counterattack by the beginning of February and both ULTRA and OSS agents in Rome revealed that their main effort, Operation *FISCHFANG*, would be launched through the small town of Campoleone.[40] The Fourteenth AOK had been deployed by Kesselring from northern Italy to prevent the fall of Rome. Son of *Generalfeldmarschal* August von Mackensen, Eberhard was straight out of Prussian central casting, complete with monocle, he was a brilliant and aggressive cavalry general, but the battles in Italy were not cavalry battles. Von Mackensen was tasked with destroying the Anzio beachhead but failed to do so.

The German counterattack was scheduled for 16 February and Clark was aware that the Germans were going to launch their main offensive on that day.[41] He had a message from the OSS in Rome on 14 February that the counterattack was imminent.[42] Therefore, if he was going to use the bombers on the Abbey, it had to be 15 February at the latest. Not only were the medium bombers required to repulse Operation *FISCHFANG*, it also required the heavy bombers which were used in the beachhead area on 17 February. In total, Allied air power conducted 54,000 sorties against German targets prior to 15 February in support of the Anzio beachhead.

37   Molony, p.645.
38   Molony, p.647.
39   TNA CAB 80/80: COS (44) 147 (O), OPERATION SHINGLE – PROPORTION OF VEHICLES – Minute By Prime Minister dated 9 February 1944.
40   AFSC:I 282/9, Chief Of Staff, 15th Army Group, Message 718 to General Wilson, 9 February 1944; Tompkins, p.83.
41   Hinsley et al, p.192.
42   Tompkins, p.103.

B-26 Marauders from 42nd Bombardment Wing. The Wing was based at the southern
Sardinian airfield at Decimommanu and operated extensively in support of the Anzio defence.
(NARA RG342-FH-000913)

The day before the bombers attacked the Abbey, Alexander had cabled London that he was
dissatisfied with Lucas as commander at Anzio.[43] Churchill reacted by telling Brooke to send
Alexander to command the beachhead directly, but the CIGS angrily told him to 'trust his
commanders...without interfering' and the Prime Minister backed down.[44] Clark received
Kesselring's orders for the planning of the *FISCHFANG* attack from ULTRA, although he
could not reveal these to Lucas or Keyes who were not indoctrinated into the secret.[45] Mackensen
submitted his initial plan to Hitler on 5 February. The date was confirmed by OSS sources
behind the lines. The operation designed to assist the breakthrough on the *Gustav* Line was
now in mortal danger and its best hope of survival was rapid success at Cassino. The fate of the
Allied corps at Anzio and the Abbey at Montecassino now became inextricably linked. The use
of 29th *Panzer-Grenadier* Division at Anzio, and the deployment of fresh forces to Mackensen
left the Cassino sector with virtually no reserves. By 15 February the die was cast. The Germans
prepared a desperate attack to push the Allies into the sea at Anzio and the measures needed to
rescue them were equally desperate. The cost was the ancient Abbey of Montecassino.

43   Danchev and Todman, p.522.
44   Danchev and Todman, p.522.
45   Bennett, pp.267-8.

5

The Forgotten Fighters: Allied Morale in Italy

The only living creatures to benefit from the holocaust that was Cassino were the rats.

J.M. Lee Harvey
'D-Day Dodger'

Morale is an intangible variable in war. Good morale engenders an offensive spirit, cohesion, and a willingness to fight. Poor morale on the other hand will certainly be a battle-loser. It can be an insidious drain on fighting quality and motivation. This can lead to disgruntlement amongst the troops, increased sickness as well as malingering and shirking. Conducting effective offensive operations can become impossible if your force has poor morale. Ultimately, poor morale leads to self-inflicted wounds, high desertion rates and, rarely, a refusal to fight. It can also lead to soldiers becoming fatalistic, taking far greater risks than they should. This was also the case for bomber aircrew, who considered that their chances of completing an operational tour were very low. There are accounts of servicemen who would prefer to be in the stockade than on the front-line.[1] Soldiers generally fight for their mates or their families, rather than for some high-level strategy, patriotism or for the greater good. They care little for buildings or culture in the cauldron of battle where only survival counts. A breakdown of the fabric of these relationships can negatively affect the ability of fighting forces to meet objectives. Losses result in emotional stress for those who remain. Despite the sadness and sense of loss, emotions cannot drive decisions at the higher levels of warfare. This is the art of generals. Generals have two major responsibilities: to their soldiers and to their political masters. They view the big picture with detachment, yet they must deeply understand the conditions that their soldiers endure. They understand they will not win if the morale of their troops is poor, yet they also have a responsibility to maintain the highest standards of behaviour. Prisoners cannot be summarily executed; civilian women and children cannot be abused; and cultural objects cannot be looted or destroyed. These responsibilities create a tension in the general's mind, and this was especially true at Cassino. As Gooderson rightly points out 'few battles have affected the minds of men in quite the same way as those fought at Cassino in 1944.'[2]

---

1   Audie Murphy, *To Hell and Back* (New York: Perma Books, 1955), p.153.
2   Ian Gooderson, *Cassino 1944* (London: Brasseys, 2003), p.8.

At the end of 1943 and into 1944, Italy was a miserable place, especially for the infantryman who was four times as likely to be injured or killed than those in other combat arms.[3] It was freezing, alternately wet, icy, muddy, and most knew that they were in the second division of the war. Casualty rates in the US Infantry divisions around Cassino were very high in the winter of 1944. Morale was already low before they entered the crucible of the Monte Cassino massif. In his request for the retention of amphibious landing ships in late November 1943, Eisenhower judged that the Anzio operation was necessary because he was concerned that the battle efficiency of his force would be at a 'low state' by January 1944.[4] Photographer Margaret Bourke-White observed conditions a few weeks before the infantry went onto the Cassino massif:

> I thought I had never seen such tired faces. It was more than the stubble of beard that told the story; it was the blank staring eyes. The men were so tired it was like a living death. They had come from such a depth of weariness that I wondered if they would ever be able to make the return to the lives and thoughts they had known.[5]

Nurse Jane Wandrey served in a Fifth Army hospital. Writing home, she said: 'I worry about those who have to bail water out of their foxholes, and don't get to take their shoes off for days at a time. Trench foot is terrible. The suffering of our young men is awful.'[6] The men were almost universally scared. The US Army asked in a questionnaire whether combat became more frightening over time and 86 percent of enlisted soldiers in Italy responded that they got more scared as time went by or that they were scared all the time.[7] The 'morale crates' sent from home to the US soldiers in December 1943, far from being filled with Christmas cheer contained mood-draining useless stuff such as ping-pong balls sent by a well-meaning, but misinformed, Washington.[8] War correspondent Ernie Pyle, who famously suffered alongside frontline soldiers, summed it up by saying 'Our troops were living in almost inconceivable misery...thousands of men had not been dry in weeks.'[9] They looked like men of prehistoric times.[10]

One sign of the poor state of morale occurred on 28 January when, prior to the ascent to the massif, troops of the 1st Battalion of the 168th Infantry ran from a key hill some 2-miles north of the town, after its capture, in a nervous panic.[11] Morale was a problem for the Americans in the first two weeks of February 1944, yet at no time did the US generals demand the boost that the destruction of the Abbey would supply. It was not that the US generals were unconcerned, the history of 135th Infantry recounts how experimental bakeries were set up in late 1943 to supplement the dreaded 'C' rations with fresh sandwiches and pastries. The trial, however, was ended on 28 January. Between the Salerno landings and Christmas 1943, US forces in

3   John Ellis, *The Sharp End : The Fighting Man in World War II* (London: Pimlico Books, 1993), p.158,
4   Combined Chiefs of Staff Memorandum CCS 379/7 dated 27 November 1943.
5   Margaret Bourke-White, *Purple Heart Valley: A Combat Chronicle of the War in Italy* (Potomac, MD: Pickle Publishing, 2015 (original text 1944)), pp.150-1.
6   Barbara Brooks-Tomblin, *GI Nightingales: The Army Nurse Corps of World War II* (Lexington KY: Kentucky University Press, 1996), p.102.
7   Ellis, *Sharp End,* p.101.
8   Duane Schultz, 'Not A Very Merry Christmas', *World War 2,* Dec 2017. p.64.
9   Ernie Pyle. *Brave Men* (New York NY: Henry Holt & Co, 1945), p.98.
10   Hapgood and Richardson, p.83.
11   Ellis, *Hollow Victory,* p.121.

Italy had suffered thousands of battle casualties, illnesses and desertions.[12] Between 15 and 20 per cent of casualties did not come from battle but from 'war neuroses.'[13] In Tunisia doctors found that after 30-days of action most men would break down.[14] Assuming similar resilience in US infantrymen, in far more appalling conditions, it is hardly a surprise that Cassino presented a morale problem. The problem was especially severe in the replacements, who could crack in a few days of combat, and many were considered neither physically or mentally capable. Once past the initial shock, veterans could stand combat

Perhaps the most celebrated war correspondent, Ernie Pyle, who shared the deprivations of US soldiers. His book *Brave Men* vividly described the hardships of the soldier in an Italian winter. (NARA RG111-SC-191705)

much longer, but their cup of courage would also eventually empty. The losses in new junior officers were especially acute. Officers were replaced at a prodigious rate, not only through combat, but also often through sickness. One officer from the 135th Infantry, First Lieutenant Robert Hunter said in his division's lessons-learned process:

> The normal tendency is to attempt to stress his ability by taking immediate initiative in the attack, an attitude of 'I'll show you all I've got what it takes.' The result is generally one officer casualty – and frequently fatal … With luck on his side he may last the week out. If he lasts the week – he will have seen enough – learned enough – and done enough – in his own natural way – to carry him through – from then on, indefinitely.[15]

In psychological studies it was estimated that no soldier could endure more than between 200 and 240-days of total combat before breaking down.[16] On 19 January, the newly arrived Commanding General of North African Theater of Operations US Army (NATOUSA), General Jacob Devers, concluded that Clark was keeping his divisions in the front line for too long.[17] The dog faces had seen much more than the recommended 21-days. On Thanksgiving Day 1943, for instance, C Company of the 1st Battalion, 135th Infantry had been in combat for

12   Shultz, p.66.
13   Brooks-Tomblin, p.108.
14   Christine Bielecki, PhD Thesis, British Morale in the Italian Campaign 1943-1945, University of London, 2006, p.24.
15   HQ II Corps 353/91 CG Lesson Learned, 16 June 1944.
16   Ellis, *Sharp End*, p.248.
17   Wheeler, p.258.

75-days straight. When relieved they were down to 28 of the original 185-soldiers. This wasn't entirely Clark's fault. The secondary nature of Italy forced his hand. Many soldiers had already, by February 1944, reached the point of exhaustion – 'the two-thousand-yard stare.'[18]

Second Lieutenant Harold Bond, a mortar section commander from the 141st Infantry experienced troops with self-inflicted injury; sickness became rife and desertion common-place. Bond's observations were supported by Lieutenant Bill Everett who spoke of soldiers shooting themselves in the fingers or toes to escape.[19] Bodies of dead Americans lay unrecovered on the slopes in full view of the Abbey and their suffering comrades. British officer Fred Majdalany, speaks of finding dead US soldiers in April 1944 that had been there mouldering for two months! Between artillery duels, black carrion crows pecked at corpses. Officers were placed on the exit trails of the massif to intercept deserters and malingerers.[20] Early in February, Alexander, concerned over American morale, sent his Deputy Chief of Staff, Brigadier-General Lyman Lemnitzer to make an assessment. He reported that morale was 'becoming progressively worse' and that soldiers were 'so disheartened as to be almost mutinous.'[21] In February 1944, there were over 500-desertion cases awaiting Courts Marshal in the British sector alone.[22]

Most units had only a small percentage of original division members. Hardly any of the soldiers in the 34th or 36th Infantry Divisions came from Iowa, Minnesota or Texas. The sons of these states had mostly been killed or injured to be replaced by green troops from the replacement depots. Many of these replacements had only received three months of basic training, and the infantry didn't attract the best recruits.[23] In a conflict of such intensity the bonds between soldiers can be brief. Why should someone make friends with his trench mate when the next day either of them was likely to be dead?[24] The way they dealt with death was to remember their fallen comrades in life. 'Remember the time when…' was a common conversation.[25] Eighty-seven per cent of US riflemen had seen a close friend killed or wounded in action.[26] Yet it is these bonds of comradeship that drive the ordinary soldier in extraordinary circumstances. The plight of the rifleman was summed up by Lieutenant General Omar Bradley, who made the following stark observation about the men he commanded:

> The rifleman fights without promise of either reward or relief. Behind every river there's another hill – and behind that hill, another river. After weeks or months in the line only a wound can offer him the comfort of safety, shelter and a bed. Those who are left to fight, fight on, evading death but knowing that with each day of evasion they have exhausted one more chance for survival. Sooner or later, unless victory comes this chase must end on the litter or in the grave.[27]

---

18   Ellis, *Sharp End,* p.251.
19   Shultz, p.66.
20   Bond, pp.82-92.
21   Atkinson, p.406.
22   Bielecki, p.235.
23   Ellis, *Sharp End,* pp.12-13.
24   Murphy, p.124.
25   Murphy, pp.153-4.
26   Ellis, *Sharp End,* p.166.
27   Ellis, *Sharp End,* p.52.

American morale on the massif diminished day by day as Bradley's thoughts proved correct and soldiers saw their friends wounded or killed and replaced by strangers. In some ways these new troops were psychologically responsible for the casualties caused, leaving them resented by those that survived.

The American soldiers on the heights above Cassino, soon to be replaced by the Indians, in early February 1944 had not had a hot meal for over a week.[28] The nightly mule trains would carry cans of Sterno, a fuel made of jellied alcohol, so that troops could make some coffee, but that was all. They would also carry mail up to the troops. On many occasions they would also carry it down again – unopened. This soaking existence resulted in many cases of trench foot, which sometimes turned gangrenous. In early February 1944, when the 34th Infantry Division had exhausted itself and was withdrawn, such was the poor physical state of some soldiers that they had to be carried down. Although they fought with pride as Pyle noted when he visited a company within the 34th Division, 'The old-timers were sick to death of battle, the new replacements were scared to death of it.'[29]

The New Zealand or Indian troops that would replace the exhausted Americans, did not have the same problems. They had seen more action, going right back to 1941, but they had not suffered the Monte Cassino massif. They had not been on that hill for weeks, under the perceived watchful eyes of the Abbey. The General Officer Commanding (GOC) 2nd New Zealand Division, Temporary Major General Howard Kippenberger, commented about how well-rested and content his troops were before the second Cassino battle. He said of his men 'daily I could see them losing that strained look…for a little while we were very content with life.'[30] Bond, the mortar section commander, had the same impression when the Indians took over his positions.[31]

In addition to the natural sources of misery there remained the tenacious defence of the Germans, resulting in the very high casualty rates. High casualties affected team cohesion, with many junior leaders being inexperienced replacements. If they could, these men would probably have blamed the generals, but they were nowhere to be seen. Chateaux leadership was alive and well in Italy in 1944. These young soldiers rarely, if ever, saw their senior leadership along the front lines. Kippenberger when talking to the 36th Division's Colonel Aaron Wyatt learned that Walker had never been to his regimental headquarters.[32] It also seems that the 36th Division's commander planned the Rapido assault from area maps within his command post and that he did not actually see the ground.[33] This was very strange to the New Zealander who was used to sharing the privations and dangers of all his men and was soon to step on a mine close to the front line. Clark was an exception to this and often visited the front lines, although even he did not set foot on Monte Cassino, distracted as he was by Anzio. There are a few eyewitness accounts of him making visits to active areas, but Clark's attitude was unusual and not replicated

28   Captain James Luttrell, 'The Operations of the 168th Infantry (34th Infantry Division) in the Rapido River Crossing, 28 January-10 February 1944' (Fort Benning, GA: Academic Department, US Army Infantry School, 1949), p.21.
29   Pyle, p.125.
30   Major General Sir Howard Kippenberger, Infantry Brigadier (London: Pickle Publishing (Kindle Edition), 2015) Kindle Location, 5445-5452.
31   Bond, p.101.
32   Kippenberger, Infantry Brigadier, Kindle Location 5459.
33   Morris, p.250.

The Abbey held all in its shadow. In a sense, it became the visible representation of the enemy. Its destruction was therefore partly to improve the morale of Allied soldiers that fought below it. (Author)

by many of his colleagues.[34] It was alien to the German commanders to hunker down in bunkers behind the lines as for the most part many of them spent much of their time in the front line.[35] Who, or what, was to blame for all the troops' suffering? The answer loomed over them all by January 1944; the Abbey. This thing that kept them in the freezing mountains, soaked to the skin, hungry and likely to be shot at any time: this thing that watched over them with an evil eye and imagined malicious intent: this thing that kept them from the warmth of the rear areas where they could rest in a proper bed and have a decent meal: this thing that was just out of reach, taunting them: this thing that had taken their buddies and would probably take them.

The German commander must have been aware of the morale effect of the Abbey, but he was also very aware that the Abbey was an important cultural artefact to be protected: 'I was glad to take charge of the neutralization of the abbey, because no-one likes to be answerable to history for the destruction of a monument of such cultural value for reasons of tactical advantage.'[36] Nevertheless, to the average soldier it was the 'source of all their misery'. It undoubtedly contributed, with the enemy and the appalling weather, to deteriorating morale within Allied ranks. Senger also understood this fact very well:

> Anyone who has ever been in a position of leading troops in an attack which is sure to be costly, while at the same time he has to protect buildings which, in the opinion of the troops, was likely to mean disaster knows the difficulty of deciding. In such cases the soldiers feel that they are being risked for the sake of preserving a monument, a monument which to them is not of the slightest importance and whose cultural significance for mankind they are unable to appreciate.[37]

34   Vernon Walters, *Silent Missions* (Garden City, NY: Doubleday and Company Inc, 1978), p.100.
35   Senger, *Neither Fear Nor Hope*, p.198.
36   Senger, *War Diary*, p.78.
37   Senger, *War Diary*, p.79.

Majdalany makes the case of the Abbey's draining psychological effect: 'In the cold desolation of winter and the fatiguing travail of unresolved battle, the spell of its monstrous eminence was complete and haunting…To the soldiers dying at its feet, the Monastery had itself become in a sense the enemy.'[38] Another Cassino veteran and author E.D 'Birdie' Smith, who served with the 7th Gurkha Rifles in the third battle of Cassino, also conflated the fact the German artillery was accurate with the Abbey's occupation. He presents no evidence for this irrational and emotive assertion beyond the usual linking of cause and effect.[39] Charles Connell made a similar point, which read like envy concerning the intactness of the Abbey, when defending GOC of the Provisional New Zealand Corps, Lieutenant General Sir Bernard Freyberg's decision to ask for the Abbey's destruction:

> He knew his men and quite rightly refused to commit the psychological blunder of launching them against a defensive system dominated by a huge building incongruously intact in an area where all else had been pounded into debris. The very fact that it was there justified his attitude. Occupied by the Germans or not, the massive structure inspired awe and uncertainty. It represented the unknown. By cutting it down to size, General Freyberg was simply ensuring that his soldiers would start the battle with the usual quota of fearlessness and confidence.[40]

The mesmerising effect of Montecassino was not restricted to the junior ranks. New Zealand Brigadier Graham Parkinson, commanding the New Zealand 6th Infantry Brigade is credited as having remarked, 'Wipers has nothing on this place', referring to his First World War experiences at Ypres on the western front.[41] Was it this psychological effect, countering what Herbert Bloch calls a 'mass psychosis', that was the main catalyst for the Military Necessity claimed for Alexander's agreement to the request to destroy the Abbey?[42] This would be a powerful reason, destroying what was undoubtedly a major contributing factor to his force's perceived poor state of mind. This argument is touched upon by US Army Major, John Clements:

> Soldiers are quick to believe and to pass along stories of enemy atrocities even in the absence of credible evidence. In the case of the Abbey of Monte Cassino, it was rumoured that the Germans had looted the monastery of all its priceless artwork. It was also commonly believed by Allied soldiers and universally reported in the Allied press that the monastery was occupied by German observers and fortified gun positions…The psychological stress of the battlefield created conditions that enhanced the suggestibility of the soldiers and shaped the seemingly inescapable conclusion that the Germans had occupied the monastery and were using it as a base of operations to systematically destroy the Fifth Army…The Abbey of Monte Cassino was not perceived as a disinterested neutral or a passive opponent. To the soldiers below, it was the enemy. And to win, the enemy had to be destroyed.[43]

38   Fred Majdalany, *Cassino: Portrait of a Battle* (London: Longmans, Green and Co., 1957), p.121.
39   E.D. Smith, *The Battles For Cassino* (Newton Abbott, Devon: David and Charles Publishing), pp.44-45.
40   Charles Connell, *Monte Cassino: The Historic Battle* (London: Elek Books Ltd) p.49.
41   TNA CAB 44/391: New Zealand War Narrative.
42   Bloch, p.14.
43   Major John Clements, 'The Necessity for the Destruction of the Monastery at Monte Cassino', United States Army Command and General Staff College, 2002, Combined Arms Research Library, Digital Library, pp.35-39.

Lieutenant Lloyd M Wells of the US 1st Armoured Division described the activity in the Abbey in the last days of January 1944. 'At sunset every evening we could hear the chimes from the Abbey tolling out vespers, but these usually pleasant sounds only added to our anger and frustration. We interpreted them as a callous pretence, a patent deception.'[44] Wells described the normal activity going on in the Abbey in the days before its destruction amidst the strangeness of battle. His twisting of normality into something sinister is indicative of the stress of Allied soldiers at the time. Many others made the subliminal connection between the German defences and the Abbey even where evidence of such a link never existed. [45]

The conclusion over the parlous state of US morale on Monte Cassino by mid-February 1944, however, does debunk many arguments that the Abbey was destroyed to improve soldiers' morale. The Abbey was not destroyed for those American soldiers who had been there for nearly 30-days and were exhausted, but it was destroyed for those Indian infantrymen who had only just arrived and were relatively fresh. In fact, the 4th Indian Division was a unit of very high morale. It had been tested sorely over the past two years and for the Indians, action increased morale. Major General Francis 'Gertie' Tuker, wrote to Montgomery:

> The esprit de corps in the Division would undoubtedly suffer if it was relegated to a peaceful theatre of war. What it requires is more fighting. Generally speaking the standard of training amongst the forces available here is not very high, but in the Fourth Indian Division this is not the case. It is well trained and fit for battle in every way.[46]

One good indicator of a division's morale is the desertion and absence record. In the first half of 1944, the 2nd New Zealand and 4th Indian Divisions had low numbers of these indicators. The morale of both divisions was much better than other British divisions under Clark's command.[47] In another example of ineffective German intelligence, on 17 January 1944, the 4th Indian Division was considered 'no great threat' because they had no combat experience!

The Abbey did negatively affect the morale of all those infantrymen who fought in its shadow, but by 15 February, that was only the Americans. It was perceived as the enemy, just as much as the German soldier. The generals knew, however, that this was an important cultural building that was protected by policy and law, and they almost certainly knew that there were no Germans inside it. This resulted in a conundrum. As Slessor pointed out in his memoirs:

> It was astonishing how that towering hill with the great white building atop dominated the whole scene in that valley of evil memory … behind those windows there must be at least an enemy observer waiting to turn the guns on him personally when the time came to attack.[48]

---

44   Lloyd M Wells, *From Anzio to the Alps: An American Soldier's Story* (Columbia MS: University of Missouri, 2004), p.48.
45   Paul A Kennedy, *Battlefield Surgeon: Life and Death on the Front Lines in World War II* (Lexington KY: The University Press of Kentucky, 2016), p.89.
46   Stevens, *Fourth Indian Division*, p.202.
47   Graham and Bidwell, p.186.
48   Vincent Orange, *Slessor Bomber Champion* (London: Grub Street, 2006), p.145.

Destroying it would raise morale and therefore improve their chances of winning this battle but as Professor Vincent Orange observes, 'commanders usually have more compelling reasons for major action than to ease the fancies of their men.'[49] This may normally be the case, but this attack appears to have been partly justified as a morale boost from the ground forces perspective. Yet its destruction was wrong and went against everything the Allies were fighting for. Its ruins would also provide the Germans with excellent defensive positions. This is an ethical dilemma, a 'damned if you do, damned if you don't' paradox.

Some argued that morale is insufficient reasoning or justification in law for destroying the building.[50] There is no doubt that Major Clements is completely correct that the perception of the soldier, British or American, was that the Abbey stood in the way of victory and that its destruction would help their cause, but this perception was a myth, and the commanders in Italy knew this. Any short-term psychological advantage gained by its destruction would soon be shattered when the soldiers realised that they were still dying on that mountain. Morale would then be sure to plummet. Majdalany, whose vivid descriptions of the Abbey, and its effects on morale, all occurred in the period after its destruction is testament to this truth. The Abbey, of course, was not 'the enemy.' It was a building, nothing more. It was its purpose and occupants that had to be determined.

---

49   Orange, *Slessor Bomber Champion*, p.145.
50   Uwe Steinhoff, 'Moral Ambiguities in the Bombing of Monte Cassino', *Journal of Military Ethics* 4:2 (2005), pp.142-143.

6

The Poor Bloody Infantry Above Cassino

Cassino, three weeks that are still a nightmare to those of us who remember them.
133rd Infantry Regimental History, 34th US Infantry Division,
Operational History, May 1945

Having failed to breach the *Gustav* Line directly into the Liri Valley, Clark decided on 22 January that Ryder's 34th Infantry Division, would strike across the Rapido to the north of Cassino, with the FEC shifting its axis of attack to the north of II Corps, closer to Cassino, aiming for the mountain village of Terrelle.[1] Fifth Army had demoted Juin's potentially profitable penetration towards Atina, which could have outflanked Cassino entirely, into a mere flank protection task. Orders to this effect were issued by Ryder with divisional objectives of Monte Castellone, Colle Sant Angelo and Albaneta Farm with the final objective of Piedmonte.

The Abbey was absent from Ryder's orders.[2] The FEC had realigned itself by 24 January after being initially successful in breaking in towards Terrelle and Belmonte. On this day there were no German reserves left to face the FEC. The attack on Monte Santa Croce by the Moroccan Division was suspended. The main attack was then switched to the southerly Algerian Division of Monsabert to attack Monte Belvedere, which caused significant logistical difficulties. He was not pleased, writing to Juin, 'Storm Belvedere? Who's dreamed up that one? Have they even looked at it? … It's pure wishful thinking! A crazy gamble, mon general.'[3]

Juin thought Monsabert 'an intrepid leader and wise counsellor' and he thought the same as his divisional commander, calling it an attack in an 'eccentric direction.'[4] Nevertheless, they got on with it and the Tunisian Tirailleurs were the main effort, starting in the Rio Secco valley around the village of Olivella on 25 January. The Rio Secco was a tributary of the Rapido some three miles north of Cassino, which ran through the narrow Belmonte Valley to Atina. Juin had recognised that the key position, what he called 'the giant enemy observatory', was not on Monte Cassino, but on Monte Cifalco (Point 947), nearly four miles north of Cassino, in

---

1   Fifth Army History, Part IV, p.50.
2   Fifth Army History, Part IV, p.51.
3   Laurie Barber and John Tonkin-Covell, *Freyberg – Churchill's Salamander* (London: Century Hutchinson, 1990), p.193.
4   Juin, pp.57, 63.

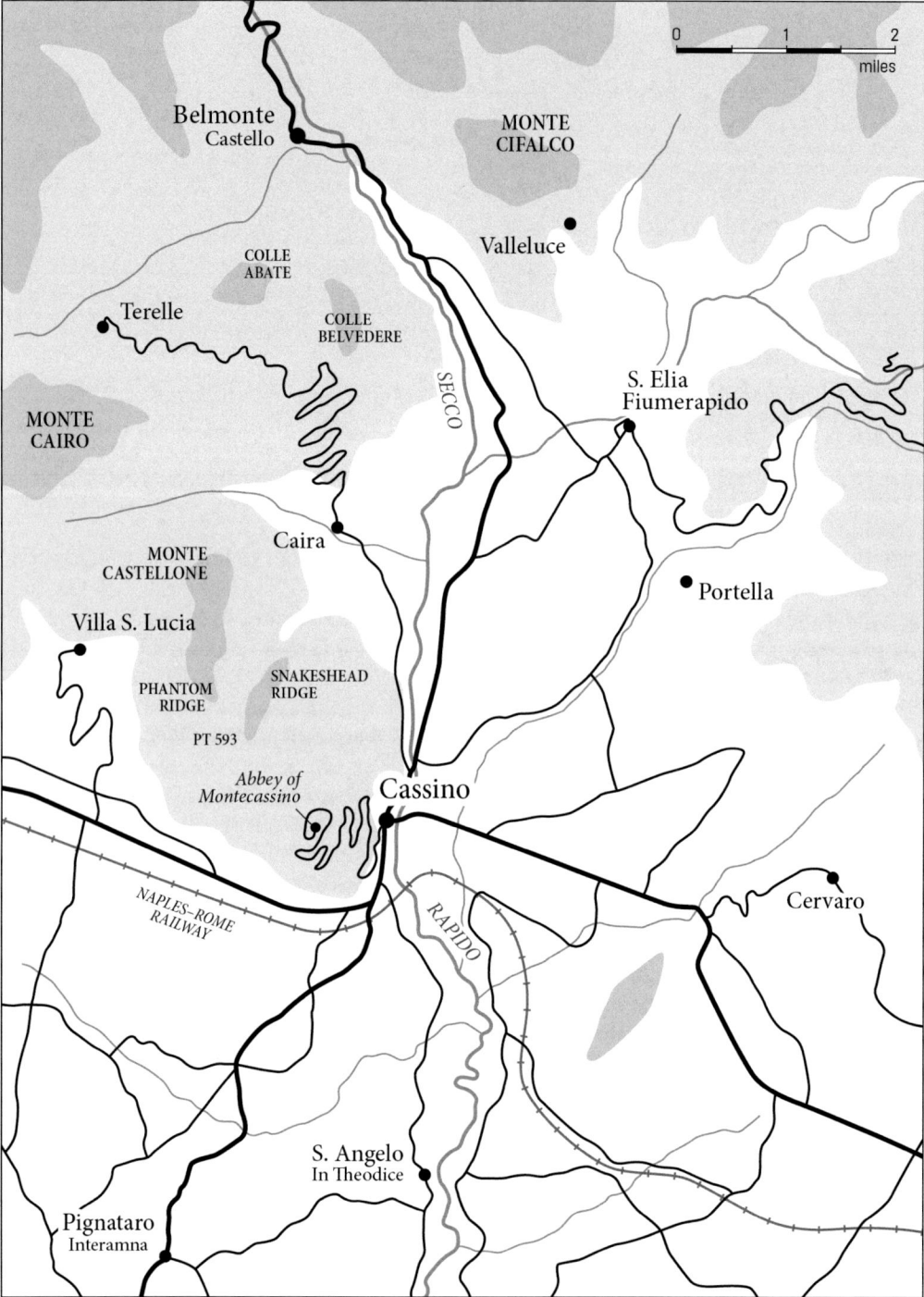

Map 3 Cassino.

Monte Castellone and the Monte Cassino massif, leading to the Abbey viewed from the excellent observation positions around Belvedere, the objective of Juin's French corps. (Author)

between the Upper Rapido and the Rio Secco, overlooking the villages and the entire Rapido valley. He aimed his forces through the mountains towards this position capturing Cifalco's lower slopes. Senger was aware of the French intent and used this excellent observation point to view the Cassino battlefield and was able to stabilise this penetration. The French retained possession throughout the next day, although they had been reduced by German counterattacks. They lost it during the night of the 25/26 January.[5]

Belvedere was a series of peaks, the most prominent, and fought over, being Point 681 and Point 862, and Monte Abate, Point 915. Pointing Juin's Corps at Belvedere and Monte Abate had the result of leaving Senger's principal observation positions intact and of exposing Juin's right flank. The attack began with the Algerians assaulting the hill of La Propaia; it was captured that evening. The Tunisians had reached the summit of Belvedere by early evening on 26 January. Senger, considered Monte Abate to be crucial to the integrity of the entire *Gustav* Line as it dominated the Belmonte Valley and the road to Atina. It fell to the Tunisian regiment early on 27 January but Point 915 was recaptured in a German counterattack later that day. German advances briefly cut the French supply lines isolating them in the mountains. By noon, Point 862 had also been lost. Had the entire Belvedere fallen, and Senger doubted whether it could be held

5   Juin, p.71.

for long, the entire line could have been outflanked from the north. Despite this, in a visit to the front opposite the French, Kesselring thought that the Allies did not have the strength to break through. The Germans attacked Belvedere the next day and the French attacked Abate; both failed. Point 862 eventually fell again to the French on 29 January, followed by Point 915 on 31 January, acts that left them exhausted. Senger juggled his very limited reserves and managed to stop further French gains, conducting a final unsuccessful attempt to recover Monte Abate on 3 February. Juin wrote to Clark on 29 January. His forces on the Belvedere were exposed due to the failure of the 34th Infantry Division to get onto the Monte Cassino massif at Monte Castellone. He told Clark that despite the Algerian and Tunisian achievements that he would be forced to withdraw from the Belvedere to the east of the road running up the Belmonte Valley unless the Americans made progress. He told Clark that whilst surrounded by enemy positions he could neither hold ground nor resupply his forward troops.[6] Fortunately, on 30 January the Americans made better progress. Monsabert's division had suffered over 2,000 casualties trying to take Belvedere and Abate, earning him the nickname, '*le boucher du Rapido.*' Two-thirds of the Tunisian Tirailleurs Regiment were lost or wounded, including its commander and all of its company commanders. In the fighting Monte Abate was taken, lost, retaken and then successfully repelled four counterattacks. On Point 862, there were 12 unsuccessful counterattacks.[7]

By the beginning of February, the German order of battle was a mixture of divisions and replacement units. From the north, the 5th *Gebirgs* Division remained in the Terrelle area. German intercepts of Allied signals indicated that the Allies were going to throw forces into the area thereby precipitating a real crisis and the 142nd Infantry's presence began to be felt after 30 January; they captured Manna Farm close to the road to Terrelle the next day. Senger withdrew elements of 90th *Panzer-Grenadier* Division from the area of the lower Garigliano in anticipation of the French and American deployment. The first reinforcements to arrive north of Cassino were from the 200th *Panzer-Grenadier* Regiment and the sister 361st *Panzer-Grenadier* Regiment, known collectively as *Kampfgruppe* Behr, that arrived on 27 January, with further reinforcements from Anzio on 31 January.[8] Von Behr's regiment was widely spread, part of the regiment was in the Minturno area with two battalions moving to Monte Castellone and a battalion initially deployed at Anzio. Baade himself took command of the Cassino position on 1 February.[9] Allied artillery was battering the German defenders, but it was impossible for them to withdraw without losing the *Gustav* Line. Inexplicably to the defenders, the attack's intensity diminished after 29 January as the Americans turned towards the village of Cairo and the Monte Cassino massif, and the French reached their culminating point on the Belvedere. Juin again did not get the extra division, although Clark sent him Walker's 142nd Infantry, but too late to allow the FEC to reach Terrelle and turn the *Gustav* Line. By the end of January both Kesselring and von Vietinghoff considered the situation to the north of Cassino as being 'dangerous but not critical.'

The objective for the 34th Division, Clark's only unused formation on the *Gustav* Line, was to strike west to secure the high ground around Monte Castellone, and south along the Cairo

6   Juin, p.74.
7   Pierre Ichac, *Nous Marchions Vers La France* (Paris: Amiot Dumont, 1954), 129.
8   Sandri, p.28; Kurowski, *Battleground Italy,* p.76.
9   Molony, p.696.

road to attack Cassino town from the north.[10] The 34th Division was not fresh and was to accrue more days in combat than any other US Army Division. It had been battered in the mountains in the *Bernhardt* Line and all three of its regiments were understrength, suffering significant losses in several encounters with the German defenders.[11] Juin considered this division as exhausted before it reached the Rapido. His French troops successfully supported the Red Bulls at Monte Pantano, which raised their standing in the mind of the Army Commander. As the battle on the massif developed over the next two weeks, the Americans appeared to be drawn towards the Abbey like a magnet, moving from a westerly to a southerly attack. This attack initially employed two regiments, the 133rd Infantry and the 135th Infantry, with the third, the 168th Infantry, held in reserve to exploit success. The attack, beginning late on 24 January, made little headway over the flooded, cleared of cover and heavily mined Rapido floodplain, overwatched by Germans on Monte Cifalco. The three battalions of 133rd Infantry, including the attached 100th *'Nisei'* battalion of Japanese-Americans,[12] had made few gains by early on 26 January holding a small bridgehead west of the Rapido, suffering over 300-casualties. The 133rd Infantry resumed its advance at midnight, and by early the next morning they had reached the base of Point 213, but didn't stay there long, being pushed back to the east of the river.[13] The plan had to be altered as the lack of progress required the early commitment of the 168th Infantry on 26 January, later postponed by a day. On 25 January the 2nd Battalion was moved to an assembly area just over a mile east of the Cairo barracks. On 27 January, the 135th Infantry managed to get a company across the Rapido slightly to the north of the town. Keyes ordered the capture of Point 213 beginning at 07:00am, with two battalions of the 168th Infantry, supported by tanks and over 5,000 rounds of artillery, leading the attack. By nightfall, all the tanks had been knocked out but the infantry had reached the base of Points 56 (actually 156 on maps), known as 'the pimple' and 213; some even made the summit of 213 early the next day, but were forced to withdraw.[14]

These attacks received immediate enemy small arms and mortar fire and the attack stalled just 200-yards across the Rapido. The 2/168 was moved to a crossroads 400-yards north-east of the barracks in preparation of an attack early on 29 January. This regiment had been heavily committed in the battles leading up to Cassino and remained at only 80 per cent strength with no replacements received.[15] After several attacks and withdrawals, the 2/168, supported by tanks, was across the Rapido in force, although the tanks had all been immobilised. A company was firm on the summit of Point 213 by that evening with another company in place before midnight. By early February, the strength of 168th Infantry was further diminished to around 50 per cent.[16] It was not until 30 January that 34th Division, reinforced by tanks and the third, and the yet unused, regiment from 36th Division began to make substantial advances.[17] On this

10   Blumenson, *Salerno to Cassino*, pp.367-368.
11   Ellis, *Hollow Victory*, p.113.
12   For some strange reason the memorial to the Nisei soldiers of 100th Battalion is located close to St Angelo where the 36th Division attempted its crossing of the Rapido on 20/21 January. The Japanese Americans were not involved in this action.
13   Fifth Army History, Part IV, p.52.
14   Fifth Army History Part IV, p.54.
15   Luttrell, p.12.
16   Luttrell, p.21.
17   Blumenson, *Salerno to Cassino*, p.373.

day the village of Cairo and the two significant high points, Point 56 and 213, were captured.[18] The secure lodgement on the west bank of the Rapido then allowed 133rd Infantry to turn south towards Cassino. The 135th and 168th Infantry climbed up the steep tracks onto the Monte Cassino massif hoping to capture firstly Monte Castellone and then to outflank Cassino by descending into the Liri Valley from the north to Piedmonte san Germano. On the same day, Clark entered the following diary entry: 'We are like two boxers in the ring, both about to collapse. I have committed my last reserve, and I am sure the Boche has done the same.'[19]

Unfortunately for Clark, they had not. Significant progress was made in the hills north-west of Cassino in the first few days of February 1944 as Monte Castellone and key heights on the Majola hill mass fell to the 3rd and 2nd battalions of the 135th Infantry respectively, taken from the remnants of the 44th Infantry Division and the 2nd battalion of the 361st *Panzer-Grenadier* Regiment. They were fortunate that on the morning of their attack a heavy fog allowed them to approach enemy positions undetected. There were several counterattacks by the Germans. Ammunition ran low and at one point on 3 February, the 2/135 Infantry was ordered to prepare to engage the enemy 'with fists and rocks if necessary.' Resupply arrived just in time as the enemy approached to within 50-yards of the battalion's positions on Majola. The Germans withdrew under cover of darkness.

The next day two companies of the 1/135 advanced to Point 445, Colle d'Onofrio, only around 500-yards north of the Abbey walls. Again, the Germans counterattacked, but the companies eventually took the hill. Only the area immediately north of the Abbey known ominously as Death Valley separated them. A platoon was dispatched southwards, across the valley, on 5 February and successfully reached the foot of the Abbey walls, capturing 14-German prisoners from various units.

These regiments were supported from the Belvedere area after 31 January by the 142nd Infantry, who arrived in the Monte Castellone area on 2 February. The next day, the 3/135 Battalion captured the key Point 706 near where the ridges divided into the Snakeshead Ridge and the Phantom Ridge, and a company got to the northern end of Snakeshead Ridge leading to the all-important Point 593. On this day, the 168th Infantry moved to the massif from Point 213.[20] Early on 5 February, the 3/135 was relieved by a battalion of the 142nd Infantry and moved towards Colle St Angelo and Phantom Ridge on the regiment's right flank.

The 2/135 reported capturing Point 593 during the night of 4 February, but in the confusion, they were mistaken and exposed to enfilade fire from the position which was now occupied by German paratroopers and panzer-grenadiers. By this time the 2/135 was exhausted and had been considerably reduced through casualties, with platoons at around half strength. The 2/135 on the left of the 3/135 struck out towards the real Point 593 from the base of Snakeshead Ridge, about two-thirds of a mile north-west of the Abbey, early on 6 February. As snow began to fall, they attacked the summit at first light with two companies, with a third providing fire support. The position, heavily shelled throughout the night, was thought to be only lightly held. The defenders had numbered only 32 on 2 February.[21] Between then and the attack by 135th

---

18   Hill 56 or 'The Pimple' is actually Hill 156 on Italian maps.
19   Blumenson, *Salerno to Cassino*, p.374.
20   Fifth Army History, Part IV, p.90.
21   Graham and Bidwell, p.170.

From a window on the northern wall of the Abbey, this modern view shows Snakeshead Ridge. German positions were located on the rocky bluff directly above the valley (Point 569) and the summit to its right is Point 593. Monte Cairo, with its observation looms over all these positions. The small building is the "Doctor's House". (Author)

Infantry, the position had been strengthened with the Germans taking cover in the deep ravines between Point 593 and the adjacent Point 569.

The 2/135 was counterattacked by at least 50-enemy as they approached the summit and were pushed off in fierce hand-to-hand fighting. However, the Germans were forced back holding only the small Bourbon fort on the summit, with the Americans holding the slopes. After withstanding at least five counterattacks, it was captured by E Company of the 2/135 who took the summit during the afternoon of 6 February. The hill was then exposed to continuous fire directed from positions on the adjacent high ground of Point 569, Colle St Angelo and Monastery Hill. It was retaken by the *Panzer-Grenadiers* at around 3:00pm, but lost again soon after. Fighting for the position continued throughout that night and the next day.

Senger's diary on 4 February reported that his 44th Infantry Division was beginning to crumble, suffering 616-casualties in the last 10-days of January from an effective strength of less than 5,000 men on 20 January.[22] It appeared to the corps commander that the position was threatened and so he reinforced it with higher quality *panzer-grenadiers* and paratroopers.[23] These were the 90th *Panzer-Grenadier* Division that had been reinstated as *Heersgruppenkommando* reserve, and the 1st *Fallschirmjager* Division in Army Reserve since 1 February. This was first confirmed on 3 February when a battalion was identified to the east of Point 593 and the next

22   Senger *War Diary*, 53; Mavrogordato, *XIV Panzer Corps*, p.57.
23   Senger, *Neither Fear Nor Hope*, p.196.

day when US soldiers captured a German paratrooper.[24] Senger fed reserve battalions into the sector as they arrived. On 31 January the 2/361 *Panzer-Grenadier* Regt arrived, followed by the 1/361 on 5/6 February and the 3/361 the next day. Throughout the next few days the other 90th *Panzer-Grenadier* Regt, the 200th also arrived. At this time Senger claimed he was losing the equivalent of one or two battalions of infantry every day, in dead, captured or wounded. The fighting on the Cassino massif was bitter, as was the weather. His fresh troops from the 90th *Panzer-Grenadiers* were successful despite many counterattacks in seizing back the key terrain of Point 593 on the morning of 7 February, suffering around 90-casualties in the attempt. It was again lost the next morning. That day the 135th's regimental headquarters moved to the Doctor's House.

The few remaining soldiers from the 2/135 were relieved by the 1/168 overnight. Following more counterattacks, the Germans recaptured Point 593 and the Americans took it back on 9 February but lost it again the next day. Further paratroopers from the 1st *Fallschirmjager* Regt reinforced the position, relieving the *Panzer-Grenadiers* from the 361st Regiment, and it was firmly in German hands from this point.[25] The hill was then held by 46-year-old Austrian *Major* Rudolf Kratzert's 3/3 *Fallschirmjager* Regiment. In the ferocity of the fighting around the hill, Kratzert received the Knight's Cross. [26]

The position changed hands six times in four days between 6-10 February. In these first few days of February, the Monte Cassino hill itself was occupied by *Major* Werner Schmidt, commander of the *Fallschirmjager* Machine-Gun Battalion. The commander of the 1/3 *Fallschirmjager* Regiment, *Major* Rudolf Böhmler, recalled that Schmidt had given strict instructions to his paratroopers that they were not under any circumstances to enter the Abbey. When he saw the leaflet dropped on 14 February, he reportedly sent a denial to the Allies in the clear, although this message has not been found.[27] His command post was located on Monte

Major Rudolph Kratzert, the Austrian officer who received the Knight's Cross for his defence of the critical point in the German line, Point 593. (Bundesarchiv Bild 146-2006-0083/Fotograf: o.Ang)

24   Luttrell, p.20.
25   Mansolas, p.54.
26   Kurowski, Battleground Italy, p.78.
27   Franz Kurowski, *Jump Into Hell: German Paratroopers in World War II* (Lanham MD: Stackpole Publishing, 2022) p.279.

Oberst Sebastian Ludwig Heilmann and *Generalmajor* Richard Heidrich of the 1st *Fallschirmjager* Division. Both officers were awarded the Knight's Cross with Oak Leaves and Swords for their defence at Cassino. (Bundesarchiv Bild 101I-577-1920-31/Fotograf Zscheile)

Cassino itself, about 400-yards from the Abbey.[28] He was the officer who gave direction as to when the civilians in the Abbey could leave, and by which route they needed to go, early on 15 February, just hours before the attack.

Senger, supported by von Vietinghoff, requested withdrawal to another defence line in the Alban Hills. He had calculated that his rate of losses could not be replenished, and that defeat was certain. The Tenth AOK had suffered 13,000 casualties in January 1944. He considered a combined defence of the *Caesar* Line by both Tenth and Fourteenth AOKs to be the only feasible way to defend south of Rome and that Kesselring was being overoptimistic in his insistence on a stubborn defence at Cassino. Should the Allies get across the German lines of communication, the defenders would be 'confronted by an impossible situation.' His request was denied.[29] Yet the Americans were also exhausted and although one patrol reached the Abbey walls, this was as far as they got and they were forced back.[30] The 168th Infantry was tasked with taking the Abbey and launched attacks against the hill on the 6 and 8 February from the direction of Colle d'Onofrio to the north of the Abbey, crossing Death Valley. Captain Jack Sheehy and his men got close to the north wall during this attempt but were quickly driven

28   Rudolf Böhmler, *Monte Cassino: A German View* (Barnsley: Pen and Sword Books, 2015), p.164.
29   Senger, *Neither Fear Nor Hope*, p.196.
30   Fifth Army History Part IV, p.92.

back. The attacking force, advancing about halfway to the Abbey from their starting positions came under withering fire from surrounding German positions including claimed machine-gun fire from Monastery Hill.[31] The arrival of the high-quality German reinforcements succeeded in halting further progress. The Americans, thinking they were close to success, added the remainder of the 36th Division to the attack despite it not being fully recovered from its efforts on the Rapido three-weeks earlier, with battalions numbering less than 100-effective men. The 1st and 3rd Battalions of the 141st Infantry were amalgamated to create a unit just bigger than a company at full establishment. The 168th Infantry made a final attempt on the Abbey and Point 593 prior to its withdrawal. The battalion ordered to make the final attack on 11 February had an effective strength of 73-men and 3-officers according to its commander.[32] These final efforts had no chance of success. The platoon officers on the massif, those that remained, were aware of the strength of their troops.[33] In total, the Americans could muster just short of 800-men for the attack, who faced around 500-paratroopers and grenadiers deployed in defensive positions between Point 593 and the Abbey.[34]

The fact that both sides could maintain themselves in the mountains above Cassino is an astounding feat. It was easier for the Germans ensconced in pre-prepared defensive positions as opposed to the temporary rock sangars used by the Americans. Nevertheless, both sides had to resupply through harrowing conditions. To get supplies onto the mountain was extremely difficult. The main US divisional supply dumps were in the rear alongside Highway 6. Supplies were taken by truck from these depots to forward supply bases; the 141st Infantry forward supply dump was near the village of Portella, 3-miles East of Caira village, in full view from Monte Cifalco. This trip, dubbed the 'Rasta Route'[35], in normal times would not take long, but with the mud, enemy and traffic congestion, could take up to 7-hours. From the dumps mules were needed to get supplies onto the mountain, and often tracks were too steep even for these. All movement on the mountains had to be carried out at night, with no lighting on precipitous trails, often through mined areas and subject to enemy fire. There were never enough mules, and many were killed or died from exhaustion. The mules could not be used to get supplies, food and ammunition, to the most forward positions. This had to be done by soldiers acting as porters. One trip would take the entire period of darkness and was a great trial for both mules and their skinners. It was not only supplies going up that taxed the logistic system, but also casualties coming down. Mules could be used, but if men were required it would take six men all night to get one casualty to a clearing station. Casualties were the one thing not in short supply, and the wounded were a far greater burden on the system than the dead.

The commanders believed they controlled heights that had been lost or had never been captured. This was to prove a handicap to the Indians when they were told of the situation prior to taking over. Because of a heavy blizzard that covered their approach the last American efforts approached to within 200-yards of the Abbey, but then the snowstorm lifted and they were forced back. Throughout these first days of February, Allied artillery regularly struck the

31   Luttrell, pp.22-23.
32   Luttrell, p.23.
33   Bond, p.93.
34   Mansolas, p.55.
35   'Rasta' simply means road in Hindustani.

Abbey, recorded by Dom Martino Matronola in the monks' diary. By 11 February the Abbey was being 'reduced to ruins.'[36]

The US II Corps' final efforts to break through at Cassino involved the 34th Division again tasked to attack Cassino town and Monte Cassino. The third infantry regiment was now back under command of the 36th Division and attacked the key terrain of Point 593 and Masseria Albaneta, 1,200yds to the north-west of the Abbey.[37] Despite the publicity given to the Abbey before and after its destruction, the key terrain, and the key to unlocking the Liri Valley was Point 593, also referred to as Monte Calvario, and the nearby Colle Sant Angelo. The ferocity of the fighting on these peaks, which included fighting with bayonets, and the fact that Point 593 changed hands several times attested to its importance. Two battalions of the recently arrived 141st Infantry could only muster 182-soldiers after defending against fierce counterattacks from 90th *Panzer-Grenadier*s near Monte Castellone on 11 February. The capture and consolidation of these positions by the Allies would have allowed Monastery Hill to be bypassed and cut-off, offering a relatively easy route down to the valley floor behind the first line of German defences. Had this position received the aerial attention that the Abbey received, the battle for the heights may have concluded much sooner. This was not to happen as the Allies, from private to general became hypnotised by the mountaintop edifice. The New Zealand Corps, swapped over from the Eighth Army sector, and specifically the 4th Indian Division, was to either exploit success, or take over from the Americans if they were unsuccessful. US II Corps had until nightfall on 12 February to capture the Abbey.[38] They failed, and despite having changed hands several times, the key terrain of Point 593 was still in German hands, still tenaciously defended by *Major* Kratzert and his paratroopers. Everyone in 34th Division command post and II Corps HQ believed that 593 was in American hands. That it was not skewed Indian planning. The Germans launched a counterattack themselves using two weak battalions of von Behr's 200th *Panzer-Grenadier* Regiment on 12 February which after initial success bogged down and a stalemate ensued.[39] The regiment suffered 249-casualties that morning. It did, however, throw-off the deployment of the Indian battalions. Having driven his US divisions to the edge of destruction, Clark admitted in his memoirs that II US Corps were down to 25 per cent effectiveness by 11 February.[40] Some rifle companies were down to their last 30-men and others were being supplemented by headquarters troops and those discharged from hospital. Ryder confessed to correspondent Sulzberger that his rifleman had suffered 65 per cent casualties.[41] The 34th Division required 1,000 mules per day to remove its wounded.[42] This period of fighting was another example of unimaginative Allied leadership. Clark's stubbornness in the face of the reality that he had insufficient force to breakthrough cost many of his soldiers' lives. Alexander was too weak to stop him. He was aware that American morale was dipping to alarming levels and that the forbidding terrain, the weather and the defences made success increasingly remote.

36   TNA FO371/60797: Vatican Secretariat of State, Monte Cassino The Last Days, p.11.
37   Fifth Army History Part IV, p.94; TNA CAB 101/229: G.R.M. Hartcup, 'The Bombing of Cassino Abbey 15th February 1944', 1965, p.2.
38   RAF Narrative – The Italian Campaign 1943-1945 – Vol. 1, p.273.
39   Senger *War Diary*, p.54.
40   Clark states that by 11 February II US Corps was at 25 percent strength. Mark Clark, *Calculated Risk* (New York: Enigma Books, 2007), p.250.
41   Casey, p.11.
42   Schultz, *Crossing the Rapido*, p.219.

Clark's ego, his suspicion of the British and his fearsome desire for an American breakthrough almost destroyed II Corps and he only reluctantly accepted that final victory would elude the Americans and handed responsibility to General Freyberg. The 'Torch was now thrown to NZ Corps' Freyberg commented in his diary on 10 February.[43]

Major Jason Merchant of the Iowa National Guard praises Ryder's use of operational art in his attempts to breakthrough to the Liri Valley.[44] The 34th Infantry Division accomplished a phenomenal feat of arms under harrowing conditions. Nevertheless, the division was destroyed, and its objectives were not met. One area where Ryder did not excel was his use of airpower to provide close air support (CAS), although to be fair to him the weather was mostly awful, and most of the XII ASC was directed at Anzio. The conditions that both sides fought through during those days is best summed up by the comments of PFC Caperton, A Company, 1/135 when he spoke in the regiment's history:

> Cassino was a nightmare. It was 14 days lying, trembling, on frozen ground with a few rocks piled up around you for protection. Sometimes you'd find yourself wishing you'd get hit, so that you'd be through. Our Battalion objective was to take the hill that had the Monastery on it. We started climbing towards it from way down in the Rapido River valley. Every move we made we were under observation. We were on the left flank of the Regiment and were also being shot at by SPs in Cassino, which was below us. We could also be seen from the Abbey, and from Hill 593. All day and night we kept getting shelled. At night, the Germans would use 'screaming meemies', and they'd almost drive you mad. During the night and before dawn, when there was a thick mist covering our positions, Jerry would sneak in on us, and you'd find yourself shooting in front of you and behind you, and just everywhere. We kept killing an awful lot of Krauts, but they still kept coming. The only one from our Battalion to reach the Monastery was a squad from Baker Company. When they finally relieved us there was 1 Officer and 26 men left in our Company. There's no question about what I remember about Cassino. I remember everything from the 'screaming meemies' to the dozens of frozen dead bodies spread out over the side of the mountains.

43   Freyberg, Bernard. *NZEF General Officer Commanding's Diary, Part IV, September 1943 to October 1944*. New Zealand National Archives, R16700590; Diary Entry, 10 February 1944.
44   Major Jason M Merchant, *The 34th Infantry Division at Cassino and Anzio: The Role of Operational Art in the Italian Campaign* (Fort Leavenworth, KS: US Army School of Advanced Military Studies, 2017), Kindle Location 577-629; Command and General Staff College, United States Army Command. 34th Infantry Division at Cassino and Anzio: The Role of Operational Art in the Italian Campaign Kindle Edition.

7

The Abbey: A Story of Europe

We are witnessing the gradual destruction of the Abbey, our hearts full of bitterness.

Dom Martino Matronola
Secretary to the Abbot of Montecassino
Diary, 11th February 1944

St Benedict of Nursia, travelled from Subiaco establishing a monastery at Montecassino around 529CE. It was built upon a rocky outcrop, formerly a temple to the god Apollo and a military acropolis, some 1,700-feet above the ancient Volsci settlement that became the Roman town of Casinum, known in medieval times as Eulogimenopolis, and then from 875CE until 1862 as San Germano, after which it was renamed Cassino. It was established in a time of great upheaval, half a century after the final fall of the western Roman Empire, when Italy was technically ruled from Constantinople, but when anarchy reigned. Its position on top of the mountain overlooked the Liri Valley, the 'land of labour', *terra di lavoro*. It had been occupied since at least the Iron Age.[1] From the original monastery, St Benedict wrote his *Rule*, the foundation document for western monasticism, becoming the dominant form of monasticism across Europe by the ninth century; by the eleventh century its monastic life was being practised in over a thousand monasteries. Benedict never again left the monastery, dying there on 21 March 547CE. Almost all of what is known of his life comes from his first biographer Pope St Gregory the Great in his *Dialogues* written in the late sixth century, nearly fifty years after Benedict's death. Gregory, who did not know him personally, spoke of Benedict as being 'renowned for his great life and apostolic virtues.'[2] Leccisotti, inmate and author in the twentieth century, speculates that St Benedict arrived at Cassino to clean up the town's idolatrous practices[3] There is no other evidence except the *Dialogues* that Benedict even lived in his Abbey.[4] Another esteemed author, and fierce critic of the destruction of the Abbey in 1944, Herbert Bloch, summed up the value of the Abbey from the time of Benedict until the present day: 'Few places in the West

1   Tommasso Leccisotti, *Monte Cassino* (Cassino: The Abbey of Monte Cassino, 1987), p.11.
2   Rennie, pp.15, 32.
3   Leccisotti, p.15.
4   Rennie, p.35.

represent the continuity of tradition between the ancient and modern world as does Monte Cassino, the foundation of St Benedict.'[5]

By the seventh century, the Abbey had achieved *locus sanctus,* enjoying freedom from local potentates and with the ability to choose its own abbots. Despite its devotion to religion and its remote location, it has always occupied a position of strategic value and has consequently been attacked and destroyed several times. These destructions have added to Montecassino's fame and have represented the suffering and resurrection of the Catholic Faith.[6] The perseverance of the Benedictines has been crucial to the continued survival of the Abbey and its significance. War and conflict have been central to its history, representing death and resurrection through destruction and recovery.[7] 'The life of the Abbey was not in the buildings and the possessions, but in the spirit that animated the community.'[8] The value of the Abbey to western civilisation can therefore be summed up as a 'universal symbol of hope, freedom, prosperity, Western culture and civilisation.'[9]

The first destruction was around 577CE when the building was destroyed by the Lombards.[10] The monks were exiled to Rome for more than a century and the subsequent fate of Benedict's body became an enduring controversy. The location of the relic is important to the tradition of Montecassino, but whether or not it remains there is contended. The opposing claim comes from the Benedictine L'Abbaye de Fleury near Orleans. The claim, supported by medieval texts, is that after being abandoned in Montecassino for nearly a century, St Benedict was transferred to France around 672CE to escape the Lombard occupation. The French Abbey claims the relics have remained there, whereas Montecassino's claim is that they never left their original resting place.[11] It is possible, though not certain, that the relics were returned to Montecassino in the mid-eighth century following Papal pressure.[12] It is important to note that the unity and tradition of Montecassino all lead back to the possession of its patron saint's relics. Their absence elsewhere, if admitted, would have serious consequences for the future influence of the Abbey. There was no physical evidence that the bones found in the ruins of Montecassino after the bombing in 1944 were those of St Benedict and his sister.[13]

Over time the Lombards, like many before them, became seduced by the Catholic Church.[14] This resulted in a flourishing religious building programme and the monastery was re-established in 718CE by the Abbot Petronax of Brescia. In the mid eighth century, Pope Zachary was successful in regaining lost church land and the Pope and the Lombard dukes competed to bestow lands and privileges to the Abbey and its reach and power grew rapidly.[15] In 787CE, the Abbey was visited by Emperor Charlemagne after his defeat of the Lombards and he was given a copy of the *Rule,* which led to it becoming normative practice in his lands. The Abbey

5   Cited by Rennie, p.15.
6   Rennie, p.16.
7   Rennie, p.17.
8   Leccisotti, p.100.
9   Rennie, p.24.
10   Rennie, p.91.
11   Rennie, pp.37-44.
12   Rennie, p.46.
13   Rennie, p.54.
14   Leccisotti, p.25.
15   Leccisotti, p.29.

was now one of the great cultural centres of the Frankish Empire, controlling over 500-square miles of land in modern-day Lazio and Campania. Despite its proximity to Rome, it remained on the borders of the Empire and was vulnerable to attacks from outside, as Charlemagne's successors failed to adequately protect the Empire's periphery. The Abbey flourished until early in the ninth century when local feudal lords forced the Abbot to pay protection money. This emptied the coffers and one Abbot, Deusdedit, died of torture at the hands of the minor Prince Zotone of Benevento in 834CE.[16] A new threat came to supplant these lords as Arabs arrived on the banks of the Garigliano around 881CE and were immediately attracted by the wealth and power of Montecassino. The Abbey had been fortified, but on 4 September 883CE it was again attacked and destroyed. The Abbot, Bertharius, was murdered a month later in a second attack.[17] The survivors exiled themselves in Teano some 18-miles to the south until 915CE, and then to Capua, at that time a major city in southern Italy, and with whose Prince's patronage the growth of the Abbey now depended and who defeated the Saracens at the Battle of the Garigliano. It was during the exile at Teano that the original signed *Rule* of St Benedict was destroyed in a fire.[18] Abbot Aligernus guided the Benedictines back to Montecassino in the mid-tenth century. He built the castle below the Abbey in 949CE on a site previously dedicated to the god Janus that was the scene of bitter fighting in March 1944.[19]

The Abbey was further fortified by the Abbot John III at the end of the tenth century.[20] At around this time the Benedictine Order was also instrumental in creating the first protections from war of churches, religious orders and women and children in the *pax dei* movement.[21] The Synod of Charroux, a Benedictine Abbey, enacted *pax dei* in 989CE, putting peasants and religious buildings under the protection of the church and offering sanctuary. The doctrine spread throughout western Europe, including the Benedictine abbeys at Cluny and the already mentioned Fleury.

Throughout the eleventh century, the Abbots had to balance friendships and loyalties, lying at the extremity of the western Empire between the Emperor, the Church, the adjacent Byzantine Empire and Norman invaders. This became as much a political task as religious and the Pope decided that piety was less important than an ability to manage conflicting relationships. In 1057, Pope Victor II appointed the Frenchman, Cardinal Frederick of Lorraine as Abbot, who then succeeded Victor as Pope Stephen IX.[22] Stephen remained as Abbot during his Papacy, but died the next year, possibly from poison. He was succeeded in 1058 by Desiderius, perhaps Montecassino's greatest Abbot. He rebuilt the entire basilica and commissioned the famous bronze doors made in 1066 in Constantinople.[23] The choice shows a positive relationship with the Byzantine Empire. He also greatly expanded the library and scriptorium, thereby increasing Montecassino's reputation as a place of learning and intellectual progress.[24] Desiderius was also of noble blood and was made a cardinal and the vicar of all southern Italy as the Abbey reached

16   Leccisotti, p.33.
17   Leccisotti, p.39, Rennie p.100.
18   Rennie, p.35.
19   Leccisotti, p.48.
20   Rennie, p.65.
21   Peace of God.
22   Leccisotti, p.54.
23   Nando Tasciotti, *Montecassino 1944: Errors, Lies and Provocations* (Rome: Castelvecchi RX, 2013), p.16.
24   Rennie, p.70.

Statue of perhaps Montecassino's greatest Abbot, Desiderius, who became Pope Victor III and adopted the Abbey as his papal seat. (Author)

the zenith of its power, siding with Rome over the Holy Roman Empire and persuading Robert Guiscard, the Norman Duke of Apulia to declare loyalty to the Pope.

Desiderius served no-one but the Pope, and he was reluctantly elevated to the Papal throne himself in 1086 as Pope Victor III.[25] Like Stephen before him he continued as the Abbot of Montecassino. For his final year of life, he relocated the Papacy to the Abbey. In 1071, Desiderius oversaw the Pope's consecration of the Abbey's Basilica, in great splendour. His bones were kept in the Abbey and were evacuated to Rome in October 1943.[26] This period was the time of Montecassino's greatest fame, with Greek and Byzantine artists brought in to decorate the church. Montecassino produced a third Pope, Gelatius II, in 1118, but he was forced to flee from Rome. The Abbey then went into a period of decline as Church and the Holy Roman Empire continued their struggle. The Abbey was placed under siege for two months in 1199 by the Empire and was occupied by imperial forces until it was retaken in 1229, whence it was turned into a fortress.[27] It was this fortification of the Abbey that was identified in 1944. After a short period of peace, the monks were driven out by the Holy Roman Emperor, Frederick II. It remained abandoned until 1265.[28]

The fourteenth century was a period of economic and social upheaval. The establishment of Montecassino as a cathedral by the Avignon Pope, John XXII in 1321 had the effect of tarring the Abbey with the unpopular and extravagant Avignon papacy. Consequently, despite a more secure

25   Leccisotti, p.56.
26   Grossetti and Matronola, p.21.
27   Leccisotti, p.65.
28   Rennie, p.105.

environment, the number of monks dwindled, and the great library went through a period of neglect. Montecassino and the town of San Germano were almost completely destroyed in an earthquake on 9 September 1349 only a year after the Black Death ravaged Italy, and although re-built for a third time at the behest of another Avignon Pope, Urban V, the Abbey's power and influence continued to diminish from the fifteenth century. During the fifteenth and sixteenth centuries, the Abbey was ruled in absentia by rentier Abbots, a period known as *commenda*, including by the child Giovanni dei Medici, who later became Pope Leo X.[29] The Abbey was caught in the middle of the war between King Louis XII of France and Ferdinand II of Aragon, which the Spanish won in another Battle of the Garigliano in December 1503, forcing Louis to cede the Kingdom of Naples to Spain. During this period the Abbey was occupied by French forces and possibly attacked by the Spanish.

War again affected the Abbey at the end of the eighteenth century when it became embroiled in the struggle between Napoleonic forces and Spanish Bourbon rulers in Naples. The Napoleonic army under French General Jean-Etienne Championnet invaded the Kingdom of Naples from the north. The army of Naples, under the Austrian General Karl Mack von Lieberich, took up defences along the Liri River. Unlike the Germans 150-years later, they occupied the Abbey, using it as a barracks with some 200 grenadiers quartered in the building.[30] Following Naples' defeat, the town of San Germano was occupied by forces under the French Brigadier General, Maurice Mathieu at the end of 1798.[31] The Abbey was again sacked in 1799 by 2,000 French troops under General Jean-Baptiste Olivier. The Benedictine Order was suppressed by the French until the Bourbon restoration in 1815.[32] Despite this restoration, the Abbey never regained the autonomy it had previously enjoyed.

The Italian Risorgimento during the 1860s further reduced the Abbey's power and influence. Following the dissolution of the Italian monasteries in 1866, and the Ordnance of 1868, it was stripped of feudal rights, its juridical power and lands, and it became a national monument with the monks as its custodians.[33] The monks' status was reduced to being caretakers, librarians and archivists.[34] In the latter part of the nineteenth century, Montecassino became the focus of British interest. It was visited by Charles Dickens who said that 'it holds the primary rank among all religious institutions.'[35] Following the dissolution, its fate and international nature resulted in a debate in the British House of Commons, where the future Prime Minister, William Gladstone, stated that the fate of Montecassino was a 'matter which went far beyond the limits of Italy, and one on which other countries were greatly interested.'[36] He called it 'an emblem of libertarianism.'

The Abbey buildings at the time of the bombing had taken form over centuries, although little visible remained of the original construction. The main Abbey was designed by the Neapolitan architect, Cosimo Fansaga.[37] The central courtyard may have dated to 1515 and the church that formed the focal point of the Abbey was started in 1649 and consecrated by Pope Benedict XIII in 1727.

29 Rennie, p.106.
30 Leccisotti, p.94.
31 Rennie, p.108.
32 Rennie, p.110.
33 Leccisotti, p.99.
34 Rennie, p.111.
35 Rennie, p.80.
36 Rennie, pp.161-163.
37 Rennie, p.145.

The reconstructed basilica of the Abbey of Montecassino. The central doors of the basilica date back to 1066 and were built in Constantinople. (Author)

The building was an unequal quadrilateral, built of Travertine stone, and was approximately 700-feet long by 360-feet wide, covering some 300,000-square feet.

Its position led the French general, Juin, to describe it as 'another Gibraltar.'[38] The Abbey belongs to Italy and is not protected by the extraterritoriality agreements of the Lateran Treaty. In a message of 10 February, just five days before the attack and before the decision was taken to attack it, AFHQ passed on to 15th Army Group and Fifth Army a list of five sites that the Vatican wished to be offered special protection. One of these was the Abbey. AFHQ, however, made it clear that these sites 'should not be allowed to interfere with bombing, artillery fire and other military operations.'[39] This message from Wilson effectively gave Alexander permission to act as he did on 15 February.

Prior to its destruction in 1944, the Abbey library contained an important archive of records and codices, dating back centuries, including some of the first ever printed works. As late as December 1942, works by Shelley and Keats were placed there for safe-keeping.[40] *Oberstleutnant* Julius Schlegel from the *Luftwaffe's* Hermann Göring *Panzer* Division who arranged their evacuation, stated there were around 80,000 documents, including the *Placito Cassinese*, which contained the first sentence written in vulgar Latin in 960CE, that was to morph into the modern

38   Rennie, p.81.
39   TNA WO 214/38: FOLIO 07519 dated 10 February 1944, AFHQ to ACMF and Fifth Army.
40   Phillips, p.201.

The Abbey viewed from Point 593. The point, a little higher than the Abbey, was the key terrain in the German defences. In bitter fighting in the first days of February 1944 it changed hands numerous times, finally being secured by the German paratroopers. It was not bombarded from the air to any great extent. (Author)

Italian language; the *Paulus Diaconus* from the eighth century, works by Pope Gregory the Great and notes in the handwriting of St Thomas Aquinas as well as the *Biblia Hebraica* and Norman documents from Robert Guiscard and Roger of Sicily who conquered the region in the eleventh century.[41] There was also an early manuscript of Dante's *The Divine Comedy*, dated to 1321 and containing handwritten notes from his son Pietro.[42] To preserve these, 387-crates of artefacts were removed to Spoleto and then transferred to the Vatican by 5 December 1943 after *Hauptmann* Maximillian Becker, a doctor also in the Hermann Göring Division, and Schlegel persuaded the Abbot that they were in danger. In addition to the Abbey's own artefacts, there were also artefacts removed from the museum in Naples following the German evacuation in September 1943. Despite Becker's honest efforts, others in the division had decided to steal objects and present them to their patron, and keen looter of art, for his birthday; a legitimate reward one officer called the theft.[43] Becker claimed that he saw Schlegel choosing items for Göring's birthday present.[44] The basilica had many irreplaceable frescoes and mosaics that could not be evacuated, including those by the seventeenth century painter Luca Giordano depicting the life of St Benedict. One

41 Julius Schlegel, Monte Cassino Treasures, *The Times*, 1951, Issue 52153, p.5.
42 Tasciotti, p.26.
43 Edsel, p.86.
44 Benedetta Gentile & Francesco Bianchini, *I Misteri dell'Abbazia* (Firenze, IT: Casa Editrice Le Lettere, 2014), p.52.

of these was first damaged on 11 January by stray artillery shells.[45] More hits were suffered on 15 January, causing serious damage, which then prompted the German photographers who had been present during the evacuation to return to take propaganda pictures of the damage. The basilica itself suffered its first damage when hit by a shell on 21 January, and more shells hit the Abbey three days later. On 25 January, the monks' diary tells of a premonition of the Abbot regarding the destruction of the Abbey.[46] Shells hit the Abbey from both sides over the next few days as the battle for the massif intensified. The evacuation of the art treasures may have been known to the Allies, but the press who first reported on the Abbey's use as an observation post on 8 February, stated that the treasures still remained within the Abbey.[47] The monks estimated that by this date the Abbey had already been struck by about 100-shells.[48]

Using the Todt Organisation to construct concrete and steel defences under the command of Kesselring's chief engineer, *Generalmajor* Hans Bessel, the area was one of the most stoutly engineered lines of defence in Europe. The Tenth AOK intention was to use infantry sparingly and to rely on the engineers for mines, obstacles and fortifications. The Abbey had a magisterial perspective on the surrounding battlefield. The hill upon which it stood, along with the surrounding terrain, certainly appeared to be an ideal defensive position, considered virtually impregnable by the Italian Staff College in a 1909 appreciation by *Generale* Alberto Pollio.[49] Surely this stone edifice, with its thick walls and unobstructed view of the valley far below, which had been labelled a 'modern fortress' by Tuker, the Allied general eventually tasked to conquer it, would be used by the Germans as a key strong point within this carefully prepared defensive system?[50] If so, then regardless of its religious nature it would possess military value to the side that occupied it. It could not be left untouched if it held up the advancing Allied army. The key question was whether the Germans honoured their promise not to use it for military purposes? Beyond that, would the Allies believe them? Its fate rested upon the validity of two words – Military Necessity, and the proof required determining it. The Abbey had in fact been used for military purposes right up until the Italian Armistice in September 1943. The Italian Air Force had made use of the Observatory as a radio transmitter, and it continued operating until 17 October on non-military tasks by the monks. The Abbey also provided accommodation for five Carabinieri. The Carabinieri, although conducting civic police duties, are part of a military force and subject to the Laws of War. The Air Force use of the Observatory was also known to the *Luftwaffe* and on 25 November 1943, a *Luftwaffe* officer visited to ask the Abbot whether they could make use of the Observatory for meteorological purposes. Abbot Gregorio Diamare wisely forbade this, as this activity would have counted as military activity. The visit appears to have triggered concerns in the Abbey that the Germans may occupy the building. This then persuaded the monks that the most important artefacts should be hidden.[51]

---

45   Leccisotti, p.118.
46   Grossetti and Matronola, p.86.
47   Monastery Used as an Observation Post, *The Times*, 10 February 1944.
48   Grossetti and Matronola, p.102.
49   Hartcup, 5; Tasciotti, p.17.
50   Memorandum No.433/1/G Operations, from Major-General Tuker, General Officer Commanding 4th Indian Division to New Zealand Corps Headquarters, 12 February 1944 In CAB 106/699 – Report on the Bombing of MONTE CASSINO ABBEY – 15 February 1944. London: Cabinet Office Historical section, 1949.
51   Gentile and Bianchini, p.39.

Gregorio Diamare, was a Benedictine priest and as well as the Abbot of the Abbey of Montecassino he was the Bishop of the Abruzzi diocese. Born in 1865, he was ordained in the Benedictine Order in 1891 and became Abbot in 1909. He was ordained as a Bishop in 1928. He reluctantly agreed to the evacuation of the Montecassino treasures. He and a few other monks remained in the Abbey throughout the Allied onslaught, and they were there when it was bombed. At 09:28am, the monks were reciting *Et pro nobic Christum exora* and Diamare and all his brothers survived due to being in the deep crypt.[52] He demonstrated great bravery during the bombing, taking time to deliver Absolution to his monks as the bombs fell. He had attempted to evacuate them and Italian civilians from the Abbey after seeing the leaflet dropped during the afternoon of 14 February. His messenger went to the nearby German position at Masseria Albaneta that evening to arrange an evacuation for the next night. This was likely the headquarters of the 1/361 *Panzer-Grenadier* Regiment.[53] He was told to come back the next morning, although before he could do so, a German officer arrived at the Abbey. Diamare suggested that the monks evacuate towards Allied lines whilst the civilians evacuated towards the German lines. This was flatly rejected by the Germans who insisted all evacuations had to be towards their lines to not provide the enemy with an intelligence opportunity.[54] Although the officer was dismissive of the leaflet, he offered the occupants of the Abbey safe passage that night from midnight to 5.00am on 16 February. The Abbey was bombed before the civilians could be evacuated. Abbot Diamare wrote the following note confirming that no Germans had been within the Abbey's walls:

> I solemnly declare that no German soldier has ever been stationed within the precincts of the Monastery of Monte Cassino; that for a while three military police were on duty, with the sole object of ensuring that the neutral zone round the Monastery was being respected. But these latter were withdrawn some twenty days ago.

As the monk's diary reveals, this statement does not exactly represent the truth. While it is true that no soldiers had been 'stationed' in the Abbey, there had been almost daily visitations. These had mostly been tourist or liaison in nature; no military activity occurred. Diamare left the ruins of his Abbey on 17 February and made the long walk down the mountain to the Liri Valley. Dom Martino Matronola could not disguise his feelings in the diary entry for that day, 'We left the house of St Benedict, destroyed by the wickedness and cruelty of men.'[55] Upon reaching a German aid station, the Abbot was taken initially to see Baade in Roccasecca and then to Senger at the former headquarters of Napoleon's brother-in-law, Joachim Murat and later of Garibaldi, in Castelmassimo, where he was interviewed by the German commander.[56]

Senger, a lay member of the Benedictine Order, tried to offer comfort, offering dinner in his headquarters. He then tried to send them on to San Anselmo in Rome, where the Head of the Order resided, but other Germans waylaid them, forcing them into another propaganda declaration. Diamare remained Abbot of Montecassino, returning in September 1944, but he

---

52   Plead with Christ our souls to spare.
53   Sandri, p.29.
54   Grossetti and Matronola, p.113.
55   Grossetti and Matronola, p.125.
56   Grossetti and Matronola, p.132-3.

was never to see it rebuilt, dying of malaria in late 1945. He remained implacable in his view of the Allied action until he died, adding to the credibility of his statement that it was not given under duress. In January 1946, an Italian liaison officer to AFHQ, *Tenente Colonello* Count de Salis wrote to AFHQ that:

> The late Abbot took the line that the destruction of the Monastery was a totally unnecessary piece of vandalism, as the Germans had never occupied the Monastery at all previous to its destruction, and that if the Allied Forces thought that if they could repair the harm they had done by just clearing the ruins, they were mistaken.[57]

In the same letter, Count De Salis recounted a conversation with the new Abbot, Dom Ildefonso Rea, regarding a publication that he was planning with regards to the Abbey during the war. Abbot Rea was no apologist for the Nazis, having been imprisoned by them in September 1943. Nevertheless, he maintained the vociferousness of his predecessor. Concerning its destruction, the publication was to state that:

> The Monastery was NEVER occupied by any German troops previous to its destruction on the fifteenth of February. The destruction was therefore not a Military Necessity, and completely unjustified.[58]

This is possibly the booklet that would be given to the US Charge d'Affaires to the Vatican, Harold Tittmann, who complained about it to the Vatican. We shall return to it later. De Salis asked that its publication be delayed so that the Allies could state their case.

Following the war, Rea was determined that Montecassino would be rebuilt faithfully, 'as it was, where it was', was what he said to Archbishop Schuster of Milan in January 1946.[59] In this he was opposed to the Vatican, which wanted a new design.[60] Schuster knew that despite Rea's desire to remain faithful to the destroyed Abbey it would never be the same:

> However, Monte Cassino is rebuilt, even if the walls are of gold and the floors of jasper, the treasures of ancient art are not rebuilt. The Cassinese basilica and the marquetry of its marbles and the gold of the stuccos that framed the paintings by Luca Giordano will no longer exist...In this respect the destruction of Monte Cassino represents irreparable damage to all Christian civilisation.[61]

The first stone was symbolically re-laid on 15 March 1945 by the Italian Prime Minister, Ivanoe Bonomi, with work beginning in earnest in June 1947. The Abbey was rebuilt for the fourth time, with the Italian Government paying the bill. A report by the Italian Ministry of Public Works spoke of the importance of the building and what its destruction signified when it said:

57 TNA WO 204/5735: Advanced Allied Force Headquarters Liaison Section, MONTE CASSINO dated 7 January 1946.
58 TNA WO 204/5735: Advanced Allied Force Headquarters Liaison Section, MONTE CASSINO dated 7 January 1946.
59 Rennie, p.148.
60 Rennie, p.185.
61 Canciani, p.192.

'Two hours of methodical bombardment that shattered a millenary tradition of meditation, of operative charity that through so many fortunate events had given inexhaustible food to the most shining and true glory of Italy.'[62]

It was reconsecrated by Pope Paul VI in 1964. The Pope in his speech this day was pointed in his views:

> It is peace that made them revive. It still seems incredible that the war acted against this Abbey, incomparable monument of religion, culture, art, civility, one of the proudest and blindest gesture of its fury, so we can't believe it is true when today we see this magnificent building revived, almost wanting to pretend that nothing happened, that its destruction was a dream, and we can forget the tragedy that had made a pile of ruins. Brothers, let us cry with emotion and gratitude…we cannot deplore that civil men had the boldness to use Saint Benedict's grave as a target for atrocious violence.[63]

It remains today an active monastery, although the number of monks has declined. Despite not being Vatican property, it retains a close relationship with the Holy See, the Abbot still oversees the Diocese of Abruzzi. On the 45th anniversary of the final battle, on 18 May 1979, the Polish Pope, John Paul II visited the Abbey, calling the destruction barbarous. His intention was 'to visit these places sacred to human pain and Christian hope.'[64] Pope Benedict XVI, named in honour of Montecassino's founder, also visited the Abbey in April 2009. The year before his visit, in April 2008, His Holiness spoke about the influence of St Benedict, and his house at Montecassino:

> The Saint's work and particularly his *Rule* were to prove heralds of an authentic spiritual leaven which, in the course of the centuries, far beyond the boundaries of his country and time, changed the face of Europe following the fall of the political unity created by the Roman Empire, inspiring a new spiritual and cultural unity, that of the Christian faith shared by the peoples of the Continent. This is how the reality we call 'Europe' came into being.[65]

This speech's veneration of St Benedict leads to one final intrigue surrounding the great Abbey. At the end of the war the United Nations established the United Nations Education, Scientific and Cultural Organisation, UNESCO. UNESCO has, following the signing of the World Heritage Convention of 1975, been responsible for the protection of sites that meet the following definition:

> Outstanding universal value means cultural and/or natural significance which is so exceptional as to transcend national boundaries and to be of common importance for present and

62   Rennie, p.112.
63   The Pope Deplores Bombing of Cassino Monastery, *The Times*, 26 October 1964, Issue 56152, p.9; Rennie, p.154.
64   Leccisotti, p.180.
65   *Benedict XVI General Audience, 9 April 2008* <https://www.vatican.va/content/benedict-xvi/en/audiences/2008/documents/hf_ben-xvi_aud_20080409.html> (accessed 5 January 2023).

future generations of all humanity. As such the permanent protection of this heritage is of the highest importance to the international community as a whole.[66]

In July 2021, there were 1,154 sites on the World Heritage list and Italy has the most sites for a single country with 58. The Abbey of Montecassino is not one of them! Examining the pages above and considering the influence of the Benedictine Order on western Christianity, western civilisation and the spread of the Roman Catholic faith globally, this is perplexing. The Benedictine Order also influenced the spread of Christianity to countries such as Britain, through monks such as St Augustine, the first Archbishop of Canterbury, and there are also those in the Orthodox Church that follow the *Rule.*

Before a country can nominate a site for inclusion on the list, the site must be nominated to a Tentative list. Italy, despite its ratification of the Convention in 1978, did not nominate the Abbey to its Tentative list until 2016. It is unclear why a gap of 38-years passed. Even then, the Abbey was not nominated under its own name, but under a collective nomination with eight other Benedictine monasteries entitled: '*The cultural landscape of the Benedictine settlements in medieval Italy.*[67] At the beginning of 2023, despite being placed on the Tentative list, Italy has made no attempt, according to the World Heritage Committee's annual decision reports, to raise the Abbey to the full World Heritage list. According to the minutes of these meetings, the Abbey has not been discussed by the Committee.[68]

Why does Monte Cassino, with all of its history and tradition, appear to have been shunned by the Italian State? It is one of the principal factors why Roman Catholicism is the largest single religion with over 1.2-billion adherents worldwide. Surely this profoundly Roman Catholic country, which possesses a rich religious history and has the Vatican within it, would have been proud to include the great Abbey amongst its finest treasures? Is it possible that the controversy surrounding its destruction in February 1944, may have influenced its non-inclusion? It clearly meets the cultural criteria, and there have been a number of inclusions of lesser sites, including by Italy, since 2016. The destruction of this culturally significant edifice has left many ashamed of what they did or did not do to prevent it. Perhaps it was just more convenient to let sleeping dogs lie for Italy, rather than raking up the controversies again?

---

66   Rennie, p.216.
67   *The cultural landscape of the Benedictine settlements in medieval Italy* <https://whc.unesco.org/en/tentativelists/6107/> (accessed 4 January 2023).
68   *UNESCO Periodic Reporting* <https://whc.unesco.org/en/periodicreporting#:~:text=Periodic%20Reporting%20is%20one%20of%20the%20core%20conservation,territory.%20Article%2029%20of%20the%20World%20Heritage%20Convention> (accessed 5 January 2023).

8

A New Broom

There is a fierce chagrin that the two best divisions in the British Army, forming a corps that seemed a perfect combination, should have achieved nothing.

Royal Artillery Officer at Cassino[1]

Clark's command was further complicated in early February 1944, when Alexander transferred divisions from the Eighth Army into his area to exploit a breakthrough at Cassino. The 2nd New Zealand Division and the 4th Indian Infantry Division were brought together as the ad hoc New Zealand Corps under Sir Bernard Freyberg on 3 February.

Born in England of German descent, Freyberg moved to New Zealand when he was two years old. He was an excellent swimmer, twice winning the New Zealand championship for the 100-yards. He left New Zealand a few months before the outbreak of war and made his way via America to England. In September 1914 he joined the Royal Naval Brigade and he first met Churchill, who later, keeping to his animal metaphor, nicknamed Freyberg the 'Salamander' – at his happiest in the heat of battle. He persuaded Churchill to award him a Royal Naval Volunteer Reserve commission. Freyberg made his name at Gallipoli, where he used his swimming skills earning the first of three Distinguished Service Orders (DSO), placing flares on a beach in the Gulf of Saros with the intent to distract defending Turks. Although he transferred to the British Army in May 1916, he remained with the Royal Naval Division on temporary secondment. As a temporary lieutenant colonel in November 1916, he was awarded the Victoria Cross for his actions on the Somme. In addition to two more DSOs, Freyberg earned the Croix de Guerre and was mentioned in despatches five times. It did not take the nine wounds to prove he was a brave man. After the war, he tried, but was unsuccessful in being elected as a British Member of Parliament for the Liberal Party in 1922.[2] This was during the period when Churchill was also a member of this Party. Heart problems forced him to retire from the British Army in 1934. He returned to active duty in 1939 as a Major General in the British Army before becoming the GOC of the 2nd New Zealand Division following an approach from the New Zealand Government and a recommendation from the War Office. Freyberg commanded

---

1   Stevens, *Tiger Triumphs*, Kindle Location 1405.
2   Laurie Barber and John Tonkin-Covell, *Freyberg: Churchill's Salamander* (London: Century Hutchinson, 1990), p.1.

Taken in March 1944 at a conference between senior officers of the US 1st Armoured Division and the provisional New Zealand Corps. From left to right the New Zealanders were Major General Parkinson, GOC 2nd NZ Division, Brigadier Ray Queree, Brigadier General Staff, NZ Corps and Lt Gen Bernard Freyberg VC wearing the B-3 flying jacket given to him by General Clark. (NARA RG 111-SC-189378)

British and Commonwealth forces in Crete in 1941, not his or the New Zealand Division's finest hour. His reputation with Churchill took a knock after a report that laid the blame onto Freyberg.[3] More recent historians have also criticised his poor use of ULTRA, but it was not intelligence appreciation that lost Crete, but a lack of air cover, a factor outside of his control. The subsequent enquiry held in Cairo in the early summer of 1941, led New Zealand's Prime Minister, Fraser to question Freyberg's suitability for command. He retained the confidence of Wavell and General Sir Claude Auchinleck and this probably saved him from dismissal.[4]

In North Africa in 1942, back in divisional command, he was again wounded and also promoted to lieutenant-general, a rank above that usually associated with a divisional commander. Prior to Montgomery taking over Eighth Army, Freyberg had disagreed with his predecessor Auchinleck and had raised the possibility that a national contingent commander had a right to disobey orders if they were not in the national interest. This threat was again apparent at Cassino, at least in the minds of Freyberg's superiors. Although a successful tactical commander he showed less aptitude at the more nuanced corps level. Montgomery said that he was 'a nice

3   Barber and Tonkin-Covell, pp.112-3.
4   Barber and Tonkin-Covell, pp.120-1.

old boy, but a bit stupid.'[5] That did not prevent him selecting Freyberg to lead the pursuit of Rommel after victory at El Alamein. His efforts in commanding at corps-level both in Crete and at Cassino were not successful, although he was more successful at this level at the Tebaga Gap action in March 1943. It was here also that he learnt the value of CAS. Following the disbandment of the New Zealand Corps after its failure at Cassino, he continued to command 2nd New Zealand Division until war's end.

At the end of January, Alexander ordered the Eighth Army divisions, to redeploy to the Fifth Army sector as Army Group Reserve.[6] Their initial task was to exploit success when US II Corps finally broke into the Liri Valley.[7] Freyberg was known to be temperamental and 'hard to handle'; Alexander, fully aware of these difficulties, was reluc-

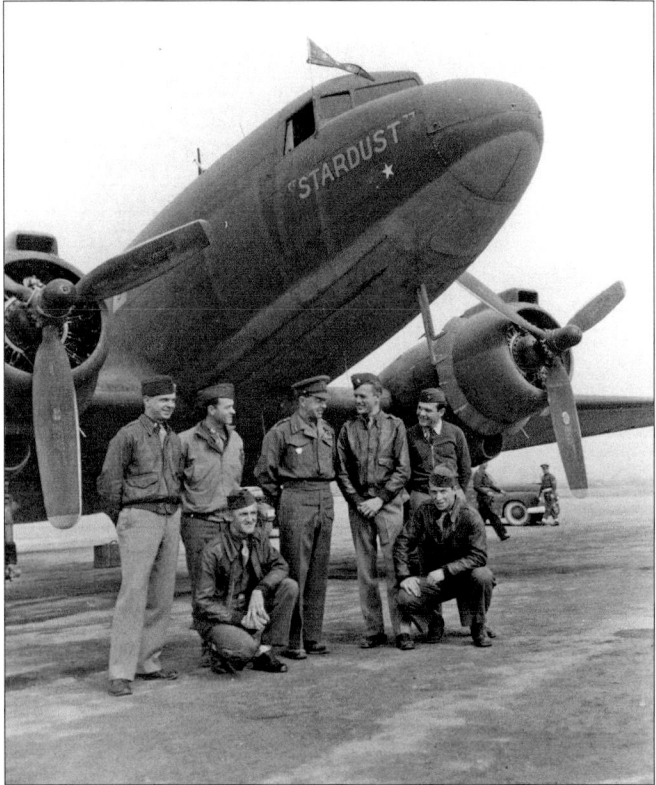

The General Officer Commanding-in-Chief, 15th Army Group, General Sir Harold Alexander chats with the crew of his personal C-47 'Stardust.' Alexander moved Eighth Army divisions from the Adriatic sector to exploit any breakthrough by Clark at Cassino. (NARA RG342-FH000065)

tant to place him under the already overstretched Clark and Alexander and Freyberg maintained personal communications throughout, often bypassing Clark.[8] This was not a surprise to him:

> I got a definite impression that 15th Army Group and Freyberg were going to tell me what to do. I objected as diplomatically as possible, pointing out that their plans for using the New Zealanders and Indian troops in the Cassino – Monte Cairo mountain sector would not fit in well.[9]

5   Douglas Porch, *The Path To Victory: The Mediterranean Theater* [sic] *in World War II* (New York: Farah, Straus and Giroux, 2003), p.162.
6   Headquarters 15th Army Group, Operations Instruction No.34, 12 January 1944. 2nd NZ Division and 4th Indian Division to be followed later by 78th British Infantry Division.
7   Fifth Army History Part IV, p.93.
8   Blumenson, *Mark Clark*, pp.180-181; Ellis, *Hollow Victory*, pp.161-2.
9   Ellis, *Hollow Victory*, p.162.

Clark didn't want British or Commonwealth troops taking the glory of breaking into the Liri Valley, a glory that had been dearly bought with American lives. Freyberg and Tuker had been informed that they would be going from Eighth Army to Army Group reserve around 21 January. This was to exploit a breakthrough rather than to fight in the mountains. Freyberg planned to use air support in the same way as he had used it at the Tebaga Gap in Tunisia, as flying artillery cab-ranking ahead of his armour .[10] Nevertheless, in his diary on 26 January, he is clear that he believes the high ground north of Cassino is where the *Gustav* Line would be broken; 'That is the key to it', he says.[11] Freyberg made an immediate poor impression with the Americans at his first staff conference on 4 February when he clashed with Keyes, whom he had first met only three days before. It did not take long for him to become critical of the Americans, although he was probably correct when he commented on their use of air support.

At a meeting of his divisional brigadiers on the day that his corps was chopped to Clark instead of as Army Group Reserve, 4 February 1944, Freyberg made it clear that his intent was to make maximum use of air support: 'I want…to get an organisation from the Americans which allows us to use their fighter bombers and their medium and light bombers for CAS during an attack.'[12] He was used to the air-land integration of Eighth Army in the North Africa set up of Montgomery and the Western Desert Air Force Commander Air Marshal Sir Arthur Coningham.

This almost seamless process was not yet well developed in Fifth Army. At this point Freyberg had no plans to seize Monastery Hill. Between being informed that he was going into the mountains near Cassino, Tuker had conducted a reconnaissance, and visited Juin.[13] Freyberg also visited his HQ and that of Monsabert's division on 31 January.[14] Freyberg thought the French had done 'quite well', all his brigadiers had a high opinion of Juin.[15] In these few days he had also visited Ryder and Walker. At a New Zealand Corps Planning Conference, Freyberg's plan was based around these discussions in that he intended a wide turning movement to the north of Cassino, intersecting Route SS 6 in the German rear.[16] He intended to move the New Zealanders to assembly areas for entry to the high ground on the night of 5-6 February and issued a Warning Order to Kippenburger.[17] Fourth Indian Division was to launch its attack well to the north of Cassino around Monte Cairo. The problem was that neither Freyberg nor Alexander thought to consult the man responsible for the attack – Mark Clark. Freyberg briefed Alexander on his plan the day before speaking to Clark, whom he first briefed on 3 February.[18] During the afternoon, Freyberg met with Clark and Alexander to discuss future operations and where he outlined his corps plan.[19] Clark was already fuming about having Freyberg foisted

10   Barber and Tonkin-Covell, pp.195-8.
11   Freyberg, Diary Entry, 26 January 1944.
12   Wright, Kindle location 700.
13   Christopher Mann, 'Failures in Command and Control: The Experience of 4th Indian Division at the Second Battle of Cassino, February 1944' in Andrew L Hargreaves, Patrick J Rose and Matthew C Ford (eds.), *Allied Fighting Effectiveness in North Africa and Italy, 1942-1945* (Leiden NL: Brill, 2014), pp.191-2.
14   Freyberg, Diary Entry, 31 January 1944.
15   Freyberg, Diary Entries, 26 January and 2 February 1944.
16   Stevens, p.275.
17   Freyberg, Diary Entry, 3 February 1944.
18   Freyberg, Diary Entry, 3 February 1944.
19   Mann, p.192.

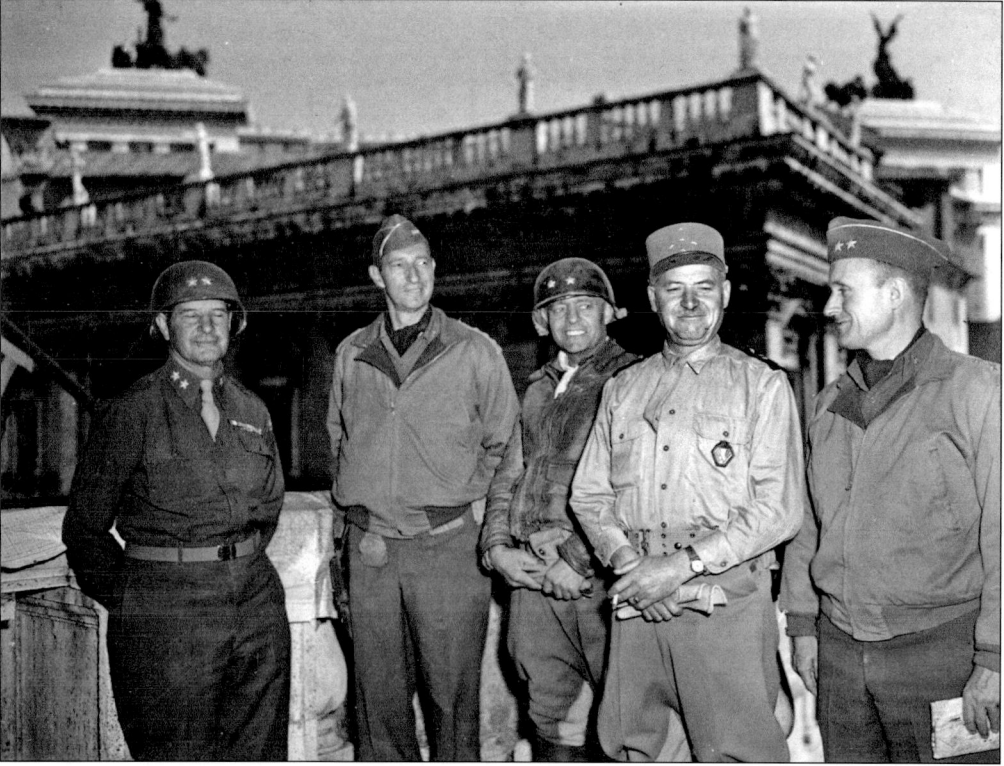

General Clark with his key officers following the capture of Rome. From l-r, US II Corps, Major General Keyes, General Clark, US VI Corps, Major General Truscott, FEC, General Juin and Fifth Army Chief of Staff, Major General Gruenther. (NARA RG80-G-252537)

on him and was clearly wary of British plotting. He was further annoyed that they had, before coming under command, conducted informal visits to his corps and divisional commanders without gaining his permission. This was despite being asked to 'give General Freyberg every facility to obtain information and carry out recces' by Harding on 30 January.[20] This annoyance further demonstrates the more formal attitude of American commanders as opposed to the relaxed attitudes of the French and British. He was not very amenable to Freyberg's plan. In his papers he recounted the incident that day:

> Freyberg had done this without reference to me. Alexander had likewise made plans, all of which quite unethically, for after all it is my job to prepare the tactical plans and conduct operations of the Fifth Army. It was apparent at the beginning of the meeting that 15th Army Group and Freyberg were going to tell me just how my next attack would be made. I objected as diplomatically as possible. Differed entirely with Freyberg's and Alexander's views on the employment of the New Zealand Corps.[21]

20   Barber and Tonkin-Covell, p.192.
21   Mann, p.193.

Clark's annoyance was justified, although Harding had informed him that Alexander would discuss Freyberg's plan with him, once made.

This shows lack of tact by the British in dealing with the different command philosophy of their ally. Consequently, he had to reject the British plan to retain credibility as the commander in charge. The British tendency was to issue an objective; how the tasked commander accomplished it was then his business. This was not the American way. There were now no other alternatives other than a frontal attack, regardless of Clark's initial intention. On 6 February, Freyberg noted that US II Corps, 'Hoped to have Monastery by dark.'[22] Clark wanted the Abbey, but he didn't want it damaged. Following the failure of US II Corps, 15th Army Group (ACMF) issued the following Operations Instruction:

OPERATIONS BY NZ CORPS IN THE LIRI VALLEY

1.   The C-in-C is naturally anxious that the advance of the NZ Corps up the LIRI Valley, astride Highway 6, should take place as early as possible. At the same time, he considers it essential to the success of that operation that the ground should be dry enough to permit the operation of armour off the roads, and that the weather, during any large scale daylight operations, should be suitable for effective air support. The C-in-C therefore orders that any major operation by NZ Corps in the LIRI Valley will not take place unless and until the physical conditions mentioned above obtain. This does not apply to the attack of 4 Ind Div to clear the high ground West of CASSINO of the enemy, or to the establishment of a bridgehead over the RAPIDO River in the CASSINO area, both of which operations will be carried out as quickly as possible, so that NZ Corps can begin to advance Westward from the CASSINO bridgehead as soon as physical conditions laid down above are fulfilled.

The C-in-C orders that, when NZ Corps is committed to an attack, all available resources will be concentrated in its support, and requests will be submitted through air channels for the maximum air effort in support of the attack.[23]

Despite the failure, both Alexander and Clark thought success was close. Slessor, the Mediterranean Allied Air Forces (MAAF) Deputy Commander, was not so confident. He wrote to the MAAF Director of Operations, Brigadier-General Lauris Norstad on the same day as the Operations Instruction from Alexander's headquarters. His views of Cassino were far less optimistic than his ground colleagues. He began his letter by saying, 'There are now 17 German Divisions in ITALY South of ROME. I do not believe the Army – even with our support – will move them.'[24]

He had concluded that the Allied Armies in Italy were not prepared to take the risks necessary, although he viewed the risks as being small considering Allied superiority. In a personal

---

22   Freyberg, Diary Entry, 6 February 1944.
23   TNA CAB 44/138: Italy Operations Winter 1943/4, Part IV – Operations in the Cassino Sector – 20 January – 31 March 1944; TNA WO 204/10402: 15th Army Group Operational Instructions, 21 Aug 43-31 Jul 44.
24   TNA AIR 75/69: Papers of Sir John Slessor, The Italian Campaign, JCS 1024 Memorandum to MAAF Director of Operations dated 11 February 1944.

Mediterranean Allied Air Forces Deputy Commander, Air Marshal Sir John Slessor awards the Commander of the Order of the British Empire to the MAAF Chief of Staff, Major General Idwal Edwards. (NARA RG342-FH-002217)

letter to the RAF's Chief of the Air Staff, Marshal of the Royal Air Force, Sir Charles Portal, on 27 January 1944, Slessor is highly critical of Alexander:

> Alexander has many excellent qualities, but it may be that the moral effect of being kicked out of two different theatres of war by superior enemies inside two years has bitten too deeply into his psychological make-up. It may be the baneful influence of a too vacant Camberley training, but whatever it is, the effect is like a quick-sand round his feet.[25]

He added his views on the lack of audacity from the ground forces:

> One very short impression I have already gained is that while the Air Forces and the Navy, British and American, are well trained and filled with a fine aggressive morale, the Armies unfortunately are no such thing …Here we are, with air superiority so complete as to be amazing – we've got more air superiority in ITALY than we have in KENT; we have great superiority on land, especially in artillery where it must be nearly ten to one; we have command of the sea, and the Army has bold and aggressive Naval support which, as a matter of fact, the value is far more moral than material…He (the enemy) is short of fuel,

25   TNA AIR 75/69: Papers of Sir John Slessor, The Italian Campaign, AOC/101/Air, Letter from Slessor to Portal dated 27 January 1944.

short of ammunition, desperately short of MT and has negligible air support. The one thing he is not short of, and we are, to put it bluntly, is guts…the air cannot win a land battle for the Army – the Army must fight.[26]

Slessor's comments must be treated with care. Airpower in winter 1944 was never consistently effective due to the very poor weather. The rain and snow, more than lack of courage, inhibited the ground forces, conditions that Slessor did not encounter. He had long been an opponent of the use of airpower as CAS.[27] He also had form when it came to criticism of his fellow officers, something his RAF superiors and Churchill were aware of.[28] Every day that German supplies were not interdicted increased their capabilities that he so admired. Being largely static, in fixed defences, the conditions affected German operations much less, something that Slessor did not appear to recognise. It was also not the opinion of Senger, the opposing German ground commander.[29] Nevertheless, his argument about ground force ineffectiveness and lack of risk-taking had a kernel of truth.

Airpower, even if used to the maximum extent at the front, would not be effective if this mindset continued. It was also perhaps an excuse for why the air forces had failed to interdict German forces around the Anzio beachhead. Slessor made the case for increasing air interdiction operations against German lines of communication saying shifting the Germans 'will have to be done by the Air making it impossible for him to stay further South, not by the Army pushing him Northwards.'[30] This letter was written during the planning for the attack on the Abbey, although MAAF may not have yet received the request. Slessor also asked whether 'medium bombers in TAF were really being used in a coordinated plan with the heavies of STRAT against the right targets?'[31] He was clearly making the case that their use in direct support of the Army was not the most efficient use of air assets and that these aircraft should be used in coordinated attacks against the enemy's lines of communication. This letter became the genesis for Operation STRANGLE, the systematic interdiction of German supply lines launched in spring 1944. What was evident is that even before the attack on the Abbey, Slessor's view was that attacks of this nature were unlikely to be successful. Despite his fame for producing a book *Air Power and Armies* in the 1930s that advocated the tactical use of airpower, he did not believe that CAS should be an air force's highest priority.[32] Both the air commander and his deputy did not believe that conducting an attack, in direct support of ground forces, against a culturally sensitive and military insignificant building for tenuous military reasons could possibly meet the requirements of Military Necessity. Why then did MAAF agree to do it?

26   TNA AIR 75/69: Papers of Sir John Slessor, The Italian Campaign, Letter from Slessor to Portal dated 27 January 1944.
27   Ian Gooderson, *Air Power at the Battlefront: Allied Close Air Support in Europe, 1943–45* (London: Frank Cass, 1998), p.35.
28   Vincent Orange, *Churchill and his Airmen* (London, Grub Street, 2013), p.197.
29   Senger, *Neither Fear Nor Hope*, p.184.
30   TNA AIR 75/69: Papers of Sir John Slessor, The Italian Campaign, JCS 1024 Memorandum to MAAF Director of Operations dated 11 February 1944.
31   TNA AIR 75/69: Papers of Sir John Slessor, The Italian Campaign, JCS 1024 Memorandum to MAAF Director of Operations dated 11 February 1944
32   Orange, p.39.

Freyberg's plan, Operation AVENGER, despite the counsel of many of his senior officers, and probably forced upon him, was to continue Clark's frontal assault and then down onto Highway SS 6. Freyberg visited Fifth Army HQ on 9 February, where he was seen by Clark and given his orders by Gruenther.[33] This was still two days before the final effort by US II Corps. The plan was first due to begin on the night of 12-13 February but was postponed to the next night and then was again delayed another 24-hours due to the slowness of the relief of US II Corps.[34] The continuance of the head-on approach was a strange decision for which there is little information on why it was made, although Clark's anger at the usurpation of his command is the most likely reason. It certainly did not meet with Britain's doctrine of an indirect approach and was very different to previous attacks by the New Zealand general in North Africa which resolutely avoided head-on attacks of German defensive positions. This way was also likely to incur the greatest casualties, something Freyberg and London were under pressure from the New Zealand Government to minimise.

33   Freyberg, Diary Entry, 9 February 1944.
34   TNA CAB 106/366.

9

The Red Eagles: Cast at Some Awful Fortress

Do not throw your weight into a stroke whilst your enemy is on guard.
Do not renew an attack along the same line (or in the same form) after it has once failed.

Basil Liddell-Hart
Strategy, 1954[1]

Prior to the New Zealand Corps moving into the Fifth Army sector there had been no recorded discussions by general officers concerning the Abbey's destruction. The order to Fifth Army as they approached Cassino on 6 January 1944 was to avoid the Abbey. On the same day, in response to a complaint by Monsignor Giovanni Montini, the Vatican Deputy Secretary of State, and later to become Pope Paul VI, regarding artillery strikes on the Abbey the following reply was sent by Fifth Army:

> There are many gun positions and installations in the vicinity of Cassino. These have been taken under fire and it is possible that erratic bursts may have hit the Abbey. If so, the damage is unintentional and unavoidable. Every effort will continue to be made to avoid damaging the Abbey in spite of the fact that it occupies dominating terrain which might well serve as an excellent observation post for the enemy.[2]

The uncertainty as to the Abbey's occupation is clear in the use of the word, 'might'. This reply was almost identical wording to the Fifth Army order and also that which was forwarded by Eisenhower to General Marshall on 8 January.[3] There was no doubt that the rank and file of both British and US Armies supported bombing it. When it was bombed the soldiers that had suffered in its shadow 'were to cry for joy as bomb after bomb crumbled it to dust.'[4]

It was not until the 4th Indian Division was planning its assault that bombing the Abbey was raised. The genesis of the idea came from the Indian commander, Gertie Tuker who was directly subordinate to Freyberg. Although he commanded an Indian Army division, Tuker

---

1   Liddell-Hart, *Strategy*, p.336.
2   Hapgood and Richardson, p.64.
3   TNA CAB 106/699: Folio No. 03977, AFHQ to AGWAR for MARSHALL, 8 January 1944.
4   Bond, p.114.

was commissioned into the British Army in 1914, but quickly transferred to the Gurkhas, then part of the Indian Army, with whom he fought in Mesopotamia in 1916. Between the wars he served in several punitive expeditions and colonial operations in the North-West Frontier Province. By the outbreak of war, he was a full Colonel and was serving as the Director of Military Training in India. His methods were not always appreciated by the more conventional British officers, and he concentrated training events on mountain and jungle warfare as well as Combined Operations. One commentator however, was far more in tune with his methods, 'General Tuker's skill and training of infantry for war and their leading in battle, is such an original yet practical kind as to border on genius.'[5] The articles he wrote for the Royal United Service Institute and other journals were done under a pseudonym in order not to raise the hackles of the Army establishment.[6] In late 1941, he was promoted to major general and appointed as GOC 4th Indian Infantry Division, the 'Red Eagles' and despatched to Egypt.[7] Prior to the second battle at El Alamein in October 1942 his division had been spread around between Tobruk, Cyprus and the Ruweisat Ridge. His 11th Indian Infantry Brigade was written off the order of battle after the fall of Tobruk in June 1942. The Division was back together in late 1942, holding part of the Ruweisat Ridge at El Alamein. Following the threat of a second dispersal, for which Tuker offered his resignation, the division fought well in Tunisia until the final German defeat, and it was his troops who took the surrender of the German commanding officer, *Generaloberst* von Arnim on 12 May 1943. Tuker requisitioned von Arnim's command caravan and used it for his remaining time in command.[8] For their efforts the division was paraded before King George VI on 13 June 1943.[9] It was recognised that Italy would offer mountainous challenges and therefore in the autumn of 1943, Tuker's 7th and 11th Indian Infantry Brigades, who would lead the assault on the Monastery and Point 593, were sent to the Mountain Warfare School in the Lebanon.[10] He moved his division to Italy in December 1943, where, despite an illness that prevented him taking full command, he remained highly influential. Just before he was about to launch his division at the heavily defended town of Orsogna, on 21 January 1944, Tuker was relieved to be told that the attack was cancelled and that his division was to be transferred across the mountains. On the news he wrote:

> I must say that I think Providence has been kind to this Division. Each time when we were about to be cast at some awful fortress something has intervened to help me fight the battle of stopping a needless sacrifice of life. I hope it is not Fifth Army's intention to use us against some impregnable place.[11]

5   G R Stevens, *The Tiger Triumphs* (London: HMSO, 1946 (2013 Kindle Edition), Kindle Location 930.
6   James Holland, *General Francis Tuker and the Bombing of Montecassino* <https://www.griffonmerlin. com/2008/08/05/general-francis-tuker-and-the-bombing-of-monte-cassino/> (accessed 27 August 2020).
7   Stevens, Fourth Indian Division, p.123.
8   Stevens, Fourth Indian Division, p.255.
9   Stevens, Fourth Indian Division, p.257.
10   Alan Jeffreys, 'Indian Army Training for the Italian Campaign and Lessons Learnt' in Andrew L Hargreaves, Patrick J Rose and Matthew C Ford (eds.), *Allied Fighting Effectiveness in North Africa and Italy, 1942-1945* (Leiden: Brill, 2014), pp.106-7.
11   Stevens, Fourth Indian Division, p. 273.

Providence was to abandon him in the coming weeks and his hopes were dashed. Another awful fortress awaited.

When he arrived in Italy, Tuker wrote to the British Deputy Commander-in-Chief in India regarding the difficulties of conducting operations. In his opinion there were significant difficulties going from south to north:

> If one looks at Italy all the way up its length one sees it to be impossible of conquest except in one tedious manner. No commander who is not either unimaginative or a time-server would accept the last direction of attack without the one and only means of conquest, great air power on the battlefield, close in.
>
> In 1914-18 in France, though the Boche had no mines and no anti-tank guns, we could not break through in spite of our huge mass of artillery of all types...Our artillery never won us a breakthrough battle in four years of war. Today, in Italy, we have less and lighter artillery as a whole: the Boche is in steel and concrete: he has anti-tank and anti-personnel mines and plenty of anti-tank guns...If we intend to put our infantry through we have only one means to do it and that is by the surprising weight of our fire. 1914-18 proved that artillery weapons will not give this effect. The only effect left to us is the weight of our air power and that must be used in its fullest weight...The blow must be in depth, division following division.[12]

He officially handed over command of his division to Brigadier Harry Dimoline on 6 February 1944, just a few days before the attack on the massif, due to a recurring bout of rheumatoid arthritis. It took him nearly a year to recover, in which time he returned to India. A renowned military intellectual, he became a prolific author on military topics. He continued to believe that had the bombing and his division's assault been properly synchronised it would have been successful.

Instructions to take-over the assault on Monte Cassino were issued following a conference between Freyberg and the caretaker divisional commander of the 4th Indian Infantry Division on 9 February in Operation Instruction No.4; a contingency plan should US II Corps fail in their assault planned for 11 February. Fourth Indian Division was tasked to capture Monte Cassino, cut Highway SS 6 and capture Cassino town from the west.[13] It must have been obvious that the casualty levels of the assaulting American divisions were extremely high and that the German defences on the massif had torn them to shreds. These casualties may have been acceptable to the Americans; they were not sustainable for the British. Using a technological approach, such as bombers to reduce the risk of casualties was preferable.

There was no mention in the operational instruction of bombing the Abbey, although Clark stated that Freyberg brought up the subject.[14] The division's mission statement did not mention the Abbey at all, just the hill upon which it sat. The hill was also only an intermediate objective as the final objective was to cut Highway SS6:

12   Stevens, *Fourth Indian Division*, pp. 277-8.
13   TNA CAB 106/699: 4th Indian Division Operation Instruction No. 3, 11 Feb 44.
14   Clark, p.251.

4 IND DIV will capture MONASTERY HILL and high feature G.835217, exploit SOUTH to cut Highway 6 and capture CASSINO from the WEST.[15]

It was clear that 4th Indian Division was given a Warning Order regarding entry into the Abbey, as 8-hours prior to Operational Instruction No.4, the division's Commander Royal Engineers, Lieutenant-Colonel Edward Stenhouse, had been informed of the possible task.[16] Stenhouse lacked information about the Abbey's construction and despatched three of his staff to Fifth Army.[17] Returning empty-handed from G-2 Intelligence, they were then sent to Naples on 10 February to scour bookshops, returning with some useful material, including a book from the Italian Fine Arts Society, an 1879 Baedeker Guide with a section on the Abbey and an Automobile Association Guide. It is not surprising that Fifth Army had little information, as no-one intended to conduct any military operations against the building. In the resulting mission analysis Stenhouse concluded that his engineers could not handle a building of this size without higher echelon support. In the 4th Indian Infantry Division's Operational Instruction No.3 dated 11 February, the following statement appears in the Air paragraph:

> Requests have been made for all buildings and suspected enemy strongpoints on and in vicinity of the objectives incl the MONASTERY to be subjected to intense bombing from now on.[18]

This is the first written request to bomb the building and was probably made on the direction of Dimoline. The request for the bombing was, in army planning terms an 'implied task', that is something the commander had inferred from his direction, as opposed to a 'specified task', something he had been ordered to do. At no point was 4th Indian Division ordered to capture or destroy the Abbey. Supporting Clark's claim that Freyberg brought up the Abbey on 10 February, the corps commander suggested to his artillery commander, Brigadier Cyril Weir, that he 'should go and see the gunners of 2 Corps re shooting up the Monastery.'[19] At this point, his Brigadier General Staff, Ray Queree, told him that this would need Clark's release. This conference is probably the genesis that led to the Abbey's destruction, although Freyberg's diary makes clear that he did not want complete demolition.[20]

The 4th Indian Division Instruction did not ask for heavy bombers. Below the above request, the instruction stated: 'One tentacle is with 7 Bde and one with Main Div HQ'.[21] A tentacle was part of the Tactical Air Force's communication infrastructure that assisted the ground forces in gaining CAS and generally referred to fighter-bombers. The forward liaison officers' tentacles could not communicate with heavy bombers and therefore the reference to it was pointless if their support was expected. The next day Tuker, still exercising influence from his sickbed, expanded on the Operational Instruction with two memoranda to New Zealand Corps. In the second he

15   TNA CAB 106/699: 4th Indian Division Operation Instruction No.3, 11 Feb 44.
16   RAF Narrative – The Italian Campaign 1943-1945 – Volume 1, p.273.
17   TNA CAB 106/699: Report on the Bombing of MONTE CASSINO ABBEY – 15 February 1944. London: Cabinet Office Historical section, 1949, pp.24, 95.
18   TNA CAB 106/699: 4th Indian Division Operation Instruction No.3, 11 Feb 44.
19   Freyberg, Diary Entry, 10 February 1944.
20   Freyberg, Diary Entry, 12 February 1944.
21   TNA CAB 106/699: 4th Indian Division Operation Instruction No.3, 11 Feb 44.

stated that he did not believe the Abbey was within the capability of divisional assets.[22] Tuker, whose name is forever linked with the decision to bomb the Abbey, was far from keen to see it attacked. 'I went through hell on earth during the early days urging desperately that no attack on Monte Cassino be contemplated.'[23] It is unclear whether Tuker knew that Clark did not want the Abbey bombed, but if he did the threat of a bombing request might have given Clark second thoughts on his scheme of manoeuvre. A student of manoeuvre, he did not want his division anywhere near Monte Cassino where it would be fixed in a head-on attack of attrition, preferring an outflanking movement to the north, like that started by the FEC in January; he had already visited Juin for discussions. This is what his doctrine told him to do and just prior to deployment, the division issued a Training Instruction, probably written by Tuker, which stated that the idea in the mountains was: 'Obtaining penetration of the enemy-occupied areas as quickly as possible and of bursting through into his gun-areas and maintenance system and cutting his roads behind him. That is, only to fight him if we cannot burst through without fighting.'[24]

He stated after the war that he 'could never understand why the US Fifth Army decided to batter its head again and again against this most powerful position, held by some of the finest troops in the German Army.'[25] Tuker was also sceptical about the military intellect of many senior British officers. He was highly critical of British generals' tactics in the desert war, and he called the period between the wars when these commanders rose to prominence the 'Ice Age of military thought.'[26] He even thought that the teaching at the staff college at Camberley was poor.[27] He was a military intellectual and 'a scholar of war'[28] and he appeared to have little time for officers such as Freyberg – 'brave as a lion but no planner of battles and a niggler in action', he said of him.[29] Some said that Tuker was 'the brains that the brawny Freyberg lacks.'[30] In contrast, he was quiet and reserved, lacking the bonhomie and affectionate relationship with his men that Freyberg excelled in building. Unfortunately, Tuker was somewhat obvious in his views regarding his seniors and therefore was sometimes overlooked for more senior posts. Clark, he considered a 'flashy ignoramus.'[31] He thought of Alexander as 'an indolent fifth wheel.'[32]

Tuker would doubtless have been a difficult subordinate. He judged people on their capability rather than their rank. He had no problem in disobeying orders if he thought that was the right course of action. Despite sickness resulting in his replacement as divisional commander, probably from the headquarters at Caserta, he continued to lobby for changes to the New Zealand Corps' orders for direct attack, suggesting an outflanking manoeuvre in his first memorandum on 12 February,[33] and in a meeting with Freyberg the same day.[34] It is important to note that in

---

22   TNA CAB 106/699: Memorandum No. 433/1/G.
23   Quoted in Raleigh Trevelyan, *Rome 44: The Battle for the Eternal City* (London: Secker and Warburg, 1981), p.132.
24   Jeffreys, p.107.
25   Quoted in Ellis, *Hollow Victory*, p.164.
26   Francis Tuker, *The Pattern of War* (London: Cassell, 1948), p.11.
27   Stevens, Fourth Indian Division, p.124.
28   Majdalany, *Portrait,* p.104
29   Quoted in Ellis, *Hollow Victory,* p.164.
30   Gervasi, p.552.
31   James Parton, *Air Force Spoken Here* (Maxwell AFB, AL: Air University Press, 2000), p.361.
32   Trevelyan, p.133.
33   TNA CAB 106/699: Main HQ 4 Ind Div No 433/G – Operations dated 12 Feb 44.
34   Ellis, *Hollow Victory*, p.164

this first memorandum to Freyberg, Tuker does not advocate bombing the Abbey referencing only 'Monastery Hill' and defences placed there and not the building itself.

1. I have today seen the officiating Comd 4 Ind Div and the Bde Comds at 4 Div HQ and there discussed the present situation in the 'Monastery' area of CASSINO in the light of our latest recces and recent activities of the 2 American Corps.

2   From NZ Intelligence Summary No.17 of 6 Feb para 3(c) it is apparent that the enemy are in concrete and steel emplacements on the 'Monastery' hill.
    From a wide experience of attacks in mountain areas I know that infantry cannot 'jump' strong defences of this sort in the mountains. These defences have to be 'softened up' either by being cut off on all sides and starved out or else by continuous and heavy bombardment over a period of days. Even with the latter preparation, success will only be achieved in my opinion if a thorough and prolonged air bombardment is undertaken with really heavy bombs a good deal larger than 'Kittybomber' missiles.

3. We have complete air superiority in this theatre of war but the 'softening' of the Monastery hill has not been started.
    An attack cannot be undertaken till this 'softening' process is complete. This has always been the view that I have voiced, and it is now confirmed by what I later hear. Already, three attacks have been put in and have failed – at some considerable cost, I am told. Another attack without air 'softening' will only lead to a similar result. The Monastery feature is a far more formidable feature than TAKROUNA and resembles the higher parts of GARCI which were rightly deemed inaccessible to infantry attack once the first initial surprise had gone. At GARCI the enemy was in field defences and not in concrete emplacements.

4. If proper air 'softening' is not possible then the alternative remains:- i.e. to turn the Monastery Hill and to isolate it.
    This course I regard to be possible as the enemy is, I believe, still only in field defences in the mountain areas to the West and S.W. of MONTE CASTELLONI. Using MONTE CASTELLONI and the area now held by the American 2 Corps as a firm base, and making it a firm base, we can attack in fast short jabs to the West and S.W> of CASTELLONI and cut No.6 road West of the Monastery Hill. With this, and an attack on CASSINO to keep that place quiet, the river can, I feel, be crossed lower down and that the crossing joined up with the cutting from the North of No.6 road, thus isolating MONASTERY HILL.

5. To go direct for the MONASTERY HILL now without 'softening' it properly is only to hit one's head straight against the hardest part of the whole enemy position and to risk the failure of the whole operation.

The references to Takrouna and Garci refer to operations around Enfidaville in the Tunisian Campaign in April 1943. This action was one where Freyberg's New Zealanders and the Indians had fought alongside each other. Neither Garci nor Takrouna were captured. Their opponents, as they had been at Mareth and in many battles in North Africa was the 90th Light Division. In May 1943, Freyberg sent their commander the message 'your position is hopeless. We have fought you for two years and have no wish to annihilate you.' In typical fashion the 90th replied, '…We appreciate your message, and we realise our position is hopeless; but we have our duty to perform.' Freyberg took their surrender at Cape Bon on 12 May 1943.[35] In his memorandum, Tuker clearly tried to persuade Freyberg through their previous experiences together, against the same foe, that the capture of the hill was a forlorn hope. If any division could have taken the Abbey it was the Indians, of whom it was said, 'The deep patrols brought out military qualities inherent in the blood of men whose ancestors have been soldiers for a thousand years.'[36] Yet Tuker knew that this was beyond even them.

Tuker's second memorandum of 12 February has been condemned as the justification for the destruction of the Abbey.[37] However, if the text is examined closely, there is an alternative analysis that considers Tuker's obvious dislike for attacking the Abbey. There is no longer any mention of 'Monastery Hill' or German defences on the hill. This memorandum was wholly concerned with the Abbey's destruction and the difficulties that this presented as if the decision had already been made:

1   After considerable trouble and investigating many bookshops in NAPLES, I have at last found a book, dated 1879, which gives certain details of the construction of the MONTE CASSINO Monastery.

2.   The Monastery was converted into a fortress in the 19th Century. The Main Gate has massive timber branches in a low archway consisting of large stone blocks 9 to 10 metres long. This Gate is the only means of entrance to the Monastery.

3.   The walls are about 15 ft high, or more where there are Monk's cells against the walls. The walls are of solid masonry and at least 10 ft thick at the base.

4.   Since the place was constructed as a fortress as late as the 19th Century it stands to reason that the walls will be suitably pierced for loopholes and will be battlemented.

5.   MONTE CASSINO is therefore a modern fortress and must be dealt with by modern means. No practicable means available within the capacity of field engineers can possibly cope with this place.
     It can only be directly dealt with by applying 'blockbuster' bombs from the air, hoping thereby to render the garrison incapable of resistance. The 1,000 lb bomb would be next to useless to effect this.

6.   Whether the Monastery is now occupied by a German Garrison or not, it is certain that it will be held as a keep by the lost remnants of the Garrison of the position. It is therefore also essential that the building should be so demolished as to prevent its effective occupation at that time.

7.   I would ask that you would give me definite information at once as to how this fortress will be dealt with as the means are not within the capacity of this Division.

35   Sandri, p.6.
36   Stevens, *The Tiger Triumphs*, Kindle Location 2210.
37   Bloch, pp.18-19.

8.   I would point out that it has only been by investigation on the part of this Div, with no help whatsoever from 'I' sources outside, that we have got any idea as to what this fortress comprises although the fortress has been a thorn in our side for many weeks.

When a formation is called upon to reduce such a place, it should be apparent that the place is reducible by the means at the disposal of that Div or that the means are ready for it, without having to go to the bookstalls of NAPLES to find out what should have been fully considered many weeks ago.[38]

Tuker was not stupid. He would have undoubtedly realised that the Abbey was an important building. His own views about the place were ambivalent – he said in his papers that, 'the smashing up of the Monastery would have been an act of vandalism if it had not been necessary. (I'm not fond of baroque but wouldn't destroy it).'[39] A potential alternative explanation is that Tuker's demand to use 'Blockbuster' bombs was an attempt to dissuade Clark from attacking the Monte Cassino feature altogether. The destruction of such a building may well be bad for your career if it goes wrong. If he could not use 'Blockbusters', he said, the 1,000lb bomb would be 'next to useless.' This was coherent with the first memorandum about softening-up. It was a tactic he had used with Freyberg before, although it appears to have been too subtle for the New Zealander. There was no time to conduct several days of bombing on the German positions on Monastery Hill and it was unlikely that the winter weather would have allowed constant bombing. If Tuker could convince him that the Abbey was beyond the capabilities of the Allies to capture or destroy, and that time was too short, the New Zealander would be forced to lobby Clark for an alternative plan not involving the Abbey. This was possibly Tuker's intention in his first memo. He would have been aware that the outflanking option only perhaps needed an extra shove to be successful as Juin would have told him. This was his preference from the beginning as can be seen from the first memorandum. Something had changed between the first and second memoranda, but unfortunately neither has an exact time when Tuker penned them so an analysis of their place in the timeline cannot be ascertained.

These Tuker memoranda may not even have been read by Freyberg. Freyberg was already of the opinion that in the event of a direct attack on Monastery Hill, the Abbey had to be neutralised.[40] He did not want it demolished. Freyberg also possibly found Tuker's advice tiresome. After the bombing, and during the Indian attempt to capture Point 593 and the Abbey, Freyberg got wind that Tuker may be going onto the massif on 17 February. He asked Dimoline, 'He is not going to give advice is he? He is not coming in on the plan. Anything like that would be very wrong. If there is anything like that it must first be reported to me.'[41]

Tuker, or his staff, had knowledge of bombs and their capabilities; the 4,000lb 'Blockbuster' was explicitly mentioned to New Zealand Corps a few days after the bombing. They were happy with the results of the heavy bombing, sending the following message:

38   TNA CAB 106/699: Memorandum No. 433/1/G.
39   Mann, p.196.
40   Phillips, p.207.
41   Freyberg, Diary Entry, 17 February 1944.

1.   In view of the precision with which heavy bombers can drop their bombs it is considered that their employment in direct close support of infantry and armour should be accepted as normal.

2.   They represent a tremendous firepower which has a devastating effect on the enemy particularly if he is in hastily constructed defences.

3.   Used together with heavy, medium and field guns in the bombardment before and during an attack they should undoubtedly clear the way for both infantry and armour and used in a counter battery role against enemy heavy calibre guns they, with their 4,000 pound bombs, should both destroy enemy personnel and equipment and also probably sympathetically detonate his ammunition dumps.

4.   Having seen the effect of this type of bombing on MONTE CASSINO where our own infantry were within 1,000yds of the target it is hard to understand why nations which possess absolute air superiority have not used such a potent and decisive weapon in the battlefield before.

5.   It is considered that the employment of heavy bombers in the direct close support role should be developed at once to form a battle winning technique the like of which the enemy has never considered possible.

This suggestion would have horrified the air generals. The last thing they wanted was to relegate their bombers to being flying heavy artillery, directly supporting a ground campaign. Bombers should be striking strategic targets and having a dramatic and direct impact on the enemy's ability to support and supply its forces. The army had a different perspective. Dimoline appeared to confuse the use of the 4,000lb 'Blockbuster' bombs with the much smaller general-purpose weapons dropped on the Abbey.

Tuker, despite his sickness, confronted Freyberg on 12 February over the direct assault plan. His demand of Freyberg on that day 'not to compromise' with Clark over the direction of the attack indicated that the idea of continuing the direct assault, was Clark's.[42] Freyberg, in conversation with Gruenther, rated his chances of success as 'not more than fifty-fifty.'[43] This did not sound like the optimism of a general confident in his mission! Tuker, however, lacked confidence in Freyberg's ability to influence Clark – he later wrote, 'I feel sorry for Freyberg, but he should never have been put in command of a corps. He had not the tactical understanding and certainly not the experience of the mountains.'[44] One officer who did have mountain experience was Alexander, who should have understood Tuker's arguments. In the second memo, Tuker outlined requirements for bombing the building. These requirements were for a head-on attack should it be ordered, rather than a statement that a head-on attack was his favoured course of action.[45] A post-war report on the circumstances surrounding the attack on the Abbey by British Cabinet Office historian, Major Francis Jones asserted that Freyberg 'agreed to General Tuker's request.'[46] The inference here was that Tuker was the driving force behind the method of attack, which he was not. We shall examine Jones' report more closely later

---

42   Trevelyan, p.133.
43   Majdalany, *Portrait*, p.107.
44   Quoted in Trevelyan, p.134.
45   Ellis, *Hollow Victory*, p.167.
46   TNA CAB 106/699: Memorandum No. 433/1/G.

Tuker did not claim that the Abbey was being used by the Germans, only that it had obvious potential as a last redoubt.[47] In the target request put forward by his divisional HQ on 14 February, the justification for the target stated that: 'Abbey is approx. 230yds long with greatest width 160yds. Walls at base probably 15-feet thick. Reports up to 14 Feb indicate Germans are living in the building including the cellar.'[48] Tuker was fully aware that once bombed the Germans would be free to use it as a defensive position, which they did. By 9 February, it was clear that his views were not being heeded. After the failure of his 12 February letters, he threw himself into the project, supporting fully a vigorous bombing with everything available. Despite his clear reservations, once the decision had been made for a head-on assault, he was determined that the job must be done properly and was pugnacious in his demands that the position should receive a proper softening-up and that the defenders should be reduced to 'imbecility.'[49] Unlike Freyberg, who wanted to breach the outer wall, he did not advocate a single attack as was carried out on 15 February, but rather a series of softening-up attacks over several days followed by a ground assault against an enemy overcome by the shock of constant and prolonged bombardment. Crisis at Anzio and the USAAF's Big Week were to ensure that this could not happen. After the war he stated that the Abbey was exposed to too little attention, rather than too much.[50] In a post-war letter to Fred Majdalany, he claimed that:

> Time and again I told Freyberg that if he were forced to attack Monte Cassino feature directly, then he should demand every bomber in Italy, the Mediterranean and Great Britain of all types to turn the garrison into a clot of imbecility, mixing and following bombs with the heaviest artillery bombardment with infantry on the heels of the bombardment at night.[51]

What is known is that Tuker initially tried to persuade his commanders not to attack the Abbey; he preferred an outflanking manoeuvre to isolate it. It was also known that he thought standard 1,000lb bombs and tactical fighter-bombers would be useless against the building. It was also known that his division was aware of High-Capacity Blockbuster bombs in Italy. He also suggested that the softening up process would take days rather than the single attack that had been suggested. All the evidence is circumstantial, but it does imply that Tuker wanted to dissuade Freyberg or Clark from conducting a head-on attack, thereby resulting in the inevitable attack on the Abbey. On 13 February, Tuker was again struck down by his affliction and took no further active part in the attack despite the rumours that he was about to trek up to the massif. Tuker was, as well as a believer in manoeuvre, convinced of an unchanging pattern of war and wrote a post-war book to this effect.[52] If forced, he saw the Abbey as a 'modern fortress' that must be 'dealt with by modern means.'[53] He was a great supporter of airpower in support of ground forces and he viewed the heavy bomber as the 'great arm of siege bombardment',[54]

47   TNA CAB 106/699, Memorandum No. 433/1/G.
48   TNA CAB 106/699, p.88.
49   Trevelyan, p.133.
50   F.S. Tuker, Bombing of Cassino, Letter to *The Times*, 21 October 1950.
51   Mann, p.202.
52   Tuker, p.1.
53   Quoted in Ellis, *Hollow Victory*, p.168.
54   Tuker, p.96.

Renowned author Professor Peter Caddick-Adams in his book on the battles made the point that Tuker had a 'profound understanding of airpower.'[55] Whilst this was true, his expertise was from the perspective of a soldier; he saw airpower as chiefly a supporting arm to ground forces.

Brigadier Osborne Lovett, whose 7th Indian Infantry Brigade would get first crack at the hill, carried out his reconnaissance of the forward areas on 11 February, telling the American staff officers that they were going to use US heavy bombers to destroy the Abbey. The US officers were less than convinced about the reliability of their bombers. Lovett, as usual for Indian Army brigades, commanded one British, one Indian and one Gurkha battalion. They began to move into the US positions on 12 February but found that the transition would not be easy. They were also unsure as to what the Americans held and what they did not. In his report Lovett told Dimoline that the Americans 'were very insecure' on both Point 593 and Monte Castellone, inferring that they held both on 12 February.[56] This was true of the latter, but not the former. This was a problem as Lovett's appreciation was that they 'must be secure on 593 before anything else can be done.'[57] The confusion was not helped by Keyes telling Freyberg on the same day that 'everything is under control.'[58] At 5:15pm Freyberg agreed that the 4th Indian Division would take over Point 593 that evening, with the plan to assault the Abbey the following night. British and American stores and ammunition were not compatible with each other meaning that the Indians could not simply use existing supply dumps for their own purposes. The American units were in very exposed positions on the massif that could only safely be approached in darkness. The ensuing delays caused handovers to be short and rushed, with greatly increased scope for misunderstanding. The Americans had been referring to the Masseria Albaneta, a German-occupied fortified house about a two-thirds of a mile from the Abbey, as a 'small abbey'.

This is not inaccurate as Albaneta had indeed once been a religious building, the Monastery of *Santa Maria dell'Albaneta*, but had ceased this function at the end of the eighteenth century, and was now ruined.[59] It was entirely possible that this information was passed on and misinterpreted by the arriving Indian soldiers. One abbey was very much like another in the dark and cold. Late on 12 February, Freyberg showed his lack of understanding of the terrain or the difficulties his troops had relieving the Americans. In a conference with Queree he complained about the slowness of the Indian takeover, and unrealistically suggested that Dimoline attacked the Abbey on a two-brigade front.[60] It had already been established that they had sufficient mules to sustain only one brigade in the mountains.

Because Point 593 was not in friendly hands it quickly became obvious that the first Indian attack on Monastery Hill could not begin until the night of the 14-15 February. However, the continuing delays, including a German counterattack from Terrelle, resulted in the 7th Indian Infantry Brigade falling further behind. Confusion reigned by the end of the day on 12 February, with New Zealand Corps realising that Dimoline probably cannot do any offensive operations before the night of 15-16 February. Meanwhile, Keyes was expecting full relief the

55   Peter Caddick-Adams. *Monte Cassino: Ten Armies in Hell* (London: Preface Publishing, 2011), p.129.
56   Freyberg, Diary Entry, 12 February 1944.
57   Freyberg, Diary Entry, 12 February 1944.
58   Freyberg, Diary Entry, 12 February 1944.
59   Alberto Turinetti, Masseria Albaneta, A place of peace, prayer and reflection (11 February to 19 February 1944) <http://www.dalvolturnoacassino.it/asp/doc.asp?id=323 > (accessed 23 April 2022).
60   Freyberg, Diary Entry, 12 February 1944.

night before this and Gruenther still thought the assault would happen over the night of 13-14 February. Gruenther was informed the next day of a new assault date, and when asked about the air plan replied, 'it would probably be okay as long as we had the weather, or something happened on the other front.'[61] The air plan for the heavy and medium bombers had been briefed to Freyberg earlier that day. It ended up that Lovett's Brigade was not in command of its sector until early on 15 February, when the 1st Royal Sussex Regiment faced Point 593 with the 4/16 Punjab Regiment on their left and the Gurkhas in reserve.

In discussion between the assaulting 7th Indian Infantry Brigade, the 4th Indian Division and New Zealand Corps on 13 February, a further delay to a time late on 16 February was decided for the attack on the Abbey.[62] A footnote to the planning note stated 'The success of this operation depends entirely on the strength of the air.'[63] Heavy bombers had not been considered by 4th Indian Division, except by Tuker, and had not been requested for the task by Dimoline or Freyberg. The use of heavy bombers required higher levels of approval to take them off their priority mission and this had not been sought from either the Commanding General of the United States Strategic Air Forces in Europe, (referred to as USSTAF or USSAFE), General Carl 'Tooey' Spaatz or the US or Allied Theatre Commander, who were the only commanders with the authority to change priorities. Eaker, the air commander in the Mediterranean theatre was in Cairo during the crucial period.

It has been suggested that Freyberg and his air officer, Lieutenant-Colonel Robin Bell were summoned to Fifth Army HQ during the afternoon of 13 February to be told that the heavy bombers were to be used on the Abbey.[64] This timeline is consistent with the Mediterranean Allied Strategic Air Forces (MASAF) planning requirements for a mission on the morning of 15 February, but the heavy bombers were also continuing to plan missions to southern Germany for this date. Freyberg, in the late afternoon of 14 February spoke to Dimoline regarding a small change to the assault plan that would require a further small delay. Freyberg at this point told him, 'we cannot go on putting it off indefinitely…the air would be playing 100% and would be doing some tomorrow which would be extra.'[65] Whether Freyberg knew of, or told, Dimoline anything more specific is not known, but the 4th Indian Division commander did not tell his forward brigade who were surprised by the attack, suggesting that the attack was not definite and that the bombers were only switched at the last minute when it became evident that their priority mission had been weathered out. Later that day, Clark confirmed the air plan to Freyberg.[66]

Poor weather and problems moving troops to a safe distance delayed the attack yet again.[67] The plan was to withdraw the forward troops to a bomb safety line, 1,000-yds from the Abbey on the night of 15-16 February in preparation for the attack. This left the Indian infantry with a problem. They did not hold Point 593, the dominating feature of Snakeshead Ridge; *Major* Kratzert was still there in strength, and this point was vital for a successful assault on the Abbey. This position had to be captured before the Abbey was assaulted but it was not targeted

61   Freyberg, Diary Entry, 13 February 1944.
62   Hartcup, p.12.
63   Hartcup, p.12.
64   Wright, Kindle Location 824.
65   Freyberg, Diary Entry, 14 February 1944.
66   Freyberg, Diary Entry, 14 February 1944.
67   Graham and Bidwell, p.198.

in the air plan, possibly because Dimoline thought it was held by the Americans when the plan was submitted. Even by the afternoon of 14 February, the caretaker divisional commander was under the impression that the air attack would take place on 16 February. He planned to assault Point 593 the night before, consolidate and then assault the Abbey on the night of 17 February. Freyberg, somewhat exasperated, said that 'the delay was making us look ridiculous.'[68] A poor weather forecast for the planned day and the knowledge from ULTRA that the Germans would attack Anzio on 16 February would advance the air attack to 15 February and ruin the plan. Dimoline could not advance the infantry attack by 24-hours due to his logistical problems and was told by Freyberg that he was unlikely to get the support from air again if he cancelled. Point 593 was not assaulted for many hours after the attack on the Abbey, an attack that was easily repulsed.

The bombing of the Abbey came as a complete surprise to those on the mountain, with Brigadier Lovett only being informed 15-minutes before, despite Dimoline knowing the previous day. Freyberg again discussed the bombing programme with Dimoline early on the morning of the attack, after which he probably told Lovett.[69] Freyberg watched the attack from 4th Indian Division HQ. The Commanding Officer of the Royal Sussex, Lieutenant Colonel Jack Glennie, famously said, 'They told the monks, and they told the enemy, but they didn't tell us.'[70] The inaccuracy of the attack, which caused 28-casualties, was described in the 4/16 Punjabi war diary:

> We went to the door of the command post, a derelict farmhouse, and gazed up into the cold blue sky. There we saw the white trails of many high-level bombers. Our first thought was that they were the enemy. The somebody said, 'Flying Fortresses'. There followed the whistle, swish and blast of the blockbusters as the first flights struck at the Monastery. Almost before the ground ceased to shake the telephones were ringing. One of our companies was within 300 yards [Point 445?] of the target and the others within 800 yards [Colle d'Onofrio?]; all had received a plastering and were asking questions with some asperity. We could not offer any explanation, we just had to grin and bear it. Luckily our casualties were under the thirty mark and were mostly bodies bruised by pieces of the Monastery hurled many yards through the air.[71] [Authors Note: Unlikely that masonry would be flung that far; likely damage caused by shrapnel and rock splinters]

The derelict farmhouse was known as the 'Doctor's House' and also acted as a first aid station. It was 1,500yds north-west of the Abbey and 500yds along Snakeshead Ridge north of Point 593. Major Reilly, the medical officer gave an account that suggested Glennie thought there were snipers in the Abbey. Reilly also claimed that immediately following the attack on the Abbey, two survivors, a 17-year-old female and a 6-year-old boy turned up at the Doctor's House claiming that there were 300-Germans in the building. It is highly unlikely that two children could have walked across that highly inhospitable terrain, including crossing Death Valley, to reach the Indian command post. The infantry attack on Monastery Hill was postponed again

68   Freyberg, Diary Entry, 14 February 1944.
69   Freyberg, Diary Entry, 15 February 1944.
70   Smith, p.90.
71   Stevens, *Fourth Indian Division*, pp.285-6.

The Mediterranean air commanders. Lieutenant General Ira Eaker, Major General John Cannon and Major General Nathan Twining. (NARA RG342-FH-000582)

late on the morning of the 14 February as it became evident that the Indians were not fully in place, and that an assault on the Abbey could not begin before the night 16-17 February – a full 36-hours after the air attack. The ground attack was postponed nearly 12-hours before the final orders for the air attack on the Abbey were issued by air commanders Major General John Cannon, Commanding General of the Mediterranean Allied Tactical Air Forces (MATAF), and Major General Nathan Twining, Commanding General of MASAF.

To add to their difficulties, the Indians discovered that *Oberst* Karl-Lothar Schultz's 1st *Fallschirmjager* Regiment of the 1st *Fallschirmjager* Division were stubbornly holding the key terrain of Point 593. Schultz was vastly experienced and battle-hardened having served in the Low Countries and Crete.[72] Since 7 February, he commanded the ad-hoc unit called *Kampfgruppe* Schultz, made up of battalions of the 1st and 3rd *Fallschirmjager* Regiments, which included Kratzert's hilltop force.[73] Without capturing this position, an attack on the Monastery would be suicidal, yet an attack during daylight hours was impossible. It had to be taken, but

---

72   Bohmler, p.149.
73   Bruce Quarrie, *German Airborne Divisions: Mediterranean Theatre 1942–45* (Oxford: Osprey Publishing, 2005), p.43; Molony et al, p.702.

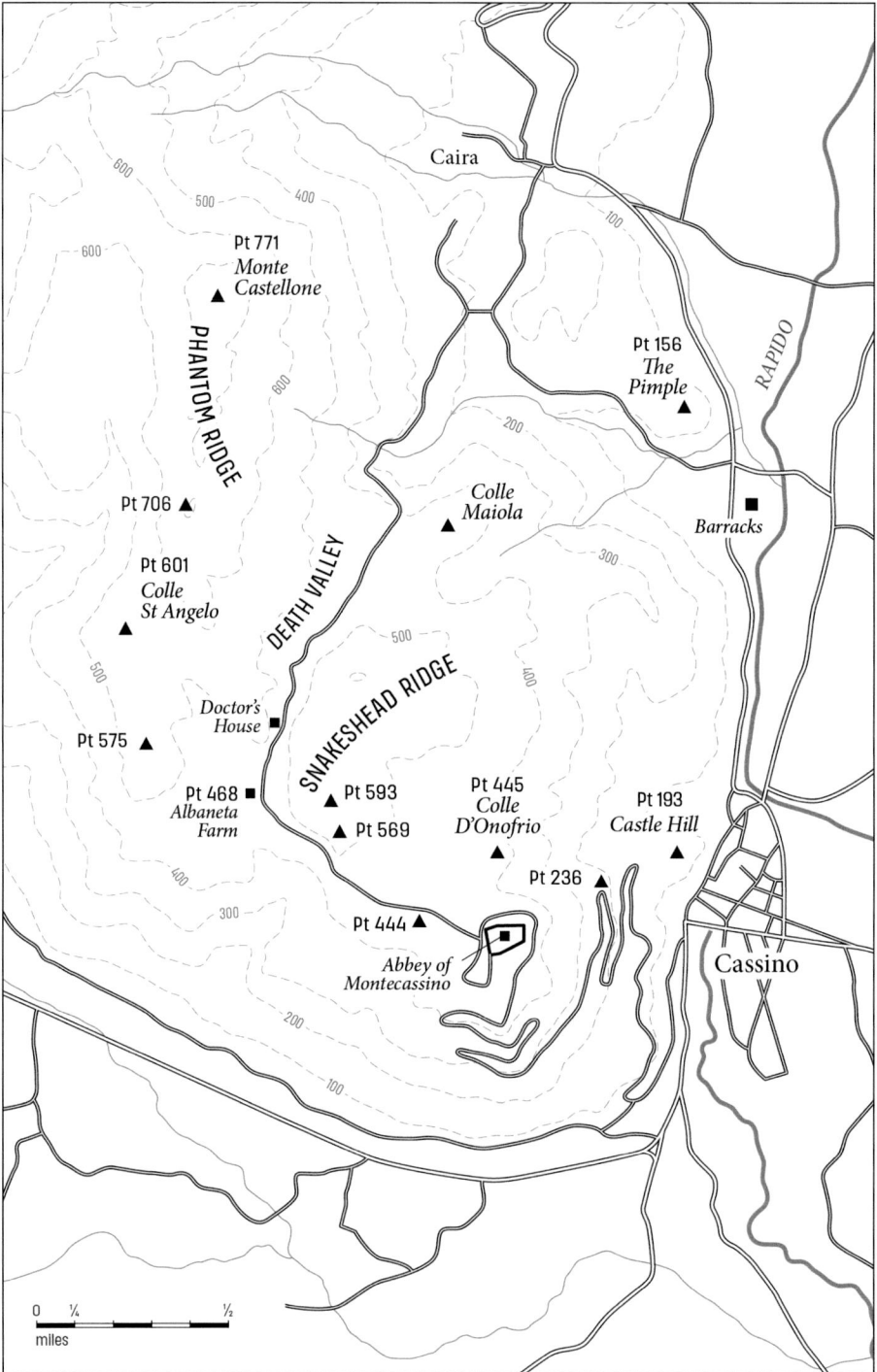

Caira

Pt 771
*Monte
Castellone*
▲

PHANTOM RIDGE

Pt 156
*The
Pimple*
▲

RAPIDO

Pt 706 ▲

DEATH VALLEY

*Colle
Maiola*
▲

■
Barracks

Pt 601
*Colle
St Angelo*
▲

SNAKESHEAD RIDGE

Pt 575 ▲

*Doctor's
House* ■

Pt 468 ■
*Albaneta
Farm*

▲ Pt 593

▲ Pt 569

Pt 445
*Colle
D'Onofrio*
▲

Pt 193
Castle Hill
▲

Pt 236 ▲

Pt 444 ▲

■
*Abbey of
Montecassino*

Cassino

0   ¼   ½
miles

Map 4 The Massif.

there were no plans for the air forces to bomb it. To attack a position before the enemy was able to recover from the shock of bombardment was a lesson that had been learned the hard way by 34th Division.

During the planning for the attack, the 4th Indian Division leadership decided that the attack on the Abbey could not be advanced, despite significant pressure from Freyberg. The two battalions needed to launch the attack, the 1/9 Gurkha Rifles and the 4/6 Rajputana Rifles were still located on the east bank of the Rapido. The Gurkhas had just completed a fifty-mile transit. The preliminary attack on Point 593 was scheduled for that evening, more than 12-hours after the bombing of the Abbey. The company of Royal Sussex tasked to capture the position got about 70-yards before succumbing to heavy machine-gun and mortar fire from the strongpoint. The Abbey, but not Point 593, was bombed again on 16 February, this time by fighter-bombers, but this failed to deter the Germans who turned the ruins into a formidable defensive position, no longer constrained by the orders not to use the site. The New Zealand Corps claimed that this attack was designed to 'throw the enemy's return into confusion.'[74] The Germans were made of stronger stuff and the Allies attacked the wrong place. Freyberg, becoming more impatient, again shows a lack of appreciation of the ground and the conditions faced by Dimoline's troops, when on 16 February, he again suggests a two-brigade frontage attack on the Abbey, ignoring Point 593.[75] Lovett makes clear that this point is the 'bastion to the Monastery.' Clark then informs Freyberg that the air priority has switched back to Anzio, so the opportunity to attack this piece of key terrain had gone. Clark said that 'I am going to give you everything I can in air support while keeping up with the battle up north.'[76] In truth this wasn't much at the height of the struggle to stay in the beachhead. Despite Freyberg's pressure, Dimoline persisted with his plan to seize Point 593 as preliminary to the assault on the Abbey. Freyberg disagreed but did not interfere in his subordinate's plan. By this time, New Zealand Corps perceived Fifth Army as becoming 'restive' and 'fed up with things.'[77] Clark was now pressurizing Freyberg for an attack on the Abbey on 17 February, and Freyberg told Dimoline that 'it must be tomorrow.'[78] The Royal Sussex Regiment again tried to secure Point 593 on the night of 16 February, beginning at 10:30pm. Again, they failed in the face of determined defence sustaining over 140-casualties.[79] Following this second failure, Dimoline bowed under the pressure from his Corps Commander saying to Freyberg, 'I am beginning to think you are right sir', regarding the direct attack on the Abbey regardless of who held Point 593. Nevertheless, this peak continued to occupy everyone's thoughts. In a conversation with his senior gunner in the hours before the direct assault, Freyberg said that 'he did not think they had any reason to be worried about 593.'[80] Weir strongly disagreed, offering the view that 'they could not hold Monastery without holding 593.'[81] The attack on the Abbey, supported by 500-guns was on for the night of 17 February. Freyberg was said to be 'edgy' and unusually slept in his uniform.[82]

74   TNA CAB 106/336.
75   Freyberg, Diary Entry, 16 February 1944.
76   Freyberg, Diary Entry, 16 February 1944.
77   Freyberg, Diary Entry, 16 February 1944.
78   Freyberg, Diary Entry, 16 February 1944.
79   2 NZEF Monthly Narrative Volume XII, Jan, Feb and Mar 44.
80   Freyberg, Diary Entry, 17 February 1944.
81   Freyberg, Diary Entry, 17 February 1944.
82   Freyberg, Diary Entry, 17 February 1944.

Overnight, and into the early morning of 18 February, the Indians continued in their efforts to capture both Point 593 and the Abbey. The supporting interlocking nature of the German defences became obvious early that morning. By 05:10am Queree believed that success had been achieved at Point 593, only for the successful troops to come under withering fire from the neighbouring Point 569, a rock bluff 200-yards to the south.[83] At around the same time the 1/9 Gurkhas, attempting to assault the Abbey directly were reported to have been caught up in a thicket festooned with wire and grenades around Point 444. This point is on the track through 'Death Valley' roughly 400-yards from the walls of the Abbey.

This news seems to have depressed Freyberg who observed, 'does not look as if they will get the Monastery.'[84] He was cheered, however, by further news that Point 593 was occupied by Indian troops and that although fighting remained confused, a company-sized force was on Point 444. The optimism was shared by Fifth Army and Gruenther was said to be 'just tickled to death about getting 593.'[85] Freyberg on the other hand, probably wisely, was not counting his chickens, and called this progress a 'partial success.' By 07:25am, Queree reported that 4th Indian Division was trying to join-up the groups on Points 593 and 444, before pressing on to the Abbey.[86]

Reports from Lovett at 08:00am suggested that a few Gurkhas had succeeded in getting into the Abbey, although how many was unknown as they had no communications. Indian troops were also observed a little later just 300-yards to the south of the main entrance. In the early morning there were reports of fighting 'all round the Monastery.' Freyberg was becoming more confident following this news saying, 'I think tonight we will bust it' and 'we have over 2,000 men on those slopes and I think the Boche is pretty well up against it.'[87] This was true, but the Germans were by no means finished and were about to recruit a significant ally – daylight. The first of Böhmler's paratroopers started to occupy the Abbey's ruins, with around 70-soldiers, three MG-42 machine-guns and mortars taking their positions on 18 February.[88] There was still fierce fighting around the summit of Point 593. The Germans were reportedly moving to counterattack and a Y intercept at 08:45am suggested that Kratzert's paratroopers still held the very top of the hill. By 09:00am, it is becoming clear that the Gurkhas cannot hold Point 444, what the Poles came later to refer to as *Dol Smirci* – The Pit of Death, in the daytime. The strong German occupation of a horseshoe of interlocking defensive positions in fixed strongpoints with mortars and automatic weapons, from Point 575 on Phantom Ridge, through the Albaneta position to Points 593 and 569 made survival impossible. Freyberg, with some impatience, appears not to appreciate that all these positions must be taken. Neutralising only one, exposes the capturing force to enfilade fire from other positions in this clever and well-protected defensive system. By 1:30pm it was reported that the Germans once again held Point 593, although nothing was certain. Freyberg returns to his idea of an assault on a two-brigade frontage but is also now thinking of other ways to crack the problem as his confidence again appears to ebb. Talking to Gruenther that afternoon about the Gurkhas reported in the Abbey, he says, 'what

83 Freyberg, Diary Entry, 18 February 1944.
84 Freyberg, Diary Entry, 18 February 1944.
85 Freyberg, Diary Entry, 18 February 1944.
86 Freyberg, Diary Entry, 18 February 1944.
87 Freyberg, Diary Entry, 18 February 1944.
88 Rennie, p.121.

has happened to them we don't know.'[89] By the afternoon, he comments that it is a 'waste of time to batter at that position from our present line.'[90]

Despite his view that the current assault was a waste of time, Freyberg was determined to persist with his two-brigade assault, in spite of protests from the division commander. The plan was to use both 5th and 7th Indian Infantry Brigades. The plan had three phases. The first was for 5th Brigade to advance to Point 445 on the Colle D'Onofrio on the northern edge of Death Valley. This point had been held by the 135th Infantry but appears to have been abandoned in the takeover or in the scramble to reach the bomb safety line shortly afterwards. It is roughly 400-yards directly north of the Abbey. Meanwhile, the 7th Brigade was to move through Point 593, which was assumed to be still held, to neutralise Point 569, which looks down into, and dominates, Death Valley and is about 1,000 yards north-west of the Abbey. The capture of Point 569 makes possible the occupation of Point 444 in daytime, which was the second phase objective of the 5th Brigade moving south down the hill into Death Valley. The second phase for 7th Brigade was to move from Point 569 in a southerly direction to intersect the track at Point 476, roughly halfway between Point 444 and the German strongpoint at Albaneta Farm. This point is around 900-yards west of the Abbey. Dimoline was supportive of the first two phases of the plan, but he thought the third phase, where both brigades move towards the Abbey eastwards along the track, had little chance of success. They told Queree that they had 'no great faith' in the plan. Even Freyberg made the entry in the diary that, 'if the Indians do their operation, they will be not worth much at the end of it.'[91]

Despite good news on 19 February that Indians still occupied Point 593, and were 'quite happy', Freyberg appeared to be grasping at straws for his next move. Bombing the Abbey had failed, and the Germans had occupied the ruins, creating yet another interlocking firing position. This position now made the third phase of Freyberg's two-brigade assault plan a very risky endeavour. Although gaining more ground than the 34th Division, probably including being firm on the vaunted Point 593, they were still no closer to breaking through. The Germans still held many key points in the town, along the river and in the high ground. Early on 19 February, Freyberg is even considering a repeat of the Rapido operation around St Angelo that had resulted in nearly 2,000 American casualties a month earlier. Fortunately, that evening Clark approved the 'big bombardment programme' for Cassino town that would become Operation DICKENS, the Third Battle of Cassino, in March. So ends the Second Battle of Cassino and Operation AVENGER.

The 4th Indian Division's inability to get itself in position to exploit the bombing within a reasonable time, and the repeated delays, negated the reason for the bombing of the Abbey. This was not Dimoline's fault. Even had his battalions been ready, the failure to attack Point 593 made a daylight assault on the Abbey a suicide mission. This point, as well as the other key points, needed to be coordinated with the air so that the air attack occurred at twilight, to allow the immediate subsequent ground attacks to take advantage of the shock of bombardment and of darkness. No ground forces received any benefit from an early morning attack in bright sunlight against the Abbey alone. After the attempt was abandoned on 19 February, observation

89   Freyberg, Diary Entry, 18 February 1944.
90   Freyberg, Diary Entry, 18 February 1944.
91   Freyberg, Diary Entry, 18 February 1944.

Cassino Italy / Monastery atop Hill – (not a house left standing for miles).

'Not a house left standing for miles.' The results of the New Zealand Corps, Operations AVENGER and DICKENS in February and March 1944. Despite the destruction, the Allies still did not hold the town, nor the Abbey and could not advance up the Liri Valley. (Library of Congress)

of the 4th Indian Division from Monastery Hill, although not from the Abbey specifically, was cited as a reason in the Corps Narrative for the failure of the assault.[92]

In a letter to his two Army commanders in late February 1944, Alexander gave the following candid assessment of why their efforts at Cassino and Anzio had failed:

> After a careful study of the fighting during the past month, I have come to the very defi-
> nite conclusion that one of the main reasons why the enemy has been able to foil us so far

92   TNA WO 204/12509: New Zealand Corps Narrative.

of victory in the battle for Rome is that he is quicker than we are: quicker at regrouping his forces, quicker at thinning out on a defensive front to provide troops to close gaps at decisive points, quicker in effecting reliefs, quicker at mounting attacks and counter-attacks, and above all quicker at reaching decisions on the battlefield. By comparison our methods are often slow and cumbersome, and this applies to all our troops, both British and American.[93]

Although all this was true, it also amounted to a shifting of blame. The failure of the Cassino battles should be squarely placed at the operational and higher tactical levels of war, where Alexander and his Army commanders resided, not blamed on the common soldier and his tactical shortcomings or the training he had received.

The capabilities of the German soldier versus their Allied counterpart were also recognised at the highest level of Allied command in the Mediterranean. In late January, Slessor and Cunningham challenged Wilson on the lack of activity at Anzio. In his letter to Portal, Slessor described the encounter:

Cunningham (who I think is good) and I, had a go at Jumbo this morning on it and told him what we thought of it. His reaction – though perhaps wise – was depressing. He said that we must face the fact that on the ground you want at least 2½ British or Americans to every Hun, and also that the stickiness of the movement was due to the commanders and to the American system of command which he said makes a quick decision impossible. I am not clear why, and still have a feeling that, if the Corps Commander and his two Divisional Commanders were told that unless they were astride the main roads to ROME by tomorrow night, they would all three be Stellenbosched,[94] it might not be too late to turn SHINGLE into a really useful turning movement.[95]

The superiority of the German soldier was somewhat of a myth. British and American soldiers, whilst they may not have the same knack of improvisation, that generally did not matter. Everywhere the Allies were on the offensive and had defeated these German 'supermen' for the last eighteen months. Offensive success is widely recognised as requiring a three to one advantage to the attacking force. If you require only two and one-half Allied soldiers instead of the doctrinal three, you are performing better than expected.

93   Nigel Nicolson, *Alex: The Life of Field Marshal Earl Alexander of Tunis* (London: Weidenfeld and Nicolson, 1973), p.232.
94   'Stellenbosched' is a term that originated in the Boer war. British officers, considered not up to the task were sent to Stellenbosch, a transit camp. See Kipling poem of same name.
95   TNA AIR 75/69, Papers of Sir John Slessor, The Italian Campaign, Letter from Slessor to Portal dated 27 January 1944.

10

Who is Responsible To Whom, For What?

Why, you may take the most gallant sailor, the most intrepid airman, or the most audacious soldier,
put them at a table together – what do you get?
A sum of all their fears!

Winston Churchill
Algiers
16 November 1943[1]

One of the driest, but most important, part of military operations is command and control and the processes that headquarters staff employ to make things happen. There are no stories of derring-do, no storming of pillboxes with only a bayonet. Wars are won by the side with the best organisation and system rather than the bravest soldiers, sailors and airmen. Wars are won or lost at the strategic and operational levels rather than at the tactical. The best tactical plan is doomed if it is in support of a flawed strategy or poor campaign management. When intending to conduct military operations, the most important question that needs to be asked is: Who is responsible to whom, for what?

This can be tricky in a large multi-national coalition where lots of people are responsible to lots of other people, sometimes several people at once, for lots of things, some of which contradict other things that they are also responsible for. Are you confused yet? Command of forces is a critical aspect in the bombing of the Abbey, in order to determine who made the decision to use heavy bombers and why. Working this out will not attribute blame, but it will tell us how the decision was possibly made and who could make it, and just as importantly, who could not! To help, it is useful to describe how military command and control is exercised and how different responsibilities are delegated to subordinate commanders.

First, terms should be defined, and the NATO glossary of terms is good enough. Command is defined as 'The authority vested in an individual of the armed forces for the direction, coordination and control of military forces.'[2] To command you must be in the military. President Roosevelt as US Commander-in-Chief could command US forces, but British Prime Minister, Winston Churchill, could not command those of Britain or the Empire. British command

1   Harold Macmillan, *Blast of War* (London: Macmillan, 1967), p.295.
2   NATO Allied Administrative Publication AAP-06 dated 2015, 2-C-8.

British Prime Minister, Sir Winston Churchill with the British Chief of the Imperial General Staff, General Sir Alan Brooke. Both Churchill and Brooke favoured operations in the Mediterranean. Brooke often had to prevent Churchill's interference in military matters. (NARA RG111-SC-190284)

Below: The commanders. From left to right: Vice Admiral H Kent Hewitt, Lieutenant General Ira Eaker, Air Marshal Sir John Slessor, General Sir Harold Alexander, Major General John Cannon, General Sir Henry Maitland-Wilson and Admiral Sir John Cunningham. (NARA RG342-FH-002215)

runs through the CoS directly to the monarch, who delegated his command authority to the Prime Minister, who controls those forces. The definition of Control is slightly different: 'The authority exercised by a commander over part of the activities of subordinate organisations, or other organisations not normally under his command, that encompasses the responsibility for implementing orders or directives.'[3]

The difference between command and control is that when in command a commander owns the resources and controls them, whereas when in control the commander uses somebody else's resources for a specific task or purpose or for a period. It is, of course, not that simple as there are different levels of command and control. These often tally with the levels of warfare, strategic, operational and tactical. Before delving into this command-and-control issue, it is worth establishing which formation in the Mediterranean Theatre operated at which level of war. There was no strategic-level command in the Mediterranean. This is reserved for the development and implementation of war strategy and therefore there are three Allied organisations that operated at this level. These were the British CoS in London, the US JCS in Washington and a combination of the two, the CCS also in Washington. What is often termed the Grand Strategic is strategy exercised by policymakers. The next level of command down, the operational level, usually includes the theatre level commanders of joint and combined forces of land, sea and air. In the Mediterranean in February 1944 this had recently changed, and one theatre command was formed. This was AFHQ. It is worth for a moment digressing to explain the operational level, as it is often misunderstood. It was not a term generally used by the Allies in the Second World War, having originated in the Soviet Union in the 1920s and 30s, but the concepts were still present. The operational level can loosely be associated with the ways in the ends, ways and means concept. It is how things are to be done, a bridge between strategy and tactics which needs to have a firm understanding of, and a relationship with both, if it is to be successful. It is not just logistics and sustainment. The operational level involves the planning, deployment, synchronisation, sustainment and redeployment of joint forces in campaigns or series of campaigns. The operational level staffs will also provide orders for what subordinate tactical formations are to achieve, but not how to achieve them, although broad guidelines in terms of scope of operations and constraints will come from the operational level to tactical commanders. For example, it was decided at the strategic level that the war was to be taken from Sicily to Italy. At the operational level, and approved by the CCS, Eisenhower eventually decided to land at Salerno. How Alexander and Clark executed Operation AVALANCHE was their business as senior tactical commanders. Sustainment of the force through assault shipping remained an operational level task, hence Eisenhower's obsession with landing ships during this period.

Confusingly, the US called their organisation that controlled the heavy bombers the US Strategic Air Forces. Despite the title, this organisation was also at the operational level because its operations were single-service but multi-theatre. Its operations were attempting to achieve strategic level effects, but they did this at the operational level of war, through high-level daylight precision bombing.

NATOUSA, commanded by Devers, was also at the operational level as although a single-service headquarters, it was responsible for the Army and Army Air Forces. All other formations from Army Group, numbered Air Forces or Fleets operated at the tactical level. These were single-service organisations that could control, but did not command, the forces from

3   AAP-06, 2-C-13.

other services. They were either given use of, or requested support from, the parent organisations.

There are several different command levels. The command relationships usually form a complicated wiring diagram, and the Italian theatre was no exception. The first level of command is full command. This is reserved for national authorities and involves every aspect of commanding a force including equipment, personnel administration, individual training and discipline. In the Mediterranean, the British (or Indian) Service Chiefs exercised full command over their deployed assets, and the American Joint Chiefs through NATOUSA did the same for their troops. When he was Chief of Staff of the USAF, General Curtis LeMay summed this up: 'the Chief of Staff can delegate authority, but he can't possibly delegate his responsibility.[4] The next level down is operational command. This allows theatre commanders to assign tasks to subordinate commanders within a theatre of operations, allocating operational or tactical control. For example, that B-17s were in the Mediterranean was a full command decision by Arnold.

How they were operated was an operational command decision exercised by Spaatz. He then delegated operational control of his bombers in the Mediterranean to the MAAF commanding general, Eaker. The US Commanding General in the Mediterranean, Devers, could take operational control of the bombers in an emergency for a specific task. This is the authority to direct assigned forces for specific missions and tasks. Devers therefore, could control but did not operationally command, Spaatz's bombers. The land commanders in Italy had neither operational command nor control of any air force assets. All the army formations in Italy, from 15th Army Group, downwards could

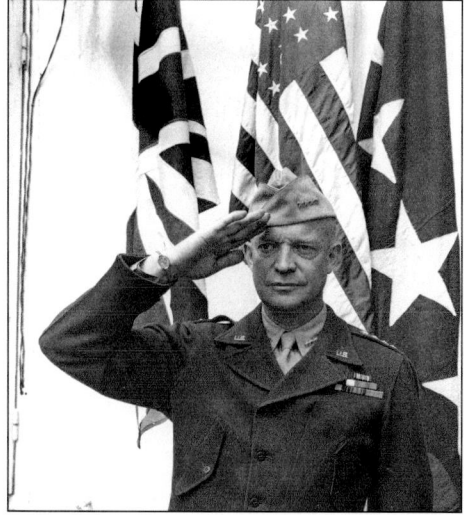

Up until the end of 1943, the Operational level commander for operations in Italy was General Eisenhower. His title was Commander-in-Chief Allied Force, not Supreme Commander Mediterranean, a position established after his departure. (NARA RG319-AP6406-SC444392)

The forgotten American. Following Eisenhower's departure, all American forces in the Mediterranean came under the Command of Lieutenant General Jacob Devers. Devers was also Deputy Commander of the Allied Force and then Deputy Supreme Commander in the Mediterranean Theatre. (NARA RG208-N-S-1938)

4   Curtis Le May with MacKinley Kantor, *Mission With Le May* (Garden City, NY: Doubleday and Company, 1965), p.512.

only exercise tactical command of land forces. They could, however, request tactical control of CAS for specific missions and tasks. In the air forces, the numbered air forces exercised tactical command of their assets.

The destruction of the Abbey could not have happened through independent tactical action alone, especially by land forces. The authorisation for the attack by heavy bombers, used tactically, had to have been agreed at a higher level than Tuker or the USAAF bombing squadrons. This decision required the entire Mediterranean command structure to enact. How did this structure work; who could have made the decisions? Until the end of 1943 the Allied Commander-in-Chief was Eisenhower, but by February 1944, Wilson had replaced him.

Wilson, known as 'Jumbo', took over as Allied Commander-in-Chief in January. Neither he nor Eisenhower was officially the 'Supreme Commander'. This title was adopted in March 1944. At the time of the bombing of the Abbey, Wilson was the Commander-in-Chief Allied Force, although this made no substantive difference, and he was often referred to by the former title.[5] His principal headquarters was known as AFHQ when the Abbey was destroyed. Wilson became the Supreme Commander Mediterranean on 4 March, a few days before he released his evidence about the Abbey bombing to the British CoS. There were important differences in the span of command and the relationships amongst the polyglot forces of AFHQ. These became more intricate under Wilson during 1944. Wilson's remit was wider than that of Eisenhower's, including all Allied forces in the Mediterranean and Middle East, not just those in Italy.[6] He also had a different command relationship with subordinate forces. Upon accession to command, he exercised operational command over all British, Dominion and Colonial troops.[7] This relationship was complicated, however, in the case of New Zealand and Canada by the administrative powers vested in the senior officers of each Dominion, who retained full command that could override the orders of the Commander-in-Chief if this was desired by their governments. This power gave Lieutenant General Freyberg far more influence than normally existed for a corps or division commander. For Indian troops, Wilson also had to consider the views of the Commander-in-Chief India, Field Marshal Sir Claude Auchinleck, who retained full command of this separate army of the British Empire. Indian commanders remained in direct contact with their superiors and an Indian Army Mission attached to Wilson's command to keep the C-in-C informed, was requested days after the bombing on 20 February 1944, although there is no evidence that this was connected to the attack.[8] Wilson did not exercise full command of US, French or other overseas troops, as these were exercised through the senior officers of each nation. He also did not command all his air forces, as the strategic air force of the USAAF were under the operational command of Spaatz. Wilson and Devers only had emergency veto powers on their use.

The first senior officer with authority to order the attack was Wilson. He had served in the British Army since before the Boer War, seeing action in the First World War at both the Somme and Passchendaele. He had served in several command appointments in the Middle

5   Allied Force Headquarters, History of AFHQ Part Three – December 1943 – July 1944 – Section 1, p.638.
6   Combined Chiefs of Staff Memorandum CCS 387 dated 3 November 1943.
7   Allied Force Headquarters, History of AFHQ Part Three – December 1943 – July 1944 – Section 1, p.695.
8   Allied Force Headquarters, History of AFHQ Part Three – December 1943 – July 1944 – Section 1, p.695.

East and North Africa, culminating in the post of General Officer Commanding in Chief (GOC-in-C) Middle East in February 1943. His was also a very sensitive command, dealing with foreign forces and the Dominions. One aspect involved the claimed wasted sacrifice of New Zealand soldiers that had prompted New Zealand's Prime Minister, Peter Fraser, to write a strongly worded letter to London after his losses in Greece and Crete in 1941. Fraser had written that 'New Zealand troops should not for the third time be committed to battle without adequate air support.'[9] The increased sensitivity to New Zealand losses, the recent 'Furlough Mutiny' and a marked decrease in New Zealanders' morale resulted in a perception that their commander was handled with kid gloves by the British. This has often been noted as a factor in the decision to allow the bombing of the Abbey.

Harold Macmillan, British Minister to AFHQ, and future Prime Minister, thought that Wilson was less adept than his predecessor in achieving consensus. US author Douglas Porch said that 'Wilson gave outsiders the impression that he was Colonel Blimp's understudy.'[10] This appears to be a view often shared by American senior officers, although not Devers who called him, 'the best British general in the whole damned war.'[11] Macmillan, who wanted Alexander for the post said, 'They call him Jumbo. I hope he is wise. He is certainly ponderous.'[12] Upon taking over, Wilson was not given a handover by Eisenhower, as he had left a few weeks prior to the official change of command. Looking at his record, it seems that Wilson was a competent, but uninspiring, officer whose background was that of a typically conservative British Army senior officer of his day, lacking in original thought or an outlook suitable for modern warfare. Whilst there is no strong evidence that Wilson was more than a rubber stamp in the Abbey's destruction, he was left to pick up the pieces, a task he did not perform well and for which he was ill-suited. Wilson was promoted to Field-Marshal in December 1944 and sent to Washington as Chief of the British Joint Staff Mission upon the death of Sir John Dill.

The next candidate is the Commanding General of all the US heavy bombers in Europe, Carl Spaatz. Spaatz had been made the commander of US Army Air Forces in North Africa in February 1943. In January 1944, he was transferred to Britain in the new post of Commanding General of the United States Strategic Air Forces in Europe. He graduated from West Point as an infantry officer in 1914, retraining as a pilot in 1915 and serving on the 1st Aero Squadron during the Pancho Villa expedition in 1916. He then commanded the American air training organisation on the western front in 1917/8, where he also gained operational experience. During the inter-war period he served in a few command and staff roles, rising to the rank of lieutenant colonel. In 1940 he was sent to Britain as an observer of the Battle of Britain. He became a Major General in January 1942 and returned to Britain, this time to command the Eighth Air Force, but was quickly transferred to the Mediterranean Theatre following Operation TORCH. As commander of the US Strategic Air Forces he, along with Air Chief Marshal Sir Arthur Harris, was nicknamed one of 'the Bomber Barons' for their confidence in destroying German war capability from the air. Spaatz's major proposal was the adoption of the 'oil plan', targeting German refining and synthetic oil production to starve their military of fuel.

9   Arthur Tedder, *With Prejudice* (London: Cassell, 1966), p.176.
10 Porch, p.109.
11 *Interview with Devers for Eisenhower Library with Dr Maclyn Burg, 5 February 1975* <https://www.eisenhowerlibrary.gov/sites/default/files/research/oral-histories/oral-history-transcripts/devers-jacob-377.pdf> (accessed 10 August 2023).
12 Macmillan, p.339.

Lieutenant General Carl Spaatz (on right with glasses) with General Sir Harold Alexander. Spaatz was the Operational Level commander of all US heavy bombers in Europe. (NARA RG342-FH-000197)

He was not a great advocate of strategic air forces supporting tactical ground operations, only accepting these tasks reluctantly. He was convinced that given time and resources the war could be won solely from the air. Promoted to full General in March 1945, he was sent to the Pacific to oversee strategic bomber operations, including the atomic attacks on Japan. Spaatz was the only general officer to attend all three surrender ceremonies. After the War, he was appointed as head of the USAAF by President Truman and became the first Chief of Staff of the United States Air Force following the National Security Act of 1947.

A third possible senior candidate was Wilson's deputy, Jacob Devers. Devers, an artillery officer, is the forgotten top American commander. He was appointed on 29 December 1943.[13] Unlike Ike, Clark or Bradley, he left no memoir, adding to his obscurity. Reaching higher positions than his peer Patton, and commanding an Army Group in France, the equivalent position of Montgomery and Bradley, he lacked their flamboyance and showmanship. Devers was the quiet innovator, responsible in part for bringing vital equipment into US military service. Without these the US Army would have found the Germans a much more difficult opponent.

13   Allied Force Headquarters, History of AFHQ Part Three – December 1943 – July 1944 – Section 1, pp.697-8.

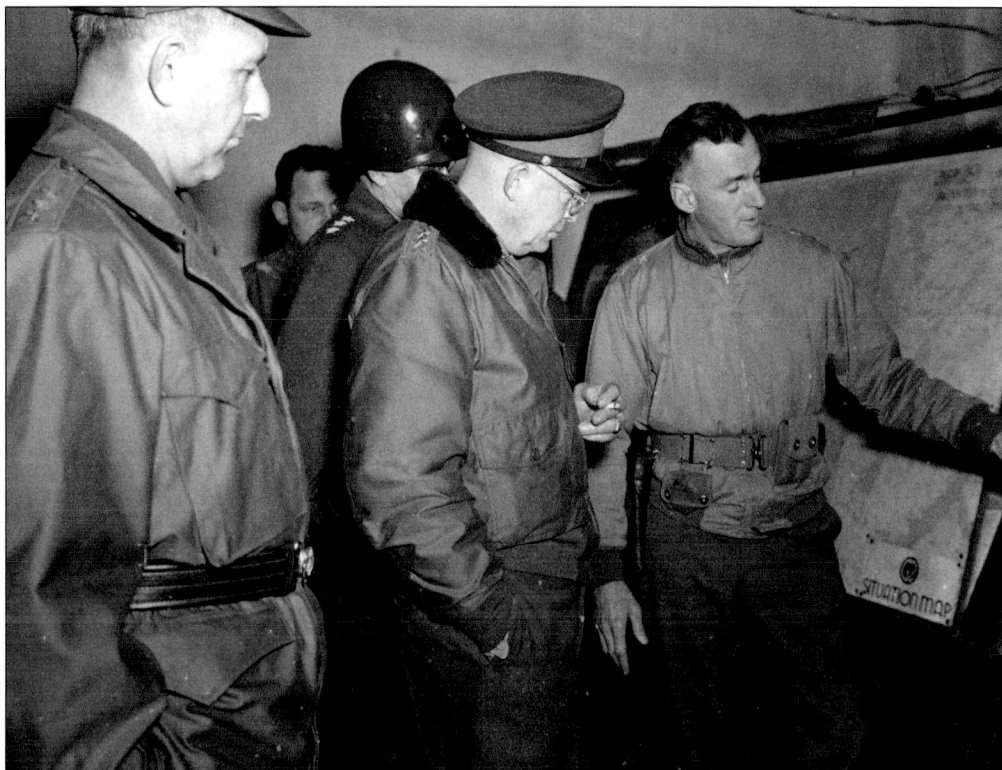

Devers and Eisenhower were both protégés of General Marshall but had completely different personalities. The two men were never close, and Eisenhower's fame may have added to Devers' future obscurity. (NARA RG319-AP-6406-SC232833)

Like Clark, although he lacked his charisma, Devers was always destined to perform well in a supporting role, never the main star. He missed action in the first war but was posted to France following the armistice. Like Eisenhower, he was a protégé of Marshall.[14] Eisenhower and Devers, however, were not close, perhaps due to their competition for Marshall's notice and their very different characters.

Devers was an innovator, creative and often heedless of accepted wisdom.[15] Sometimes this paid off, as with the medium tank, an innovation which Eisenhower at first disapproved. Occasionally, Devers came unstuck as with his decision to press for the Rhine in late 1944, a decision that created the Colmar Pocket and went against his orders. Eisenhower was a by-the-book, solid dependable pair of hands with an affable collegiate approach, ideal for running a potentially fractious coalition. Unlike Clark and Eisenhower, Devers had more than just staff experience commanding various US Army formations. As well as being an artilleryman, he had commanded an infantry division and armoured forces. Whilst in this job he may have

14 Martin Blumenson and James Stokesbury, *Masters of the Art of Command* (Boston, MA: Houghton Mifflin, 1975), pp.173-176.
15 Adams, Kindle location 1719.

influenced his mentor Marshall into approving the radical air doctrine, that made air and ground commanders equal.[16] His first contribution to the war was being sent by Marshall to replace General Frank Andrews in England following his death. His main task was Operation BOLERO, the build-up of US forces for the invasion of France. It was during this period that Devers and Ira Eaker, then Eighth Air Force commander, may have ruined their chances to command in OVERLORD, although there was no way either could have known it. Before Devers arrived in England, on 30 April 1943, Eisenhower asked the CCS for two B-17 bombardment groups to support the operation in Sicily.[17] Eaker fought to keep the bombers and the CCS refused Ike. During July 1943, Eisenhower again demanded four bomber groups from Eaker's Eighth Air Force to support Operation AVALANCHE. Eaker's priority, in line with CCS direction, was the strategic bombing campaign to which the Americans were just beginning to make a meaningful contribution. He was very reluctant to give up his bombers. Devers, now the US commander in Britain, agreed with Eaker, saying later that there 'wasn't a more fool idea thought up in the world' and the bombers stayed in England.[18] Eisenhower was clearly irked by the decision and complained several times to Marshall. Keeping to the CCS priority, he refused to intervene, writing, 'Devers is right, and the heavy bombers have to stay in England.'[19] He also tried with the entire CCS on 28 July, again without success.[20]

Eisenhower didn't forget, serving his revenge cold a few months later when both Eaker and Devers were exiled to the secondary Mediterranean.[21] To get him out of the way he insisted Devers replace him in the Mediterranean, when he took over as the senior American officer, although he offered Marshall the option that if left in the UK, he would find Devers a 'useful job', although he would be 'superfluous' if he remained.[22] Marshall was surprised by this decision but allowed it.[23] Devers accused Eisenhower of 'bypassing him.'[24] In a scheme to have Devers demoted, Ike suggested to Marshall that he be offered an Army command, but the Chief of Staff continued to protect his other protégé by sending him to the more senior, yet less glamorous number two slot in the Mediterranean. Devers did not, unlike Ike, become the Commander-in-Chief, and his move, which he discovered from the *The Times*, embittered him, and his relationship with Ike remained frosty thereafter.[25] Both he and Eaker, who were good friends despite

16   Daniel Mortensen, 'Getting Together', in Daniel R Mortensen (ed.), *Airpower and Ground Armies – Essays on the Evolution of Anglo-American Air Doctrine, 1940-43,* (Maxwell AL: Air University Press, 1998), p.123.
17   Chandler et al, *Eisenhower Papers, Vol II*, p.1106.
18   *Interview with Devers for Eisenhower Library with Dr Maclyn Burg, 5 February 1975* <https://www.eisenhowerlibrary.gov/sites/default/files/research/oral-histories/oral-history-transcripts/devers-jacob-377.pdf> (accessed 10 August 2023).
19   Chandler et al, *Eisenhower Papers, Vol II*, 1269-70; Wilbur Morrison, *Fortress Without A Roof* (London, W H Allen, 1982), p.128.
20   Chandler et al, *Eisenhower Papers, Vol II*, p.1296.
21   Adams, Kindle location 1844.
22   Chandler et al, *Eisenhower Papers, Vol III*, p.1604-1612.
23   Wheeler, p.242.
24   *Interview with Devers for Eisenhower Library with Dr Maclyn Burg, 5 February 1975* <https://www.eisenhowerlibrary.gov/sites/default/files/research/oral-histories/oral-history-transcripts/devers-jacob-377.pdf> (accessed 10 August 2023).
25   Adams, Kindle location 2141. Wheeler, 242. Interview with Devers for Eisenhower Library with Dr Maclyn Burg, 19 August 1974. < https://www.eisenhowerlibrary.gov/sites/default/files/research/oral-histories/oral-history-transcripts/devers-jacob-377.pdf > (accessed 10 August 2023).

only meeting for the first time in England, were deflated by postings 'away from the big leagues.'[26] On arrival, he was uncomplimentary about Eisenhower's management, calling it 'pretty much of a mess…there was chaos all over the place', which was leaked to the press, eventually getting back to Eisenhower, souring the relationship further.[27] He was again, perhaps unsurprisingly, uncooperative when Eisenhower demanded his best combat commanders, such as Truscott, then commanding the US 3rd Infantry Division. He called Eisenhower's poaching of the best staff 'scandalous' and it also worried Marshall who wrote to Eisenhower on 24 December 1943 concerning the subject.[28] He again tried unsuccessfully to get Truscott a number of times prior to OVERLORD. Marshall, despite their diametrically opposed and often feuding characters, continued to have confidence in both Eisenhower and Devers. Had Marshall commanded OVERLORD, Devers would probably have been selected ahead of Bradley as Army and subsequently Army Group Commander in Normandy. He saw the Mediterranean posting somewhat differently to Devers, although it had taken some persuasion for him to agree to it. Marshall had been impressed by his handling of the British. He wanted someone in the Mediterranean who would not stand for pointless excursions and he needed a trusted insider who would inform him of diversions of effort to the Balkans as Marshall suspected to be Churchill's intention. Devers had proven himself able in handling the difficult 'limeys' and would probably be able to do the same with the even more awkward French. He was primarily responsible for the administration of the US Army and for equipping and training French divisions in Italy. Although this was to his credit, it came back to bite him when he commanded a French Army in southern France in late 1944 and early 1945. Unfortunately for him at this time, he was under the command of his old 'friend' Eisenhower. To be fair to both men, Eisenhower had been supportive of Devers to command 6th Army Group prior to the landings in southern France, and Devers had sent warm congratulations to Ike when he was appointed to command OVERLORD. Like many other senior commanders in Italy in early 1944, including Eaker, Devers had only just arrived when the Abbey was attacked. It was not a surprise that Devers took a dislike to Clark, as he was not impressed by his self-publicity, although he rated him 'superior' in his fitness report. Before he went to southern France he wrote of Clark: 'Noted two cables from Clark to me which show quite well his lack of judgement and tact and indicate definitely that he is not a team player nor has he the instincts of a fighting soldier and a gentleman.'[29] Another diary comment from Devers reveals the power of the US Army Chief of Staff over his subordinates, even those that have his favour: 'He (Clark) is a headache to me and I would relieve him if I could, but I can't. Marshall wouldn't let me relieve him.'[30] The feeling was mutual; Clark referred to Devers once as 'that dope.'[31] Clark's sympathetic biographer, Blumenson, appeared to dislike Devers calling him 'inarticulate', 'something of a big kid', and an officer whose 'star seemed on the wane'.[32] There is no recorded evidence that Devers took any active part in the decision to bomb the Abbey, but he will always be associated with it. This is because many histories include details of

26   Adams, Kindle location 2186.
27   Adams, Kindle location 2230.
28   Wheeler, 246. Chandler et al, *Eisenhower Papers, Vol III,* p.1614fn1.
29   Adams, Kindle location 2287.
30   Adams, Kindle location 2287.
31   Adams, Kindle location 2287.
32   Blumenson, *Mark Clark,* p.166.

the flight by Eaker and Devers that saw Germans in the Abbey before it was bombed. In fact, as we shall see, this flight never took place.

Officially, the authority of one of these three senior generals must have been gained before the Abbey could be attacked with USAAF heavy bombers, but was it, and by which one?

Before discussing the events that led up to the bombing, it is worth looking at how the Allied Army Group in Italy was organised. The command-and-control arrangement of the Fifth Army was unusual. In North Africa, following Operation TORCH, the Allies had been organised under Eisenhower as Commander-in-Chief in often mixed units with the British First and Eighth Armies and the US II Corps. This was not always successful and often caused confusion because of different supply systems and doctrines. The Americans had much to learn, and their progress was often hindered by poor interpersonal relationships. One officer, Truscott, talked of his peers' 'bitterness, personal and professional jealousy, the complete lack of understanding and even hatred.'[33] The next hop took the Allies to Sicily for Operation HUSKY, where the jealousies could become multi-national.

The two armies of 15th Army Group in Sicily, were the Seventh US Army (Patton) and British Eighth Army (Montgomery). These were separated along US/British and Commonwealth lines. Alexander, supposedly Churchill's favourite general, served as GOC-in-C throughout Sicily, the invasion of Italy and the Cassino battles. Prior to January 1944, as well as commanding the Army Group as overall land force commander, he was also Deputy Allied Commander-in-Chief to Eisenhower, although Ike viewed him as only his land commander.[34]

He was an Ulster aristocrat, and because he was not the inheritor of his father's title, he was destined for the army, commissioning into the Irish Guards in 1911 after leaving Harrow. Alexander's upbringing at Caledon, County Tyrone, was in a strong Protestant environment,[35] although he demonstrated no sectarian bias towards the Roman Catholics he commanded. Many soldiers in the Irish Guards were Ulster Catholics.[36] He was not academically gifted and was initially a slow learner, being poor at reading and writing during his early school years. Despite this, Harrow held fond memories for him, mainly due to his sporting prowess. At Sandhurst, he displayed far greater ability at practical subjects than military academics. He was near the top in riding, shooting and military skills, but always in the bottom half of his class for law, history and administration.[37] This was irrelevant to his career, as someone of his aristocratic background was assured of success in the Edwardian British Army. As Lord Louis Mountbatten stated:

> He had almost every quality you could wish to have, except that he had the average brain of an average English gentleman. He lacked that little extra cubic centimetre which produces genius. If you recognise that, it's perhaps a greater tribute to what he did achieve by leadership, courage and inspiring devotion in those who served under him.[38]

---

33   Truscott, p.533.
34   Chandler et al, *Eisenhower Papers Vol III*, p.1421.
35   Nicolson, p.7. An interesting aside is that the US 34th Infantry Division, one of the units intimately involved in the battle for Cassino, was the first US Division to cross the Atlantic, assembling in Northern Ireland on 28 May 1942 at Alexander's home at Caledon.
36   Nicolson, p.35.
37   Nicolson, p.22.
38   Nicolson, p.239.

The Irish Guards saw its first action in the First World War, having been raised after the Boer War by Queen Victoria. Alexander was a natural leader, popular with his men and superiors. Officers were expected to lead their troops without much training in the art or science of leadership. He served as a regimental officer, and was known as daring and courageous, rising to the rank of temporary lieutenant colonel. He saw war as a gentlemanly pursuit and, 'enjoyed the war and was not ashamed to admit it,' and he was not at all reflective about its causes or results.[39] Afterwards, still keen for active service, he served in the Baltic, commanding the Baltische Landeswehr, a predominantly German force in the Latvian War of Independence, but the rite of passage to the highest echelons of the British Army begins with the Staff College,

Overall land commander in Italy, General Sir Harold Alexander examines some photographic reconnaissance photographs with President Roosevelt's son, Elliot. (NARA RG342-FH-000408)

either at Camberley or Quetta and Alexander had chosen the Baltic and was over-age and too senior to be selected. He failed to get accepted in 1924 and only passed the entrance exam in 1926. To attend he took a reduction in rank. He again excelled at leadership and socially; predictably less so academically.

In the first years of the Second World War, now a major general, he served in France and Burma, supervising British retreats on both occasions. Despite his first two commands ending in defeat, Alexander's career blossomed, and he was seen as an inspiring leader, unflappable and calm. He was sent to oversee Montgomery as GOC-in-C Middle East, although he remained mostly in the shadow of his more illustrious subordinate. Nicolson, in his largely favourable biography, suggests this was a deliberate policy, although it would be very unusual for an Army Group commander to give all the credit to his subordinate. Montgomery considered him a friend, but never rated his abilities. Following the joining of Eisenhower's TORCH forces and Montgomery's Eighth Army, he became commander of the 18th Army Group. Alexander probably accepted the political nature of Eisenhower's appointment, but he must have been disappointed not to have been given command in the Mediterranean, especially considering

39   Nicolson, p.33.

the American's lack of experience. Upon the German defeat he sent the famous message to Churchill: 'Sir: It is my duty to report that the Tunisian Campaign is over. All enemy resistance has ceased. We are masters of the North African shores.'

The scale of this victory has often been underestimated. His role in the Sicilian and Italian campaigns was to command all land forces, an increasingly difficult task as these were denuded from late 1943 onwards. Again, he was not given the top job after Eisenhower's departure, that position going to the lesser-known Wilson. The principal reason for this was CIGS in London. Brooke had long held the view that Alexander wasn't up to it; his diary entry on 19 June 1943, suggested that Eisenhower also shared his views on Alex's suitability.[40] Eisenhower wrote to CIGS two weeks later with a glowing assessment, but in a diary entry the week before this letter he questioned his ability to deal firmly with subordinates.[41] He rated Alexander only third in his list of British subordinates behind Cunningham and Tedder. Brooke considered neither Ike nor Alex a big soldier', although his diary was a release valve and he often gave colourful descriptions of his fellow commanders.[42] During the Quebec Conference, Churchill suggested to Brooke that Alexander replace Eisenhower.[43] This was still the case when he and Brooke met with him in Malta on 18 November 1943, but Brooke remained unconvinced about Alex, writing:

> Alexander charming as he is fills me with gloom, he is a very, very, small man and cannot see big. Unfortunately, he does not recognize this fact and is oblivious to his shortcomings! But I shudder at the thought of him as a Supreme Commander! He will never have the personality or vision to command three services! It is hard to advise him as he fails to grasp the significance of things.[44]

Brooke felt his words were harsh, but he judged that he would not alter them.[45] Alex had no experience commanding air forces, and Brooke thought that he would do it badly, writing an exclamation mark after the comment regarding his ability to command jointly. Brooke persuaded Churchill on 4 December 1943 that Wilson should take over as Commander-in-Chief in the Mediterranean.[46] This was then promptly unagreed by Churchill after an intervention by Macmillan.[47] Macmillan liked Wilson but disagreed that he should be the Commander-in-Chief.[48] He makes the point in his diary that not only Brooke, but the Air Force and Navy favoured Wilson. Macmillan, however, felt that Wilson was too old, and that the public would not understand if the dashing Alexander was passed-over.[49] Someone far more important had doubts about his suitability. Roosevelt was concerned that Alex would be too dominated by Churchill and would pursue his policies in the Mediterranean, rather than those agreed.[50] By

40   Danchev and Todman, p.422.
41   Chandler et al, *Eisenhower Papers, Vol II*, p.1236.
42   Danchev and Todman, p.452.
43   Danchev and Todman, p.441.
44   Danchev and Todman, p.473.
45   Danchev and Todman, p.473.
46   Danchev and Todman, p.491.
47   Danchev and Todman, p.493.
48   Macmillan, p.321.
49   Macmillan, p.322.
50   Matloff, Kindle loc 8176.

12 December, Wilson was again in the chair and Alexander had been informed by Churchill, although the confirmatory signal was not sent until 18 December.[51] Although there is no indication of disappointment, not being selected for OVERLORD and not being in overall command in the Mediterranean were bitter blows. Clark sensed a listlessness in him after the decision and assumed it was due to his disappointment.[52] He was also no longer Deputy Commander because when Wilson took over, this job was passed to Devers on 8 January 1944. In Italy, he did not control the air forces, as these were independent entities under the air commander. He was a tactical commander of land forces and not the overall Italy commander as many authors, mainly land warfare historians, suggest. Despite his reputation, Alexander's style was not always suited to his command; he often struggled to control his senior subordinate commanders, vindicating Brooke's judgement. He said of Alexander's handling of Montgomery, 'He wants guiding and watching continually and I do not think that Alex is sufficiently strong and rough with him.'[53] Some that worked for him considered him somewhat lazy, using his charm and delegation where forceful and energetic decisiveness were required. The eminent historian and British officer, Sir Michael Howard compared Alexander to the hapless commander at Gallipoli, Sir Ian Hamilton, a 'gallant gentleman, far out of his depth.'[54] Commander of 56th Infantry Division at the Garigliano and Anzio, Major General Gerald Templer said of him, 'He was lazy, but not over the essentials. He relied on his staff. If they did something wrong, he would pull them up. His laziness was a virtue. It meant the capacity to delegate, and in wartime it became a tremendous asset, because it meant that he could relax and unhook.'[55]

This 'virtue' was naïve and was savagely exploited by the extremely strong personalities that were his subordinates. It also has a tinge of damnation by faint praise. He acquiesced to both Montgomery and Patton in Sicily, possibly delaying the German defeat, and arguably allowing their escape. At Salerno, he should have vetoed the inexperienced Clark's flawed plan of landing his weak Fifth Army either side of a river with a large gap in between his corps. Instead, his lack of a firm grip barely avoided disaster as the Germans nearly exploited the over-extension of Clark's army. Throughout the Cassino battles, the Army Group lacked concentration of force until the arrival of Harding as his COS. Anzio was an operation that Alexander should never have agreed to. Despite this, Truscott, one of the commanders in the 'beached whale', greatly admired him, saying 'he had all the personality and drive of Patton and Montgomery, without any of their flamboyance'.[56] He considered him an outstanding leader. Despite this, Clark virtually ignored his orders in the Anzio break-out to be the first into Rome, a decision Truscott strongly disagreed with. The military commentator Liddell-Hart accurately sums him up when he wrote:

> He had good intelligence and an exceptionally open mind, but success came so quickly and continually that there was no compelling pressure to set him to the grindstone of hard application that sharpens the edge. He was a born leader, but the ease with which he had always won men's confidence provided no incentive to increase his magnetism by applying

51   Danchev and Todman, p.497 and p.502.
52   Blumenson, *Mark Clark*, p.162.
53   Fraser, p.319.
54   Orange, *Churchills' Airmen*, p.227.
55   Nicolson, p.79.
56   Truscott, p.547.

the arts of leadership. But beyond that he had an innate reluctance to exert more power over others than the minimum necessary for the performance of his task, and sometimes it was not enough for the purpose. Eminent as his record was, he might have been a greater commander if he had not been so nice a man, and so deeply a gentleman.[57]

Brooke continued to struggle to hide his weaknesses from Churchill, his poor grasp of strategy and his inability to control his subordinates.[58] Some were even more scathing than Brooke. After the war, Slessor, described Alexander to Auchinleck as 'quite the stupidest man who has ever commanded more than a division… he owes his position entirely to Churchill's occasional gross misjudgement of men.'[59]

Despite being an inspirational leader, Alexander owed his very high rank more to his breeding and connections than to his ability or intellect. A successful career in the British army at this time depended on the right school and the right regiment and family connections. Brilliance in military thought was a distant second to bravery, if not a hindrance to success.[60] Being a 'good chap' was paramount and the 'old school tie' remained influential; both Alexander and Churchill were Old Harrovians. He could not take this relationship for granted and Churchill had to remind him that he could give orders to Americans. The Prime Minister sent messages to his senior commanders via what were known as Special Unnumbered Messages. These were sent from Bletchley Park by secure one-time-pad. This 'unpleasant habit' of Churchill's used to infuriate the CIGS and they often contained issues upon which he and the Prime Minister disagreed.[61] This signal is undated but contemporaneous as Churchill mentions Freyberg's upcoming attack and remarks on Lucas at Anzio, putting it around 5 February 1944. The Prime Minister gently rebukes Alexander throughout, especially in his handling of allied commanders:

1. I do not wish you to be worried during the Battle by anything except the enemy. But I am sure you realise how great a disappointment was caused at home and in the USA by standstill at Nettuno. I do not of course know what orders were given to General Lucas, but it is a Root principal to push out and form contact with enemy… The ease with which the enemy moved their pieces on the board and rapidity with which they adjusted perilous gap that they had to make on their Southern front is most impressive. It all seems to give us very awkward data in regard to OVERLORD.
2. I have a certain feeling that you have hesitated to assert your authority because you were dealing so largely with Americans and therefore urged repeat urged advance instead of ordering it. You are however quite entitled to give orders and I have it from highest American Authorities that it is their wish that their troops should receive direct orders. They say their Army has been formed more on Prussian lines than the more smooth British lines and that American Commanders expect to receive positive orders which they will immediately obey. Do not hesitate therefore to give orders just

57   Nicolson, p.120.
58   Danchev and Todman, p.519. Graham and Bidwell, p.244.
59   Orange, *Slessor Bomber Champion*, p.140.
60   Porch, p.297.
61   Fraser, p.519.

as you would to our own men. The Americans are very good to work with and quite prepared to take the rough with the smooth.

3. I am naturally looking forward to the news of Freyberg's attack. If some of our troops are tired enemy must be equally so. I trust that you are satisfied with leaving Lucas in command at Bridgehead. If not you should put someone there you can trust.[62]

Alexander, despite his seniority to Monty and experience as an Army Group commander in two large operations was not selected to command the 21st Army Group in Normandy, despite Eisenhower's preference. The reason given was that Italy could not lose its two most senior commanders. Brooke would probably have preferred Alexander in Normandy than as Mediterranean Supreme Commander, although he wanted Monty for OVERLORD.[63] Montgomery's public persona, his battle experience and Brooke's long-standing patronage carried the day, although he was fully aware that the Americans did not like Monty, whose lack of tact had earned him several reprimands. Brooke partly blamed Alexander's lack of strength in controlling Monty.[64] Although he showed no resentment, he was probably overlooked for more than reasons of continuity. Perhaps it was a mistake not to appoint the more congenial British general? Bradley certainly thought so:

Had Alexander commanded the 21st Army Group in Europe, we could probably have avoided the petulance that later was to becloud our relationship with Montgomery. For in contrast to the rigid self-assurance of General Montgomery, Alexander brought to his command the reasonableness, patience and modesty of a great soldier. In each successive Mediterranean campaign he had won the adulation of his American subordinates.[65]

Ambassador Robert Murphy, Macmillan's US counterpart, described him as 'the ablest of British generals in the Mediterranean theatre of war'.[66] There is no doubt that Alexander was a people person, a great leader of men in battle. He was not, however, a master of strategy and his limited intellect did not always give him insight in deciding where, when and how those battles should be fought.

Alexander's principal subordinate in the west of Italy was Lieutenant General Mark Clark. The two invasions of Italy in September 1943; Operation AVALANCHE at Salerno by US Fifth Army and Operation BAYTOWN at Regio di Calabria by British Eighth Army were differently formed than the Sicily operation. Whilst the Eighth Army remained largely a British Empire affair, the Fifth Army he commanded was much more polyglot. Clark, known as 'Wayne', remains a controversial figure. His senior aide in late 1944, and later US Ambassador to the United Nations, Vernon Walters, described him in soldierly terms, 'Clark was a commanding figure. He was six feet three inches tall, slender with a hawklike nose and was an impressive figure of a soldier...He was not an easy man to work for, very demanding and less than polite.'[67]

62   TNA WO 214/14: Churchill Undated Special Unnumbered Message to Alexander in Alexander's Papers.
63   Danchev and Todman, p 496.
64   Danchev and Todman, p 417.
65   Nicolson, p 174.
66   Adleman and Walton, p.100.
67   Walters, p.91.

He was the second generation of his family to attend West Point. He briefly served in the US Expeditionary Force in France in 1918, where he was wounded whilst in command of an infantry battalion. He first met Eisenhower at West Point and the two men shared a lifelong friendship. Marshall became aware of Clark as early as 1937 when he was an operations officer for the division in which Marshall commanded a brigade.[68] In 1940, Marshall had asked for him to be directing staff at the Army War College in Washington. He never took the post, however, and was picked for a brigadier-general's post in the General Staff, skipping the rank of colonel in autumn 1941. At the outbreak of the Second World War, he was in G-3 Operations in Washington and was two months senior to Eisenhower. In charge of training the US' mass-produced army under Army Ground Forces commander, Lieutenant General Leslie McNair, his growing reputation depended upon success. It was McNair that accidentally reintroduced Clark to Marshall. McNair was profoundly deaf, unable to hear what

Clark in a typically posed publicity photograph aboard USS Ancon on 12 September 1943, a day before crisis struck his Army at Salerno. Clark liked his photographs to be of his better left visage. (NARA RG80-G-087335)

was being said at important conferences. Clark represented him and impressed the chief.[69] He was, at 45, made the US Army's youngest major-general in April 1942, being sent to England alongside Eisenhower to assess the feasibility of a cross-channel invasion, before being appointed as the Commanding General of II US Corps. He met Churchill many times during this visit, who referred to him as 'The American Eagle', a code name revived by Eisenhower in correspondence prior to TORCH.[70]

He was, at first, in absolute awe of the British leader and his ability to get things done. He said of him, 'I feel that one of the greatest privileges of my life was the fact that I was able to know Churchill. He was a great man. A great man.'[71] This positive relationship was not to last.

Having ruled out the cross-channel operation in 1942, for which Eisenhower was happy to allow Clark to command the US element of what would have been a primarily British operation[72], Clark remained briefly in command of II US Corps before being sent as Deputy Commander for TORCH; he was now three weeks junior to Eisenhower whose progression had been even

68   This was prior to the wartime organisation of the US Army. Brigades had been replaced in the triangular divisions by RCTs.
69   Adleman and Walton, p.39.
70   Chandler et al, *Eisenhower Papers Vol II*, p.673.
71   Adleman and Walton, p.45.
72   Ferrell, p.72.

faster than his own. As part of this task, he was sent covertly to Vichy North Africa to negotiate with pro-Allied French officers to ease the entry of US forces to Algeria. He famously lost his trousers evading a patrol on an Algerian beach. He did not hide the story and could be self-deprecating if he thought an incident was humorous. This mission even made the cover of a patriotic US comic called *True Comics* in April 1943. Despite this accolade he was never to receive the fame and adulation of Eisenhower. His task, like Eisenhower's was not entirely military and he quickly learnt diplomacy and political acumen, especially in his dealings with the French. Murphy, the American political representative to the French in North Africa had to rein in Clark on occasions. These early dealings with the French may have coloured his later view when they came under his command in early 1944.

Clark became the US Army's youngest three-star general in November 1942 and was assigned command of the US Fifth Army in January 1943. His promotion

Nicknamed the 'American Eagle' by Churchill, Clark retained this name as his codename in correspondence with Eisenhower. (Library of Congress)

was enthusiastically supported by Eisenhower in a letter on 11 November 1942.[73] According to Brooke's diary, not always an unbiased judge, Clark's reassignment from Deputy Commander to Army Commander may also have been due to Eisenhower discovering his scheming with the French to obtain command in Tunisia, although there was no hint of this in Eisenhower's letters to Marshall regarding Clark.[74] On the same day, in a letter to his son John, Eisenhower spoke of Clark as 'one of my dearest friends in this Army and my principal assistant in this show.'[75] Four days later, however, Clark's ego earned him a warning from his commander as he planned a live broadcast to the US in which Eisenhower seriously doubted the wisdom of participating.[76] Eisenhower was delivered a rocket by Marshall on 21 November following exaggerated press accounts of Clark's exploits. Ike did not accuse him directly but was undoubtedly suspicious as he knew of Clark's penchant for self-publicity.[77] Did this incident plant a seed of doubt in Eisenhower's mind over Clark's judgement? Perhaps the first doubts about Clark were dawning? In a diary entry on 10 December 1942, he calls Clark, despite their long association, an 'unusual individual' whose command ability was as yet unproven.[78]

73   Chandler et al, *Eisenhower Papers Vol II*, p.690.
74   Danchev and Todman, p356.
75   Chandler et al, *Eisenhower Papers Vol II*, p.696.
76   Chandler et al, *Eisenhower Papers Vol II*, p.721.
77   Chandler et al, *Eisenhower Papers Vol II*, pp.747-8.
78   Ferrell, p.84.

Nevertheless, in his January 1943 efficiency report, Eisenhower stated that he had 'performed brilliantly as Deputy Commander-in-Chief.'[79] Clark had to wait until September 1943 to lead his Army into battle, but Eisenhower may have preferred Patton to Clark as Fifth Army commander.[80] In a comment made in a letter to Marshall on 27 August 1943 he stated that, ' I had no recourse except to name Clark to command that expedition.'[81]

One of Eisenhower's regular activities in his letters to Marshall was his assessments of his senior staff and recommendations for promotions and appointments. In a letter dated 17 August 1942, he wrote of Clark, 'I know of no one upon who you can depend with greater confidence and assurance, no matter to what post you may eventually raise him.'[82] A year later, Eisenhower rated his senior generals in rank order. He did this because at the time he thought that Marshall would command OVERLORD and he wished to inform him of his best men for command positions. Clark was ranked third, behind Patton and Bradley. If he knew, this must have been a blow,

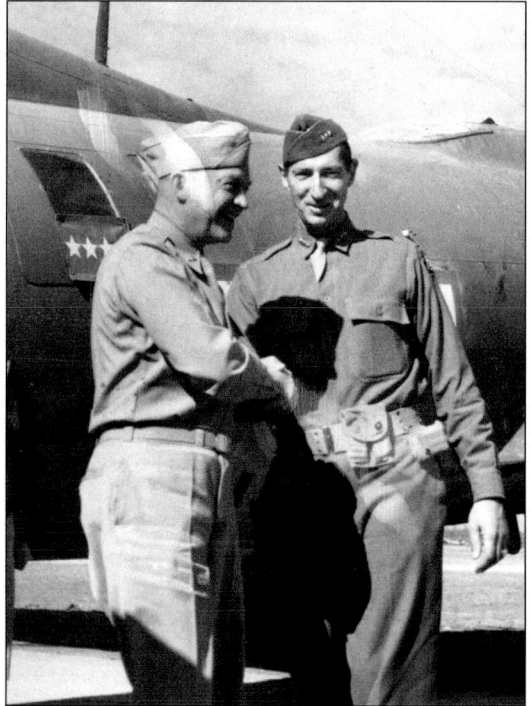

Despite their long relationship, Eisenhower rated Clark behind Patton and Bradley and made no efforts to take him to Normandy.
(NARA RG342-FH000405)

considering their longstanding friendship. This assessment, if Marshall was influenced by it, and considering his mentorship of other officers such as Devers, would almost certainly have discounted Clark from Normandy. In military reporting, an officer's performance is often judged with a great deal of nuance. What is not said can be more important than the words themselves. Those in positions to affect their subordinates' career learn to carefully word appraisals to always be encouraging to the subject, but always passing on their candid views of an officer's potential. For very senior posts this meant potential for high command in battle. Eisenhower was a master of this skill. In an appraisal of Montgomery in June 1943, Ike suggests that 'the only thing he needs is a strong immediate commander', implying obliquely that he lacked this in Alexander.[83] In one appraisal of his Chief of Staff, Walter Beddell-Smith, he told Marshall that 'Frankly he comes close to being the ideal Chief of Staff.'[84]

79   Chandler et al, *Eisenhower Papers Vol* II, p.898.
80   Atkinson, p.315.
81   Chandler et al, *Eisenhower Papers, Vol II*, p.1357.
82   Hobbs, p.37.
83   Ferrell, p.91.
84   Hobbs, p.68.

This sounds extremely positive, but reading between the lines, this describes a good number two. Beddell-Smith was never given a position of high command. In another damned with faint praise piece, he stated of Clark,' the best organiser, planner and trainer of troops I have met.'[85] Patton and Bradley were praised for their battle command and leadership; Clark was not, although Eisenhower expressed his confidence in him. He, like Devers, remained in the secondary theatre of war, despite his enormous attempts at self-publicity. Why, considering, his previous closeness to Eisenhower was Clark not whipped away to England in early 1944? It was possibly Clark's pride and ego that turned Ike off.[86] In the dark days of Tunisia in December 1942, before the Kasserine Pass, Eisenhower wanted Clark to command US forces in south-central Tunisia. This would have been his first senior combat command. Clark, already in command of the US Fifth Army in Morocco, was asked to take a subordinate corps-level command under a British Army commander in a situation where success was far from guaranteed. He refused; a mistake that eventually pushed him down the pecking order and that may have cost him the fame he craved. Fredendall, then in command of US II Corps, took the job instead, but his poor personality cost him his job after Kasserine. Ike said of the incident in his diary entry of 11 June 1943:

> His only drawback now is a lack of combat experience in a high command position. This I tried to give him in the early days of organising an American task force in the central Tunisian front. He rather resented taking any title except that of army commander; and since I could not at that time establish an American army command on the Tunisian front, I had to place another in charge of the American effort. This was a bad mistake on Clark's part, but I still think that he could successfully command an army in operations.[87]

Eisenhower then gave the job to Patton and subsequently fought hard to get him to Normandy. Patton passed that command to Bradley in Sicily, who also went to Normandy. For Clark, his old friend, he fought not at all. Even after Clark led his Army into combat in September 1943, and after Patton's indiscipline over accusations of malingering to soldiers with battle shock, Eisenhower preferred Patton. In another letter to Marshall on 20 September, Ike again used his wordsmith skills to keep Clark in the Mediterranean. He said:

> Events have progressed here in such a way that it looks like Clark would be my American Army Commander for the fall and winter. He is not so good as Bradley in winning, almost without effort, the complete confidence of everybody around him, including his British associates. He is not the equal of Patton in his refusal to see anything but victory in any situation that arises; but he is carrying his full weight and, so far, has fully justified his selection for his present important post.[88]

While Patton and Bradley were in England over the winter preparing for OVERLORD, Clark remained in his 'present important post', but away from the glory, in the secondary theatre of

85   Hobbs, p.121.
86   Blumenson and Stokesbury, p.186.
87   Ferrell, p.94.
88   Hobbs, p.129.

Italy. Nowhere in his letters to Marshall does Eisenhower even raise the prospect of Clark joining him. Although not necessarily reflecting the views of the father, Eisenhower's son John, in his account of the Anzio battles viewed Clark as an egotist, always 'looking for someone to blame.'[89]

He was initially inexperienced in combat command, never having commanded troops at regimental, division or corps level. This lack of experience was to lead him to clash with battle-hardened British senior officers. He led the international Fifth Army onto the beaches at Salerno, but to keep them there he relied very much on air and naval gunfire, and the fierce German resistance nearly forced re-embarkation of the Allied force. Clark, despite showing considerable personal courage, was accused by some detractors of panic. He had a reputation as being arrogant and egotistic, only letting US press photographers take publicity shots of his left side – his good side. He admitted the truth of this many years later.[90] Some, such as Patton, believed that he had been promoted too quickly and to a level beyond his experience due to the nepotism of senior US generals.

Many authors, as well as number of his subordinate officers, have been critical of his performance as a commander and of his personality, often making the mistake of conflating the two. One of his subordinates in Italy, Truscott, had this impression of his boss, 'He lacked Alexander's training and experience in high command...His concern for personal publicity was his greatest weakness. I have sometimes thought it may have prevented him from acquiring that 'feel for battle' that marks all top-flight battle leaders.'[91]

Was he impetuous at Salerno, too timid at Anzio and impetuous again at the Rapido? Walker, the officer to whose division he gave the task of crossing the Rapido River in January 1944, thought that his flaws as a commander were obvious:

> I have no confidence in Clark's ability to select and assign proper missions to combat divisions. The same goes for Keyes (US II Corps commander at Cassino). I do not wish to be subjected to more official insults from Clark similar to the one I had to take after the Rapido, when he relieved my key officers, over my objections and without any specific charges against them.[92]

Walker was not the only one who thought Clark unfit for Army command. After the war the 36th Division Association launched a complaint that went before the US Congress. The resolution against Clark's command originated without Walker's knowledge in March 1944, but was not publicised during the war. The President of the Association, Colonel H Miller Ainsworth, had the following to say regarding Clark's leadership:

> This is the eve of the second anniversary of the crossing of the Rapido River, a military undertaking that will go down in history as one of the colossal blunders of the Second World War.

89   Cole Kingseed, Review Essay, The Anzio Campaign, *Parameters*, Winter 2008-9, pp.126-7.
90   Adleman and Walton, p.5.
91   Truscott, p.547.
92   Major General Fred L Walker, *From Texas To Rome* (El Dorado Hills CA, 2014) Kindle loc 7013.

Every man connected with this undertaking knew it was doomed to failure because it was an impossible situation. Contrary to the repeated recommendations of the subordinate commander, Gen Mark W Clark ordered the crossing of the Rapido. The results of this blunder are well known.

Resolved, that the men of the 36th Division in convention assembled at Brownwood, Texas, petition the Congress of the United States to investigate the Rapido River fiasco and take the necessary steps to correct a military system that will permit an inefficient and inexperienced officer such as Gen Mark W Clark in a high command to destroy the young manhood of this country and to prevent future soldiers being sacrificed wastefully and uselessly.[93]

In giving evidence to the Congressional investigation, the commander of the 143rd Infantry Regiment, said of him: 'It was obvious even to an inexperienced soldier that an attack such as the one ordered had practically no chance of success.'[94]

Despite the testimony from many members of the 36th Infantry Division, Clark was exonerated, and the senior ranks pulled together. Nevertheless, the fact that he lost the confidence of many of his senior subordinates must weigh against him. As for his decisions at Cassino with regards to the bombing of the Abbey, his judgement as a three-star general officer must also be questioned. He was not perceived as a likeable individual. That his character, and the way people viewed him changed as his career progressed was not lost on him. Whilst commanding Fifth Army he wrote to his wife, 'The more stars a man gets, the more lonesome he becomes… they used to come around in the evening, but they don't anymore…I wish, Renie, you would send me Pal.'[95]

At the darkest point of the Cassino campaign, he was reunited with his black cocker spaniel. Pal was terrified by the accidental bombing of Clark's headquarters in Presenzano during the Abbey attack. This vulnerability was not something he ever showed in his Army career. Perhaps if he had shown the softer side reserved for his wife, children and dog, he would be remembered more affectionately. At this point, most things were going wrong, he was out of the main fight, and he was under enormous pressure in his command. He was a senior officer that gave the impression that he would sacrifice anything for his career, he would readily blame subordinates for his mistakes, and he rarely put the needs of his men first. Intellectually capable, under great pressure, he perhaps lacked the human empathy and emotional intelligence required to be an effective leader at the highest level. What Alexander had too much of, he had too little. Clark's personality and ambition may have cost him the ultimate career fillip, that of US Army Chief of Staff.[96] Some commentators have suggested that his personality should not be mistaken for his military ability. Whilst correct, great commanders possess both empathy and an ability to motivate their men to carry out impossible tasks. The commander cannot be fully divorced from his personality. A comment that he made to his aide, Walters, suggests that his attitude may have been a device to protect himself from the loneliness of his command:

93   Schultz, *Crossing The Rapido*, p.245.
94   Schultz, *Crossing The Rapido*, p.252.
95   Maurine Clark, *Captain's Bride, General's Lady* (New York NY: McGraw-Hill Book Company, 1956), pp.114-5.
96   Adleman and Walton, p.3.

Sometimes if I appear unreasonable, you must remember the burdens I bear are very heavy. The time comes when I have to give orders that will result in the death of a large number of fine young men – and this is a responsibility I cannot share with anybody. I must bear it by myself. So you just see that you remember that when you think I am being unreasonable.[97]

His relationship with Alexander was fractious following the Salerno landings when Alexander tried to enhance the role of Montgomery at the expense of Clark's army. He came to dislike the British and as the campaign progressed, he became more obsessed with seizing Rome, generating maximum publicity for Mark Clark's Fifth Army. Every move that the British made became another scheme to rob him of his reward. His stubbornness in continuing to destroy his American divisions on the massif prior to the bombing, rather than asking for the help of the New Zealanders may be another example of his determination not to allow his British, Dominion and Empire allies any credit. A vignette of Clark's style may be seen during the final operation for Rome. During the switch from Valmontone to Rome, his 'hard-luck' division, the 36th Infantry, found a route through the German lines, thereby opening the approach to Rome. Walker was sure of his plan, Clark less so. Eventually he told Walker that he did not officially approve the plan and that if it failed, he would 'bear the brunt of what comes with failure'.[98] Clark did not want to be tarred with failure; it would be bad for his career. The plan succeeded spectacularly, and Clark took all the credit driving into the centre of Rome on 4 June 1944 to the adulation of Roman crowds. Walker was reassigned and sent to a training post at Fort Benning. The letter from Clark relieving him was delivered six days after the fall of Rome.[99] Walker, belatedly fired for the failure to cross the Rapido four months previously, was Clark's third major general to be fired in nine-months. His ability to shift the blame for reverses can also be seen in the previous dismissal of the Commanding General of US VI Corps at Salerno, Major General Ernest Dawley, following a poor performance, and the stripping out of the leadership of 36th Infantry Division following the Rapido fiasco. Dawley froze at Salerno, but his predicament was caused by Clark's poor planning and his overextension of the beachhead. The dismissal of Dawley was also encouraged by Alexander, Clark's immediate superior.

Alexander was keen that Clark got rid of Dawley and the latter duly obliged. The sacking of Dawley's successor at VI Corps, Lucas, was also blamed on Alexander by Clark. Lucas, although less than inspirational, was made the scapegoat for the ensuing, but probably inevitable, siege. Both Churchill and Marshall were livid at the performance of Allied troops in the beachhead. Someone had to pay, and Clark and Alexander could be in the firing line for the chop. The generals danced about and when the music stopped, Lucas was without a chair to sit on. One dismissal of a principal subordinate could be said to be misfortune; two unlucky; but three showed either poor judgement in his choice of commanders or a tendency to find scapegoats.

On entering Rome, Clark held an impromptu press conference where according to Sevareid his words managed to annoy almost every journalist with his self-congratulatory attitude, where he gave no credit to anyone but himself. Another correspondent commented, 'On this historic

---

97   Walters, p.109.
98   Adleman and Walton, p.13.
99   Walker, Kindle 7081.

occasion I feel like vomiting.'[100] The majority of reporters with Fifth Army had come to loathe his self-serving publicity stunts, his wearing of a forage cap in photographs immediately replaced by helmet as soon as the photographers had finished and his tactless self-adulation. None of this, however, was reported at the time as it would never have got past his censors who vigorously removed any criticism of the Army Commander.[101]

Not all biographers and commentators are critical of Clark. Jon Mikolashek defended his record, arguing persuasively that although Clark had faults and was clearly over-ambitious, he was a fine combat commander. Pitted against Germany's greatest defensive general, with limited resources and in terrain that did not suit US doctrine, he performed well.[102] He could be ruthless and did not accept failure lightly. From Slessor's perspective Clark was viewed positively, if also slightly damned by faint

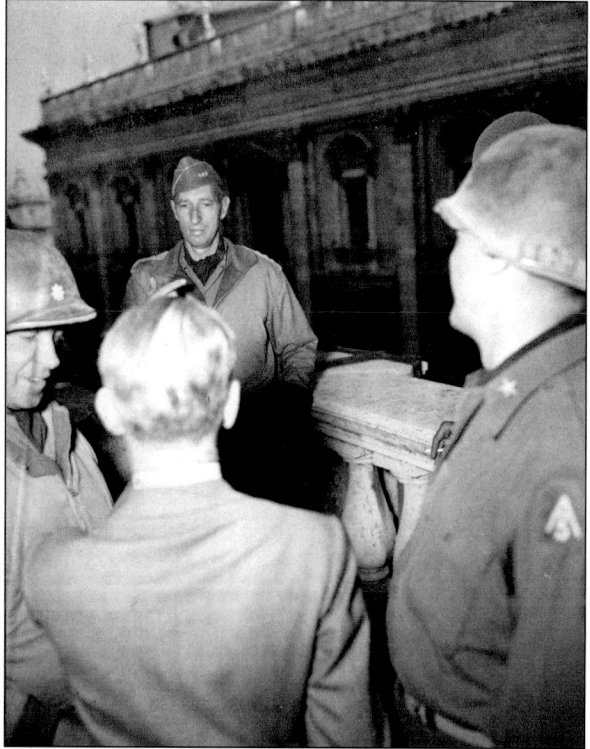

General Clark delivering his Press Conference to journalists on 5 June 1944 in Rome. Clark constantly annoyed the pressmen with his publicity stunts. (NARA RG80-G252537)

praise in his letter to Portal at around the time of the German counterattacks at Anzio:

Clark impressed me favourably. I should say good hunter, fair turn of speed, jumps well, likely to win a point to point but am doubtful if he is prospective winner in a good class under National Hunt rules. I think he is a good chap and a very fair commander who is handling competently a situation which would probably have never arisen if we had shown a bit more initiative and taken more risks at the very beginning.[103]

Considering his disdain for the British, one can only wonder what he would have thought of this assessment?

100 Sevareid, p.530-1.
101 Casey, p.21.
102 Jon B. Mikolashek, *General Mark Clark Commander of America's Fifth Army in World War II and Liberator of Rome* (Havertown, PA: Casemate Publishers, 2013), pp.164-5.
103 TNA AIR 75/69: Papers of Sir John Slessor, The Italian Campaign, JCS 183 Personal Letter from Slessor to Portal, February 1944.

Macmillan considered him one of the most intelligent officers he encountered. Not all agreed. Harry Sions from *Yank* magazine said of him:

> I guess the word 'stupid' is wrong to use to describe Clark. He was unsophisticated. Maybe unimaginative. One of the things that bothers me about the military mind is that many of them are so square. A lot of brass are easily corrupted by power. They develop a fantastic sense of their own importance. They read the reports, and they start to believe that they really are these heroic figures that the newspapers are writing about. These guys get to feel that they are goddamned bloody Caesars.[104]

Sions was, however, pleased with the support that he gave to *Yank* and *Stars and Stripes* as outlets for his troops' feelings. Clark was also protective of cartoonist Sergeant Bill Mauldin whose cynical drawings often drew criticism, but whose wit assisted troops' morale.[105] In judging Clark, we should remember that America had fought no wars in twenty years. Few of his peers had combat experience, and his limited combat command was no different to anyone else in the US Army's higher echelons. Only Patton had the natural instinct of successful command in the crucible of battle. The others had to learn. Clark replaced Alexander as Commanding General 15th Army Group in December 1944, after a recommendation from Churchill. He accepted the German surrender in Italy in May 1945. Clark was a victim of the Italian campaign as well as its victorious general. He never quite attained the fame of Eisenhower, Patton or Bradley, nor did he receive a fifth star. His personality flaws did not endear him to his fellow commanders and his inflexibility and his willingness to accept high casualties did not endear him to the men. As a commander he was the equal of Bradley and Montgomery, but he always remained tainted by the struggle for the soft underbelly. He remains an enigma. He was victorious; he was trusted to command and was promoted to the highest army level, that of Army Group commander. He kept together a dizzying coalition of nations. All this is to his credit, yet he could not rid himself of the controversies of the Rapido and the bombing of the Abbey. Ultimately, he was a good planner and staff officer, but lacked the feel and creativity to be a great commander.

Perhaps Clark's biggest challenge was reconciling command systems and operating philosophies. He had commanded British X Corps since Salerno and was used to the British. The New Zealanders were not used to him and were culturally different from their British cousins. A study of British and US Army command culture in the Italian Campaign, concludes that both Armies operated a command-led system where commanders decided what was to be done.[106] Most British and some US commanders, among them Devers, preferred 'mission type' orders, where they trusted subordinates and even tolerated the odd mistake.[107] Devers was a rarity, as most US generals couldn't help dabbling directly in their subordinates' business. Eisenhower summed up most US generals' philosophy in March 1943:

104 Adleman and Walton, p.138.
105 Morris, p.198.
106 Patrick Rose. 'Allies at War: British and US Army Command Culture in the Italian Campaign, 1943-1944', *Journal of Strategic Studies* 36:1 (2013), pp.42-75.
107 Adams, Kindle Location 582.

Discipline is that quality in an organisation that gives the commander the assurance that every man in it will do exactly as he is told and will not deviate from that path, except under circumstances that he knows his commander could not have foreseen.[108]

The British system interpreted the Commander's intent and translated this into orders. The tensions between the different command systems were evident long before the Italian Campaign. In February 1943, in a letter to Marshall, Eisenhower commented on how the British commanded 'by committee'; he viewed all decisions to be his responsibility. This was difficult for Eisenhower as his principal subordinates were British:

I am thinking of the inevitable trend of the British mind toward 'committee' rather than 'single' command…In the HUSKY paper, the CCS directed Alexander to take over planning details, yet they expect Alexander to *cooperate* with Cunningham and Tedder in executing this project. Manifestly, responsibility again falls directly on me and though, in this particular instance…I would consider it a definite invasion of my own proper field if they attempted to prevent me…from setting up a Task Force commander…it seems impossible for the British to grasp the utter simplicity of the system that we employ…I will be constantly on my guard to prevent any important military venture depending for its control and direction upon the 'committee' system of command.[109]

The Americans had unified command whereas the British used cooperation and suggestions rather than giving direct orders. The notion of a single 'Supreme' Commander was most definitely American. Whilst Alex's affable attitude may have endeared him, it also made him liable to be ignored by more belligerent subordinates such as Clark and Montgomery. Graham and Bidwell in their analysis of the failure at Anzio commented, 'Commanders are not intended to follow the letter of their orders, but the spirit of them.'[110] This was true of British but not American commanders. The British system of command and Alexander's flexible and indecisive character were a principal reason why the Abbey was bombed. He was simply too nice, and too wedded to his system, to directly interfere with assertive subordinates and would have seen any counter-orders as outside his purview, sticking his nose into a subordinate's 'mission command'. In short, Alexander's view of command made him incapable of taking a grip of events and he therefore allowed tactical events to go ahead, regardless of the larger consequences that then occurred.

The US command system was centralised, rigid and involved the Commander himself issuing orders that affected all levels, including minor tactical plans. The British operated a system where lower-level commanders were allowed to use their initiative. British officers were told what needed doing; how it was done was, within reason, not their Commander's concern. In a conversation with the 141st Infantry commander, Kippenberger, explained that he told his subordinate commanders what to do, not how to do it. Colonel Wyatt was 'astonished when I told him that Division with us would never do more than tell me what to do, leaving me to

108 Chandler et al, *Eisenhower Papers Vol II*, p.1050.
109 Hobbs, pp.99-100; Chandler et al, *Eisenhower Papers Vol II*, pp.943-4.
110 Graham and Bidwell, p.139.

decide how, and similarly that I would never tell battalions how to carry out a task, that I might advise and suggest and support in every way possible, but nothing more.'[111]

The US system involved the decisive point and attacking it with decisive force; the US Army was willing to suffer high casualties to see the job done. They initially considered a force of 215 divisions, although this was unrealistic even considering the US' vast resources.[112] Considering the size of the US Army and the speed with which it was grown a regimented process was inevitable. The US system produced an industrial process where replacements were treated as plentiful spare parts that could just fit into units as a one for one exchange. Many US soldiers fought with complete strangers at their side, and some had never met their squad leader or platoon officer before going into battle. The British system involved the construction of a team, where each member filled a place within that team.[113] The US system was easier to follow in that there were strict chains of command and clear roles and responsibilities. Everything was run by the book; that was Field Manual (FM) 100-15. The British were less good with books, although they had plenty. The individualist command structure, which offered flexibility, also relied on intellect. This had not been a strong suit in the British Army thus far in the war, and they had suffered some grievous defeats due to poor leadership. The years between the end of the First war and the beginning of the Second had not seen innovation in military command, and many senior British officers failed to appreciate the impact of new technology including armour, airpower and the importance of intelligence.[114] The Army had been the poor relation as politicians such as Churchill favoured the RAF and Royal Navy and the 'ten-year rule' stymied growth. Influential British thinkers such as Fuller or Liddell-Hart made their mark with the Germans more than with the British army, who had remained stuck in class-ridden time warps throughout the inter-war years. Clubability and character were more important than intellect and ability. British senior officers could not believe that their old ways could be bettered; many Americans thought the same.[115] Training and education were seen as no substitute for breeding and the ability to muddle through. They were unprepared for the rigours of three-dimensional mechanized warfare.

The Americans had only the manual. Clark had not commanded anyone in battle; he was not alone in the higher echelons of the US Army. He was a talented staff officer but had no command experience. He had little natural feel for battle. Dealing with a highly decorated warrior, with little time for staff work, like Freyberg must have been difficult. An additional problem was that the rank system of commanders was different. In the British system a corps commander was a lieutenant-general and an army commander was a full general. In the US system a corps was commanded by a senior major-general and an army by a lieutenant-general. Freyberg and Clark were equals, both highly egotistical and likely to clash. They were not, however, equal in experience with Freyberg toting a chest full of medals including the VC. He was several months senior to Clark. At least Clark had a war wound, something Freyberg respected! More importantly, Freyberg felt no compunction about cutting Clark out of the command loop, going directly to Alexander. This is one of the reasons why the Abbey was bombed. In January, operations in the

111 Kippenberger, *Infantry Brigadier,* Kindle Location, 5466.
112 Blackwell, Kindle location 534.
113 Graham and Bidwell, p.135-6.
114 Blackwell, Kindle location 992.
115 Blackwell, Kindle location 1037.

Cassino sector were an all-American show and despite the troops' thoughts, Clark saw no reason to bomb the Abbey and the Abbey was not bombed. No US corps or divisional commander dared go over Clark's head to Alexander. Freyberg had no such qualms and probably considered it completely within his initiative to conduct his assigned task in any way he wished, including going around the obstacle of Clark.

The British, had an institutional memory of the Somme and Passchendaele, and were less accepting of high casualties than the Americans. After four years of war, they were running out of people. They respected the power of the *Wehrmacht* and instinctively knew that man for man the German soldier was better. At the tactical level the perception was that the German soldier had greater understanding, acted with greater initiative, was generally more aggressive and could spot and exploit opportunities more effectively. This was true of the *Fallschirmjager* and *Panzer-Grenadiers*, but it was not the case when fighting the lower-quality German units. The Allied system was superior to the German, and it was this that mitigated their weaknesses and ensured success. The British did not wish to face the German army on equal terms, preferring fighting with machines rather than people. British tactics involved greater artillery preparation and the use of infiltration and manoeuvre rather than a head-on approach. This was what Keyes, not in a complimentary way, called a 'gradualist' approach. The US approach was that the quickest way to defeat Germany was not to nibble away but to use mass and industrial might to decisively attack the centre of gravity directly. With their manpower and industrial resources, America could do this. Britain could not. Nevertheless, Keyes' own brute force direct approach at the Rapido in January 1944 did not prove to be more effective, although he was hardly keen on Clark's plan. Kippenberger was shocked by how the US Army was handled by its senior officers and implied that they had little regard for their soldiers' safety or morale. He informed US commanders that their troops were in no condition to fight. It was clear that no American commanders had been to see for themselves.[116] The task came first, whatever the consequences. The Americans were not the only ones to say things that were bound to annoy their Allies. In November 1943 a letter sent by Montgomery to Brooke said that:

> So long as you fight an army in combat teams and the big idea is that every combat team should 'combat' somebody all the time, then you don't get very far...Clark would be only too delighted to be given quiet advice as to how to fight his army; I think he is a very decent chap and most co-operative. If he received good and clear guidance he would do very well.[117]

To receive such condescending treatment from what many considered to be an unimaginative plodder whose progress in Italy was no better, would not have endeared the British to their American allies. It is not surprising that Clark loathed some British generals.

A summation of the different war philosophies of Britain and America was summed up by General Sir Leslie Hollis who put it:

---

116 Kippenberger, *Infantry Brigadier,* Kindle Location, 5487.
117 Brian Holden-Reid, 'The Italian Campaign 1943-45: A reappraisal of allied generalship', *Journal of Strategic Studies* 13:1 (1990), pp.128-161.

The reasons for the clash between America and Britain over the best way to conquer Germany were really psychological.

America, a large country, adopted – like a large man – frontal tactics. They wanted quick and terrible hammer blows that would speedily finish the fight: in this case, a very early landing in Europe, and then on down through France into Germany, and so over with the war.

Britain, a small country, with a long history of frequently successful engagements against opponents that could have overwhelmed her with their numbers, adopted – like a small man faced by a large enemy – more subtle tactics. Over the centuries we had established an Empire by a policy of small operations which could be consolidated. Frequently we had gone 'in at the back door'. For instance, we had beaten Napoleon by going through Spain. In Churchill's view (and mine) we could have destroyed Germany in the First War had the back door at Gallipoli been less ineptly opened.[118]

These differences were also known on the other side of the Atlantic. Maurice Matloff, the US Army Official Historian on war strategy, sums up the American philosophy:

The US Staff believed that only by massing the great vigor and might of the two countries under overwhelming mastery of the air could Germany be defeated. The British theory was that Germany would be beaten by a 'series of attritions' in the Mediterranean and the Balkans. The USSR, to which both the United States and Great Britain were pledged to open a second front, would not be fooled by 'pinprick warfare.'[119]

118 James Leasor and Leslie Hollis, *War At The Top* (London: The Companion Book Club, 1959), p.239.
119 Matloff, Kindle loc, 5189.

11

What is the Price of Our History?

Where once stood a peaceful Abbey, in which no military element was to be found, there is an enormous heap of ruins which are easily defended and whose conquest may involve great loss of human life.

Archbishop William Godfrey
Apostolic Delegate to Great Britain
22 March 1944

Concern over the Abbey began before October 1943. The monks had a cordial relationship with the Germans, at least until the evacuation. Before going to Sicily, Senger's predecessor as commander of the German XIV *Panzerkorps*, *General der Panzertruppen* Hans-Valentin Hube, visited in May 1943 and again at the end of June.[1] Even then there was concern. Hube wrote on 8 July, 'With renewed wishes that your excellency and the fine monastery of Monte Cassino may successfully survive the onslaught of war.'[2] Kesselring himself visited the Abbey on 19 September, as the Allies broke out of the Salerno beachhead.[3] Before the evacuation on 17 October, Hube again expressed concern:

> May I be permitted to express a prayer of my own; the ever greater aerial incursions of the enemy could eventually compromise the security of the Abbey of Monte Cassino. I would therefore be deeply grateful to Your Excellency if the safety of your great works of art could be secured, wither by transfer to Rome or in some other appropriate fashion.[4]

The superintendents of Italy's historic monuments were facing land combat in the south as well as aerial bombing. Italian Minister of National Education Carlo Biggini received a note that said, 'Now that the war is being fought inch by inch on our national territory and without any

---

1   Grossetti and Matronola, p.28 & p.183.
2   Grossetti and Matronola, p.185.
3   Tasciotti, p.17.
4   Grossetti and Matronola, p.187.

immune or less jeopardized areas, shelters situated for the most part in the countryside run the risk of finding themselves …in the very midst of the battlefield.'[5]

As the Allies battled northwards, two German officers from the Hermann Göring *Panzer* Division arranged for the evacuation of the Abbey's treasures.[6] The majority of accounts suggest that this was an altruistic act to save Montecassino's treasures. More recent investigations have uncovered the possibility that Schlegel, although not Becker, had ideas of larceny rather than altruism.[7] *General* Hube was apparently unaware of the mission of Schlegel and Becker. Diamare informed him in his letter of thanks. The movement of Montecassino's artefacts was, at the beginning, a private venture by these officers, without the support of their division's commander. It was carried out without consulting Minister Biggini or any other Italian or German official. This explanation does appear fanciful, in that military units in the teeth of battle rarely think of such things without direct orders from their commanders. It is very likely that at either Conrath or Hube were aware, and unlikely that Becker or Schlegel acted on their own. Hube's note to Diamare seems too coincidental with the movement of Montecassino's artefacts. Kesselring, a devout Roman Catholic, had promised Diamare that the Abbey would not be used for military purposes.[8] Becker was aware that the chances of damage to the Abbey were great, but he never imagined that the Allies would wilfully destroy it. Nor did Diamare who initially rebuffed the German offer, trusting to both sides' word saying: 'What harm could come to this holy place?' Eventually, he succumbed to persuasion from Becker, who used the bombing of Rome in July 1943 as a potential outcome for the Abbey, and more coercive behaviour by *Oberstleutnant* Schlegel, a card-carrying Austrian Nazi.[9] It may be that Diamare was given little choice. Becker, whose initial approach to the Abbot was suggested by two Franciscan friars, was not linked to that of Schlegel, was clearly suspicious of his colleague's motives. [10]

The artefacts were initially moved, not to Rome, but to the division's depot in Spoleto. From there it now seems likely they were destined for Germany, until Senger and Kesselring intervened in early November 1943. All the Montecassino treasures were then moved to Rome in two shipments in December 1943 and January 1944. Abbot Diamare presented Schlegel with the following script in December 1943 in gratitude, although not all of the monks trusted him:

> In the name of our Lord Jesus Christ, to the illustrious and beloved Tribune, Julius Schlegel, who saved the monks and possessions of the holy monastery of Monte Cassino, these monks of Cassino give their heartfelt thanks and pray to God for his future well-being.
>
> Monte Cassino, in the month of November 1943.
>
> Gregorius Diamare
>
> Bishop and Abbot of Monte Cassino[11]

5   Marta Nezzo., 'The Defence of Works of Art from Bombing in Italy during the Second World War' in Claudia Baldoli, Andrew Knapp and Richard Overy (eds.), *Bombing, States and Peoples In Western Europe 1940-1945* (London: Continuum International Publishing, 2011), p.110.
6   Hapgood and Richardson, p.31.
7   Gentile and Bianchini, p.10.
8   Hapgood and Richardson, p.9.
9   Gentile and Bianchini, p.23.
10   Grossetti and Matronola, p.258. Gentile and Bianchini, p.22.
11   Rennie, p.119.

Obserstleutnant Julius Schlegel, credited with saving Montecassino's treasures in October 1943, although his efforts may not have been entirely altruistic. He is pictured here with an officer from the Hermann Göring Panzer Division and *General* Kurt Malzer, Commandant of Rome.
(Bundesarchiv Bild 101I-729-0004-18/Fotograf:Linke)

The soon to be fired Italian Superintendent for Fine Arts, Marino Lazzari, was opposed to the removal of the art from Montecassino, possibly fearing, perhaps correctly, that it would be looted by the Germans.[12] The monks' diary describes extremely good behaviour by the soldiers of the Hermann Göring *Panzer* Division.[13] In the end they stole 15-crates of treasures from the Naples Museum as a fiftieth birthday present to Göring, but none from the Abbey. There is no evidence to connect Becker with the theft. Lazzari wrote to the head of the new Salo Republic Fascist Party, Alessandro Pavolini, referring to the removal of art in November 1943 with the concern that:

> I do not doubt that the Germans want more than just to save the works. It is a fact, however, that a group of very valuable objects, taken by foreigners from their shelter, is now being moved across Italy without the office responsible for its reception having been given due notice or even knowing where it will arrive. The German authorities must understand that none of us is reckless and irresponsible enough to want Italian art treasures to be captured by the British or Americans, and that we want these treasures out of the war zone, and

12   Nezzo, p.111.
13   Grossetti and Matronola, p.20.

therefore in the North, but that we should be the ones to take them from their shelters, protect them en route, and decide on the most suitable destination…we are dealing with the only possession that we Italians still have, and as it is a spiritual one it must be saved at all costs.[14]

Had Lazzari had his way, the great treasures would probably have been destroyed alongside their shelter three months later. The Secretary General of the Ministry of National Education – General Directorate for the Arts, wrote to the Superintendent of Antiquities for Rome, Professor Alfonso Bartoli in gratitude for the German action. [15]

Bartoli, on 31 December 1943 expressed profound thanks for the safeguarding of 'national artistic patrimony.'[16] Following the evacuation, on 8 November 1943, two *feldgendarmes* were posted to the Abbey. This duty was picked up by soldiers from Fries' 29th *Panzer-Grenadier* Division on 17 November. Fries' Chaplain made contact with the Abbey two days later when he brought items from a church in the local village of Sant Elia. Fries visited the Abbey himself on 24 November.[17] The guards were there to stop German soldiers from damaging the Abbey or harming its occupants. Their utility was proven the day following Fries' visit when they ejected German soldiers trying to kidnap Italian female refugees. Throughout the autumn and winter, there was a regular stream of German visitors. From the monks' diary, there was a visit by senior German officers on 2 December and the local Commandant, *Oberst* Pollack, visited on the 7 December.[18] The next day the Abbey was visited by the Bauhaus artist, Wilhelm Wessel, who wished to make sketches of the landscape.[19] It was on 9 December, that the monks believed that munitions were placed in a cave below the Abbey. Diamare spoke with Pollack regarding the military emplacements being built close to the Abbey.[20] Following more senior visits on 11 December, a junior officer from Kesselring's headquarters turned-up to tell the Abbot that the Vatican had demanded the guards' removal, as they gave the impression that the Abbey was occupied by the military. This led to the establishment of the 300-metre exclusion zone. The Abbot complained about the munitions stored in the cave and the officer promised that they would be removed and that further visits would be forbidden. Neither of these things happened immediately.

Fries again sent Chaplain Meyer to discuss the exclusion zone on 13 December. Diamare was happy with the guards staying and Fries did not initially arrange for the zone to be measured out or enforced. The monks themselves put up neutral zone signs. This 300-metre zone was perceived as a safe haven and more and more civilians began to seek refuge. Fries had some correspondence with Diamare in the weeks leading up to the bombing of the Abbey. His chaplain again visited the Abbey in mid-December and the Abbot asked Fries to have the ammunition removed from the caves on 17 December. This was now becoming a major issue for the monks, which was sharpened on 18 December when shells hit the Abbey for the first time. The next day fighter-bombers possibly targeted the munitions cave. The

14   Nezzo, p.111.
15   Grossetti and Matronola, p.201.
16   Rennie, p.118.
17   Grossetti and Matronola, pp.36-7.
18   Fritz Pollack commanded the *29th Panzer Grenadier Artillerie* Regiment.
19   Grossetti and Matronola, p.43.
20   Grossetti and Matronola, p.44.

German Propaganda Ministry sent photographers to the Abbey. They took photos, 'in case it is hit, when it will be good for us to be able to show the…Anglo-American barbarities.'[21] Diamare wrote to Fries on 22 December, again regarding the cave, and again asked for the munitions to be removed when Senger visited on Christmas Day. On 26 December Fries replied that munitions were not placed there by troops under his orders, although he would 'make it my duty to ensure the munitions are removed.' He added, echoing *General* Hube, and his successor, Senger, that, 'It is vital that the monastery, which represents an inesti-mable value both for art and for the history of culture, should pass unharmed through the difficult times of this war.'[22]

Fries' division, however, was in need of recuperation and was being moved into the rear. Fries told the Abbot on 29 December that he could not move the ammunition from the cave. That day the Abbey was visited by an *Oberst* from the new 44th Infantry Division. He was told that the Germans were not respecting the exclusion zone. This was due to the activity in the cave, as the monks were happy to host visits and had a tour that afternoon.[23] By 1 January, the guards from the 29th *Panzer-Grenadiers* had been replaced by those from the 44th Infantry Division. That was the only thing that changed as officers continued to make tourist visits to the Abbey almost daily and the munitions in the cave were not moved. The relationship with the 44th Division was never as good as with the 29th Division, and their commander did not visit. Diamare considered it a discourtesy when the division sent over a junior interpreter on 5 January to tell the monks that the 300-metre exclusion zone would no longer be respected.[24] A German *major*, in charge of the cave, visited the Abbey on 10 January; others from the cave visited on 12 January. The cave was then raided by US soldiers on 5 February and prisoners were taken. This event was observed from the Abbey by Brother Zaccaria. On the same day, a German medical officer asked whether the Abbey could be used as an aid station. Matronola agreed.

Senger confirmed Kesselring's order not to use the Abbey for military purposes.[25] Roosevelt had written to the Pope on 10 July 1943, and although not specifically referring to the Abbey, he wrote that 'Churches and religious institutions will, to the extent that it is within our power, be spared the devastations of war.'[26] Tittmann was contacted by the Vatican following the inva-sion of Italy. He sent a message to Cordell Hull on 9 September regarding the protection of the Papal retreat at Castegandolfo.[27] According to author Gianfranco La Vizzera, an arrange-ment was being negotiated to safeguard the monastery. This deal, which came to nothing, was arranged by the good offices of Archbishop Spellman in New York, via an exiled Italian priest with connections to OSS, Father Don Luigi Sturzo, with the Pope and Roosevelt, and with the consent of Hitler. The agreement was to create a neutral zone, guaranteed by the Archbishop of Naples, Alessio Ascalesi.[28]

21   Grossetti and Matronola, p.53.
22   Grossetti and Matronola, p.197.
23   Grossetti and Matronola, p.58.
24   Grossetti and Matronola, p.65.
25   Senger *War Diary*, p.78.
26   Quoted in Combined Chiefs of Staff message R-8408/7777. FAN 322. to Supreme Commander Mediterranean, 22 January 1944.
27   AFHRA Reel A6338 Message from Secretary of State dated 9 September 1943.
28   Canciani, p.166.

Archbishop Francis Spellman, Archbishop of New York and to the US Armed Forces often represented President Roosevelt around the world. Spellman assisted in an abortive attempt to save the Abbey.
(NARA RG111-SC-192047)

Marshall was not in complete accord with his Commander-in-Chief regarding cultural property protection. In June 1943, whilst in the Mediterranean with Churchill, he urged that Rome should be bombed into submission. He observed, 'I consider the blood of the present to completely outweigh the desire to preserve the historical treasures of antiquity.'[29] His views were vetoed by his colleagues and the widespread bombing of Rome was not approved. It was, however, selectively attacked. The first attack on 19 July 1943 was against a marshalling yard in the San Lorenzo district, close to the city centre. The US bomber crews were warned not to miss the target and that 'The Vatican City was not to be hit at any cost'.[30] Despite this order, there was damage to an adjacent church, the *Basilica di San Lorenzo fuori le Mura*, parts of which dated back to Emperor Constantine, and a large number of civilian casualties.

The district commemorates 1,674 dead, although reports of exact numbers vary.[31] The attack also partly demolished the Institute of Public Health and damaged the University of Rome. It was not wholly successful, failing to cut the rail lines leading to the north-west. This mission was led by Major General James Doolittle, commanding the US Twelfth Air Force. It was the first indication in the Vatican that the Allies may not spare Italy's treasures. The Pope, who watched the bombing through binoculars, left the Vatican for the first time since 1940 to inspect the damage, which included his own family's burial plot. It occurred only nine days after the President's promise and less than a week later Mussolini was removed by King Victor Emanuel

29   Morris, p.27.
30   Charles W Richard, *The Second Was First* (Bend OR: Maverick Publications, 1999) p.36.
31   Robert M Edsel, *Saving Italy* (New York: WW Norton & Co, 2013), 13. Chadwick, p.242.

III, who also watched the bombing from the Quirinal Palace. The King's jest that the Pope was 'the best anti-aircraft battery he had for the defence of the capital' was suddenly not so funny.[32] Pope Pius XII wrote to the President but kept his protest informal to not offer the Germans a propaganda opportunity.[33]

The bombing of San Lorenzo disturbed the Catholic world, bringing damage to religious buildings up the priority list for Allied leaders. In the US, which had a large and influential Catholic population, it was especially sensitive. Roosevelt and Pius were not strangers. In November 1936, they met in at the end of the then Cardinal Secretary of State's tour. Pius, then just plain Eugenio Pacelli, assisted the President by helping rid him of a turbulent priest, an influential anti-New Dealer named Father Charles Coughlin whose popular radio show was a thorn in Roosevelt's side.[34] The visit culminated with an agreement to re-establish limited US diplomatic representation after a gap of 70-years. Despite this positive relationship, Roosevelt put war success first. This was confirmed on 23 July 1943 when the President made a broadcast justifying the bombing of Rome. In the USAAF classified magazine, *Impact*, an article highlighted the precision of the attack, claiming not to have hit any 'religious edifice.'[35] The fate of the church and people of San Lorenzo were not included in the piece. On 11 September, Brigadier-General Charles Born, sent the following message regarding bombing in Italy, 'Present political situation in Italy makes it imperative that we do not, repeat, do not bomb non-military objectives. In event objective is obscured by clouds wings will not, repeat not indiscriminately bomb Italian cities unless it presents target of military value.'[36]

British Minister to the Holy See Sir Francis D'Arcy Osborne, whilst having little sympathy for the Vatican's position, asked London not to bomb Rome again.[37] Both he and Tittmann felt the silent disapproval of their diplomatic colleagues. Just a couple of weeks later on 8 August, the northern city of Milan was targeted by RAF Bomber Command nearly resulting in the loss of Da Vinci's *The Last Supper* and damage to the *La Scala* opera house through incendiary attack.[38] Rome was bombed again on 13 August and yet another church was badly damaged. Osborne's diary in response to the Milan bombing said that 'It is all too beastly … this detestable bombing.'[39] In addition to Rome and Milan, the Allies also bombed Turin and Genoa in August 1943; an inducement to the new government to accept unconditional surrender, then under secret negotiation. His diary entry gave a clear picture of Osborne's personal views about the use of air power and the damage it caused prior to the bombing of the Abbey.

The Allies were keen to protect Italy's artistic heritage if possible. In December 1943, the Deputy Permanent Under-Secretary at the Foreign Office, Sir Orme Sargent, wrote a note regarding the protection of objects in Italy:

32   Canciani, p.13.
33   Chadwick, p.242.
34   John Cornwell, *Hitler's Pope: The Secret History of Pius XII* (London: Penguin Books, 2000), pp.176-7.
35   Conrad Crane, *Bombs, Cities and Civilians* (Wichita KS: University of Kansas, 1993), p.60. *Impact* was a project began in January 1943. The idea originated in a similar publication from the RAF, *Evidence in Camera.*
36   AFHRA Reel A6338, Message, Northwest African Strategic Air Force ACOS A-3 to 5th, 42nd and 57th BWs dated 11 September 1943.
37   Chadwick, p.243.
38   Edsel, p.36.
39   Chadwick, p.244.

Brigadier-General Charles Born (centre), the Chief of Operations at Fifteenth Air Force, warned aircrews about damaging Italian cities. It was Born who would have approved the target selections for the B-17 bombers on 15 February 1944. (NARA RG342-FH-0000

The Secretary of State for Air and the Chief of the Air Staff gave an assurance that full consideration had been and was being given by the authorities concerned to the avoidance of damage to historic and artistic buildings in Italy. Moreover, he knew that the Air Officer Commanding in Chief the Mediterranean (Slessor) would do all in his power to attain the necessary military objectives without bombing this city.[40]

In the US, Secretary of State, Cordell Hull, suggested to the President that a commission was required to protect Italian art.[41] Roosevelt established this commission to oversee the protection 'so far as consistent with Military Necessity, works of cultural value.'[42] It was chaired by Associate US Supreme Court Justice, Owen J Roberts and was established on 20 August 1943 in the National Gallery of Art in Washington. In late 1944, Roosevelt's Papal liaison, Archbishop Francis Spellman of New York was appointed as a commissioner after conducting visits to the

40   TNA FO371/43817 dated 28 December 1943.
41   Ilaria Dagnini Brey, *The Venus Fixers* (New York: Picador Books, 2009), p.42.
42   *The Roberts Commission,* Report of the American Commission for the Protection and Salvage of Artistic and Historic Monuments in War Areas (Washington DC, 1946), p.2.

Pope on Roosevelt's behalf in 1943. Spellman had such influence that Clark dined with his Army's Roman Catholic Chaplain, Colonel Patrick Ryan, with the intent that Ryan should inform Spellman of Clark's opposition to the bombing of the Abbey.[43]

Protection of Italian art and monuments was also being considered across the Atlantic. Following activity in North Africa, around ancient sites such as Leptis Magna, requests for the protection of archaeological sites were made to the Minister of War, P J Grigg, and to Churchill himself. The eminent archaeologist, Sir Leonard Woolley, already a lieutenant-colonel in the War Office, was appointed to take on the role in November 1943.[44] Woolley was not a man for detail, or administration, and he quickly realised that the Roberts Commission, stuck in Washington bureaucracy was not going to work. The US Army would simply not allow their influence, and they remained in Washington. Woolley fought the British art history establishment vigorously, a group to which he did not belong, to prevent a similar committee being formed in Britain. In this he succeeded; the British staff remained under War Office control. In the early months of 1944, when sites such as the Abbey were under threat, the Roberts Commission and Woolley seemed more concerned with bickering over whether the establishment of a British Commission would be beneficial.

The Roberts Commission met nine times, the third meeting being just 12-days before the bombing of the Abbey.[45] Its first substantive act was the sponsorship of the 'Harvard Lists'. These were lists of monuments, churches and works of art, prioritised by their artistic importance. They were placed on complicated maps called Frick Maps, produced by the American Council of Learned Societies.[46] The maps were named after Helen Clay Frick, founder and Director of the Frick Art Reference Library in New York. The problem with the lists was that there were too many sites that would require protection, even with the priority system. The lists were compiled, and the sites plotted on the Frick maps in New York, a task not completed until 4 January 1944, some four months after the Allies set foot in Italy. By January, the Allies were only about five miles from the Abbey which had already been placed on a list by Eisenhower. Its inclusion on any of the 'Harvard Lists' was overtaken by events. The use of Frick Maps was reported in the US press in March 1944, but clearly a month earlier the landmark of the Abbey was what the airman were trying to destroy so its presence on a map was somewhat beside the point:

> NEW YORK, March 16 – (AP) – When Allied bomber crews start on destructive missions over Axis-held territory they carry with them treasure maps made in the United States.
>
> Devised by some of this nation's foremost historians, geographers and art authorities, these treasure maps show locations of art treasures, shrines and landmarks with a view to preventing their destruction.
>
> President Raymond E Fosdick of the Rockefeller Foundation reported that maps are being prepared at the Frick Art Reference Library in New York, under the direction of the Commission for Protection and Salvage of Artistic Monuments. The latter group was appointed by the State Department last August.[47]

43   Tasciotti, p.108.
44   Dagnini-Brey, p.53.
45   Roberts Commission, p.7.
46   Dagnini-Brey, pp.44-5.
47   Help Avoid Shrines, *Pittsburgh Post-Gazette*, 17 March 1944, <https://artsandculture.google.com/exhibit/the-frick-during-world-war-ii-frick-art-reference-library/pQISdZwnX7otIg?hl=en>

The Commission's final report made no mention of whether the Abbey was discussed. As they established a military government, so experts in fine arts and cultural heritage were sent to the country. Mostly British and American academics, these men formed the Monuments, Fine Arts and Archives (MFAA) organization, better known as the Monuments Men, or more informally in Italy, the 'Venus Fixers.'[48] This was the operational arm of the Commission, although their influence was slight. Despite the Harvard Lists and Frick maps, the MFAA staff spent more time cataloguing damage and to a certain degree repairing it, than advising commanders or campaigning for the prevention of damage. The MFAA Director in Italy led a joint US/British team whose mission was:

1.   Mission
     To prevent as far as possible destruction of and damage to historical monuments, buildings, works of art and historical records of Italy; to safeguard and preserve them and to give first aid in repairs when needed…
2.   Major Functions
     a)   Advises on orders to be issued by commanders to their troops for the protection and safeguarding of monuments, buildings, works of art, etc.
     b)   Maintains liaison with ground and air forces in order to furnish them with information concerning historical monuments within their respective theaters of operation.[49]

It was the responsibility of the MFAA to provide advice and guidance to commanders when there was a risk of damage to buildings of cultural importance. There is no evidence that the experts on the MFAA were consulted during the decision-making process that led to the destruction of the Abbey. At the time of the bombing, MFAA staff were not allowed to leave Naples. Despite their extensive academic qualifications, they were given lowly ranks, mostly lieutenants and captains, which prevented their attendance at important planning meetings. Support for the protection policy in theory came from the highest levels of command. In November 1943, Monuments Man Major Norman Newton issued a list of sites of cultural importance as directed by the US JCS. Newton's list had an introduction from Alexander,[50] who was an art aficionado. He even wrote a letter to all commanders two days after the Abbey bombing concerning damage to art in Italy. He said:

Concern has been caused at home by reports of damage done to property of historical and educational importance in Italy…

I wish to impress on all officers how vitally necessary it is that the troops under their command behave in a manner which safeguards the good name of our armies and brings credit to their race.[51]

(accessed 8 July 2021).
48   Edsel, p.61. Dagnini-Brey, p.87.
49   Roberts Commission, p.60.
50   Roberts Commission, p.61.
51   TNA WO 204/3692: Alexander Letter dated 17 February 1944, Property of Historical and Educational Importance in Italy – Preservation of.

A sketcher and painter, he appreciated the debt to civilisation owed to Italy that gave the world great masterpieces, archives and architecture, but clearly not Abbeys!

As a building of great importance to Christianity and western monasticism, the attack on the Abbey received perfunctory coverage in the Roberts Commission's final report. The comments could be described as offhand or even callous – 'so long as these things are not lost or destroyed, the loss of material objects should not be too distressing, for new buildings can be erected to house the indestructible heritage of Saint Benedict.'[52] The Roberts Commission was disinterested in the destruction of the monks' home or the final refuge of several hundred Italian civilians, as long as the art survived.

In late October, Leccisotti was sent by Diamare to the Vatican to plead the case of the Abbey to Pope Pius XII, possibly taking St Benedict's relic with him.[53] He met with Monsignor Montini. The Vatican agreed to intervene and on 23 October, a note was sent to the German Ambassador.[54] On 25 October messages were also sent to the British and American representatives. The British message read thus:

> The Secretary-General of His Holiness has the honour to call upon the good offices of the Legation of England near the Holy See for the following case.
>
> As the theatre of war approaches more and more of the historic Abbey of Monte Cassino, we are justified in fearing that this splendid monument, venerable by its antiquity and by its memories not less than by its artistic value, to suffer destructions consecutive to military operations.
>
> The Secretary of State would therefore be very grateful to the Legation of England if it could, by its intervention with the competent English authorities, obtain that all possible respects be employed towards the abbey in question.
>
> A similar communication is made at the same time as the other belligerent party.
>
> The State Secretariat, thanking the Legation of England in advance for its courteous intervention, seized the opportunity to renew to it the assurance of its high consideration.[55]

Osborne, Britain's Envoy Extraordinary and Minister Plenipotentiary in February 1944 was a British aristocrat and diplomat and was an experienced Vatican hand, taking up his post in February 1936.[56] On his arrival relations were poor and Osborne was not asked, nor expected, to improve them. He was polite, formal and an Italophile. To avoid any conflict of loyalties, Osborne had to be a Protestant.[57] He was friendly with King George VI having known him and the Queen since before the war. He was to ask many of the most awkward questions about the justification for bombing the Abbey. Despite British expectations, he used diplomatic skill within the Vatican to become one of the most important British conduits to Europe in the war. By 1940 he was 'adored' in the Vatican and his relationship with the French ambassador, the most important non-Italian voice pre-war, came to be influential as war approached.[58] British

52   Roberts Commission, pp.67-68.
53   Gentile and Bianchini, p.44.
54   Tasciotti, p.31.
55   TNA FO371/37330: Folio R12578, Note 70279/S dated 25 October 1943.
56   Chadwick, p.13.
57   Chadwick, p.14.
58   Chadwick, p.15.

intelligence had realised by this time that the Vatican could perhaps be a useful conduit to Roman Catholic anti-Nazis within Germany. As Minister, Osborne assisted with the conceal-ment of almost 4,000 escapees and Jews from the Nazis and was also privy to a plot by German Generals to kill Hitler in 1940. He remained in his position until 1947.

The Vatican has been accused of doing too little to oppose the Nazis, with some justification. The Papacy was viewed by Britain before the war as a supplicant to Mussolini; Pius XI was seen as 'a fascist Pope'.[59] In an unusually long interview with Osborne at the end of 1938, and just two months before his death, Pius XI, in a less than neutral conversation, told him that 'Nazi Germany has taken the place of Communism as the Church's most dangerous enemy.'[60] The Lateran Treaty of 1929 was seen by the British Foreign Office as pulling the Vatican closer to the Italian state, although by 1939 Fascism too was beginning to concern the Papacy.[61] Many of the same King Charles Street officials were to play a hand in the aftermath of the Abbey's bombing. By the time of his death, Pius XI was in open conflict with Nazism and was well on the way with fascism as well. The Secretary of State to Pius XI, Cardinal Pacelli, became Pope Pius XII in 1939.

He was Britain's and France's choice as they thought he would continue his predecessor's poli-cies on Germany. Both Hitler and Mussolini were also satisfied with his election. He was less strident than his predecessor coming to an accommodation with the Nazis to prevent church persecutions and to maintain a neutral stance. Just days after his election he penned an affirma-tion of Hitler's leadership.[62] He made great efforts to protect the church's cultural property, but this came at a cost. The Vatican had a narrow path to tread. There was a threat that Hitler, in a fit of rage, could order the *SS* into the Vatican should Papal protests become too vociferous. Hitler planned to send 3,000 *SS* troops into St Peter's following the deposition of Mussolini.[63] The Vatican was at the time shielding several thousand Jews, including the Italian Chief Rabbi and Allied POWs in the Vatican itself and in its estates in Rome and wider afield. In this it was encouraged by the German ambassador to the Vatican, and battle of Jutland veteran, Baron Ernst Freiherr von Weizsäcker, a less than fanatical Nazi.[64] Pius, himself however played a minimal role in the protection of Jews.[65] Weizsäcker even warned one of the Vatican's prin-cipal plotters, Monsignor O'Flaherty, not to leave Vatican property as the *Geheimstatspolizei (Gestapo)* would arrest him.[66] Weizsäcker and some of his staff within the Villa Napoleon used a Swiss League of Nations official to alert Roman Jews to flee or hide when he learnt that they were to be rounded-up in September 1943.[67] Pius' attempts to walk the tightrope resulted in accusations of weakness and indifference to their fate. He never made any open protests against Nazi atrocities. The French ambassador said of his actions, 'his initiatives are timid, his results insignificant.'[68] In December 1942, Osborne, also becoming frustrated by the Pope's atti-

59   Chadwick, p.7.
60   Chadwick, p.25.
61   Chadwick, pp.9-10.
62   Cornwell, p.208.
63   Lamb, Kindle location 1074.
64   Lamb, Kindle location 1049.
65   Kertzer, p.380.
66   Trevelyan, p.63.
67   Katz, pp.55-56.
68   Kertzer, p.477.

Pope Pius XII meets Allied soldiers following the capture of Rome in June 1944. Pius was highly critical of Allied bombing, less so of German atrocities (NARA RG80-G-059409)

tude wrote to Maglione stating, 'instead of thinking of nothing but the bombing of Rome (the Vatican) should consider their duties in respect of the unprecedented crime against humanity of Hitler's campaign of extermination of the Jews.'[69]

The Vatican, although not the Pope himself, saved many lives; greater stridency in protest may have resulted in a German entrance to Vatican territory. Weizsäcker, and his First Secretary and fellow anti-Nazi, Baron Albrecht von Kessel, warned them:

> The Curia and the Pope himself against rash utterances. To offer any opinion on a question of martyrdom would have been entirely out of place for us Germans, whose Head of State was a criminal…would it not have been better from the point of view of human dignity, of Christendom and the Catholic Church, if Pius XII had assumed the martyr's crown even without achieving any practical results…I was convinced then and am still convinced today that he almost broke down under the conflicts of conscience. No one could relieve him of the responsibility.[70]

The political leanings of senior German diplomats, or at least the views they claimed to hold after the fact were anti-Nazi, and therefore they had little reason to provide the Nazis with

69   Cornwell, p.291.
70   Lamb, Kindle location 1049.

a propaganda victory that the bombing of the Abbey would offer, although Weizsäcker continued to effectively represent Germany if not the Nazi state.

Von Kessel, however, was anything but loyal to Hitler, taking an active but peripheral role in the assassination plot that year.[71] The British and American diplomatic representation to the Vatican, must have been aware of liberal German diplomatic loyalties, although von Kessel claimed that all approaches were rebuffed by 'unconditional surrender' responses. The Vatican was being given advice that Hitler was 'a criminal' by his own diplomatic representatives, although again, we do need to take post-war claims from German wartime officials with a large pinch of salt.

All Allied messages from the Vatican had to be hand-carried to Switzerland before they could be transmitted to London or Washington. This could involve significant delay. Osborne would send messages twice a week via the Papal Diplomatic bag where it would be handed over and transmitted to London.[72] Nothing of any great sensitivity was passed as the British were never convinced about its security nor about the German inability to break their

German ambassador to the Vatican, Baron Ernst von Weizsäcker. Weizsäcker was never a keen Nazi and was possibly a participant in efforts to rid Germany of Hitler. He had no reason to offer the Nazis the propaganda victory destroying the Abbey would provide. (NARA RG306-NT-222A-7)

cyphers. The Vatican sent messages to their Apostolic Delegates, Archbishop William Godfrey in London and Archbishop Amleto Cicognani in Washington DC regarding the Abbey in October 1943.[73]

Probably as a result, Sargent in London asked Macmillan to remind Eisenhower why the Abbey was 'particularly important.'[74] In a message to 15th Army Group on 4 November 1943, Eisenhower added it to his list of protected places.[75] The next day he informed Marshall, that 'consistent with Military Necessity all precautions to safeguard works of art and monuments are

---

71   Sulzberger, pp.289-90.
72   Chadwick, p.181.
73   Tasciotti, p.32.
74   TNA FO371/37330: Folio R10960, Foreign Office To Resident Minister's Office Algiers No 2483 dated 2 November 1943.
75   TNA CAB 106/699: Folio No 02003 AFHQ to 15 Army Group, 4 November 1943. Montecassino, unlike Castelgandolfo was not Papal property, but belonged to the Italian state. Under the Lateran Treaty of 1929, Papal property attracts extraterritoriality and should be treated as neutral territory.

being taken.'[76] The order adding the Abbey to the protected list was sent to Fifth and Eighth Armies on 5 November 1943.[77] In a message on 6 January, Fifth Army claimed no record of the 5 November message, learning of it from MAAF.[78] Cicognani, the Apostolic Delegate to Washington DC wrote to Maglione on 8 November to inform him that the US Deputy Secretary of State, Edward Stettinius, had confirmed that Eisenhower had been properly apprised of the historical importance of Montecassino and the Holy Father's anxiety.[79]

Earlier that week, Macmillan received correspondence from Osborne that the Vatican had asked the British to ensure the Abbey's safety. He added that requests had also been sent to Weizsäcker.[80] Osborne speculated that 'the Germans had already occupied Monte Cassino and sent the monks away.' He added that 'if the Germans make use of the Monastery the Allies will be obliged to take whatever counter-measures, aerial or otherwise, that their own military interests may require.'[81] He was probably referring to the recently completed operation to secure the evacuation of art and inmates, when German transport and manpower was used to move the Abbey's contents. The second comment exposes the importance of the Abbey's occupation and places German military use of the building as the defining justification. It can be inferred, as a reflection of British Government policy, that the Military Necessity for attacking the Abbey would only occur if it was occupied by the Germans.

The British response to the Vatican's Note Verbale of 25 October was received on 4 November. Maglione wrote the following in response:

> We have received a response from London stating that the Holy See's appeal for Monte Cassino has been forwarded to the Allied High Command. As Sir D Osborne has already verbally stated, if the German military authorities use the Abbazzia or its territory for military purposes, the Allied military authorities will be forced to take any countermeasures that their military interest may dictate. At the same time, His Majesty's Government instructed His Majesty's Minister in Algiers to remind General Eisenhower of the reasons that make Monte Cassino particularly venerable and important.[82]

On 7 November, Osborne sent a telegram stating that the Vatican had received an assurance that the 'Abbey of Monte Cassino 'will not be occupied by regular German troops.'[83] The Vatican's Note Verbale 72939/S observed:

> The German Embassy to the Holy See, which has been approached at the same time as the British Legation in regard to the Abbey of Monte Cassino, has now informed the Secretary

---

76   TNA CAB 106/699: Folio No 02542 AFHQ to US War Department, 5 November 1943
77   TNA CAB 106/699: Message Ref 0-1478 Date Time Group 051910A November 1943.
78   TNA WO 204/3692: Dated 6 January 1944.
79   Tasciotti, p.37.
80   TNA CAB 106/699: JCH/DW/jw, MGS 619.3 – Monuments and Fine Arts – Monastery of Monte Cassino, AFHQ Military Government Section, 5 November 1943.
81   TNA CAB 106/699: JCH/DW/jw, MGS 619.3 – Monuments and Fine Arts – Monastery of Monte Cassino, AFHQ Military Government Section, 5 November 1943.
82   Tasciotti, p.34.
83   TNA CAB 106/699: Telegram No. 410, HM Minister to Holy See to Foreign Office, 7 November 1943.

of State that they 'are glad to be able to declare that the Abbey of Monte Cassino will not be taken over by German troops.'

The Secretariat of State takes this opportunity to acknowledge with cordial thanks their receipt of the Note Verbale No 3/130/43, of November 4th, whereby the British Legation, on instruction from their Government, gave courteous assurances on the latter's part regarding the said Abbey.[84]

This German promise was a local initiative taken by Weizsäcker with no authority from Berlin. He had overstepped his authority. There had been no official promise from the Nazis.[85] This telegram was passed from the Foreign Office to AFHQ at Algiers and to Washington on 10 November.[86] It reached Alexander on 15 November 1943, although Osborne had asked for a clarification of what was meant by 'regular German troops.'[87] A similar message was given to Tittmann, on 8 January 1944.[88] Tittmann took up his post when the US Embassy in Rome was closed in December 1941. In his memoir of his time in the Vatican, he recounted how he spent the majority of his time dealing with the after effects of Allied air activity on Church property.[89] It was discovered after the war that 95 per cent of damage to Italian monuments was caused by aerial bombardment.[90] Osborne forwarded a complaint from the Vatican on 7 December that the Abbey had been badly damaged by Allied artillery directed against German positions around Castle Hill (Point 193/Rocco Janula).[91] Weizsäcker then delivered a message to the Vatican on 18 December that gave an update from the Abbey, stating that there had been no damage to the building. The Papal Secretary of State had no direct communication with the Abbot and therefore no way to confirm reports:

According to uniform reports received from various German Command Posts, it is not true that the Abbey of Monte Cassino has been damaged by enemy shell-fire.

The only incident was the explosion of two shells on the hillside a short time ago, no serious damage being done.

As stated in the Note Verbale of November 7, the Abbey is not occupied by German troops. There is a special guard, outside the Monastery, whose duty it is to see that both now and in the future any occupation, even temporary, be avoided...

The Secretariat of State will conclude from the foregoing statements – as the German Embassy sincerely hopes – that everything possible is being done by the German military authorities to protect the Abbey of Monte Cassino from war damage now as well as in the future.[92]

84   TNA FO371/7330: Folio R12785, Note Verbale No 72939/S, 7 November 1943.
85   Tasciotti, p.37.
86   TNA FO371/37330: Folio R11534, Minute 1, 10 November 1943.
87   TNA CAB 106/699:Folio No.05697, AFHQ to 15th Army Group, 15 November 1943.
88   Trevelyan, p.25.
89   Harold Tittmann Jr, *Inside The Vatican Of Pius XII* (New York: Doubleday, 2004), p.199.
90   Dagnini-Brey, p.255.
91   TNA FO371/37330: Folio R12950. Holy See To Foreign Office Telegram 461, 7 December 1943.
92   TNA FO371/60797: Vatican Secretariat of State, Monte Cassino The Last Days, p.7.

Weizsäcker was a career diplomat, and although a reluctant Nazi Party member, he was associated with an anti-war faction, including some within the 20 July assassination plot, although he denied this after the war. He met with William Donovan in the Vatican just days before the attempt, telling the OSS man of the plot. He had personally selected von Kessel to the Vatican Embassy, probably saving his life. Since 1938 he was in contact with the plotters including Canaris, *General* Ludwig Beck and *Oberst* Hans Oster, placing anti-Nazis into key positions within the German Foreign Ministry. A little later, he was also associated with another plot led by the Army Chief of Staff, Franz Halder. He was State Secretary at the *Willhemstrasse* until he asked to move to Rome, becoming disillusioned with Germany's war. In the Vatican he aimed to use the Holy See as a conduit for peace, a hopeless task after Casablanca.[93] He remains a controversial character and was sentenced to seven years in prison at Nuremburg, although in most counts against him he was acquitted. He was not convicted for anything he did in the Vatican. Weizsäcker painted the Pope to Berlin as pro-German and actively opposed any occupation of the Vatican City. Nothing that Weizsäcker said in his communiques with the Vatican during this period regarding the status of the Abbey was false, and his actions encouraged the protection of historical locations. The note above could have easily taken advantage, to create a propaganda coup that the Allies had damaged the Abbey. Weizsäcker did not take this opportunity. Instead, he positively debunked it. Following the bombing, many British commentators thought that the Germans used trickery, and accused the German diplomatic denials of being worthless. They attempted to convince popular opinion that the Germans were simply exploiting the Abbey as a tool of propaganda. Why would the German diplomatic authorities manufacture a position when they could have the same benefit without doing so?

The Allies were becoming more concerned about the reputational damage that excessive destruction of historic and religious buildings would cause, especially in Catholic neutral countries in Latin America, Spain and Portugal. On 9 December a message was sent to Macmillan asking what instructions had been given concerning the protection of the Abbey.[94] On 29 December, Eisenhower issued his order regarding historical monuments and Military Necessity, known as General Order 68. This order was probably drafted for Eisenhower by Woolley, who was visiting Italy for a progress check.[95] He was clear, through Eisenhower, that where possible, monuments were to be spared, but that Military Necessity was paramount. He warned that necessity was not the same as convenience.[96] The Eisenhower order was forwarded to the British Foreign Office by AFHQ Resident Minister's staff on 5 January 1944.[97] It was registered in London on 13 January 1944. The full text of Eisenhower's order is as follows:

> Today we are fighting in a country which has contributed a great deal to our cultural inheritance, a country rich in monuments which by their creation helped and now in their old

93   Katz, p.52.
94   TNA FO371/37330: Folio R12785, Foreign Office To Resident Minister in Algiers Telegram 2950, 9 December 1943.
95   Dagnini-Brey, p.83.
96   TNA CAB 106/699: AG.000.4-1, Allied Force Headquarters, Office of the Commander-in-Chief, Historical Monuments, 29 December 1943.
97   TNA FO371/43817: Folio R627, Letter from Roger Makins to Sir Anthony Rumbold, 5 January 1944.

age illustrate the growth of the civilization which is ours. We are bound to respect those monuments as far as war allows.

If we have to choose between destroying a famous building and sacrificing our own men, then our men's lives count infinitely more, and the buildings must go. But the choice is not always so clear-cut as that. In many cases the monuments can be spared without any detriment to operational needs. Nothing can stand against the argument of military necessity. That is an accepted principle. But the phrase 'military necessity' is sometimes used where it would be more truthful to speak of military convenience or even of personal convenience. I do not want it to cloak slackness or indifference.

It is the responsibility of higher commanders to determine through A.M.G. officers the location of historical monuments whether they be immediately ahead of our front lines or in areas occupied by us. This information passed to lower echelons through normal channels places the responsibility on all commanders of complying with the spirit of this letter.

Why did Eisenhower feel the need to express this view? The Law was clear, and his senior commanders must have understood its restrictions? If, as Eisenhower suggested, Military Necessity is an accepted principle, why did he feel the need to remind his senior decision-makers that their actions should not be disguised under Military Necessity? It is now clear that his political masters were concerned that the explanation of Military Necessity was being used too liberally. Eisenhower was asked to issue the decree by the US Assistant Secretary for War, John McCloy.[98] The British interest through Macmillan was also an influence on Eisenhower. McCloy wrote the following to the Commander-in-Chief:

> _Crimes are being committed in the name of military necessity_ (emphasis added) that I think could be avoided with a pronouncement by you. We have been running many articles in the States as to the good work of the Armies in Italy are doing toward respecting the great monuments of Italy, but I was a bit shocked at the way the thing was operating in Naples itself. Could not some expeditious method be setup whereby the military government people could have authority to veto the use of great monuments for billeting unless overruled by the Commanding General?[99]

Woolley, during his visit in November and December 1943, realised that the protection of monuments and art was not working. The staff were stuck in Naples. None were anywhere near the fighting, offering advice to commanders as their orders required. The Venus fixers were fixing nothing.

It was eventually Woolley that gave them the impetus that the brilliant minds in London and Washington could not, but this was after the bombing. Quoting the full text of Eisenhower's 29 December 1943 order is vital. Many authors, keen to justify the attack, use the first sentence of the second paragraph as their justification. The second part concerning military or personal convenience is sometimes omitted. This order should have allowed the Monuments Men more power to prevent the destruction of important cultural objects. These experts should have been consulted if commanders planned to attack buildings of cultural significance. It placed the

98   Ronald Schaffer, _Wings of Judgement_ (Oxford: OUP, 1985), p.50.
99   Edsel, p.66.

protection of these objects firmly in the hands of the Army commanders. Sevareid passed a stinging judgement on Allied attitudes towards art and historical buildings. 'We had destroyed them simply because we didn't care what they were, and it required effort to spare them…it had become a kind of obsession to destroy, to fire for the sake of firing.'[100]

Six weeks after this Order, its effectiveness would be tested. It would fail! It failed after just three days. On New Year's Day, Tittmann sent a message following a conversation with the Vatican Secretary of State regarding an errant artillery round that struck the Abbey.[101] Woolley's efforts had simply not had the time to take effect, and Sevareid was right; they didn't care enough. Eisenhower's order was confirmed by Wilson on 16 January in a message to Marshall.[102] The MFAA staff did not overcome US War Department rules of not allowing non-tactical trained officers near the front lines until spring, still at Cassino, but long after the Abbey was bombed.[103] Eisenhower's directive was made public on the day of the Abbey's destruction by Roosevelt himself in a White House press conference.[104]

Another tactic for hearts and minds over the damage being caused to cultural sites in Italy was to distract criticism of Allied damage by emphasizing German damage. The first and best opportunity was in early October 1943 when they found the Italian Royal Society Library and State Archives in Naples destroyed. In early January, Foreign Office officials found that the British Political Warfare Executive and the Ministry of Information were struggling to obtain further evidence of 'German acts of looting and terror destruction in Italy.'[105] In a letter to Woolley, it was suggested that the Germans were sensitive to the publicity that they were destroying Europe's civilisation, referencing the manuscripts at Montecassino specifically. The Foreign Office's Sir Anthony Rumbold thought that any evidence of this kind would help to 'hit back' as the Germans were exploiting every Allied bombing error in this regard. Surely not making these errors is a better solution.

In London, Archbishop William Godfrey, the Papal Apostolic Delegate wrote to Sir Alexander Cadogan, the Permanent Under-Secretary at the Foreign Office, on 28 December 1943 and again on 6 January 1944. Archbishop Godfrey reiterated the anxiety felt by the Vatican over the great Benedictine Abbeys. These were not his first pleas for their preservation; his first letter to Sir Alexander was in October 1943.[106] By November 1943, the MFAA was subordinated to the Allied Military Government.[107] The MFAA had presented Professor Solly Zuckerman, Tedder's scientific adviser, with a list of 50-cities which should be spared aerial bombardment. It is not clear whether Cassino was on this list, although Zuckerman claimed that he was approached by an unnamed US Officer who asked him to make representations about the planned bombing. Zuckerman said, 'this time I failed'.[108] This approach must have

100 Sevareid, pp.536-7.
101 TNA WO 204/3692: Msg AGWAR to Fifteenth Army Group, Ref 22236, 1 January 1944.
102 TNA WO 204/3692: Msg Wilson for Marshall ref W309, 16 January 1944.
103 Dagnini-Brey, p.109.
104 Roberts Commission, p.49.
105 TNA FO371/37330: Folio R12393, Letter to Sir Leonard Woolley.
106 TNA FO371/37330: Folio R10941, Letter from Archbishop Willian Godfrey to Sir Alexander Cadogan dated 28 October 1943.
107 HQAMG Monuments Fine Arts & Archives Sub-Commission, First Monthly Report for November 1943 dated 4 December 1943.
108 Solly Zuckerman, *From Apes to Warlords* (London: Collins, 1988), p.211.

come after he returned to the UK as part of Tedder's OVERLORD staff on 30 December 1943.[109] Assuming that Zuckerman's memory was correct and that he was not contacted in England from Italy, this request for help must have been made by someone who knew the Abbey was to be bombed and who was in the UK. The most likely source would have been from within the US Strategic Air Forces in Europe and the most likely person that Zuckerman would have gone to was Tedder. If this was the case, the discussion over the Abbey's fate must have reached the UK in the 13 or 14 February timeframe.

On 8 January 1944, the Vatican Secretary of State passed another Note Verbale (74804/S) to Osborne regarding the use of the Abbey by the Germans. This is the second communication from the Germans that claimed they were not using the Abbey, and the wording is like that delivered to the Vatican by Weizsäcker on 18 December:

> The State Secretariat of His Holiness, following his Note Verbale No. 70279 / S of October 23, 1943, concerning the Abbey of Monte Cassino, has the honour to bring to the attention of the Legation of Great Britain that the German Embassy has just communicated, on this same subject, that 'on the side of the German Military Authorities we are doing everything possible so that the Abbey of Monte Cassino is preserved, now and in the future, from the damages of the war.[110]

Nevertheless, the Vatican Secretariat of State felt it necessary to communicate with the Germans on 8 January in Note Verbale 73821/S. He asked Weizsäcker:

> The Secretariat of State takes the liberty of insisting upon the necessity of avoiding every-thing that might furnish an excuse for a possible attack upon the historic monastery.
>
> It is in fact obvious that its security would not be effectively safe-guarded if works of a military character, such as gun-emplacements, observation posts, etc, were to be carried out in the immediate vicinity or, which would be even worse, if the Monastery itself should be used as an ammunition dump.[111]

The Germans replied on 12 January:

> The German Embassy has clearly explained on several occasions – beginning with its Note Verbale of November 7 – that the Abbey of Monte Cassino is not occupied by German troops, nor will it be used for military purposes.
>
> Nevertheless, the above-mentioned Note from the Holy See (No 73821/S of January 8) says that the Abbey could be used by the Germans as an ammunition dump.
>
> The German Embassy is surprised to note that its formal assurances have been placed in doubt.[112]

109 Zuckerman, p.214.
110 TNA FO371/43817: Folio R1991, Preservation of the Abbey of Monte Cassino, Note 74804S of 8 January – Secretary of State to British Legation to the Holy See.
111 TNA FO371/6079: Vatican Secretariat of State, Monte Cassino The Last Days, p.7.
112 TNA FO371/60797: Vatican Secretariat of State, Monte Cassino The Last Days, p.8.

It was now that a new German division took over the defence of Cassino. This was the 44th Infantry Division which moved into the *Gustav* Line in the first week of January 1944. The Abbot reportedly spoke to an officer from the division around 7 January and was told that the Abbey itself would remain unoccupied by German forces. The German military policemen were removed from the Abbey around 10 January. The first Allied shell hit the Monastery on 13 January 1944.

The Abbey was a sensitive site, both politically and religiously, and it would not be unusual for military commanders to require higher authority before such sites are attacked. No request from Wilson is recorded in the archives. Having been turned down before, he may have thought that offering an apology was preferable to asking permission. However, an intriguing piece of evidence was unearthed in 2007, when New York judge and former member of USAAF intelligence staff in the Mediterranean, Justice Bentley Kassal, wrote to the *New York Times* regarding his part in the attack on the Abbey. 'I was the air combat intelligence officer who prepared the aerial bombing of the Abbey on Monte Cassino.' he said[113] He probably served in XII ASC because of the award of the Bronze Star by General Saville, its commander at the time of the attack. Kassal claims, although provides no solid evidence, that the decision went all the way up to Roosevelt. One of many obituaries of Kassal also claimed that he was tasked to brief Arnold directly on the situation, although Arnold did not visit Italy during the critical period. XII ASC attacked the Abbey on 16 February, and it is possible that Kassal was referring to this event.

As January passed, and the fighting got closer to the Abbey, Allied shelling struck the building more regularly. On 25 January, as the 34th Infantry Division was scaling the heights to the Cassino massif, Tittmann gave the following message from the US State Department:

> General Eisenhower [sic] has reported that in the neighbourhood of Monte Cassino many German gun positions and installations have been taken under fire. The report goes on to say that it is possible that the Abbey was struck by erratic bursts; that if any damage occurred, it could not be avoided and was not intended, and that the appropriate commanders have been issued instructions to make every effort to keep from harming this hallowed place.[114]

The reference to Eisenhower in January 1944, after he had departed to the UK, was probably a mistake. The German Embassy in the Vatican also reported damage to the Abbey caused by Allied shelling in its message of 31 January again claiming that they were not using the Abbey for any military purpose:

> According to reports by the German military commands based on appropriate investigation, the Abbey of Monte Cassino has been damaged by Anglo-American artillery fire. It received a direct hit on January 24 and previous to that the courtyard of the Monastery had been hit three times.

113 Justice Bentley Kassal, 'Fog of War' Letter to the Editor, *New York Times* dated 7 October 2007. <https://thaa.org/pg/hof-bkassal.html > (accessed 11 October 2022).
114 TNA FO371/60797: Vatican Secretariat of State, Monte Cassino The Last Days, quoting US Dept of State Note 34 dated 25 January 1944, p.10.

The bombardment of the Abbey occurred in spite of the fact that it had not been utilised by the Germans either as a billet for troops, or as a support position or as an observation post.

The German Embassy deplores the fact that it has not been possible to preserve that famous monument from enemy bombardment, although the German military commands did everything in their power to render unnecessary such methods of procedure on the part of the Anglo-Americans.[115]

Nothing more was heard from the Vatican, but by the end of January 1944 journalists were reporting that the Abbey was being used for military purposes. Sulzberger accused the Germans of using the Abbey as an observation post on 29 January and by 9 February Anne O'Hare of the *New York Times*, declared a German presence. A London *Times* correspondent reported on 10 February 1944 'wireless aerials established on the roofs and telescopes at the windows.'[116] The same correspondent upped the ante the next day, claiming that Fifth Army troops had 'seen machine-guns along the abbey walls.'[117] Both these reports bear a marked similarity to elements of the evidence used to justify the attack following the bombing. Who had seen machine guns? The journalist, or was this 1940s spin, attempting to pre-justify an upcoming controversial event? Even the day before the attack, the British *Daily Mail* added to the propaganda narrative:

Nazis Turn Cassino Monastery Into a Fort
Allies May Shell It
From Daily Mail Special Correspondent

Fifth Army Front, Wednesday (delayed)
The Allies may, I believe, be changing their policy towards the **notorious** Abbey of Monte Cassino, which although **being used as an observation post** by the Germans has been banned as a target for our artillery in view of its historic importance.

Such a change in policy should produce something effective on this front within 48-hours. The Abbey, birthplace of the Benedictine Order, has so far been spared even though **this consideration has cost soldiers' lives. Information brought in by Italian civilians today may end its immunity.**

This makes it fairly certain that the Germans have already **wrecked much of the Abbey's interior** themselves by **dynamiting the feet-thick stone floors** and walls to **turn the building into a fortress**. Until recently, said the Italian who had crawled over minefields into our lines early this morning civilians from Cassino were allowed by the Germans to use the Abbey as a refuge during heavy artillery bombardments. But one day recently, when the civilians made their way to the Abbey, they found the entry barred. But from the main gateway **they could see many machine-guns** being placed into positions which gave the gunners 100 per cent cover but which controlled all the approaches to the building.[118] [emphasis added by author].

---

115 TNA FO371/60797: Vatican Secretariat of State, Monte Cassino The Last Days, p.10.
116 *The Times,* Monastery Used as an Observation Post, 10 February 1944.
117 *The Times,* Monastery Used as Gun-Post, 11 February 1944.
118 Canciani, p.113.

Maglione was warned the same day by Cicognani that similar reports were appearing in the US press. Christopher Buckley explained that many of the news reports came from correspondents in the headquarters press corps, a long way from the front, who had no way of verifying what they were told. These reports were popular with editors as they arrived sooner than those of front-line reporters, whose news was often stale when despatched.[119] The *Daily Mail* piece covers all the emotive excuses needed to justify the building's destruction. Similar press reports had been drawing questions from the British Foreign Office. On 8 February, official, Geoffrey McDermott, had referenced press reports of the Germans using the Abbey as an observation post and asked whether the War Office, through Brigadier Hollis, could ascertain the truth.[120] Osborne referred to an undated BBC report from correspondent Rupert Dowing when sending the following message on 11 February:

> I have thought it well to remind the Vatican, both verbally and in writing, that I had warned them that if the Abbey <u>or</u> its territory were used by the Germans for military purpose, the Allied military authorities would be obliged to take necessary counter measures; also that I have never received any reply to my suggestion…that the Vatican should ascertain from the Germans whether their assurance that the Abbey would not be occupied by German troops covered occupation or utilisation of the Abbey or its territory for any military purpose.[121]

From HM Government's point of view, occupation remained paramount. In response the German media through the Berlin International News Agency wrote in its 11-12 February edition that, 'In response to the false statements made by the Anglo-Americans, competent Germanic circles point out once again that the famous abbey of Monte Cassino is not actually used for military purposes by the Germans. American troops are themselves planning something deliberately.'[122]

This was four days before the Abbey's destruction; had the Germans discovered Allied plans? On the same day Benedictine monk Leccisotti, still representing the Abbot, wrote a pessimistic outlook to Diamare;

> I knew that leaving would already have been suggested to the monks. But, although greatly wishing that you were in safety, it was not the case of thinking of *totally* abandoning the site. With a few staying there, a chance still remains, since, despite all the concern – and it is intense – war is war, and diplomatic weapons cannot match military requirements. We are still hoping the monastery will be spared any direct attack, but it would be wise to take every possible precaution and to use the very greatest prudence in your actions. The consequences could be irreparable.[123]

On 12 February the Germans rebuffed Allied press claims stating 'competent German circles point out once more that the celebrated Benedictine Abbey of Montecassino is not in fact being

119 Buckley, p.132.
120 TNA FO371/43817: Folio R1991 Minute 1 dated 8 February 1944.
121 Telegram No. 87 HM Minister to Holy See to Foreign Office, 11 February 1944.
122 Tasciotti, p.124.
123 Grossetti and Matronola, p.202.

used for military purposes by the Germans.'[124] The Foreign Office received Osborne's message on 13 February and the next day Rumbold forwarded it to Hollis in the War Cabinet Office and Woolley amongst others.[125] The German Embassy in the Vatican made a final communication on the 14 February, this time to Baron von Stotzingen:

> According to German military information, statements regarding German defence equipment in the Convent of Monte Cassino are false. It is absolutely untrue that cannon, mortars or machine-guns are there. No large-size concentrations of troops are there (that is to say, of course, not in the neighbourhood of the Monastery). Moreover, everything within the limits of the possible was done to prevent Monte Cassino from becoming a transit centre.[126]

After the bombing, the Vatican wanted to bring to the attention of the Allies further sites of historical value. The first of these was the Cathedral at Orvieto, a city north of Rome and an important rail junction. The Vatican Secretariat of State asked Osborne on the 22 February to impress the importance of the city being spared 'any hostile action which might endanger its religious and artistic treasures.'[127] Perhaps the use of the word 'hostile' by the Vatican is an indication of their attitude towards the Allies?

On 23 February, Norstad issued a Directive to MAAF regarding the bombing of historical monuments. The Directive listed three categories of 'historical, cultural and religious importance'. Category A was the most important, with Rome, Florence, Venice and Torcello (island near Venice) as the only members. Targets in this category could not be attacked without MAAF's authority. Category B locations were on a much longer list of Italian and Dalmatian towns where bombing could be undertaken for essential operational reasons. Category C locations were places where there were important military objectives in or near the town and where damage could be accepted. The Directive gave instructions to MAAF commanders. It showed little remorse for damage already done and its restrictions continued to stress Military Necessity and crew safety as the overriding factors. [128] The Directive also placed greater protection on Vatican properties, stressing their 'diplomatic immunity' and 'accorded the rights of a neutral and independent state.'[129] The overflight of the Vatican was prohibited and extra protection for Papal properties such as Castelgandolfo was put in place. Even so, the Directive stressed that Papal and Irish properties 'will not be allowed to interfere in any way with the attack of military objectives.'[130] As we will see, a military objective was often defined as anything it needed to be.

Following the bombing, the Allies continued to target areas close to important heritage sites. Alexander asked Wilson in mid-January for the restrictions on bombing targets in Florence to be lifted.[131] He explained that some bombs would hit the city as well as the communication targets he was requesting. At this point Wilson turned him down, saying that the required

124 TNA FO371/60797: Vatican Secretariat of State, Monte Cassino The Last Days, p.11.
125 TNA FO371/43817: Folio R2320 dated 13 February 1944.
126 TNA FO371/6079: Vatican Secretariat of State, Monte Cassino The Last Days, 12.
127 TNA FO371/43817: Folio R2998, Holy See To Foreign Office Telegram No115 dated 23 February 1944.
128 TNA WO 204/1077: MAAF, Historic Monuments dated 23 February 1944.
129 TNA WO 204/1077: MAAF, Historic Monuments dated 23 February 1944.
130 TNA WO 204/1077: MAAF, Historic Monuments dated 23 February 1944.
131 TNA WO 204/3692: Msg ref MA1001 dated 14 January 1944, Alexander to Wilson.

B-26 Marauders from the 42nd Bombardment Wing bomb rail facilities in Florence in March 1944. The bombing of Florence was of deep concern to Mediterranean Allied Air Forces Deputy Commander, Air Marshal Sir John Slessor. (NARA RG342-FH-000408)

effects could be achieved without attacking the city.[132] Just two weeks after the bombing of the Abbey on 29 February, Alexander once again requested the bombing of Florence[133] and on 1 March, Slessor requested permission from the British CoS, agents for operations in Italy, that the Florence *Campo di Marte* marshalling yards be bombed. The reason given was that the yard was only a mile from the famous Duomo and the Cathedral of *Santa Maria del Fiore*. In mitigation Slessor proposed 'to use only the most experienced and accurate bomber squadrons, if permission to bomb these yards was given. It would therefore be very bad luck if any of the really famous buildings were hit.'[134]

It would luckier not to hit a large building a mile away, considering the inaccuracy of Allied bombers in early 1944. The Florence request, put into the committee by Portal, makes the sensitivity of the target clear that, 'In view of the political implications, the matter had been referred to the Secretary of State for Air, who might wish to raise it with the War Cabinet.'[135] The CoS

132 TNA WO 204/3692: Msg ref 26928 dated 15 January 1944, Wilson to Alexander.
133 TNA WO 204/3692: Msg ref MA1123 dated 29 February 1944, Alexander to Wilson.
134 TNA CAB 79/71/12 dated 1 March 1944.
135 TNA CAB 79/71/12 dated 1 March 1944.

recommended that their approval of the attack was sent to the Prime Minister. Wilson agreed that the marshalling yards could be bombed after consulting Eaker on 2 March.[136] Why was a similar process not followed, or has been removed from the records, in the case of the Abbey, an equally famous Italian building? In the subsequent attack, the 'bad luck' fell on people as stray bombs killed 215-civilians.

The Vatican feared that if the Allies would bomb the Abbey, they would also bomb Rome. After Rome was liberated, Abbot Diamare in a conversation with Monsignor Lombardi from the Vatican Secretariat of State, said that he thought they had exploited the Abbey's destruction with world public opinion in order to save Rome.[137] On 28 February, Maglione linked the Abbey with Rome in a letter to Archbishop Cicognani: 'What happened at Montecassino is very painful and arouses serious fears for the future.' That the Abbot formally assured the Holy See that within the enclosure of the monastery, there were never any weapons posts, nor German soldiers, nor even observation posts.[138] Around the end of February, Monsignor Domenico Tardini, the Undersecretary of State for General Affairs at the Vatican, produced an internal Vatican note regarding the bombing of Rome and the belligerents' intentions. Despite his cynicism, the note strikes a note of truth, at least from the Vatican view:

> Basically both belligerents have no respect for monuments and works of civilisation. The only thing that matters is the military interest. The only tactic is to get the other party the blame. If the Germans decided to defend Rome, they would blame the Allies because they would be the attackers. These, in turn would accuse the Germans because they would make Rome the cornerstone of their defence.[139]

Rome was bombed again several times. The Vatican newspaper, *L'Osservatore Romano* appealed to the belligerents to spare Rome and its population. In a reference to one incident, labelled 'of particular secrecy' dated 7 March and received in London the next day, Osborne relayed the distress that Maglione felt about the loss of civilian life. Maglione was viewed by the OSS as being the most pro-American senior official within the Vatican. He was a keen military historian who kept track of the war's events through a map in his office.[140] They also believed that his influence with His Holiness was declining due to differences of opinion with Pius' policy of silence over German atrocities.[141] Osborne dutifully justified the attacks because the Germans continued to use Rome's rail facilities. He also described the propaganda advantage exploited by the Germans when Allied raids struck civilian objects.[142] Maglione complained to Osborne that one Allied raid on Rome had affected the city's water supplies. The Foreign Office was less than sympathetic. [143]

The Vatican was a neutral state and should be 'spared the horrors of war.' Despite the offhand dismissal of concerns over Rome, the pressure on the Allies intensified. Another message by

136 TNA WO 204/3692: Msg ref 59209 dated 2 March 1944, Wilson to Alexander.
137 Gentile and Bianchini, p.75.
138 Tasciotti, p.198.
139 Tasciotti, p.200.
140 Cornwell, p.221.
141 Katz, p.369.
142 TNA FO 371/43870: Folio R3867, Telegram 146, Holy See To Foreign Office, dated 8 March 1944.
143 TNA FO 371/43870: Folio R3868, Minute 1 dated 13 March 1944.

Osborne received in the Foreign Office on 14 March, and following more civilian deaths on 10 March after marshalling yards were targeted in Rome, reported increased German propaganda in the Italian press. On 16 March 1944, Osborne reported a conversation he had with an intimate of the Pope where the view was that the bombing of Rome was a greater propaganda coup to the Germans than it was a military advantage to the Allies.[144] This conversation followed yet another Allied bombing raid on 14 March. Again, the Foreign Office, this time McDermott, brushed Osborne's point aside.[145]

There was greater interest from Sir Orme Sargent who thought the matter worth discussing further. Osborne wrote to the Foreign Office on 18 March, although the message was not received until the 23 March, that Allied bombing was resulting in a loss of support from the Italians. He said that 'All reports tend to indicate that the destruction of civil life and property is altogether disproportionate to military results obtained.'[146] He added that some Italians thought 'that German occupation is almost the lesser evil, generally detested as the Germans are, than Anglo-Saxon liberation.' He made the same points again on 21 March when reporting civilian deaths from the Allied raid of 18 March. Much of what Osborne reported is anecdotal, but it offered a flavour of public opinion. He also made the point that it wasn't only German propaganda that was hitting home. Italian communists were also taking advantage. [147] In the view of the Minister, Allied bombing was driving the Italian public into the arms of Moscow. On 28 March, Churchill asked the Chief of the Air Staff to comment upon Osborne's reports.[148]

Tardini's solution to the warlike intent of both belligerents was 'to get Catholics from all over the world to move, especially those from neutral countries and those united with the Allies.'[149] This happened over the next few weeks. The Catholic Church's response to the threat to Rome started to spread, perhaps in part fuelled by the damage done to the Abbey. On 20 March the British Ambassador to Uruguay received notice from the Archbishop of Uruguay that he was going to write to Churchill and Roosevelt directly to plead for an avoidance of the bombing of Rome. The Foreign Office had also received telegrams from Peru, Ecuador and Argentina in what appears to have been a coordinated campaign. This campaign was sent from London to Osborne on 30 March.[150] Further evidence of an orchestrated Vatican campaign was received on 23 March when a letter to the Dominions Office was sent to the Prime Minister from the Irish Taoiseach, Eamon De Valera. De Valera's letter to Churchill expressed distress at the threat to Rome stating that unless measures were taken that 'its destruction was inevitable.' This he called 'a major calamity for the human race.' There was also what could be termed veiled threats when he stated, 'Millions of Catholics would risk their lives to save these memorials, symbols of the Eternal things which alone give meaning to human life.' He also made it clear that should the city be destroyed, future generations would not forget.[151] The campaign continued when the Spanish Embassy wrote to Cadogan at the Foreign Office with an appeal to avoid 'irreparable

144 TNA FO 371/43870: Folio R4294, Telegram 167, Holy See To Foreign Office, dated 16 March 1944.
145 TNA FO 371/43870: Folio R4294, Minute 1, dated 18 March 1944.
146 TNA FO371/43870: Folio R4709, Telegram 174, Holy See To Foreign Office, dated 18 March 1944.
147 TNA FO371/43870: Folio R4709, Telegram 174, Holy See To Foreign Office, dated 18 March 1944.
148 TNA FO371/43870: Folio R4763, Telegram 183, Holy See To Foreign Office, dated 21 March 1944. Minute by PM to CAS dated 28 March 1944.
149 Tasciotti, p.200.
150 TNA FO371/43870: Telegram 103, Foreign Office To Holy See, dated 29 March 1944.
151 TNA FO371/43870: Folio R4558, Message from Mr De Valera, dated 17 March 1944.

damage being done' to Rome. Spain offered to act as an intermediary with the Germans.[152] On the 27 March another letter arrived at the Foreign Office. This time it came from the Roman Catholic Bishops and Archbishops of Australia.[153]

At around the same time, Foreign Office official Peter Scarlett wrote to the War Cabinet Office's Chief of the JIC, Victor Cavendish-Bentinck following correspondence with the Vatican Secretary of State through Archbishop Godfrey, that concerned the Vatican's views on Montecassino and their fears over Rome. Scarlett is clearly concerned that the standard answer that the Germans are using Rome as a rail hub, whilst true, was no longer sufficient and that it was likely that any blame for damage to Rome would be placed at the Allies' door. The 'damage to Rome will, I fear, long be remembered against us not merely by Italians but all over the civilised world.'[154]

Scarlett suggested that a neutral power, probably Switzerland, perform a monitoring mission to ensure that Germany did not use the city in exchange for a cessation of bombing. Another Foreign Office official, Roger Allen, replied on 26 March:

> I have tried this proposal on the JPS (Joint Planning Staff). Their first reaction was not very favourable. They felt that if by any chance the Germans accepted and withdrew their forces north of Rome, we should be in a quandary, since the inability to use communications through Rome would hamper us greatly in following them up.[155]

Regardless, the Allies last bombed Rome on 18 March 1944. By 3 June 1944, the battles of Cassino were over, although the Allies had not yet reached Rome. On that day, the German High Command passed on an order from Hitler to Kesselring that there should be no battle for Rome. It was abandoned to the Allies and declared an open city. Ironically, in 1965 Ira Eaker, in a late 1960s interview with *American Heritage*, 'Italy is the world's greatest jewel box of art and architectural treasures. To me it is a miracle of the Italian Campaign, and a great tribute to the carefulness of the Allied Commanders, that there was so little damage.'[156]

152 TNA FO371/43870: Folio R4733, Letter Spanish Embassy to PUS Foreign Office, dated 23 March 1944.
153 TNA FO371/43870: Folio R4944, Australian High Commission To Dominions Office, dated 27 March 1944.
154 TNA FO371/43870: Folio R4552, Minute 1, dated 23 March 1944.
155 TNA FO371/43870: Folio R4552, Minute 2, dated 26 March 1944.
156 AFHRA Roll 23324, Eaker interview with *American Heritage* in response to Martin Blumenson account for US Army Official History, *Salerno to Cassino*.

12

The Law of War and Military Necessity

If International Law is the Weakest Point of all Law, then the Law of War is its Vanishing Point
Sir Hersch Lauterpacht

As Professor Geoffrey Best argues in *War and Law*, the Law of Armed Conflict has serious weaknesses in that States often ignore it with impunity, or selectively follow the rules.[1] Yet even during the greatest war, when the temptation to abandon the rules was at its greatest, all belligerents kept to some rules at least most of the time. In the case of incidents such as the Abbey bombing, when the rules were stretched or broken, the warring sides made some pretence of acting within international behaviour, for example citing Military Necessity. Even atrocities committed by Germany were largely hidden or denied, thereby presenting a tacit acceptance that rules existed even if they had no intention of following them. The British hid the Lindemann 'dehousing' plan, effectively the terror-bombing of German civilians, for nearly 20-years. This can be judged by the unguarded comment from an RAF officer after the bombing of Dresden, 'Allied war chiefs have made the long-awaited decision to adopt deliberate terror bombing of German population centres as a ruthless expedient to hasten Hitler's doom.'[2]

Best suggests that the law on bombing was vague and open to wide interpretation.[3] His opinion was that warring parties followed many of the battlefield principles for most of the time. The Red Cross flag was mostly respected, prisoners were usually treated in an approved manner and neither side resorted to the battlefield use of chemical or biological weapons, at least in Europe. The targeting of civilians, either directly or indirectly through methods such as area bombing, or the V-weapons, was far less respected, especially if the belligerent was under military pressure. In the case of the Abbey, the Allied land commanders were under pressure, not of being defeated, but of being thwarted in their desire to avoid irrelevance when larger events overshadowed their importance. The capture of Rome in mid-June would hardly have raised a footnote in the newspapers; before OVERLORD it was front page news.

The best place to start is to define a war crime. This gives the argument a yardstick upon which to base conclusions as to the legality of attacking the Abbey. The most appropriate definition is

---

1   Geoffrey Best, *War & Law Since 1945* (Oxford: Oxford University Press, 1997), pp.5-6.
2   Veale, p.186.
3   Best, p.51.

that used to convict German war criminals at the International Military Tribunal at Nuremburg. Sanford Levinson, writing on where the responsibility for war crimes laid, quoted directly from the statute establishing the court. Under Article 6a, a war crime is defined as:

> Violations of the laws or customs of war. Such violations shall include, but not be limited to, murder, ill-treatment or deportation to slave labour or for any other purpose of civilian population of or in occupied territory...plunder of public or private property, wanton destruction of cities, towns or villages, or devastation not justified by military necessity.[4]

The question is whether the Allied action on 15 February 1944 was a lawful act of war or whether it was unlawful and a war crime? If the attack can be justified by Military Necessity, then the destruction of the building and the deaths of civilians may be judged as a tragic, but acceptable, by-product of a terrible war. It would be within the laws of war as they stood in 1944. However, without Necessity, the destruction of the Abbey would be a war crime under the above definition, which was the Allied contemporary definition. The deaths of hundreds of civilians in this case would not fall within incidental damage and would be murder. Levinson continued by stressing that for an individual to be a war criminal the act must be 'a breach of some moral obligation fixed by international law, a personal act voluntarily done with the knowledge of its inherent criminality.'[5] For any of the officers involved to be guilty of a war crime, the presence of *mens rea* is necessary; they must have known what they had ordered was unlawful. This rests on the proof of Military Necessity.

How did the Allies view the legality of bombing civilian targets? Before the war there was a very clear British view of what was allowed during aerial bombardment. In June 1938, Neville Chamberlain proposed three rules to guide bombardment in a statement to the House of Commons:

1. It is against international law to bomb civilians as such and to make deliberate attacks upon civilian populations.
2. Targets which are aimed at from the air must be legitimate military objectives and must be capable of identification.
3. Reasonable care must be taken in attacking those military objectives so that by carelessness a civilian population in the neighbourhood is not bombed.[6]

In the same speech he admitted that there were no agreed rules for air warfare, but that the principles of the Hague 1907 Convention were applicable.[7] If we apply Chamberlain's rules to the Abbey, it is clear that the attack broke them all. The Abbey was a civilian building, occupied by monks and civilians, mostly women, children and old men. These had been protected

---

4   Sanford Levinson, 'Responsibility for Crimes of War', *Philosophy and Public Affairs*, 2:3 (1973), pp.244-273.
5   Levinson, p.257.
6   Tami, Davis-Biddle. 'Strategic Bombardment: Expectation, Theory and Practice in the Early Twentieth Century' in Matthew Evangelista and Henry Shue (eds.), *The American Way of Bombing* (London, Cornell University Press, 2014), p.39.
7   Peter Gray, *The Leadership, Direction and Legitimacy of the RAF Bomber Offensive from Inception to 1945* (London: Continuum International Publishing, 2012), p.137.

in customary law as non-combatants since at least the eighteenth century.[8] The British adoption of these rules can be traced back to the abortive Hague Rules of 1923. Despite this Treaty not being ratified, its articles appear to form the basis of the British interpretation of the law. In 1924, British lawyer, Air Ministry employee and prolific airpower commentator, J M Spaight, published his views on *Air Power and War Rights* which articulated the rules of air warfare based upon the Hague Treaty and on precedent from the First World War upon which he drew widely.

Spaight was hopeful in 1924 that the Hague Rules would be adopted; he was a member of the British delegation to the discussions. Despite this, Britain was one of the principal opponents to the adoption of these rules.[9] He produced a second edition of his work in 1933 which was a text for the new RAF Staff College,[10] and a third following the Second World War. These works were the most influential pre-war British academic interpretations of the unregulated war in the air, and they provide a contemporary view on how warfare in the third dimension could be regulated. There were a few elements within Spaight's work that were relevant to the bombing of the Abbey. Many post-war commentators have speculated that the Abbey was bombed for psychological or morale purposes. Spaight agreed that airpower's moral and psychological effect was often greater than its physical effect. He described the potential for air bombing to destroy towns and cities. These thoughts were generally restricted to the great airpower theorists, but many others believed that airpower's future was to lay waste to enemy cities, destroying their infrastructure and will to resist.[11]

Many commentators also realised that what one side could do, the other could also do. Some definition and regulation was required. Without regulation, airpower would 'destroy civilization itself.'[12] Spaight analysed the concepts of 'defended' as defined in the Hague Convention of 1907, considering it redundant if any town or city could quickly be 'defended' from the air, regardless of its military occupation. The new Hague Air Rules replaced this with the concept of the 'military objective'. In the Second World War, the military objective is of far greater relevance, but it was a term that had no strength in law. Spaight also recognised the Principle of Proportionality where bombarding a military objective could result in incidental damage to civilians and their morale to gain military advantage. He added that an attack delivered merely to gain psychological advantage would 'unquestionably be a breach of international law.'[13] Best takes this further by warning that a psychological advantage is a dangerous path to tread as it transferred justification from 'the purportedly rational and objective towards the probably irrational and admittedly subjective.'[14] On balance this is a strong argument. Who was to know how or whether an act offered psychological advantage? How could this be measured? How long would it last? What are the effects on subsequent morale if it failed? Regarding the Abbey, Best added, 'What was important for the infantry was the subjective psychological boost of seeing the buildings being spectacularly destroyed. Restraint and rationality will not be promoted by

---

8   A P V Rogers, *Law on the Battlefield* (Manchester: Manchester University Press, 2004), p.8.
9   Gray, p.53.
10   Gray, p.55.
11   J.M. Spaight, *Air Power and War Rights* (Milton Keynes: Gale MOML Print Editions, 2010 (reprint of 1924 Edition)), pp.5-18.
12   Spaight, p.18.
13   Spaight, p.18.
14   Best, p.275.

bringing the appeasement of one's own side's psychological needs within the definition of a military objective.'[15]

When discussing the rules regarding the bombardment of civilian property, Spaight predicted quite accurately the methods that would be used to gain moral advantage through bombing military objectives in highly populated areas that incidentally affect the civilian population.[16] The bombing of the Abbey was the reverse of the Hague Air Laws; bombing a civilian structure to incidentally affect military objectives. This was in direct contravention of the principle of Double Effect that forms the basis of Proportionality. With regards to historic and religious buildings, military commanders must observe the rules of Hague 1907 to spare these buildings 'provided they are not being used for military purposes.'[17] These rules remained the same in the moribund 1923 Hague Air Rules. The use of protected buildings must be known as a fact before immunity is lost. In his third edition of *Air Power and War Rights*, he lamented the lack of improvement in the bombing record of protected buildings.[18] His views on the bombing by the Allies of Italy in general and of the Abbey in particular were therefore surprising. Spaight called the bombing of Italy 'poetic justice' as he justified the bombing as retribution for the damage meted out on Malta. On the Abbey, he justified the destruction as legitimate because the Germans had turned the Monastery into a fortress.[19]

In addition to his published works, Spaight also produced a secret supplement for the AHB in 1946. One of the chapters dealt with the legal development of British bombing policy. Between 1939 and 1944 when the Abbey was bombed at the request of a British general and with the approval of several superior British officers, there had been no changes to the Laws of War regarding the bombardment of civilians. If the deliberate bombardment of civilians was considered illegal by the British Government in 1939 it remained so five years later. Spaight thought that pre-war it was in the British national interest to restrict bombing because the larger *Luftwaffe* could inflict more damage than the RAF.[20] In November 1937, the Secretary of State for Air, Lord Swinton, wrote to the new Chief of the Air Staff, Air Chief Marshal Sir Cyril Newall, that:

> I suggest we frame our proposal on the maximum of immunity, eg, you may bomb purely military objectives and nothing else. By this I mean warships, troops, whether in camp, barracks or on moving to the field of battle, aircraft and aerodromes and airmen. This means that you can always try to kill the fighting men; you must not try to kill the civilian.[21]

This memorandum would have raised consternation amongst the largely Trenchardian RAF hierarchy, who slavishly followed his war methodology for the aeroplane. The overwhelming school of thought amongst senior officers at the time was that the air instrument should be used as a weapon against morale and that meant centres of population. In June 1938, three

---

15   Best, p.275.
16   Spaight, *Air Power and War Rights*, p.239.
17   Spaight, p.260.
18   Spaight, p.286.
19   Spaight, p.287.
20   J.M. Spaight, *International Law of the Air, 1939-1945 – Confidential Supplement to Air Power And War Rights* (London: Air Ministry – Air Historical Branch, 1946), Section D, British Bombing Policy.
21   Spaight, British Bombing Policy.

weeks before Chamberlain's statement, the Foreign Office wrote to the Committee for Imperial Defence regarding the restriction of air warfare. The result was a committee, chaired by the Foreign Office's Senior Legal Adviser, Sir William Malkin. His initial report on 15 July 1938 addressed the Prime Minister's points and reached two solutions. These were:

The total prohibition of bombing.
The restriction of bombing to the area of sea and land fighting.

Neither of these was considered satisfactory and therefore the committee produced its own rule for consideration:

Air bombardment is only legitimate in the following circumstances: -

1. Against warships, including transports and fleet auxiliaries, at sea;

2. On land, in accordance with the following rules:
    Any objective on land which may legitimately be bombarded under the rules applicable to land warfare, may be bombarded from the air if it is within range of medium artillery, which for this purpose should be taken as ten miles from any of the forces of the belligerent who affects the bombardment or his allies.
        In addition, the following objectives on land may be bombarded provided that they are either anywhere on territory occupied by an invader or within a radius of fifty miles of the nearest troops or air forces of the belligerent carrying out the bombardment or of his allies:-
        In addition, the following objectives on land may be bombarded provided that they are either anywhere on territory occupied by an invader or within a radius of fifty miles of the nearest troops or air forces of the belligerent carrying out the bombardment or of his allies:-
    a) Enemy troops and air forces;
    b) Ammunition dumps, military supply depots, artillery parks and similar well-defined aggregations of distinctively military equipment, stores or supplies;
    c) Supply columns and other means of transport which are engaged in transporting supplies to or from the depots etc mentioned under (b).

Even though Malkin's committee had membership from the Air Staff, there were objections to such a 'tactical' use of airpower. The report was considered by the Ministerial Limitations of Armaments Sub-Committee, chaired by Sir Thomas Inskip, on 18 July 1938. Its conclusion was considered not to be in Britain's interests, and it decided to recommend no further work on the subject to the Prime Minister.[22] The Air Officer Commanding-in-Chief (AOC-in-C) of RAF Bomber Command, Air Chief Marshal Sir Edgar Ludlow-Hewitt, wrote to the Air Council on 30 August 1938 to ask for guidance regarding attacking German aircraft factories where bombs could cause incidental civilian casualties. The Air Council reiterated Chamberlain's three

22   Spaight, British Bombing Policy.

principles. As there were no deliberate civilian casualties, Bomber Command's query could be within this guidance. However, the Air Council added the additional caveat that:

> For reasons of policy, however, which the Council feel sure you will readily understand, it is essential that in the opening stages of a war your action should be rigorously restricted to attack on objectives which are manifestly and unmistakably military on the narrowest interpretation of the term; and that even such objectives should not be attacked initially unless they can be clearly identified and attacked with a reasonable expectation of damage being confined to them.

A statement of policy rather than law, the Air Council was concerned about British reputation in the eyes of neutrals, mainly the Americans. Any bombing seen to be targeted at the civilian population could result in retaliation. The RAF did not 'readily understand', with Ludlow-Hewitt saying to Lord Swinton in early September 1938 that, 'I feel sure that this restriction will not last very long, but we obviously cannot be the first to 'take the gloves off.'"[23] Many in the Air Staff had long advocated the bombing of civilians.[24] They, however, didn't make the ultimate decisions. The next event where bombing policy was expressed was a meeting in August 1939, again chaired by Malkin, which delivered the opinion, agreed with the French, that 'the Allies would not initiate air action against any but purely 'military' objectives in the narrowest sense of the word…and would confine it to objectives of which attack will not involve loss of civil life.'[25] Malkin's committee report to the Committee for Imperial Defence accepted that the restrictions placed on bombing were more restrictive than the current law, the Hague Convention of 1907. At the end of the list of permissible target sets, the report gave the British view on bombing civilians when it stated, 'Thus it is clearly illegal to bombard a populated area in the hope of hitting a legitimate target which is known to be in the area, but which cannot be precisely located and identified.' British officers were aware that the Abbey was occupied by monks and civilian refugees and had not to a reasonable level of satisfaction established whether the enemy also occupied the building. The Malkin Committee Rules, slightly amended but with no substantive changes, were issued as Air Council Instructions on 22 August 1939. On the same day the RAF issued its Air Ministry Instructions and Notes on the Rules to be observed by the RAF in war. As well as reiterating Chamberlain's three points as the British interpretation of International Law, these instructions discussed the definition of 'legitimate military objective' which the RAF considered ill-defined. It gave the following direction:

> A difficulty which arises in attempting to translate these principles into practical rules is that there exists no internationally agreed definition of what is to be regarded as a 'legitimate military objective'. It is, however, possible to divide targets broadly into three categories as follows:-

23   Spaight, British Bombing Policy.
24   Alex Bellamy, 'The Ethics of Terror Bombing: Beyond Supreme Emergency', *Journal of Military Ethics*, 7:1 (2008), pp.41-65.
25   Spaight, British Bombing Policy, COS Meeting 915 Annex I.

Category A: targets which, by reason of international agreements such as the Red Cross
    Convention (author's note– presumably Hague 1907), or the accepted customs and
    usage of war, must be regarded as definitely illegitimate;
Category B: targets, the legitimacy of which could not be questioned even in the present
    unregulated state of air warfare;
Category C: targets as to whose legitimacy it is impossible to set down a hard and fast rule;
    the legality of attacking these targets may depend upon the circumstances and the
    manner in which the attack is made. The selection of targets in this category will…
    depend upon the policy of His Majesty's Government at the time.

As regards Category A, it is clear that attacks upon the civil population as such, or upon
hospitals, hospital ships, and other places where the sick and wounded are collected, are
definitely forbidden. Attacks upon buildings devoted to religion, art, charitable purposes,
or science, and upon historic monuments must also be regarded as illegal provided these
buildings are not being used for military purposes.[26]

By these Air Ministry instructions, British Government policy and its interpretation of the
Law of War in 1939 was that religious buildings could only be attacked if they were being
used for military purposes. Commentators have made the point that occupation of the Abbey
was irrelevant to the decision to destroy it. The occupation by military forces is the only legal
criteria upon which its destruction could be warranted. As the war progressed, more and more
Category C targets were attacked in the area offensive that resulted in great losses of civilian
life. This expansion did not change the British interpretation of Category A entities. On 2
September 1939, after an appeal to belligerents by Roosevelt, the British and French reiterated
their intention to restrict air warfare to military objectives 'in the narrowest sense of the word.'
This meant abiding by the direction given in the Air Ministry's instructions. On the same day
the Committee for Imperial Defence discussed Britain's response to unrestricted air attacks.
The CID decided that in that event Britain would broaden its military objective definition
to 'objectives vital to Germany's war effort, and in particular her oil supplies.' This would fall
within the Category C target definition. Category A targets would remain protected.
    As the Chief of the Air Staff predicted, it did not take long for the 'gloves to come off.' He
wrote to the RAF commander in France, Air Marshal Sir Arthur Barratt, on 16 October 1939
relaxing some of the restrictions:

Owing to German action in Poland, we are no longer bound by restrictions under the
instructions governing naval and air bombardment of 22/8 nor by our acceptance of
Roosevelt's appeal. Our action is now governed entirely by expediency, i.e. what it suits us
to do having regard to (a) the need to conserve our resources, (b) probable enemy retali-
atory action, and (c) our need still to take into account to some extent influential neutral
opinion.[27]

26 Spaight, British Bombing Policy.
27 Spaight, British Bombing Policy.

By its words, this note allowed almost limitless power to attack any targets with all previous instructions, and by inference, the Law of War being null and void. This was not the case. Barratt asked CAS whether he could 'start bombing targets behind the line regardless of civilian ban?' CAS replied that bombing was still subject to the principles stated by Chamberlain in his speech in June 1938. The British still considered the deliberate targeting and bombing of civilians and civilian structures as illegal. A week later the position was clarified by the British Government. If Germany were to use indiscriminate methods against France, Belgium or Britain, the vital industries of the Ruhr would be attacked by the RAF. The death of civilians in this case was to be expected, but the target would be against Germany's industrial power; the deaths of civilians would be incidental.

Following the invasion of the Low Countries, France and Norway, new bombing instructions were approved by the British CoS and issued to RAF commanders in June 1940. These instructions directed that:

> 3. Bombardment by naval and air forces is to be confined to military objectives and must be subject to the following general principles:-
> a) The intentional bombardment of civil population as such is illegal.
> b) It must be possible to identify the objective.
> c) The attack must be made with reasonable care to avoid undue loss of civil life in the vicinity of the target.
> d) The provisions of the Red Cross Conventions are to be observed.

The instructions proceeded to describe what constituted a legitimate military objective. For the Abbey, the pertinent instruction is that 'Provided that the principles set out in paragraph 3 above are observed, other objectives, the destruction of which is an immediate military necessity, may be attacked for particular purposes.'[28]

On 30 October 1940, the Air Ministry directed Bomber Command to attack the morale of the German people. It did not allow attacks directly on the civilian population. The aim was to 'demonstrate to the enemy the power and severity of air bombardment and the hardship and dislocation that will result from it.' The method for achieving this was to attack oil, aluminium and component factories, not civilian areas. There was an acceptance that some profitable military targets would be in populated areas, although civilians were considered incidental to the objectives. It was recognised that there would be heavy civilian loss of life, but this was not the prime purpose, at least in official documents. The exception to this policy was reprisal attacks. In April 1941, Downing Street issued the following statement regarding their intentions should the Germans bomb cities in the Mediterranean:

> In view of the German threats to bomb Athens and Cairo, His Majesty's Government wish it to be understood that if either of these two cities is molested they will begin the systematic bombing of Rome. Once this has begun it will continue as convenient till the end of the war. The greatest care will be taken not to bomb the Vatican City and the strictest orders to that effect have been issued.[29]

28   Spaight, British Bombing Policy.
29   TNA CAB 69/2: Meeting at 10 Downing Street dated 18 April 1941.

The British Defence Committee, however, backed away from this position in July 1941, when they discounted bombing Naples in response to an attack on Alexandria.[30]

This remained British bombing policy until 9 July 1941 when the Air Ministry issued Bomber Command with instructions that authorised area bombing of German cities when precision attacks were impractical. The policy continued suggesting that targets were the rail centres in German industrial cities; it also accepted that the area attacks would be against populous working-class areas where 'the psychological effect would be the greatest.' This was still viewed as a secondary and incidental effect of bombing. Considering the inaccuracy of RAF bombing and the use of unaimable incendiaries, the distinction between bombing rail centres and civilians was opaque and the attacks should be viewed as indiscriminate. No British bombing instruction up to July 1941 called for direct targeting by air bombardment of the civilian population or civilian infrastructure. On 21 July 1941 in a Defence Committee meeting British Foreign Secretary Sir Anthony Eden advocated bombing centres of population after night-precision attacks on the German oil industry proved ineffective.[31] His view was supported by Churchill. The Committee decided to give oil one more chance, but the writing was on the wall.

The Rubicon was crossed when area bombing policy was formalised on 22 February 1942. Harris was appointed AOC-in-C RAF Bomber Command, and the British government adopted the Lindemann 'dehousing' plan on 30 March 1942 that directly targeted civilian dwellings. As the bomber campaigns intensified, the US Eighth Air Force joined the campaign in late 1942 and through 1943, the acceptable threshold of German civilian casualties became higher and higher. British Army lawyer Major General A P V Rogers offers the view that the relaxation of the rules is a result of confusion over the definition of the term 'undefended' and whether a town in general became defended when the military were located within it or whether only the military entities became valid objectives.[32] This rationale is not sustainable if one reads Spaight's work and did not apply in the case of the Abbey. It remained the case that although the primary effect was the erosion of morale, this effect was not realised through direct attack on civilians, although there it was true that many civilians contributed to the war effort through their employment. In August 1942, the Air Ministry insisted on changing the directive from reading 'industrial populations' to 'industrial centres' to avoid the impression that Bomber Command was targeting civilians.[33] The British kept secret the policy of deliberate targeting of civilians until 1961 when it was revealed by Sir Charles Snow.

This policy did not apply to the occupied territories, to which Italy could be added after September 1943. On 21 April 1943, CAS, now Air Chief Marshal Portal wrote to Eaker of the US Eighth Air Force regarding French civilian casualties:

> I am sure that the high standard of accuracy achieved by your bomber crews in recent operations is generally realised. It is clear, however, from the diagrams which we recently examined in connection with your new plan that in spite of this standard of accuracy, high altitude bombing in heavily populated areas must inevitably result in considerable civilian

---

30 TNA CAB 69/2: DO (41) 45th Meeting of the War Cabinet Defence Committee (Operations) dated 3 July 1941.

31 TNA CAB 69/2: DO (41) 52nd Meeting War Cabinet Defence Committee (Operations), dated 21 July 1941

32 Rogers, p13.

33 Richard Overy, *The Bombing War* (London: Penguin Books, 2013), Kindle Edition Location 5321.

British Chief of the Air Staff and agent for strategic bombing on the Combined Chiefs of Staff, Air Chief Marshal Sir Charles Portal. Although an area bombing advocate, Portal warned Eaker regarding excessive civilian casualties outside Germany. (NARA RG80-G-042146)

casualties. We can accept this fact in attacks on Germany, but we cannot accept it in enemy occupied countries unless the objective is of outstanding economic or military importance.

We will examine the 'high standard of accuracy' later, but this letter reaffirmed that the Allies had a lower appetite for allied and neutral civilian casualties. The civilians in the Abbey on 15 February 1944, were neither of economic nor military importance and they were from a country that was officially a co-belligerent, partly occupied by the Germans. This was recognised by Eisenhower in September 1943 when he wrote of the capitulation of Italy:

My views are summarized as follows. In our future relations with Italy there are only two courses:

1. To accept and strengthen the legal government of Italy under the King and Badoglio; to regard this government and the Italian people as co-belligerents…
2. To sweep this government aside, set up an Allied military government of occupied Italy…

Of these two courses, on military grounds, I strongly recommend the first.[34]

34   Chandler et al, *Eisenhower Papers Vol III*, p.1435.

Eisenhower's recommendation was accepted; Italy became a co-belligerent on 23 September. Portal was the agent of the CCS for the strategic bombing campaign and therefore his views reflected Allied policy. Although his letter to Eaker was in reference to northwestern Europe, his statement regarding enemy occupation was not specific and a few months later would include Italy and the Abbey.

The British bombing campaign eventually descended into an attack, if still veiled, onto Germany's civilian population. The Americans mostly refused to follow this path in the European War. This was surprising considering that the US Army generally followed the strategy of annihilation. This meant that they tried to win wars 'in the shortest time, with the most efficient use of resources and the fewest possible American casualties.'[35] Laws or morality would usually be secondary to that aim, but the USAAF adopted a precision bombing doctrine from the beginning and could not be persuaded to join the British. Although the weather in the European theatre often meant bombing through clouds, this was hidden through use of the English language. In the first six weeks of 1944, the US heavy bombers flew 21-missions, only six of which were visual due to poor weather.[36] The US doctrine of precision attack and therefore fewer civilian casualties developed from the pioneers in the Air Corps Tactical School (ACTS) in the early 1930s.

Many graduates of the school went on to high command, including Ira Eaker, Carl Spaatz and Harold George. George was the mastermind behind Air War Plans Division Plan 1 (AWPD-1), the bible of USAAF precision attack in the Second World War. By 1939, the Army War College taught that attacking civilians was 'butchery in the eyes of a trained soldier.'[37] There was little difference between the US and Britain in their viewpoints on the deaths of civilians. From this point, the costs of defeat to Britain became vastly more than to the Americans and the willingness to go further to achieve victory diverged. The US followed this path in late 1944 and 1945 when trying to defeat Japan from the air. They had little hesitancy in conducting area attacks in these circumstances.

The USAAF doctrine regarding the bombing of civilians was generally supported by US public opinion. The plea from Roosevelt to the belligerents in 1939 reflected the American desire to limit the damage. This is not to say that American leaders, both civilian and military, were all morally repulsed by the area offensive, but they believed that precision was likely to result in the quick victory that their philosophy demanded. Arnold supported this strategy, but had few moral issues with the Tokyo fire-raid in March 1945. His public utterances did not always reflect his private beliefs.[38] He always went to great lengths to keep US public opinion on the side of his force and laying waste to German cities would have been counterproductive. Not all senior Americans thought this way. Secretary of War, Stimson, a gentleman in every way, was morally repulsed by the thought of attacking civilians. The greatest advocate of the precision approach was Spaatz. He knew that the available technology did not allow for great precision, but instead of opting to follow the RAF route, he pressed for improvement through training and tactics. Spaatz like his chief, showed little moral or legal angst when he commanded the force that used the atomic bombs. The air commander in the Mediterranean was Eaker. Despite

---

35   Crane, pp.8-9.
36   David R Mets, *Master of Airpower: General Carl A Spaatz* (Novato CA: Presidio Press, 1997), p.191.
37   Crane, p.23.
38   Crane, p.33.

convincing Churchill at Casablanca that daylight precision bombing was an effective counter-foil to the RAF's night efforts, he was not as wedded to the doctrine as Spaatz, although he did speak out against 'throwing the strategic bomber at the man in the street.'[39] To all the US commanders the concept of Military Necessity had little to do with civilians, nor ethics, nor morals, nor Law; it was a ruthless desire to win and the key to the independence of their force. Attacking civilian areas was not the way American airmen believed they would be successful.

Why did British and Commonwealth commanders judge that this building's destruction was necessary? It was stated at the time,[40] and in post-war publications such as the Air Historical Branch (AHB) Narrative and in a report for the British Official Historian by the AHB's Guy Hartcup, that the German military occupation was not the major reason. It was rather that its physical location, its dominating position and its potential for use in the future, or as a last redoubt were more important and therefore it was 'destined to be a target.'[41] The US Judge Advocate General's,1943 training manual, quoting from International Court of Justice lawyer, Sir Hersch Lauterpacht, questioned this reasoning, stating that, 'it has been denied that such a force may destroy provisions in the possession of private enemy inhabitants in order to prevent the enemy from using them in the future.'[42] Soldier and author Majdalany called occupation 'the great red herring.'[43] A more recent historian, Peter Caddick-Adams called the argument an 'entirely fatuous debate.'[44] Carlo D'Este called the occupation irrelevant; Eaker, after firstly claiming that intelligence confirmed its occupation, then called it 'immaterial'. Another British author, Colonel J H Green, belittled those who disagreed with the Abbey's destruction by implying:

> To the critics, mainly non-military, the question was as straight forward as it was naïve. Were the Germans in the Abbey before 15th February? If not, its destruction was totally unjustified and to be condemned. It was one thing to sit in an armchair making lofty pronouncements and another to have to make decisions on which hundreds of soldiers' lives depended.[45]

Freyberg, commander of the assaulting ground forces, asserted that the building was defended and therefore a valid target whether occupied or not. The 'occupation doesn't matter' defence has been a regular argument made by those wishing to justify the attack. It is neither fatuous nor a red herring and ownership of an armchair does not preclude a reasoned opinion. Who occupies a target, and to what purpose they put it, is the only relevant consideration when destruction is contemplated. To say anything different is to show a serious misunderstanding, if not contempt, for the Laws of War. To fulfil the definition of 'Military Necessity' as it was applied at the time, there must have been solid proof that the building was 'defended' for it to be a legitimate target.

---

39   Crane, p.41.
40   TNA CAB 106/699: Memorandum No. 433/1/G.
41   Hartcup, 12 and 23. RAF Narrative – The Italian Campaign 1943-1945 – Volume 1, 281. Also see John Strawson, *The Italian Campaign* (London: Secker and Warburg, 1987), p.150.
42   Judge Advocate General's School. Law of Land Warfare. Ann Arbor MI: United States War Department, 1943, p.46.
43   Majdalany, *Portrait*, p.118.
44   Caddick-Adams, p.139
45   J.H. Green, *Cassino 1944* (Cassino: Lamberti Editore, 1989), p.45.

Freyberg's use of the word 'defended' is ambiguous. Did he mean that the building itself was defended by German forces inside it, or did he mean that it was defended by the Germans that occupied Monastery Hill outside the Abbey? It is not clear. The US War Department Field Manual FM 27-10, The Rules of War, published in 1940, and the most up-to-date US interpretation of the Laws of War in 1944, defined a defended place as:

> A place that is <u>occupied</u> by a combatant military force or through which such a force is passing.[46]

In addition, FM 27-10 stated that:

> In sieges and bombardments, all necessary steps must be taken to spare, as far as possible, buildings dedicated to religion, art, science, or charitable purposes, historic monuments, hospitals… provided that they are not being used at the time for military purposes.[47]

From the definition, Freyberg was wrong to call the Abbey 'defended' unless there were German troops occupying it, rather than in its proximity. It is equally wrong, as Freyberg's countryman and close colleague Howard Kippenberger argued after the war, to justify the attack based upon its potential for military use:

> As Commander of 2 NZ Division I said that the Abbey must be destroyed. It was a *place d'armes*, a potential fortress and observation post which could not be left intact on the crest of a hill our troops were required to storm. Whether occupied or not didn't matter. If not occupied today, it might be tonight or while the assault was underway.[48]

Kippenberger was correct that the Germans could have occupied the Abbey and that this may have been disadvantageous to the assault. The Law made no mention of potential, only of actual occupation. This argument could be used to justify an attack on any building and is therefore as absurd as saying that anyone is capable of committing a future crime and should be locked up, just in case. The Germans did not occupy the Abbey during the 34th Division assault and there was no intelligence that they would. In a letter to Kippenberger, Freyberg gave his definition of defended to be where 'any soldier is denying a dominating feature to the enemy.'[49] This definition did not correspond to the Law of War in 1944. Freyberg argued against himself when stating, 'nobody wants to sit on an obvious target.'[50] In November 1949, writing to Brigadier Harry Latham of the Cabinet Office and the originator of the report written by historian Major Francis Jones that shall be examined later, Kippenberger rationalised the Abbey's destruction not on facts but on what the soldiers thought, 'every soldier in the Divisions held up at Monte

---

46   US War Department Field Manual FM27-10, *The Laws of War* (Washington DC: United States War Department, 1940), 12, Paragraph 47c. <http://www.loc.gov/rr/frd/Military_Law/pdf/rules_warfare-1940.pdf > (accessed 5 May 2010).
47   FM27-10,14 para 58.
48   Harper and Tonkin Covill, Kindle loc 770. Quoting from: Kippenberger letter to J.L. Scoullar, 6 January 1956, WAII 11/6, Archives of New Zealand.
49   Lord Freyberg, Letter to HK Kippenberger, 11 August 1950 in Jones, p.180.
50   Lord Freyberg, Letter to HK Kippenberger, 11 August 1950 in Jones, p.180.

Cassino believed implicitly that the Abbey was being used as an observation post and as a fortress. They would have been disgusted with their Commanders if it had been left alone.'[51]

Others, like Spaight, have jumped upon the suggestion that it was a 'fortress'. The dictionary definition of fortress is:

A military stronghold, especially a strongly fortified town.[52]

Former RAF bomber pilot Andrew Brookes made this assertion for the prestigious Royal United Services Institute.[53] The implication of the word 'fortress' is that the building has a military function and was a valid military target. At no time in its recent history was the Abbey used as a defensive position or a garrison. Its occupation by military forces in the distant past had been for defensive purposes when the Abbey lay at the periphery of unstable regimes. The use of the word 'fortress' thereby implied 'fortified' which thereby led to 'defended', making it a lawful military objective.[54] Its origin as a fortress probably came from the books on the Abbey obtained in Naples a few days before the bombing, which has been said to state that the monastery was turned into a fortress in 1230.[55] Except that it did not say any such thing. This book is almost certainly the 1879 Baedeker Guide to Southern Italy, which says: 'The extensive edifice, the interior of which resembles a castle rather than a monastery.'[56] There is no mention of any military fortifications in this guide, beyond the reference to a castle.

There were two questions. Were all necessary steps taken to preserve this building or was its destruction vital to military success? Was the building being used for military purposes, and was it defended as Freyberg claimed? The FM 27-10, although applicable to US forces was still relevant because even though the destruction of the building was requested by a British unit, the force that carried it out was entirely American and the commander of the MAAF was also an American and subject to his nation's interpretation of the relevant International Law customs and conventions which are laid out in this Field Manual.

In addition to Chamberlain's statement in 1938, the British officers were subject to the *British Manual of Military Law*, Chapter XIV (The Laws and Usages of War on Land), revised in 1940. Neither of these military manuals, constituted Law, but were reflective guides to the rules of The Hague Convention, the overarching legal instrument. It has been argued that the Hague Convention only applied to warfare on land and not to attack from the air. It was true that no specific treaty existed on the regulation of air power, but it is true that the Hague Rules were applied to air warfare against land targets, as confirmed by the British Prime Minister in 1938. Both Britain and the US accept that there are two applicable Laws of War. These are Customary and Treaty laws. Customary Law is not necessarily articulated in a Treaty or Convention but is accepted by most nations. The white flag of Truce is an example of a Customary Law of War. Treaty Law is law that has been formally codified and ratified in a Treaty or Convention such as

51   H.K Kippenberger, Letter to Brigadier H B Latham dated 3 November 1949 in Jones, p.179.
52   *Concise Oxford English Dictionary, Eleventh Edition* (revised) (Oxford: Oxford University Press, 2006), p.560.
53   Andrew Brookes 'How Precious is Culture?', *RUSI Journal*, 145:5, (2000), pp.53-58.
54   Judge Advocate General's School. Law of Land Warfare. Ann Arbor MI: United States War Department, 1943, p.40.
55   TNA CAB 106/699, p.96.
56   Karl Baedeker, *Baedeker's Southern Italy and Sicily* (Leipzig: Baedecker's, 1880), pp.5-6.

The Hague or Geneva Conventions. Treaty Laws are only applicable to states that have signed and ratified them whereas Customary Law applies to all. When sufficient States have signed a Treaty, it may be considered Customary.

What is Military Necessity? In his account of the moral decisions made by American airmen, Schaffer made the point that there was 'substantial dispute' over these two words.[57] There is also a problem of perception. The principle may be viewed through opposing lenses. The first, often favoured by the military, was a permissive lens in that any act that furthers military progress is necessary. This view was used to carry out activities that could have been done differently, but which were less convenient. The second lens is restrictive, where the literal meaning of the word 'necessity' is rigorously applied. This view is favoured by those whose priority is humanitarian. In this view Military Necessity does not mean, 'safer' or 'easier' or 'quicker'. It means no other way. Military Necessity has become a caveat, a pathway to action that would otherwise be unlawful. This avoidance of otherwise inconvenient rules has been enshrined in almost every piece of law that protects non-combatants. It still trumps everything else.[58]

The principle can be traced in codified law back to the American Civil War. In 1862, a lawyer, Professor at Columbia University and Prussian émigré, Francis Lieber, was asked to draft a set of laws to guide Union officers unaccustomed to warfare and its customs in the expanded army. The Lieber Code was formally accepted by President Lincoln in April 1863. The Code was the first modern attempt to control actions through a set of written rules, based on the principle of Military Necessity. The definition articulated by Article 14 of the Code is as follows:

> Military Necessity, as understood by modern civilized nations, consists in the necessity of those measures which are indispensable for securing the ends of the war, and which are lawful according to the modern law and usages of war.

Analysis of this definition reveals two words critical to the investigation into the bombing of the Abbey. These are 'indispensable' and 'lawful'. Lieber said that for an action to be necessary there must be no other way of 'securing the ends of the war.' He added that the action must be lawful. He used 'and', not 'or' and both must be proven for an act to meet the principle of Military Necessity. Lieber's Code was echoed by General Eisenhower in his order of 29 December 1943 where he argued that Military Necessity should not be confused with military convenience, echoing the humanitarian interpretation.

Article 15 then states what is permissible under the principle of Military Necessity:

> Military Necessity admits of all direct destruction of life or limb of armed enemies, and of other persons whose destruction is incidentally unavoidable in the armed contests.[59]

The key words here are 'incidentally unavoidable'. Was the Abbey's destruction an unavoidable act and were the deaths of civilians and the destruction of civilian property incidental? Were there no reasonable alternatives?

---

57   Ronald Schaffer, p. xii.
58   Craig Forest, 'The Doctrine of Military Necessity and the Protection of Cultural Property During Armed Conflicts', *The California Western International Law Journal)* 37:2 (2007), p.43.
59   Gary Solis, *The Law Of Armed Conflict* (Cambridge: Cambridge University Press, 2012), p.42.

As military lawyer and scholar Air Commodore William Boothby pointed out, the Lieber Code had no power in international law, but it formed the principles from which Treaty Law was drawn.[60] Following Lieber, the concept of Military Necessity was further developed by the 1868 St Petersburg Treaty where the necessity of small calibre exploding bullets was questioned and the weapons banned. The definition of Military Necessity was also exported, with Prussia adopting it in 1870. The Germans subverted the humanitarian principle, turning it into the military doctrine of *kriegsraison*, arguing that anything was justified to achieve advantage and that the rules ceased when required by the situation. This culminated with German reprisals and atrocities in the Second World War. In response to this argument, referring to destruction of property, the International Military Tribunal stated:

> The destruction of property to be lawful must be imperatively demanded by the necessities of war. Destruction as an end in itself is a violation of international law. There must be some reasonable connection between the destruction of property and the overcoming of the enemy forces…Military necessity or expediency does not justify a violation of positive rules. International law is prohibitive law.[61]

Military Necessity has been used as an excuse for action based upon a commander's desire to see progress, regardless of how tangential to the ultimate ends that may be. Hilaire McCoubrey, using examples at Nuremburg made it clear that: 'Military necessity is a doctrine of self-defence which is only capable of being pleaded where no reasonably practicable alternative course of action has existed'[62]

For the Abbey there were a few practicable alternatives and therefore the attack may not be seen as necessary. Military Necessity is also a movable principle. What might not be militarily necessary today may be tomorrow, depending upon the circumstances. It is judged upon the level of warfare that the decision-maker is considering the necessity. What may be necessary to achieve a tactical objective in a single encounter may not be so important at the operational level and may be almost irrelevant at the strategic level. Wherever and whenever it occurs, Military Necessity did not equate to 'whatever it takes.'[63] The key point is that Lieber and Lincoln developed the principle to <u>limit</u> military acts to those that are necessary <u>and</u> those that are lawful. It is a restraint on destructive activities rather than a permissive principle. Rogers takes the reader step by step through the principle's development, coming to the conclusion that Military Necessity is 'the principle that forbids destructive acts unnecessary to secure a military advantage.'[64] The principle should be a guide for military commanders to constrain their activities. It was not an either-or principle which justified acts that would be unacceptable merely because they are considered necessary. The argument of Military Necessity could not justify breaking the Laws of War.[65] Some

---

60   William Boothby, *The Law of Targeting* (Oxford: Oxford University Press, 2012), p.15.
61   United States v. List (The Hostage Case), Case No. 7 (Feb. 19, 1948), reprinted in 11 TRIALS OF WAR CRIMINALS BEFORE THE NUREMBERG MILITARY TRIBUNALS UNDER CONTROL COUNCIL LAW NO. 10, at p.1253–56.
62   McCoubrey, pp.201-202.
63   Solis, p.259.
64   Rogers, pp.6-7.
65   UK Ministry of Defence, *The Manual of the Law of Armed Conflict* (Oxford: Oxford University Press, 2005), p.23.

have argued that in dire emergency this was the case, but it could not be argued that the bombing of the Abbey would fall into this category even if it were accepted as valid. There was no dire emergency; the Allies would not suffer any defeat in front of Cassino.

Both Allied manuals articulated the requirements of the Hague Convention of 1907, to which the US, Britain and Germany were all ratified signatories.[66] Article 27 of The Hague Conventions was the latest in several international treaties dealing with the destruction of culturally important property. It read as follows:

ARTICLE 27
In sieges and bombardments all necessary steps must be taken to spare, as far as possible, buildings dedicated to religion, art, science or charitable purposes, historic monuments, hospitals, and places where the sick and wounded are collected, provided they are not being used at the time for military purposes.

It is the duty of the besieged to indicate the presence of such buildings or places by distinctive and visible signs, which shall be notified to the enemy beforehand.[67]

The principle of sparing religious property dated back to the *pax dei* of the late tenth century but was first written down in the Brussels Declaration of 1874. The Hague Conventions of 1899, updated in 1907, governed hostilities in Europe in the Second World War. These were laws written for warfare in a bygone age. The Laws of Armed Conflict in the first half of the twentieth century were still appropriate for the American Civil War.[68] The only mention of war in the third dimension was a temporary ban on military balloons firing projectiles! Despite the removal of the balloon ban in 1907, the jurists added to Article 25 when considering bombardment, the words 'by whatever means', which covers air bombardment, although Germany declined to sign this clause. These laws were out of date in 1914, never mind 1944.

The destruction of the Abbey was not incidental to an attack on any military objective, or to use more modern language, it cannot be argued that it was collateral damage. The deaths of several hundred Italian civilians could only be viewed as collateral damage if the Abbey was a legitimate military target. Collateral damage is not a term used in 1944, but is defined as:

Unintentional or incidental injury or damage to persons or objects that would not be lawful military targets in the circumstances ruling at the time. Such damage is not unlawful so long as it is not excessive in light of the overall military advantage anticipated from the attack.[69]

66   Convention (IV) respecting the Laws and Customs of War on Land and its annex: Regulations concerning the Laws and Customs of War on Land. The Hague, 18 October 1907. International Committee for the Red Cross. <http://www.icrc.org/ihl.nsf/FULL/195?OpenDocument> (accessed 5 May 2010).
67   Laws and Customs of War On Land (Hague IV), Article 27, Signed 18 October 1907, <https://www.loc.gov/law/help/us-treaties/bevans/m-ust000001-0631.pdf > (accessed 1 March 2010).
68   Solis, p.80.
69   Chairman of Joint Chiefs of Staff, United States Department of Defence, Joint Publication 3-60 – Joint Targeting, dated 13 April 2007, GL-6. <https://www.dtic.mil/doctrine/new_pubs/jp3_60.pdf > (accessed 15 July 2010).

The term has been deemed dehumanising, an antiseptic and euphemistic description of accepting civilian deaths and damage for a greater military outcome. It can either be inflicted accidentally, through malfunction or mistake, or incidentally through the positive acceptance of civilian casualties. That damage to civilian property or loss of life is accepted as a cost does not pass moral judgement on the validity of the attack in the first place. Although the term is recent, the principles associated with it are as ancient as the Abbey itself and ironically were developed by a local. Catholic doctrine speaks of a set of moral principles called Double Effect, devised by St Thomas Aquinas in the thirteenth century as a device to reconcile the pacifist Christian faith with violent acts committed in its name.[70] Aquinas was born in Aquino, less than 10-miles from the Abbey. His birthplace, the Castle of Roccasecca, was near Baade's headquarters when the Abbey was bombed. Double Effect's first principle is that actions should not intentionally harm innocent people. Actions should intend to achieve a good result. The Doctrine accepted, however, that well-intentioned actions may have foreseeable incidental negative results other than those intended. The action was morally acceptable if that bad result did not outweigh the good intended.

The argument that the damage to the Abbey was incidental is problematic because it was clearly wrong that the destruction was 'collateral damage,'[71] proportional to the military advantage accrued. There are two reasons for this: its destruction was not incidental to an attack on a military target because the Abbey was the target. It is this that sets it apart from other damage to religious or cultural sites. In bombing offensives by both sides, sites such as Cologne or Coventry Cathedrals were badly damaged. These were not the target of the attack, but were damaged incidentally.[72] Hartcup made a related point in the conclusion to his report to the British Official Historian: 'Its dominating position was vital to the defence… if the Germans were not in the Abbey, their positions were in close proximity to it. In order to neutralise these positions by aerial or artillery bombardment the Abbey would inevitably suffer damage.'[73]

Everything Hartcup says is true. Had German fighting positions close to the Abbey been targeted, and had the Abbey suffered incidental damage, even including destruction, that could have been a lawful and necessary action if the damage had been judged against the military advantage. But it was not these positions that were targeted; the Abbey itself was targeted and it was damage to German positions that was incidental. A second problem with the collateral damage argument is that there was no military advantage anticipated as the Germans quickly occupied the ruins, thereby improving their defences before ground forces attacked the position. Evidence that military commanders judged that they would do so was plentiful and no reasonable commander could anticipate any concrete and definite military advantage.[74] German propaganda leaflets following the attack had no difficulty in making this point very clear:

70   David Oderberg, 'Doctrine of Double Effect' in Timothy O'Connor and Constantine Sandis (eds.), *A Companion to the Philosophy of Action* (London: Blackwell Publishing, 2010), pp.324-330..

71   Nigel De Lee, 'Moral Ambiguities in the Bombing of Monte Cassino', *Journal of Military Ethics* 4:2 (2005), pp.129-38.

72   The target of the RAF's night area bombing offensive was the morale of the German population. Whether this was a valid target set under the Hague Convention IV, 1907, is beyond the scope this book, but the aim was not to destroy Germany's cultural and religious infrastructure. See Arthur Harris, *Bomber Offensive* (London: Greenhill Books, 1998), p.77.

73   Hartcup, p.26.

74   FM27-10, p.82 para 324.

By violating this sanctuary of Christianity, your bombers have given us full right to incorporate the ruins of the monastery into our defensive system. The ruins have been transformed by our men into a formidable fortress which has wasted all your efforts during the last few weeks and caused an indefinable number of dead and maimed.[75]

Permissible devastation under the Laws of War could only be taken against buildings, not against civilians.[76] For their actions to be legal, Allied commanders must have proven occupation by the enemy, and then once the building was attacked taken immediate steps to destroy the enemy. They did neither. The postponements of the ground attack were known prior to the final orders for the air attack being issued. The air attack could have been cancelled when commanders knew the attack did not support immediate ground manoeuvre. Because no advantage could be gained, the attack must be viewed as unnecessary and consequently unlawful.

The bombing of Monte Cassino has also been justified by comparing it with the bombing of road communications in Albano within the Papal Estate at Castelgandolfo on the 1-2 February, arguing that the same principles applied and therefore precedent was set. The discussion by Eaker of the MAAF was set forth in a telegram on 2 February.[77]

Gould and later Hartcup of the AHB both made this comparison, using Alexander's decision to bomb the Papal estate to justify the subsequent attack at Montecassino.[78] This comparison is not valid. All targets must be judged on their own circumstances. The casualties and damage at Castelgandolfo should be seen as incidental to an attack on German military facilities, not an attack on the estate itself. This may be described as 'collateral' and therefore possibly proportionate. Proportionate damage to one civilian object does not set a precedent for the lawfulness of another similar object. As the US Judge Advocate General's 1943 manual pointed out, 'Deliberate or reckless bombing of non-combatants is forbidden as is bombardment for terrorizing the civilian population.'[79] At Castelgandolfo the civilian population was not targeted, at Montecassino it was. The relative values and the costs must be weighed for each. There was a distinct difference in the object of each of these attacks, although both were on Eisenhower's list of protected sites. The Castelgandolfo, Papal buildings were not the target. The target was a road junction within the estate, which was being used by the Germans. This junction was a military objective, for which there was Military Necessity, as it was being used in German operations against the Anzio beachhead. It was reasonable to assume that the successful interdiction of this junction would accrue a definite military advantage by disrupting logistics. Any civilian damage was incidental to the attack rather than the object of it.[80] We can say this because Fifth Army intelligence knew that civilians were in the Abbey, and they knew that the Germans were not.

That does not mean, however, that the attack on the extraterritorial property at Castegandolfo was lawful. This target was not in Italy, but in Vatican State territory, a sovereign nation with which the Allies were not at war. That the Germans had pursued an aggressive act in using Vatican territory did not excuse the Allies doing likewise. Two wrongs do not make a right. The

---

75 Tasciotti, p.185.
76 Spaight, *Air Power and War Rights*, p.257.
77 TNA CAB 106/699: MEDCOS 27, 2 February 1944.
78 Hartcup, p.19.
79 Judge Advocate General's School. Law of Land Warfare. Ann Arbor MI: United States War Department, 1943, p.43.
80 TNA CAB 106/699, pp.15-18.

1 February attack on targets in the area of Castelgandolfo, laid the mental foundations for the justification for bombing the other protected site on Eisenhower's list. The Rubicon of protection for religious sites was crossed on 3 February when the British CoS Committee approved Eaker's orders.[81] The attack was also vindicated by the Foreign Office when on 8 February Rumbold wrote to the CoS Committee secretary regarding immunity to attack of Vatican property:

> It follows that if the Commander-in-Chief is allowed this latitude in the treatment of Vatican properties in Rome during the assault on Rome, he should be allowed a similar latitude in regard to these similar properties during the assault on the localities in which they are situated. In other words, the Commander-in-Chief was not only within his rights, but within his instructions in permitting such action to be taken as resulted in bombs falling on these two properties (ie at Castel Gandolfo).[82]

As Jones pointed out in his 1949 report on the bombing at Cassino, the case of Castelgandolfo and the continuing support for air activity in its vicinity offers the Commander-in-Chief reassurance that:

1.   General Wilson could attack Papal property if in his opinion the situation warranted such action.
2.   That General Wilson was supported by the Government and the Chiefs of Staff in this action.[83]

The conclusion that can be drawn is that Allied governments had given permission to the Allied Commander-in-Chief to break International Law by conducting military operations against a State with which they are not at war. If they were happy for commanders in the Mediterranean to do this, they must have had the confidence that support would be forthcoming in the attack on the Abbey.

81   TNA CAB 106/699, p.16.
82   TNA CAB 106/699, p.17.
83   TNA CAB 106/699, p.18.

13

What is the Right Thing to be Done?

Even in destruction there's a right way and a wrong way – and there are limits.

Albert Camus
The Just Assassins
Act 2[1]

In addition to the law, which was opaque in 1944, there was also the moral aspect of bombing the Abbey. One of the differences between the law and ethics is that the law articulates what can and cannot be done, ethics tells us why. Was it the right thing to do? In his book *Just and Unjust Wars*, a standard text in the field, Michael Walzer made the following observation about the killing of civilians in battle:

> A soldier must take careful aim at his military target and away from non-military targets. He can only shoot if he has a reasonably clear shot, he can only attack if a direct attack is possible. He can risk incidental deaths, but he cannot kill civilians simply because he finds them between himself and his enemies.[2]

In the chapter on the law, the Abbey as a cultural and religious building was the main focus. In this section on morals and ethics we will look more closely at the civilians inside the Abbey and their rights. Civilians started to seek shelter from the fighting after an Allied air raid on Cassino on 10 September 1943; the number possibly reached up to 1,000 at its height. By 5 February 1944, the Abbot's secretary believed that around 800 were in the Abbey with another 200 in the adjacent rabbitry.[3]

The generally accepted traits of Just War theory are *jus ad bellum;* that war should only be fought for a just cause and *jus in bello;* that the participants in war fight justly. These are connected but independent principles. Just because states fight for a just cause, does not mean unjust methods of fighting are permitted. A soldier fighting for his country in an aggressive war or unjust cause should expect to be treated justly if his individual conduct has been correct. 'Just

---

1   Quoted from Michael Walzer, *Just and Unjust Wars* (New York: Basic Books, 1992), p.199.
2   Walzer, p.174.
3   Grossetti and Matronola, pp.96-7.

Italian civilians in Cassino. Several hundred, mostly women, children and the elderly were in the Abbey on the day it was bombed. It is likely that several hundred were killed in the attack, although the exact figure is unknown. These are the survivors. (Bundesarchiv Bild 101I-310-0889-30A/Fotograf: Schmidt)

War Theory insists on a fundamental moral consistency between means and ends.[4] The Just War theory accepts that non-combatant damage is inevitable and morally acceptable if it is proportionate to achieving definite military gains. To be a just war, Walzer suggested that it must be a limited war, where there are rules to prevent the violence being directed at civilians.[5] The Allied cause in Italy was undoubtedly a just one. However, as the war progressed the just ends were sometimes not matched with just means. The limited nature of this war was, by implication, ended with Roosevelt's Unconditional Surrender statement, although it has been suggested that the statement was more rhetoric than reality, with contentions that 'there can be no such thing as a morally mandated unconditional surrender.'[6] It fed the emotional cravings of public opinion in the democratic societies, where great sacrifices were required and where demonising the opponent was a vital political lever to galvanise public opinion.[7] Liddell-Hart describes the policy as 'a deepening danger to the relatively shallow foundations of civilised life.'[8] Allied policy was not truly unconditional, but this statement opened the way to unlimited means to reach the ends, culminating in the atomic attacks.

4   Brain Orend, *The Morality of War* (Plymouth: Broadview Press, 2006), p.105.
5   Walzer, p. xvii.
6   Orend, p.164.
7   Armstrong, p.165.
8   Liddell-Hart, *Revolution in Warfare*, p.74.

Germany surrendered before this crescendo reached its peak, but the atomic bomb project was to be used against Berlin rather than Hiroshima and in Just War theory it is intentions that count. Almost the only means not used by the Allies were biological and chemical warfare. The norm of not bombing civilians cracked quite early.[9] The reason was that the Allies felt that the rationale for holding back had diminished and there was little possibility of reciprocal consequences. After the Blitz ended in May 1941, it was clear that Germany did not possess the strategic air weapon to defeat Britain. Policy from 1938 was written with the *Luftwaffe* in mind and this fear was now gone. Long keen on strategic bombing, Britain could attack Germany with few domestic civilian consequences. The Americans, whom the Axis could also not attack, could also loosen their adherence to the bombing norm. The precision targeting in Europe by the USAAF as opposed to the RAF's area offensive was not a moral choice, as demonstrated by their incendiary attacks on Japan. Their doctrine of precision, though preferable, still resulted in many civilians dying by their hands. The willingness of the Allies to kill hundreds of thousands of civilians was therefore a result of the absolute imbalance of aerial superiority.

Had the atomic bomb been ready a few months earlier it would, in all probability, have been used against Germany and would have been delivered with massive loss of civilian life. Instead, the Allies initially planned under the Morgenthau Plan to turn Germany into an agrarian economy, until the opposition from politicians on both sides of the Atlantic put a stop to this unlimited and wholly unjust proposal that could have resulted in extreme poverty and possibly mass starvation. These two events were as close to unconditional as it is possible to be. As Anne Armstrong stated of the Unconditional Surrender policy, 'the Allies adhered to the strategy of pursuing an unlimited objective with unlimited means.'[10] The attack on the Abbey of Montecassino was a tactical symptom of this slide towards unlimited means to reach victory.

The unassailable nature of the state has meant that world order is generally self-policed in a moral sense, and only barely enforceable legally. Nevertheless, the Second World War was still a limited war, despite its many horrors. Both sides acknowledged limits and to some small extent limited their actions. That is not to say that the actions of the *SS* or *Gestapo* were just, nor some would argue, was the use of the heavy air weapon against civilian populations. But neither side used the most horrific and indiscriminate weapons in their arsenals, at least not until the atomic bomb. The Germans made attempts to destroy the evidence of their death camps; an indication that they knew the immoral nature of this policy. In Italy, for the most part, the fighting between fighting forces was within the rules. The same is not true for German activity against Italian partisans. Reports suggested, despite their ferocious defence at Cassino, the *Fallschirmjager* meted out the worst treatment to Italian civilians.[11] The bombing of the Abbey is a notable exception, where the Allies acted outside norms and conventions by deliberately attacking a protected building and the innocent civilians within it on the flimsiest of evidence and with no reasonable expectation of military gain.

There has been debate and controversy concerning the justification for the use of heavy bombers in the Second World War. Most of the literature is a criticism placed at the feet of the Allies, and in particular the RAF's area bombing campaign. It should not be forgotten that this activity was carried out by the Germans and Japanese as well. The scale of the British bombing

9   Ward Thomas, *The Ethics of Destruction* (Ithaca NY: Cornell University Press, 2001), p.90.
10   Armstrong, p.164.
11   Dagnini-Brey, p.118.

surpassed all but the American efforts against Japan. In the occupied nations, including Italy, it was often the US bombing that was seen to be more indiscriminate by the civilian population.[12] To the Italians, the RAF was perceived as the 'gentlemen of the air', when compared with the seeming indiscriminate nature of American daylight bombing.[13] The Americans were far more feared than the British. This was despite the fact that Italian morale, as predicted by the Italian air doctrine pioneer Emilio Douhet, had begun to collapse under British night bombing and battlefield defeat by the end of 1942. The Americans bombed by day and could be seen in the skies above. Authors such as the British philosopher A C Grayling and German historian Jorg Friedrich have both made the link between area bombing and genocide. The vastness of city bombing and the arguments concerning its usefulness have effectively buried moral and ethical discussions surrounding more isolated events such as the bombing of the Abbey of Montecassino.

Was Eisenhower right when he said that 'If we have to choose between destroying a famous building and sacrificing our own men, then our men's lives count infinitely more and the buildings must go?' This question wasn't only about buildings. It was also about people. The Allies knew that there were several hundred civilians within the Abbey, as well as a few monks and laymen. Their deaths were a foreseeable event. Does Eisenhower's argument stand scrutiny? Eisenhower painted the war as a battle between good and evil, where there can be no compromise in the defeat of evil, by inference an unlimited aim. In effect he made it a religious crusade, refusing to meet the defeated German generals. His memoir is entitled *Crusade in Europe*. The defeat of 'evil' was all that counted and was any contribution therefore an acceptable act? Eisenhower's viewpoint conflates a just war and a war fought justly. Morally, this attitude, suggesting that America's opponents are 'evil', in effect denies them the rights of the *jus in bello* as 'evil' cannot be treated as an equal to 'good', and 'evil' can have no rights. This destruction of an evil enemy inevitably leads to unlimited and unrestrained warfare based on vengeance and hatred.[14]

Is an Allied soldier's life worth 'infinitely more' than the life of an Italian peasant or a Benedictine monk? The Just War tradition is far older than the legal constraints on warfare, reaching back into antiquity, and is a commentary on the morality of war. Within it, combatants are afforded equivalence, regardless of their cause. They are not considered 'evil', merely for fighting for their country or cause. A German soldier had no fewer rights or less value than a British soldier, despite the heinous crimes of the Nazi state. Most soldiers were coerced into fighting through conscription; given the choice neither Tommy nor Fritz would be fighting in the mountains of Italy. Their contribution to the fighting, if it was within the rules, was not a crime and nor was it immoral. The justice of their cause was irrelevant: it is only how they fought that counted. This standpoint is not agreed by all scholars. Some, such as Jeff McMahan, agree that there is a legal equivalence, but that this cannot be stretched to a moral equivalence to those

12 Richard Overy, 'Introduction' in Claudia Baldoli, Andrew Knapp and Richard Overy (eds.), *Bombing, States and Peoples In Western Europe 1940-1945* (London: Continuum International Publishing, 2011), p.16.
13 Gabriella Gribaudi, 'The True Cause of the 'Moral Collapse': People, Fascists and Authorities under the Bombs. Naples and the Countryside, 1940-1944' in Claudia Baldoli, Andrew Knapp and Richard Overy (eds.), *Bombing, States and Peoples In Western Europe 1940-1945* (London: Continuum International Publishing, 2011), p.223.
14 Basil Liddell-Hart, *The Revolution in Warfare* (London: Faber & Faber Ltd, 1946), pp.42-44.

whose cause is unjust.[15] He argues that the equivalence is legally pragmatic, rather than morally correct.

Should a civilian life be considered of less value than a soldier's life? A soldier gives up certain rights and gains others, the right to kill other combatants for example. In Italy some soldiers perhaps found this a little too easy. In Rome in June 1944, Sevareid in conversation with a US paratrooper from the Special Service Force recorded him saying, 'You know it kind of scares me. It's so easy to kill. It solves all your problems, and there's no questions asked.'[16] The civilian does not give up any rights, but in turn they cannot lawfully participate in combat, except in self-defence. It is not very surprising that a general would favour his soldiers over enemy civilians. Although the Principle of Proportionality as a legal term was not part of the law until after the war, there has been a principle of moral proportionality for centuries. Even had a few Germans occupied the Abbey, could the small effect that they could have inflicted on the attacking force have warranted the deaths of hundreds of civilians? The answer to this has to be No. In all the deaths of late January and early February on the hills behind Monte Cassino, not one American soldier died from fire from the Abbey. A civilian's life is just as worthy of consideration in any moral decision as that of a combatant and should be protected from the results of combat to the greatest extent. There were never any thoughts that the building was strongly held by the Germans. The damage upon the attacking force from within the Abbey, had it occurred, would have been minor. Allied casualties would have been taken from the surrounding peaks, not from the Abbey itself. Killing hundreds to save dozens could never be deemed as morally acceptable or legally proportionate.

The Doctrine of Double Effect has been briefly described when considering the lawfulness of the attack. There are four key principles for Double Effect as an ethical and moral judgement and this forms the basis of the modern legal principle of Proportionality:

> The principal effect intended must itself be morally acceptable.
> The evil effect is not intended by the agent, but merely (regrettably) foreseen.
> The evil effect cannot be the means of achieving the good effect.
> There must be an acceptable proportionality between the good effect achieved and the amount of undesired evil effects.[17]

It is one of the measures by which any act that results in foreseeable harm can be judged ethically and morally. The problem applying the Double Effect to the Montecassino attack was that the Abbey's destruction, and therefore the 'evil effect' was not incidental to an attack on adjacent German units, the 'good effect.' All evidence shows that the Abbey itself was the target and therefore the good effect, defeat of Germans, was to be achieved because of the evil effect, rather than vice versa.

This doctrine is based around the intentions of an actor rather than the consequences of the act. The philosophy of Double Effect is often used to justify actions, and although not

15   Jeff McMahan, 'The Sources and Status of Just War Principles', *Journal of Military Ethics* 6:2 (2007), pp.91-106.
16   Sevareid, p.533.
17   Martin L Cook. 'Ethical Issues in Targeting' in Paul A.L. Ducheine, Michael N Schmitt and Frans P.B. Osinga (eds.), *Targeting: The Challenges of Modern Warfare* (The Hague: Asser Press, 2016), pp.151-4.

universally accepted by scholars, it is one benchmark upon which to base the justification of the attack on the Abbey and especially the moral rightness of the deliberate killing of hundreds of innocent civilians taking refuge. Apologists for the attack have claimed that the civilians were offered the opportunity to leave and were warned of the attack by leaflet. By staying, they accepted the consequences and absolved the Allies of moral responsibility for their safety. The dropping of leaflets demonstrated that the Allied intention was not to kill civilians. This argument is flawed because the leaflets were dropped into an active and very intense battle zone less than 24-hours prior to the attack. The warning was vague and gave no indication of timeframe or means. Vicious artillery duels continued throughout the warning period, and there was no truce to allow non-combatants to leave. By leaving without planned arrangements, the monks and the civilians were condemning themselves to certain death or injury. Their opportunity to escape was illusory. The soldiers could not storm the Abbey immediately after it was bombed, and these civilians all died in vain. The Germans then made better use of it which was predictable and anticipated. Even though the stated intended effect was good, the overcoming of an enemy position in a just conflict, the fact that it was impossible to meet and that this was known beforehand negated that positive intention. An act with a stated good intention that was impossible to achieve cannot be a genuinely intended effect. The other difficulty in this case is that the Allies knew the civilians and monks were there beforehand. Their death or injury was more than foreseen, it was certain. Therefore, the validity of the statement that death and injury was unintended is unsustainable.

This argument is that the attack did not intend to kill hundreds of civilians. The victims in the Abbey were guilty of nothing. The attack resulted in no war crimes accusations, but the Allies deliberately killed Italian civilians. Morally, it is difficult to square this circle. The civilian deaths at Montecassino, although not the intention, were a certain and deliberate consequence. They were not merely foreseen, they were unavoidable. The deaths were disproportionate to the military value of the Abbey and were certainly greater than any military casualties that could have been inflicted by soldiers possibly in the Abbey. The military legitimacy of the attack was slight, and many senior officers did not support it. Why should the deaths of innocent civilians inside be anything other than murder? It makes little difference to the victims whether their death is caused by a bullet to the back of the head or by a 500lb bomb. For the executioners, however, it is much easier to kill from 18,000 feet! Perhaps it is the detachment of the bomber crews, where the victims are rarely viewed as individual human beings, that colours our judgement of the crime. As Professor Ward Thomas recounts when discussing the moral anomaly of Churchill's abhorrence at Stalin's idea of executing German Officers and his apparent ambivalence in ordering the raid on Dresden, 'Mass executions, even of those bearing a large measure of responsibility for the war, were unthinkable, whereas the norm against the aerial bombing of noncombatants was an early, if unfortunate, casualty of the exigencies of war.'[18] Is it that moral norms were only followed where they gave the belligerents some military advantage? There was little complaint from the Allies about 'Strategic' bombing of civilians, because they benefitted the most from it.

In a 2009 essay, Tony Coady described combatants' attitudes to the deaths of non-combatants in four categories:

18   Thomas, p.29.

1. Sadistic contempt for non-combatants' lives and well-being, leading to the intentional killing of them.
2. Instrumental disdain for them, leading again to the intentional killing of them.
3. Indifference to their lives and well-being, leading to a casual attitude to collateral damage.
4. Concern for their lives and well-being, leading to attempts to avoid or limit the collateral damage.[19]

The Ardeatine massacre, a month after the Abbey attack without doubt should be placed squarely within Category 1, although not all of the 335-victims should be considered 'non-combatants,' although most were *hors de combat*. The attack on the Abbey is more difficult as tokenistic attempts were made to warn, however vaguely, the civilian occupants. Their escape was impossible, and the Allies went through the motions. The concern after the attack has been mostly for the building rather than the people, and therefore an indifference to their fate is apparent. Consequently, the attack on the Abbey and its occupants falls into Category 3. The only morally acceptable course of action would have been to follow the considerations of Category Four.

Some scholars added that it is insufficient merely to intend a good effect; some positive action has to be taken to reduce unintended bad effects, including accepting increased risks to military forces.[20] The harm meted out to the monks and civilians was disproportionate to the gain that could have been made had a ground assault been possible. Hundreds of dead civilians are not a morally worthwhile cost to remove a few lightly-armed enemy soldiers from an observation position. There have also been attempts to revise the doctrine to add a final condition which is particularly relevant: 'Where there are other feasible ways of achieving the good end that do not involve the harmful side effects or involve fewer or less grave such effects, the agent should choose the event where the alternatives involve somewhat higher costs to the agent.'[21] One potential measure is that the heavy bombers were so inaccurate because of their high altitude. To fly lower would have entailed more risk from anti-aircraft fire, the higher cost to the agent, but the bombing would have been more accurate. This would be valid mitigation if the civilian casualties were outside the Abbey, but as they were inside greater accuracy would have resulted in more deaths and therefore this is not a valid mitigation measure.

There were several alternatives not involving heavy bombers against the Abbey and the civilians inside. This does not rely on hindsight; all these were options considered at the time. The most obvious would have been an agreement with the Germans, using the Vatican as an honest broker, that the Abbey would be considered neutral territory. This was effectively done unilaterally by the Germans, but a reciprocal arrangement was not adopted. The weight of bombers could have been used against the positions surrounding the Abbey that were definitely in German hands and where few civilians were present. Carrying out precision attacks against Point 593, Albaneta Farm and Colle San Angelo could have resulted in shock and possibly a breakthrough.

19 C.A.J. Coady, Bombing and the Morality of War', in Yuki Tanaka and Marilyn B Young (ed.), *Bombing Civilians: A Twentieth Century History* (New York: The New Press, 2009), p.214.
20 Peter Olsthoorn, 'Intentions and Consequences in Military Ethics', *Journal of Military Ethics*, 10:2 (2011), pp.81-93.
21 Anne Schwenkenbecher, 'Collateral Damage and the Principle of Due Care', *Journal of Military Ethics* 13:2 (2014), pp.94-105.

This was not seriously considered due to an increased risk of fratricide. Is fratricide of a few more morally acceptable than the killing of hundreds? The Abbey could have been bypassed by concentrating attacks through Terrelle or Atina as Juin and Tuker wanted. There would have been logistic and time difficulties, but it would have resulted in fewer grave effects on the affected civilians. The Allies could have delivered bombs via fighter-bomber as Freyberg requested. This would have produced some innocent victims, but far fewer than with an intense heavy bombardment. There are no circumstances where the attack passed the tests required of the Doctrine of Double Effect, so under this benchmark it should be judged as militarily unethical.

This not the only moral and ethical yardstick upon which the morality of the act can be judged. Controversially, the 'Supreme Emergency' is possibly a valid justification for conducting what otherwise would be an unjustified act.[22] It offers a paradox, where a decision-maker in dire circumstances has a right to do something that is otherwise morally unacceptable. The RAF's strategic bombing campaign up until 1942 is a possible example. In normal circumstances direct attack on the civilian population of Germany could not be morally countenanced. However, Britain had no other effective weapon to defeat the monstrously evil outcome of Nazi victory, an outcome that looked probable in the first years of the war. To avoid annihilation, the act of city bombing could be the lesser of the two evils. Whether this is a valid argument has been hotly contested since *Just and Unjust Wars* was published. The danger to Britain had largely passed when the RAF began the dehousing campaign in 1942, so the argument appears invalid. How does this argument relate to the attack on the Abbey? Walzer argued that once the dire emergency had been lifted, the British area bombing campaign should have stopped because a 'Supreme Emergency' no longer existed. There was no exceptional reason to deny those within the Abbey immunity. In Italy, in 1944, the Allies were winning. Progress may have been slow, but there were no circumstances that the Germans could have made a recovery, and the fate of the Abbey would not change this. The argument of 'Supreme Emergency' or the commitment of a wrongful act for the greater good is also invalid.

There is the notion that an unethical or immoral act could be accepted if the result was necessary to end the war as quickly as possible. The soldier has no moral requirement to sacrifice himself for civilians as their lives have a moral equivalence. His moral duty is to his comrades and his family at home rather than to some faceless stranger. Some scholars claim this to be flawed morality, but it is real nonetheless. This realist or utilitarian approach is that adopted by the Germans as *kriegsraison*. The necessity of the act justifies it. Good intentions are not relevant to this approach; consequences are more important. Why should generals run higher risks of casualties and operational failure for the sake of saving a few civilians? The old saying, 'all's fair in love and war', suggests that war is no place for the law or morals. Walzer uses Sherman's famous adage, 'war is hell', to explain the doctrine that if on the side of good, anything is acceptable to defeat evil.[23] Eisenhower and the US philosophy of war fits hand and glove with this doctrine. This moral justification is highly dubious and has generally been discredited but was alive and well in 1944. Nevertheless, even the utilitarian morality has limits in its proportionality. Walzer again:

> For then we must grant that soldiers are entitled to try to win the wars they are entitled to fight. That means that they can do their utmost, so long as what they do is actually related

---

22   Walzer, p.251.
23   Walzer, p.32.

to winning. Indeed, they should do their utmost, so as to end the fighting as quickly as possible. The rules of war rule out only purposeless or wanton violence.[24]

In the case of the Abbey, the moral necessity rests on the use made of the attack in subsequent actions. Did the attack contribute to winning or was it 'purposeless?' What were the consequences of the attack? It was a one-off attack, considered necessary on 15 February 1944, but never repeated despite the Germans being unarguably present in the ruins. Repeated attacks until victory was assured could be justified. It was a single attack that failed, carried the appearance of a demonstration of power or a show of force rather than a serious attempt to overcome the enemy. If it was not necessary to attack the position again with such force, even though its status in enemy hands remained the same, how necessary was it in the first place? The fact was that the attack did not further the Allied cause and was never likely to do so. Even on a utilitarian judgement, the consequences of the attack on the Abbey were that it failed, a famous building was destroyed and the people within it died unnecessarily. The consequential as well as the anticipatory justification both failed the ethical test.

A final moral argument is that of *tu quoque* or 'you too'. This essentially stresses that the bad actions of Germany justified the Allies in acting similarly. The Germans had no right to judge Allied actions. This argument is of course fallacious because each act should be judged upon its own merits and morality. One bad act does not justify another. It was noticeable that despite direct attacks on civilian targets by the *Luftwaffe*, only three officers (not including Kesselring) were convicted of war crimes. None of these was for bombing civilians. Perhaps the accusation of *tu quoque* against the RAF contributed to this decision?

Eisenhower's theme in the December order was carried on by British Labour Party peer and Chairman of the British Civil Defence Committee, Lord Charles Latham, representing the British Government in the House of Lords on 16 February 1944 when he quoted three airmen who supposedly criticised clerical opponents by saying, 'These Bishops think buildings are more important than we are.'[25] Perhaps true regarding bricks and mortar, but not correct regarding innocent civilians. The war convention stressed the protection of the innocent even if that meant increased risk to combatants. Father of the RAF, Viscount Hugh Trenchard, defended the action by telling the House how hazardous the airman's job was. Of course, this was irrelevant as to whether the Abbey was being used by the Germans, but it unsurprisingly put Trenchard into the bombing camp. He also used the concepts of 'good' versus 'evil' as an excuse for Total War, just like Eisenhower, dressing all activity as justified as part of a moral crusade. Viscount John Simon, the Lord Chancellor, was equally emphatic that the utilitarian view of Military Necessity counted far more than the preservation of art or culture:

> It is universally accepted and everywhere understood that the necessities of war must be put far in front of any consideration of special historical or cultural value at all…the necessity of getting victory – victory as complete and as quickly as possible – make it ridiculous to compare the needs of that claimant with any artistic or cultural matter whatever.[26]

---

24 Walzer, p.129.
25 House of Lords Debate, Preservation of Art and Historical Treasures, *Hansard*, 16 February 1944, p.820.
26 Viscount Simon, *Hansard*, 16 February 1944.

Simon thought that the 'buildings themselves are of small importance.' He added that all the treasures had been removed, thereby diminishing the building's importance. Simon's utilitarian viewpoint assumed that the Abbey's destruction was a necessary act to achieve complete victory and his opinion on the Abbey's importance would probably not be shared by the monks, the Vatican or by many experts and scholars. He then tries *tu quoque* with the story of how the Germans played a duplicitous game, turning the Abbey into a fortress. In another standard line of defence, the Lord Chancellor then called those that disagreed with the decision 'amateurs.' Finally, Simon stated falsely that the 'monks are not there.'[27] There was no mention at all of the Italian refugees. Of course, Simon was making all this up. He had no information about whether the Germans were in the Abbey. Wilson did not provide his evidence for several weeks. Simon was relying on the BBC like everyone else. In the same debate on 16 February, Conservative Party peer Lord Geddes broadened the utilitarian justification when he said:

> Yet we do not want to use any expression here that would discourage in any way whatever or limit the initiative of our commanders, soldiers, sailors and airmen in winning that victory which we know to be essential, which we know we cannot do without, without which we know if we were not to win the war, there would be no value left in any of the cultural monuments of Europe for our time and probably any other time.[28]

His Lordship is using a similar moral argument to Walzer's Supreme Emergency and *Kreigsraison*, in that the gravity of the situation makes anything that adds to victory necessary, as defeat would be morally worse. Both these justifications are invalid in this case; although the outcome of the war was far from clear, the Allies were winning in all theatres globally. The probability of victory was growing by the day and no existential emergency existed that justified abandoning the laws and ethics of warfare. *The Times*, in reporting the same debate in the House of Lords, followed the same theme:

> Such historic sites as Monte Cassino, though ravaged by successive barbarians from the Lombards to the Nazis, belong to the central deposit of Christian civilization, and the loss of them impoverishes all subsequent ages. On the other hand that which is at stake in this war is the survival of civilisation itself, which is incomparably greater than any of its material expressions. The necessity of victory is paramount over the preservation of any monument, however beautiful, however historic, however sacred. No British or American general is likely to be indifferent to the fate of the precious monuments that lie in the path of war; but neither will he willingly contemplate the sacrifice of more men than strategic necessity makes unavoidable.[29]

The *Times* angle was that the Abbey had been destroyed many times before and that one more destruction hardly mattered. The comment that civilization itself is more important than its material expressions is rich for a paragon of the English Establishment. It is also wrong more

---

27   House of Lords Debate, Preservation of Art and Historical Treasures, *Hansard*, 16 February 1944, p.857.
28   Rennie, p.179, citing *Hansard*.
29   War and Art, *The Times*, 17 February 1944, Issue 49782, p.5.

fundamentally, for what is civilization if it is not the expressions of progress and rich history? The editorial comment read the same as the necessity of *Kriegsraison* where any destruction may be morally justified if it does not increase the sacrifice we ask of our soldiers. This viewpoint was expressed whilst the battle continued to rage and was possibly tinged with the emotion and fervour of the moment. It suggested that rules shouldn't count and that if a general considered it necessary, anything may be destroyed.

Lord Simon's views were not, of course, 'universally accepted'. Former Archbishop of Canterbury, Lord William Lang of Lambeth, put the view that 'The loss of some temporary military advantage … could not be compared with a loss of civilisation and religion which would be for all time, and irreparable.'[30] He was supported by Liberal Lord Samuel in the Lords debate. Having said this, the venerable Lord Lang argued that the German occupation of the Abbey justified the attack. The Bishop of Birmingham was also doubtful making the point that 'Christian people are gravely troubled by the direction the war was taking.' He was perturbed that the Allies were adopting the 'necessity of retaliation' in that if the Germans did unlawful acts, it was okay for the Allies to do so. Or, as stated by British Member of Parliament, diplomat, former Minister and friend to Winston Churchill, Sir Harold Nicolson in an article in *Spectator* in late February 1944:

> I am not among those who feel that religious sites are, as such, of more importance than human lives; nor should I hesitate, were I a military commander, to reduce some purely historical building to rubble if I felt that by doing so I could gain a tactical advantage or diminish the danger to which my men were exposed. Works of major artistic value fall, however, into a completely different category. It is to my mind absolutely desirable that such works should be preserved from destruction, even if their preservation entails the sacrifice of human lives. I should assuredly be prepared to be shot against a wall if I were certain that by such a sacrifice I could preserve the Giotto frescoes; nor should I hesitate for an instant (were such a decision ever open to me) to save St. Mark's even if I were aware that by so doing I should bring death to my sons. My attitude would be governed by a principle which is surely incontrovertible. The irreplaceable is more important than the replaceable, and the loss of even the most valued human life is ultimately less disastrous than the loss of something which in no circumstances can ever be created again.[31]

Sir Harold was strongly against the Abbey's destruction. His assertion that human lives were replaceable whereas the art and culture are not a fringe position whereas Military Necessity does not enter the discussion. Most people would disagree with Nicolson, but one must question what wars are fought for, if they are not fought for is the preservation and values of civilisation? A similar question was asked by the Vatican's *L'Osservatore Romano*:

> There is the debate, point of divergence, lives or stones? That is: are the lives of so many young people who are the present and tomorrow or are the relics of the past more precious? If the necessities of war, if the demands of strategy required the attack of glorious cities…

30   Edsel, p.100.
31   Sir Harold Nicolson, Marginal Comments, *The Spectator*, Feb. 25, 1944, reprinted in full in J. MERRYMAN and A. ELSEN, supra note 17, at 1-85

234   Plumes of Smoke

one should prefer an immunity that would cost a greater sacrifice of human lives or a sacrifice of monuments and memories that was worth less price of crushed existences?[32]

Was anything necessary in order to win? One interested party who took a similar position to Sir
Harold was Slessor. Just a few days later, on 22 February, he wrote to two of his senior officers,
Air Marshal Sir John Linnell and Air Vice Marshal James Robb. Although referring to saving
Florence, Slessor's views were possibly influenced by distaste for the destruction of the Abbey:

> On the question of principle. We say we are fighting to preserve civilization. FLORENCE
> is one of the shrines of European civilization and in my view is of more permanent value to
> the cause for which we are fighting, than a few British or American lives. If we are prepared
> to be killed in defending these things, we should, if necessary, be prepared to accept a small
> added risk of being killed in preserving them from destruction by our own action. [33]

This letter was written when the Germans were making maximum propaganda advantage
from the Abbey. Although not specifically mentioned in the letter, its shadow hangs over it.
He wished to protect the reputation of the Air Forces, something that had been damaged.
His letter, so soon after the Abbey's destruction, offered an insight into the thought processes
following the bombing and may contain an element of hindsight. It did not have to mention the
Abbey for it to loom over these thoughts.

32 Tasciotti, p.82.
33 TNA AIR 75/69: Papers of Sir John Slessor, The Italian Campaign, letter to A.M. Linnell and
    A.V.M. Robb dated 22 February 1944.

14

Our Eyes and Ears: Do They Deceive Us?

---

*A balance is required between necessary flexibility in practical operation, without which the law
becomes unworkable, and the need to avoid subversion of the whole humanitarian enterprise at the
arbitrary discretion of military convenience.*

Hilaire McCoubrey
International Humanitarian Law, 1990.[1]

It is evident from the differences of opinion of the Allied commanders at all levels, that no
consensus was reached as to whether the Abbey was occupied, or that there was wilful ignorance
to justify the decision, or even that there was a deliberate discounting of the evidence. One of
the key weaknesses of intelligence is that it is a human activity that suffers from the veering
and hauling of human biases. Intelligence officers whether they admit it or not, often reflect the
views of their commander. The information, processed and turned into actionable intelligence
does not stand on its own. Headquarters personnel, regardless of the fidelity of their information, never have a complete understanding of their enemy. Some things remain permanently
unknown such as the feelings or thoughts of an enemy general. Information that is analysed
and the story passed on always has an element of opinion or judgement. Because of this, senior
officers are likely to interpret their intelligence in a way that meets the intent of their operations.
Cassino was no different.

   That the Abbey was having a detrimental psychological effect on Allied forces was not in
doubt, but did its destruction meet Eisenhower's definition of necessity or convenience? The
claimed irrelevance of the Abbey's occupation is largely a post-bombing phenomenon and does
not reflect most opinions beforehand. The view of the *Daily Telegraph* correspondent L Marsland
Gander in his 1946 article is typical: 'Frankly, I do not know whether they did in fact occupy
it before the bombardment; but there was always a strong likelihood that, sooner or later, they
would. It is certain that they were using sangars in the vicinity of the Monastery buildings.'[2]

---

1   McCoubrey, p.199.
2   L Marsland Gander, *Cassino: Ypres of the Second Great War,* War Illustrated, Vol. 10 No. 246, pp.483-4,
    22 November 1946 <http://www.thewarillustrated.info/246/cassino-ypres-of-the-second-great-war.
    asp> (accessed 5 March 2019) .

Apart from Tuker, who was ambivalent, German occupation was the key factor in the opinions of all the Allied commanders. On what bases were opinions formed? There have been arguments put forward that put the blame for the bombing on faulty or insufficient intelligence. After the war an Italian President blamed the bombing on 'a tragic error, the result of poor intelligence.' Bradford Evans, the pilot who led the attack, also claims that intelligence at Cassino was poor, leading in the heat of battle to poor decisions.[3] Both are wrong. It has always been easy for commanders and politicians to blame their intelligence for a bad decision. Intelligence lives in a secret world where the revelation of sources could be deadly to future exploitation. Intelligence organisations are usually not able to defend themselves as this threatens sources and methods. At Cassino, intelligence from multiple sources was plentiful and generally accurate. Historian Ronald Lewin contended that 'no previous commander was informed so extensively and as accurately as Alexander.'[4] The argument is strong to suggest that none have since. Were there sources of intelligence available to Alexander and Wilson that were not available to Clark and lower-level commanders that had a bearing on the decision? Or as seems likely, was it the interpretation of the information and the decisions based upon it that were faulty? To determine who knew what and when, it is necessary to examine the sources of intelligence that were available to Allied commanders.

The first source is Signals Intelligence or SIGINT. SIGINT is a cover term for two forms of intelligence, only one of which was relevant to the Abbey. Of little importance is Electronic Intelligence or ELINT. Of far greater importance was Communications Intelligence or COMINT. This is the interception and exploitation of transmitted communications. It also covers the discipline of Traffic Analysis, which is the discovery of how enemy communications networks function, rather than their content. This includes radio, wireless telegraphy and landline or cable interception. There were generally three methods by which communications were transmitted; by Morse Code, non-Morse text and voice. Communications were encrypted depending upon their vulnerability, security classification and time sensitivity. The landline was the most secure means of communication as any intelligence organization had to physically tap into telephone lines to exploit the communications. British Mediterranean cables were cut early in the war by the Italians which resulted in reliance on radio signals that could be intercepted. Whilst landline interception was possible against German communications, especially when partisan groups controlled more and more territory, getting the intercepted communications back was difficult as the Germans also had an active counter-intelligence organization that could detect the necessary transmissions. As many German operational headquarters were static in Italy, landline was the primary and most secure means of communicating. Westphal made the point in his memoirs that the telephone lines were often damaged by Allied air raids. The use of radio in southern Italy could be difficult due to atmospheric interference.[5] The Germans made much use of the Fiesler Storch aircraft for important communications, although these were often shot down. It is a myth that British codebreaking revealed all German plans.

For forward headquarters that relocated regularly, landline communications were often impractical. These required a secure, yet mobile means of receiving orders and sending reports. For this they used Morse and non-Morse teletype machines. These provided a secure and mobile

3   Evans, p.7.
4   Ronald Lewin, *ULTRA Goes To War: The Secret Story* (London: Book Club Associates, 1978), pp.286-7.
5   Westphal, p.151.

system for headquarters, but the machines were bulky, and transmissions were slow. They were not much use to the agile front-line fighting unit. These relied on smaller, but less secure systems to transmit operational information. Finally, although voice transmissions could be scrambled, as in the transatlantic scrambler, this did not happen close to the front line. Generally, voice communications such as those between artillery spotters and their associated gun batteries were transmitted over radio nets and in the clear, using veiled language and cover terms to add a basic level of security. For instance, US VI Corps referred to Cassino as ROCHESTER.[6] Field telephones using flimsy wire to connect positions were also common, although the wires were often cut by artillery.

The Germans also transmitted signals from observation posts to their artillery units using flashing lights.[7] The observation post reports from 34th Division regularly report seeing lights and flares and intelligence reports suggested different colour flares had different meanings. This is an inefficient way to pass detailed and time-sensitive information to firing units often well to the rear of the front-line, whose movement was regular and who would struggle to see light messages in daylight. Flares could be used by both sides, and therefore messages to one side may be misinterpreted as a message to the other. This occurred in the battle for Point 593 in February 1944 when the German paratroopers were under attack by the 4th Indian Division. They fired a flare pattern to call for reinforcements. The same flare pattern was used by the Indians as a withdrawal signal resulting in a termination of promising attack on a difficult and important piece of terrain. To prevent this sort of occurrence happening, radio was needed. However, transmissions were vulnerable to exploitation. As well as being intercepted and translated, it was possible for SIGINT units to triangulate and locate radio transmissions using direction-finding (DF) equipment. The higher-level Morse and non-Morse transmissions were intercepted and transmitted back to Bletchley Park in Britain for exploitation, whereas tactical communications would be exploited by specialist teams attached to the Army HQ.

COMINT has distinct advantages for the intelligence officer trying to work out what the opponent is going to do. Unlike photography which shows a snapshot in time, interception of communications can provide indications of both the enemy's capability and, most importantly, their intentions. Whilst what is happening now is important, what will happen next is invaluable to the commander or decision-maker, allowing action inside the enemy's decision-making cycle. COMINT also provides an accurate transliteration of what has been sent. Even if the actual communications cannot be decrypted the analysis of communications traffic allows the analyst to build an accurate picture of who is communicating with whom, generating valuable command and control and order of battle information. Like all sources of intelligence, COMINT has disadvantages. The most obvious is its fragility and the ease of countermeasures should an opponent realise that communications are compromised. There are several measures they could take. They could change the equipment with which they encrypt communications making decryption more difficult. Alternatively, if a target realises that communications have become non-secure, deception could be fed though false messages into the opponent's intelligence machinery. A countermeasure for these weaknesses brings another disadvantage of COMINT. It remained very highly classified and narrowly disseminated making operational exploitation problematic. Acting

---

6   Operation SHINGLE Plan – Appendix 2 to Annex I dated 7 January 1944.
7   David Colvin and Richard Hodges, 'Tempting Providence The Bombing of Monte Cassino', *History Today*, 44:2 (1994), pp.13-20.

directly on it may result in the target realising that communications are unsafe. The opposite of this is the example of the US intelligence failure at Pearl Harbor. The US could read the Japanese diplomatic code known as 'Purple' and nicknamed 'Magic'. This breakthrough was highly classified with only a very few people having knowledge. Although Magic did not warn of the attack directly, Japanese diplomatic communications offered clues and because of its compartmentation Magic was poorly fused with other sources. One final disadvantage of COMINT is obvious. The intelligence could only be gained if the target transmits it. It was a passive gatherer.

COMINT in Italy was divided into the two parts: high-level and tactical. Most prominent was a source named ULTRA, the results of breaking cryptographical keys in the German *Enigma* machine. ULTRA started to become available to the British as early as 1940. The risks associated with the unintentional dissemination of highly sensitive ULTRA intelligence were considered when it was decided that overseas commands needed access. Special units were required to ensure its integrity and the first of these, Special Signals Unit (SSU) No 1 was set up in the Middle East in April 1941. Its job was to receive enciphered ULTRA from Hut 3 at Bletchley Park, decipher it and maintain strict control of dissemination.[8] To maintain a level of anonymity these were renamed Special Liaison Units and their commanding officers had absolute authority over ULTRA, often having to remind senior officers of their responsibilities. These were usually RAF officers, which in Army headquarters could attract attention, especially as they were usually not pilots. To allow control of 'source' the SLUs were independent of the commands they served, working directly for the Directors of Intelligence and 'C', the Chief of the Secret Intelligence Service (SIS). This independence was 'jealously guarded'.[9] In day-to-day command was Group Captain Frederick Winterbotham, an RAF officer attached to the SIS. As the organisation grew it was divided into the SLUs, which handled liaison, ciphers and security, and Special Communications Units (SCU) that conducted signalling and transport.[10] The British used a machine called the TYPEX to send ULTRA messages, whereas the Americans used a similar machine called SIGABA. The security rules regarding ULTRA were stringent and applied to all Allied personnel: the main points are as follows:

a.   No action could be taken on Ultra information, unless this could have been obtained from some other source or adequate cover manufactured eg by arranging for a recce flight over some area, containing a target already disclosed by Ultra.

b.   No Ultra records could be kept at a lower formation than Army Group.

c.   A list of authorised recipients was available at each SLU and Ultra information could only be discussed with and by such persons.

d.   New readers could only be admitted if they held positions authorised by the Regulations to admission or if special permission had been granted by Home.

e.   All new readers had to be guaranteed by their commanders; they had to be briefed by the Senior SLU Officer or an officer of the rank of Brigadier (or equivalent) already in the picture; and they had to sign a declaration that they had read and understood the Regulations.

8   Fifth Army History Part IV, 242. TNA HW 49/1, The History of the Special Liaison Units –
     Mediterranean and Western Europe, Government Codes and Cypher School, p.2.
9   TNA HW 49/1: History of SLUs, p.9.
10   TNA HW 49/1: History of SLUs, p.3.

f.   Readers who left such positions had to sign a declaration that they realised that they were no longer entitled to see or discuss Ultra and that they would not divulge its existence. They were debarred from taking on any position which might involve their capture by the enemy. They were never to take part in operational flights.

g.   The use of the telephone was only permitted in the UK and even then a scrambler had to be used.[11]

In addition, ULTRA could not be intermingled with lower grades of intelligence unless it retained the ULTRA security caveat. It could not be passed by any code or cipher that could be read by non-authorised personnel.

ULTRA was not a single source. It was a cover term for a whole range of German communications, covering both Morse and non-Morse transmissions. ULTRA was derived from German high-grade ciphers that were transmitted via Wireless/Telephony (W/T) over the *Enigma* encryption system. Because ULTRA was associated with W/T, with an *Enigma* machine encrypting and decrypting messages, the Germans were aware that their messages were being intercepted. They were confident that these messages could not be decrypted, except by another *Enigma* machine with the correct daily settings. They were wrong. Additional high-grade ULTRA was gained from non-Morse teleprinters that connected headquarters with Berlin, codenamed FISH, using the Lorenz SZ40/42 *Geheimschrieber* enciphering equipment. ULTRA was largely decrypted using an electromechanical machine called a Bombe. In February 1944, the bombers were joined by an even more powerful machine, the Colossus, that could read 25,000 bits per second.[12]

ULTRA provided valuable insights into German intentions and orders of battle, but like any single source of intelligence it did not stand alone. It needed to be fused with other sources to be completely effective. This presented problems due to the limited distribution of ULTRA even within Intelligence sections. The volume of non-ULTRA intelligence was great; the addition of this source to often single individuals could easily overwhelm their ability to make sense of it in conflicting, ambiguous and fast-moving situations. Between 1943 and the end of the war in Europe, Bletchley Park produced nearly 84,000 *Enigma* decrypts per month.[13] In Fifth Army only two officers in the G-2 section were able to perform this very large task. One of these was the commander, who obviously had considerable responsibilities other than ULTRA, the other was his deputy, another very busy man. This situation often resulted in commanders being their own intelligence analysts. ULTRA had to have a cover story. It was often hidden through tactical COMINT or 'Y' or Photographic Reconnaissance. Most famously, the British used the codename BONIFACE to indicate that ULTRA was derived from a human source, although this codename was discontinued earlier in the war.

Hunt, an Intelligence Officer to Alexander stated that, 'it was the greatest secret of the war.'[14] The *Enigma* machine had originally been broken in 1932 by the Polish Cipher Bureau, but following the invasion of Poland and later France, Britain was left as the sole recipient. It is wrong to assume that ULTRA was an all-seeing eye that allowed commanders total clarity

11   TNA HW 49/1: History of SLUs, Chapter II. Security.
12   Putney, p.77.
13   Putney, p.xii.
14   Hunt, p. x.

on their enemy. ULTRA was a cover-term for a wide range of wireless signals transmitted via the *Enigma* or *Geheimschreiber* machines. The Germans used lots of different *Enigma* 'keys', each associated with its service or function. Each presented a separate puzzle, and each was broken at different times and with differing delay. Some keys could only be broken occasionally. Some keys remained secure, especially those that were only sporadically used. The exploitation of these keys, if possible, would take varying amounts of time depending on whether GC&CS could decrypt the messages easily or not. In Italy, *Enigma* communications within German Tenth AOK used a key codenamed ALBATROSS, and communications between *Oberkommando des Heeres* (OKH) in Berlin and Kesselring's *Heersgruppenkommando* used a key codenamed PUFFIN.[15] Neither of these were regularly broken because there were insufficient 'cribs' developed because the keys were only sporadically used. A 'crib' is a clue or a template that assists the cryptanalysts. It may be that the *Enigma* operator used the same phrase at the start of every message, or it may be that a portion of the code book had been captured, or that the same message was transmitted via different exploitable means which acted as a template. Allied messages warned recipients that they should not make an exact copy of the signal for this reason. GC&CS made a breakthrough in January 1944 when they succeeded in breaking a Tenth AOK key codenamed BULLFINCH, which reported order-of-battle information to OKH.[16] This source allowed Allied commanders full knowledge of the German order of battle at Cassino. Unfortunately, BULLFINCH became unbreakable again on 6 February resulting in a marked decline in high-level SIGINT.[17] There were only small changes to the Cassino sector order of battle between this date and 13 February when the decision to bomb the Abbey was made. Two sources of ULTRA continued uninterrupted throughout, providing considerable intelligence. These were the *Luftwaffe* keys codenamed RED and PUMA, issued to air liaison officers (*flivos*) at army units. PUMA was the key used by *Luftflotte* 2 and Vietinghoff's headquarters and RED was a more general key. Also intercepted was the FISH link between Kesselring's headquarters and OKH, codenamed BREAM and which was decrypted via the Colossus computer.[18] In February 1944, the Germans introduced a new cryptologic security device that resulted in only half the normal decrypted messages.[19] The *Luftwaffe* RED key had been exploitable by Bletchley Park since the Battle of Britain and could be decrypted quickly providing close to real-time intelligence. It was this key that provided a high proportion of *Enigma* intelligence during the Cassino battle period.[20]

Because of its great value, and inherent fragility, ULTRA intelligence was retained in a very restricted compartment, with great care taken over its distribution and use. It remained largely unknown to the general public until Winterbotham published *The Ultra Secret* in 1974. Generally only distributed to formations at Army level and above, there were some exceptions with some corps and air forces having access. In Italy some commanders at lower levels were aware of ULTRA. For instance, Freyberg had commanded Crete in 1941 and had been given

15   Hinsley et al, p.175fn. OKH was German Army Command located at Zossen outside Berlin.
16   Hinsley et al p.185-6.
17   Hinsley et al, p.190.
18   Hinsley et al, p.175fn, p.182.
19   Hinsley et al, pp.481-2.
20   TNA HW 11/5: Air And Military History, Vol.5, Italy 1943-1945, Bletchley Park: Government Code and Cypher School, p.95.

access. He was only told that this intelligence came from 'most secret sources' and he believed it to be from an Allied agent.[21] It is not clear whether he retained this informally, but his corps had no SLU, the conduit for ULTRA to the operational user. The ULTRA keys in Italy, apart from the *Luftwaffe* keys would have been different. It is possible that Alexander divulged relevant facts from ULTRA to Freyberg, at least verbally, in their numerous meetings, although there is no evidence either way.

ULTRA was a British intelligence source and its existence had been shared with the Americans since March 1941. Agreement to share the actual intelligence with the US War Department only came on 17 May 1943 when the head of GC&CS, Commander Edward Travis and the head of the US Signals Security Agency (SSA), Arlington Hall, Colonel Preston Corderman, signed the formal agreement.[22] The Americans developed their own Bombes, slightly faster than those at Bletchley, under what was known as Project Yellow. The arrangements with US agencies and Bletchley Park were arranged separately as US Army and Navy SIGINT organisations jealously remained apart.

Each organisation authorised to receive ULTRA had to have its own SLU, identified by a digraph. Clark, as an Allied Army commander, had formal access to ULTRA through the Fifth Army SLU (Station KQ).[23] The Fifth Army SLU arrived at Caserta before the 15th Army Group SLU and for a brief time served as a surrogate until the Army Group's SLU arrived from Bari. It was only staffed by officers, the commander did not want senior NCOs, mainly because he considered that they would find it more difficult to stand up to very demanding senior officers. Considering Clark's intense dislike and distrust of the British and his overbearing personality, this was probably a sensible decision. ULTRA was delivered to Clark via his intelligence officer, Colonel Edwin Howard or the deputy, Colonel Wells. This procedure was at odds with Winterbotham's instructions as the SLU officers were supposed to always retain positive control of ULTRA. They should have delivered the intelligence to Clark directly, although other indoctrinated persons could be present.

Although collocated with 15th Army Group (Station SB) briefly until late January 1944 when Clark moved his Command Post to Presenzano, the Fifth Army SLU was separate after 20 January.[24] A second SLU was set-up at Anzio (Station GW) on 25 January. This was the most exposed SLU, being at times only 3-miles from German lines.[25] Unusually, ULTRA was also released to Lucas from this station. Both received ULTRA messages via a Secure Communications Unit directly from GC&CS. The SLU and SCU were British manned in their entirety, with the SLU staff posted to MAAF and then detached to the various units.[26] There were American officers in similar positions. One of these, Major Lewis Powell, a future Associate Justice in the US Supreme Court, worked at Spaatz's USSTAF in England and was known as a Special Security Officer (SSO).[27] Powell worked for the US Army's Military Intelligence Service's Special Branch under Colonel Alfred McCormack who ran the US

21   Hinsley et al, Vol 1, 417 and Anthony Beevor, *Crete* (London: John Murray Publishers, 2005), pp.88-89.
22   Putney, p.81.
23   TNA HW 49/1: History of SLUs, 36. The US called ULTRA Special Intelligence A and 'Y' Special Intelligence B. It is unclear which this is as it has both letters within the unit title.
24   TNA HW 49/1: History of SLUs, p.39.
25   TNA HW 49/1: History of SLUs, p.36.
26   Fournier 152-154; TNA HW 49/1: History of SLUs, p.10.
27   Putney, p. xiii.

Army's access to ULTRA.[28] Americans were either indoctrinated into ULTRA via their own SSOs or, as in the case of Fifteenth Air Force, deputy A2, Lieutenant Colonel Robert Storey, through the British SLU.

Whether Clark received the same ULTRA traffic as Alexander is unknown, but he probably did. Distribution of ULTRA during early 1944 was limited to the SLU/SCU staff and just four Fifth Army officers; Clark, Gruenther; Howard, the G-2 and his deputy, Colonel Wells.[29] Unlike the Fifth Army SLU, located in a truck, Alexander's SLU was within the plusher surroundings of the Caserta Palace.[30] ULTRA was managed in the war room, entry to which was limited to a small number of indoctrinated persons. These were Alexander, Harding, Lemnitzer, Brigadier Terence Airey the 15th Army Group Assistant Chief of Staff Intelligence, Brigadier R B Mainwaring the G-3 Operations Chief, Lieutenant Colonel David Hunt, the General Staff Officer Intelligence and possibly Captain Rupert Clarke, Alexander's aide-de-camp.

ULTRA was a closely guarded secret even within the Intelligence sections of the higher headquarters. Major Powell, when part of Spaatz's intelligence staff in Tunisia in late 1943 had never heard of ULTRA and only vaguely knew what the SLU was involved with.[31]

In the MAAF, considering that the attack on the Abbey was carried by USAAF bombers, only a single US officer within MAAF A-2 Intelligence, Colonel Harris Hull, a journalist in civilian life, was cleared to see ULTRA. Hull arrived on 10 January 1944 as part of Eaker's advance party to find that the Fifteenth Air Force had a number of important posts vacant, including the targets officer.[32] No US targets officer was cleared for ULTRA, even its section chief.[33] The only other ULTRA-cleared MAAF staff officers were all British, including Chief Intelligence Officer, Air Commodore Frank Woolley and his British deputy Group Captain J C E Luard. Powell considered that the headquarters was dominated by RAF officers.[34] The SCU/SLU (Station LM) was only set-up in the grounds of Caserta Palace by 12 February, too late to influence the attack on the Abbey, although MAAF did receive ULTRA through the 15th Army Group beforehand.[35] Similarly in MATAF, only a single US officer in the A-2 section was cleared.[36] No-one in the US Fifteenth Air Force targets section had access to ULTRA, although Twining did have a SLU attached to his headquarters. (Station JY).[37] As late as May 1944, many senior officers in the Mediterranean Theatre considered ULTRA to be purely a British affair. This was highlighted in a report from Major Powell, an indoctrinated US Special Branch officer and former intelligence officer of the 319th Bombardment Group.[38]

28   Putney, p.14.
29   Fournier, p.153. This list is correct to December 1943. By July 1944, a fifth authorized person, the G-3 Brigadier-General Brann had been added. It is not known whether Brann was added before or after 15 February 1944.
30   Lewin, p.282.
31   Putney, p.11.
32   James Parton, *The History of the Mediterranean Allied Air Forces – 10 December 1943 to 1 September 1944* (Caserta Italy: Headquarters Mediterranean Allied Air Forces, 1945), p.12.
33   John F Kreis, *Piercing The Fog* (Washington DC: Air Force History and Museum Program, 1996), pp.179-180.
34   Putney, p.13.
35   TNA HW 49/1: History of SLUs, p.38.
36   The 12th AF A-2 also served as Deputy MATAF A-2
37   TNA HW 49/1: History of SLUs, p.37.
38   Putney.

In *The ULTRA Secret,* Winterbotham accused Clark of not making best use of ULTRA. Arthur Fournier presents evidence suggesting that he took it very seriously.[39] Sir Harry Hinsley in his Official History of Intelligence in the Second World War argued that Clark became convinced of the value of ULTRA when on 3 February he received the message from Station GW indicating Kesselring's counteroffensive intentions at Anzio.[40] He was informed of Kesselring's final preparations a few hours after the attack on the Abbey.[41] In a 1970 interview with Nigel Nicolson, and before the ULTRA secret had been revealed, Clark knew from broken codes that Hitler wanted to 'drive us into the sea and drown us.'[42] In the subsequent decision to bomb the Abbey, it is the intelligence relating to the timing of German ambitions at Anzio that is crucial, as ULTRA had nothing to say about the Abbey.[43] ULTRA must have added to the momentum to break the *Gustav* Line, playing a part in Clark's reluctance to adopt the time-consuming outflanking option. The majority of his subordinate commanders were not cleared to receive ULTRA and would therefore have been unaware. It may have led to the abandonment of this option on 4 February and to his subsequent insistence on a more attritional but potentially quicker head-on attack. The overall importance of ULTRA can be summed up by Eisenhower wrote that:

> The intelligence which has emanated from you before and during this campaign has been of priceless value to me. It has simplified my task as commander enormously. It has saved thousands of British and American lives and, in no small way, contributed to the speed with which the enemy was routed and eventually forced to surrender.[44]

The second major source of SIGINT was much more tactical, accessing battlefield communications. These lower-level tactical messages were transmitted either in the clear or using less secure cryptographic means. These were intercepted and exploited by the 'Y'-Service. Although suffering a slow start in Italy, lower-grade communication interception and direction-finding was, by February 1944, performing well after regaining its ability to intercept German VHF signals. Fifth Army was well established and carried out by US Signals Intelligence Service (SIS) units and British Special Wireless/Telegraphy units. These were the US 849th Signal Intelligence Service and until January 1944 the British 105th Special W/T Section, replaced by 3rd W/T Section.[45] Direction-finding was also carried out by British and American units, with detachments deployed to corps level.[46] After January, Detachment A of 128th Signals Company supported Fifth Army. Detachment H of the 849th SIS and a detachment of 128th Signals Company supported collection at US II Corps HQ and Detachment D was sent to Anzio. The

39   Fournier, 2; TNA HW 49/1: History of SLUs, p.36.
40   Hinsley et al, p.190.
41   Hinsley et al, p.192.
42   Nicolson, p.233.
43   TNA DEFE 3 Jan-Feb 1944. W.T. Beckmann, G. Church, W. Coombs, L.S. Hawthorn, R. Horstmann, Norton, HW 11/5: Air And Military History, Vol.5, Italy 1943-1945, Bletchley Park: Government Code and Cypher School, pp.95-101.
44   Letter from Eisenhower to Menzies, 12 July 1945 in Putney, p. xiii.
45   TNA HW 41/125: History of Signal Intelligence in the Field – Europe and Africa – 1939-1945, pp.101-115.
46   TNA HW 41/125: History of Sigint in the Field, p.112.

123rd Radio Intercept Company and Detachment F of 849th SIS supported MAAF signals intelligence collection.[47] Collection facilities were mobile and were conducted from the back of a 2 1/2-ton truck. Direction-finding was extremely important in identifying the location of military units even if their radio messages could not be read. D/F in the case of the Abbey could have provided *prima facie* evidence of German occupation. Three mobile teams carried out D/F concentrating on German division and regiment traffic.[48] Analysis of the collected signals was carried out at Fifth Army headquarters, US II Corps and a small team detached with the FEC. Results were codenamed THUMB. The French did not get access to ULTRA at the insistence of the British. At the beginning of February 1944, an ad hoc unit was established to support the New Zealand Corps.[49] British 'Y' units supported 15th Army Group.[50]

'Y' was the source of the greatest amount of tactical intelligence, with 60 per cent coming from the German VHF tactical radio net, hence the preference of Fifth Army to deploy its 'Y' units at corps level and below where they could intercept line-of-sight VHF communications.[51] The corps SIGINT detachments were made up of around 120-officers and men, split down into 8 or 10-positions. Soldiers from 849th Detachments were able to recognise enemy networks and carry out simple decryption tasks on low grade traffic – codenamed PEARL.[52] That the Germans were using radio in addition to landlines and possibly flashing light signals to direct fire onto the Cassino massif was confirmed when a German radio operator was captured on 1 February.[53] This operator was captured by the 2/135 Infantry on the Majola hill mass about a mile north of the Abbey. When the monks and surviving civilians left the Abbey on 16 February, they met some German soldiers near Albaneta Farm. The soldiers said that they couldn't get in touch with their command post because the 'telephone lines were down.'[54] Despite this evidence of landline use, all German divisions in the Cassino area were regularly intercepted.[55] It was claimed that as much was known about German formations by the Allies as by the Germans themselves.[56] Tighter radio security procedures were introduced across German units on 15 February, which made 'Y' staffs' task more difficult, in that frequencies were changed three times daily, and a new codebook was introduced.[57] This had no impact on the decision to bomb the Abbey. The use of VHF communications increased in the days before the bombing during the period of US II Corps activity in early February, with the paratroopers from the 1st *Fallschirmjager* Division who occupied Montecassino being 'almost continually active.'[58] Until early February the Abbey area was the responsibility of 44th Infantry Division. From then

47   AFHRA Reel A6030, History of MAAF, December 1943 – September 1944, Volume 1, Chapter II, p.119.
48   George F Howe, *United States Cryptologic History: Sources in Cryptologic History Series IV Volume 1 – American Signal Intelligence in Northwest Africa and Western Europe* (Fort Meade; Maryland: National Security Agency, 1980 (published 2010)), p.84.
49   TNA HW 41/125: History of Sigint in the Field, p.113.
50   British 1st and 3rd Spec W/T Sections TNA HW 41/125, History of Sigint in the Field, p.115.
51   Hinsley et al, 178-182. TNA HW 41/125: History of Sigint in the Field, p.90.
52   Howe p.83.
53   Breit, *'Phase VIII 135th Infantry Regiment History'*, p.15.
54   Leccisotti, p.150.
55   Fournier 150, TNA HW 41/125: History of Sigint in the Field 105, p.116.
56   TNA HW 41/125: History of Sigint in the Field, p.91.
57   TNA HW 41/125: History of Sigint in the Field, pp.115-116.
58   TNA HW 41/125: History of Sigint in the Field, p.116.

onwards, the 90th *Panzer-Grenadiers* took over and at the time of the attack, the Abbey and the Key Terrain at Point 593 were the responsibility of the 3rd Battalion, 3rd Regiment, of the *Fallschirmjager* Division. The 90th *Panzer-Grenadier* Division, commanded by Baade, the eccentric Anglophile who may have deliberately sent radio messages to the Allied side, was in overall command of the Cassino hill mass where an eclectic mix of units from several German divisions were brought together.

The second primary source was photographic reconnaissance (PR). Since the dawn of military operations, commanders have always wished to know what was on 'the other side of the hill'. Observing the enemy from a high vantage point such as a hill or tree allowed military leaders to make informed decisions. The ability to conduct such operations and obtain intelligence was the original task of military aviation before and during the First World War. It remained a critical, yet less glamorous element of airpower. As the name implied, PR was the collection of aerial reconnaissance photography and its subsequent analysis by photographic interpreters. Like SIGINT, PR had advantages and disadvantages. The first and greatest advantage was the old saying that 'a picture paints a thousand words.' If the Abbey was occupied, photography should have been able to see this, especially when air supremacy allowed regular and unhindered coverage. Aircraft were not limited by the altitude they could fly, and they could use cameras with long focal-length lenses to give maximum detail. Photographs could be taken vertically from high-altitude or obliquely from lower altitude, generally below 5,000ft, a task known as 'dicing' as they diced with the danger of German flak.

Imagery could be taken at varying scales, depending on the use to be made of the photographs. High-scale imagery (1:5000) would be needed to determine individual activity within the Abbey's precincts. Low oblique pictures, images where the horizon is not visible, normally taken from low-level, would also offer great detail, allowing greater perspective on elevation and terrain, but much would be obscured by walls or other obstacles. Frames were produced with 60 per cent overlap producing a stereoscopic image.

All vertical images were to have this level of overlap. This allowed analysts to judge the effect of terrain.[59] Both types were taken of the Abbey on 15 February. Another advantage was that aircraft could gain photography from every aspect of the building to give an overall picture of activity. Photography was seemingly intuitive; everyone could look at it and see what was there. This final advantage could be a double-edged sword in that the old saying was not always true – the thousand words can be the wrong words or words in a different language. This is why imagery is analysed and interpreted by highly trained photographic interpreters who look for details by analysing the photography systematically, looking at size, shape, shadow, tone and other associated features to extract the maximum amount of information.

A disadvantage that should not be underestimated was the tendency for the untrained general to be his own photographic interpreter. People tend to see what they wish to see, and not necessarily what is there. Many senior officers and politicians insisted on seeing raw information. As Strong made clear this was not a bad thing if the professional intelligence adviser was on hand to provide context.[60] This is true for all raw intelligence, not just PR.

US Army PR doctrine was cumbersome and was written in three separate field manuals: FM 1-20, FM 1-35 and FM 30-21. FM 1-20 offers a general, and by today's standards rather

59   FM 1-35, pp.12-13.
60   Kenneth Strong, *Intelligence At The Top* (London: Doubleday, 1969), pp.118-9.

A high-oblique image of the destroyed Abbey. Photographic Reconnaissance missions such as this were called 'dicing' sorties as the pilots considered them more dangerous than high-level sorties. (NCAP)

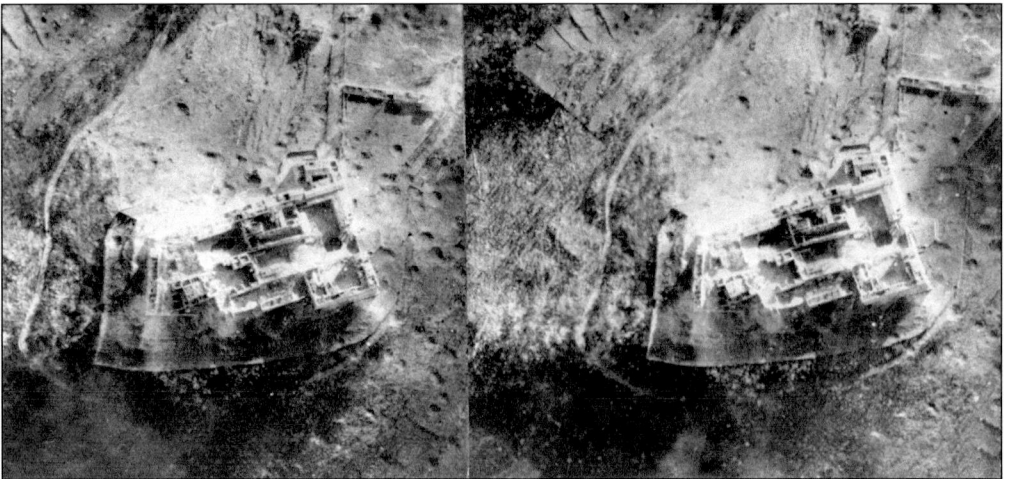

A high-level stereo-pair image of the destroyed Abbey, possibly taken by Lieutenant Hersey on the afternoon of 15 February 1944. (NARA RG342-FH-000157)

basic, description of the uses of aerial photography whereas FM 1-35 is a much more detailed technical manual. Perhaps the most important was the Role of Aerial Photography in FM 30-21 of November 1940 (updated in 1942).[61] The Field Manual stressed the importance of aerial photography in that it can 'frequently reveal the most carefully guarded secrets in hostile territory.'[62] Whilst this may be an exaggeration, it did reveal the value placed on this intelligence source. The manual also recognised that photographic reconnaissance was highly dependent on other sources to act as context or as collateral cueing to allow analysts to narrow down their search. This doctrine placed responsibility for aerial photography on the G-2 of the army formation that required it, in the case of Fifth Army, Colonel Howard. The Field Manual reflected theoretical photographic interpretation, based largely on the US Army's experiences in the First World War. It would require significant modernisation, often influenced by more advanced British practices, during the first few years of war.

PR missions were as much about luck as good judgement. In 1944, there was plenty to go wrong. The camera lens was often obscured, and any untoward aircraft vibration could ruin the photography. The reconnaissance pilot flew at high altitudes with only a map to navigate and often the target was obscured by cloud, especially in the winter. He had to fly straight and level with the correct settings between exposures, often in hostile airspace where he was the favourite prey of German fighters – 'the most survivable photo-recon pilot was the one who was most scared.'[63] Merely getting good photography was a challenge. Photographs would only show the analyst what was there at that point in time. There may be some indications of future or past activity, but the analyst could only see what was there or what was not there. Regular coverage of a static target such as the Abbey would offer the ability to compare coverage over time. It was very difficult to hide activity over a period; this may be things such as tyre tracks, footprints or other patterns of life that can be discerned by lengthy and systematic examination.

Today's analysts can look at digital full-colour electro-optical, synthetic aperture radar or infra-red imagery in either still or video formats giving a dynamic day and night, all weather capability with almost instant dissemination. Modern systems offer almost an airborne observation post as long endurance allows almost persistent surveillance. In 1944 it was different as the reconnaissance aircraft often collected only a single frame of the target every few hours or days. The photographic interpreters were limited by the wet film that required the reconnaissance aircraft to return to base safely before a lengthy processing which only worked when light levels were sufficient or when there was no cloud. The disadvantages of PR in the case of the Abbey were twofold. Firstly, the weather was often poor, which precluded the relatively high-level PR sorties from taking pictures. In addition, the photo-light in the Italian winter only allowed effective photography from 10:00am to 2:00pm each day.[64]. In February 1944, all reconnaissance imagery was monochrome, although by June 1944 the 90th Photo Reconnaissance Wing had started to experiment with colour film.[65]

---

61 US War Department, Basic Field Manual FM 30-21, *Military Intelligence – Role of Aerial Photography,* 1940.
62 FM 30-21, p.1.
63 Barrett Tillman, *Forgotten Fifteenth: The Daring Airmen Who Crippled Hitler's War Machine* (Washington DC: Regnery Publishing, 2014), p.163.
64 3 Photo Group, p.22.
65 AFHRA Reel C0043 Frame 0063, 90th PRW Wing History Apr-Jun 1944. The first colour recce mission was flown on 24 June 1944.

In a 1978 interview, Clark's Intelligence Chief, Howard, confirmed the importance of PR in determining the Abbey's status;

> I had the place photographed every day. We studied the photos. We pinpointed every single weapon and overprinted them on maps.' I can't say they didn't have an OP up there...A photo wouldn't necessarily show one man...There might have been Germans in there, but no defence installations...To take a million-dollar plane and drop a million dollars' worth of bombs on a place like that, you've got to have more reason than a few Germans standing around.[66]

Howard's claim of photographing the Abbey daily was an exaggeration as the weather prevented effective PR on many days of early 1944. His conclusion is the right one. Even if they were there, a few Germans in the Abbey hardly affected the outcome of the battle.

The organisation of PR and its analysis in the Mediterranean Theatre was complicated, with collection being conducted by several MAAF units and interpretation being carried out by different organizations both land and air. The overall management and governance of PR analysis was formalised on 1 February 1944 when the Mediterranean Photo Intelligence Centre (MPIC) was established. The MAAF history states that it had two tasks:

> Receiving, coordinating, allotting priorities to all requirements for aerial photos, aerial photographic intelligence and material within the Mediterranean Theatre.
> Directing and coordinating the distribution of aerial photos, aerial photo intelligence and material within the theatre to authorized agents outside the theatre.[67]

The first task of the MPIC was an audit of the existing collection mechanisms. Collection of PR was the responsibility of MAAF and was conducted by an inter-Allied organization formed by President Roosevelt's son, Colonel Elliot Roosevelt, the Mediterranean Air Photographic Reconnaissance Wing (MAPRW).[68] MAPRW was officially formed in January 1944.[69] It was directly subordinated to MAAF, not to the component air forces or the ground formations. By the time of the Abbey bombing, Roosevelt, who had a somewhat colourful and chequered career and who had unabashedly used his family connections, had been poached by General Carl Spaatz to run the PR organization from England. He was a popular commander and his men often enjoyed themselves. US intelligence officer and future notable history professor, Leland D Baldwin made the following diary entry concerning the PR organisation at La Marsa in October 1943:

> Saturday 23 October La Marsa
> Last night the Photo boys had another wild party, with loud music and squealing nurses, but no shooting, apparently, they were celebrating Elliot Roosevelt's return after his several

---

66   Hapgood and Richardson, p.168.
67   Parton, *MAAF History*, pp.114-115
68   Roosevelt had been poached by Gen Carl Spaatz to run the US Strategic Air Forces in Europe PR organization. He departed MAAF at the beginning of 1944. The MAPRW is also called the MAPRC (Command), but this seems to be the same organisation as MAPRW.
69   Hinsley, p.465.

At the beginning of 1944, command of the Mediterranean Allied Photographic Reconnaissance Wing passed from Colonel Roosevelt to Colonel Karl Polifka. (NARA RG342-FH-002302)

months in the States. This morning about 0430 I was awakened by the voice of a drunken argument. A brassy, youthful voice was saying over and over, 'I'm running this goddamn show, and you'll do what I say.' The someone else would chime in, 'Well, I don't like the way you're doing it.'[70]

Roosevelt departed MAAF at the beginning of 1944 to be replaced by the Wing Executive Officer, Colonel Karl Polifka, although he continued to visit Italy regularly and attended a dinner with Spaatz, Eaker and Polifka a week after the bombing.[71]

USAAF PR for MAPRW was conducted by the 3rd Photo Group of the 90th Photo Reconnaissance Wing flying F-5 aircraft, the reconnaissance version of the P-38 and the pilots were known as 'Photo Joes.'[72]

70   AFHRA Reel 23111, Diary of Leland D Baldwin dated 23 October 1943.
71   Kreis, p.180. AFHRA Reel C0043 Frame 0070. HQ 90th PRW A-2 (Historical Section), 90th PRW Monthly Historical Report for May 1944 dated 30 June 1944; AFHRA A6030 MAAF CINC Diary entry – 22 February 1944.
72   F-5 was the PR version of the P-38 Lightning.

In total MAPRW flew 336-reconnaissance sorties in February 1944 and produced over 1-million interpretation products.[73] This was the lowest monthly total during the first half of the year, due to the poor weather conditions. Nevertheless, 33.5 per cent of all PR was allocated to Fifth Army during January and February 1944 and nearly 350,000-products were provided to the Fifth Army Photographic Intelligence Centre (FAPIC). The 3rd Photo Group was subordinated operationally to the MATAF and had supported US Army and USAAF forces since their arrival in North Africa in late 1942.[74] Processes and relationships had developed from a difficult beginning through the battles in Sicily and Salerno. The Fifteenth Air Force had no independent PR organization until October 1944, although the 5th Photo Group supported it through most of 1944. In addition to its strategic duties the 5th Photo Group also supported PR tasks at Anzio and Cassino.[75] By early 1944, PR was an efficient business where the needs of armies and air forces alike were well understood. The static nature of the *Gustav* Line and the Anzio beachhead during the early months of 1944 simplified the reconnaissance task. Nevertheless, as with the allocation of airpower generally, the Anzio crisis resulted in a greater apportionment of reconnaissance effort than to other areas of the Fifth Army front.

Many of the processes were informally developed; 'the product of trial, error and bitter experience'. In May 1944, the wing received a Presidential Unit Citation for its outstanding performance of duty.[76] In March 1945, Clark wrote to the commander of the 3rd Photographic Reconnaissance Group: 'During our operations in Italy we have found aerial photography to be the most accurate, rapid, and comprehensive means at our disposal for obtaining information on the enemy.' [77]

The USAAF also operated a squadron of P-51/F-6 Mustang aircraft, which were subordinated to XII ASC rather than MAPRW, flying armed reconnaissance.[78] This was the 111th Tactical Reconnaissance Squadron. The 111th was often used to fill in coverage gaps and conducted a lot of the oblique coverage. The RAF also contributed two squadrons of PR Spitfire XIs.[79] These were 682 Squadron and 683 Squadron flying from San Severo close to the Adriatic coast.

In addition, 60 Squadron South African Air Force (SAAF) flying from Trigno on the Adriatic operated Mosquito PR aircraft. For more tactical fighter-reconnaissance work the RAF operated Spitfires VCs from 285 Wing under the command of Group Captain Geoffrey

73   AFHRA Reel C0043, Frame 0340, Operational Statistics for MAPRW 1 January 1944 thru 31 May 1944, dated 15 June 1944.
74   *Photo recon for MATAF and 15th Army Group, 3rd Photo Group – World War II Operational Documents – Ike Skelton Combined Arms Research Library (CARL) Digital Library (oclc.org)* <https://cgsc.contentdm.oclc.org/digital/collection/p4013coll8/id/2903/rec/8> (accessed 1 July 2010).
75   Maurer Maurer, *Air Force Combat Units of World War II* (Washington DC: Office of Air Force History, 1983), p.40.
76   AFHRA Reel C0043, Frame 0070.
77   *Foreword to Photo Recon for MATAF and 15th Army Group – 3rd Photo Group, 6 March 1945, Combined Arms Research Library, Digital Library* <http://cgsc.cdmhost.com/cdm4/item_viewer.php?CISOROOT=/p4013coll8&CISOPTR=3299&CISOBOX=1&REC=11#metajump > (accessed 1 July 2010).
78   Chris Staerck, *Allied Photo Reconnaissance of World War Two* (San Diego CA: Thunder Bay Press, 1998), p.71.
79   Denis Richards and Hilary St. G Saunders, *Royal Air Force 1939–45 Volume II, The Fight Avails* (London: Her Majesty's Stationery Office, 1954), pp.395-6. 682 Squadron appears to be the main squadron supporting Italian operations.

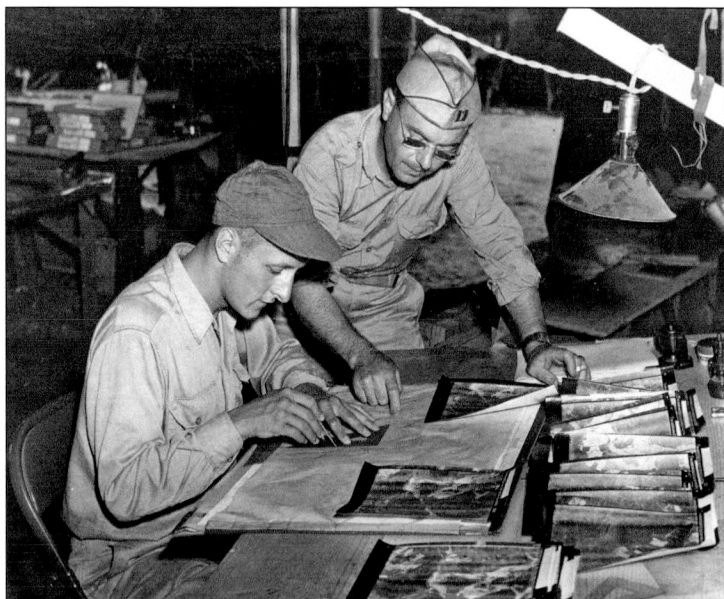

Photo Interpreters work on prints at the Mediterranean Allied Photographic Reconnaissance Wing. (NARA RG342-FH-000205)

Two Royal Air Force technicians prepare to fit a reconnaissance camera to a Spitfire aircraft. (NARA RG342-FH-000142)

Millington.[80] The RAF and SAAF Squadrons flew the most sorties of all the reconnaissance aircraft during this period, with 225 Squadron, flying from an airfield near Naples, allocated to the Fifth Army area of operations. The PR Spitfires flew at high altitudes, usually alone, whilst the 285 Wing aircraft were not dedicated reconnaissance aircraft and could also conduct artillery spotting. They usually flew in pairs at lower altitudes than those from the PR squadrons. Demands for PR were made through the inter-Allied MPIC.[81] A final, less coordinated, form of PR was flown by the bombers themselves. Mainly used for bomb damage assessment, they had cameras fitted to allow post-flight analysis of bombing results. This form of PR often suffered because the bombers' imagery could not confirm the level of damage due to smoke and dust.

The 3rd Photo Group was equipped with three squadrons, two of which, the 5th and 23rd Reconnaissance Squadrons, were assigned to XII ASC for support to MATAF, and one, the 12th Reconnaissance Squadron, was assigned directly to Fifth Army. Each squadron was equipped with 16-aircraft.[82] Demands for PR for US Fifth Army were coordinated by the Photo Recce Unit (PRU) within Army G-2 Intelligence. Overall guidance to PR army demanders was given by 15th Army Group. The PRU was the main link between the Army and the 3rd Photo Group and was also responsible for the dissemination of photographs and reports. To support Fifth Army, 3rd Photo Group deployed liaison officers to the FAPIC, located 30-60 miles behind the front line.[83] Tasking of PR missions began when requests came from subordinate units to the G-2 (Air) section.[84] This offered several advantages including fusion with other intelligence sources and coordination of reconnaissance and attack assets. Counter-battery operations were generally considered the highest priority for PR followed by rear area observation to determine enemy lines of communication and activity that may reveal future intentions.[85] The G-2 (Air) Air Liaison Officers at the FAPIC were in direct contact with PR squadrons, issuing tasks via telephone without going through official chains of command.[86] In addition to the PR squadrons, Fifth Army also employed liaison and spotter aircraft in the tactical reconnaissance and observation role with handheld cameras up to an altitude of 6,000ft.[87] These spotter aircraft worked directly for the Army and were the responsibility of Clark's chief artillery officer. They did not work for the USAAF and reported their results directly to artillery units.[88]

Central management of interpretation of photography was attempted, with the establishment of the Mediterranean Army Interpretation Unit (MAIU). This centralisation of interpretation

80   Millington, p.104.
81   Hinsley et al, 465. MPIC worked directly for MAAF Operations and Intelligence. Parton, *MAAF History*, pp.117-18.
82   3 Photo Group, p.9.
83   A Military Encyclopaedia Based on Operations in the Italian Campaigns 1943-1945. Prepared by G-3 Section, Headquarters Fifteenth Army Group, Italy, Chapter 2 – Intelligence, 57-58. Military History Network, <http://www.milhist.net/docs/milencyc/MilEncyc.02G2.pdf > (accessed 15 July 2010); AFHRA Reel, A6111 Scope, Responsibility and Function of the G-2 TARGET Section, HQ Fifth Army, 27 May 1944, Frame 1225.
84   David, Dengler, *Seeing The Enemy: Army Air Force Aerial Reconnaissance Support to US Army Operations in the Mediterranean in World War II* (Fort Leavenworth KT: US Army Command and General Staff College, 1998), p.148.
85   3 Photo Group, p.17.
86   3 Photo Group, p.18.
87   Fifteenth Army Group Encyclopaedia, p.62.
88   Bourke-White, p.171.

was a British method as the US tended to rusticate its interpretation closer to the demanding formation down to division level. MAPRW had several interpretation sections including a Second Phase Reporting Section manned with 12-officers (six British and six US). There was also 'D' (Bomb Damage) Section which would have conducted post-attack interpretation on the Abbey, comprising RAF, USAAF and French officers. Centralisation appeared to have met mixed success as interpretation of tactical PR was conducted at least divisional level in Fifth Army. The FAPIC, which was responsible for interpretation, was staffed with British photo-interpreters from MAIU (West), and Americans from 3rd Photo Interpretation Detachment of the 3rd Photo Group.[89] There were also interpreters in Fifth Army whose role was entirely devoted to Target Intelligence. Their role was to find ground targets either directly from photography or by using collateral intelligence sources, issue target graphics and to produce battle damage assessment reports.[90] The G-2 Target section, according to its procedures, had little ability to coordinate its activities with the strategic air forces. It provided targeting support mainly to XII ASC and occasionally to MATAF when medium bomber support was required.

The collation of the various intelligence sources for targeting purposes was lacking in Fifth Army. Although this function had been informally conducted since the days of the Volturno crossings, no targets section formally existed with Army G-2 until 10 March 1944, nearly a month after the attack on the Abbey. The informal Targets Section was very successful at finding targets for air attack in the Anzio area but struggled to coordinate between G-2 and A-2 at XII ASC.

The MAIU War Diary states that in early 1944 the MAIU (West) was commanded by Lieutenant Colonel C J F Ashby.[91] Ashby had detached a General Staff Officer Grade 2, to be in command of the interpreters at FAPIC. He was supported by a junior staff officer and 102-other ranks. From these, five interpreters had been deployed to US II Corps and the FEC to provide interpretation support.[92] The streamlined system of control often resulted in the interpreted photographs being delivered within 24-hours of the demand and verbal results could be delivered within 6-hours of the photography being taken. Photographs were produced by a developing facility in FAPIC called 'The Blue Train' and delivered to the customer via Jeep.

Unannotated prints in small numbers and without interpretation could be made available within 2-hours.[93] Interpretation was also carried out by divisional photo-interpreters detached from FAPIC whose analysis of minor defensive positions was accepted by Army out to a depth of about 5,000yds.[94] There was also a corps Photo Intelligence Section that performed intermediate coordination. This function was more controlled in Fifth Army than in Eighth Army. The New Zealand Corps was a temporary formation and it remained unclear what photo-intelligence capability it had. The 2nd New Zealand Divisional interpretation set-up would probably have been used. They may not have been used to the more rigid control methods employed by Fifth Army, having only recently crossed the Appenines.

89   3 Photo Group, p.18.
90   AFHRA Reel A6111 Frames 1215-1216. Scope, Responsibility and Function of the G-2 TARGET Section, HQ Fifth Army, 27 May 1944.
91   TNA WO 170/118: MAIU (West) War Diary.
92   TNA WO 170/118: MAIU (West) War Diary.
93   FM 30-21, p.8.
94   Fifteenth Army Group Encyclopaedia, pp.57-58.

Interpretation reports were delivered to customers as first, second or third phase. This was a British process that was adopted by the US. First phase reports were despatched to around twenty customers within four to five hours of the aircraft landing.[95] The 3rd Photo Group defined First Phase reports as:

> These may be either verbal, or radio or telegraphic signals. They come from a quick survey of the photographs to discover a few important bits of intelligence upon which an operation may be waiting. They do not aim to be thorough – SPEED is their essence.[96]

Second phase reporting was more detailed and more likely to be written down in Photographic Interpretation Reports that have been retained in archives. They do not, however, deal with targets in minute detail. The distribution of second phase reporting was also greater with about 180-customers receiving the reports. These reports were delivered to the customer the day after they were flown, and each report usually covered an average of 10-targets.[97] Greater levels of detail were considered in third phase interpretation where installations are studied in great depth, possibly over weeks or months. The 3rd Photo Group was responsible for the collection of battle damage assessment. This was considered separately to other interpretation and was generally the highest priority for the USAAF in terms of flying the mission and assessing the results. Effective assessment could determine whether a bombing mission had been a success or whether it needed to be flown again. Occupation of potential defensive positions, such as the Abbey and the hills surrounding it would be overlaid on defence overprints. All enemy defensive positions identified on air photographs would be marked on the overprint in red and all other sources reporting defensive positions would be shown in purple.

The importance of PR was also supported from the German viewpoint. A captured German document gave the following powerful indictment of Allied PR and the effect upon its operations:

> Enemy aerial reconnaissance detects our every movement, every concentration, every weapon, and immediately after detection, smashes every one of these objectives. This is accomplished by a close coordination of Air Force and Artillery. Every soldier must be made to realise that the enemy's present superiority in the air is not of temporary duration – subject to time and location – but rather that it is part of a permanent set of conditions that must be faced by our troops. Experience demonstrates that the enemy knows how to reconnoitre and destroy our every concentration. Every weapon detected by the enemy is destroyed by coordinated fire directed by his OPs. The enemy can conduct his artillery reconnaissance observation completely unhindered.[98]

That the Germans displayed excellent camouflage discipline was testified to by the Commanding Officer of the 285 Wing of fighter-reconnaissance aircraft, Millington:

---

95   AFHRA Reel C0043, Frame 0247, Types Of Photographic Interpretation Done By MAPRW Interpretation Sections, Headquarters 1944, 90th PRW A-2 Historical Section.
96   Photo Recon for MATAF and 15th Army Group – 3rd Photo Group, 6 March 1945, Combined Arms Research Library, Digital Library <https://cgsc.contentdm.oclc.org/digital/collection/p4013coll8/id/2903/rec/8> (accessed 10 July 2010).
97   AFHRA Reel C0043, Frame 0247.
98   AFHRA Reel A6112.

On the subject of concealment, we always knew when we were flying over the front line either when starting out on a reconnaissance mission or when returning: the contrast was astonishing, for in the German occupied territory not a thing moved; perhaps a solitary vehicle would be observed, but as soon as the driver or look-out saw an aeroplane the vehicle stopped.[99]

If the Allied PR organisation was as good as the Germans suggested, how likely was it that it would not have been able to ascertain whether a very large building was occupied by a military force? And, if the German discipline was as good as the Allies witnessed, how likely was it that any Germans in the building would have exposed themselves to detection by standing around in the courtyard, or hanging out their washing?

The final major source of intelligence used to determine the German occupation of the Abbey was Human Intelligence (HUMINT). This incorporated a number of sub-sources including: agents, escaped or rescued Allied POWs, refugees, partisans, prisoners and friendly force patrolling.

As the name suggests HUMINT is the intelligence function that dealt with the extraction of information from people. This is not just the enemy. Information came from friendly and neutral sources. Just like SIGINT and PR, HUMINT has a few advantages and disadvantages. The first advantage is that human sources can have direct contact with the intelligence that gave a contextual richness not available to the other sources. Unlike SIGINT that relied on transmission, a human source could be more proactive, gleaning intelligence through subtle questioning, through visual means or by the acquisition of documents. Human sources were more likely to gain a good feel of an enemy's intentions or the atmospherics of a situation than other sources.

There were, however, a few traps with HUMINT that intelligence staff needed to know when dealing with this information. Very few people had a broad knowledge of what was going on in a very complex and naturally secretive environment. They saw information from a narrow perspective. They may have risked their liberty or their life to obtain it and therefore from their point of view it had great value. In the case of agents or spies, the motivation of someone willing to betray their own side needs to be assessed. Why were they doing it? Money, belief, fears, the thrill of it, or are they being forced through exposed weaknesses? There were a host of reasons why a person would become an intelligence source. Could they be trusted? Any source, if exposed, could be used to pass false and damaging information. The collection of information from spies often conjured up a seductive allure to commanders and intelligence analysts alike. The adventure and derring-do of the secret services often presented a more credible picture than the evidence warranted. Human intelligence was possibly the most likely to be wrong, or at least contextually in error, due to the vagaries of human nature. It should not be trusted unless supported by other forms of intelligence, but it often sat on the top of the intelligence reports that decision-makers read. Successful analysis and assessment dealing with such potentially volatile intelligence sources relied on ensuring that each piece of information is supported by other sources. All intelligence is vulnerable to deception activity and clever deceivers could make it incredibly difficult to differentiate the signal from the noise. Use of all sources, each interlocking and providing collateral support for the other was really the only way to pierce the fog.

99   G Millington, *The Unseen Eye* (London: Panther Books, 1965), p.127.

The Fifth Army history, between January and March 1944 accounts for a total of 1,535 prisoners that were captured from the three German divisions directly defending the Monte Cassino area; these were the 1st *Fallschirmjager* Division, the 44th Infantry Division and the 90th *Panzer-Grenadier* Division.[100] The vast majority were from the 44th Infantry Division, responsible until 7 February for the defence of Monte Cassino and the surrounding hills. The large number of prisoners captured by Fifth Army, a total of over 8,500 between January and March 1944, meant that not all could be interrogated by the Fifth Army Interrogation Center.[101] It was vitally important that prisoners were quickly interrogated in order to exploit the so-called 'shock of capture'. Each prisoner was classified by his rank, unit, whether he was likely to cooperate and how intelligent he was. Interrogation was carried out by US II Corps down to regimental level.[102] This allowed interrogators to benefit from the initial shock of capture, when prisoners were most likely to talk.[103] Each corps and division had six-man interrogation teams. Information gleaned was then passed through subsequent levels to assist interrogators to sift the most likely subjects of intelligence value. There was considerable use of aerial photography to assist prisoners in providing information on enemy dispositions.[104] A captured document exploitation team was attached from AFHQ to examine every scrap of paper.[105] German army prisoners were generally willing to speak, especially those from other nations forced to serve. This was supported by war correspondent Ernie Pyle who visited a POW camp in Italy early in 1944. He said that all but the hardened Nazis were talkative and that many were Austrians or Poles.[106] It seemed likely that from the 1,300 or so prisoners captured on the Cassino massif from a non-native unit, the 44th Infantry Division, someone would have mentioned any German defensive positions within the Abbey. Included in these prisoners was at least one regimental commander captured on 30 January 1944 in the Cairo village area.[107] The 44th was an Austrian Division, which was only partially trained in mountain warfare and whose lack of efficiency had been identified by the corps commander and logged in his war diary. Gaining an accurate picture of dispositions, and occupation or otherwise of the Abbey itself from prisoners from this lesser quality division, should have been a routine task.[108]

The British SIS established itself at Bari by October 1943.[109] This unit's pseudonym was No1 Intelligence Unit and it was run by James Bruce Lockhart. Its task was twofold; to establish an independent network of agents, and to establish a relationship with Italian Military

100 Fifth Army History Part IV, pp.226-7. Totals: 1st Parachute Division – 116, 44th Infantry Division – 1303 and 90th Panzer Grenadier Division – 166.
101 Fifteenth Army Group Encyclopaedia, p.32.
102 Fifteenth Army Group Encyclopaedia, p.36.
103 Lessons in Combat, November 1942 to September 1944, Headquarters 34th Infantry Division, Chapter VII – Intelligence, PW Interrogation, September 1944. <http://www.34infdiv.org/history/34div/LessonsLearned.pdf > (accessed 15 July 2010).
104 Fifteenth Army Group Encyclopaedia, p.36. Lessons in Combat 34th Infantry Division, Chapter VII.
105 Fifteenth Army Group Encyclopaedia, p.41.
106 Pyle, p.86.
107 Luttrell, p.19.
108 See Jackson, p156. Doubts about its reliability may also be found in Ellis, *Hollow Victory*, pp.114-5 and Senger, *Neither Fear nor Hope*, p.186.
109 Hinsley et al, 178. Keith Jeffrey. *MI6: The History of the Secret Intelligence Service 1909-1949* (London: Bloomsbury Publishing, 2010), p.500.

Intelligence.[110] Its focus was penetrating Northern Italy, Central Europe and the Balkans rather than supporting the Allied armies.[111] By the beginning of 1944, most SIS staff had relocated to Naples.[112] The Bari unit had established about five agents and wireless-telegraphy operators in enemy-held territory. At AFHQ, SIS was also known as the Inter-Service Liaison Department.[113] Little survived of what they produced, but its 'intelligence on German order-of-battle and troop movements was well received.'[114] This assertion is contradicted by Hunt, in 15th Army Group intelligence at the time. On intelligence received from 'various special organizations', code for secret services, he bluntly stated that 'Results were miserable and never looked like being anything else. The trouble is that the organisers, more often than not, had no military background and did not realize what sort of rubbish they were purveying.'[115]

A far more influential critic of SIS was Brooke. In March 1943 he visited SIS in London and noted that at that time there were no agents in Sicily, Sardinia or Italy. In his view, this was due to an over-reliance on ULTRA.[116] Another of what Hunt called, perhaps unfairly, 'these naive and useless organizations', was the American OSS, the forerunner of today's CIA. Despite SIS' hand in establishing OSS, the two organizations had a strained relationship.[117] OSS acted independently and often in competition with SIS despite the 'necessity for harmonious collaboration.'[118] Even Eisenhower had noticed problems with the two organisations. In a letter to Marshall on 28 August 1943, before Allied forces landed on mainland Italy, he complained:

> I have always believed in Donovan's organisation which represents also a high level intelligence gathering agency in which the British have been particularly proficient, and in which we have sadly lacking in our own organisation. However, there is great competition and much jealousy between Donovan's organisation and the corresponding British set up. We have managed to get them pretty well integrated in this area, although this has been done only by knocking their heads together and putting them under the direct control of G-2.[119]

Even internally problems were very apparent. OSS officer Peter Tompkins, a pre-war journalist, thought the OSS was rife with 'injustice, corruption, incompetence and political machinations.'[120] The British and American spies worked alongside each other, but would not merge. In one important aspect OSS had the edge in that it could make use of Italian Americans who often spoke fluent Italian, retaining familial and business contacts. The British ceded the Rome networks to OSS. Following victory in Sicily the Italian OSS, known as the 2677th Headquarters Company, was divided into detachments, with a unit concentrating on Italy in general and another providing specific support to Fifth Army's G-2 Branch.[121] Elements landed

110 Jeffrey, p.500.
111 Jeffrey, pp.500-1.
112 Hinsley et al, p.178.
113 Max Corvo, *OSS Italy 1942-1945* (New York: Enigma Books, 2005), p.333.
114 Hinsley et al, p.178fn.
115 Hunt, p.241.
116 Fraser, p.313fn.
117 Hinsley et al, p.464.
118 Jeffrey, p.499.
119 Chandler et al, *Eisenhower Papers, Vol II*, p.1361.
120 Tompkins, p.12.
121 Corvo, p.100.

with the infantry on the Salerno beaches.[122] By January 1944, OSS had 46-agents behind enemy lines in Italy.[123] Several, controlled by Tompkins in Rome, were passing valuable military data.[124] Tompkins had been assigned to Rome by Donovan in January 1944, 'to act as intelligence officer for the Fifth Army and coordinate sabotage and counter sabotage activities with the resistance movements.'[125] He arrived in Rome late in January 1944 just hours before the Anzio landing.[126] Soon, Tompkins had taken over a clandestine radio, Radio Vittoria, the only intelligence source transmitting from Rome. The radio network was operated under the supervision of agent 'Cervo.' Also working for Giglio was Franco Malfatti, a suave socialist resistance member, whose 'Socialist Intelligence Service' worked with Tompkins, and used his extensive network to provide accurate military intelligence. His intelligence was so extensive and accurate that Tompkins initially thought that he must be a double-agent.[127] He accurately identified the *panzer-grenadier* divisions heading south to reinforce Senger following McCreery's assault on the Garigliano.[128] His sources correctly identified the German first attempt to quash the Anzio landings and also identified Operation *FISCHFANG* by 5 February.[129] He knew about the total number of German troops being thrown against the beachhead by getting hold of their bread ration figures.[130] One of his main sources was an Italian officer named Ottorino Borin from the Alto Adige region of Northern Italy, who spoke perfect German and worked in the Rome headquarters of the military commander of the city, *Generalleutnant* Kurt Mälzer.[131] Malfatti may also have had a source from within Kesselring's headquarters.[132] Tompkins sent his Radio Vittoria messages both to Caserta and directly to the Anzio beachhead.[133]

Tompkins, although an American educated in England, was well-connected in Italy and spoke the language like a native. He was the godson of Osborne, British Minister to the Holy See.[134] Unlike other operatives, Tompkins worked directly to Donovan through Colonel Ellery Huntington, the OSS' head of Special Operations.[135] The Fifth Army OSS unit was not a harmonious organization, with individual rivalry being rife. One detachment commander, Donald Downes, told Donovan, 'the quality of those directing OSS in the field was appallingly low.'[136] Within three weeks of the Salerno landing, the Fifth Army detachment commander, possibly Captain Andre Pacatte, had been changed and was changed again several times thereafter.[137] Pacatte was transferred to Corsica by January 1944 where he was a key OSS figure until

122 Corvo, p.112.
123 TNA WO 204/12836 OSS Operations, Letter Off Special Detachment G-2, Fifth Army to Colonel Glavin Commanding Officer OSS, AFHQ, 12 January 1944.
124 Trevelyan pp.106-7
125 Katz, p.373.
126 Katz, p.144-5.
127 Tompkins, p.61.
128 Tompkins, p.60.
129 Tompkins, pp.77, 90.
130 Tompkins, p.83.
131 Tompkins, p.104.
132 Katz, p.165.
133 Tompkins, p.63.
134 Katz, p.49.
135 Katz, p.96.
136 Anthony Cave-Brown, *Wild Bill Donovan: The Last Hero* (New York: Times Books, 1982), p.503.
137 Corvo, p.139.

1945.[138] It wasn't only OSS that was involved. Tompkins was inserted into Italy via an OSS network ran by a professional French *Deuxieme Bureau* officer called Captain A who ran a rival network.[139] The OSS in Rome was fractious with several individuals claiming command; this would eventually result in disaster and Tompkins was forced to go on the run. Following the collapse of Tompkins' network and another crisis with British Intelligence over the reliability of the OSS agent Princess Pignatelli, who turned out to also be a Fascist and SD informer, the interest of Devers was aroused.[140] He asked his senior staff to investigate the amount of money OSS was spending. In a conversation with the man Donovan had sent to sort out the mess, Colonel Edward Glavin, he said the OSS seemed to be 'expending greater sums than were warranted by the achievements.'[141]

The Fifth Army unit was commanded by Captain Vincent Abrignani in February 1944. He was asked to investigate following the bombing of the Abbey but could find no evidence of German occupation. The conclusion from this is that if Abrignani could not find any OSS intelligence after the bombing, he could not have supported the decision to bomb it. OSS Intelligence was transmitted daily from field agents all over Italy to Fifth Army, much of which concerned the German order of battle at Cassino.[142] They did not only operate in Italy. In Berlin, in the German Foreign Ministry, the OSS had a spy named Fritz Köibe, who was passing German cables, including those from the Rome Embassy to Allen Dulles in Switzerland.[143] In addition to OSS and SIS collaboration, Fifth Army established direct contact with the Italian service through its G-2 Italian Liaison Section.[144]

Finally, from the middle of January 1944, Allied soldiers were near the Abbey. Contact with the enemy was constant and patrolling and direct observation was fundamental to discovering German dispositions and intentions. As Lieutenant Harold Bishop of 168th Infantry Regiment stated, 'it is of great importance in defensive positions to gain intelligence through reconnaissance and combat patrols.'[145] The US Army suggested that observation positions contributed more than half of all operational intelligence to divisional and higher headquarters.[146]

138 Claudia Nasini, *The OSS in the Italian Resistance: A Post Cold War Interpretation* <http://eurostudium. eu/rivista/monografie/Nasini%20OSS.pdf > (accessed September 2021).
139 Tompkins, p.17.
140 Cave-Brown, p.504.
141 Cave-Brown, p.504.
142 Corvo, p.162.
143 Katz, pp.80-1.
144 Fifteenth Army Group Encyclopaedia, pp.46-8.
145 34th Inf Div, *Lessons Learned*, para 1g 'patrol operations.'
146 TNA CAB 106/361: US Army Lessons from Italy, 1 Feb-30 Sep 1944, p.121.

15

Making the Decision

The Anglo-American gentlemen have treated Monte Cassino like a potato field, and it looks here just like any other place they have given their special attention.

Dom Martino Matronola
Secretary to Abbot Diamare
9 February 1944[1]

Before examining the final decision to destroy the Abbey of Montecassino, it is worth making clear that those involved in the process were all experienced men with very great responsibilities. They were all under extreme pressure by the time of the second battle of Cassino. They were under political pressure, under time pressure as OVERLORD approached and their time in the sun diminished, under practical pressure as the casualties mounted and under psychological pressure as their soldiers' morale sagged as they failed again and again. Others such as Arnold were under different pressures, striving for great ambitions of independence from the Army. He suffered several heart attacks in pursuit of his vision. The decisions they made must be judged with these pressures in mind. The human is fallible, it makes mistakes. This fallibility should, perhaps, be an alternative principle of war. Even the most talented, and the leaders in this theatre were all talented, make mistakes. They make decisions that they would have made differently under different circumstances. This will not stop us from critically analysing the decision, but the often-harrowing circumstances in which it was made must not be forgotten.

If Tuker did not use occupation by the enemy as a reason for the Abbey's destruction, Freyberg did, and it is reasonably clear that the impetus to attack, if not destroy, the Abbey came from him. Like the soldiers with which he had a great affinity, Freyberg was convinced the Germans were using the building, although how he drew this conclusion is unclear. There had been plenty of Germans in the Abbey over the past few months, but they did not occupy it or conduct military operations from it. In the New Zealand Corps intelligence summaries from 2-14 February, it was not assessed that they occupied the Abbey.[2] In his despatch to his government on 4 April, he reported: 'The Benedictine Monastery was destroyed by heavy air bombardment, a

---

1   Grossetti and Matronola, p.103.
2   TNA CAB 44/138: Italy Operations Winter 1943/4, Part IV – Operations in the Cassino Sector – 20 January – 31 March 1944, Appendix 27.

step which was forced upon us because, despite enemy protests to the contrary, it was being used as an observatory for military purposes.'[3]

Freyberg's statement is inconsistent with research unearthed by historian of New Zealand's war, Matthew Wright, in his 2003 study of the decision. He claims that occupation of the Abbey 'was irrelevant to Freyberg's plan.'[4] Wright makes strong arguments, using primary sources from the New Zealand archives to suggest that the Abbey was incidental to his attack and that he was prepared for damage to the building but that he did not plan the direct targeting of it. In Freyberg's diary, in the entry for 11 February he said that: 'GOC said we are going on with our bombardment and if the monastery is hit, it cannot be helped. Same thing applies to dive bombing.'[5]

Freyberg did not intend to target the Abbey directly, but he had judged that damage to it was an acceptable risk in the attack on German positions. The final sentence in the above quotation inferred that Freyberg had only fighter-bombers and dive bombers in mind, not strategic bombers, and that damage was to be restricted to one of the thick walls to effect entry for the Indians. His diary entry of 12 February states at his 8.00am air conference that, 'air not available – wall of Abbey is so thick that bombing of it is not looked upon as much use. The wall is really the only military objective.'[6] This statement is key to the Necessity argument and if this was his intent, the blame for the attack on the Abbey itself as the principal target lies elsewhere. However, Wright also cited Freyberg's conversation with one of his senior officers, Queree later on 11 February. The Official History suggests it was Queree, who called the Abbey 'the wee white hoose', that began the process that culminated with its bombing.[7]

Freyberg was concerned that his soldiers could be picked off by Germans retreating into the Abbey, hence his request to bomb it. He had no evidence that they were occupying it. There was no intelligence to suggest that they would occupy it and the orders not to use the Abbey, issued by Kesselring, remained in place. Kippenberger said that the decision was taken on 12 February, but that he did not want to destroy the Abbey, but only to 'soften resistance.'[8] Freyberg accepted the responsibility stating: 'I will take full responsibility. I am perfectly certain that if it were put to an adult audience the decision would be to bomb it; if it means lives can be saved.'[9] He attended an official handover with US II Corps early on 12 February, where notes were taken by the New Zealanders, based upon conflicting reports concerning occupation of the Abbey that 'some have said that Germans are lying there but this is not supported by others. It is very difficult to say whether it is being put to any military purpose at this time.'[10] Despite this lack of clarity, Freyberg's formal request for air support was made late on 12 February, for the next day. He asked for fighter-bomber attacks of German positions close to the Abbey. His air staff officer, Robin Bell, made the observation that: 'The difficulty about bombing at present is that whole of air effort at present is concentrated on the beachhead.'[11] The request for air support

3   Peter Singleton-Gates, *General Lord Freyberg VC* (London: Michael Joseph, 1963), p.277.
4   Wright, Kindle location, p.738.
5   Wright, Kindle location, p.756.
6   Freyberg, Diary Entry, 12 February 1944.
7   Phillips, p.205.
8   Wright, Kindle location, 788.
9   Freyberg, Diary Entry, 11 February 1944.
10   Wright, Kindle location, 764.
11   Freyberg, Diary Entry, 11 February 1944.

and the decision to use heavy bombers are therefore unconnected. The next statement could be considered contradictory to that claim. On 9 February, Freyberg spoke to Clark about striking the Abbey with a 'token bomb' as a show of force. Clark, however, said that only heavy bombers would do.[12] Freyberg was reported to have said, disingenuously considering Tuker's reluctance to attack the Abbey, that 'I want it bombed. The other targets are unimportant, but this one is vital. The division commander who is making the attack feels that it is an essential target and I thoroughly agree with him.'[13] This statement is based on oral testimony and not through written records, so it cannot be verified whether it was said at all or whether the memory is faulty about what was actually said. He may have been referring to Dimoline, who was in temporary command of the Division due to Tuker's illness. He had been up on the massif that day to ascertain the division's requirements and had reported that evening to Freyberg.

Freyberg should have known that the other targets were far from unimportant. His entire scheme of manoeuvre depended on control of the key terrain, although he did not fully appreciate this. Holland suggests that Tuker asked for Point 593 to be attacked by air as well as the Monte Cassino feature. He did not ask in his two memoranda and there is no other documentary evidence that he did so.[14] It was from this point that Dimoline planned to send his infantry to seize the Abbey. As of 9 February, it was controlled by the German defenders, although the situation remained confused. There was never any order to use CAS against this strong defensive position, yet without it, Freyberg could not assault the Abbey as German positions were mutually supporting. Considering Freyberg's previous observations regarding the Americans' poor use of air power in support of assaulting forces, it seemed a strange omission. The failure to attack Point 593 and other terrain made the bombing pointless because the Germans would occupy its ruins, strengthen them into a more formidable position than they could have been when the Abbey stood. Merely damaging the Abbey in a 'token effort' as was Freyberg's stated intent was equally pointless, would soften up no-one and would in not support the Indian assault unless the surrounding German positions were also attacked. Gaining entry by using fighter-bombers to breach the Abbey wall could have been effective, had Germans been present in the Abbey. The heavy and medium bombers could not achieve the accuracy to accomplish this task.

Freyberg was unusual for a subordinate general in that he was also the representative of a Dominion Government, who could recommend the withdrawal of his country's contingent in the event of excessive casualties. This point has been made often in the chronicles of the battles. He was handled carefully by Alexander. Clark claimed of the New Zealanders that 'they have always been given special considerations which we would not give to our own troops.'[15] In his diary he called the attitude to Freyberg 'political daintiness'.[16] Freyberg was a 'man of great bravery and limited intellect who had been placed in a position of great political subtlety.'[17] Yet the national position of Freyberg was only relevant when New Zealand forces were involved.

12   Hapgood and Richardson, p.158.
13   Trevelyan, p.131.
14   James Holland, *General Francis Tuker and the Bombing of Montecassino* <https://www.griffonmerlin.com/2008/08/05/general-francis-tuker-and-the-bombing-of-monte-cassino/> (accessed 27 August 2020).
15   Blumenson, *Salerno to Cassino*, p.402.
16   Atkinson, p.435.
17   Hapgood and Richardson, p.149.

They were not used in the attack on the Monte Cassino massif, which involved only Indian troops. Freyberg had no national responsibility for the Indians and could not dictate what Indian forces could do beyond his normal command responsibilities. In military command and control terms he had Operational Control (OPCON) of the Indians, rather than Full Command which was retained by C-in-C India. This command level remained with Auchinlek. Perhaps as relevant as Freyberg's military position was his political connections in that he was on first name terms with Churchill.[18]

The request for air support should not have included an explicit request for a specific target or the use of a specific weapon or aircraft. Ground forces should ask the air force for an effect on the ground that helped to achieve their aims; how air forces achieved this was up to them. This was the practice in early 1944 according to an AFHQ Operations Memorandum dated 6 May 1944 which reflected US air doctrine, and summarised how air power had been delivered:

> It is the duty of the Army Commander to indicate to the Air Force Commander the effect he wants achieved to further the operations of the land forces, and when he wants that effect achieved. The method of achieving it in the actual selection of targets is the responsibility of the Air Force Commander, who will make appropriate use of the available expert advice and information from ground forces and other intelligence sources. Success in a modern battle on land, however, involves a combined land air plan. Army and Air Force Commanders therefore must work in the closest consultation throughout all stages of the formulation and execution of the plan, to ensure that the land and air operations interact to the best advantage.[19]

Reading this guidance, the target selection of the Abbey should have come from Saville or Cannon rather than from the land commanders. The ground generals should have asked their air counterparts to deliver the effect of clearing the route for Fifth Army into the Liri Valley, the aim of the Cassino battles. Had that task required the seizure of Monte Cassino or the Abbey, then Cannon should have made the judgement of whether that task was within his force's capacity to achieve and what other targets would be necessary, for example Point 593. He may have made the decision that the light and medium bombers could not destroy the targets and he could then have referred the target to Eaker, who could either on his own initiative or by gaining the agreement of Spaatz have tasked Twining's heavy bombers if they were available. This is not, however, what appears to have happened. The target was entirely selected by ground commanders with little idea or knowledge of the air effects that could be achieved.

Despite Tuker's request for 'Blockbuster' bombs, Freyberg's first request to Gruenther at 7:00pm on 12 February was for 36-'Kittybomber' sorties, each delivering only single-1000lb bombs.[20] This request, at odds with his divisional commander, probably confirmed that he had not yet read Tuker's memos on the subject, or if he had, chose an alternative plan. Tuker's letters are regularly seen as an important step in the destruction of the Abbey. Freyberg's request casts

18 David Reynolds, *In Command of History* (London: Penguin Books, 2004) Amazon Kindle Location 4303-4308. Singleton-Gates, pp.66-72.
19 AFHQ Operation Memorandum No 54 dated 6 May 1944 – The Employment of Bombers and Fighter-Bombers in Co-Operation with the Army in AFRHA REEL A6111 Frames 1114-1115.
20 Blumenson, '*Salerno to Cassino*', p.403.

Decisionmakers. Major General John Cannon, Lieutenant General Carl Spaatz, Lieutenant General Mark Clark and General Henry Arnold. (NARA RG342-FH-000584)

Forward Air Controllers in light aircraft assisted fighter-bombers in target location. This L-5 aircraft is accompanied by P-40 Kitty bombers. (NARA RG342-FH-000588)

A pre-attack reconnaissance image of the Abbey. This is probably taken shortly before the attack as damage to the Basilica can be clearly seen on the image. Note that there are only a few craters around the Abbey. (NARA RG342-FH-000143)

doubt on their importance. The Kittybomber aircraft could deliver up to 2,000lb of ordnance using bombs between 250lb and 1,000lb. He did not at this point mention that the actual target was the Abbey. Apart from the clear inappropriateness of the request if the intent was to flatten the Abbey, Gruenther doubted whether the support would be available on 13 February as a counterattack was expected at Anzio which would require considerable air support and Clark had ordered prioritisation for the beachhead. All he could offer was a squadron of A-36 Mustangs, each with single-500lb bombs, a less effective solution.[21] This request came on the heels of a visit to Freyberg's headquarters by Alexander and Harding in the afternoon of the 12 February.[22] Neither Freyberg's request nor Gruenther's offer was going to knock the defenders, if there were any, into 'imbecility.' It may never have been Freyberg's intention to do so. In Freyberg's aide's log he said the aim was to 'soften the people who are there.'[23] It was at this point that Fifth Army learned that he wanted to attack the Abbey itself rather than the surrounding

21   Blumenson, '*Salerno to Cassino*', p.404. The A-36 is the attack aircraft that was developed to become the P-51 Mustang, a very light tactical aircraft for Close Air Support use.
22   Phillips, p.207.
23   Graham and Bidwell, p.197.

positions. Gruenther could not find the Abbey on the target list, but Freyberg argued, 'I am quite sure it was on my list, but in any case, I want it bombed.'[24]

This list, as with many documents related to the bombing has not been found. As it was on the list of protected sites, Gruenther did not have authority to approve the request without consulting Clark, who was at Anzio. Unable to contact him, he stated that he contacted Harding, for the opinion of 15th Army Group.[25] Blumenson's Official History stated that Gruenther told Harding the following:

> General Freyberg has asked that the Abbey of Monte Cassino be bombed tomorrow. General Clark will not be available for about an hour, so he does not know of this request. General Clark has spoken to General Freyberg on at least two occasions concerning the advisability of bombing the Monastery. He told General Freyberg that after consulting General Keyes, the II Corps Commander, and General Ryder, the Commander of the 34th Division, he considered that no military necessity existed for its destruction. General Freyberg expressed to General Clark his considered opinion that the destruction of the Monastery was a military necessity, and that it was unfair to assign to any military commander the mission of taking the hill, and at the same time not grant permission to bomb the Monastery. I am quite sure that General Clark still feels that it is unnecessary to bomb the Monastery. However, in view of the nature of the target, and the international and religious implications involved. I should like to get an expression of opinion from ACMF as to the advisability of authorizing the bombing.[26]

When Gruenther told Freyberg that Clark was 'not anxious to bomb the monastery.' Freyberg replied:

> The General who had to do the attack considered that if the place was not softened the most difficult feature…would be an obstacle which might cause the attack to fail. Gen G(ruenther) said that the Army Comd had pointed out that the fact it was demolished would not necessarily lessen its value as an obstacle. The GOC said he did not think the bombing and shelling would demolish it. They would damage it. The thing was that they would soften the people who are there. Gen G mentioned reports that there are possibly civilians there and said 'But if your judgement is that you think it should be done, it shall be done.[27]

The visit from Alexander and the subsequent request by Freyberg to Clark, suggests that these two had made the decision and that Clark's nod was to keep the decision within the chain of command. Neither Freyberg nor Alexander could be seen to bypass Clark. His position was supported by those American commanders most intimately associated with the battle. These were Major-Generals Keyes, Ryder and Walker Commanding US II Corps, 34th and 36th

24 Blumenson, 'Salerno to Cassino', p.404.
25 Strangely, as with Wilson's memoirs, Harding's biographer (Field-Marshal, Lord) Carver fails to account for the decision. See Michael Carver, Harding of Petherton (London: Wiedenfeld and Nicolson, 1978), pp.125-6.
26 Blumenson, Salerno to Cassino, p404. ACMF refers to 15th Army Group.
27 Wright, Kindle location, 806.

Divisions respectively as well as their Chief Intelligence Officers.[28] Juin, who considered Monte Cifalco to the northwest a far more important observation position, was also opposed.[29] In his memoir he called the attack an *'essai 'bille en tête''* – 'a reckless test.'[30] He viewed the attack as isolated, carried out whilst all the other forces looked on impotently – part of Clarks 'pitiful' plan.[31] It had no chance of success as the Germans would shift their defences to meet it. Even the *Times* correspondent, who had been reporting the German use of the Abbey, in his report of 28 January identified Monte Cairo as having 'direct observation over the valley from a vantage point not merely hundreds, but thousands of feet high' and 'Every movement would be clear through field glasses by day.'[32] Destroying the Abbey would have no effect on the German ability to direct its guns from observation posts, regardless of how it was being used. Juin, like Tuker had always advocated a mountain strategy swinging round behind Cassino and isolating it rather than attacking it head-on, although he would have faced severe logistical difficulties getting supplies and men through the fierce slopes and bitter winter weather. He had come very close to succeeding in the last days of January, but Clark's inability or unwillingness to trust or reinforce the French resulted in exhaustion. Eaker and his British deputy, Slessor, also shared Clark's doubts.[33] In his memoirs Sir John stated that the airmen were 'strongly opposed' to the bombing. In his script for the British Official History, kept with his papers, he made a handwritten comment in the section dealing with the bombing of the Abbey. He has underlined the piece which stated, 'Freyberg believed…was a Military Necessity' and placed an X beside it. He also added in the same section that decisions were made 'All without consulting Air.'[34] This was nearly 30-years later. His disapproval was not evident in a letter he wrote to his wife on 16 February in which he shared his 'joy' at American bombing.[35] He tempers that view that whilst accepting the Germans were not occupying the Abbey, he stated that this 'was beside the point.'[36] He also uses the morale argument to justify the building's destruction.[37] If Eaker was not in Italy to make the decision to use the strategic bombers, Slessor as his deputy could have been responsible for the final decision. This is not mentioned either in his memoir or by his biographer. However, in a correspondence with the RAF's Official Historian in 1948, Slessor claims to have had a part in the decision to bomb the Abbey.

> I was very much in on it all at the time and discussed it with Mark Clark, who, as you may remember, was the American Army Commander responsible for the Cassino operation. We (the Air Forces, and particularly the RAF) were always anxious to avoid bombing the Monastery if we possibly could. We were not convinced that the Germans were actually holding it and, in fact, I remember Clark telling me at the time that the American

28   Blumenson, *Salerno to Cassino*, p.404. Green, p.44.
29   Ellis, *Hollow Victory*, p.166; Hapgood and Richardson, p.124.
30   Juin, p.81.
31   Juin, p.83.
32   *The Times*, US Attack North of Cassino, Issue 49765, p.4.
33   Richards and Saunders, p.359; Aileen Clayton, *The Enemy is Listening* (New York: Ballantine Books, 1980), p.346.
34   TNA AIR 75/38, Papers of Sir John Slessor, Draft Official History of the Mediterranean and Middle East Campaign, Chapter XVIII, p.1074.
35   Orange, *Slessor Bomber Champion*, p.145.
36   Sir John Slessor, *The Central Blue* (London: Cassel, 1956), p.577.
37   Slessor, p.578.

Plumes of Smoke

Divisional Commander from whom Freyberg took over did not believe the Monastery was held. Freyberg however incidentally in a very insubordinate manner which put Mark Clark in a difficult position, declined to attack unless the Monastery was first destroyed by bombing.[38]

In his letter, he again makes the point, even after stressing the lack of Germans in the Abbey, that its occupation was 'academic'. Slessor observed that 'we could never have forced the Cassino position without destroying the Monastery.'[39] This opinion makes little sense because the Germans occupied and strengthened the ruins making it an even more formidable obstacle. In his reply Saunders answered Slessor on this point and stated that 'the bombing of the Monastery seems to me to have prolonged the battle and not to have shortened it, for the Germans occupied the ruins.'[40] In a comment piece to *American Heritage* in 1967, Eaker expressed the opinion that he thought fighter-bombers were better for the task. Why he, or his deputy, did not order the fighter-bombers, as was their right as overall air commanders, is an unanswered question. Only the Commander-in-Chief or his American deputy could order the heavy Air Forces to attack the Abbey. Alexander, Clark, Freyberg or Tuker did not have this power. Therefore, the airmen's claims of disagreement do not stand-up.

Before Harding received his instructions from Alexander, Gruenther managed to contact Clark who, as expected, judged no Military Necessity to destroy the Abbey. At around 9:30pm on 12 February, Harding informed Gruenther that Alexander had decided that the Abbey should be bombed if 'Freyberg considered it a Military Necessity.'[41] In his memoirs, Alexander's opinion was that he had deliberately spared the Abbey 'to our detriment', but he also said, 'whether the Germans took advantage of its deep cellars for shelter and its high windows for observation, I do not know.'[42] This was highly improbable. What detriment was Alexander referring to if he remained unsure whether the Germans occupied the Abbey? Besides, he almost certainly did know! His Deputy Chief of Staff, Lemnitzer was closely associated with planning for the attack on the Abbey. In a letter written in 1982 in response to criticism of the decision, he, accused the author of using hindsight saying that: 'Military operations have to be conducted based on intelligence at the time, not on what history shows to be the case forty years later.'[43]

Lemnitzer made a very valid point regarding hindsight. Of course, it is easier for historians to ascertain the facts many years later. His views, admittedly given when memories have dimmed, were not as clear cut as it seemed. He justified the attack on intelligence available that the Germans were occupying the building. He did not say that the building occupied or not, forms part of a defensive position. Nor did he claim it was destroyed for some psychological boost. Lemnitzer also directly contradicted his boss, Alexander, who clearly stated that he wasn't sure whether it was being used as an observation post. Finally, what intelligence did Lemnitzer see

38 TNA AIR 75/69: Papers of Sir John Slessor, The Italian Campaign, Letter to H A St G Saunders Esq dated 19 July 1948.
39 TNA AIR 75/69: Papers of Sir John Slessor, The Italian Campaign, Letter to H A St G Saunders Esq dated 19 July 1948:
40 TNA AIR 75/69, Papers of Sir John Slessor, The Italian Campaign, Letter from H A St G Saunders Esq dated 20 July 1948.
41 Blumenson, *Salerno to Cassino*, p.405.
42 Alexander, *Memoirs*, p.119.
43 L. James Binder, *Lemnitzer A Soldier For His Time* (Washington DC: Brassey's Inc., 1997), p.121.

A post-war picture of Alexander with his former Deputy Chief of Staff, General Lyman Lemnitzer. Lemnitzer claims to have had a part in the planning for the bombing of the Abbey with General Lauris Norstad. (NARA RG73-2355)

that others did not? The intelligence was gathered after the attack to justify it to national capitals, the press and the Vatican. None of it firmly indicated that the Germans were using it. The intelligence of occupation was weak and was rejected by London as valid evidence.

Alexander apparently claimed later that the decision to bomb the Abbey 'had been the most difficult he had ever made.'[44] George Forbes, a British officer present and a post-war contributor to the Catholic *Ampleforth Journal*, in a 1969 article, disagreed. He claimed that Alexander was quite flippant about the Abbey, hearing him say:

> Before the bombing of the Abbey I had a good look at it through my field-glasses and I came to the conclusion that it was not, architecturally, very impressive. Now that it has been destroyed, they will be able to get lots of dollars from America and will be able to put up something really good![45]

In his memoirs, published in 1962, Alexander justified the decision largely on the morale effect rather than occupation by the Germans. He suspected when he sent Lemnitzer to Cassino to review Allied morale whilst the 34th US Infantry Division fought on the Cassino massif that

---

44 Tony Williams, *Cassino: New Zealand Soldiers in the Battle for Italy* (Auckland: Penguin Books, 2002), p.119.
45 Alexander to George Forbes OSB MBE MC <http://www.monlib.org.uk/papers/aj/aj1969-forbes-monte-cassino.html> (accessed 27 April 2017).

morale was poor. There was no immediate attempt to improve American morale by attacking the Abbey prior to their withdrawal on 11 February or even to support their final effort with the ultimate show of force. He must have considered that the destruction of the Abbey could have been the boost in morale required to get the US troops to the prize of Montecassino? But he waited until asked to bomb it by Freyberg, whose Indian troops had just arrived on the massif and whose morale had not yet been affected by the looming presence of the Abbey. He said the following in his memoirs:

> In the context of the Cassino battle, how could a structure which dominated the fighting field be allowed to stand? The monastery had to be destroyed. Withal, everything was done to save the lives of the monks and their treasures: ample warning was given of the bombing.[46]

Clark knew exactly who was in the Abbey when it was bombed. If Clark knew, Alexander knew as well. He made no mention of the hundreds of refugees inside the Abbey in his memoir. How its continuing existence was disadvantageous to the Allies is explained by its morale effect on his troops that has already been discussed.[47] How the Abbey weighed against human lives, when it was just a building that had no Germans in it and had hurt no-one was again a statement that strove to justify an invalid action later rather than a valid reason to do it in the first place. Perhaps more importantly Alexander's handling of the campaign was under constant scrutiny from an impatient Churchill, whose project the Mediterranean had been and who was keen for success before the Americans completely lost interest.[48] The Americans had never been that interested in the first place. Alexander knew what happened to generals who failed Churchill. Churchill was also under pressure to get the stalled campaign going and he faced disaster at Anzio, for which he was the grand architect. Comparisons with Gallipoli were already being made. This was seeping out of the beachhead with CBS' John Daly reporting that 'the situation on the beachhead is grim.'[49] NBC news called the Anzio situation 'desperate'. This pressure was intensified on 11 February when Roosevelt made an uncharacteristically candid and gloomy assessment of the Italian campaign.[50] As OVERLORD approached, Alexander's resources were going to reduce. He needed success and he needed it quickly. Alexander also judged that the Abbey's occupation was an important factor when he stated, through Harding, that 'if there is any reasonable probability that the building is being used for military purposes, General Alexander believes its destruction is warranted.'[51] The decision to bomb the Abbey sounds like an act of desperation, Alex clutching at straws.

Clark wilted under great pressure from above and below; it was made clear to him by Freyberg that he would take the blame if things went wrong. He agreed 'to defer to General Freyberg's judgement if Freyberg had evidence that indicated that the monastery should be bombed'.[52]

46   Alexander, *Memoirs*, p.121.
47   Alexander, *Memoirs*, p.121.
48   Martin Gilbert, *Churchill: A Life* (London: Heineman, 1991), 767; Churchill, pp.380-1; Molony, p.705.
49   Casey, p.5.
50   Casey, p.4.
51   Blumenson, *Salerno to Cassino*, p.405.
52   Blumenson, *Salerno to Cassino*, p.406.

Freyberg was informed at around 10:00pm on 12 February. Yet, Freyberg's diary entry for this decision does not suggest that either Clark or Gruenther had any strenuous objections. The entry at this time stated that:

> Gruenther had raised it with Clark who reluctantly concurred if Freyberg thought it a military objective.
> Clark pointed out that if Abbey demolished it would not necessarily lessen its value as an obstacle.
> Freyberg did not think the attack would demolish it, only damage it.
> Gruenther mentioned the civilians but said 'If your judgement is that you think it should be done it shall be done.'[53]

Clark was against the assault, of that there is little doubt. This is supported by a number of contemporary sources. Yet the orthodox view, largely contained within Blumenson's Official History and Clark's memoir is that he was pushed kicking and screaming by the British into the attack. Freyberg's contemporary diary entry, written before the act and subsequent controversy suggests much less resistance at Fifth Army.

Gruenther was told not to order the bombing before 10:00am on 13 February to give Clark time to dissuade Alexander. Gruenther passed this message to the Fifth Army Operations Officer, Donald Brann late on 12 February.[54] On the morning of 13 February, at around 09:15am, Clark spoke directly to Alexander; he explained that he did not support the bombing, and that the Germans were not using the Abbey. The US Army Official History claims that Alexander agreed with Clark, but said 'if Freyberg wanted the monastery bombed, the monastery would have to be bombed.' Freyberg told Gruenther that he had gone into the matter and was quite convinced of the necessity. Clark 'was never able to discover on what he based his opinion.'[55] Nonetheless, Freyberg's request was approved. Although Gruenther approved the target's attack, at this point it was still only the squadron of A-36s that could be allocated. Had the weather not been poor on 13 February, the Abbey would only have been attacked by fighter-bombers as requested by Freyberg. In his memoir Clark, when faced with the decision to attack the Abbey decided that 'we will put everything into it.'[56] This suggested that he wanted to employ the heavy bombers to attack the Abbey, although this was not within his command authority to order. That morning there was a meeting between the HQ Fifth Army, 7th Army Air Support Control (AASC) and HQ New Zealand Corps to discuss arrangements for the bombing of the Abbey and the coordination of the subsequent ground attack.[57] In his diary, Freyberg and Bell visited Fifth Army to be told at 1:50pm that the air plan was 'to smash Monastery in one blow, 700-odd tons in 1,000, 2,000lb bombs.'[58] This appears to be the first time that the use of heavy bombers was mentioned. At 2:00pm on this date, the approval to bomb the Abbey had not yet been received from Clark. The decision had been made by the evening of 13 February as Clark had written the following resigned entry into his diary:

53   Freyberg, Diary Entry, 12 February 1944.
54   Clark, p.253.
55   Clark, p.253.
56   Clark, p.302.
57   Hartcup, p.12.
58   Freyberg Diary Entry, 13 February 1944.

For religious and sentimental reasons, it is too bad unnecessarily to destroy one of the art treasures of the world. Besides we have indications that many civilian women and children are taking shelter therein. The extent of our air effort which we can put on it will not destroy the building but will merely give the Germans an excuse to use it.[59]

Clark gave a lengthy explanation of the decision to the US Army Heritage and Education Centre in 1972. Despite the passage of time from the decision and the likelihood that Clark would paint himself in a positive light; the piece is worth quoting in full:

They had fought in Egypt and so forth and they had fought all the way through, and they took one look at the thing, and they said, 'God we can't take that thing.' The Indians said, 'Hell.' The Indians are a little better on defence than they are on offence anyhow. And the New Zealanders had been used to a lot of air support and stuff. And so I was up at Anzio when I got word from Gruenther that Freyberg had come in and wanted to talk to me about air support and Al (Gruenther) was surprised. It developed that he wanted the monastery destroyed, and then he would attack. I came back and got into it and I said: 'All my intelligence indicates that there are no Germans in the Abbey'…and so I said, 'Nothing doing, I'm not going to do it.' So he went to Alexander, which is what I supposed he would do, and Alex came to me, and Harding got into the act and everything, and I said that I didn't think it should be bombed at all. Gruenther, who represented me when I was away at Anzio, said the same thing. We didn't see the necessity. It was not a military target. He said it was. And so finally I said, 'Well, Alex, it's your decision. If you order it to be done, we do it, but I don't believe in it.' So that's what happened, and we did destroy it and then they didn't attack promptly as they should have, and they were unsuccessful in their attack. There we were sitting with the Germans holding a beautiful defensive work up there, much better off in the rubble and heaping propaganda on us for destroying something they have saved. It was just all wrong, all wrong. [60]

This piece creates an impression of a beleaguered Clark, forced into the decision. The Freyberg diary entry, however, suggests that he put up much less resistance at least to his subordinate than this piece portrays.

For heavy bombers to have been generated to bomb the Abbey, the official method was to declare an 'emergency' situation to the Theatre Commander or to Eaker, who would authorise the bombers to switch tasks on Spaatz's authority. It is not certain how Wilson or Devers justified this diversion as an 'emergency' and no evidence has been found that one was ever declared, or whether they informed the CCS as orders required; there was no mention of it in Brooke's diary.[61]

The official switch from tactical fighter-bombers was probably suggested by MAAF, approved by Wilson and then orders were transmitted to Cannon and Twining who carried them out. A

59   Mikolashek, p.106 citing Clark diary, 13 February 1944.
60   Glynn Harper and John Tonkin-Covell, *The Battles of Monte-Cassino: The Campaign and its Controversies* (London: Allen and Unwin, 2013), Kindle loc 653.
61   Arthur Bryant, *Triumph in the West* (London: Fontana Books, 1965), 120. Danchev and Todman, p.521. Nor is it mentioned in First Sea Lord, Admiral of the Fleet Sir Andrew Cunningham's memoirs. Andrew Cunningham, *A Sailor's Odyssey* (London: Hutchinson and Co., 1952), pp.589-595.

Commanding General of the Mediterranean Allied Strategic Air Forces, Major General Nathan Twining delivers briefing to General Maitland-Wilson on bombing targets in Italy. Wilson could not routinely task Twining's heavy bombers. (NARA RG342-FH-000474)

letter sent by the British CoS to Wilson on 4 March inferred that he had informed them; that it was his decision; and that the claim of the occupation of the Abbey by German forces was the deciding factor.[62] Alexander wrote a long letter to Churchill and Brooke on 11 February, which went into great tactical detail on the Italian campaign.[63] On Freyberg's plans he reported to the Prime Minister that, 'Freyberg hopes to have both his divisions in positions so that we can begin on the night of February 11. The fighting will be very hard as the Germans are fighting as hard and bitterly as I have never seen them do before.'[64]

He did not mention, then or later, any intention to destroy the Abbey. It may have been that he was not aware of Freyberg's intent, but Churchill specifically asked Alexander about the New Zealand Corps attack in a letter of 14 February.[65] He did not mention the Abbey to the Prime Minister on this occasion either, an act of which he was by now undoubtedly aware. This is unusual, especially considering the Prime Minister's thirst for details and his interest in the Mediterranean. Remarkably, there is no evidence that Churchill or Brooke was informed of this highly controversial and politically sensitive act. The next War Cabinet meeting was held on 21 February. The destruction of the Abbey was not mentioned. The Minutes of the Meeting say that: 'On our main front our attempts to take the Cassino monastery had not yet succeeded.'[66]

---

62   TNA CAB 106/699: 35. Message from British Chiefs of Staff to General Wilson, COSMED 51, 4 March 1944. See Jackson, p.194.
63   TNA WO 214/14: Alexander's Correspondence with Prime Minister and CIGS, letter time 111740A February 1944.
64   Tasciotti, p.75.
65   TNA WO 214/14: Alexander Correspondence with Prime Minister and CIGS, letter PM to Alexander 14 February 1944.
66   TNA CAB 65/41/23: War Cabinet Minutes 23 (44) dated 21 February 1944.

Alexander wrote directly to Brooke on the day of the attack, undoubtedly after the attack itself. He made no mention of it, apart from a vague statement about Freyberg's operation starting which presumably was a reference to the bombing as Freyberg had done nothing else by this stage. [67]

It stretched credibility that Churchill was interested in the number of drivers at Anzio, but not the destruction of priceless art and an irreplaceable building. Why would Alexander not even remark that it had happened or give a reason? One possible reason is that Britain's principal policy adviser in AFHQ, Macmillan, was absent from the theatre during the period of decision-making. He had returned to Britain on 12 February, not returning to Algiers until 9 March. A politician as astute as Macmillan, who was in regular receipt of Foreign Office correspondence, would surely have ensured that a decision of such high political potential was referred to Churchill or at the very least senior Foreign Office officials.[68] Churchill forwarded a note to Wilson on the day of the bombing where he discusses Balkans operations. Nowhere in the note does he ask Wilson about the bombing, although he does admonish him for continuing the use of American spellings in his telegrams![69] Again on 19 February Churchill wrote a note to the CoS regarding Italy operations with no mention of the bombing.[70]

67   TNA WO 214/29: Italian Campaign January-February 1944, Signal Alexander to Brooke, 15 February 1944.
68   Macmillan, p.481.
69   TNA CAB 80/80: Annex To COS (44) 167 (O) dated 15 February 1944.
70   TNA CAB 80/80: Annex To COS (44) 177 (O) dated 19 February 1944.

16

The Making of an Air Force

Don't get the notion that your job is going to be glorious or glamorous. You've got dirty work to do, and you might as well face the facts. You're going to be baby-killers and women-killers.

Colonel D H Alkire
Commander, 100th Bombardment Group (Heavy)
Addressing the Group on 15 November 1942 at Wendover Field, Utah[1]

The United States Army Air Corps, despite the fact that America pioneered powered flight and was by far the greatest industrial nation, entered the Second World War disadvantageously when compared to the airpower of its European Allies and its Axis foes. Although the ACTS at Maxwell Field developed innovative theories and the US had the best bombsight in the Norden, the high priest of US military aviation, General Billy Mitchell, had been court-martialled, marginalised and was now dead. The concept of American strategic bombing had been developed after a study in 1917 by Lieutenant Colonel Edgar Gorrall, but after the end of the war strategic bombing found disfavour with the Army, politicians and public opinion. Newton Baker, the Secretary of War, called it a 'manifestation of inhumanity.'[2] Pursuit aviation was seen as the base of airpower until around 1930.

Even as early as 1919, there were official discussions and investigations into an independent air arm, but opposition remained intense, and the air services had until recently been hamstrung by doctrine that restricted airpower only to direct support to its terrestrial masters. In the 1920s air service regulations clearly stated that, 'all air action is auxiliary to the ground battle.'[3] By the time of the Air Corps Act in 1926, the positions of ground and air officers were highly polarised, but the infantry retained the power.[4] Therefore, despite an increasingly dominant bomber doctrine from within the Air Corps and the ACTS specifically, the direct support of ground forces remained the official air doctrine of the US Army. Nevertheless, a concept for decisive airpower employment took shape throughout the 1930s and this doctrine would also, it was

---

1   Edward Jablonski, *Flying Fortress* (Garden City NY: Doubleday Publishing, 1965), p.174.
2   Thomas Greer, *The Development of Air Doctrine in the Army Air Arm, 1917-1941* (Washington, DC: Office of Air Force History, 1985), p.15.
3   Greer, p.16.
4   David E Johnson, *Fast Tanks and Heavy Bombers: Innovation in the US Army 1917-1945* (Ithaca NY: Cornell University Press, 1998), p.102.

hoped, secure Air Force independence. The next step towards autonomy was the establishment of the GHQ Air Force in 1935, which removed all but observation from the control of the corps commanders.

Despite having some of the most modern and innovative aircraft producers, in 1941 most of the Air Corps' equipment was inferior. The B-17 was given to the RAF, but as a day bomber, especially without the Norden bombsight which remained an American secret, the aircraft was too vulnerable to fly over Germany. It was unsuitable as a night bomber with a small bomb load. The RAF rejected the B-17 as a frontline bomber when the Air Staff stated of the E-model:

a)   Defensive power is too weak to afford reasonable protection, the tail-gun position being cramped and the belly turret so awkward as to be useless.

b)   4000lb bombs cannot be installed and bomb loads in any case are small unless the bomb-bay fuel tanks are removed at the expense of range.[5]

It was quickly demoted to a Coastal Command patrol aircraft, which ironically is what the US Army Air Corps stated was its original role – hemispheric defence. The editor of *Jane's All The World's Aircraft*, Charles Grey, lambasted the aircraft, calling it 'just a huge flying target.'[6] Even aircraft with more successful reputations such as the P-38 were not taken up due to safety and power reasons. The famous P-51, built specifically for the RAF with its original Allison engine, was underpowered and ineffective at altitude. It was Rolls Royce that fitted the Merlin engine. Had the aircraft been a USAAC project, history may have been very different. Grey stated, 'To order American airplanes of any sort is an imbecility.'[7] Churchill was scandalized, but one suspects this was due to political embarrassment rather than Grey's statements being untrue! Grey received equal treatment in the British press. He was supported by the Commander in Chief of the RAF's Bomber Command, Air Marshal Sir Richard Pierse, who in December 1941 announced that the Fortress was unsuitable as a day bomber. Arnold had a tough job bringing his force up to scratch, although if decorated pilot and air power author and critic, Alexander de Seversky, was to be believed, he was at least partly responsible for its poor state at the beginning of 1942.

General Henry Harley Arnold, known as Hap, short for Happy, although he had little sense of humour.[8] He graduated from West Point in 1907, and was a mediocre cadet, who failed to make any cadet rank and who finished in the bottom half of his class. He was sent to the infantry, which he hated. After a tour in the Philippines, he was asked to become an army pilot trained by the Wright brothers themselves, although he never flew with them.[9] In 1911, he became the second Army officer to hold an official pilot's licence.[10] As such, he was somewhat of a celebrity, setting three altitude records in 1911 and 1912. He quickly learned the value of

5   Weigley, p.338.
6   Magazine Extracts, Volume 7, Issues 16-18, United States Office of War Information, 21 April 1941.
7   Magazine extracts.
8   Geoffrey Perret, *Winged Victory The Army Air Forces in World War II* (New York: Random House, 1993), p.15.
9   Dik Alan Daso, *Hap Arnold and the Evolution of American Air Power* (Washington DC: Smithsonian Institute Press, 2000), p.48.
10 Richard Davis, *HAP. Henry H Arnold: Military Aviator* (Washington, DC: Air Force Museums and History Program, 1997), p.3.

General Henry 'Hap' Arnold, Commanding General of the USAAF. Arnold could be called the 'father of the modern air force.' He drove his staff hard. (NARA RG342-FH-000373)

using the media to his advantage. In 1914, Arnold met First Lieutenant George Marshall at Fort McKinley in Manila and made a favourable impression. Both men rose to five-star rank and their relationship was a key factor in Allied victory. Arnold did not see combat service in the First World War, much to his frustration, but by August 1918 he had been promoted to colonel, the youngest in the Army.[11] This didn't last as peace brought demobilisation and he was reduced to major as air power languished. In the 1920s Arnold used his connections with politicians and the press to advance aviation. He also appeared, risking his career, as a defence witness in the Courts Martial of Mitchell. Mitchell was a legendary figure within the embryonic US Army aviation services, whom Arnold first met in 1912, and his thoughts on the application of air power to twentieth-century warfare had influenced Arnold and most other airmen. Arnold also learnt how not to influence people after Mitchell was sent into obscurity, considering that his tactics had hardened the conservative War Department against radical air doctrine.[12]

Arnold supported the Air Service chief Major General Mason Patrick and his efforts to obtain greater independence for the Air Service in the mid-1920s. Patrick preferred evolution to revolution and did not like Arnold. When he overstepped the mark, zealously lobbying the case to Congressmen and the papers, Patrick offered him Courts Martial or resignation. He chose the former and Patrick backed down, wishing to avoid a repetition of Mitchell. Arnold

11   Daso, p.86.
12   Greer, p.17.

was then despatched to a remote outpost where he could do no harm and was denied attendance of the staff college at Fort Leavenworth.[13] Perhaps the only victory, albeit a minor one and down largely to Patrick's moderate diplomacy, from the Mitchell affair was that the Air Service was expanded, and in the 1926 Air Corps Act, changed its name to the United States Army Air Corps. When Patrick was replaced by Major General James Fechet, Arnold flourished. He continued to be a networker par excellence, cultivating influential contacts in Hollywood and the aviation industry. He also maintained close relationships with his future Army Air Force commanders, Eaker and Spaatz. In many ways Arnold was a lucky officer as well as a talented one. He had been noticed by several Army Chiefs of Staff, MacArthur, Craig and Summerall during his formative years in different ways. Arnold was a golf partner to General Malin Craig but could not dissuade him that the basic combat element of the Army was still the infantry division. Once the gates had been opened to bomber production, Arnold became Craig's principal adviser.

By the mid-1930s Arnold was a wing commander and in 1936 became a Brigadier-General and Assistant Chief of the Air Corps. After the death of the Chief, Oscar Westover in 1938, and following the public moderation of his radical airpower theories, Arnold was appointed as Chief of the Air Corps in September 1938, over Frank Andrews whose more open sponsorship of four-engine bombers made him unpopular with the General Staff.[14]

Finally, in 1939 his old neighbour and friend Marshall succeeded Craig to the top spot. That is not to say that Arnold was a yes-man or sycophant, but Marshall was a keen advocate for air power and Arnold was his man. Despite the changes, Air Corps historical attitudes to fighters and the War Department opposition to heavy bombers had left American airpower in an unenviable position.

Hap's unstinting, public, and radical support of Mitchell and his difficulties with Patrick had both threatened to torpedo his career, but he had survived. He was an early airpower zealot, whose trajectory was propelling him towards an independent air force, something that to most in the US Army of the 1930s was an anathema. Against his usual form of behaviour, Arnold tempered his views on independence, showed great patience and became a loyal Army officer, keeping his powder dry throughout these years and during his time as Chief of the Air Corps.

When he took over, there was little enthusiasm in the conservative War Department for four-engine bombers. The Air Corps was there to provide direct support to ground forces, nothing more.[15] The tactical thinkers during this time were thinking beyond the support of ground forces, a relative backwater in air thinking in the US as it was in Britain. The bomber culture shaped its future. In the first quarter of 1940, his force numbered just 47,936. In 1940 and 1941, whilst Arnold was trying to build-up the force, he opposed the President's plan to provide Britain with aircraft.[16] Roosevelt threatened to fire him, for amongst other things his leaks to the isolationist press.[17] He also delayed his third star, instead promoting a major general junior to Arnold.[18] Hap had to await Pearl Harbor before receiving his promotion when the President decided not to

13   Perret, p.20.
14   Perret, pp.31-32.
15   H H Arnold, *Global Mission* (Blue Ridge Summit PA: TAB Books, 1989), p.166.
16   Henry. H. Arnold, *American Airpower Comes of Age: General Henry H 'Hap' Arnold's World War II Diaries – Volume 1* (USA: Progressive Management Publications, 2002), p.70.
17   Perret, p.36.
18   Perret, p.56. The officer was Delos C. Emmons, two years junior to Arnold.

Pilot, engineer and airpower commentator, Alexander de Seversky. De Seversky was a major critic of Arnold's management of US airpower, especially upon his failure to deliver a balanced force.
(NARA RG58-753-01)

change horses in light of the attack. After a visit to Britain in early 1941, Arnold worked hard to regain his Commander in Chief's confidence, coming to an agreement with the RAF's Sir Charles Portal.[19] After his period of wilderness, he was eventually readmitted to the top tent following Japan's attack. Under Marshall's tutelage and with the solid support of the President, Arnold oversaw the rapid expansion of America's airpower as war loomed. In 1941 he had a programme of 45 Groups; by September of 1942 this had grown to 273 Groups.[20] At the end of 1941, his force had grown to over 350,000. He was criticised by those who considered he had betrayed the Mitchell idea. Most notably by de Seversky in his book *Victory Through Air Power.21*

De Seversky advocated Mitchell's ideas of a balanced force of fighters and bombers rather than the absolute focus on strategic bombers that seemed to be the trend within the Air Corps. Arnold also talked of a balanced force, but by early 1942 the bombers were far ahead of the fighters in technology and priority. Although unnamed, Seversky was clearly referring to Arnold when he said, 'the officer with a happy talent for handshaking and back-slapping normally rises to power. But that sort of politically minded personality rarely, if ever goes with military or aviation genius.'[22] This was an influential opponent, who thought that an independent US Air Force

19   Arnold Diary Vol 1, p.162.
20   Arnold Diary, p.356.
21   Alexander de Seversky, *Victory Through Air Power* (New York: Simon and Schuster, 1942), pp.250-1.
22   De Seversky, p.220.

was a critical precondition if America was to develop airpower free of stifling Army and Navy bureaucracy. Arnold made it his business to discredit de Seversky, but his efforts were mostly ineffective. Some of his ire came from de Seversky's insistence on escort fighters for the bomber force. In time, de Seversky was proven right and Arnold wrong; the bombers could not defend themselves. His dislike of Arnold was longstanding, and the feeling was mutual. He said of US military aviation in 1942:

> We have no air power. We have only army and naval aviation developed and used primarily as auxiliary weapons for surface operations...Worst of all, our aviation equipment is built without specific relation to strategic and tactical problems facing us; it has not the range for independent action in the ever-widening theatre of operations, being normally an appendage to slow-moving surface forces. We lack even a vestige of unity of command in the aerial sphere. As a matter of plain fact, we have neither air power nor airmen, but only flying soldiers and flying sailors who do not even speak the same military language.[23]

De Seversky was perhaps somewhat harsh on Arnold, but his views were certainly enhanced by US aviation's performance up to early 1942 and no part of the above statement could be deemed untrue. He had many supporters within the higher echelons of Arnold's force. At the Battle of Midway, Arnold's B-17 force failed to hit any Japanese warship. Change was on the way but airpower was 'little more than an 'oxymoron', prior to Arnold taking over as Chief.'[24] It didn't seem much better after four years of his tenure if Pearl Harbor, the Philippines and Midway were anything to go by. By the Autumn of 1941, the *Luftwaffe* and the RAF had proven that the self-defended day bomber could not defeat the single-engine day fighter on home turf. The performance of Midway rapidly improved and the USAAF would gain much greater independent freedom of action. Nevertheless, de Seversky's book remains the best-selling book on airpower; even though a polemic on America's pre-war malaise and a criticism of war leaders in time of war, it sold 400,000 copies in just a few months.[25] The book remained at the top of the *New York Times* bestseller list for four-weeks and spawned a Walt Disney film in 1943. Arnold refused to watch it, but it was seen by both Roosevelt and Churchill, who then made Arnold and the CCS watch it.[26]

Although a little xenophobic, he was impressed by the RAF's pioneering use of the heavy bomber and the blockbuster bomb.[27] He continued to work towards the loosening of the bonds between his force and the ground forces and in March 1942, the newly designated Army Air Forces achieved parity with the Army Ground Forces. He also masterminded the Army Air Force's plan to defeat the Axis, one of the seminal documents in modern airpower, AWPD-1, a manifesto of strategic bombing and known by one of its authors as *'The Air Plan That Defeated Hitler.'*[28]

23   De Seversky, pp.151-2.
24   Francois Le Roy and Drew Perkins, Visionary Leadership – Henry H. 'Hap' Arnold, in Harry S Laver and Jeffrey J. Matthews (eds.), *The Art of Command: Military Leadership from George Washington to Colin Powell* (Lexington KY: The University Press of Kentucky, 2017) p.157.
25   Libbey, p.197.
26   Brian D Laslie, *Architect of Air Power: General Laurence Kuter and the Birth of the US Air Force* (Lexington KY: The University Press of Kentucky, 2017), p.100.
27   Arnold, p.222.
28   Haywood S Hansell Jr, *The Air Plan That Defeated Hitler* (NT: Arno Press, 1980). Johnson, pp.172-3.

The plan called for a total of 6,860 bombers in the European Theatre alone.[29] In March 1943, the USAAF issued a handbook called *The Air Force in a Task Force*. Chapter five dealt with the subject of The Bomber Command and laid out the purpose of bombing:

> The air forces serve to assist the other arms, but they also are the only arm which is capable at all times of penetrating directly to the heart and other vitals of the enemy. The nervous system of the enemy will eventually lose its virility from a long accumulation of surface hurts, but it will more certainly and more quickly collapse from blows directly at the brain and nerve centers. When that collapse occurs, openings will appear in the skin, and the other arms can accomplish the final result with a minimum of effort and loss.[30]

Arnold became a full member of the JCS and the CCS in December 1941. He also became the Chief of the Army Air Forces and Deputy Chief of Army Staff for Air. He had to juggle the demands of Pacific versus Europe, Army versus Navy and tactical versus the strategic use of airpower. His advocacy of the Europe First strategy and his unstinting support of Marshall made him an adversary of the US Navy's irascible chief, Admiral Ernest King. Alongside the other Chiefs, he strongly objected to the Mediterranean strategy, convinced that the direct route was best. Above all, his strategic aim was the ultimate transformation of his force into the United States Air Force.

He drove his operational commanders hard, not only to achieve operational success, but also to provide justification for the force's utility as a separate arm. Guilt over his own lack of combat experience may have contributed to the pressure he placed upon himself and his men. He constantly pressed for examples he could use with the US media to highlight the force's effectiveness. In this he sometimes undermined the wishes of his boss and friend, Marshall. A keen advocate of precision bombing, he was perturbed by the failure to seriously affect German industry and by the losses incurred in the attempt. He drove his commanders remorselessly and his friendship with Eaker became strained through the latter half of 1943. Eaker gave as good as he received offering veiled criticism of Arnold for diverting his bombers to North Africa and the Mediterranean, filing his nagging letters in 'the nut file.'[31] The build-up in England was slower than promised and in a visit in September 1943, Arnold saw for himself the Eighth Air Force – he was not impressed.[32] Despite a historically close relationship with Eaker, including the co-authorship of several books on airpower, he had little hesitation in moving him on from England, although he tried to shift the responsibility onto Eisenhower.[33] Eisenhower denied that Eaker was unacceptable, telling Eaker that it was Arnold that had proposed him for command of MAAF.[34]

He also pushed for the swift introduction of long-range escort fighters and blind bombing-aids as his original support of unescorted daylight precision bombing became untenable in summer 1943. In a response to some searching questions by Arnold in mid-1943, Eaker told him that

29   James Gaston, *Planning the American Air War – Four Men and Nine Days in 1941* (Washington DC: National Defense University Press, 1982), p.58.
30   AFHRA A1592, *The Air Force in a Task Force*, Chapter V: The Bomber Command dated March 1943.
31   Perret, p.280.
32   Arnold Diaries Vol 2, p.27.
33   Arnold, p.475.
34   Chandler et al, *Eisenhower Papers, Vol. III*, p.1615.

The Top Table. Arnold on the CCS at Casablanca. Also visible at the top are Generals Marshall and Brooke and opposite Air Chief Marshall Portal, Field Marshal Dill and Admiral Pound. Dill was quite critical of Arnold's staff work. (NARA RG342-FH-000812)

Kindred spirits. Arnold and Eaker pose with the daughter of Air Chief Marshal Sir Arthur 'Bomber' Harris. The longstanding relationship between the two men became strained in late 1943 as Arnold failed to deliver the resources and Eaker failed to deliver the results. (NARA RG342-FH-000039)

bombers using the GEE blind-bombing aid were more accurate than using the Norden. Even though Arnold was the supreme administrator and chief executive of his force, he had not attended the prestigious ACTS, and did not know what his commanders were going through. He could not understand their difficulties, seeing all problems as mere administrative hurdles. The strategic bombing campaign was underperforming due to the enemy and the weather. He also deflected blame towards the RAF's night bombing efforts and RAF Fighter Command for not supporting his bombers, despite the RAF continuing to carry out the bulk of the strategic bombing effort in 1943, to the annoyance of Portal. Arnold had approved the diversion of American fighters earmarked for England to support Eisenhower in Italy. On 24 October 1943, a week after 'Black Thursday', Portal wrote to Arnold 'candidly':

> With regard to your statement as to our failure to employ our forces in adequate numbers against the German Air Force in being, I do not know the extent to which your statement is based on precise figures, but I would like you to be aware of some facts in regard to the operation of the various forces engaged.[35]

Portal's facts were that 76 per cent of offensive fighter sorties were to protect bombers, with one in three sorties supporting Arnold's aircraft. He made it clear that the Germans waited for the day bombers to penetrate their airspace before attacking. Portal obliquely criticises him for his opposition to the P-51, saying that 'unfortunately there was a great deal of prejudice in the early stages in accepting the virtues of this aircraft.'

Arnold's disappointment at the performance of his main strike force was down to circumstances beyond anyone but Arnold's control, but he needed someone to blame, and that became his old friend Ira Eaker. Later, Eaker called Arnold's criticisms the 'petulance of an overworked man.'[36]

His desire to see an independent United States Air Force was based around his belief in the capability of airpower to affect the outcome of a war without ground or naval forces. In this he was supported by his principal subordinates. Spaatz, one of these, and his ultimate successor as Chief of Staff, commented in mid-1943 to the British scientific adviser, Solly Zuckerman, 'there was one 'A' too many in the designation of USAAF – the 'A' which stood for Army.'[37] To reach this freedom, forward thinkers within the Army Air Forces had concluded that the strategic use of airpower against targets that directly impacted an enemy's war production and fighting capability should be attacked in a systematic fashion. The RAF thinkers had also reached the same conclusion, and in the early months of the war had tried daylight precision bombing against key German industries. They had quickly discovered that they had neither the number nor size of bombers, nor the ability to defend themselves against fierce German air defences. Their leader, Sir Arthur Harris, made the point, seemingly lost on the Americans, that 'One cannot win wars by defending oneself.'[38] Their daylight efforts were quickly switched to the night area bombing of key German industrial cities in the early months of 1942. They did this not because they wished to terrorise the civilian population, although a reprisal for the Blitz was on their minds,

---

35   AFHRA Reel A1372, Letter Portal to Arnold dated 24 October 1943.
36   AFHRA Iris No 1036066, United States Air Force Oral History Program, Interview of Lt Gen Ira
      C Eaker by Hugh N Ahmann, dated 10-11 February 1975, p.392.
37   Zuckerman, p.195.
38   Charles Webster and Noble Frankland, *The Strategic Air Offensive Against Germany Volume I,
      Preparation* (London: HMSO, 1961 (Kindle Edition)), Kindle Location 7610.

Slightly xenophobic, Arnold tried to blame the RAF for his bomber force's failure in late 1943. When presented with the facts by Portal he turned his ire on Eaker instead. (NARA RG342-000562)

By the end of 1943, the doctrine of unescorted high-level daylight precision bombing had become untenable. Results were poor and losses unsustainable. This formation bears the markings of the 5th Bombardment Wing of the Fifteenth Air Force. (NARA RG342-FH-000907)

but because they could do nothing else with the technology of the time. Not to be dissuaded, the Americans still believed that using massed bombers in unescorted daylight precision attacks against industrial targets was possible. It formed the keystone to their operational doctrine and, in Arnold's mind, the most effective route to full independence. De Seversky realised in his book a year earlier that 'massed daytime bombing without fighter convoys proved futile and costly.'[39] His views were dismissed by Arnold as 'tactical heresy.'[40]

Churchill was unconvinced by American day doctrine. By September 1942, he was trying to persuade Roosevelt to join them in the night offensive.[41] He adopted this view largely because of Portal, who was not convinced that the USAAF could penetrate deeply into Germany in daylight without fighter escort. At that time, it was thought that a single-engine escort that could go deep into Germany was impossible. Without this escort, the losses would be unacceptably high; Portal also was aware that precision was a relative term and that most bombs would fall harmlessly awry.[42] By October 1942, Churchill mused to the British CoS that US-day bombers would 'probably experience a heavy disaster.'[43] In the months to come he was to be proven correct. He could not press his case too hard as he feared the Americans switching their efforts to the Pacific or tactical airpower. Ironically, it was Portal who chose what he considered the lesser of two evils and persuaded Churchill to tolerate the daylight campaign.

Spaatz wrote to fellow USAAF general, George Stratemeyer in February 1943 that 'it was hard to treat aviation as co-equal with the Army and Navy in our set-up, whereas the RAF will not submit to it being considered in any other way.'[44] Everything changed for the USAAF in July 1943:

> The command of air and ground forces in a theatre of operations will be vested in the superior commander charged with the actual conduct of operations in the theater, who will exercise command of air forces through the air force commander and command of ground forces through the ground force commander. The superior commander will not attach army air forces to units of the ground forces under his command except when such ground force units are operating independently or are isolated by distance or lack of communication.[45]

This is from US Army Field Manual FM 100-20 which was issued to provide doctrinal guidance to US commanders as to how air forces were to be used offensively. This replaced the defensively focused FM 1-5 – Army Air Forces Field Manual – Employment of Aviation of the Army.[46] FM 1-5 made clear in its first paragraphs that tactical air units could be assigned to ground task force commanders. FM 100-20's most important statement was to replace this by stating that 'LAND POWER AND AIR POWER ARE CO-EQUAL AND INTERDEPENDENT

39 De Seversky, p.37.
40 De Seversky, p.230.
41 Webster and Frankland, *Volume 1, Preparation*, Kindle Location 7878.
42 Webster and Frankland, *Volume 1, Preparation*, Kindle Location 7974.
43 Webster and Frankland, *Volume 1, Preparation*, Kindle Location 7994.
44 Vincent Orange, 'Getting Together', in Daniel R Mortensen (ed.), *Airpower and Ground Armies: Essays on the Evolution of Anglo-American Air Doctrine, 1940-43* (Maxwell AL: Air University Press, 1998), p.35.
45 US War Department Field Manual FM 100-20, July 1943.
46 US War Department Field Manual FM 1-5 Army Air Forces Field Manual – Employment of Aviation of the Army, US War Department, Washington DC, 18 January 1943.

Major General Laurence Kuter (centre). Kuter was the architect of the USAAF doctrine, Field Manual FM 100-20. This was essentially the air's declaration of independence from the ground forces. It meant that targeting decisions were made by airmen rather than soldiers. (NARA RG342-000451)

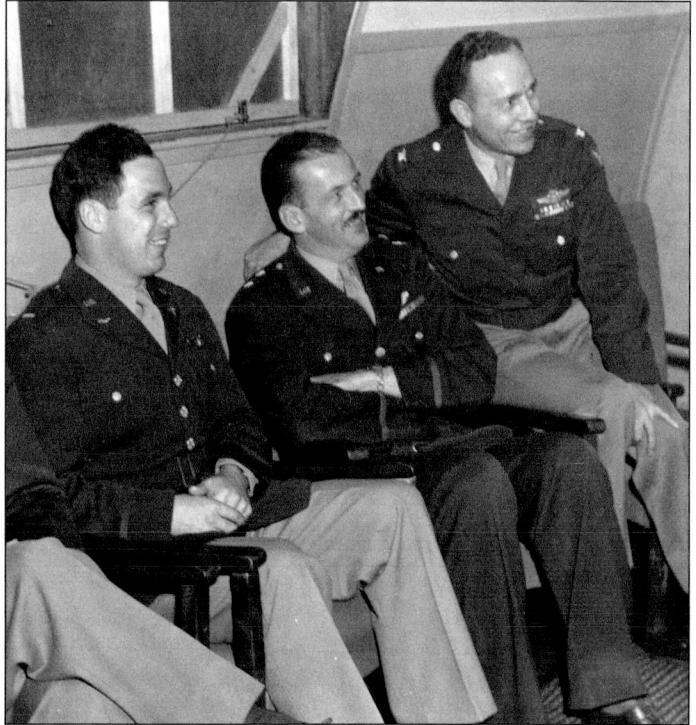

FORCES; NEITHER IS AN AUXILIARY OF THE OTHER.' This statement, in upper-case typeset, signed by Marshall established the command relationships, specifically the unity of command for air forces that existed in Italy. This doctrine explained how strategic and tactical air operations were to be conducted, establishing the core principles of US airpower doctrine. It also prioritised air operations, putting support to ground forces at the bottom of the list! The USAAF somewhat bundled through this capstone doctrine when the ground forces weren't looking. This short document lacked detail and was mostly unremarkable. The first two pages, however, were explosive, chiefly for Clark's mentor, General McNair, the Commanding General of ground forces. His staff were not sent a draft copy of the new doctrine to review.[47]

In a reference to the ground forces, Kuter wrote to RAF air commander, Coningham, in June 1943, 'More people were defeated in Tunisia than Germans and Italians.'[48] FM 100-20, although not copied from the British had been influenced by the independent RAF. The success of British airpower in North Africa was seen as an exemplar to the Americans as to how the relationship should work. It was not that US air commanders had not realised how to use their weapon to the best effect, they had worked that out on their own long before, but it took British success, and American failure, to convince traditional US Army voices.[49] The US already had worked out the theory, but practice is often different, and in this they learnt from the British. It did not, however, convince all the old-stagers, including in Italy.

---

47   Mortensen, p.134.
48   Mortensen, p.134.
49   Robert S Ehlers, *The Mediterranean Air War: Airpower and Allied Victory in World War II* (Wichita KS: University Press of Kansas, 2015), pp.257-8.

The heavy bombers were used in the furtherance of strategic objectives and were usually a responsibility of the theatre commander.[50] This was not so in the Mediterranean Theatre as all USAAF strategic bombers were under the control of Spaatz, who was the Commanding General of all US Strategic Air Forces in Europe. Doctrinally, the tactical air forces were tasked with three missions. These were in priority order, attaining air superiority, conducting interdiction within a theatre of operations and direct support to ground forces as the lowest priority. The doctrine conceded that this third priority is the most difficult to control and that it is only profitable at critical times.[51] The detail of how these operations should be conducted was contained within another US Army manual, FM 31-35.[52] This manual was initially a subordinate manual to FM 1-5, prior to July 1943. This latter manual when talking about air support to Ground Forces makes the following observation:

> 39. OBJECTIVES NORMALLY UNSUITABLE FOR HEAVY AND MEDIUM BOMBARDMENT
> a) *Fortifications.* Fortified positions, consisting of small, heavily fortified, dispersed positions are not suitable for attack by level bombing for the following reasons:
> 1. Velocity required for penetration of the structure by a bomb requires a high release altitude.
> 2. At high altitude the chance of hitting an object less than 200 feet square is quite small. However, in the exceptional case of a large permanent fortification, valuable support can be rendered.[53]

A conclusion from the above statement is that heavy bombers should not attack targets such as the Abbey. Bigger than 200-feet square, it would still be hard to hit as an 'exceptional' target, and the aircrew would not have practiced against such small targets. A lot of these procedures were developed on the hoof and as Wilson stated in his Dispatch, 'The Mediterranean Theater had been the primary laboratory for the use of airpower to assist ground advances.'[54] This statement would no doubt have annoyed the Prime Minister, for its spelling at least.

The USAAF required a few things to make its principal doctrine work. In the late 1930s the US Army Air Corps was controlled by the Army General Staff. It danced to the Army's tune and this meant that its accepted doctrine was, like the *Luftwaffe* and the Soviet Air Force, as a direct support to ground operations. The change came in 1940 when the Air Corps' role was changed to 'hemispheric defense and offensive strategic bombardment.'[55] This change was supported by Roosevelt and the Army was forced to relent. By 1941, close support of ground forces was no longer the primary mission of the Air Corps, soon to be renamed the USAAF. The first thing the USAAF needed was an effective plan for its daytime precision strategic bombing.

---

50   US War Department Field Manual FM 100-20, July 1943, Chapter II, para 11.
51   US War Department Field Manual FM 100-20, July 1943, Chapter II, para 16.
52   US War Department Field Manual FM 31-35, Aviation in Support of Ground Forces dated 9 April 1942.
53   FM 1-5, para 39, p.27.
54   TNA AIR 75/138 – Allied Force Headquarters, Supreme Allied Commander's Despatch – Italian Campaign 10 May 1944-12 August 1944, p.10.
55   Stephen L McFarland, *America's Pursuit of Precision Bombing, 1910 -1945* (Washington DC: Smithsonian Institution Press, 1995), p.100.

This was developed from the ACTS at Maxwell Field in Alabama, who had maintained the shadow doctrine in the face of official Army opposition throughout the 1920s and 30s. Precision bombing, they thought, was the answer to public opprobrium to the mass destruction theories of men such as Douhet. The focus of the air service moved from 1925 from pursuit to bombardment and by the mid-1930s the former had ceased to have any meaningful importance, especially the escorting of bombers. This was something the American airmen would come to bitterly regret in the skies over Germany. By the late 1930s, the ACTS under Lieutenant Colonel Donald Wilson had firmly adopted the doctrine of high-level precision daylight bombing.[56] Graduates of the school became the nucleus to produce the AWPD-1 that planned to defeat the enemy through the destruction of its industrial might rather than attacking cities and civilians to break the enemy's morale. This plan was asked for by the President and was delivered in the autumn of 1941. It was largely written by six men; four ex-ACTS instructors and two businessmen co-opted into the Army Reserve to identify and target key German industries. The ACTS had become somewhat of a one-trick pony – bombing. Fighter, attack or transport aviation were largely ignored, and this shortfall helped to blinker USAAF thinking when unescorted bombing over Germany was proven to be unsustainable. Arnold and principal pursuit advocate Clare Chennault were fierce rivals. A battle initially won by Hap, the pursuit doctrine of Chennault proved to be of vital importance over Germany:

> Attachment to this commitment was, however, so inflexible that it inhibited the development of tactics for escort, for air defence, for support of ground forces and for reconnaissance and transport aviation. Thus the school's greatest achievement as a laboratory for Air Corps thought prevented the full accomplishment of the purpose designated by the name, the Air Corps Tactical School.[57]

The arguments made by de Seversky in *Victory Through Air Power* were to be proven substantially correct, yet the 'Bomber Mafia' was to rule the independent USAF for the next 20-years.

In early 1944, the USAAF hierarchy of combat units began with the numbered Air Forces. In total the USAAF had 16-numbered Air Forces of which two were in the Mediterranean Theatre; these were the Twelfth Air Force, a tactical air force under MAAF, and the Fifteenth Air Force, a strategic air force under the US Strategic Air Forces in Europe. Below the Air Force was the Command. Commands were based upon function with the main Command titles being fighter, bomber, air support, troop carrier etc. Below the commands were the Wings. These were formed within the commands and were often aircraft specific. For instance, the 5th Bombardment Wing within Fifteenth Air Force was equipped with the B-17 bomber; there was no XV Bomber Command. The 42nd Bombardment Wing of XII Bomber Command of Twelfth Air Force was equipped with the B-26 Marauder medium bomber. Subordinate to the Wings were the Groups, again largely type-based. Bomber Groups would have the suffix (H) for Heavy (B-17 and B-24) or (M) for Medium (B-25 and B-26). The 2nd Bombardment Group (H) of B-17s that led the attack on the Abbey had a provenance that preceded the above structure in that it was created as the only Bombardment Group when the US-based Air Service

---

56   Perret, p.26.
57   Perry McCoy-Smith, *The Air Force Plans for Peace* (Baltimore MD: Johns Hopkins Press, 1970), p.33.

consisted of just four Groups.[58] When the US entered the war the USAAF had 67 Groups; this had increased to 269 by the end of 1943, with 218 of these combat Groups.[59] Each Group, depending on type, comprised a number of Squadrons.

The second thing the USAAF required was the right aircraft in the right numbers. In the late 1930s, the Army was uninterested in a high-level strategic bomber as it was of little use in supporting troops on the ground. Only a small number of large bombers such as the B-17 had been ordered. Only 13 of these aircraft were ordered in 1939 and 38 the next year! The loudest proponent of the B-17, General HQ Air Force commander Lieutenant General Frank Andrews was removed from post and sent into a backwater posting in Texas.

This aircraft had a troubled birth as the Air Corps were forced to hide the development of offensive heavy bombers under the defensive role of hemispheric defence that supported the pre-war National Defense Policy. The ploy was transparent to the War Department, who wanted twin-engine medium bombers, and who tried to stymie air plans. They would have succeeded had it not been for a Presidential order to prioritise heavy bombers.[60]

The final element was the ability to conduct precision bombing from high altitude. Arnold could have all the clever plans, and all the big aircraft, but if they could not hit their targets, they would not serve the nation's purpose. The USAAF struggled to develop an effective aiming mechanism that gave the precision they required. For that they had to go cap in hand to the US Navy and Karl Norden.

Arnold's Chief of the Air Staff in Washington and Deputy Commander of the Army Air Forces, Lieutenant General Barney Giles, called the attack on the Abbey, 'the finest example of bombing that I have ever seen.'[61] Arnold himself called the damage, 'monuments to the destructive force of Air Power' when he overflew the ruins of the building in June 1944.[62] There was no contrition at the destruction of a culturally important site. Arnold's favouring of precision bombing should not be taken to mean that he was squeamish about the deaths of civilians or about conducting area bombing if necessary. The opinion of Giles was not a statement that could be regularly made about the performance of American heavy bombers, either in Italy or in the Eighth Air Force in England. By the beginning of 1944, the daylight precision bombing concept was failing and was in somewhat of a crisis.[63] The USAAF had successfully attacked the periphery of the Reich but had failed to destroy the U-Boat pens in Western France. Deep penetrations into Germany usually resulted in great losses and limited effectiveness, most clearly identified by the two attacks on ball-bearing works at Schweinfurt in August and October 1943, when 120-bombers and over 1,000-lives were lost. In the second week of October losses were 148-bombers; this was unsustainable and the USAAF was hurtling towards defeat by the end of 1943. As Curtis LeMay observed in response to the loss statistics, 'In the end everybody was going to get shot down.'[64] There was a consequent sag in crew morale until fatalism took over. Only following these disasters did Arnold order all P-51 production to be sent to Eaker. It was

58   Maurer, p.5.
59   Maurer, p.7.
60   Greer, pp.98-100.
61   Schaffer, p.51; AFHRA Reel A6030, MAAF C-in-C Correspondence, Giles to Eaker dated 25 April 1944.
62   Schaffer, p.52.
63   Tillman, p.13.
64   Le May, p.278.

this level of loss in 1940 that drove the RAF to the 'safety' of the night. The USAAF did not want to follow the same route. It may have been the case that Eaker had persuaded Churchill at Casablanca that round the clock bombing was the best way to achieve victory, but so far, his claims seemed more like empty boasts. His promises ran into trouble in less than a month. On 5 February 1943, Eaker's Army boss, Andrews, who until his death in May commanded all US Army forces in the European Theatre, wrote to Marshall, highlighting his concerns. There is one remarkable aspect to this cable; Andrews was an AAF officer, a supporter of daylight precision bombing and air force independence:

> Bomber strength deteriorating rapidly to point where raids cannot be made in sufficient strength to disperse anti-aircraft strength of enemy. Please transmit message to Arnold important he visit this headquarters for discussion on build-up of Eighth Air Force before his return to US. Reputation US Air Forces adversely involved unless better results can be obtained.[65]

Marshall was sympathetic to Andrews' plight answering:

> We are in full agreement with you that it is excessively costly and relatively ineffective to use your present inadequate forces on deep penetration daylight missions. Therefore, we will support any decision reached in your theatre involving either postponement of effort until proper sized force is accumulated or pending that time for use against objectives in France and Low Countries or in experiments with night bombing...Build-up of force considered adequate for deep daylight penetration against German targets will take many months.[66]

Marshall's response, drafted by Arnold's then Chief of the Air Staff, Major General George Stratemeyer, would have sent shivers down the spines of the other advocates of daylight precision bombing. Neither of Marshall's suggestions to Andrews were remotely attractive.

The road to an independent air force was dependent on the doctrine working. Stratemeyer wrote to Colonel Charles Cabell, part of Arnold's Advisory Council, on the same day suggesting that Eighth Air Force bombers should be fitted with flame dampeners to allow night operations. These should be undertaken until the force can be built-up to the numbers required.[67] Eaker pressed on, with the results already discussed, although he did allocate a small number of aircraft for night missions with the RAF. He also put an over-optimistic spin on the success of his missions. In a press conference on 10 June 1943, he was very positive about the performance of his force, and he wrote a letter to Washington on 26 June 1943 concerning the raid the previous day on Bremen and Hamburg, in which he made extravagant claims of the success his crews were having in destroying enemy fighters and the accuracy of bombing.[68] To the press he said:

65   AFHRA Reel A1372, Memorandum for General Marshall, Bombing Units for United Kingdom date 5 February 1943.
66   AFHRA Reel A1372, Memorandum for General Marshall, Bombing Units for United Kingdom date 5 February 1943.
67   AFHRA Reel A1372, Memorandum from Chief of Air Staff to Colonel Cabell dated 5 February 1943.
68   AFHRA Reel A1592, Eaker Letter, 8th Air Force Attack on 25 June dated 26 June 1943.

With Air Chief Marshal Sir Arthur Harris are Lieutenant General Frank Andrews, then in Command of all Americans in Britain and Ira Eaker. The case for air force independence relied on its bombing doctrine. The US did not want to join the RAF night area campaign. (NARA RG342-FH-000591)

> We have found that a formation of about 100 of our heavy bombers can be guaranteed to saturate and obliterate the normal industrial target. We have found also that a formation of this size can defend itself and that it will sustain, normally, 5% losses or less.[69]

Much of what Eaker said was untrue. He tried to claim that 100-B-17s would be at no more risk than 500 – 'he only has so many rounds of ammunition' he said. In the months ahead, he would be found out and in protecting his boss, whose responsibility it was, he would lose his job for the backwater of the Mediterranean.

In May 1943, Arnold wrote to Giles who had replaced Stratemeyer, instructing him on how bombers would be allocated. Giles was Arnold's right-hand man and often acted as the attenuator of Arnold's temper. His priority was to maintain combat units at full strength, regardless of the impact on training, or the establishment of new groups.[70] He was also to aim for a 50 per cent reserve as soon as possible. However, Arnold did not tell Giles which combat theatre was to be prioritised. By June 1943, Arnold had ordered escort fighters with an operating radius of 600-miles to be developed, but these had not materialised by autumn 1943. Eaker and Arnold

---

69   AFHRA Reel A1592, Transcript of Press Conference of Maj Gen I C Eaker dated 10 June 1943.
70   AFHRA Reel A1372, Memorandum for General Giles, Allocation of Heavy and Medium Bombers, dated 6 May 1943.

wanted to avoid the failure of switching the attack to night bombing. Excuses such as airspace congestion, lack of training in night operations and unsuitable aircraft were all used to maintain the day assault. These reasons all gave the impression that to give up now would cause unacceptable delay to the Combined Bomber Offensive. Lack of escort fighters and very poor weather restricted bombing operations after October 1943, despite Eaker having 759-heavy bombers by mid-month.[71] In that month, Portal, in a clear the air letter to Arnold, blamed the Eighth Air Force's failure, not on Eaker, but indirectly on Arnold himself saying, 'we have been unable to carry out the plan mainly because the aircraft strength of this force has only been 70% of that planned, and because the crew strength has been only 70%.' The allocation of bombers to England was entirely Arnold's responsibility. Portal added even more pointedly:

> The great tactical advantage, including the element of surprise which your heavy bombers had at the start of their operations in this theatre, have therefore been largely thrown away by the slow rate of the build-up which you have achieved. This has enabled the enemy to handle the small force put over whilst he developed countermeasures. As a result, unless we are to continue to accept a high proportion of casualties, we now need greater numbers than those stated in the Plan, in order to achieve the same effect.[72]

The American public would not stand for the losses for long and 1944 was an election year. Proof was required that the bombers had the power to defeat the Germans and the Abbey offered a convenient demonstration of that power when the entire world would be watching. It also offered an opportunity for MAAF, for whom Italy was a proving ground for air support to ground forces, to prove its utility. The Chief US intelligence officer in MAAF, Harris Hull, was a professional journalist in civilian life. He was a key Eaker staff officer, one of the first six officers to go with him to England to set up VIII Bomber Command. He performed a similar role when he pioneered Eaker's move to MAAF. He had experience when it came to stunts designed to enhance the reputation of the air force. In 1938, while again working for Eaker as a reserve second lieutenant, Hull came up with the idea for B-17s to intercept the Italian liner *Rex* some 400-miles from the US coast.[73] If he had an idea once, why not again?

There is indeed a long history of the American air services using staged publicity events to further their cause. In the 1920s, the sinking of the *Ostfriesland* under Mitchell in 1921 was widely publicised as the end of the battleship. The Barling bomber was produced around the same time, widely publicised as the future of heavy bombers, which alongside the slightly later *Question Mark* flight flown by Spaatz and Eaker demonstrated to an eager public the key strengths of airpower. This was a proof of concept that bombers could defend the continental US, much to the annoyance of the US Navy. Even as the war began for America there were propaganda myths the perpetuate. A well-known instance is that of Captain Colin P Kelly Jr. Kelly's bravery, although real enough, in destroying a Japanese warship near the Philippines a few days after Pearl Harbor, was greatly exaggerated in subsequent press reports, and which the

71 AFHRA Reel A1372, HQ AAF, Office of Management Control, Combined Allied Serviceable Air Strength dated 16 October 1943.
72 AFHRA Reel A1372, Letter Portal to Arnold dated 24 October 1943.
73 AFHRA Iris No 1036066, United States Air Force Oral History Program, Interview of Lt Gen Ira C Eaker by Hugh N Ahmann, dated 10-11 February 1975, p.187-8.

Key Eaker staff officer Colonel Harris Hull chats with veteran journalist William Shirer. The USAAF had a long history of enhancing its reputation through what could be described as 'publicity stunts'. (NARA RG342-FH-000794)

Army Air Forces cleverly exploited to create America's first war hero.[74] Arnold was not satisfied for long, writing to Eaker in England in June 1943 that the Army and Navy had more heroes than the USAAF. Couldn't Eaker find him a hero?[75] The recruitment of Hollywood 'heroes' James Stewart and Clark Gable helped raise the AAF's public profile. The myth of the infallible Norden bombsight was also heavily sold to the American public.[76] In 1942, American author John Steinbeck was commissioned by Arnold to produce the patriotic book *Bombs Away: The Story of a Bomber Team,* boosting the morale and increasing the recruitment to the USAAF.[77] Finally, Arnold put a stop to the term 'blind bombing' as this did not portray the bombers as precision instruments. Instead, he insisted that press releases used the terms 'overcast bombing technique' or 'bombing through overcast.'[78] In reality these missions were area bombing, little different to those of the RAF. In early 1943, Arnold instigated a project to use aerial photography as part of a public relations effort to enhance his force's reputation.[79] This was to be run by former *Life* magazine journalist E K Thompson.

74   Stewart Halsey Ross, *Strategic Bombing by the United States in World War II: The Myths and the Facts* (Jefferson NC: McFarland and Co., 2003), pp.55-6.
75   Johnson, p.207.
76   Halsey-Ross, p.130.
77   Johnson, p.202.
78   Halsey Ross, p.139.
79   AFHRA Reel A1592, Frame 016, Letter from Major General Davenport Johnson, Evidence in Camera, dated 2 January 1943.

Planning for the divorce from the US Army was well under way. By April 1943, Arnold had established his Special Projects Office within AAF HQ to assist with post-war plans.[80] A few months later head of AAF Plans, Major-General Laurence Kuter established the Post-War Division (PWD) within his directorate and this work continued in AAF HQ throughout that year and into the next. It was the PWD that drew up plans for Air Force autonomy and on the very day of the attack on the Abbey, they outlined their initial policy plans:

FROM THE PLAN FOR INITIAL POST-WAR AIR FORCE OF 15 February 1944

1.   To maintain an Air Force strong enough to provide for the military protection of our future global air commerce.
2.   To sustain an up-to-date, well trained, well equipped force of highest military quality.
3.   To maintain a strong 'M' day Air Force, strategically deployed for prompt striking action against a new outbreak of hostilities in areas within range of its bases, of defending the integrity of the US and its possessions, of enforcing the US foreign policy, and of supporting ground and naval forces similarly engaged.
...

17. That the Air Force is to be an autonomous division of a new Department of War, the other three being the (1) Army, (2) Navy, (3) Joint Production. Procurement and Resources Division. (Emphasis by Author).[81]

There was also political support for the independent post-war air force before the war was won. In September 1944, Robert Lovett, the Assistant Secretary for War wrote to Spaatz:

Naturally, everything must be subordinated to the goal of winning the war at the least cost and at the earliest possible date. However, the whole future security of this country depends, I believe, on a proper recognition of Air Power in our national defense setup and the acceptance of the demonstrated fact that its striking power is at least equal to that of land or sea forces and probably greater than either since it is a prerequisite to successful offensive operations.[82]

Lovett was a strong supporter of independence but had also served as the political brake during wartime.[83] Arnold, Spaatz, Eaker, Kuter and his successor at Plans, Norstad, all believed strongly that strategic airpower should dominate and even supplant the other services. Norstad in a directive in late 1945 made his views crystal clear: 'Although the conception of a tactical air force was one of the greatest developments of this war, it is now as old-fashioned as the Maginot Line.'[84]

80   McCoy-Smith, p.6.
81   AFHRA Reel A1372, Frames 377-8, AAF Policy Book dated February 1945.
82   Mets, p.293.
83   Perret, pp.56-7.
84   McCoy-Smith, p.100.

This comment, although made after the end of war did not reveal new thoughts. All USAAF leaders, especially those in the 'Bomber Mafia' strongly believed that the Air Force would not only achieve independence and equality but that they would dominate warfare. The plan above called for a peacetime Air Force of 105-Groups and 1,000,000-men, the same size as that planned for the other services combined.[85] Arnold was playing for high stakes. He was trying to turn his force from being subordinate to the Army to being not only a competitor but a dominant force. The post-war planners aimed to make US strategic bombardment capability into the guarantor of world peace.[86] According to a long-standing member of Arnold's Advisory Council, autonomy was the post-war priority for Arnold and AAF leaders during the final years of the war. This planning, and even the conduct of bomber operations, was a means to an end. This end should have been victory and the US' future security. Instead, the AAF leadership saw their goal as a large and independent United States Air Force based around the strategic bombing mission.[87] Although an independent US Air Force would flow from the powers given to Arnold by Roosevelt and by the approved doctrine FM 100-20, ultimate success could only be achieved through congressional approval and the passing of legislation, which would remove scarce money from the Army and Navy. The Army was supportive, but the Navy was vehemently hostile. To win this battle, visible and public proof of success needed to be demonstrated. By the autumn of 1943, this was far from secured as the US daylight bomber force failed to substantively affect German output and suffered horrendous casualties. High-level precision daylight bombing was the supporting foundation upon which all of Arnold's plans for autonomy were built. Failure in this respect weakened the case for independence. Not only this, but as Norstad identified, tactical air power was having substantial success supporting land forces in Italy through CAS and interdiction. In a bizarre twist, this tactical success, where air forces supported land forces, weakened the case for autonomy.[88] The use of heavy bombers in support of ground operations offered a powerful alternative to tactical airpower with the agility to switch from tactical to strategic targets. The theory, however, was not proven in battle in 1944. The failure of their heavy bombing doctrine to be a decisive operation in war would seriously undermine post-war plans for supremacy.

Arnold was ultimately a highly successful commander. When he took command, the Army Air Corps had just over 20,000 personnel. By the end of 1944, it had more than two million and controlled the skies. February 1944 saw both the zenith and the nadir of his force. It had reached the astounding maximum of 2,411,294, people but by this month it had also sustained 12,544 battle deaths and, in the Mediterranean, only 60 per cent of bomber sorties were effective, the worst month of the war.[89] The strain of his responsibilities took its toll. He suffered several heart attacks during his period in command and he eventually succumbed in 1950. His legacy was profound, and the National Security Act of 1947 resulted in the establishment of the independent United States Air Force, with Spaatz as its first commander. If Trenchard was the father of the independent air force, Arnold was the father of the modern air force. He wore his unique blue USAF General of the Air Force uniform seldomly; lastly, in his coffin.

85   McCoy-Smith, p.57.
86   McCoy-Smith, pp.16-17.
87   McCoy-Smith, p.114.
88   McCoy-Smith, p.27.
89   Army Air Forces Statistical Charts, 1940-45.

17

The Most Powerful Force

Close air support of heavy and medium bombers was an untested novelty on the battlefield.

Guy Hartcup
Royal Air Force, Air Historical Branch[1]

Mediterranean command and control arrangements beyond land forces, and the personalities involved in February 1944 needs to be discussed in greater detail. Many accounts of the Abbey's destruction place the final decision with Alexander.[2] In fact, all ground force commanders could only request strategic air support, not order it. In AFHQ, following the British pattern and the new US Army doctrine, the Air Forces were independent, not within the chain of command of the land force commander. The various tensions between ground forces and air forces and between the air forces themselves can be summed up by a comment from USAAF officer Laurence Kuter: 'Since all ground officers are expert Air Chief Marshals, ...my job is to keep ground forces from swallowing the air forces, to keep the RAF from swallowing AAF, etc. Nice bunch of cannibals in Africa! And Casablanca. And London. And Washington.'[3]

Other than the Commander-in-Chief, only Eaker, commander of the Mediterranean Allied Air Forces could order air support, but even he did not exert total control of all air assets in Italy. Eaker had been in post as Commanding General MAAF for barely a month when the Abbey was destroyed. Prior to this he had been in command of the Eighth Air Force, which he had inherited from Spaatz in 1942. Eaker had developed the USAAF Bomber Command in Britain, but was not to see the rewards of its success. Had it not been for Eaker's stubborn support of day bombing, the B-17s may have joined the RAF in night area attacks, or they could have turned away from strategic bombing in the European Theatre altogether. He managed to persuade Churchill that around-the-clock bombing was a more effective strategy. Had he not done so, the heavy bomber forces to bomb the Abbey would not have been available. Despite his success, Eaker still hedged his bets, placing a few B-17s under RAF Bomber Command for night operations in summer 1943.[4]

---

1   Hartcup, p.28.
2   For Example, Rupert Clarke, *With Alex At War: From the Irrawaddy to the Po, 1941-1945* (Barnsley: Leo Cooper, 2000), pp.135-6; Green, p.43; Singleton-Gates, pp.278-9.
3   Orange, *Getting Together*, p.34.
4   Charles Webster and Noble Frankland, *The Strategic Air Offensive Volume II, Endeavour* (London: HMSO, 1961 (kindle Edition)), fn. 130.

Heavy losses in bombers without escorts and the desire of Eisenhower to bring in his own team, consigned Eaker to the secondary Mediterranean by the end of 1943. Eaker had joined the US Army Air Service in 1917 and did not serve in the First World War. Trained as a pursuit pilot, in the inter-war years, he served in several posts where his face became known to Air Corps senior officers. He first met Arnold in 1919 and had the dubious distinction of occupying the office between General Patrick and General Mitchell as an executive assistant when the latter was preparing for his Court Martial. In oral testimony in 1975, Eaker described a close relationship with Mitchell, including support for his combative methods to ensure the future of airpower in America.[5] After this, he made a few record-breaking flights including in 1929, an endurance record where he, Carl Spaatz and three other pilots kept the aircraft *Question Mark* aloft for over 150-hours using primitive air to air refuelling. On the outbreak of war, he was sent to Britain alongside Spaatz in January 1942. On 1 July, the first B-17 was delivered to Europe. Working directly to Spaatz, Eaker initially commanded the VIII Bomber Command of Eighth Air Force until December 1942 when Spaatz went to North Africa and he moved into the Commanding General's position. Before this happened, Spaatz had to diplomatically manage the expectations of an impatient Arnold. Although B-17s were in England, they were not ready and the first USAAF bombing operation, planned for the 4 July had to be completed by RAF aircraft with American crews. Arnold wanted the B-17s and by 11 August Spaatz told him that the 97th Bombardment Group was combat ready.[6] The European weather delayed their first mission until 17 August 1942.

Eaker personally observed that first bombing raid onto mainland Europe to the rail marshalling yards at Stoneville near Rouen, when a mere 18-tons of bombs were dropped. He flew that day in the B-17 *'Yankee Doodle'*. Also flying this mission was Major Paul Tibbetts, then commander of the 340th Bomb Squadron in the 97th Bombardment Group, and the pilot who would carry out the atomic raid on Hiroshima less than three years later.

His Group was to take part in the bombing of the Abbey 18-months later. At first things went well; bombs were dropped, losses were low, and the claims appeared justified. It would be another seven months, in March 1943 until the Americans first conducted deep penetration into Germany, attacking the Hamm marshalling yards.[7] His losses when he turned his force to Germany were then grievous. USAAF raids into Germany were curtailed until effective fighter escorts could be obtained, although very poor weather over Europe in late 1943 also impacted his ability to operate. By this time, the USAAF's, strategic bombing doctrine was proving to be a dismal failure, and the considerations regarding fighter escort in the 1930s and supported by Arnold and the 'bomber mafia' were failing badly. More than this, the thoughts of many of these men bordered on arrogance and hubris. They seemed to think that their interceptors would easily shoot down the enemy's bombers, whereas there was a feeling 'bombardment invincibility' amongst the advocates of their own high-level precision daylight bombing.[8] Unfortunately, both Japan and Germany were very capable of destroying unescorted American bombers. During the period between February and October 1943, there were three times as many RAF night

5   AFHRA Iris No 1036066, United States Air Force Oral History Program, Interview of Lt Gen Ira C Eaker by Hugh N Ahmann, dated 10-11 February 1975, pp.29-31.
6   Mets, p.133.
7   John McCrary and David Shermann, *First of the Many* (London: Robson Books, 1981), pp.6-7.
8   Greer, pp.83-84.

sorties as US-day sorties, and Eaker only had just over half the aircraft required to enact the Combined Bomber Offensive in October 1943.[9] That month his bombers only dropped 5,500 tons compared to nearly 14,000 by the RAF. In a briefing to the CCS in Cairo, Portal defended Eaker and made the most of his efforts, but the failure to curtail the rise in German fighter production, his main effort, could not be hidden.[10] By December 1943, Eaker had only achieved 54 per cent of the results expected and was three months behind schedule.[11] The great USAAF daylight precision bombing experiment was failing by the time Eaker left England. There were not enough four-engine bombers; the Norden bombsight could not put a bomb in a 'pickle barrel' in European conditions and the aircraft were incapable of defending themselves with an acceptable and sustainable loss rate. Eaker's crews had only around a 20 per cent chance of finishing their 25-missions.[12] In just October 1943 the Eighth Air Force lost 9.1 per cent of its entire force, with 45.6 per cent damaged.[13] Regarding the Norden bombsight, Eaker at least was realistic about its potential and performance, admitting that many of the accuracy claims were little more than air force propaganda:

> Under ideal conditions of visibility and ideal operational conditions, it was very satisfactory. It was the best we had, and we did some very accurate bombing. We did exaggerate the excellence of the bombsight and the capability of the bomber with it. Part of it was by design. In order to get bombers at all, we had to prove that they could do the job, and all of the stories about pickle barrel bombing – an expert bombardier with the bombsight in an excellent condition with nobody shooting at him could do a pretty precise bombing job, certainly good enough to hit the smallest target – a factory. It was quite different operating a bombsight in training and under operational conditions.[14]

Eaker's subordinate, Colonel Curtis LeMay, serving in Eighth Air Force, made the comment about bombing efficacy, 'These people didn't know where half their bombs fell. And most of the bombs didn't hit the target anyway.'[15] General Arnold was not as forgiving as Portal for the Eighth Air Force's failure to meet its timeline, and Eaker had clearly lost his confidence, contributing to his transfer. The Commanding General of the Army Air Force had been demanding higher rates of performance from Eaker's force since his inspection visit in September 1943.[16] Arnold had been critical of Eighth Air Force performance and had made this clear at the Allied Cairo conference on 4 December 1943. Eaker was accused of a 'lack of flexibility in operations.'[17] He could not be blamed for the fact that the USAAF had not provided his full complement of heavy bombers, something for which Portal had been critical of Arnold for the preceding months. Sir Archibald Sinclair, the

9   Combined Chiefs of Staff Memorandum CCS 403 dated 21 November 1943.
10   Combined Chiefs of Staff Memorandum CCS 403 dated 21 November 1943 – Enclosure.
11   Minutes, 134th CCS Meeting, Mena House Cairo, 4 December 1943.
12   Morrison, p.187.
13   Webster & Frankland, *Volume II, Endeavour,* Kindle Location, 1438.
14   AFHRA Iris No 1036066, United States Air Force Oral History Program, Interview of Lt Gen Ira C Eaker by Hugh N Ahmann, dated 10-11 February 1975, p.461.
15   Le May, p.231.
16   Richard G Davies, *Carl A Spaatz and the Air War in Europe* (Washington DC: Smithsonian Institution Press, 1992), p.273.
17   Davies, p.271.

Secretary of State for Air, recounted how Portal gave Arnold a 'salutary drubbing' over the issue.[18] Arnold successfully deflected the blame to his operational commander. This was not all. The failure of the Eighth Air Force to meet its POINTBLANK targets threatened the invasion timeline. The USAAF Chief blamed not only Eaker but RAF Fighter Command and RAF Bomber Command. Arnold had decided to move Spaatz to the UK to command both his strategic air forces. This meant a new commander for MAAF, and Spaatz, supported by Tedder, recommended Eaker. Eaker was told that Spaatz was coming to the UK by Portal on 14 December rather than by Arnold.[19] He was shocked to be informed via cable on 19 December that he was going to Italy and saw it as a dismissal. He fought his boss, and appealed for allies, but it was no good. Marshall, blaming pressure from Tedder and Spaatz, thought the move 'selfish and not purely objective', but he did not intervene.[20] Even Portal, the ultimate authority in the CCS for bombing could not dissuade Arnold, although he called the decision 'a grave mistake'.[21] Eaker was relieved of command on 23 December 1943 effective 1 January 1944. Portal continued to hear reports of Arnold 'struggling to face the facts and live up to the extravagant prognostications which he had made.' Field Marshal Sir John Dill, the British representative on the CCS, wrote to Portal on 23 January 1944 and accused Arnold of being 'slapdash in both what he says and writes.'[22]

It was abundantly clear from his personal letters that Eaker did not have the same enthusiasm for Italy that he did for the Eighth Air Force and saw his transfer as his 'darkest hour.'[23] His new command, however, was the largest air command in existence; he was in charge of two US Army Air Forces, allied commands, over 320,000 personnel and well over 4,000 combat aircraft. He was reminded of this in a personal meeting with Churchill in Morocco on the way to his new command. Nevertheless, he saw it as being 'kicked upstairs' and he was being sent to the second division of military operations. He remained at MAAF until the Germans in Italy surrendered when he was posted to Washington as Deputy Commander of the USAAF still in the rank of Lieutenant General. He was not promoted again and retired in 1947 but was belatedly awarded his fourth star in 1985 by President Ronald Reagan.

Later, his friend and boss, Jacob Devers said of Eaker, 'I consider him the man that carried the heaviest load for the Air Force.'[24] Another reluctant addition to the MAAF command team was Slessor, Eaker's British deputy. He was sent to the Mediterranean at the same time from command of RAF Coastal Command. Slessor dearly hoped to be part of OVERLORD.[25] He was to be disappointed, possibly due to his very poor relationship with Tedder, the Deputy Supreme Commander. The posting made little practical sense as Slessor had been successful in the U-Boat war and had no experience in the Mediterranean, but Eaker who knew him from England was glad to have him saying, 'I can't think of anyone I'd rather have.'[26]

---

18   Webster and Frankland, *Volume II, Endeavour*, Kindle Location 866.
19   James Parton, *Air Force Spoken Here* (Maxwell AFB AL: Air University Press, 2000), pp.335-6.
20   Chandler et al, *Eisenhower Papers, Vol III*, 1614 fn.2 and Mets, p.181.
21   Davies, p.276.
22   Webster and Frankland, *Volume II, Endeavour*, Kindle Location, 2061 fn169.
23   AFHRA Reel 23268, Ira C Eaker, Personal Letters.
24   *Interview with Devers for Eisenhower Library with Dr Maclyn Burg, 5 February 1975* <https://www. eisenhowerlibrary.gov/sites/default/files/research/oral-histories/oral-history-transcripts/devers-jacob-377.pdf> (accessed 10 August 2023).
25   Orange, *Bomber Champion*, p.123.
26   Morrison, p.176.

When created, the MAAF's priorities were as follows:

> The Mediterranean Allied Air Forces have four primary tasks. The first with the Strategic Air Force is to bring maximum pressure on German industry. The second is to support, with the Tactical Air Force, the land armies in battle. The third is to assist in keeping the sea lanes of communication open, protecting our shipping, our harbours and our rear establishments from enemy air action. The fourth major task is to supply the maximum cooperation to the Partisans in the Balkans.[27]

It was established in December 1943 as an allied unified command of all air forces in the Mediterranean theatre of operations, simplifying the command-and-control structure. Originally to be commanded by Tedder with Spaatz as his deputy, the command arrangements were quickly altered as these officers were posted to England. Spaatz was the ultimate arbiter of what operations the US strategic air forces in Europe conducted. Nevertheless, in a conversation with British Secretary of State for Air, Sir Archibald Sinclair on 7 January 1944, Spaatz made it clear that he did not expect to exercise much control over the Fifteenth Air Force.[28]

Eaker arrived at MAAF HQ in Tunisia on 17 January 1944. He stayed one night before moving to Caserta in Italy to be with the other theatre commanders stating, 'There is no war going on here, General. I am going over to Italy to find a headquarters.'[29] He officially set up shop in Italy on 20 January. Caserta, ironically, was the hometown of the bombing prophet, Guilio Douhet. Prior to his arrival he had despatched several staff officers from England whom he planned to use in the Mediterranean. These officers were perturbed at the lack of organisation.[30] Eaker had command of three air commands, tactical, strategic and coastal, of which the MATAF and the MASAF are relevant to the bombing of the Abbey. These when added to the mostly British Balkan Air Force (BAF) fulfilled his priorities. MATAF was an Allied command and comprised two national elements, the British Desert Air Force and what became rebadged as the US Twelfth Air Force. It was located alongside Alexander's 15th Army Group at Caserta and was considered by the armies to be the equivalent of a corps level formation, commanded initially by Air Marshal Coningham and then by Major General Cannon, reflecting the differing ranks used by the Allies for this level of command. The Twelfth Air Force, provided tactical support to Fifth Army, with fighter bombers of XII ASC, initially commanded by Major General Edwin House, soon to be replaced by Gordon Saville, giving direct support. This support was usually obtained through the 7th AASC which was collocated with Clark's command post. This arrangement was consistent with US Army doctrine.[31] Nevertheless, according to Truscott, 'Air Support was the subject of many stormy conferences.'[32]

27   Air Power in the Mediterranean, November 1942-February 1945. <https://cgsc.contentdm.oclc.org/digital/collection/p4013coll8/id/1418/rec/1>

28   Webster & Frankland, *Volume II, Endeavour,* Kindle Location 2042 fn159.

29   AFHRA Iris No 1036066, United States Air Force Oral History Program, Interview of Lt Gen Ira C Eaker by Hugh N Ahmann, dated 10-11 February 1975, p.253.

30   AFHRA Reel A6030, History of MAAF, December 1943 – September 1944, Volume 1, Chapter II, p.10.

31   US War Department Field Manual FM 31-35, Aviation in Support of Ground Forces dated 9 April 1942, Chapter 1, paras 1-6.

32   Truscott, p.353.

Commanding General of the Twelfth Air Force's Air Support Command, Brigadier General Gordon Saville and his boss Lieutenant General Ira Eaker visit Major General Lucian Truscott in the Anzio beachhead. Saville did not see eye-to-eye with Eaker over air support. (NARA RG342-FH-002344)

This was probably mostly down to Truscott himself. He was a vigorous advocate of the ground commander owning his air support and a constant thorn in the side of Eaker and his air commanders. In the end, according to Eaker, even Truscott had a road to Damascus moment.[33]

Cannon's twin-engine B-25 and B-26 tactical bombers are widely credited with doing most of the damage to the Abbey. Cannon was commissioned in 1917 and served as an infantry officer until 1921 when he retrained as a pilot. He served in various flying, and staff posts in the inter-war years and was a full colonel when the US entered the war. Quickly promoted to brigadier general in February 1942, he was the Commanding General of XII ASC for the Operation TORCH Western Task Force, moving to Algeria to command XII Bomber Command once it was established. In May 1943 he was appointed Deputy Commander of the Northwest Africa Tactical Air Force, the predecessor of MATAF, under Coningham, supporting the Sicily and Italy invasion campaigns. He became the commander of Twelfth Air Force in June 1943 on promotion to major general and succeeded Coningham to become commander of MATAF in January 1944, when the latter was pulled for OVERLORD by Eisenhower. By February 1944, according to Cannon's immediate superior, he had made a very good impression as Twelfth Air

---

33   AFHRA Iris No 1036066, United States Air Force Oral History Program, Interview of Lt Gen Ira C. Eaker by Hugh N Ahmann, dated 10-11 February 1975, p.378.

Force commander, establishing 'tremendous influence' with Alexander and 'trusted implicitly' by Clark.[34] Cannon commanded all Allied air forces involved with Operation DRAGOON in August 1944 and was promoted to lieutenant general in early 1945. After the war he served as Commanding General of the United States Air Force in Europe (USAFE) and upon promotion to four-star general, USAF's Tactical Air Command.

At least in public, the relationship between Fifth Army and the air forces was appreciative and cordial. In an exchange of letters in April 1944 Clark and Arnold thanked each other profusely for the mutual support.

Arnold wrote on 19 April,

> Dear Wayne,
> A letter has just arrived from Ira Eaker which again speaks of the wholehearted coopera-
> tion which you have given the Army Air Forces. We've sent you our very best men, but I
> hold it no coincidence that Cannon, House and Saville have all spoken in such high terms
> of the understanding and friendship found at the V Army. The battle of air against ground
> has been fought on many fields. It is unusual and reassuring to find the kind of confidence
> that has been established at Caserta without even a reconnaissance in force.
>
> I know how difficult and disappointing the campaign in Italy has been. I know the
> restrictions and shortages that have so influenced the results. But above all, I want you to
> know how thoroughly aware, we of the AAF are, of that fine, disciplined, Fifth Army that
> you and your staff have created.
>
> Please convey to General Gruenther and your staff my appreciation of their excellent
> teamwork to date.[35]

A week later, Clark replied,

> Dear General:
> Your letter of April 19 reached me today. It was thoughtful of you to write me concerning
> the splendid way in which the air ground forces have been working together over here.
> Cooperation is a two-sided thing, and I cannot praise too highly the magnificent way the
> Air Corps has responded when we have called upon them for either close-in support or
> strategic missions.
>
> Generals Eaker, Cannon, House and Saville have shown themselves completely coop-
> erative and a great share of the credit for the harmonious conduct of Air Corps jobs with
> the Fifth Army goes to them. Gordon Saville was a fine replacement for Ed House and
> he has carried on the splendid air support that Ed started. I confer several times a week
> with Gordon, and he has given me wise counsel and one hundred per cent cooperation. I
> also see Ira and Joe occasionally. Personal contact means a great deal. You can be certain
> that there will be no conflict between air and ground when these matters involve the
> Fifth Army.[36]

34   AFHRA Reel A6030, MAAF C-in-C Correspondence, Eaker to Arnold 21 March 1944.
35   AFHRA Reel A1376, Letter Arnold to Clark dated 19 April 1944.
36   AFHRA Reel A1376, Letter Clark to Arnold dated 26 April 1944.

In June 1944, following the successful entry into Rome, Clark and Alexander wrote to the air generals, with letters praising the performance of air forces.[37] There was a difference in style between the two letters. Clark's was more of the superior to the subordinate. The USAAF remained part of a greater US Army so this tone was not a surprise, and was also directed specifically at American units, not at MATAF more generally. Alexander's note was more collegiate, treating the tactical air forces more like a partner than a subordinate and inclusive of the air forces of both Britain and America.

Overall control of MATAF remained with Eaker, not Clark or Alexander, as both FM 100-20 and FM 31-35 dictated that control by ground commanders should be granted only in exceptional circumstances or where the air support commander could not effectively control his command. Neither condition existed at Cassino. At the time, the medium bombers came operationally under the Allied, but mainly British manned, Tactical Bomber Force (TBF). This force had been set-up in 1943 to coordinate light and medium bomber support between the Desert Air Force supporting Eighth Army and the XII ASC supporting Fifth Army. A lack of resources made the provision of separate bomber forces to each Army impossible. This again demonstrates the favoured doctrine for air forces of centralised control, decentralised execution. It also had the task of separating targeting responsibility with the heavies of the strategic air forces. The deployment of the two forces was described in a note:

> The general policy laid down by the Commander-in-Chief is that Tactical Air Force will be responsible for the dislocation and attack of communications in the area South of a line running approximately from ROME to the North-east. Strategic Air Force will be responsible for attacking objectives North of this line.
>
> This division of responsibility is not of course absolutely rigid. Nevertheless, if Strategic Air Force is to fulfil its proper function, it must be relieved of attacking targets which can be hit by Tactical Bomber Force. Therefore except in an emergency, or against targets which Tactical Bomber Force are not capable of attacking effectively, Strategic will not normally be asked to operate in the tactical area.[38]

This policy was issued on 23 October 1943 by Air Commodore Edward Hudleston, the TBF's Senior Air Staff Officer and highlights the 'emergency' use only of the strategic air forces for tactical targets. The Abbey was clearly within the capability of the TBF's B-25s and B-26s and they did the majority of the damage on 15 February. What was the 'emergency' that required heavy bombers? There was none declared, and this adds to the speculation that these bombers were used as a demonstration of airpower rather than through tactical necessity.

All US Medium bombers from the 42nd and 57th Bombardment Wings were reorganised as the XII Bomber Command as of 1 January 1944, which retained national administrative control over the wings. The 57th Wing was inactive between January and March 1944, although most histories continue to credit it as the organisation that commanded the B-25 Bombardment Groups.

---

37   AFHRA Reel B0949. War Diary of 42nd Bombardment Wing, Entry for 5 and 6 June 1944.
38   AFHRA Iris No 2000469, Note On The Deployment Of Tactical Bomber Force, dated 23 October 1943.

B-25 Mitchell medium bombers of 57th Bombardment Wing of the Tactical Bomber Force. The TBF was disbanded in March 1944. (NARA RG342-FH-000192)

Conveniently, the attack on the Abbey is not included in its history as the bombardment groups were directly subordinated to the XII Bomber Command and the TBF. This was a clumsy arrangement and only lasted until 1 March when the wings came under MATAF for operational control and Twelfth Air Force for administration. The order for this change was issued by Hudleston two days before the Abbey attack on 13 February.[39] The 42nd Bombardment Wing, commanded by Brigadier-General Robert Webster, an original ACTS precision bombing theoretician, was in Sardinia. The units of this wing had been in action since late 1942 and the Tunisia campaign. The B-26 units were initially formed into what would become the 42nd Bombardment Wing in April 1943, although the numbered wing came later.[40] Their first mission was the bombing of the island of Pantelleria in early June 1943. They then supplied medium bomber support to Sicily operations during July and August, attacking mainly airfields and interdiction targets. The wing was also tasked to interdict communications infrastructure and airfields in mainland Italy. The unit was renamed the 42nd Bombardment Wing (Medium) on 24 August 1943 and remained in Tunisia until

39   AFHRA Iris No 2000469, Letter A106, Letter MATAF to 12th Air Force dated 13 February 1944.
40   AFHRA Reel B0948 Frame 1435, A Short History of the 42nd Bomb Wing.

October when it moved to Sardinia. During the crisis following the German counterattack after Operation AVALANCHE, it conducted direct support to ground forces for the first time in the area of Battipaglia and Eboli to the east of Salerno. Following the capture of Naples, the wing reverted to bridge busting, mainly over the Volturno River. Whilst this prevented German reinforcements moving south, it also left the Fifth Army with no intact bridges on their movement northwards. The wing was also the pioneer of cutting rail communications by attacking bridges. Zuckerman, had concluded that attacking marshalling yards was the most effective way of interdicting Italy's railways. Many disagreed, thinking that the geography of Italy meant that bridges would be more effective targets. Bridges, however, were harder to hit than large marshalling yards. These were the major targets of the wing from late 1943 onwards, culminating with Operation STRANGLE in spring 1944. Poor weather hindered their activities at Anzio, but what bombing occurred in early February 1944 was largely targeted at German road communications feeding their frontline units rather than direct support to the beachhead. In the second counteroffensive between 16-20 February, the B-26s provided direct bombing support to ground forces. The wing's operational record prior to the Abbey bombing shows that despite the stated priority of MATAF to support the land battle, the B-26s had very little experience of this. Unlike the strategic bombers, the 42nd Bombardment Wing did have an army liaison officer sent from TBF. By February 1944, a British officer was assigned to the wing, working in the intelligence section, providing valuable information and insight into ground operations. Training for USAAF officers for these important posts was lacking. Fifteenth Army Group wrote to Cannon on 18 February to initiate a plan to replace British officers with Americans when sufficient trained personnel became available.[41] MAAF Deputy Commander, Slessor considered the 42nd Bombardment Wing, 'probably the best day-bomber unit in the world.'[42] They certainly outperformed all other bombers on 15 February, hitting the Abbey more than both the heavies and the B-25s. As one B-26's bombs made a direct hit on the Abbey, one watching soldier shouted, 'Touchdown.'[43]

The 57th Bombardment Wing started life in Egypt when the 8th Fighter Wing was re-designated on 15 May 1943. It was part of the Ninth Air Force and when that Air Force transferred to England the personnel of the wing followed. The unit, however, remained under the command of the Twelfth Air Force. It was almost immediately moved from Egypt to Sicily where it arrived in early September 1943. New personnel began to be assigned shortly after. By the end of October 1943, it had moved again, this time to the Foggia airfield complex that had been captured by the British. By the end of 1943, the wing was once again declared inactive, with all personnel transferred to the XII Bomber Command. It was this unit, usually called the 57th Bombardment Wing, but directly part of XII Bomber Command that took part in the bombing of the Abbey.[44] By 4 January 1944, the headquarters of XII Bomber Command had been moved to a location near Mount Vesuvius. One of the bombardment groups, the 321st, that was involved in the Abbey attack, was relocated on the same day as the attack from Foggia

41   AFHRA Iris No 2000469, HQ ACMF to CG MATAF, ACMF/9018/G(Air), Air Liaison Officers, dated 18 February 1944.
42   Richard P Hallion, *Strike From The Sky: The History of Battlefield Air Attack, 1911-1945* (Shrewsbury: Airlife Publishing Ltd, 1989), p.182.
43   Canciano, p.158 citing *Time Magazine*, 28 February 1944.
44   AFHRA Reel B0996, A History of the 57th Bomb Wing to November 1944, pp.2-4.

to an airfield near Salerno.[45] The order from MATAF reactivating the 57th Wing and assigning the B-25 groups to it was issued on 13 February.[46] By 1 March 1944, and commanded by Brigadier-General Robert Knapp, it was again officially called the 57th Bombardment Wing, although Knapp had commanded the units since 5 December 1943. The 57th Bombardment Wing HQ was in the Foggia complex of southern Italy.

The TBF was disbanded on 1 March 1944, with all medium bombers coming under direct MATAF control. This decision was announced by Cannon's deputy, Air Vice Marshal John D'Albiac, in a note issued on 9 February 1944.[47] The MATAF was given the following offensive priorities by HQ MAAF on 18 February 1944:

a.   The first priority object for the Tactical Air Force will be operations in support of the land battle.

b.   Second priority objectives for the Tactical Air Force will be marshalling yards, railroad repair facilities and other railroad targets south of, but not including, the Pisa-Rimini line, but exclusive of marshalling yards located within the city of Florence. The purpose of these operations is, first, to destroy railway facilities in that area and, second, to stop rail movements...

c.   Third priority for the Tactical Air Force will be ports on the east coast of Italy which are being used as terminals for the coast-wise shipping traffic supporting the German forces in Italy. Operations in this category will be closely coordinated with the Coastal Air Force.[48]

The US medium bomber force began 1944 with tasking to support the amphibious operation at Anzio. Tasking was issued to both wings on 4 January, with the primary mission to interdict Italian rail communications in west and central Italy, south of 44º North latitude.[49] Use of the mediums in direct support of Fifth Army ground operations was a second priority, only to be conducted if the weather precluded interdiction of rail targets. The 42nd Wing was the principal unit used in the interdiction plan, with marshalling yards being the primary targets. Although the attack on marshalling yards was favoured following the analysis of Zuckerman, the damage was only short-term, whereas attacks on bridges, viaducts and tunnels resulted in more permanent blockages. Of the 50-targets allocated to 42nd Wing, 31 were marshalling yards. The B-25 Groups as well as servicing targets in Italy were tasked against Balkan targets. In addition to interdiction missions the mediums supported the Anzio operation by conducting offensive counter-air missions against *Luftwaffe* airfields in Italy. February 1944, however, was a poor month for weather, with only about a third of the month being flyable.

The amalgamation of all Allied strategic bombers under a single command was suggested to the CCS by Arnold, who wanted an American commander. Not surprisingly, RAF Bomber

45   Medium Bomber Operations 1 Jan-28 Aug 1944 Medium bomber operations, 1 January--28 August 1944. – World War II Operational Documents – Ike Skelton Combined Arms Research Library (CARL) Digital Library (oclc.org) [accessed 11 May 2017].
46   TNA AIR 51/81: MATAF message DTG 131425A Feb 44.
47   TNA AIR 51/81: Loose Minute AVM D'Albiac TAF/7/Air dated 9 February 1944.
48   AFHRA Reel A6377, Frame 1434. HQ MAAF Bombing Directive dated 18 February 1944.
49   *Medium Bomber Operations 1 Jan – 28 Aug 1944*, p.5 <https://cgsc.contentdm.oclc.org/digital/collection/p4013coll8/id/1386/rec/1> (accessed 13 October 2023).

Command objected and remained separate, but the US Strategic Air Forces were brigaded under Spaatz, with Portal retaining the position of CCS agent for strategic bomber operations. The recommendation was put before the CCS in a memorandum of 18 November 1943.[50] Eaker and his deputy, Slessor, had administrative responsibility, but the RAF's AOC-in-C Middle East and Spaatz had overall operational responsibility for the British and American strategic bombers respectively. Slessor filled the British position as well as his Allied role in MAAF. The relevant CCS text to this effect is below:

a. That control of all U.S. Strategic Air Forces in the European-Mediterranean area, including the control of movement of forces from an area to another, should be vested in a single command in order to exploit the flexibility of U.S. heavy bomber capabilities most effectively and that these forces should be employed primarily against POINTBLANK objectives or **such other objectives as the Combined Chiefs of Staff** [author emphasis] may from time to time direct.

b. That such a command should likewise be charged with the coordination of these operations with those of the R.A.F Bomber Command.

c. That the responsibility for over-all base services and administrative control of those Strategic Air Forces should remain with the appropriate commanders of U.S. Army Forces in the United Kingdom and in the Mediterranean area.

d. That provision should be made to assure that assignment of resources, supplies and other services between tactical and strategic operations so as to bring the required support to POINTBLANK as the air operation of first priority.

e. That the Headquarters of such U.S Strategic Air Forces should be established in the United Kingdom because of the facilities available, the existing weight of the respective bomber forces, and the necessity for continuous integration of operations with the R.A.F.

f. That the Commanding General, U.S. Army Air Forces should continue to have direct channels of approach to the U.S. Strategic Air Force commander in order to provide direct technical control and insure that operational and training technique and uniformity of U.S. tactical doctrine are maintained.[51]

The MASAF was also an Allied command comprising 205 Group RAF and Fifteenth Air Force USAAF. The Fifteenth Air Force was created on 23 October 1943 to deliver the Combined Bomber Offensive from Italian bases and was formally activated on 1 November.[52] The decision to raise a second heavy bomber air force in Europe was opposed by Portal, Harris and Eaker in the UK, but strongly supported by Arnold and Spaatz.[53] Those in England believed that its establishment diverted effort from POINTBLANK for only minor gains.[54] It was Arnold that insisted upon its creation. In conversation with Air Marshal Sir William Welsh in August 1943, subsequently passed to Portal, Arnold explained that he did not want the Mediterranean

50 Combined Chiefs of Staff Memorandum CCS 400 dated 18 November 1943.
51 Combined Chiefs of Staff Memorandum CCS 400/2 dated 5 December 1943.
52 Kevin Mahoney, *Fifteenth Air Force Against the Axis* (Plymouth: Scarecrow Press, 2013), p.2. Chandler et al, *Eisenhower Papers, Vol III*, p.1546 fn4, referencing FAN254.
53 Mets, p.168.
54 Webster & Frankland, *Volume II, Endeavour*, Kindle Location, 2035.

to become a tactical-only campaign, subservient to the land campaign. The Fifteenth Air Force's role was not defined by the situation in Italy, but by the CCS at the Cairo conference in December 1943. Its commander, Nathan Twining, came from a famous military family. He graduated from West Point a week before the end of the First World War serving for three years as an infantry officer before transfer to the Air Service, winning his wings in 1924. For the next 15-years he flew fighter aircraft. Alongside many of the bomber generals in the Second World War, Twining was a graduate of the ACTS at Maxwell Field Alabama. Between 1940 and 1942 he worked directly for Arnold as part of his Advisory Council. Promoted to major general in January 1943, his first major command in the Second World War was as Commanding General of the Thirteenth Air Force in New Caledonia in the Pacific. Despite being a fighter pilot, he was then reluctantly sent to the Mediterranean to command the strategic bombers of the Fifteenth Air Force at the insistence of Arnold. He commanded that force in February 1944 when the Abbey was bombed and probably issued the final orders to the B-17s, although unlike others he gave no opinion publicly of his views. After Germany's defeat he went to the Pacific to command the Twentieth Air Force's B-29 bombers. Twining stayed in the newly independent USAF after the war, ultimately becoming USAF Chief of Staff in 1953. In 1957, he was appointed Chairman of the JCS by President Eisenhower.

His priorities were similar but slightly different to those of MAAF:

1. To destroy the German Air Force in the air (by making it come up to fight) and on the ground, wherever it might be located within range of Fifteenth planes.
2. To participate in POINTBLANK (the Combined Bomber Offensive), which called for the destruction of German fighter aircraft plants, ball bearing plants, oil refineries, rubber plants, munition factories, sub pens and bases etc.
3. To support the battle on the Italian mainland (mainly by attacking communications targets – In Italy, along the Brenner Pass route and also in neighbouring Austria).
4. To weaken the German position in the Balkans.[55]

MASAF's principal function was to conduct 'Operation POINTBLANK as the air operation of first priority.' Strategic bombing operations from or against Italy were not initially part of the POINTBLANK Directive; this was added during the QUADRANT Conference in August 1943.[56] Throughout the remainder of 1943 and early 1944, the Fifteenth Air Force was often switched between competing priorities of strategic bombing, interdiction, and close support of threatened ground forces. The first two stated priorities supported the strategic aim. POINTBLANK was the highest strategic priority in the first months of 1944 and it was vital to the invasion plans that air superiority be achieved by April 1944.[57] The directive was initiated on 11 January 1944 with the following strategic mission.

55   Kenn C. Rust, *Fifteenth Air Force Story* (Temple City CA: Historical Aviation Album, 1976), p.7. See also, HQ MAAF Bombing Directive dated 18 February 1944.
56   TNA CAB 80/74/513: COS (43) 513 Part A, QUADRANT Record of Plenary Meetings and the Proceedings of the Combined Chiefs of Staff, Quebec, August 1943, dated 11 September 1943.
57   Matloff, Kindle loc, 3322.

The progressive destruction and dislocation of the German military, industrial and economic system, and the undermining of the morale of the German people to a point where their capacity for armed resistance is fatally weakened.[58]

Norstad continued to stress the priority of destroying the *Luftwaffe* when he wrote to Twining on 3 February 1944 that the Fifteenth Air Force's bombing priorities must be to most effectively support Operation OVERLORD and that to do this the force should be used primarily against fighter airframe and component targets and ball bearing plants as target systems of 'first and equal priority.'[59] This was confirmed by the CCS on 13 February 1944, just two days before the Abbey attack, when they issued an order, the concept of operations of which was:

The overall reduction of German air combat strength, in its factories, on the ground and in the air, through mutually supporting attacks by both strategic air forces, pursued with relentless determination against the same target areas or systems, so far as tactical conditions allow, in order to create the air situation most propitious for OVERLORD, is the immediate purpose of the bomber offensive.[60]

Because of the primary task, Eaker had only administrative command of MASAF and could not divert heavy bombers to Italy if higher priorities existed elsewhere. The strategic air forces in the Mediterranean Theatre did not come under the operational control of Wilson. In a post-war interview, the MASAF commander thought that this was sound policy, as he suspected that had his force come under Wilson it would have neglected more strategic targets in favour of greater support to land forces. In practice Spaatz probably left most decisions to Eaker's judgement, reflecting their close personal relationship. The following message signed by Spaatz formalised this chain of command in his operational directive of 11 January:

HQ USSAFE will exercise operational control over the Fifteenth Air Force. This control will be exercised through HQ MAAF. All matters will be coordinated with HQ MAAF, and unless specifically excepted by joint directive, all communications will be routed through Commanding General MAAF.[61]

If the Fifth Army required direct support from the strategic bombers the request usually went through Cannon, as the action officer for CAS, to Eaker.[62] This arrangement was confirmed by Eaker in a letter to Alexander on 4 February, where Eaker noted that 80 per cent of MAAF operations had been devoted to supporting 15th Army Group.[63]

---

58   AFHRA Reel A6377, Frame 1420. USSAFE Operational Directive to CG 15th Air Force dated 11 January 1944.

59   AFHRA Reel A6377, Frame 1430, HQ MAAF Strategic Bombing Directive to 15th Air Force dated 3rd February 1944.

60   AFHRA Reel A1376, FACS8, CCS for General Eisenhower dated 13 February 1944.

61   AFHRA Reel A6030, History of MAAF, December 1943 – September 1944, Volume 1, Chapter II, p.19.

62   W.M. Gould, *The Italian Campaign Volume 1* (London: Air Historical Branch, 1948), p.246.

63   TNA WO214/29, Italian Campaign January-February 1944. Letter Eaker to Alexander, 4 February 1944.

The element of the Fifteenth Air Force tasked by Twining to carry out the attack on the Abbey was the 5th Bombardment Wing. This was the only wing within the Fifteenth Air Force equipped with the B-17. The other six heavy bombardment wings were equipped with the B-24 Liberator. The wing was an original unit of the Fifteenth Air Force being transferred from the XII Bomber Command when the air force was stood up in November. The wing comprised four B-17 Heavy Bombardment Groups, the 2nd Bombardment Group, commanded by Colonel Herbert Rice, 97th Bombardment Group commanded by Colonel Frank Allen, the 99th Bombardment Group, whose commander Lieutenant Colonel Ford Lauer took command on the day of the Abbey attack. Lauer had previously served under Robert Olds in the 2nd Bombardment Group and had commanded that group in 1943. The final unit was the 301st Bombardment Group, which was commanded at the time by Lieutenant Colonel Karl Barthelmess, after its commander was killed on Christmas Day.[64] Barthelmess was one of the USAAF's most experienced operational B-17 commanders, having as a lieutenant, landed his aircraft at Hickam Field, Hawaii, during the Japanese attack on Pearl Harbor.[65]

Two B-17 groups, the 97th and the 301st had been in the theatre since November 1942, when they transferred from Eighth Air Force. They were joined by the 99th in March 1943 and finally the 2nd in April 1943.[66] Each Group was equipped with around 50-aircraft.[67] The Fifteenth Air Force was still growing in February 1944, with approaching 60,000 officers and men. It would not reach full operational strength of 21-Bombardment Groups and 80,000 personnel until May. As the growth of the air force continued, the B-17s took the weight of the operations, including the mission to Montecassino. Upon establishment, its headquarters was in Tunis, but by February 1944 it had relocated to an Italian Air Force building at Bari. The B-17 units were also based in Tunisia in November 1943 at airfields near Tunis. In December 1943, they moved to airfields in the Foggia area of southeast Italy, Amendola, Tortorella and Lucera.

These airfields, some previously used by the *Luftwaffe*, were not at first suitable and much work had to be done to enlarge them. The headquarters of 5th Bombardment Wing was relocated to Foggia.[68] Tortorella, new home of the 99th Bombardment Group, was an abandoned *Luftwaffe* airfield whilst Amendola was built in 1931 for the Italian Air Force and Lucera was a new airfield, built by US engineers. At Amendola, the 2nd Bombardment Group arrived in December 1943, but the second unit, the 97th Bombardment Group only arrived at its permanent base two weeks before the attack on the Abbey, although they relocated temporarily to San Giovanni near Cerignola in December 1943.[69] Their existence was miserable. The entry of the 341st Bomb Squadron historian for 22 December 1943 summed up life in the Foggia complex: 'Seldom within the memory of this recorder of history has he seen a country that rained less and still stayed so wet. Life has become a constant struggle to stay warm and dry.'[70] The 97th Bombardment Group then wholly relocated to Amendola on 17 January 1944. Getting away from San Giovanni elicited the comment 'Praise Be', from the 341st historian. Similarly, the 301st Bombardment Group initially moved to Cerignola in December 1943 but was again

64   William Hess, *B-17 Flying Fortress Units of the MTO* (London: Osprey Publishing, 2003), p51.
65   Jablonski, p47.
66   Hess, p25.
67   AFHRA Reel A6377, History of Fifteenth Air Force, p.23; Maurer, p171.
68   AFHRA Reel A6377, History of Fifteenth Air Force, p.48.
69   AFHRA Reel A0583, 340th Bombardment Squadron History, December 1943.
70   AFHRA Reel A0583, 341st Bombardment Squadron History, December 1943.

Eaker and Twining talk to Colonel Herbert Rice. Rice commanded the 2nd Bombardment Group that led the attack on the Abbey on 15 February 1944. (NARA RG342-FH-000442)

moved to occupy Lucera at the end of January to make way for a B-24 unit at Cerignola. After a few missions Lucera was then temporarily abandoned due to poor facilities and deep mud on the runway, being reoccupied by the 301st Bombardment Group in April 1944.

By mid-January 1944, Eaker had 499-operational heavy bombers in his command.[71] During the week ending 20 February he had 206-operational B-17s, 181-B-25s and 167-B-26s. Arnold wrote an 'eyes only' letter to Eaker expressing his thoughts as to how the air forces should be employed. The letter is undated, but is probably sometime in February or early March 1944:

Dear Ira,
We are all very greatly disturbed here at the apparent 'bogging down' of the Italian Campaign. I admit that I am looking at this from a great distance away from the actual scene of battle. However, if we in the Air Forces accept this situation, I have reason to fear that we will be dragged down to the level and outlook of the Ground Forces. A situation such as exists at present in Italy furnishes ammunition to the advocates who decry the use

71   AFHRA Reel A6030, History of MAAF, December 1943 – September 1944, Vol. 1, Chapter II, p.5 fn.2.

of air power except as artillery. As soon as a Commander finds himself at an impasse, it puts him in a position to demand that all facilities – land, sea and air – be under his control. I am convinced that one solution is to ensure that our Air Commanders feel their responsibility for employing their Air Forces correctly and to their full capability. This responsibility cannot be delegated.

I am going to put down various thoughts that occur to me and would welcome your frank comments.

The Ground Forces are at almost the exact position which they found themselves during my last visit. The hill overlooking Cassino is still in German hands. That hill apparently dominates the military situation in that it must be taken before we can hope to affect a juncture between the main Army and the beachhead force. With different terrain, the desert force found itself in similar positions during its fight across the top of Africa. They solved the problem, I believe, by convincing the Ground Forces that they could and would blow a hole through the opposition, providing those Ground Forces were ready and set to take advantage of the opportunity. I am of the opinion that Air Marshal Coningham refused to allow his Air Forces to be attritted by daily meaningless battles. Is not that happening to your Tactical Air Force at present? I understand that part of our Ground Forces are engaging the enemy in the vicinity of the town of Cassino. Is it not possible that similar to the following could be employed to ensure the advance of the Ground Forces?

a)   Withdraw all of our coastal Air Force aircraft from their present normal operations; gather in all of our night fighters; gather up all of our heavy bombardment crews and aircraft, including those in rest camps, those not yet considered ready for battle, those in Africa (if any); the same with our medium bombers and with our fighter aircraft; and establish a force which, for one day, could really make air history.

b)   Withdraw our Ground Forces, temporarily, from such a place as the town of Cassino at a given time or given signal, and utilising all this assembled air power, break up every stone in the town behind which a German soldier might be hiding. When the smoke of the last bombers and fighters begins to die down, have the ground troops rapidly take the entire town of Cassino.

c)   Again, by utilising this force and in consultation with the Ground Forces, completely blast every inch of the hill behind Cassino. I firmly believe that this could be done as a shuttle proposition with heavies, mediums and fighters operating as many missions that day as feverishly working ground crews and pilots could accomplish for a short period. And, when the smoke clears off, have a Ground Force ready to exploit the resulting devastating barrage and take the hill.

I believe that I am correct in stating that the history of the Desert Campaign and the Tunisian Campaign are replete with such examples. I invite your attention to the Medjez-el-Bab operation, the Kasserine Pass operation, and others. Unless some such drastic action is taken in a limited area – where resistance is such that no other methods will avail – I fear that the Strategic Air Force's part of the combined bomber offensive will be sharply reduced, if not stopped entirely. Truly – the whole future of the Air Forces is closely knit into this whole problem.

I have seen a report which indicates to me that one possible reason for a lack of inge-nuity in the air action is due to the assumption of tactical air operational control by the Army G-3s, apparently with your knowledge and agreement. While I cannot credit such an explanation since I have received no intimation from you of such a situation, neverthe-less I would appreciate your thoughts on this subject also. Our airmen thoroughly know the capabilities of their Arm. They, and they alone, must control the operations of their Air Forces. It is, in my opinion, impossible for Ground Force officers to fully utilise vision and imagination in air action, since they are not well acquainted with air capabilities and limitations. We have fought for twenty years to get the principles of FM 100-20 accepted. We must go forward, not backwards.

In order to break this stalemate, I believe it depends upon the initiative of the Air Forces. Am anxiously awaiting a reply from you.[72]

This articulates a similar plan to Arthur Harris's '1000 Bomber raid', Operation MILLENIUM in mid-1942. The Official Historians of the RAF's bomber offensive describe these raids as, 'an impressive demonstration of what Bomber Command might achieve if it was expanded.'[73] Arnold's thoughts may have been the sapling of a seed planted in his mind by Eisenhower a few months previously when still in command in the Mediterranean. On 1 May 1943, he wrote to Arnold regarding the visibility of air support to the soldier on the ground:

You do not need to sell me any bill of goods on the Air Force. So far as I know, Spaatz and I see eye to eye on every single thing that comes up; and we believe that we have learned lots of things that were, before the war, either not understood or not fully appreciated either by our Ground Forces or our Air Forces. For example: The tremendous value of an occa-sional operation so staged that the man on the ground can actually see his brother in the air doing something effective in the battle. It is impossible to get down to the last soldier in the ranks, who may be sweating and struggling up a hill 1500ft high in the face of machine gun fire, that friendly planes off on a very important mission are contributing something to his immediate problem. **An occasional bit of 'stage management' pays huge dividends.** (author emphasis added)[74]

Was the attack on the Abbey the piece of 'stage management' on a hill 1,700 feet high that was needed? Or, as Juin put it 'the reckless test.' Even the German military, writing after the end of the conflict in 1958, considered that the attack on the Abbey achieved no military advantage beyond the fleeting psychological boost and the demonstration of what airpower could do when in command of the air.[75]

The timing of Arnold's letter is vague but important. It was later than 22 January when the Anzio beachhead was formed and earlier than 6 March when Eaker responded. The mention of the 'hill behind Cassino', but not of the attack upon it, may infer a date earlier than 15 February.

72   AFHRA Reel A6030, MAAF C-in-C Correspondence, undated letter.
73   Webster & Frankland, *Volume I, Preparation*, Kindle Location, 7578.
74   Chandler et al, *Eisenhower Papers, Vol II*, p.1107.
75   AFHRA Reel K1026Y, Frame 1022. Wolfgang Pickert. The Impact Of Allied Air Attacks On German Divisions And Other Army Forces In Zones Of Combat.

This and the preceding sub-paragraph concerning Cassino town could have been viewed by Eaker as an indication of his Chief's intention and direction. The reference to 'our' Ground Forces probably meant US rather than Allied. The New Zealand Corps relieved US II Corps around 11 February, so the letter is most likely to have been penned between the 24 January when the 34th Division attacked the Cassino massif and the town and the 11 February when they were relieved. Arnold stresses the importance of succeeding at Cassino for the future of his air force. In an oddly contradictory letter on 28 January, one of Arnold's principal air advisers, Kuter warns him that the strategic bombers keep being diverted to 'strategically less important tasks.'[76]

> Every day on which we fail to bomb the German aircraft industry or the German Air Force in being – either because of weather or because of diversion to some relatively non-important mission – allows Göring to add some thirty more aircraft to his single engine fighters. From past statistics these thirty aircraft airborne on one mission will cost us three flying fortresses.[77]

Kuter was right. In January 1944, Fifteenth Air Force only attacked POINTBLANK targets four per cent (137 sorties) of the time.[78] Spaatz was clearly concerned that the Fifteenth Air Force was spending too much time attacking targets in the Anzio beachhead area. Kuter made the following recommendation:

> The US Strategic Air Forces in Europe devote, from February 1 until the time it passes to the control of the Supreme Allied Commander AEF, 100% of its effort to the destruction of the German Air Force, all other targets notwithstanding, except only when weather conditions prevent so doing.[79]

Arnold was being pulled in two directions. Firstly, from his airpower experts who advocated the strategic mission and secondly, he was concerned that the AAF would receive harsh criticism if they did not pull out all the stops to support the armies on the battlefield. Arnold fears that the old-guard would succumb to the temptation to use the airpower as 'flying artillery', but he also shows that despite his enthusiasm he does not really grasp the practical difficulties. In it, he essentially recommended that Eaker consider implementing air operations that are remarkably similar to both the 15 February and the 15 March air attacks at Cassino, both of which failed to shift the impasse and gave sceptical army officers ample ammunition to blame air ineffectiveness rather than ground commander ineptitude. Arnold's plan of action at Cassino was supported by the US JCS.[80] This letter was the probable catalyst for MAAF to use the heavy bombers at Cassino. The letter, although asking for Eaker's thoughts, was also admonishing him for his

---

76   AFHRA Reel A1376, Memorandum For The Commanding General, Army Air Forces, *Diversion from Mission of Strategic Air Forces* dated 28 January 1944.
77   AFHRA Reel A1376, Memorandum For The Commanding General, Army Air Forces, *Diversion from Mission of Strategic Air Forces* dated 28 January 1944.
78   AFHRA Reel A1376 Letter Spaatz to Arnold dated 5 February 1944.
79   AFHRA Reel A1376, Memorandum For The Commanding General, Army Air Forces, *Diversion from Mission of Strategic Air Forces,* dated 28 January 1944.
80   Wesley Frank Craven and James Lea Cate, *The Army Air Forces In World War II, Volume Three, Europe: ARGUMENT To VE Day – January 1944 To May 1945* (Washington DC: Office of Air Force History, 1983), p.365.

failure and for passing responsibility for air use to the ground forces. This would not have been lost on Eaker, who according to Saville, was especially keen to use the heavies in the March attack on Cassino town. Especially significant was Arnold's dramatic claim that the future of the Air Forces is at stake; Kuter made the same claim, but for different reasons. This was Arnold's real strategic end-state; shaking the Army shackles from his Air Force.

Eaker addressed Arnold's concerns in a lengthy reply where he managed his commander's expectations whilst describing the upcoming operation to destroy Cassino town; he explained that his air forces are concentrating on interdicting German supplies and educated him on the difficulties of an Italian winter. He used the Abbey bombing as an explanation why using mass airpower against ground force targets was unprofitable unless the Army is able to exploit the air's activity; 'It was clearly demonstrated in the bombing of the Abbey that little useful purpose is served by our blasting the opposition unless the army does follow through' he said,[81] adding:

> I am anxious that you do not set your heart on a great victory as a result of this operation. Personally, I do not feel it will throw the German out of his present position completely or entirely, or compel him to abandon the defensive role, if he decides and determines to hold on the last man.[82]

In an interview after the war Norstad, said that 'it was clear to me that the fundamentals of air power were around bombers.'[83] Can the hidden hand of Arnold be detected? Norstad, a few years previously, when he was a colonel, had been a key informal adviser to Arnold in his private think-tank known as the Advisory Council. Norstad was one of the first members and joked in a 1979 oral history interview that, 'he was always going to fire me for something. If a day passed when Hap wasn't going to fire me, then I knew that I was falling flat on my face.'[84] In the biography of Kuter, another favoured son, the point was made that there were two men whom you never wanted to see; the first was Kuter, the second Norstad.[85] These officers were the eyes and ears of Arnold. Officers in the Council were known as 'The Heavenly Twins,' the representatives of God. This Council was formed by Arnold within 60-days of the attack on Pearl Harbor. Members had unlimited access to him, and their job was to conduct the deep thinking about the Army Air Force, its role and future. Norstad as one of the first members, would have had an instinctive feeling for the thoughts and intent of his boss.[86] Arnold was aware that he lacked creativity, and had reportedly said to Norstad and the others 'your job is to do my thinking for me.'[87] He thought very highly of Norstad saying one night to him after another gruelling workday:

> You think I am pushing you pretty hard sometimes, don't you? Well don't think this is just by accident, this is just on whim and fancy. But it's time I told you, I have been meaning to

81   AFRHA Reel A6030, MAAF C-in-C Correspondence, Letter Eaker to Arnold dated 6th March 1944.
82   AFRHA Reel A6030, MAAF C-in-C Correspondence, Letter Eaker to Arnold dated 6 March 1944.
83   Robert Jordan, *Norstad: Cold War NATO Supreme Commander* (New York: St Martin's Press, 2000), p.37.
84   AFHRA Iris No 1077003, USAF Oral History Program, Interview with Gen Norstad, 1979, p.483.
85   Laslie, p.88.
86   Henry. H. Arnold, *American Airpower Comes of Age – General Henry H 'Hap' Arnold's World War II Diaries – Volume 2* (Progressive Management Publications, 2002), p.8.
87   Howard D Belote. *Once in a Blue Moon: Airmen in Theater Command* (Maxwell AFB AL: Air University College of Aerospace Doctrine Research and Education, Air University Press, 2000), p.13.

tell you for a long time. You are special. There aren't very many special people, but you are one of them. It's my responsibility to see that you get a wide range of training, get the best background we can give you, and also that you have pressure on you.[88]

Norstad, as Chief of MAAF Operations, probably saw Arnold's letter. There is no hard evidence of how the Abbey attack became what it was, but this letter could have given Norstad the idea of using the B-17s. Maybe he continued to think for Arnold on this occasion? In Lemnitzer's biography, he and Norstad are credited with conducting the planning for the attack on the Abbey.[89] He was the primary recipient of special intelligence within Eaker's headquarters.[90] Norstad was therefore in the best position to change the 36-fighter-bombers into the heavy bomber armada, especially during Eaker's absence in the days before the attack. In whodunnit terms he was one of the few officers with motive, means and opportunity. He remained close to Arnold and was rewarded with a meteoric rise through the ranks. Many Advisory Council members achieved four-star rank and Norstad was one of the very few USAF generals to become a Joint Combatant Commander when he took over as Supreme Allied Commander of Europe in NATO and the US's European Command in the 1950s. Airmen have rarely attained such joint responsibility in the US system. Only four USAF officers have held this position – Norstad was the first.

In his time in the Mediterranean Norstad was responsible for planning air operations supporting Ops TORCH and ANVIL. He developed the plan for the Italian air interdiction mission, Op STRANGLE, as well as delivering air support to the Anzio beachhead and the *Gustav* Line.[91] It is almost certain that he had a major role in plans to bomb the Abbey and was one of the MAAF officers deployed forward to Caserta. As we have seen Arnold was very keen to see the USAAF used to its greatest extent. He had bigger strategic fish to fry than merely winning the war. A demonstration of awesome air power in a blaze of publicity would do his campaign no harm. It is unlikely that Norstad would have had specific instructions from Arnold, but he had several opportunities to directly gauge his intent. In Tunis on 20 November 1943, while on his way to the Cairo conference, Arnold met with his air commanders, including Norstad.[92] Arnold's diary does not divulge details of the discussion, but it is probably safe to say that bombing effectiveness came up. When this meeting occurred the Fifth Army was approaching the Mignano Gap, barely 10-miles from the Abbey. He met Norstad again on 8 December; Fifth Army were at San Pietro, eight miles from Cassino. They had moved at a rate of a mile a week, battling the weather and fierce opposition. Arnold went to Bari the next day, where he was briefed by Fifteenth Air Force on the state of the war in Italy and presumably their part in it.[93] Then, on 11 December, Arnold took a flight over the front line in a Piper Cub aircraft where he would have observed the great Abbey from just a few miles away.[94]

Hap referred to the lack of progress on the ground in his letter to Eaker.

88   AFHRA Iris No 1077003, USAF Oral History Program, Interview with Gen Norstad, 1979, p.484.
89   Binder, p.120.
90   Putney, p.13.
91   Belote, p.16.
92   Arnold Diaries Vol 2, p.48.
93   Arnold diaries Vol. 2, p.56.
94   Because he was in receipt of ULTRA and aware of OVERLORD plans, Arnold would not have flown over the Abbey, still in enemy territory in mid-December 1943.

Marshall and Arnold with Brigadier-General Lauris Norstad. As one of Arnold's first Advisory Council members, he was given great latitude to do Arnold's thinking for him. Did he continue this role in Italy when Eaker was absent? (NARA RG18-2772a)

Arnold took a ride in an L-4 Cub artillery spotting aircraft in December 1943. It is likely that he saw the Abbey during this trip. (NARA RG342-FH-000588)

18

The Flight of General Eaker

Possibly there exist men with infallible memories, but it so happens that I have never met one.
General Curtis LeMay USAF
Mission With LeMay[1]

A piece of evidence used widely by historians to explain the attack, although not included on the list of evidence sent to the British CoS, but which, has been suggested was pivotal to the decision, was a flight on 14 February by Eaker and Devers.[2] Sources differ as to the exact date and even Eaker was unsure. In a 1975 letter to columnist Vincent Flaherty, Eaker said it was a 'couple of days before the attack,'[3] but in his piece for *National Security Affairs* the year before he stated the day before.[4] He made no comment as to the altitude at which he flew in either letter, although the USAAF Official History stated 200-feet. In an oral history interview the same year, Eaker stated he flew at 1,500-feet over the Abbey.[5] The standard operating procedure for the spotter pilots upon crossing into enemy territory was to fly at around 3,000-feet to avoid small-arms fire, which supports the second claim. They would fly very low, however, to avoid German fighters. Despite claims that placed this flight on 13 February, the weather on that day was very poor. It could only have occurred on 14 February when the weather was fine.

The request to bomb the Abbey may have offered an opportunity to Eaker who, like Alexander had been coming under increasing pressure, even though he had only been in post for a few weeks. Eaker, himself a trained journalist who like his boss and friend Arnold and senior intelligence officer Harris Hull, had a nose for a good story. When Assistant Chief of the Air Corps, Arnold had sent him to the Information Division where one of his principal responsibilities was to nurture relations with newspaper publishers, editors and reporters. High-altitude precision bombing was failing with unsustainable loss rates and minimal effect on the enemy. Most of the blame for this failure would be placed on Ira Eaker and other members of the bomber mafia

---

1   Le May, p.vii.
2   Gervasi, p.558.
3   AFHRA Reel 23268, Eaker letter to Vincent Flaherty, 9 January 1975, in Eaker Correspondence, Frame 1400.
4   Ira C Eaker, Why We Bombed Monte Cassino, *National Security Affairs*, 28 April 1974
5   AFHRA Iris No 1036066, United States Air Force Oral History Program, Interview of Lt Gen Ira C. Eaker by Hugh N Ahmann dated 10-11 February 1975, p.445.

Devers and Eaker stated that they flew over the Abbey in a spotter aircraft on 14 February 1944. Neither man was in Italy at the time and neither corrected their story before their deaths. (NARA RG342-FH-000571)

who had championed this form of bombing. Eaker needed a success, a tangible example where the doctrine they had long espoused, which seemed on the verge of disaster could be resurrected in the minds of the American public and sceptical allies. A trained journalist would know all this. As we shall see, however, this flight is a myth – it never happened. The key question is why Eaker has always claimed to have made it?

The problem with the story was that Eaker was travelling most of the time that the decision was being made in Caserta and he may not have been aware of the bombing until after it had occurred, although he claimed to have consulted widely on its merits. The pressure for increased air support in Italy came from Arnold, who wanted Eaker to make better use of the 4,062 operational aircraft under his command, and, we should remember, whom Eaker had already displeased due to his lack of success the previous year when he was in charge of Eighth Air Force.

Arnold wrote the following to Eaker on 10 February:

A serious crisis appears to be imminent for our troops in the Beachhead South of ROME and for our Fifth and the British Eighth Army.

In view of this, information is requested as to why every airplane that is flyable and has a crew is not used against German personnel, equipment and installations. By staging units through forward fields and all other possible means it should be possible to exert maximum air effort in support of these ground battles and seriously interfere with German disposition (?).

Your comments desired.[6]

This note offers a similar solution, but with less detail, than his long letter to Eaker in the previous chapter. Was this note before or after the long letter? It is uncertain because the latter is undated, but a follow-on seems more likely. That places the long letter somewhere between 22 January and 10 February 1944. Arnold's guidance was in direct contradiction of Spaatz's theories of the use of airpower, but as the Commanding General, he could not be ignored. Despite his lack of direct influence, he held full command of his force and more importantly the career prospects of his subordinates. His correspondence was contradictory from an operational perspective, but made sense from a public relations perspective, considering that above all else Arnold wished for independence. Any successful air force action was a positive contribution in the eyes of the President, Congress and the public; doctrine be damned. The timing of Arnold's note and letter and the decision to use the heavy bombers to showcase their capability against an 'easy' target, guaranteed to attract world attention, was probably not coincidental. Considering Eaker's hectic schedule in the week of the bombing it is uncertain he read either prior to the bombing, but his principal subordinates probably did. Not only would an attack on the Abbey with his heavy bombers offer a highly visible opportunity to relieve the pressure from above, but it gave Eaker, or bomber advocates in his staff, an opportunity to prove that strategic airpower could effectively support ground operations, or even possibly supplant them.

This note and letter suggest that Arnold, far from advocating that strategic air power be used only in Op POINTBLANK missions, was keen to use it selectively in support of ground forces, where it would have most impact and enhance air's public profile as a battle winner. The letter was in direct conflict with his communication with Eaker the day before, where he reiterated the 'tactical emergency' policy by telling Eaker that he should not receive directives for the Fifteenth Air Force from Wilson.[7] This order was not within Arnold's power as he had no direct operational command over Eaker's air forces. He could fire him again, however.

In a correspondence with Mr Brian Burke in March 1965, Eaker claimed that he knew from intelligence sources that Germans were in the Abbey and that they used it for an observation position and that radio direction finders indicated heavy traffic from there.

No evidence has been found that this is true in February 1944 although it was true in March 1944. Eaker also said to Burke that Clark strongly recommended to Devers that it be bombed. Again, there was no evidence for this, and Clark was strongly opposed to bombing the Abbey, although he did support bombing the town of Cassino a month later. All those involved knew Clark's position as being against the attack. Eaker stated that the 'New Zealand' Brigade had planned to storm the Abbey one minute after the bombing. This showed that he had his facts wrong in that it was an Indian Brigade and there was never a plan to storm the Abbey in daylight straight after the bombing. More likely, the intervening twenty years had dimmed

---

6   AFHRA Reel A6060, Figures from MAAF aircraft (US, UK, Fr) dated 6 February 1944. Frame 0447; AFSC N 1144/10 Message from General Arnold to Lieutenant-General Eaker, 10 February 1944.
7   AFHRA Reel A6030, History of MAAF, December 1943 – September 1944, Volume 2, AFSC N1187/9 dated 9 February 1944.

Eaker's memory, and he was mixing-up the assault on the Abbey with the New Zealanders' assault on the town and castle on 15 March.[8]

The diaries of Eaker and Devers had been analysed and it was discovered that both officers had appointments in North Africa on 14 February. Devers should have met with Wilson in the morning and was due to give the opening address at a boxing tournament in the afternoon. Eaker was at conferences and then touring Army Air Force facilities near Cairo.[9] Examining Eaker's appointments calendar, it is certain that Eaker did not fly over Montecassino Abbey on either 13 or 14 February, or on any other day during the decisive period. Slessor arrived in Caserta from MAAF HQ to stand-in for Eaker on 8 February. The last daily staff meeting Eaker attended was on the morning of 9 February. Early on 10 February, the day of Arnold's note, he flew to Algiers with the AFHQ Chief of Staff, Lieutenant General Sir James Gammell, arriving just after 2:00pm. Eaker had dinner with Wilson that night. They could not have discussed the destruction of the Abbey, as this dinner was prior to the first known request, which came the next day from 4th Indian Division. That day he remained in Algiers and attended a cocktail party that evening, but the request had probably not climbed to AFHQ by then. The next morning, he flew back to Italy in his new B-17, RAINBOW GIRL. He may now have learned of Arnold's scolding note and the request to bomb the Abbey, but again the timeline suggests that discussions between the New Zealand Corps and Fifth Army were still continuing on 12 February. Cannon and Saville, the new XII ASC commander, were probably aware and they may have informed MAAF, but there is no correspondence found supporting this, and Slessor wrote in his copy of British Official History draft that air was not consulted about the decisions made by Freyberg and Alexander on the afternoon of 12 February.

Eaker again left Italy early on 13 February, flying to Cairo, where he stayed all day and the next. Cairo is at least an 8-hour flight from Naples or Foggia, avoiding German-held territory such as Crete. This flight was before the proposed attack was discussed by Clark and Alexander for his final approval that morning and Eaker could not have been involved. Eaker's presence in Cairo on 14 February, when his flight over the Abbey was supposed to have occurred, is confirmed because he attended a dinner party that evening with the AOC-in-C Middle East Command, Air Marshal Sir Keith Park and the Commanding General of the United States Army Forces in the Middle East (USAFIME), Major General Ralph Royce.

Eaker's presence in Cairo on the crucial days was confirmed by a message sent by Park to Slessor on 13 February which confirmed that Eaker had arrived in Cairo and that he would be looked after by Royce during his stay.[10]

In his letter to Saunders in 1948, Slessor claimed to have spoken to Clark during the discussions prior to the bombing, with both men being against the attack, which implied his presence in Italy on the key dates. Whilst his aircraft were destroying the Abbey, Eaker and Royce were enjoying lunch at Shepheard's followed by a bit of sightseeing. They visited the bazaar and climbed the Great Pyramid, where they bumped into King Peter of Yugoslavia at the top.[11]

8   AFHRA Reel 23324, Ira C Eaker, Letter to Mr Brian Burke, 29 March 1965.
9   Glyn Harper and John Tonkin-Covell, *The Battles of Monte Cassino: The Campaign and its Controversies*, passim.
10 TNA AIR 23/888: Message Reference AOC 599, Personal For Slessor from Park dated 13 February 1944.
11 AFHRA Reel A6030. CINC MAAF Diary Entries and Daily Staff Meeting minutes – 8-15 February 1944.

Personal message from the RAF's Air Officer Commanding Middle East, Air Marshal
Sir Keith Park to Air Marshal Sir John Slessor, dated 13 February 1944, confirming that
Lieutenant General Eaker had arrived in Cairo. (UK TNA)

On the day of the bombing, Eaker's diary shows that whilst his aircraft destroyed the Abbey he
was having lunch with Ralph Royce followed by a trip to the bazaar and the Pyramids. (AFHRA)

The next day, Eaker inspected a B-25 unit near Benghazi, before returning to Italy that afternoon. Devers' biographer, John Adams, described the Abbey flight but then proceeds to quote Devers' diary from 15 March rather than 15 February.[12]

The implication is that not only did Eaker not fly over the Abbey with Devers to confirm that the Germans were there, but also that he was not in Italy when the decision was made. From this evidence it was unlikely that Eaker had anything to do with the order to use heavy bombers against the Abbey, and that he had delegated this responsibility to a subordinate, most probably Slessor, his deputy, or Norstad, his Chief of Operations. No personal REDLINE message between Norstad and Eaker that discussed the Abbey bombing has surfaced. Eaker was back at Caserta by 17 February and was present at a Commander-in-Chief's Conference the next day.[13]

In 1975, Eaker again states that he was involved in the decision and that he informed Giles in Washington beforehand in order that he may keep Arnold informed of the decision. He said the following:

> I wanted General Arnold to have a thorough understanding about the Cassino bombing. I called Giles as soon as we finished the conference and decided we were going to bomb Monte Cassino. I gave Giles, for his and General Arnold's information, the whole story. It would be very easy for them to go to Marshall and the President even and condemn us for a course of action in the theatre unless they were thoroughly briefed on all the reasons and who took what position and everything. So, I kept them constantly advised of what went on with General Devers and Field Marshal Wilson, Field Marshal Alexander, Mark Clark.[14]

This explanation from Eaker raises more questions than it answers. When was the conference? The archival records contain no messages between Eaker and Giles or Arnold that give notice that the Abbey will be bombed or of the circumstances behind the decision. There is no doubt that he was in Cairo in the few days before the bombing when the final decision was made. Devers was elsewhere in North Africa, and Wilson was in Algiers. Clark and Alexander were both in Italy. On the morning of the 14 February, there was no intent to bomb the Abbey with heavies who, were still planning to strike targets in Germany, although some planning had been undertaken and a tasking order issued. There is no time during these few days when the officers mentioned could possibly have met and none ever mention a senior conference in their memoirs and nor is it in Eaker's appointments calendar. There can be only two possibilities. They decided that the Abbey was to be bombed before the requests from the Army or, Eaker is again mixing up the operations of 15 February with the town bombing on 15 March. There is no evidence for the first possibility. Eaker's memory of an event more than 30-years previously has sometimes been faulty. Nothing else meets the known timeline of events. He added the following startling comment in his 1975 oral recollection:

12   Adams, Kindle loc 2530.
13   TNA WO 214/30, Minutes of Commander-in-Chief's Conference on ANVIL dated 18 February 1944.
14   AFHRA Iris No. 1036066, United States Air Force Oral History Program, Interview of Lt Gen Ira C Eaker by Hugh N Ahmann, dated 10-11 February 1975, pp.421-2.

Some Germans came out of the cave halfway down Monte Cassino where they had been in hiding. A few machine-guns opened up, and troops dived off the road into the cover of the bombing craters, and so did the tanks. They never went forward. It would have been easy; I could have taken a squadron of air forces and captured the town at Cassino that day. Many people have asked me how I knew that, and I said, 'I had a photographer walk all over Cassino that afternoon grinding his camera, and nobody paid any attention to him.'[15]

The claims in this statement also support a March event rather than a February event. Operation AVENGER on 15 March was launched into Cassino town, along the road. It was initially supported by tanks, but these had considerable problems with bomb craters, especially after it started raining that evening. The operation on 15 February did not use a road, did not involve any tanks, was not aimed at the town and the attacking troops did not encounter bomb craters. Sending a photographer into Cassino or onto the mountain on 15 February would have been foolhardy.

War Correspondent Frank Gervasi clearly remembered a flight on 14 February, but these spotter flights were a regular occurrence, happening multiple times daily when the weather permitted. Eaker's biographer claims that he had refused to be briefed into ULTRA so that he could go on operational missions, something that the British would have forbidden had he been indoctrinated.[16] He claimed in an interview in 1975 that it was Spaatz that advised him not to be ULTRA indoctrinated.[17] He did, however, know about OVERLORD, another reason to bar him from flying over enemy territory. The same rules would have applied to his flight over the Abbey.

Eaker claimed that he saw a radio mast and German uniforms on a washing-line in the Abbey courtyard.[18] It is implausible that Eaker could have distinguished German tunics from 200-feet above as some have claimed was his altitude, never mind the 1,500-feet altitude as he stated in 1975. Why would a German observation position, a key element of which is conceal-ment, be hanging its washing out for all to see, especially when the German leadership has been vociferous for months over its desire to save the Abbey and has claimed that no German soldier was there? A fighting position, as the ruins became, would not be so concerned about the enemy locating its whereabouts. The mast, although conceivably a German radio mast, would have been there in March. If it was a German radio mast, the Allied Y service has no record of any transmissions being intercepted from it in February 1944. Both of these things, however, were far more plausible if the Eaker flight had been after the Abbey's destruction because the Germans were indeed in occupation, and they now had no need to hide themselves. Eaker's supposed observations were also not in harmony with other intelligence as identified by Italian historian Livio Cavallaro who said that the Eaker flight:

was not supported by any photograph and gives rise to suspicion, considering that it was formulated by the leading American proponent of high-altitude precision bombing. What

---

15   AFHRA Iris No 1036066, United States Air Force Oral History Program, Interview of Lt Gen Ira C. Eaker by Hugh N Ahmann, dated 10-11 February 1975, p.448.
16   Parton, *Air Force Spoken Here*, p.145.
17   AFHRA Iris No 1036066, United States Air Force Oral History Program, Interview of Lt Gen Ira C. Eaker by Hugh N Ahmann, dated 10-11 February 1975, pp.327-8.
18   Hapgood and Richardson, p.185.

makes General Eaker's statement uncertain is the series of aerial photographs that the 5th Army command took of the abbey in the first two weeks of February. From those photos the intelligence officers were able to locate some German positions on the ground outside the building, but never detected the presence of military installations or German soldiers inside the building.[19]

Eaker's story changed over the years. In some accounts he flew with Devers, and they saw Germans in the Abbey grounds. In a comment piece to *American Heritage* magazine when asked about a piece by Blumenson, Eaker suggested there were two spotter planes and that he saw aerials and 'machine-gun nests less than fifty feet from the walls of the ancient Monastery.'[20] Eaker was generally ambivalent about the bombing, although his comment about the waterlogged Liri Valley below suggested that by the 1970s he was confused over the 15 February attack on the Abbey and the 15 March attack on Cassino town. It was these bomb craters that held up the New Zealanders after the attack on the town on 15 March. No tanks were used on the massif in February when he said in a 1975 correspondence to columnist Flaherty:

> Devers' and my position was that if it would save the lives of our soldiers we could and would bomb it, but the bombing would only be effective if the attack followed immediately. I also pointed out that the Liri Valley, at that time of year, was very marshy; that our bombs would create water filled craters and might impede the US and British tanks, which was exactly what happened.[21]

Much of the story of Eaker and Devers flying over the Abbey in February 1944, originated from the former in interviews and correspondences with various people in the late 1960s and 1970s, although it is included in the Official History which was written long before. He said almost the same in his oral history interview the same year as the Flaherty interview.[22] The elapsed time and his advancing years may have dimmed his memory, but its inclusion in the Craven and Cates history adds suspicion that Eaker has sustained a story which is suspicious. It may be that Eaker saw German soldiers and aerials in the Abbey; he did not see them in February but in March when Böhmler's paratroopers were occupying the ruins. His diary entries from 13-15 March 1944 place him in Italy and there are gaps in his normal routine on both 13-14 March when he could have flown over Cassino.

In his oral history interview, he mentions a few conferences he attended with Devers and others. These could not have occurred in February as neither officer was in Italy, but these could have happened in March. The diary entry of 15 March placed him in Cassino to observe the bombing of the town. That evening he went to Naples to give an interview to the NBC News

19   In Tasciotti, p.99.
20   AFHRA Reel 23324, Ira C Eaker Comment on Monte Cassino and the Bombs by Martin Blumenson.
21   AFHRA Reel 23268, Eaker letter to Vincent Flaherty, 9 January 1975, in Eaker Correspondence, Frame 1400.
22   AFHRA Iris No 1036066, United States Air Force Oral History Program, Interview of Lt Gen Ira C. Eaker by Hugh N Ahmann, dated 10-11 February 1975, p.446-7.

This picture of General Eaker was taken at Cassino on 15 March 1944 when the town was bombed.
It proves he was in Cassino for the town bombing. He was not in Italy on 15 February.
(NARA RG342-FH-000472)

Network and gave a 'bird's eye description' of the Cassino bombing.[23] This phrasing hints that Eaker had flown over the town.

According to Hughes Rudd, a US Army spotter pilot who also claims to have flown over Cassino on 15 February during the actual bombing, the Germans generally fired at these aircraft with small-arms fire if they came within range.[24] Eaker mentions that the reason they did not do this on his flight was the flight of P-47s that were escorting him. Rudd was tasked with spotting flak batteries shooting at the heavy bombers that day, flying over the area at around 3,000-feet. It could have been his aircraft that was seen by Gervasi. The distances that Eaker claimed are well within rifle or machine-gun range of the Abbey, yet he did not report being fired upon. Eaker, when interviewed in 1977 said that he was certain of what he was going to find even prior to going. If the ruins were occupied by the paratroopers in March, it makes sense that he would have known. Another senior officer, US II Corps commander, Keyes, also claimed

23   AFHRA Reel A6030. CINC MAAF Diary Entries and Daily Staff Meeting minutes – 13-15 March 1944.

24   Hughes Rudd, *When I Landed the War Was Over*, American Heritage, Vol. 32, p.6, 1981. <http://www. americanheritage.com/content/when-i-landed-war-was-over?page=7> (accessed 24 January 2019).

to have flown over the Abbey on 14 February and saw nothing unusual, although he is equally susceptible to anchoring albeit in the opposite sense.[25] Rudd, the spotter pilot, claimed that he saw machine-gun tracer fire from the northeast corner of the Abbey, but was unsure whether it was from inside or by the exterior wall. His evidence was also not used by AFHQ in their 'irrefutable evidence'. Neither were the pieces of evidence that originated in the US II Corps Intelligence Summaries of 14 February which reported friendly artillery engaging an 'enemy gun' at a location very close to the position given for the Abbey (G846207).[26] Senger made it clear that not a single German soldier was killed or wounded during the attack on the Abbey.

Regardless of what he did or did not see, or whether his flight occurred at all as the records place him over 1,000-miles away, Ira Eaker's personal reconnaissance could not have had a substantial impact on the decision to bomb the Abbey for a simple reason. He was still suppos-edly in the air when Fifteenth Air Force had its 11:00am Targeting Meeting that decided the next day's targets and when the order was being written. Based on the 1977 interview, his aircraft landed at around noon on the 14 February.[27] He was actually in Cairo at this time. The air tasking message to destroy the Abbey was issued by the 5th Bombardment Wing only 30-minutes later. It would have been impossible for the wing to plan the mission and issue the orders through the chain of command in such a short time had Eaker recommended the use of heavy bombers.[28] It is far more likely that the flight of Eaker and Devers occurred in March and had absolutely nothing to do with the Abbey's bombing. It was hardly surprising that this event has become one of the major planks of the Military Necessity argument when it has been used by the US Army Air Forces Official Historians.[29] This mythical flight was also used as evidence and justification by the semi-official Air Force History and Museums Program in its1994 publication, *With Courage*.[30] This piece of evidence, like many of the others, failed to stand up to scrutiny by being out of kilter with the known timeline of events that led to the destruction of the Abbey. Eaker and Devers stood together on the 15 March, witnessing for themselves the inaccuracy of the B-17s. He took a transcript of his NBC broadcast to Devers' office early on 16 March 1944, as well as sending a copy to Clark. They did not, however, fly together the month before. The only solid contemporary evidence that Eaker and Devers ever flew together over the Abbey came from a report Eaker sent to Arnold on 22 May, four days after the Abbey's capture.[31]

Despite Eaker being a model officer of undoubted integrity, the question must be raised over whether he became mixed-up or whether he deliberately misled the historical record? Many of his comments on the event that claim he flew with Devers came from interviews during the 1960s and 1970s, at least 20-years, and sometimes much more, after the event. Because this is a great span of time, and there is little evidence that Eaker kept a personal diary of events, and he was becoming elderly, he can be excused for a lapse in memory. The attacks are only a month

25   Hapgood and Richardson, p.169.
26   The National Archives and Records Administration (NARA) RG338, NND 903618, II Corps Records, Intelligence Summary No 89 dated 14 February 1944, Para 5b.
27   Hapgood and Richardson, p.186.
28   5th Bomb Wing Operation Order 341, 14 February 1944.
29   Craven and Cate, p.363.
30   Bernard C Nalty, John F Shiner and George M Watson, *With Courage: The US Army Air Forces in World War II* (Washington DC: Air Force History and Museums Program, 1994), p.219.
31   AFHRA Reel A6030, MAAF CinC Correspondence, Eaker to Arnold dated 22 May 1944.

apart, they both occur on the 15th of the month, and both are against targets in Cassino. The problem, however, is with the Official History. Craven and Cate gathered their evidence for a third volume, in which the attack on the Abbey is recounted, in the late 1940s as the 900-page volume was first published in 1951. In the notes to this volume, Eaker was interviewed by USAF historian Dr Albert Simpson on 24 January 1950, less than six years after the event, when his memory should have been fresh and his mind sharp.[32] It was during this interview that Eaker claimed to have flown over the Abbey the day before the attack. This makes Eaker's mixing up of the events more problematic and more difficult to believe, raising the possibility that he deliberately claimed to have undertaken his flight to exculpate his force from the controversial act. The note in the Official History quotes British and American documents from Gould, Saunders and Osborne regarding the occupancy of the building; however, this note muddies the water over whether the occupancy was clear at the time, but concludes that no German occupied the Abbey. Because of this, the Official History does not appear to have contributed to any misinformation of the bombing. The editors took Eaker's claim at face value when evidence to the contrary was available; no attempt to fact-check the illustrious general appears to have been made. One further element is the silence of Jacob Devers. Both men lived for more than 30-years after the event, yet Devers, as far as I have been able to ascertain, never contradicted Eaker's account or date. That two men both have the same memory lapse stretches credibility. Whether General Eaker misspoke, misremembered or simply lied over his role in the Abbey attack will probably never be proven.

---

32   Craven and Cate, *Volume III*, p.847.

19

Sledgehammer to Crack a Nut?

'It takes close coordination with the Army to obtain maximum misuse of air power.'
General Carl Spaatz
Battle of Britain Diary,
28 August 1940[1]

Throughout its history airpower has struggled to break from the shackles, as the airman saw it, of supporting land operations as their primary duty. The Army has been equally convinced that they should have first call on supporting airpower and has been as determined as the airmen to retain its services, preferably under command: 'most soldiers believe their air-support requirements will only be met when army commanders have 'air resources at their disposal which are adequate for the operations at hand.'[2] Armies, especially the dominant branches of Infantry and Armour, were used to having everyone else support operations unquestioningly. Many expected the same from the air services, often not accepting or recognising their wider responsibilities. Air forces, sometimes behaving like newly free adolescents, resisted fiercely. The differences in cultural and doctrinal approaches were apparent even during the First World War and they increased in the inter-war years as the competition for very limited funding intensified. It was perhaps fiercer in Britain due to the independent nature of the RAF, which remained in doubt in the early 1920s, but also in America the air service struggled against the 'big army'. It was not unusual for soldiers to blame the failure of armies on the ground on their air support.

From 1941, and especially after the publication of FM 100-20 in mid-1943, the direction of travel was towards the airman as far as air support was concerned. In September of 1941, Churchill issued the following directive:

> Never more must the ground troops expect, as a matter of course, to be protected against the air by aircraft. If this can be done, it must only be as a happy make-weight and a piece of good luck. Above all, the idea of keeping standing patrols of aircraft over moving columns must be abandoned.[3]

---

1   Davies, p.37.
2   David Hall, *Learning How to Fight Together: The British Experience with Joint Air-Land Warfare* (Maxwell AFB AL: Air University – Air Force Research Institute, 2009), p.2.
3   Tedder, p.161.

It was a hard task to ween generals from their aircraft. In one encounter with General Alan Cunningham in North Africa, Tedder recalled that the British Army would 'feel lonely and unsupported unless they had a fighter and a bomber squadron at their personal beck and call.'[4] Throughout Britain's travails in the western desert, the lack of direct air control was used as a scapegoat for defeat. This, with a little help from army voices whispering in the hacks' ears, filtered back to the British press. Tedder, the air commander, spent much of his time defending his service and its doctrine. In January 1942 he wrote to Secretary of State for Air: 'The RAF have on this occasion given the Army, at great sacrifice, all the air support and protection they required. The German Air Force has interfered little with Army operations. Yet the Army continues to withdraw; therefore, the RAF crews are perplexed and feel that their efforts have been wasted.'[5]

Despite personal antipathy, one area where Tedder and Slessor agreed was their disdain for the fighting abilities of the British soldier and the competency of their commanders. The differences in outlook were not just doctrinal or technological, although both played a part, but there were large cultural differences. By mid-1942, Tedder was the architect of the methodology of both British and American air forces' support to the land battle for the rest of the war. He had also found a general with whom he could work in Auchinleck. Tedder's problem was that although the Auk was enlightened, he was losing and was soon to be fired. As Tedder saw it, this was down to his senior staff and he commented, 'He was badly served. With few exceptions his senior staff and commanders were useless 'good fellows'. No-one could expect to win a war against professionals in these circumstances.'[6] Tedder had low confidence in his replacements, Montgomery and Alexander, whom he considered unlikely to take 'inspired risks'.

One US Army report suggested that CAS had become the 'tactical stepchild' of air power.[7] Despite advances in doctrine, the lessons accrued in the desert had not been wholly learned during the final battles in North Africa despite the successes of the RAF's Western Desert Air Force and Eighth Army. Following victory in Tunisia, Group Captain Kenneth 'Bing' Cross, Commanding Officer of No 242 Group RAF, wrote in September 1943 that:

> It is no use the Army producing a plan in which the air's role is visualised as sort of super artillery to be laid on as and when the Army is held up, for more often than not, the target is unsuitable for air attack and the hold up might never have occurred if the air forces had been operating continuously since the commencement of the attack, instead of waiting for calls. The airman understands the possibilities and limitations of his weapon, the soldier does not, and providing the soldier remembers this, he will bring the airman in before his plan is made so that the airman can advise in their making to allow the air to be used to its maximum capacity. If necessary, prior to the battle and providing the air forces are strong enough, the Army Commander must be prepared to change his plans to suit the Air Commander always supposing other more important factors don't make this impossible.[8]

4   Tedder, p.175.
5   Tedder, p.243.
6   Tedder, p.314.
7   US Army Close Air Support Requirements Board, Close Air Support History, Command and General Staff College, Fort Leavenworth, 29 Aug 63, p.23.
8   AFHRA Reel A6111, Group Captain Cross, Lesson Learned Report of No. 242 Group RAF, Report to AOC DAF, 18 September 1943, p.10 in Frame 0197.

Tedder saw all operations as 'a joint campaign that demanded the utmost interservice cooperation.'[9] Levels of cooperation between the army and the air forces remained fraught at times. Cooperation between Montgomery and Coningham in Eighth Army in North Africa were well-developed and successful, but these procedures were local rather than doctrinal. The battle for Tunis saw the airmen working with General Sir Kenneth Anderson's First Army and cross-fertilisation of how to use them effectively had not yet occurred. The USAAF, less experienced than the British, were far more wedded to the ground forces than the RAF.[10] The commander of the USAAF 33rd Fighter Group, Colonel William Momyer, complained of flying 'umbrella patrols' over Allied units instead of seizing control of the air.[11] Momyer's complaint was reiterated after the war in a talk by Kuter, one of Arnold's closest advisers:

> Tactical air units were parcelled out among the ground forces, and so scattered that their inherent flexibility and mobility were lost. Fighters were used almost wholly in local defensive cover and the capability of those air forces to strike the enemy was ignored. No use was made of opportunities to take the initiative. The air forces were tied to the local interests of divisions and corps, and no attention was given to the task of winning control of the air or assisting the theatre as a whole.[12]

The impression in Washington was that, like the British, US airmen had no interest in CAS. Following a visit to North Africa in late 1942, US Assistant Secretary of War, John McCloy wrote, 'It is my firm belief that the air forces are not interested in this type of work, think it is unsound, and are very much concerned lest it result in control of air units by ground commanders. Their interest, enthusiasm and energy are directed to different fields.'[13]

Perhaps the nadir, between air and ground, US and UK, came in April 1943 when Patton's US II Corps, recently mauled at Kasserine Pass, complained of a lack of airpower in a situation report with a wider than usual distribution. Nearly as abrasive as the American, the tactical air commander, Coningham, was irritated by Patton's complaints, especially as they were not true. Patton was an old-fashioned army man who wanted to control air support. Coningham lit the fuse with a fierce, sarcastic rebuttal to an equally wide distribution list, accusing II Corps of being 'not battleworthy in terms of present operations.'[14] Spaatz came down on Coningham's side. Alexander telephoned Patton saying, 'he had read Coningham's message, that he had asked for it and got just what he had asked for.'[15] Tedder had foreseen such incidents, writing to Portal months earlier that 'Coningham is not going to have an easy time to get rid of the fantastic ideas of soldiers controlling aircraft.'[16] Tedder thought his response lacked judgement, and placated Eisenhower, who favoured and protected Patton, although he admonished him in a

9   Hall, p.15.
10 Ehlers, p.257.
11 Orange, 'Getting Together', p.25.
12 US Army Close Air Support Requirements Board, Close Air Support History, Command and General Staff College, Fort Leavenworth, 29 Aug 63, p.20.
13 US Army Close Air Support Requirements Board, Close Air Support History, Command and General Staff College, Fort Leavenworth, 29 Aug 63, p.19.
14 Vincent Orange, Coningham (London: Methuen, 1990), p.147.
15 Orange, Coningham, p.147.
16 Tedder, p.398.

letter on inter-allied cooperation.[17] To smooth over a potential Allied crisis, over which Ike had threatened to resign, Tedder compelled the New Zealander to apologise.

Truscott, Commanding General of the US 3rd Infantry Division and the US VI Corps at Anzio, commented in his memoir that in late 1943:

> So far in the Italian campaign there had been little direct air support for the divisions. It is true that the fighter planes of the 12ASC were attacking enemy troops and other targets which assisted the advance of the ground forces, but there was little or no coordination between the air and ground effort at the division level. A division selected targets which it wished to have attacked and submitted the list to the Army G-3. A Committee of Army and Air Force staff officers coordinated these requests…12ASC allocated the missions to the air sqns which were to fly them. The division rarely knew whether its requests had been accepted, and never knew whether or not the missions would be flown. Since the requests for air support always had to be made 12 hours or more before they were to be flown, there was no way to obtain air support quickly in case of need.[18]

The lessons identified by Cross and Truscott had not been fully rectified months later and were especially prevalent in cooperation with strategic bombers. Unfortunately, Cross' report was not widely distributed because a senior officer considered his conclusions 'impulsive and will lead to an amount of controversy and bad feeling.' A handwritten note, probably from the AOC, circles the word 'impulsive' and states 'not so much' although he does agree that Cross' report is not circulated. Tedder had already reached similar conclusions to Cross on Anderson's use of his air resources. Cross had identified many of the most pertinent lessons that could have prevented events such as the bombing of the Abbey had they been implemented. The US Fifth Army in its Training Manual No. 7, *Air Support of Ground Forces*, and possibly using a quote from Montgomery, recognises that air power used properly can be a battle-winning weapon:

> Any officer who holds high command, or who aspires to hold high command, must understand clearly certain basic principles regarding the use of air power. The greatest asset of air power is its flexibility, and this enables it to be switched quickly from one objective to another in the theatre of operations. So long as this is realised, then the whole weight of the concentrated use of the air striking force is a campaign-winning factor of the first importance.
>
> The command of all air forces allocated to assist land operations is vested in an independent air commander. With limited air resources, there is a definite requirement for this centralised control to achieve the necessary measure of concentrated effort. Nothing could be more fatal to successful results than to dissipate the air resources into small packets, placed under command of division or corps commanders, with each packet working on its own plan.[19]

17   Chandler et al, *Eisenhower Papers Vol II*, pp.1073-4.
18   Truscott, p.279.
19   AFHRA Reel A6111, Tactical Air Command's Close Support of the Fifth Army, HQ MAAF, Frame 1104-5.

Commander in Chief of the Mediterranean Air Command until the end of 1943, Air Chief Marshal Sir Arthur Tedder and his Chief of Staff, Brigadier General Patrick Timberlake visit the photo interpreters at the Mediterranean Allied Photographic Reconnaissance Wing. (NARA RG342-FH-002386)

Whilst Fifth Army accepts the independence of air forces and the doctrine of 'centralised command, decentralised execution', one still the senses in the text that the air supports or assists land forces. This was not the view of air forces, as close support was a third priority behind air superiority and air interdiction. The overall control of tactical air forces by Army commanders remained a part of US Army doctrine despite Fifth Army policy. This doctrine consigned the air force to a shield for the ground forces, under the control of corps commanders.[20] In truth, as Gooderson notes in his CAS study, the relationship remained strained as neither service showed much inclination to educate themselves about the other.[21] By the end of the Tunisian campaign Eisenhower had recognised that an air force fighting a separate war in support of its own ground formations was inefficient. He established the Mediterranean Air Command, and a unified air commander in Tedder. He did not, however, allow the airmen to have it all their own way and was emphatic that at times all air forces, including strategic bombers, must support

20   Hall, p.21.
21   Gooderson, *Battlefront,* pp.35-9.

ground operations.[22] The relationship between the USAAF and the RAF was far more cordial throughout the period than that between the US and British armies, despite the egos of some of the principal airmen. The creation of a unified, independent air commander was an important milestone in the creation of air doctrine, especially for the Americans.[23]

Tedder, agreeing to this unified air command and control gave the following speech to his senior staff:

> You know we British are intensely proud of our Air Force. We think it is the very best in the world, and that it saved England and the world – all of us. We have our own way of doing things and I suppose we feel we are justified in keeping these ways. But we also know that you Americans are equally proud of your splendid Air Force, of your magnificent aeroplanes and equipment, and that you feel justified in doing things your way – as well you are. However, it will be the fusion of us, the British, with you, the Americans, that is going to make the very best Air Force in the world. And now, gentlemen this is the last time I shall ever speak of 'us' the British and 'you' the Americans. From now on it is 'we' together who will function as Allies, even better than either of us alone.[24]

These sentiments galvanised the relationship between allied tactical air operations for the rest of the war, both in the Mediterranean and later. There were disagreements aplenty, but these were never allowed to get in the way of Tedder's driving focus.

In all but name FM 100-20 created an independent US Air Force. That this was a wise decision can be judged from the Germans. By mid-1944, the *Luftwaffe* was almost unable to operate, and it was the denial of resupply to units at the front due to Allied air interdiction that most concerned German commanders at OB SUED.[25] The US Army commanders in the Mediterranean were not yet wholly convinced. Early in his period in charge of Allied air forces, Tedder struggled to convince them that they did not have 'a divine right to command his own private air force, and incidentally a divine inspiration by which he knows better than anyone else how those air forces should be used.'[26] Despite Tedder's suspicions of Montgomery and Alexander, on 21 July 1943, just a few days after the launch of Operation HUSKY, Alexander's 15th Army Group issued their pamphlet *Employment of Air Forces in Support of Land Operations*.[27] The implication in the title was that air forces are there to support land forces, but the pamphlet accepts the independence and decentralization of air power, and that the independent air commander is responsible for all air plans. It even accepts that direct air support to the land battle is a secondary task. Giving with one hand, Alex's pamphlet takes away with the other stating that air planning will be determined 'within the framework of the Army-Air plan approved by the army commander.' The pamphlet provides ground commanders with guidance in how to employ air forces with the striking exception of the use of heavy bombers, the subject of which is not addressed.

---

22   Chandler et al, *Eisenhower Papers Vol III*, p.1446.
23   Edward T Russell & Robert M Johnson, *Africa To The Alps: The Army Air Forces in the Mediterranean Theater* (Air Force History and Museums Program, 1999), pp.6-8.
24   Tedder, p.398.
25   Westphal, p.163.
26   Tedder, p.404.
27   AFHRA Reel A1372, Employment of Air Forces In Support of Land Operations – 15AG/2055/G (Trg), dated 21 July 1943.

By 1944, despite Army doctrine, the Air Forces in Italy had greater independence considering their multi-national composition and the recognition at the highest levels of Allied Command that airpower was a weapon to be wielded at all levels of war. In Russia and Germany, the air arms were seen only as tactical. Even though the USAAF failed to achieve its independence until 1947, the views of its senior commanders were like the British; that air forces could be a decisive weapon if applied strategically and operationally. Tuker's philosophy and 4th Indian Division's tactical ideas were unattractive to them. In one of his letters to Portal, Slessor gave his opinion that bombers should only be used to directly support ground forces in a defensive emergency.[28] The US Army's FM 31-35 emphasized teamwork and training to ensure good cooperation between the air and ground forces.[29] It also made the point that the 'timing of the air attack is of primary importance in securing the maximum effect.'[30] The strategic air forces could not fulfil the doctrinal air requirements of the US Army because that was not their job. They had no direct communication or liaison, no experience of, or training in, support to ground forces and the choreography was poor, ensuring no advantage to the ground units. The failures of bombing over Cassino were viewed as being a failure of the concept of air as artillery. It was a display of what air power cannot do.[31] The USAAF had adopted FM 100-20 as their doctrine, whereas the ground forces considered FM 31-35 as their doctrinal approach. FM 100-20 did not replace FM 31-35, both documents existed side by side; one document described the overall doctrine, the other offered instruction as to how part of that doctrine should be executed. These manuals, in places contradictory, could not have resulted in harmonious cooperation. FM 31-35 emphasis was on the supporting role of air power rather than equality.[32] Another air power expert Richard Hallion makes the point that its concentration on corps level support made it 'cumbersome and flawed in both concept and execution.'[33] Slessor summed up the problem as he saw it in Italy a couple of weeks prior to the bombing of the Abbey:

> We must face the fact that our Armies in ITALY or elsewhere will not fight unless they have complete air superiority. What a dreadful legacy this is of the old days when Ironside (CIGS 1939-40) and Massey (presumably Montgomery-Massingberd CIGS 1933-36) and even Brooke were always clamouring for more air support and crying from the house tops for every subaltern to hear that the Army could not fight without it. And I'm afraid the Monty regime has not improved matters in that respect.[34]

Senior commanders in the German Army, although ravaged by Allied air power, considered artillery more effective in support of ground forces. In a post-war interrogation, commander of

28 Sir John Slessor, *The Central Blue* (London: Cassel, 1956), pp.570-576.
29 US War Department Field Manual FM 31-35, Aviation in Support of Ground Forces dated 9 April 1942, paras 10 and 25 <https://archive.org/details/FM31-35> (accessed 13 October 2023).
30 US War Department Field Manual FM 31-35, Aviation in Support of Ground Forces dated 9 April 1942, para 39 <https://archive.org/details/FM31-35> (accessed 13 October 2023).
31 AFHRA Reel A6030, History of MAAF, December 1943-September 1944, Volume 1, Chapter IX, p185.
32 Ehlers, p.256.
33 Hallion, p.163.
34 TNA AIR 75/69, Papers of Sir John Slessor, The Italian Campaign, Letter from Slessor to Portal dated 27 January 1944.

the 26th *Panzer* Division, *Generalleutnant* Viktor Linnarz gave his view of the relative importance of air power:

> The effect of air bombardment on ground troops is not so great as commonly imagined, as the troops can always move out of their shelters immediately after the air raid. Men accustomed to continuous artillery barrages for days on end are not likely to be absolutely demoralized by an air bombardment lasting 15 minutes…the really demoralizing experience for the ground soldier is the sight of the artillery-directing aircraft circling over our positions for hours…in an aerial bombardment you do not feel that an attack is personally directed against you. Jabos (fighter-bombers) and artillery-directing aircraft on the other hand seem to have a personal grudge against you.[35]

The majority of MASAF operations were against northern Italy, southern German, Balkan and Austrian targets too far away from UK airfields.

The Fifteenth Air Force had no tasking to directly support ground forces with CAS. It lacked ground liaison officers or communications links to the ground armies, although the 5th Bombardment Wing sent two officers to observe the Abbey bombing.[36] Nevertheless, the Fifteenth Air Force conducted eight per cent or 11,281 of its total sorties in support of ground forces, dropping over 25,000 tons of bombs in this role.[37] Orders and priorities should have prevented the Fifteenth Air Force being used against the Abbey if the POINTBLANK weather had been acceptable during mid-February. The decision to go-ahead with the primary target was decided at Twining's weather conference at 6:00am each day. This was based upon the forecast from 6:00pm the day before. The REDLINE messages leading up to 15 February support this conclusion. There was certainly no defensive emergency to justify the diversion.

Inevitably, there were times when the strategic bombers were required to support tactical operations. The first of these arose in the most difficult phase of Operation AVALANCHE. Heavy bombers were employed against German thrusts against the beachhead at Battipaglia and Eboli on 13-15 September 1943, with over 500 sorties flown on 14 September 1943 alone.[38] It was concluded afterwards that a mechanism for diverting them from their primary mission in an emergency was required. Eisenhower, at the height of the crisis on 13 September wrote to General Albert Wedemeyer, 'I would give my next year's pay for two or three extra heavy groups right this minute.'[39] Despite all Clark's beach difficulties, Eisenhower put his faith in air power, calling it the 'great hope' in a letter to Marshall.[40] This optimism, however, required procedures. At the Cairo conference, some control of the strategic bombers was delegated to the Mediterranean Theatre Commander only, and only 'should a tactical or strategic emergency arise,' although the definition of an emergency was

---

35 Opinions of Lieutenant General Linnarz, HQ USAAF Report, *Defeat* (Washington DC: Headquarters Army Air Forces, 1946), p.4.
36 AFHRA Reel B0897, Frame 0992, 5th Bombardment Wing War Diary, Entry for 15 February 1944.
37 AFHRA Reel A6377, History of the Fifteenth Air Force, pp.302, 452, 491.
38 Kit C Carter and Robert Mueller, *US Army Air Forces in World War II: Combat Chronology 1941-1945* (Washington DC: Center for Air Force History, 1991), p.217.
39 Chandler et al, *Eisenhower Papers Vol III*, p.1408.
40 Chandler et al, *Eisenhower Papers Vol III*, p.1411.

not specified and the use was at the Theatre Commander's 'discretion.'[41] Most writers have assumed that this referred to Eisenhower and then to Wilson, but this is not completely clear. The Theatre Commander could take operational control of the US strategic bombers by the CCS for a specified purpose. Permission of the USSTAF was not required, although the directive required the Theatre Commander to inform Spaatz and the CCS. Eisenhower was informed of this authority through US channels before the conference in October 1943.[42] He disagreed with the formation of USSTAF, something he called 'unthinkable.'[43] Arnold had proposed the idea in July 1943 but official discussion of this proposal within the CCS began on 18 November with a memorandum from the US JCS named CCS 400. It is specific that the 'emergency' powers were to be retained by the US Theatre Commander.[44] The draft directive at the appendix to the US proposal is unclear whether the authority had been given to the Allied C-in-C or just the US Theatre Commander (NATOUSA), in this case Devers, although the wording suggests that the 'emergency' powers were delegated within the US national chains of command rather than Allied.

> The Commanding General, USSAFE (*Spaatz*), will employ six heavy bombardment groups and two long-range fighter groups of the Fifteenth Air Force to meet the requirements of the Commanding General NATO (*Devers*), in operations against objectives other than those prescribed for POINTBLANK, until such time as the air base objective area, north and east of Rome, is secured, in accordance with the provision of the directive issued by the Combined Chiefs of Staff on 22nd October. (Italics added by author for clarity).[45]

The appointment of Wilson had not yet been confirmed. The British responded to the US proposal on 26 November.[46] The British thought that the plan to coordinate the two US Air Forces was impractical and that 'the results would not justify the effort involved.' They also thought that there would be a 'conflict of interest between the commander of the Strategic Air Force on the one hand and the UK Government and theatre commanders on the other.'[47] The proposal would place US heavy bombers under CCS oversight in Washington, rather than under the British Chief of the Air Staff, the arrangement thus far. They also saw the proposal as a way to divert the heavy bombers from their principal task to the support of the Supreme Allied Commander when appointed. Although vociferous in their disagreement with the US proposal, the British made no complaint concerning the 'emergency' powers given to a Theatre Commander. The British did not usually use the term Theatre Commander, sticking to the term Commander-in-Chief. As the proposal only affected US assets it was judged to be a national issue and the US JCS dismissed the British complaints and drafted a directive to enact the joining of the two US strategic air forces. The CCS deferred the decision on 4 December 1943;

41   CCS 387/3 (Sextant) dated 5 December 1943. See also, Ambrose, p.270.
42   AFHRA Reel A6030, History of MAAF, December 1943 – September 1944, Volume 2, FAN 254 CCS to Eisenhower, 23 October 1943.
43   Chandler et al, *Eisenhower Papers Vol III*, p.1477.
44   Combined Chiefs of Staff Memorandum CCS 400 dated 18 November 1943, Enclosure.
45   Combined Chiefs of Staff Memorandum CCS 400 dated 18 November 1943, Appendix.
46   Combined Chiefs of Staff Memorandum CCS 400/1 dated 26 November.
47   Combined Chiefs of Staff Memorandum CCS 400/1 dated 26 November.

it was adopted at the CCS meeting in 7 December[48] despite continuing British disagreement and the order was issued by the US JCS on 5 January 1944 as follows:

> Should a strategic or tactical emergency arise requiring such action, Theatre Commanders, may, at their discretion utilize the Strategic Air Forces, which are based in their Theatres, for purposes other than their primary mission, informing the Combined Chiefs of Staff and the Commanding General USSAFE of the action taken.[49]

At no point from 18 November to when the order was issued on 5 January does the CCS give the Allied C-in-C 'emergency' powers to use the strategic bombers and the change was entirely an American change to which the British were in no position to veto despite their disagreement. Portal made clear on 4 December 1943 that he strongly disagreed with the proposal but that he would make sure it was implemented 'as smoothly as possible.'[50] Portal did agree that the Theatre Commander, mentioning Eisenhower by name, would be allowed to use Fifteenth Air Force 'in an emergency'. As the decision to appoint Wilson had not been taken it is unclear whether that right would also apply to him. The directive, however, was not sent to Wilson; it was kept in US channels and sent to Devers, Spaatz and Eisenhower only. Direction was given that 'the Commanding General USSAFE will coordinate his operations with those of the Allied
 Commander-in-Chief in the Mediterranean.'[51] The final CCS directive does include Wilson as having the 'emergency powers.' The execution of 'emergency' powers principally lay with Devers, CG NATOUSA -what we call today a national 'Red Card'. This was supported by Eaker in his 1975 interview with the oral history project. When asked how conflicts over bomber use were resolved in the Mediterranean he said:

> The final decision maker is the supreme commander. Down in Italy. For example, General Devers was the overall commander of US forces. He was the Deputy to Field Marshal Wilson in that capacity. For example, shortly after we made the Anzio landing, the commander up there was wanting to have all the air in the theatre come right in and kill those Germans who were shooting at him out front. General Devers said he would like to see me give more air support to the Anzio beachhead. I said, 'Let's go up and talk to him.' We flew up in a little plane and landed on the airdrome on D-plus-2, and it was true that Truscott wanted to get heavy bombers. I pointed out to Truscott – and Devers was listening – I said, 'Heavy bombers are not what you want. The heavy bombers are knocking down bridges so that this division out in front of you here is not going to get any ammunition or any replacements.'[52]

Whilst Eaker's memory may be fuzzy about the exact date when he visited the beachhead; his description suggests later than D+2, the narrative implies that Devers was a key decision maker

48   Minutes, 138th CCS Meeting, Mena House Cairo, 7 December 1943.
49   James Parton, The History of the Mediterranean Allied Air Forces (1945), pp.18-19.
50   Minutes, 134th CCS Meeting, Mena House Cairo, 4 December 1943.
51   Combined Chiefs of Staff Memorandum CCS 400/2 dated 4 December 1943, Enclosure.
52   AFHRA Iris No 1036066, United States Air Force Oral History Program, Interview of Lt Gen Ira C Eaker by Hugh N. Ahmann, dated 10-11 February 1975, pp.375-6.

on air support and that Eaker went to some length to avoid using heavy bombers in direct support to the ground commander.

The procedure for using heavy bombers in support of ground forces in Italy was confused at the beginning of 1944. Despite separate chains of command, General Cannon was responsible for sorting this confusion out, probably at the instigation of Alexander. Prior to the Anzio operation, on 14 January 1944, Cannon wrote to Norstad to clarify a few points. He identified that the Fifteenth Air Force was operating to three different directives. He wished to assist, but that he was 'somewhat confused as to just what they should do.'[53] Cannon and Alexander had discussed the use of the heavy bombers for support at Anzio, but there is no mention of an emergency situation. He suggested that pre-Anzio interdiction of Italian communication networks would require the 'entire strategic and tactical bomber forces'.[54] He then made the point that the heavy bombers were not operating with Anzio as their priority, and he then asked for clarification from Norstad. Norstad replied the next day, telling Cannon that MAAF should be informed of all bombing plans and that once approved coordination for bombing by Twelfth and Fifteenth Air Forces should be direct between them. He also made it clear to him that MAAF was responsible for issuing all 'Orders, Instructions and Directives to the Tactical and Strategic Air Forces.'[55]

It did not detail which of the air forces had primacy of planning. This direction was probably still valid a month later for the bombing of the Abbey, although no detailed plans have been located. Norstad finished his message by confirming that the Fifteenth Air Force participation in Operation SHINGLE had been approved by Spaatz.

Although no documentary evidence has been discovered, MASAF strategic bombers were not used against tactical objectives without higher level approval or without tacit agreement from Spaatz, although almost all operational decisions that did not impact Op POINTBLANK regarding Fifteenth Air Force were delegated to Eaker. As soon as he arrived in the Mediterranean Theatre, he reached an arrangement with Wilson that no emergency should be declared and that he had Spaatz's confidence to act appropriately.[56] Devers and Eaker were already friends, so the former probably trusted the airman's judgement – Devers was that sort of General. In a press conference in the UK in June 1943, Eaker said the following about Devers: 'In all my 26 years of service I have never worked for a military commander and staff which gave me stronger direction, abler decisions, or firmer support than this Air Force of ours is getting now from General Devers and his Staff.'[57]

Eaker relocated a small forward headquarters staff to Caserta by mid-January to be alongside Alexander and he remained there for a few weeks. The main headquarters moved from near Tunis to Caserta only after the bombing on 23 February.[58] AFHQ was not located in Italy, so it is unlikely that they gave verbal 'emergency' approval. This approval may have been communicated via REDLINE personal message, but no such message has been found, and this

53   TNA AIR 51/81/184 – Redline Message Cannon/Norstad dated 14 January 1944.
54   TNA AIR 51/81/184: Redline Message Cannon/Norstad dated 14 January 1944.
55   TNA AIR 51/81/184: Redline Message Norstad/Cannon dated 15 January 1944.
56   Parton, *Air Force Spoken Here*, p.356.
57   AFHRA Reel A1592, Transcript of Press Conference of Maj Gen I C Eaker dated 10 June 1943.
58   History of Allied Force Headquarters, Part 3, Section 2, December 1943-July 1944, Combined Arms Research Library, US Command and General Staff College, Fort Leavenworth KS, <http://cgsc.cdmhost.com/cdm/singleitem/collection/p4013coll8/id/2452/rec/8> (accessed 22 January 2019)

communication means was internal to the USAAF. Wilson and Devers were both in Algiers during the critical decision-making period; it is possible that both officers gave their assent from there although no written record has been discovered. Eaker suggested that the agreement was verbal and informal many years later, although as already discussed it was certain that Eaker himself was not there and that he was never in the same place as Wilson or Devers at the critical times. He may again be referring to the attack on Cassino town on 15 March. Hartcup claimed that Alexander gained Wilson's concurrence in his account for the British Official Historian, but again we lack documentary evidence.[59] Wilson would probably have wanted to give approval of a controversial act regardless of the planned method.

This would have come afterwards, and Devers would not turn him down. There is no surviving evidence that either were forced to declare a 'tactical emergency' that would authorise the use of heavy bombers. Such an emergency did not exist at Cassino. Eaker, in a piece for *National Security Affairs* magazine, confirmed that the decision to attack the Abbey was taken by Wilson, but his recollection, so long after the event, should not be trusted.[60] He was keen to avoid an official demarche from Wilson or Devers, usually opting for more gentlemanly agreements. Considering the final decision to divert the heavy bombers on 15 February resulted in one of the most controversial acts of the Second World War, it is hardly mentioned in Wilson's memoirs.[61] In his official despatch, he cited the occupation of the Abbey as an important justification. He stated that the Abbey was 'occupied and fortified…and formed the pivot on which the German defensive system was based.'[62]

Evidence that Eaker favoured an informal agreement can be seen in his correspondence with Spaatz after the Abbey was bombed on 19 February 1944:

> Re your mission assignment to Fifteenth for tomorrow, here is our situation: a. Clark and Cannon believe tomorrow will be critical day in beachhead; both hope for full heavy bomber help. Cannon believes some heavies must help. b. Our weather prophets believe we have little chance for visual targets in South Germany. You speak of area targets. We have no H2X as you know. In view of the foregoing we have this problem: Shall General Wilson declare an emergency under CCS Directive and employ heavies. I hope to avoid this. Will you therefore tell me as soon as possible whether your other planned attacks require our help as diversion even with no prospect of visual bombing. In that event we must make a split and send five or six groups on one or two targets for you and put four on beachhead support. In view of our dilemma please give me desires. Request earliest possible reply.[63]

This correspondence highlighted Eaker's wishes to come to an acceptable compromise informally through the command chain, rather than go through the formal process of the emergency

59   Hartcup, p.12.
60   Eaker, Why We Bombed Monte Cassino.
61   Henry Maitland-Wilson, *Field-Marshal Lord Wilson of Libya: Eight Years Overseas 1939-1947* (London: Hutchinson, 1951), p.195.
62   Henry Maitland-Wilson, *Report by The Supreme Allied Commander Mediterranean to the Combined Chiefs of Staff on The Italian Campaign 8th January 1944 to 10th May 1944* (London: HMSO, 1946), pp.30-1.
63   Personal Redline No. 29 Eaker/Spaatz in Parton, The History of the Mediterranean Allied Air Forces, p.24.

declaration. Eaker informed Spaatz when he believed that a conflict could occur between strategic operations and tactical support to ground forces. On 19 February, Spaatz planned to conduct a joint Eighth/Fifteenth Air Force attack from which any deviation would have required his permission – hence Eaker's note. The day before, MAAF had issued a new bombing directive confirming the priority of POINTBLANK.[64] This directive closely mirrored the priorities articulated in FM 100-20. This operation began the often-delayed Operation ARGUMENT, also known as 'Big Week', the USAAF's major effort to seize air superiority in preparation for the OVERLORD. MAAF should have followed the same procedure for the Abbey attack, although there was no possibility of attack north of the Alps on 15 February due to weather in Germany. There was no reason for any senior officer delegated by Eaker in his absence, to consult Spaatz. Spaatz left most things to Eaker's discretion and in the next nine-months of operations, agreement to use the heavies outside their priority tasking was always informal. Wilson or Devers were never required to declare an 'emergency'.

Eaker did not have complete *carte blanche*. In response to the use of heavy bombers against German advances on the Anzio beachhead, Spaatz wrote to Eaker, probably in response to his previous correspondence above, and reminded him of the need to keep more strategic priorities in mind:

> I am greatly concerned at the possibility of continuous emergency in battle situation preventing proper application of our forces to insure reasonable success of POINTBLANK. Weather conditions may improve for the next two or three days, giving us one of few opportunities to strike blow for which we have been waiting for three or more months. I fully realize that in emergency conditions heavy bombers must be used in beachhead support and therefore concur with you that such action is indicated for tomorrow. My personal number 12 releases you from participation in tomorrow's operation. However, I hope critical nature of beachhead will not be continuous problem which will prevent heavy force of Fifteenth Air Force from being utilized against POINTBLANK targets Monday and Tuesday if weather permits.[65]

The next day, following Eaker's decision to divide his force between Anzio and POINTBLANK, Spaatz again reiterated the importance of 'Big Week' operations, with reference to OVERLORD. His overriding priority during this period of the war was to seize control of the air through the strategic use of the air weapon. To do this he required the maximum force of bombers from both his strategic air forces to attack Germany's air production. This was how air forces could play their part in decisive victory. Against this everything else was secondary; the measure of his success was that the *Luftwaffe* was wholly ineffective over the beaches of Normandy and for the remainder of the war. Eaker's discretion to use the heavies for a tactical situation was accepted, but was clearly not without limits:

> …I believe we are in midst of most decisive action of entire war and that appropriate priority must be given to taking advantage of an opportunity that experience proves to be most rare.

64   TNA WO 204/1066, MAAF Bombing Directive dated 18 February 1944.
65   James Parton, The History of the Mediterranean Allied Air Forces, 1945, p.145.

I fully realize that against this must be weighed any critical situation in beachhead area and of course extent of your participation can be decided only in Mediterranean.[66]

Similar discussions over Cassino may not have occurred but the proximity of the two operations, only four-days apart, gives a flavour as to how decisions were made at the time and where the priorities lay.

The escalation from 36-single-engined fighter-bombers to an air armada of heavy and medium bombers remains unclear without the associated operation orders. It may have originated with Alexander's desire to consult Wilson, although Freyberg has credited Clark for the idea in a letter to Howard Kippenberger in 1950.[67] Clark confirmed that he made such a suggestion, but there is little evidence that he acted upon it.[68] Again to Kippenberger, Freyberg said, 'Mark Clark was shifty and wanted it both ways. It was he who decided to use the heavy bombers. I made a definite point at one of the conferences that I did not like the operation. It had elements of a failure and an expensive one.'[69]

The problem with Freyberg's perception is that it was not within the gift of Clark to demand heavy bombers, nor does he make his point in his operational diary. Nowhere in this diary does he mention that he did not like the operation, although he did not request heavy bombers. The final decision remains opaque, but probably lay within the USAAF command chain. The standard operating procedure in place was that the army told the air force what they wanted doing, but not how to do it. Therefore, the method of attack should have been an air decision, albeit with the final say of operational level commanders, but there is no surviving paperwork. There are several USAAF officers who could have made that decision. These were: Generals Spaatz. Eaker, Cannon, Twining and possibly the Chief of Operations, Norstad. Also included in this list is Slessor.

One officer who certainly did not make, or approve of, the decision was the new Commanding General of XII ASC, Brigadier-General Gordon Saville. On the very day of the attack, Saville wrote to his boss, Cannon, with a new plan, the purpose of which is shown below, heavy bombers were kept well away from the front-line:

15 February 1944
MEMORANDUM
TO: Commanding General, Mediterranean Allied Tactical Air Force.

1.   The purpose of this paper is to present a plan of air operations in support of the advance of the Fifth Army with a view to releasing Army forces into the LIRI VALLEY, and thus expediting the join-up with forces in the ANZIO BEACHHEAD...
GORDON P SAVILLE
Brig General, USA
Commanding.[70]

66   James Parton, The History of the Mediterranean Allied Air Forces, p.145.
67   Letter from General Freyberg to Major General Kippenberger, 11 August 1950.
68   Clark, p.254.
69   Wright, Kindle location, 833.
70   AFHRA Iris No 2000472, HQ 12 ASC Memorandum to CG MATAF dated 15 February 1944.

The draft plan tells us firstly, that whilst a contingency, Saville was planning for the failure of the large operation carried out on that day. It is an accurate representation of the current situation and offers a conventional approach to the delivery of battlefield air support. The positions around Cassino, including the Abbey and the surrounding peaks are not planned to be attacked by either heavy or medium bombers. Saville was leaving these positions to ad-hoc targeting by fighter-bombers. In his air estimate of the problem, he actively discounts the use of air support of any kind to the battlefield apart from in a 'defensive emergency'.[71] There is no mention of the heavy bomber attack on Cassino town that ultimately occurred when the weather at last cleared on 15 March 1944, which Saville also strongly opposed. XII ASC was collocated with and worked closely alongside Clark's Fifth Army, and it is completely in keeping with what is known of how Clark wished to use airpower to support his operations. Cannon forwarded Saville's plan, with some targeting additions, to Eaker on 21 February. His memorandum also limits the use of medium and heavy bombers to the isolation of the Cassino battlefield. There is no mention of a re-attack on the Abbey or of an attack on the town.[72]

Permission from Spaatz was unnecessary to use the B-25 and B-26 medium bombers, as these were directly under Cannon's command and could be directly tasked in support of ground forces. The order to attack the Abbey with the medium bombers was issued by Cannon at 9:50pm on 14 February.[73] This timeline was possible because the mediums were more reactive to ground forces' needs than the heavies, although it did appear to be a late request, one that supports a late cancellation of the heavy bomber's original mission

Despite Eaker's willingness to support ground forces with heavy bombers, he was not keen that this support be offered too eagerly. He is strongly criticised by Saville in a 1970 interview. Saville's criticism is of the 15 March attack on Cassino, rather than on the Abbey, but his general comments about bombing religious sanctuaries are equally valid. He said, 'I am in the school of not bombing, unless there is something there that you know is there. I don't believe in bombing from fear. I believe in bombing when you can find something to hit, and then you can hit it.'[74] This statement is not specifically about the Abbey of Montecassino, but it is hard to believe he was not thinking of it. He did, however, specifically mention Castelgandolfo and Monte Cassino in the interview:

> The intelligence people were telling me all the time that these guns were taking advantage of this religious sanctuary. I didn't know how to find out. I didn't believe them. I didn't know what to believe, where they are. I couldn't find them. We didn't know where they were shooting from, and I had airplanes looking for them all over. So I went to see the local Catholic priests and said: 'Look you guys have got contact back there. All I want to know is this, are they taking advantage of a religious sanctuary, or are they not?' And these guys independently came back and said: 'They're not.' And I believed them, just like I knew the Germans were not taking advantage of Monte Cassino, and I knew it the same way, because if you want to know something about a Benedictine Order, where do you go?

71 AFHRA Iris No 1040018, HQ 12 ASC, Air Estimate and Plan for Support of 5th Army in the Present Situation dated March 1944.
72 AFHRA Iris No 2000472, HQ MATAF Memorandum to HQ MAAF dated 21 February 1944.
73 Hartcup, p,15.
74 AFHRA Iris NO 1103217, Interview with Major General Gordon Saville, San Antonio, Texas, dated 9 February 1970, p,45.

You don't go to the New York Times; you go to a Benedictine monk and ask him…they confirmed what I believed that the Germans were not violating the Conventions.[75]

Saville, the brash young fighter pilot disliked Eaker questioning his technical competence, saying 'part of my bias against Eaker is that he doesn't know his business.' Or to use less restrained language, he said 'Eaker was a bull-shitter.'[76] Throughout his career Saville had been a single-engine advocate, although an avid supporter of an independent air force, who often opposed the 'bomber mafia' that dominated the higher echelons of the USAAF. This included Eaker, although he too was a fighter pilot. Saville would not have asked for, or approved of, the use of heavy bombers to attack the Abbey, preferring to use his own fighter-bombers as requested by Freyberg from the beginning.

Saville commented that the command-and-control set-up between the ground and tactical air forces was complex, calling it a 'Rube Goldberg' set-up, far more complicated than necessary.[77] He considered the attack on Cassino town on 15 March 1944 with the heavy bombers to be 'totally unworkable' and considered Freyberg 'incompetent'. He is clear that in his view both Clark and Cannon were against the use of the heavies, saying that Clark considered the operation the most 'suicidal and nutty operation' that would end up killing Allied soldiers. It was Eaker that approved the air plan for 15 March, against the advice of his subordinate air commanders. Why would he do this if he was against using heavy bombers in support of ground forces? Saville rightly thought that the mass use of bombers would create so much dust and smoke that the target would be totally obscured after just a few bombers.

He protested to Cannon, developing a much more normal air plan using fighter-bombers. Saville, the tactical air commander, recalled that Clark supported the more limited plan, but Eaker was insistent in using the heavies, stating in his order, 'You will have saturation bombing; you will employ all of the resources of the theatre.' He considered that the heavy attack would be a failure and would exacerbate the difficulties faced by the ground forces, 'this air bombardment is going to create the greatest tank trap the world has ever seen.' Saville was so irate that he claims Cannon sent him on leave to Algiers, probably for his own good.

A possible clue to Eaker's determination to use the heavies is revealed by Saville. He said that the same evening Eaker went onto the radio to say that 'this was the greatest concentration of air power that had ever been put on anything.' Saville states that this was to the BBC, although this was probably his broadcast on NBC radio already mentioned. The use of the heavies against the town was as much a demonstration as it was to provide support to the ground forces, especially as many of those involved strongly opposed it. Did the air forces wish a similar demonstration a month earlier, one which was not realised and had to be repeated to justify continuing the doctrine of high-level daylight precision bombing? This was the impression of journalist Frank Gervasi who reported, 'Apparently the US Army Air Force was going all out to demonstrate the efficacy of high-level 'pinpoint' saturation bombing

75 AFHRA Iris NO 1103217, Interview with Major General Gordon Saville, San Antonio, Texas, dated 9 February 1970, pp.45-46.
76 AFHRA Iris NO 1103217, Interview with Major General Gordon Saville, San Antonio, Texas, dated 9 February 1970, p.65.
77 AFHRA Iris NO 1103217, Interview with Major General Gordon Saville, San Antonio, Texas, dated 9 February 1970, p.33.

in battlefield conditions, something never before attempted, and the monastery provided a perfect laboratory case.'[78]

The ground forces failed to make the breakthrough and once the newspapers picked up on this failure and related it to Eaker's claims, Arnold received the fallout in Washington. Saville, still on 'leave' in Algiers claimed to have received a personal REDLINE message from Arnold stating, 'We are in trouble. We've advertised this thing, and I and the AF are being attacked in the newspapers.' This message shows that some bombing operations were initiated for public relations purposes. Arnold asked if Saville could rescue the situation. He returned to Italy, claiming that Eaker had been 'whipped down' by Arnold. There is no supporting evidence for this; Saville and Eaker disliked each other, and Saville's account may be self-promotion as the returning hero, coming to the rescue after his boss made a mess of things. He also claims that he got Clark to send another REDLINE to Arnold, exonerating him from any blame for the failed Cassino air plan. This message has not surfaced in the USAAF REDLINE archive.[79]

Eaker expressed his opinion in a report to Arnold in April 1944 that 'Heavy and medium bombers should very rarely be used on the battlefield. Exceptions include a critical situation in defence, as at Salerno, or to precede a large-scale amphibious landing against beach defences.'[80] To Wilson he commented, 'Heavy bombers should, as a matter of principle, never be employed in close support operations where there is an adequate Tactical Air Force present for the task.'[81] If Saville is to be believed this may not have been his opinion before the attacks. In the lessons learned report from the Cassino operations he made the following observations and recommendations:

1. Unless otherwise indicated, the following points are extracted from the report of the air commander.
2. In the CASSINO operation both the Tactical and Strategic Air Forces were employed. The Tactical Air Force gave better performance and results, largely because close support is a normal operation for this type of air force. Conversely, close support missions are rare operations for the Strategic Air Force, which had little training and experience in such operations.
3. In general, heavy bombers should not be used in close support operations when there is present an adequate Tactical Air Force.
4. When operations require the use of the heavy bombers in close support of ground operations, the following recommendations are advanced by the air commander:
    a) When practicable. Bomb leaders and leading navigators should make a previous flight over the target area.
    b) Bombing altitudes should be specified. The heavy bombers showed a tendency to bomb from too high an altitude.
    c) Angles of approach should be specified, especially when ground troops are close to the target area.

78   Gervasi, p.560.
79   AFHRA Iris NO 1103217, Interview with Major General Gordon Saville, San Antonio, Texas, dated 9 February 1970, pp.33-38.
80   AFHRA Reel A6024, General Eaker to General Arnold – The Employment of Bombers and Fighter-Bombers in Co-operation with the Army. April1944, Para 11c, Frame 0654.
81   AFHRA Reel A6030, MAAF C-in-C Correspondence, Eaker to Wilson dated 12 April 1944.

d)   Intervals between bomber groups, especially when the wind is sufficiently strong to clear the smoke from the targets, should be decreased. The whole bombing operations should be concentrated in the briefest possible time.

e)   A member of the Strategic Air Force Commander's staff should be present in position to observe the bombing action of his units and should have radio communications with his units in the air.[82]

This report was written following the Cassino town attack on 15 March. All the points made by Eaker are relevant to the Abbey. Even Brooke in London commented after the operations in Cassino that, 'I am not a believer in the use of heavy bombers on forward defences, it is a great pity that Freyberg did not make a freer use of infantry.'[83] These lessons were ignored, and the problems came to the fore again when US bombers supported the American break-out in Normandy in July 1944. They were not even then persuaded that this was not an effective operation of war. Ground commanders continued to be addicted to the potential of technology over human beings that the heavy bomber promised but rarely delivered.

Alexander, however, also considered heavy bombers an inappropriate weapon for battlefield support. Two weeks after Eaker's report, he wrote, 'While bombardment of tactical land objectives by formations of heavy bombers undoubtedly causes many casualties and has a considerable effect on enemy morale, it is not sufficiently accurate for general use in the tactical area of the land battle.'[84] Freyberg put it a little more bluntly: 'Thank you for the air effort. Please don't send anymore Forts.'[85] This was not the view of all those involved. Dimoline reported to Freyberg that the medium bombers in the afternoon carried out 'the finest bombing he had ever seen.'[86] In their monthly war diary, the 4th Indian Division judged that, 'If this form of bombardment in support of ground troops is to be developed fully, and its potentialities are enormous, it is essential that the bomber force concerned and the ground troops should be under one commander and that the plan should be fully co-ordinated.'[87] This was the old British Army view of airpower in that the air force is considered as a supporting arm to ground manoeuvre. The cynic may suggest that the 'one commander' they had in mind would be wearing khaki rather than blue!

Alexander and Eaker's views were accepted by AFHQ and included in its Operations Instruction on the employment of bombers on 6 May 44:

Except to retrieve a critical situation in defence, when it is vital to use every available means to stop enemy movement on the battlefield, heavy and medium bombers should very rarely be used on the battlefield itself.

In the attack, our aim being to move ourselves, the use of heavy or medium bombers on the battlefield, so far from being a help to the land forces, is definitely liable to be a hindrance. By demolishing buildings, blocking roads with debris and making deep craters,

82   TNA WO 204/4354: Lessons Applicable To The Air Operations.
83   Fraser, p.375.
84   AFHRA Reel A6024 Cassino Operations letter to AFHQ, HQ AAI 48/1/G(Ops) dated 4 May 1944. Frame 0662.
85   Freyberg, Diary Entry, 15 February 1944.
86   Freyberg, Diary Entry, 15 February 1944.
87   TNA CAB 106/699, p.93.

air bombardment tends to create obstacles to movement by our infantry and tanks – obstacles which are still suitable for defence by determined infantry and anti-tank gunners.[88]

On 18 April 1944 Slessor informed Eaker from Algiers that his lessons had been taken as recommendations by Wilson's Joint Planning Staff to inform Operation OVERLORD planning. This was that 'heavy bombers should only be employed in battle area in emergency.'[89] Slessor, however, was sceptical and lacked confidence that this agreement would survive. In his opinion, 'I suspect that on resumption of battle these sort [sic] of principles will be thrown overboard and we shall be subjected to the usual pressure to use every sort of aeroplane on gun positions, strong points, troop concentrations etc on the field of battle itself.'[90]

Following the attack on the Abbey, on 4 March 1944, Norstad formalised the process and issued MAAF Operations Instruction No 11 – *Employment of Fifteenth Air Force in Assistance of Land Battle in Italy*.[91] This instruction was written to provide guidance on procedures to be used in the light of the use of heavy bombers at Anzio and Cassino. The instruction was only sent to air addressees and not to the ground formations. The instruction implicitly recognised that MASAF did not have the situational awareness of the land battle and MATAF was officially tasked with passing details of the ground situation and the bomb safety line. The process for using heavy bombers tactically began with Cannon. He was responsible for tasking them via Norstad, who would approve the request. Orders would then be passed to MASAF, also informing Spaatz. MASAF would then issue orders to its bombardment wings to plan and carry out the task, informing MATAF of the plan. Cannon would then inform ground forces of the strategic bombers' intentions. All of this would leave a reasonably large paper trail, yet that none of this trail for the bombing of the Abbey has survived.

Late in 1944, Arnold produced a glossy report for the Secretary of War. Each Air Force contributed its activity through 1943 and 1944. In the Twelfth and Fifteenth Air Force contribution, which was detailed on air operations, there is no mention of air support in the Cassino battle or of the attack on the Abbey. In a document produced near the end of the war by HQ MAAF on the achievements of airpower in the Mediterranean, with a foreword by Eaker, he did not count the attack on the Abbey as one of its 'more significant achievements.'[92] This pseudo-advert mentioned neither the attack on the Abbey nor any heavy bomber support to ground forces. The History of MAAF written by Eaker's subordinate, biographer and close friend, James Parton, devoted an entire chapter to the bombing of Cassino town on 15 March 1944. It devoted one line within that chapter to the attack on the Abbey. Were they so ashamed of what they had done that they had chosen to expunge it from the written record?

After the dust had settled at Cassino, Arnold visited in June 1944. When he met with Slessor, the Briton was convinced that his understanding of the application of airpower in Italy was not as thorough as it should have been. Slessor must have been present, or at least aware, of the times when Arnold had criticised Eaker's performance, and he perhaps wanted to put the record straight. He wrote a long review of the effects of airpower in support of the land operation in

88 AFHQ Operation Memorandum No 54 dated 6 May 1944 – The Employment of Bombers and Fighter-Bombers in Co-Operation with the Army in AFRHA REEL A6111
89 TNA AIR 23/884: JCS 625 dated 18 April 1944 Personal for Eaker from Slessor.
90 TNA AIR 23/884: JCS 625 dated 18 April 1944 Personal for Eaker from Slessor.
91 TNA AIR 51/81: MAAF Operations Instruction No. 11 dated 4 March 1944.
92 Air Power in the Mediterranean- November 1942 to February 1945, HQ MAAF, 27 February 1945.

Italy. It is not clear from his papers whether Slessor penned his report on his own initiative, or whether he was asked to do so by Eaker. What is clear is that Slessor, a very busy man, took considerable time to explain the issues faced by this massive force. Slessor had known Arnold for some time having accompanied him for his first visit to CAS in April 1941.[93] He started by addressing some of the things that air power could not achieve, perhaps in counterpoint to some of Arnold's earlier complaints and certainly a lesson learned from the bombing of the Abbey at Cassino:

> It cannot by itself defeat a highly organised and disciplined Army, even when that Army is virtually without air support of its own. The German will fight defensively without support or cover and does not become demoralised by constant air attack against his communications or back areas. The heaviest and most concentrated air bombardment of organised defensive positions cannot be relied upon to obliterate resistance and enable our land forces to advance without loss.[94]

He then explained over five pages the devastating effects that airpower had inflicted upon Kesselring's armies. Slessor carefully explained the nature of teamwork with ground forces to achieve the desired result. He used the letter as the basis for his 1948 Royal United Services Institute article on *The Effect of Air Power in a Land Offensive*. He was not alone regarding the use of air power and heavy bombers. His boss, Portal, in a letter to Tedder in late 1944 passed the following assessment, based upon the use of heavy bombers both in Italy and in support of ground forces in north-western Europe:

> I believe that the constant application of heavy bomber power to the land battle, when it is not essential and its only purpose is to save casualties, must eventually lead to the demoralisation of the army. If one division captures an objective with strong heavy bomber support and loses only a few men, other divisions will naturally be reluctant to attack without similar support, and we shall sooner or later reach a stage where almost the whole of the heavy bomber effort has to be frittered away in small packets if the army is to attack at all.[95]

Tedder, who was to become CAS after Portal responded, 'The Army having been drugged with bombs; it is going to be a difficult process to cure the drug addicts.'[96]

The words of Great Britain's most effective CAS and its best fighting airman echo through the decades to their modern counterparts as they struggle to define a meaningful role. The British Army of today is no less addicted to the air support drug than its ancestors. If an air force the size of the RAF today succumbs to assuaging such withdrawal symptoms, it will be rapidly consumed just as Portal predicted.

---

93   Daso, p.65-6.
94   TNA AIR 75/69: Papers of Sir John Slessor, The Italian Campaign, Report to General Arnold – The Effect Of Air Power In A Land Offensive dated 18 June 1944.
95   Tedder, p.605.
96   Tedder, p.606.

20

Bombs and Bombing

The air gives uncurbed bestial instincts a wider field of expression, leaving only humanity and common sense to dictate limitations. Law cannot limit what physics makes possible.

Major General Frederick L. Anderson
Commanding General, VIII Bomber Command, January 1944[1]

Even before the First World War had finished it was clear that for offensive air power to be effective, bombs dropped must be able to hit and destroy targets. The best aircraft in the world, crewed by the most courageous and well-trained airmen, counted for little if the weapons are ineffective.[2] The Bombing Problem was essentially a battle between gravity, forward momentum and air resistance or drag. Mathematically straight-forward, the task of releasing a bomb from the single point in the air from where it would strike the ground in the correct place was a complicated practical task. Bombs are not released directly above their targets, but from a considerable distance away. A bombardier's principal task is to turn his direct line-of-sight view of a target into the correct bomb trajectory, taking into account a host of often unknown variables.

Getting a bomb to target was only part of the problem. What it did when it got there was also vital to success. Aerial bombs generally produce several damage mechanisms; blast, heat, fragmentation and penetration/perforation being the major effects. Perforation involves going through the target's construction material and detonating internally. Different targets require differing ratios of these mechanisms to be effective, and specific weapons are designed to accentuate effects most likely to be successful.

Most bombs dropped in the Second World War by the USAAF, and those used against the Abbey, were of the General Purpose (GP) type. These weapons were a compromise, a balance between blast and fragmentation and with limited penetration.

Most GP or fragmentation bombs had scoring inside the casing that allowed the bomb case to fragment uniformly upon detonation. The detonation pushed small pieces of sharp, hot metal at great speed in a calculated fragmentation pattern. This pattern changed depending on the angle of impact and the velocity of the weapon at detonation. Fragmentation is the principal

---

1   From Humanitarian Aspects of Air Power, Papers of Frederick L Anderson in Crane, p.164.
2   John MacBean & Arthur Hogben, *Bombs Gone: The Development and Use of British Air-dropped Weapons from 1912 to the Present Day* (Wellingborough: Patrick Stephens Ltd, 1990), p.12.

SIGHT ∠   WR∠   DROP ∠

TRAIL
subtracted from
WR by bombsight

ACTUAL RANGE
solved by bombsight and
subtended by dropping angle

WHOLE RANGE
solved by bombsight from GS x ATF

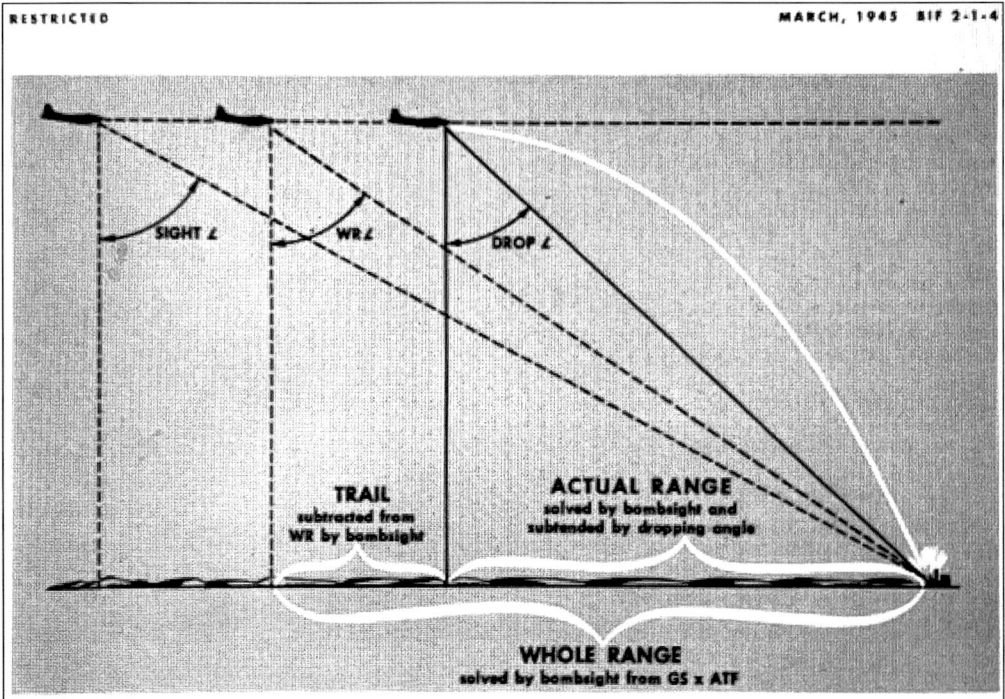

The Bombing Problem. The Norden bombsight was designed to solve the complex task of placing a bomber in the exact spot in the sky from where, given the aircraft's speed, altitude and environmental conditions, a bomb would strike accurately a target on the ground. (Bombardier Information File)

Although the USAAF had bombs of different sizes, these were mostly General Purpose. Unlike the RAF they had developed few specialist weapons for different target types. (NARA RG342-FH-000903)

B-26 Marauder from the 42nd Bombardment Wing of the Mediterranean Allied Tactical Air Forces
releasing 4 x 1000lb General Purpose bombs, the same as delivered against the Abbey.
(NARA RG342-FH-001110)

mechanism for the destruction of personnel and soft-skinned vehicles such as trucks in the open as opposed to buildings with thick walls, as the metal fragments bounced off leaving little damage. A study by the USAAF found that these fragments, from their 500lb GP bombs, had an initial high velocity at detonation of around 7,390-feet/second, but that this rapidly degraded to about 300-feet/second at 1,000-feet from the detonation. The effect of the fragments was small, in that at 20-feet they struggled to perforate ½-inch steel and that at 200-feet from the detonation there was virtually no effect, and any effect would not be felt by a fragment weighing less than three-ounces. The study also looked at how many fragments would strike a target with different deliveries. If an aircraft dropped a 500lb GP bomb from 20,000ft, it would impact the ground at up to a 75⁰ angle at an impact velocity of around 900-feet/second. An object 40-feet from the detonation would receive one fragment hit per square foot. This would diminish rapidly, with at 110-feet distance the object could expect to have one fragment per 10-square feet.[3] With a direct hit, these bombs could expect to perforate no more than 1½-feet of concrete.

The 1,000lb GP bombs delivered by the medium bombers were better, but not much, achieving around 2-feet perforation.[4] These bombs were moderately effective against most targets, but were not effective against specialised targets, as they required a direct hit to cause significant damage, something that was difficult to achieve. Considering that Freyberg's initial request was to gain

3   Terminal Ballistic Data Volume 1 – Bombing, Office of the Chief of Ordnance, Washington DC, August 1944, p.72.
4   Terminal Ballistic Data – Vol 1, p.62.

entry to the Abbey by using airpower to breach the walls, these weapons were inadequate for the task, as the walls of Montecassino were at least 15-feet thick at the bottom, and still beyond the GP bomb capability at the top. To achieve Freyberg's needs, the bombers would have to perform what is known as 'consecutive miracles', putting numerous bombs down the same hole.

The opinion of Tuker was that only 'Blockbuster' bombs would be sufficient against the Abbey. What was this wonder weapon? 'Blockbuster' bombs were also known as the 4,000lb canisters, Cookies or High Capacity (HC) bombs. Containing 3,000lbs of explosive, they first entered RAF service in the Spring of 1941.[5] The canisters were nearly 10-feet long and 2-feet in diameter and were used by the RAF to create blast waves that would remove roofs allowing access to buildings for incendiaries. The problem for the Americans was that due to their size, the RAF's 'Blockbusters' could not be carried by American bombers, and the only aircraft in the theatre that could carry them was the RAF Wellingtons. These were employed largely in medium bomber support and although part of the strategic air forces, widely used in support of ground forces. Cookies were available to the Wellingtons of No.205 Group but could only be carried on modified aircraft. Only two aircraft per squadron were modified, a total of 12-aircraft.[6] In a message sent by Norstad on 25 January, the Wellingtons were to be tasked against tactical targets until further notice.[7] The USAAF, in their handbook, claimed that two of their 2,000lb General Purpose (GP) weapons, that could be carried by the B-17, were a better solution than the 4,000lb Blockbuster, but the claim has an odour of jealousy about it.[8] There is no doubt that 'Blockbusters' were used in Italy. In April 2001, 77,000 inhabitants of Vicenza were evacuated whilst one was defused in the town's central cemetery. They were also used on 15 February, just not in Cassino, with several weapons dropped between Rome and the Anzio beachhead that night. There was also a larger 8,000lb HC bomb, but this was only carried by RAF Halifax and Lancaster aircraft, and it too had been used in Italy. These massive bombs had first been dropped on Turin in late 1942, by the Lancasters commanded by the future dambuster, Guy Gibson.[9] Only Gibson's 617 Squadron could carry the ultimate Blockbuster, the 12,000lb weapon in specially modified Lancasters. First used in September 1943, these were available for use against the Abbey.

That this was feasible can be judged by a similar operation that had been conducted by the squadron three months previously. On 11 November 1943, 617 Squadron aircraft attacked the Antheor viaduct near Cannes in Southern France with these bombs. The aircraft landed at Blida Airfield in North Africa.[10] Did Tuker know these types of bombs existed and, as a keen student of warfare, did he know that a method to deliver them had been recently proven? His division was in nearby Tunisia when the Lancasters landed at Blida in Algeria and it is possible that Tuker, always interested in airpower, learnt of it. This is, of course, speculative theory as no evidence has been found that he did or that it was his intention to use these bombs. But, if it became necessary, a repetition of the viaduct attack seems a perfect solution to the problem of the Abbey. Why was it not considered?

5   MacBean and Hogben, p.74.
6   Hilary St. G. Saunders, *Royal Air Force 1939–45, Volume III: The Fight Is Won* (London: Her Majesty's Stationery Office, 1954), p.223.
7   TNA AIR 51/81/184 – Message from Norstad to MASAF and MATAF dated 25th January 1944.
8   AFHRA Reel A1592, The Air Force in a Task Force, Chapter V – Bomber Command dated March 1943.
9   MacBean & Hogben, p.79.
10   Webster and Frankland, *Volume II, Endeavour*, Kindle Location, 3835.

The ultimate 'Blockbuster.' This 12,000lb weapon could only be carried by RAF Lancasters of 617 Squadron. Its thin casing and high charge to weight ratio of explosive ensured a large blast effect. This effect is what is required to knock down buildings. (NARA RG342-FH-000919)

In his second memorandum, Tuker specifically referred to 'Blockbuster' bombs being required to destroy the Abbey due to its robust construction. He called the 1,000lb bomb 'useless' for this task. Presumably, he had no faith in the 500lb that was eventually dropped by the heavy bombers. Other types of bombs were used for heavily reinforced targets such as submarine pens. These required a bomb such as the 12,000lb TALLBOY which had a very thick bomb casing so that it survived the immense forces placed upon it when striking reinforced concrete at great velocity. It was classified as a Medium Capacity (MC) weapon with a 50 per cent charge-to-weight ratio (CWR). This metal to explosive ratio was lower than that for GP, resulting in greater penetration and large fragmentation, but relatively little blast effect, which manifested itself as ground shock. The strength of the MC weapon allowed it to penetrate concrete and a delayed fuse resulted in the weapon perforating the walls and detonating inside the structure. In RAF service these MC bombs were favoured over the GP bombs, but this was not the case in the USAAF. The RAF and USAAF also possessed Armour Piercing or Semi-Armour Piercing (AP/SAP) bombs with even more metal to explosive CWR. Today these weapons are often called 'bunker-busters'. The HC bomb, 'Blockbuster', had the opposite effect and was particularly useful in destroying buildings, as the principal mechanism required to knock down unhardened masonry walls and roofs is blast. Tuker's staff considered these blast bombs to be the most effective for the Abbey. The weapons, although large, had a thin bomb casing of 8mm steel, and a high explosive to iron ratio, around 75 per cent, that produced high blast effects but limited fragmentation. Tuker was right, these weapons were the most appropriate for the Abbey, and therefore the building should have been attacked by the RAF, not the USAAF. There is

NOMENCLATURE AND OPERATION

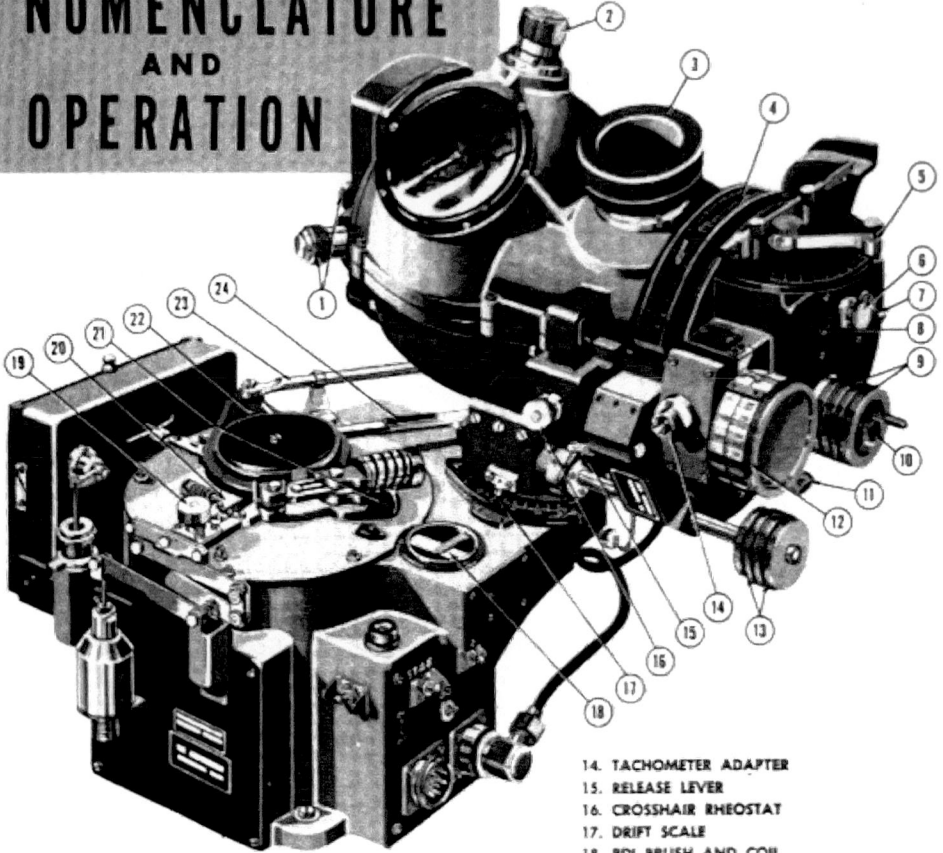

1. LEVELING KNOBS
2. CAGING KNOB
3. EYEPIECE
4. INDEX WINDOW
5. TRAIL ARM AND TRAIL PLATE
6. EXTENDED VISION KNOB
7. RATE MOTOR SWITCH
8. DISC SPEED GEAR SHIFT
9. RATE AND DISPLACEMENT KNOBS
10. MIRROR DRIVE CLUTCH
11. SEARCH KNOB
12. DISC SPEED DRUM
13. TURN AND DRIFT KNOBS

14. TACHOMETER ADAPTER
15. RELEASE LEVER
16. CROSSHAIR RHEOSTAT
17. DRIFT SCALE
18. PDI BRUSH AND COIL
19. AUTOPILOT CLUTCH ENGAGING KNOB
20. AUTOPILOT CLUTCH
21. BOMBSIGHT CLUTCH ENGAGING LEVER
22. BOMBSIGHT CLUTCH
23. BOMBSIGHT CONNECTING ROD
24. AUTOPILOT CONNECTING ROD

The bombsight has 2 main parts, **sighthead** and **stabilizer**. The sighthead pivots on the stabilizer and is locked to it by the dovetail locking pin. The sighthead is connected to the directional gyro in the stabilizer through the **bombsight connecting rod** and the **bombsight clutch**.

RESTRICTED

The Norden M-Type bombsight. The promise of 'pickle barrel' accuracy was pivotal to America's high-level daylight precision bombing doctrine. Unfortunately, the accuracy of the testbed did not always transfer to operational use. (Bombardier Information File)

nothing to suggest that this was ever an option; the US air generals preferred to use their own bombers, even though the weapons they carried were highly sub-optimal.

The Americans were determined to do it themselves. The journey undertaken by the US Army to deliver weapons accurately from high altitude was long and painful. The US Navy's interest in precision bombing stemmed from a requirement to attack manoeuvring warships. The Army, concentrating on CAS, made only minor efforts to secure accurate bombsights for its bombers. The US Navy had been working with a Dutch citizen named Carl L. Norden in New York since 1918.[11] Dodging Congressional rules of fair competition, the US Navy worked exclusively with Norden Inc to produce bombsights and in 1931 Norden delivered two proto-types of the Mark XV.[12]

The Mark XV, or the M-Type as the USAAF would call it, was revolutionary, offering the first automatic bomb release system that eliminated human error from the delivery. It didn't take long, despite Navy secrecy, for the Air Corps to make enquiries. The relationship between the US Army and Navy was famously poor and the tale of the Norden bombsight is no exception, but one made more difficult because of the presence of Norden, nicknamed 'Old Man Dynamite' by his US Navy interlocutors. The relationship remained difficult throughout, and despite all requests Norden refused to supply its bombsights to the Army without going through the US Navy Bureau of Ordnance, even though the Navy had decided that dive-bombing was superior to level-bombing and had less use for the Norden. Norden was a stickler for precision and each bombsight was hand-made. Many were rejected by quality control. It seemed an impossible expectation that these instruments could be mass-produced to service the thousands of bombers that would be needed to achieve AWPD-1 and its successors. As Army aircraft production increased dramatically to meet the war requirement, the bombsight production could not keep up, largely due to the slowness of producing high-quality bearings. There was only one month between the US entry into the war and May 1943 when there wasn't a shortfall against the Army's bombsight requirement.[13] By 1944, bombers were being produced faster than bomb-sights. In order to meet demand, the bombsight was then produced at several sites, but this came at a cost of quality. By late 1944, 75-80 per cent of bombsights did not meet the specification.[14]

Although they claimed that they could conduct effective 'precision bombing', the USAAF delivered poor results, especially for the heavy bombers. The inaccuracy of bombers was well known even prior to the US' entry into the war. In an ACTS lecture, given in 1939 by Captain Laurence Kuter, soon to be one of Arnold's advisory council members and a driving force behind FM 100-20, he stated:

> In the preceding three periods and in our two Practical Bombing Probabilities Problems, we have not only found the potential power of Bombardment Aviation tremendously restricted by bombing accuracy (better called bombing inaccuracy in this case), but we have also uncovered some valuable suggestions as to means of remedying this very severe limitation.[15]

11 McFarland, p.58.
12 McFarland, p.70.
13 McFarland, p.136.
14 McFarland, p.145.
15 Phil Haun, *Lectures of the Air Corps Tactical School and American Strategic Bombing in World War II* (Lexington KY: The University Press of Kentucky, 2019), p.118.

Kuter's student problems identified that a small target, that in theory could be destroyed by a single aircraft, would, due to bombing inaccuracy, require more bombers than the service possessed in 1939 to guarantee success. This was the result for bombers without a Norden bombsight, and Kuter had great hopes for it; hopes that often proved illusory in Europe. This was not an unknown problem. In 1918, the RAF's Sir John Salmond had identified that the damage from daylight bombing would remain minor if bombs were dropped from high altitudes.[16] Even the USAAF's AWPD-1 planners knew that a single bomber had only a one per cent chance of hitting a 100-feet by 100-feet target from an altitude of 20,000 feet.[17] There is an important difference between 'precision' and 'accuracy'. Accuracy is the measurement of delivery error from the target, whereas precision is the repeatability of the delivery.

Apart from the pilot, the key member of the bomber crew was the bombardier. USAAF bombardiers were trained to deliver their payload to a Circular Error Probable (CEP) of 230-feet. The CEP is the general term for precision and is a statistical measurement that measures the average distance away as a radius from the aiming point that 50 per cent of bombs will impact. In 1944, CEP was defined as:

> Circular probable error (CEP) is the radius of a circle circumscribed about the point of aim within which circular area 50% of all bombs individually sighted and released under similar conditions will fall – provided the number of trials is large.[18]

For example, if an aircraft dropped 100-weapons and the 50th farthest weapon's distance from the point of aim was 100-feet, then that weapon's CEP would be 100-feet. Between 100-feet and 200-feet another 43-weapons would fall. The accuracy of a weapon is determined by the probability that it will hit the target P^{Hit}. The distance from the aimpoint is the radial error, and a direct hit continues to have an element of luck. Knowing the CEP and the P^{Hit} and the target type allows planners to determine force levels required by calculating the Single Shot Probability of Damage (SSPD). This is the probability that a single bomb type will cause the percentage desired level of damage against a specific category of target. If the requirement is to inflict 50 per cent demolition of a building and one bomb has an SSPD of 0.1per cent, then 500-bombs are required to achieve 50 per cent destruction or 50-B-17s loaded with the same bomb load as they carried to strike the Abbey. Planners, however, also needed to take into account all the reasons why a bomber may not drop its bombs, including the enemy, maintenance issues, the weather, dud weapons and crews getting lost. The number of aircraft flown could easily exceed the number required by 50 per cent. In 1944, the USAAF used only 'dumb bombs', unguided once they left the aircraft, relying on a ballistic trajectory. For instance, the atomic weapon dropped on Hiroshima was aimed by one of the best bombardiers in the USAAF, Major Thomas Ferebee, in good weather conditions and with no opposition. 'Little Boy' missed its aimpoint by around 800-feet. Two days later over Nagasaki, Fat Man missed by 1,500-feet. Both bombs were aimed with the Norden bombsight and the

16   MacBean & Hogben, p.31.
17   Gaston, p.56.
18   AFHRA Reel A1592, AFDIS-ID/3B Selection of Circular Probable Error (CEP) Applicable to Combat Bombing at 25000ft Altitude by Heavy Bombardment Units of the VIII Bomber Command.

miss distances hardly mattered.[19] In the case of the Abbey, a much smaller target area with much smaller bombs, these distances were critical.

According to figures obtained from ACTS records, by 1938 bombers were achieving average radial errors of around 235-feet and a CEP of 438-feet from 15,000-feet in ideal conditions and using the best bombardment units.[20] This was accurate enough to hit the Abbey with a large number of bombs, but this performance was to prove illusory under war conditions where the errors would be much greater. This had been recognised by ACTS instructors by the late 1930s.[21] The crews from the 2nd Bombardment Group should not have been surprised by this either. One of the premier bombardment groups within the USAAF, they had been one of the first deployed across the Atlantic and had also been the first group equipped with the Norden in its B-17s. Another former ACTS instructor, Lieutenant Colonel Robert Olds, commanded the group from 1935 to 1940. He tested his aircraft and their crews in more demanding conditions, where clouds and overcast conditions were present. Instead of 235-feet, the errors were vastly greater, both in range and deflection. He realised, as did Kuter, that in wartime European conditions hitting a target would take great fleets of bombers.[22] In Operation Training Units in 1942, in almost perfect conditions, bomber crews were achieving no better than a CEP of 563-feet from an altitude of 25,000-feet. From this, a combat and practice factor of 1.8 was applied, bringing the CEP for combat crews to just over 1,000-feet. This was believed in early 1943 to be a 'conservative estimate'. Kuter also had access to reports from the Japanese bombing in China and from the Spanish civil war. The Japanese results were almost three times the CEP for their bombing than the US bombers in bombing trials. Instead of putting this down to operational conditions, Kuter made the ethnocentric mistake of assuming this was down to Japanese incompetence. His conclusion was that, 'We have proof that the bombardiers in the Army Air Corps can hit small targets. We believe that United States Army Air Corps bombardment units can be counted upon to hit and destroy small vital hostile objectives, whatever they may be.'[23] It is amazing how one's mind can be changed merely through elevation in rank! He was right, they could hit small targets, but the effort expended to do so was very large.

The conditions in Italy were not those of the training syllabus. The USAAF struggled with accuracy throughout its time in Europe, largely due to challenging meteorological conditions, where cloud and poor visibility hampered bomb-aiming; so different from the training environment. Bombing inaccuracy reportedly caused terror amongst the Italian civilian population. SOE operative Major Barton, behind enemy lines in Italy, said the bombing was 'wanton jettisoning' and that the population was 'terribly frightened of the Allied air force.'[24] The Norden bombsight, in perfect weather conditions with no flak could achieve 'pickle barrel' accuracy, but as spotter pilot Captain Rudd pointed out 'there were no pickle barrels in the Liri Valley that day.'[25]

The bombardier took control between the aircraft's Initial Point (IP), when the pilot placed the aircraft at the final bombing speed, heading and altitude, and the calculated bomb release point. This IP was decided in the planning and is dependent on the wind conditions, usually

19   McFarland, p.2-3.
20   McFarland, p.95. Haun, p.122.
21   Haun, p.124.
22   McFarland, p.96.
23   Haun, p.135.
24   Lamb, Kindle location 5280.
25   Hughes Rudd, *When I Landed the War Was Over*, passim.

around 15-20-miles from the target. Whether the formation remains on an even heading and speed up until the final bomb run depended on the anticipated defences around the target and on the route to it. As these were minimal at Cassino, a long final bomb run was carried out.

The first production Norden M-1 bombsight was delivered to the Air Corps in 1933. The Norden allowed the bombardier, through the aircraft's Automatic Flight Control Equipment (AFCE), to control the aircraft in its final bomb run, considering the drift of the aircraft and the rate of the aircraft's movement towards the target. The cross-hairs remained motionless on the target and the bombs dropped automatically at the calculated release point.[26] The bombsight was a very complex piece of equipment and misuse of it under combat conditions could result in large bombing errors. This was in sharp contrast to the claims made by the Norden company, whose president, Theodore Barth, claimed that 'we do not regard a 15-foot square…as being a very difficult target to hit from an altitude of 30,000-feet.'[27] In European conditions, hitting a target of that size would not only be extremely unusual, but it would also be pure luck. In 1946, Democrat Senator Elbert D Thomas wrote that precision bombing was 'one of the outstanding hoaxes of military history.'[28]

The Norden bombsight was a difficult piece of equipment for the bombardiers to master and only the most experienced bombardiers in the lead aircraft used it well. Its complex gears, knobs and discs could compensate for aircraft drift by working out the wind at the aircraft's altitude. This was vital in the calculation of ground speed; the speed calculated when true air speed and wind speed are combined. One of the first tasks of the bombardier was to calibrate the bombsight in flight by stabilising the gyroscope to the true vertical. This was called 'chasing the bubble' or, 'bubble, bubble toil and trouble' by Fifteenth Air Force.[29] To align the gyros the bombardier had to get two bubbles, lateral and fore and aft, directly over a 'lubber line'. This was a difficult task, in which small bubble alignment errors could result in bombing errors, in deflection and range respectively. An automated system for this task had earlier been abandoned.

Wind was a large problem in accurate bomb dropping as a cross wind could cause errors in deflection and errors in wind speed could cause errors in range. The speed and direction of the wind would determine the speed of the aircraft across the ground and therefore the point where the bombs should be released. If there was a tail wind the bombs were released further from the target than for a head wind. Because the wind was not constant at all altitudes, bombardiers used a mean constant wind, known as the ballistic wind, in their calculations. Whilst this made calculations simpler, it also introduced variance, and hence small errors, from reality.[30] The tables used by bombardiers mostly had measured data based upon releases from lower altitudes.[31] The atmospheric conditions produced something called trail or the distance between where the bomb lands and where the aircraft has reached in the air at the same time. Trail was the difference between the natural trajectory of the weapon in a vacuum with the actual trajectory it was forced to take by air resistance. Trail was concerned with the effects of gravity, air resistance and the true air speed of the aircraft at release. The higher and faster an aircraft flies the greater the trail of the dropped weapon and the greater the inaccuracy. The final determinant of the amount

26 McFarland, p.74.
27 John T. Correll, 'Daylight Precision Bombing', *Air Force Magazine*, October, (2008), pp.60-64.
28 Jablonski, p.293.
29 McFarland, p.128.
30 Terminal Ballistic Data – Vol 1, p.17.
31 Halsey Ross, p.132.

of trail is the bomb itself. Some bombs have a high ballistic coefficient which means they offer less air resistance through a more aerodynamic shape. Lower resistance results in a shorter time of flight and therefore less trail.

A cross wind adds the problem of drift. The aircraft would have to offset its desired heading to account for the wind, meaning that it flew slightly sideways along its track to maintain a heading. This generated another source of potential error called cross-trail, or the distance a bomb travels downwind from its release point. The greater the crosswind component, the greater the heading differential required to keep the aircraft on the desired track when drift is accounted for. The bombsight calculated cross-trail automatically using the inputted wind.[32]

The Norden could only account for conditions at release. It could not account for factors such as air density or wind speed following weapon release. As with ballistic wind, bombardiers also simplified air density, using a figure called ballistic density difference. Tabular evidence calculates that every 10 per cent error from the real air density would result in a 50-feet error on the ground.[33] With the Abbey sitting on a 1,700ft hill, the air density would be lower than in the valley, where measurements would have been taken. The bombsight also could not consider inherent errors such as ballistic dispersion error; the slight but important differences in each bomb's manufacture tolerances, such as centre of gravity, weight and slight surface deviations. Very few 500lb bombs weighed exactly 500lbs. A 500lb AN-M43 weapon with an Amatol explosive fill weighed on average 508lb; with a TNT fill this was 514lb. The 1,000lb AN M65A1 weapon dropped by the medium bombers weighed between 997 and 1,039lb depending on the explosive fill.[34] These differences resulted in a slightly different ballistic trajectory. The bomb-bay and the bombsight were not in the same place, being 30-40-feet apart, inducing another small error. There was also a minor time lag between the bombsight releasing the bombs and the bombs leaving the aircraft. This was known as rack lag and could be a half a second or about 100-feet of error at impact.

In the Eighth Air Force they adopted the policy of drop on the leader, but Fifteenth Air Force may have started with individual aiming. A bombardier, of the 454th Bombardment Group said that the 'drop on lead' policy was in operation in Italy by August 1944.[35] This was the case in the B-17s of Fifteenth Air Force as recounted by John Muirhead in his memoir.[36] The lead aircraft of each box formation would identify the target and use the bombsight to determine weapon release. When the lead dropped, the others followed, in what was ingenuously referred to as formation precision bombing.[37] This resulted in small inaccuracies because only the lead aircraft placed a bombsight on the target, yet each aircraft in the formation was in a different location in the air. Practically, it was possible for each half-bombardment group formation to have a lead bombardier. According to author Wilbur Morrison, the Eighth Air Force, went as far as having the bombsights removed.[38] This was a practice developed in the first attempt on a raid on St Nazaire on 3 January 1943. It was adopted due to the low competency of bombardiers. It produced increased precision, but not always increased accuracy. A

32   *Bombardiers Information File*, HQ USAAF, Washington DC, 1944, 2-1-4.
33   Terminal Ballistic Data – Vol 1, p.23.
34   Terminal Ballistic Data – Vol 1, p.116.
35   Tillman, p.134.
36   John Muirhead, *Those Who Fall* (London: Bantam Press, 1986), pp.108-10.
37   Halsey Ross, p.133.
38   Morrison, p.75.

This post-attack image of the Abbey shows the inefficiency of pattern bombing. While clearly the Abbey has been hit and badly damaged, there are many craters around the building that have made no contribution to the damage. (NARA RG342-FH-000151)

delay of just one second between aircraft releases resulted in bombs going 220-270-feet long on average, depending on altitude and speed.[39] All the bombing aircraft would be slightly different in either range or deflection. If the lead missed, so would all the others. Major Edgar Pewitt, a staff bombardier of the 319th Bombardment Group, a medium bomber unit, stressed that this error was accounted for by the lead aircraft releasing its weapons slightly early. From

39   McFarland, p.171, Ross p.135.

the ground the Abbey looks like a very large building; but to the bomber it was a very small target. Research suggests that bombing on lead diminished bombing accuracy by one-third.[40] The bombers were used to peppering large industrial facilities many times larger than the Abbey. The result was known as pattern bombing and it was the favoured methodology.[41] AFHQ in May 1944 recognised that pattern bombing was very wasteful when used against pinpoint targets as most of the bombs did not strike the target or indeed damage it.[42] This tactic was more efficient when used against area targets and was advantageous when facing opposition from fighter aircraft. Pattern bombing ensured some success, but for a single small target it guaranteed that most of the bombs would fall harmlessly onto the hillside, although ironically at Cassino that was where the Germans were!

This was different to the RAF, where all aircraft aimed their own weapons, although they were often aimed at target flares dropped by Pathfinder aircraft.

Altitude awareness was also a critical factor in achieving accuracy. The altimeter was an aneroid barometer that measured altitude at sea level based upon a standard atmospheric pressure and temperature. These conditions were rarely met and were certainly not those of 15 February 1944 as this standard temperature was 15°C, far warmer than on that winter's day. The altimeter was fine for maintaining a standard formation altitude, but bombing accuracy is based upon the actual altitude, with real air pressure, rather than a convenient standard. A 2°C difference versus the standard temperature would result in a 1,000 feet differential between indicated altitude and actual altitude.[43] A typical February day in Italy was probably around 5°C at sea-level (colder at a height of 1,500 feet, where the Abbey lay, possibly by 1-2°C). This gives more than a 10°C differential in temperature, or up to 5,000 feet between indicated and actual altitude. This difference would induce large bombing errors due to increased real air density in colder conditions. To overcome this error, it was necessary to know the barometric pressure and air temperature. This was problematic when the target is in enemy-held territory and on top of a large hill where the pressure and density would be lower. Although ground meteorological units could help, the accuracy of their pressure readings from the valley floor would be doubtful and there is no evidence that it was requested on 15 February by the Fifteenth Air Force.

In the 5th Bombardment Wing's bombing order, the Abbey is at a height of 1,750-feet. Maps show that the Abbey is located on Point 516. This indicates an elevation of 516-metres or 1,692-feet. We do not know which is right, but the difference would have resulted in delivery error because the bombardiers' bombing tables would have given a different trail offset, resulting in the bombs falling long. This level of altitude error would result in an inaccuracy of nearly 280-feet on the ground.[44] It was also not known where this height was referenced from. Was it above mean sea level or above ground level and from which geographic datum was the elevation drawn? Determining elevation is a complicated business. By 1944, radio altimeters could measure the altitude above the ground relatively accurately, but the target was not at ground level, and this the altimeter could not account for. To overcome the elevation problem, weapons should be delivered with high impact angles to offset vertical errors. In 1944, the ballistic nature

40   Haun, p.207.
41   Bombardiers Information File, HQ USAAF, Washington DC, 1944, 8-6-1.
42   AFHRA Reel A6111, AFHQ Operation Memorandum No 54 dated 6 May 1944 – The Employment of Bombers and Fighter-Bombers in Co-Operation with the Army.
43   Bombardiers Information File, HQ USAAF, Washington DC, 1944, 3-3-2.
44   Ross, p.136.

of the weapon resulted in lower impact angles. The bombs would have achieved around a 65^0 impact angle from its delivery altitude. The mediums, bombing from lower, achieved around 60^0.[45] Small errors in elevation could result in weapons missing by a considerable distance. If the target's elevation is lower than measured, the bombs would go over the target and impact long and vice versa if the target is higher than measured. This error was compounded if the aircraft did not fly at the correct altitude. Small discrepancies would result in large errors on the ground. The USAAF's Bombardier Information File, the instruction manual for bombardiers, stresses that the cooperation between pilot and bombardier in maintaining the correct airspeed and altitude was critical to successful bombing.[46] Evans' aircraft released its bombs from an indicated altitude of 17,000-feet, which resulted in a five-mile and roughly 35-second journey from the aircraft to target, where the bomb travelled through differing air temperatures, density and currents, all of which may have fractionally altered the trajectory of the weapons. Calculating the Actual Time of Fall (ATF) of the bombs was a key calculation for the bombardier which, when combined with the groundspeed calculation would determine whole range, the distance the aircraft travels between release and impact.[47] The ATF is translated from the bombing tables into something called disc speed on the Norden bombsight. If the disc speed was too slow, the bombs would fall short; if too fast, they would be long.

Another source of error, one that would have affected the Abbey bombing is not technical, but procedural; that is the 'bomber box.' Heavy bombers adopted several formations, the smallest of which was the *Element*, a vee formation of three aircraft. Two or three Elements made up a *Box* and four boxes made up a *Group*. Two or more Groups constituted a *Combat Wave*, with a minimum of 48-bombers.[48] Each bombardment group had two formations of up to 28-aircraft in named boxes, where each box is at a slightly different altitude. These boxes comprised 'Able Box' with the lead aircraft at the front. There are a few possible formations. One is that the B-17 formation would form a group diamond with four boxes of six or seven-aircraft. The formations would have been separated in altitude to allow mutual protection from enemy fighters. This was the most common formation later in 1944, but was not the one flown by Evans, who flew in a formation called a group stagger. Evans' aircraft would have led 'Able Box' of the 2nd Bombardment Group. His deputy commander would have been his wingman in case he was shot down. To Evans' right would have been the seven B-17s of 'Baker Box', slightly higher, and to his left seven B-17s of 'Charlie Box', slightly lower in what was known as 'Purple Heart Corner.'[49] Immediately behind Evans would have been 'Dog Box' also comprising seven aircraft. The Group adopted a six Box formation, with 'Easy' and 'Fox' Boxes mirroring the first formation on 'Dog Box' for a total of 39-bombers.[50] Three aircraft from the 2nd Bombardment Group failed to reach the target. Although the aircraft wingtips were only a few feet apart, a formation three Elements wide, that is nine aircraft, would produce a wide swath of bombs, wider than the Abbey's perimeter. Evans gave instructions to his fellow pilots to fly with no more than five feet between wingtips in order to maximise the damage. Despite this, the B-17's wingspan is 103-feet, the formation nearly 1000-feet wide. The outlying bombers were incapable of hitting

45   Terminal Ballistic Data Vol 1, p.35.
46   Bombardiers Information File, HQ USAAF, Washington DC, 1944, 1-1-1.
47   Bombardiers Information File, HQ USAAF, Washington DC, 1944, 2-1-2.
48   AFHRA Reel 25169. Formations in the Fifteenth.
49   McCrary and Shermann, p.114.
50   Tillman p.34-35.

Whilst a useful tactic for large industrial complexes, or when mutual self-defence is a necessity, the bomber box ensured that for pinpoint targets such as the Abbey, most bombs would fall astray.
(NARA RG342-FH-001688)

the Abbey if Evans got his box into the right location. This formation guaranteed that many bombs fell nowhere near the mean point of impact. This flaw for pinpoint targets was eventually recognised and the Fifteenth Air Force switched to the diamond formation. The Fifteenth Air Force also developed a six-aircraft front formation or a three-aircraft front 'column of Boxes' formation for smaller targets, but these were not adopted for the Abbey.[51]

All these errors added up. Typically, in operational conditions the USAAF B-17 achieved a CEP of 1,300-feet or a quarter of a mile, although in the clear skies that day on a sortie with no German air opposition, little flak and only a short, less fatiguing flight, it is probable that they achieved better results than the average, although exact figures have not been found. A similar sortie, although with many fewer bombers and with greater opposition, against the submarine pens at Lorient in late October 1942 attained a CEP of around 750-feet from 17,500 feet altitude and this seems a reasonable comparison. In a letter to Devers on the performance of heavy bombers against the town of Cassino on 15 March, Eaker claimed that 47 per cent of bombs fell within 1,000-feet of the aimpoint.[52] There is no reason why the figure would not be similar a month before. It is a reasonable assumption, therefore, that the Abbey attack would have achieved a CEP of something around 750-875-feet.

51   AFHRA Reel 25169. Formations in the Fifteenth.
52   AFHRA Reel A6030, MAAF C-in-C Correspondence, Eaker to Devers dated 6 April 1944.

The first aircraft over the target would generally be the most accurate. The dust and obscurants thrown up reduce the accuracy of succeeding waves. (NARA RG342-FH-000147)

Eighth Air Force statistics showed that by December 1943 its bombers were getting around 23 per cent of their bombs within 1,000-feet of a desired mean point of impact.[53] Overall, in the entire period of strategic bombing during the war, the Fifteenth Air Force achieved 30.78 per cent of its bombs within 1,000-feet of the aimpoint.[54] This roughly equated to the 1,300-feet CEP. The first aircraft in the formation, that flown by Evans, was likely to be the most accurate. The simple reason for this was that they could see the target. As the first formation struck the Abbey and the mountain around it, a large cloud of smoke and dust was thrown up. From Evans' testimony this was what happened. The Norden bombsight was an optical device, requiring a clear view of the target. None of those that followed Evans' formation would have had this view as the wind moved the obscurants around the mountain top.

The bombing order stated that 108-B-17 aircraft would have 12 x AN-M-43 or M-64 500lb GP bombs each – a total of 1,296-weapons for the attack on the Abbey plus 36-aircraft with incendiaries. However, records reveal that only 107-aircraft were available in the 2nd, 99th and 301st Groups and 35-aircraft from the 97th Group loaded with incendiaries. Despite its

53   McFarland, p.173.
54   McFarland, p.186.

size, the B-17 carried only a small number of bombs compared to its RAF four-engine equiv-
alents. One B-24 Liberator Group Commander, Colonel Edward Timberlake, commented
sarcastically, 'Listen, there is nothing wrong with the Fortress. It's a damn good medium
bomber.'[55] Six aircraft did not make the target, resulting in a maximum total of 1,212-
bombs dropped from 101-B-17s. Statistically, only a maximum of 606-bombs would have
fallen within 1,300-feet of the aimpoint, which presumably was the centre of the Abbey.
The distribution of these bombs would have a normal gaussian distribution in that more
of them would have fallen closer to the aimpoint than far away. This is an area of more
than 5-million square feet. The remainder should statistically have landed more than 1,300-
feet away, with about 521-bombs falling between 1,300 and 2,600-feet from the aimpoint,
causing no damage to the building but possibly hitting friendly infantry units. The USAAF
know all about CEP in 1944. Nearly a year earlier in the *The Air Force in a Task Force* handbook the HQ AAF commented: 'How, then can we justify average error of over a thousand
feet, meaning that less than fifty percent of all bombs dropped will be within a circle having
a two-thousand-foot diameter?'[56]

The USAAF thought British bombs were ballistically inferior to their own but, when interrogated shortly after the war, Albert Speer said American 500lb bombs were much less effective.[57]
The USAAF were delusional in their view of the effectiveness of their weapons, saying in their
handbook that when compared with British bombs, 'carrying the given amount of explosive on
missions may require twice the number of airplanes that would be required to carry the same
amount in American bombs.'[58] In one of its standard configurations the RAF Lancaster could
carry a 4,000lb Cookie and up to 18 x 500lb MC bombs. In another it could carry 14 x 1,000lb
MC bombs. The RAF had dispensed with their own GP bombs due to poor effectiveness,
replacing them with MC weapons with a higher CWR. The US opinion on British bombs was
outdated by February 1944. These MC bombs had a 50 per cent CWR whereas the British GP
bombs were around 30 per cent.[59] The US GP bombs, however, had a similar CWR to the British
MC bombs, with an explosive fill of around 260lbs and 528lbs respectively for 500 and 1,000lb
weapons.[60] Had Lancasters with their normal bombloads, delivering in a stream with individual
aiming, carried out the attack with the same number of aircraft, the damage would likely have
been far greater. By Spring 1944 Lancaster crews used Master Bombers and a technique known
as offset marking to attain accuracy at night down to as low as 855-feet, much better than the
daytime B-17 accuracy.[61] By February 1944, 617 Sqn was using the Stabilised Automatic Bomb
Sight (SABS) to drop its 12,000lb weapons with great accuracy in daylight. Accuracy still
depended very much on the weather, but also upon the skill of the Master Bombers dropping
the markers carried on the aircraft. An attack just before dawn would have allowed the infantry
to attack with the benefit of darkness.

55   McCrary and Shermann, p.188.
56   AFHRA Reel A1592, The Air Force in a Task Force, Chapter V, Bomber Command dated March 1943.
57   Albert Speer, Interview with the US Strategic Bomber Survey, 17 May 1945, in MAAF Air
     Surrender Documents, TAB I, p.37-8.
58   AFHRA Reel A1592, The Air Force in a Task Force, Chapter V, Bomber Command dated March 1943.
59   MacBean and Hogben, p.43.
60   Terminal Ballistic Data – Vol 1, p.116.
61   Charles Webster and Noble Frankland, *The Strategic Air Offensive, Volume III: Victory* (London:
     HMSO, 1961 (Kindle Edition)), Kindle Location 3242.

The USAAF thought that training and practice would reduce the errors; they were wrong. The Abbey was approximately 700-feet long by 362-feet wide, an area of roughly 300,000-square feet. The weapons that missed were too small to have any blast effects on a strongly built building and fragmentation effects would do little more than break windows and remove roof tiles. The 500lb bomb had a lethal blast radius of around 60-90-feet.[62] A 500lb bomb created a crater of around 30-32-feet in diameter and a 1,000lb GP bomb created a 32-35-feet crater, depending on the ground composition.[63] The prevailing thinking in the USAAF and the RAF since the 1930s was that it was better to drop a large number of smaller bombs than a smaller number of larger bombs.[64] The reasoning seemed to have been that the airmen were more interested in hitting the target than destroying it. The more bombs that were dropped, the greater percentage of hits and the better the performance of the mission. This is a false statistic in that if the weapon used is incapable of achieving the desired effect it mattered little how many hits you obtain. There is no indication in the 5th Bombardment Wing's bombing order of the percentage of damage required to achieve the ground commander's desired effects. Using statistics and assuming all the bombs were normally distributed the Abbey was probably only struck by around 10 per cent of the bombs dropped. Assuming 1,212 weapons were delivered, with an average Fifteenth Air Force precision of 30.78 per cent within 1,000-feet, 373-bombs would have fallen within 1,000 feet of the centre of the Abbey. The Abbey area filled eight per cent of the 1,000-feet radius. If an equal distribution is assumed for simplicity, a maximum of around 141 bombs could have statistically hit the Abbey from the B-17s. The PHit has been calculated at 11.695 per cent. This figure does not take into account those bombers on the outside of the formation whose bombs could not possibly have hit the Abbey if Evans had done so. This figure was consistent with actual data in that out of 16-bombardment groups sent against the Schweinfurt ball-bearing works in October 1943, only around 63-weapons struck the target.[65] One account from the Fifteenth Air Force estimated only 35-direct hits on the Abbey buildings were observed.[66] Only those weapons that struck the Abbey directly would have caused damage and it is likely, given manufacturing standards in 1944 that at least a few weapons would not have detonated. At least one unexploded bomb was found in the rubble of the Abbey when the renovation began.[67] The average for Army Air Force was around 12 per cent duds, and some from the medium bombers had long delay fuses.[68] The number of duds had been a constant irritant since 1942. To minimize duds, the 500lb bombs had been fitted with a tail fuse and a nose fuse.[69] Ironically, the original request from Freyberg for 36-Kittybombers would probably have produced more hits than the B-17s. The dive-bombing single-engine Kittyhawk could carry two 500lb bombs, opposed to the 12 on the B-17. They would, however, have been much more likely to hit the Abbey from much closer range. On 16 February these aircraft attacked

62   McFarland, p.225.
63   AFHRA Reel A6112 Frame 0064, and, The Relative Effectiveness of Various Types of Bombs and Fuses, AAF Evaluation Board in ETO, 1 June 1945.
64   McFarland, p.94.
65   Ross, p.54.
66   AFHRA Reel A6377, Frame 1408, Fifteenth Air Force Operations – 1 November 1943–1 March 1944, p.23.
67   Leccisotti, p.154.
68   Tillman, p.255.
69   George Parris, *Memoirs of Foggia Book III 1943-1944*, Kindle loc 2060.

the Abbey claiming 43-hits with 500lb and 1,000lb bombs. This is roughly the same number of hits by all the B-17s, but with half the number of aircraft.[70] The majority of the damage to the building came from the medium bombers. These dropped larger more damaging weapons from a lower altitude with greater precision. That lower altitude bombing produced better results was well known. In his Practical Bombing Problems, Kuter had identified that a 33 per cent reduction in altitude produced a 66 per cent reduction in the force required to destroy a pinpoint target.[71] Reducing altitude as a practical solution to inaccuracy was dismissed due to anti-aircraft defences. This is not pertinent to the Abbey where flak was present but negligible, yet the bombers remained at high altitude. This suggests a dogmatic following of procedure by the heavy bombers instead of the adoption of tactics offering greater prospects of success.

The inappropriateness of this method of bombing for this target should not have been a surprise. In November 1943, the Operational Research Section of VIII Bomber Command carried out an in-depth study into bombing results for the first ten months of 1943.[72] It is possible that the study's results were not shared with Fifteenth Air Force. The subject of this report was one of the Eighth Air Force Commanding General's top priorities. If the daylight strategic bombing campaign could not hit its targets, the pressure to join the RAF would grow. The Eighth Air Force's Commander was the chief supporter of this campaign and would have seen this report. In November 1943, this was Lieutenant General Ira Eaker.

The report judged the results of B-17 attacks based upon the pattern bombing of each bombardment group of up to 21-aircraft. It was not concerned about whether individual aircraft hit their targets, but whether the pattern of bombs from the group achieved the desired effects. The study used photography taken by each group as they dropped their bombloads to determine individual group patterns. The group pattern was measured by placing a 1,000-feet circle that covered the greatest density of impacts. This was known as the pattern centre. This demon-strated the precision of the group rather than its accuracy. Accuracy was measured by how far the pattern centre was from the aimpoint. The analysts were looking for compact patterns, with a centre close to the aimpoint. A perfect attack is where the pattern centre and the aimpoint are the same. The report had good data for 285 of the 615-recorded attacks in the period. Bombing errors were divided into 'normal' and 'gross' errors. Normal errors (radial error of less than 3,000-feet) were those that could be expected in standard operations where the bombs formed a spread, but where the bombardiers had carried out operating procedures correctly. Gross errors (radial error of more than 3,000 feet) were outside normal errors due to several factors including, excessive defensive manoeuvring, weather or navigation errors. Both types of errors occurred at Cassino on 15 February 1944. The report ignored gross errors which accounted for nearly 30 per cent of all attacks.

They recognised that 'bombing on lead' methodology caused large errors because only the lead aircraft in each group delivered at the right time in the right place. The other aircraft dropped at varying times and locations, affecting range and deflection depending on the delay between the leader, and the subordinate aircraft's position within the Combat Box. The study

70   RAF Narrative – The Italian Campaign 1943-1945 – Volume 1, p.288.
71   Haun, p.120.
72   VIII Bomber Command Operational Research Report, Analysis of VIII Bomber Command Operations From The Point Of View of Bombing Accuracy – 1 January 1943 to 15 October 1943, dated 1 November 1943.

found that despite being the only aircraft that aimed its weapons, the leader's delivery rarely constituted the pattern centre. The report suggested that the leader's bombs should be dropped a few hundred feet short of the aimpoint. In Evans' account, some of his bombs hit the Abbey, meaning that most of his group's bombs may have been long of the target. The mean aiming error for over 200-aiming events was 150-feet short and 167-feet to the right of the aimpoint. The average pattern for 1943 in VIII Bomber Command placed most bombs in a box 3,700-feet long and 2,500-feet wide with the lower limit of pattern size being 2,000-feet by 2,000-feet. Considering a pinpoint target like the Abbey, which was 700-feet by 360-feet, we can begin to confirm that most bombs missed even when only normal and unavoidable errors are accounted for. The study concluded that group impacts would have been normally distributed with the peak of the gaussian curve being around the 800-1000-feet; this accounted for around a quarter of attacks. If we interpolate the VIII Bomber Command histogram to make a judgement of the percentage that would have a better than 600-feet radial error it can be seen that this is no more than 15 per cent. The pattern density was only effective if it is close to the aimpoint. The study discovered that in late 1943, B-17 bombers with a pre-assigned aimpoint in a group attack were placing their bombs within 1,000-feet of that aimpoint on 28.7 per cent of occasions, roughly equivalent to the Fifteenth Air Force average of 30.78 per cent. The best Bombardment Group in VIII Bomber Command achieved 41 per cent within 1000-feet of the aimpoint, whereas a less experienced group, only achieved 16.7 per cent. It was clear from the report that where waves of group attacks were conducted the best results were always achieved by the leading group, and bombing performance declined in successive waves. This is supported operationally as the lead bombardment groups were usually the most experienced, suggesting that the later groups in the Abbey attack would have been less likely to hit the building than Evans' group.[73] The study also concluded that by the time the fourth Group released its weapons, the misses were largely due to gross errors, more than 3,000 feet from the aimpoint.

The Norden was connected to the aircraft's intervalometer. This was the device that allowed bombardiers to release weapons at specific intervals between each bomb, thereby determining how close they fell to each other. These intervals would be larger for area targets and smaller for pinpoint targets; these were between one twentieth and one half a second interval and were called a train release. In a train release the intervals are timed so that the middle of the train hits the desired point of impact.[74] The bombardier would set the interval of bomb release in feet, the number of bombs to be released and the expected ground speed. There was also a salvo setting where the bombs could be all released simultaneously. The choice of interval was a balancing act. The salvo would achieve greater destruction in one place, whereas a train would spread the bombs. If a salvo missed, then all the bombs missed; with an interval there was a greater chance of a hit but with less destruction. The interface between the Norden and the intervalometer had been causing automatic release interference since September 1943 and may not have been used on the Abbey attack.[75]

The bombing order for the Abbey ordered all aircraft to use the minimum intervalometer setting – that is that each bomb would leave the aircraft at one-twentieth of a second after its predecessor. For 12-bombs that is nearly a second from start to finish, a distance of around

73   Analysis of VIII Bomber Command Operations, p.25.
74   Bombardiers Information File, HQ USAAF, Washington DC, 1944, 7-4-6.
75   Albert Pardini, *The Legendary Norden Bombsight* (Atglen PA: Schiffer Military History, 1999), p.205.

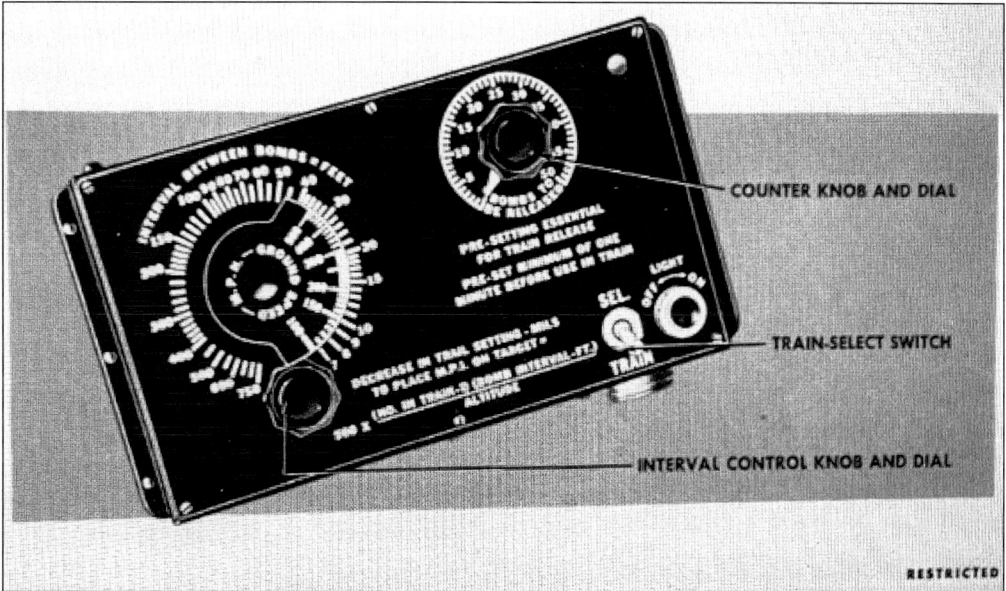

COUNTER KNOB AND DIAL

TRAIN-SELECT SWITCH

INTERVAL CONTROL KNOB AND DIAL

RESTRICTED

The intervalometer. This equipment allowed the Bombardier to drop all the bombs at once – the salvo setting, or to space them out to increase the chances of a hit. (Bombardier Information File)

200-feet. This setting guaranteed that some bombs would miss as a single second of error was larger than the target area. The aircraft could have delivered their loads simultaneously using the salvo setting, but this risked all the bombs missing. It had been proven by Eighth Air Force operational analysts that a salvo had a greater chance of hitting a pinpoint target than a minimum intervalometer setting in train.[76] Had this lesson had been transferred? They did not follow the advice in the Abbey attack.

The later waves of medium bombers had smaller bomb loads, but they dropped from lower altitude, resulting in a smaller CEP and a greater chance of hitting the target. They also dropped 1,000lb GP bombs that had greater destructive power, but that still required a direct hit on the Abbey to do significant damage. The greater accuracy of the mediums was borne out by the statistics, in that aircraft that dropped from 12,000-feet had 44 per cent of bombs within 1,000-feet of the aimpoint whereas this plummeted to 21 per cent at 18,000-feet. These figures again came from Eighth Air Force Operational Analysis.[77] The statistics were available from November 1943, but the Fifteenth Air Force heavies, despite no aerial threat and little flak still bombed from the higher altitude. The B-26 was more accurate than the B-25 because it had the Norden bombsight, whereas the B-25 received it in April 1944. In a May 1944 report on bombing accuracy from the Mediterranean Theatre, the CEP of a medium bomber, dropping from 10,000-feet, was 900-feet for the B-25 and 650-feet for the B-26.[78] The 42nd Bombardment Wing claimed in its post-war report that in February 1944

76   McFarland, p.172.
77   McFarland, p.174.
78   AFHRA Reel A6030, MAAF C-in-C Correspondence, Eaker to Arnold dated 7 May 1944.

its mean CEP was 953-feet but this is for all bombs regardless of the altitude from which they are delivered.[79]

Eaker was not impressed with the performance of the Fifteenth Air Force. In a report to Arnold, dated 21 March 1944 he referred to it as a 'disorganised mob', although he accepted that it contained some very good men, but the change from a tactical to a strategic air force was proving difficult. The Fifteenth Air Force was short of key officers. There was no Deputy Commander until the first week in March when Brigadier-General Joseph Atkinson arrived from 5th Bombardment Wing. The key role of deputy Operations Officer was filled by Lieutenant Colonel Curtis Sluman who had been in his post for a month. The Fifteenth Air Force struggled to hit pinpoint targets, although it proved 'fairly acceptable' at large targets such as marshalling yards. Spaatz too was 'depressed' at the performance of the Fifteenth Air Force in early 1944.[80] He had warned Twining about 'promiscuous attacks' after Florence was accidently bombed. In the report he suggested that the heavy bombers were having difficulty training the new crews that were now rapidly arriving and that they were struggling to adapt to the rigours of strategic bombing. A B-17 pilot of the 301st Bombardment Group, John Muirhead, recounted that many of the new co-pilots were so poorly trained that they were incapable of keeping formation.[81] Twining specifically mentioned that bombing was inaccurate for pinpoint targets such as the Abbey.[82] An embarrassed Eaker, after witnessing the bombing of Cassino town in mid-March, and having to write an apology to British Eighth Army Commander, General Sir Oliver Leese, for the errant bombs that destroyed his command vehicle, ordered Twining to investigate. In a letter dated 17 March, Eaker compared the heavies and the mediums, saying of the heavy bombers that, 'By contrast with the Mediums, however, they looked very bad, and everybody commented on it. The mediums formation was precise; they passed over their targets exactly on time, and their air discipline was perfect.'[83]

Twining found that poor air discipline and smoke over the target were the main causes for the inaccuracy. He did not take any disciplinary action but established an in-house bombardier school to correct the training inadequacies.[84] This measure supplemented the already existing Staff Bombardier position, a senior bombardier on each squadron, group or wing who maintained the formation's training standards and performance records. He was also responsible for spreading best practice and for ensuring that the bombing instruments were properly calibrated. The performance took some months to improve. In a letter to Kuter, Assistant Chief of the AAF Air Staff for Plans, on 9 April, Norstad reported a 'definite improvement' in accuracy.[85] On the same day the Fifteenth Air Force was officially commended, with laudatory comments from Eaker, Spaatz, Wilson and Arnold. Arnold's impatience with progress was probably not assuaged by the bombing of the Abbey. In his New Year message to Fifteenth Air Force he

79   AFHRA Reel B0949, History of 42nd Bombardment Wing (Medium), Appendix J – Chart Of Bombing Accuracy.
80   AFHRA Reel A6030, History of MAAF, December 1943 – September 1944, Volume 1, Chapter II, p.48.
81   Muirhead, p.23
82   James Parton, The History of the Mediterranean Allied Air Forces, p.48.
83   AFHRA Reel A6030, History of MAAF, C-in-C Correspondence, Eaker to Twining dated 17 March 1944.
84   Tillman, p.37.
85   AFHRA Reel A1372, Letter Norstad to Kuter dated 9 April 1944.

believed that both strategic air forces conducted too many 'diversionary attacks' rather than concentrating on the main effort which was destroying the *Luftwaffe*.[86] The attack on the Abbey was clearly another diversion, and possibly an experiment for the tactical use of long-range bombers, although Arnold's messages were clearly contradictory as he sometimes demanded that Eaker commit all his forces to assisting the land forces, bogged down in the Italian winter.

The implications for the bombing of the Abbey are clear. Use of heavy bombers would result in most bombs missing the target. Many would miss by a long distance and that this was the case was known by air planners. There was no indication in the bombing study that it was distributed to MASAF, and it was written before the unified command of USSTAF came into being, but its conclusions cannot have been a surprise. Eaker would not have approved a mission which he knew would be spotlighted and which the statistics suggested would fail. The only conclusion is that Eaker did not approve the mission to bomb the Abbey. The bombload, the formation and the delivery altitude of the heavy bombers that day were not just inappropriate, but incapable of doing great damage to a small target. They were prepared for an attack against a much larger target in Germany or Austria and were switched when the weather became unfavourable. The late hour of this switch meant that they had to go with what they had. There was no time to completely re-plan for this new tactical target. In a way they were lucky; they struck the ammunition stored in the cave close to the Abbey's walls. This accidental strike caused a very large explosion which probably contributed more to the damage than the later waves of heavy bombers. The heavies were overshadowed by the medium bombers, which from the surviving available film footage caused the greatest amount of damage.

As one of the original six officers who were the architects of AWPD-1, and head of the Eighth Air Force's Operational Planning Section, Colonel Richard Hughes stated: 'Contrary to all expectations with a few notable exceptions, the strategic bombers of Eighth and Fifteenth Air Forces seldom succeeded in achieving real precision bombing.'[87] The attack on the Abbey was not one of these 'notable exceptions'.

86   Gould, p.230.
87   McFarland, p.170.

21

Una Giornata da B-17

The air arm should be our most effective weapon in bringing home to the German people and the German Army the futility of continued resistance

General George C Marshall
Chief of Staff
United States Army[1]

Newsweek's John Lardner christened it 'the most publicized bombing of a single target in history.' It was one of the most controversial bombings of the Second World War. The Abbey had not been targeted throughout the campaign, yet in hindsight, its destruction seems pre-ordained, almost providential. Normal procedure for the use of air power in support of Fifth Army was from XII ASC, and the evidence suggests that this was all the ground commanders asked from the air force. Fifteenth Air Force was always unsuitable for this task. It lacked Ground Liaison Officers (GLOs) that were present in XII ASC to ensure smooth coordination between land and air. The GLOs were vital, the conduit between the 7th Army Air Support Command (AASC) at Fifth Army and the squadrons and groups. The XII ASC was also collocated with Fifth Army HQ whereas Fifteenth Air Force was miles away in Bari. The battle rhythms of the tactical and strategic forces were never synchronised. Everything about the bombing of the Abbey was ad-hoc. The standard process whereby Fifth Army gained air support was through a daily operations conference held each afternoon which discussed activity in the past 24-hours and plans for the next 24-48-hours. In addition to Lieutenant Colonel O'Hare, the commanding officer of 7th AASC, the conference was attended by Fifth Army air operations officer, Lieutenant Colonel John Hansborough and XII ASC intelligence and operations staff. No Fifteenth Air Force personnel were present. By the time this conference sat on 14 February, an order to attack the Abbey had already been drafted by Fifteenth Air Force, whose own daily targeting conference finished around midday.

This mission was also unusual for the medium bombers. Their primary task had always been interdiction missions, targeted to prevent German freedom of movement within Italy. Over the previous few weeks, they had concentrated on preventing a quick German redeployment to the Anzio beachhead. On this day, they too were given the task to directly support the struggling

---

1   Matloff, Kindle Location 9649.

Allied ground forces south of Rome. Both forces were to conduct a mission that today would be characterised as CAS, something neither force was used to or trained for. This air support skill was with the light fighter-bombers of the RAF's Desert Air Force and the US XII ASC. Despite Freyberg's request, someone thought that this target needed considerably more firepower.

Major Francis Jones wrote in his report of 1949 that the final decision to bomb the Abbey was taken on the afternoon of 14 February, but several events strongly suggest that a decision of sorts was made earlier than that, although the participation of the heavy bombers may have been a later addition as the Abbey was a secondary target only to be attacked if the weather further north was poor. The first indication of an earlier decision was the dropping of leaflets at around 1:00pm on 14 February. On 15 February, *The Times* reported that these were dropped the day before, thereby giving an impression that the occupants had more time than in reality they had.[2] An honest mistake or a deliberate lie? The leaflet was suggested to Freyberg by Gruenther in a meeting in the early afternoon on 13 February.[3] The monk, Leccisotti, wrote that the leaflets, none of which actually landed within the Abbey walls, were taken there by three young men, Fulvio de Angelis, Antonio Miele and Nino Morra, at about 2:00pm.[4] The leaflet said the following:

> Italian friends, beware! We have been until now especially careful to avoid <u>shelling</u> the MONTE CASSINO Monastery. The Germans have known how to benefit from this but now the fighting has swept closer to its sacred precincts. The time has come when regretfully we must <u>train our guns</u> on the Monastery itself. We give you warning so that you may save yourselves. We warn you urgently: Leave the Monastery!! Leave it at once!! Respect this warning, it is for your benefit.
>   Signed FIFTH ARMY[5]

The leaflet is vague. It does not claim that the Germans are occupying the Abbey, just that they are taking advantage of it. It also did not say that the Abbey was to be bombed; it refers to artillery or direct fire weapons. No time limit is given. The leaflet was an indirect admission that the Allies knew that Italian civilians occupied the Abbey. Why else would it be written in Italian, but not in German?

The Fifth Army produced 11,000 leaflets and delivered them via a modified artillery shell. This was an inexact science due to the difference in weight of shells and the leaflets could be delivered from up to eight-miles away.[6] Although the exact timing or method of the attack may not have been decided upon when these were produced, there must have been a time lag between the decision to attack and the ability of the Fifth Army propaganda unit to receive orders, design the leaflet, get it approved, have it delivered to the guns and its delivery to the target audience. These leaflets were produced by the AFHQ Psychological Warfare Branch, 5th Army Combat Team, commanded by Lieutenant Colonel Buck Weaver. Leaflets were either printed in Naples

2   *The Times*, Shelling Of Monte Cassino Abbey: 'The Time Has Come', 15 February 1944, Issue 49780, p.4.
3   Freyberg, Diary Entry, 13 February 1944.
4   Leccisotti, p.120.
5   Freyberg, Diary Entry, 17 February 1944.
6   TNA WO 204/6420: AFHQ Psychological Warfare Branch: Combat Propaganda – Leaflet Distribution To Date, 1 February 1944.

or at the Fifth Army's own printing press, where they had a Crowell mobile printing unit.[7] This was run by its civilian manufacturer, Tom Crowell. Nearly five million leaflets a week were produced across the front in February 1944.[8] Assuming that the leaflets were printed by Fifth Army, the quicker option, their printer could print 2,000 sheets per hour (each sheet has four leaflets). Therefore, 11,000 leaflets would have taken around 90-minutes to print, an hour to set-up and an hour to cut into four – a total of around 3½ hours. From production the leaflet was approved by Weaver, Greunther and by the intelligence section. Once approved, Weaver issued an operations memorandum to the relevant corps artillery officer for action. The leaflets then needed to be packed into shells at an ammunition dump and collected by the Base Ordnance Service and delivered to the firing units. Approximately 750 x 5-inch by 8-inch leaflets could fit into a 105mm shell case. This process could take up to five hours.[9] The trip to the firing units could take hours along the crowded and often under-fire Route 6. From beginning to end it was unlikely that these leaflets could have been designed, written, approved, produced, packed and delivered in less than 24-hours, putting the very latest time for the decision to attack the Abbey by some means as early to mid-afternoon of 13 February, shortly after Freyberg met Gruenther. A vexing question following the delivery of the leaflet is why the Allies and Germans did not try to negotiate a truce period when the trapped civilians could escape? Truces to collect the dead and wounded were commonplace. There was a truce that day on Monte Castellone, requested by the 90th *Panzer-Grenadiers*, which had ended two hours before the leaflet drop.

This truce was for three hours, enough time to evacuate the civilians and less than two miles from the Abbey. In 1947, von Vietinghoff claimed that he tried in vain to get a truce for the Abbey's inhabitants, but this claim has little supporting evidence.

The second indicator was the issuing of an air tasking message at 12:30pm on 14 February by the 5th Bombardment Wing. This implies that a decision to use the heavy bombers was taken that morning at the latest, although top-priority POINTBLANK missions further north were also being planned. Fifteenth Air Force standard target selection procedures support this time-line. Mission planning usually began at 6.00am with the day's weather, followed at 8:00am with the A-2 Intelligence staff briefing the Assistant Chief of Staff for Intelligence, Colonel Charles Young, on the previous day's events. This briefing would be passed to Twining each morning. At 10:30am A-2, with the support of Targets Officers and meteorologists, would select the target priorities to be presented to the A-3 (Operations) Director. Each day at 11:00am a group of 30-officers held a Targeting Meeting where these targets were presented by A-2 (Intelligence) and approved by the A-3 (Operations) Director, Brigadier-General Born.[10] Once approved, the operational order for the targets was written by the A-3 Division. This would normally take between 12 and 18-hours to produce, meaning that a time lag of 24-hours was usual between the decision and the execution of the mission.[11]

7   *Functions of the Fifth Army Propaganda Team* <www.psywar.org/psywar/reproductions/5ACPTPWB. pdf> (accessed 10 October 2020).
8   TNA WO 204/6420: AFHQ Psychological Warfare Branch: Combat Propaganda – Leaflet Distribution To Date, 1 February 1944.
9   NARA RG 208-AA-49, (3 March 1944) <https://www.psywar.org/pwbAfhq03.php> (accessed 10 October 2020).
10   Kreis, p.180-190.
11   AFHRA Reel A6377. History of 15th Air Force, p.223.

Truce on Castellone. On 14 February, the 36th US Infantry Division and the 90th *Panzer-Grenadier* Division agreed a truce to remove their dead from Monte Castellone. The same day the leaflet was dropped on the Abbey. No truce was offered to allow the brothers and civilians to leave.
(NARA-RG111-SC-421528_001)

The REDLINE messages up until late on the 14 February continue to suggest a POINTBLANK mission for the B-17s, so the Abbey must have been an alternate target, only to be executed in the event of poor weather at the primary targets. The weather was often poor that winter, so contingency plans would be produced routinely.

The original target was still being planned for a time-over-target of 1:00pm on 15 February, so definitely not the Abbey. The message initially suggesting possible cancellation of the primary mission was sent to Spaatz at 4:30pm on 14 February and the final cancellation message was received by Spaatz from MAAF at 7:00pm.[12]

The planning of the alternate mission, its formations, tactics by the 5th Bombardment Wing and coordination with the medium bombers would take time. The bombardment groups were required to assign aircraft and crews, service the aircraft and make them ready with fuel,

---

12   AFHRA Reel A5548. REDLINE IE187NT, CS95NT dated 13 February 1944, REDLINE CS99NT dated 14 February 1944, REDLINE CS100NT dated 14 February 1944 and REDLINE CS99IE dated 14 February 1944. These messages are personal messages with the recipient (e.g. CS – Carl Spaatz) followed by the message number and then the sender (e.g. IE – Ira Eaker). NT is Nathan Twining.

ammunition and desired bomb loads. Execution of the mission would be carried out by A-3 combat operations from the control room at Bari. Hartcup stated in his 1965 piece, quoting from an earlier AHB document that Major-General Nathan Twining ordered the attack at 1:14am on 15 February.[13] This order was probably Twining's final confirmation after a weather forecast received earlier that evening ruled out the primary targets, rather than the beginning of the process, which must have begun considerably earlier. The tasking order was issued over 6-hours before the primary target's cancellation and 12-hours before Twining's order and was signed on behalf of the Wing Commander, Colonel Charles W Lawrence:[14] Lawrence was another of the key commanding officers who had been in command for only a month.

HEADQUARTERS FIFTH WING (US)

APO520
14 February 1944 1230A

OPERATIONS ORDER:) (ORDER 341)
MAPS: Italy, 1:100,000, Sheets Nos. 160, 161 and 172.

1. a. See attached Intelligence Annex.
    b. No change.

2. Thirty-six (36) B-17s each of the 2nd, 99th, 301st and 97th Bomb Gps will attack and destroy at 15 minute intervals, the MONASTERY (41 deg 29 min N, 13 deg 49 min E)(G843209), ¾ mile due west of CASSINO, ITALY on 15 February 1944.
    SET COURSE FROM FOGGIA: 0830A – 2nd Bomb Gp at 10,000 ft.
                                   0845A – 99th Bomb Gp at 10,000 ft.
                                   0900A – 301st Bomb Gp at 10, 000 ft.
                                   0915A – 97th Bomb Gp at 10, 000 ft.
    ORDER OF FLIGHT: 2ND-99TH-301ST-97TH Bomb Gps.
    ROUTE OUT: FOGGIA to BENEVENTO to I.P to TARGET.
    INITIAL POINT: VAIRANO (K-110035)(41 deg 20 min N 14 deg 08 min E)
    AXIS OF ATTACK: 305 degrees.
    BOMBING ALTITUDE: Above 16,000 ft.
    TARGET ELEVATION: 1750ft
    RALLY: Right turn.
    ROUTE BACK: Direct.

3. a. The 97th Bomb Gp will load M47-A1 Incendiary with the M126-A1 fuse.
    b. (1) The bomb load for the 2nd, 99th and 301st will be 500s with .1 second nose fuse and .01 second tail fuse.
    (2) It is important to set course at prescribed time.
    (3) Must be sure of target before bombing as target is very close to the front line.

13 Hartcup, p.15.
14 TNA CAB 106/699, p29. HQ 5th Bombardment Wing Operation Order 341, 14 February 1944.

(4) Initial point and axis are planned so as to make bombing run parallel up highway #6.
(5) The bend in the VOLTURNO RIVER where it is joined by the River LIRI and high hill should be good landmarks for identification of I.P.
(6) If necessary, 'stooge' around over friendly territory until target is clear and definitely identified.
(7) Target is a group of buildings on a hill approximately ¾ mile due West of CASSINO.
(8) This is a definite pinpoint target and intervalometer setting should be minimum.

4.   No change.

5.   No change.

By Order of Colonel LAWRENCE:
STEPHEN W. HENRY
Major, Air Corps
Ass't A-3 Officer.

The discussions were over, the decision had been made, the orders issued. The fate of the Abbey was now sealed. There was nothing left but the execution of the order. It was now in the hands of the mission commander and the aircrews.

The pre-mission briefing occurred several hours prior to take-off, between 4:00am and 4:30am after Twining issued his final go-message early on 15 February. The mission commander was the Commanding Officer of the 96th Bombardment Squadron, based at Amendola in South Eastern Italy. The squadron had been at this airfield, 12-miles northeast of Foggia, since early December 1943, and had been commanded by Major Evans since its arrival. This was the first time that Evans had flown this aircraft, one of 12,731 B-17s built, and nicknamed 'Miss Laid' with the ominous tail-number of 42-31666 – the number of the beast. 'Miss Laid' was a brand-new aircraft, a B-17G with a chin turret to counter head-on attacks, the scourge of previous models. This model, because of the increased drag of the turret had a slightly lower top speed and ceiling when compared to the B-17F but had three extra 50-calibre machine-guns. It was so new that the aircraft's name and nose art had yet to be applied. The aircraft had been delivered by Boeing to the USAAF in Denver on the 2 December 1943 and had arrived at Amendola on 12 January 1944. It was one of the first batches of B-17Gs off the production line and its first operational mission was on 28 January 1944. It had conducted just a handful of missions.

Evans had an experienced crew. In addition to him and his co-pilot Second Lieutenant Benjamin Nabers, there was bombardier Lieutenant James Harbin with nearly 50-missions, navigator First Lieutenant Sam Mayer was on his 25th mission; engineer and top turret gunner, Technical Sergeant Hermann Sussman was on his 29th mission; radio operator Staff Sergeant Edward Bennett was on his 47th mission as was waist gunner Staff Sergeant William Richardson; the other waist gunner, Staff Sergeant Oscar Rome was on his 38th mission; the tail gunner Staff Sergeant Joseph Peters was just one behind. Finally, ball turret gunner Staff Sergeant Karl Letters was on his 42nd mission. Nine days and five missions later the aircraft was lost during Big Week over Austria, still without nose art. Six of Evans' crew remained on 'Miss

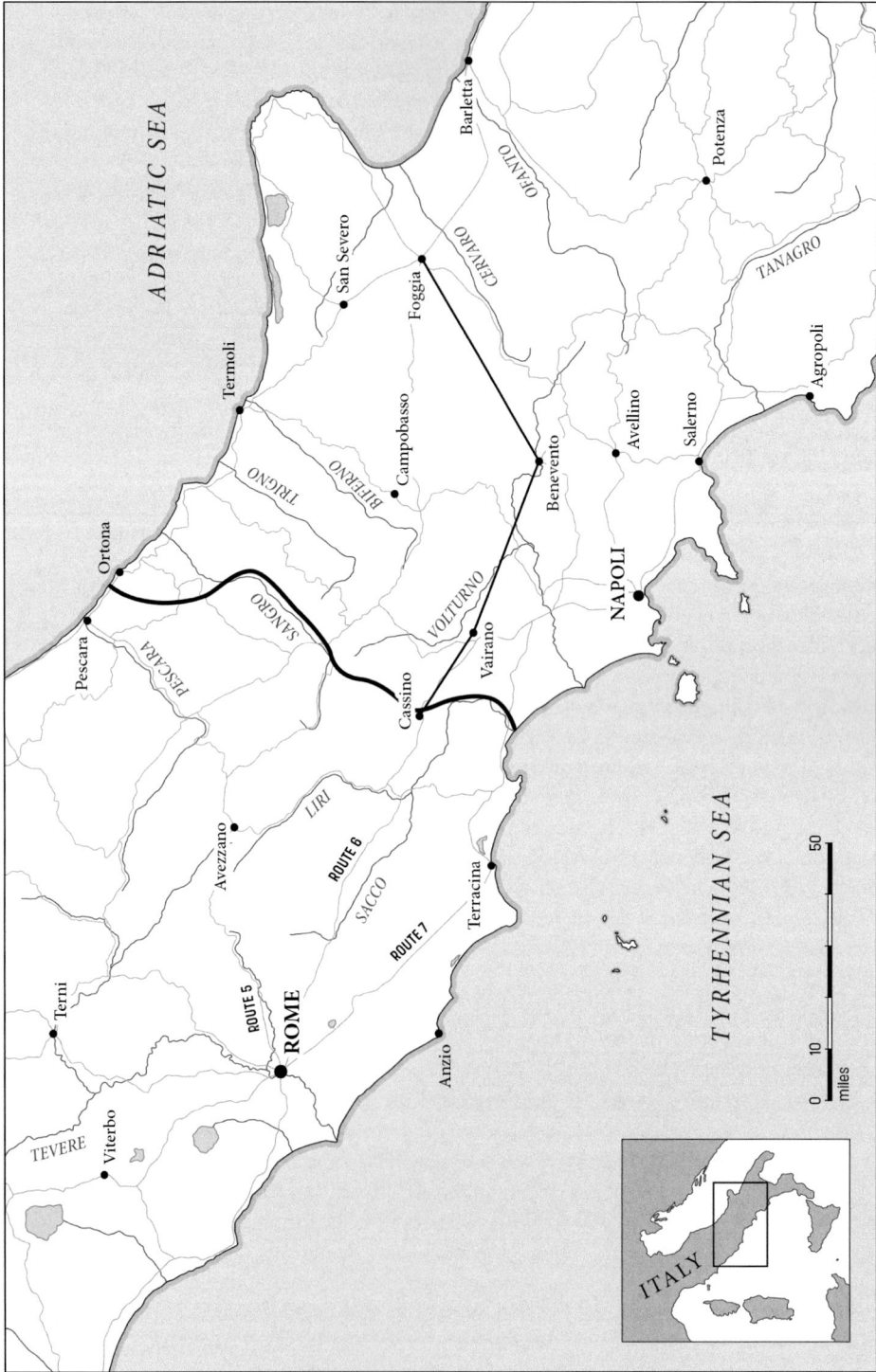

Map 5 The Route.

Commanding Officer of 96th Bomb Squadron and leader of the Monte Cassino attack, Major Bradford Evans lands his B-17 with one engine on fire at the end of his 46th mission. He eventually completed 53 missions. (NARA RG342-FH-000663)

Laid', although fortunately for Bennett and Richardson, they reached their 50-missions on 22 February. Much less fortunate were Mayer, Sussman, Letters and Peters who were all on board over Steyr. All survived and were taken prisoner near Linz. The sergeants were sent to Stalag Luft IV and Mayer to Stalag Luft III, of Great Escape fame. This was Nabers' 15th mission. He would be killed on his 21st, two weeks later, after ditching in the sea near Anzio. Nabers drowned trying to rescue a stricken crew member. Sergeant Rome was not on that mission but was killed in action over Klagenfurt Austria on 19 March when just seven short of his 50.

The intelligence issued to Evans can be judged by the Annex to Operation Order 341, issued by Headquarters 5th Bombardment Wing, A-2 Intelligence Division:

> The target is a huge ancient monastery which the Germans have chosen as a key defense point and have loaded with heavy guns. It is located about 1 mile West of Cassino on a hill and stands out as a perfect target for heavy bombers. Those crew members who have served through the African campaign will remember how we did not bomb mosques because of the religious and humanitarian training all of us have received from our parents and our schools. Because of that and because the Krauts and the Eyties know this they lived in these mosques. They knew we would not bomb these places. The Germans are still capitalizing on this belief in our avoiding churches and hospitals. In the past few days this monastery has accounted for the lives of upwards of 2,000 American boys who felt the same as we do about church property and who paid for it because the Germans do not understand anything human when total war is concerned. This monastery <u>MUST</u> be destroyed and everyone in it as there is no one in it but Germans.[15]

15   Intelligence Annex to Operations Order 341, Headquarters Fifth Wing (US), 14 February 1944.

The report breaks all the basic rules of intelligence analysis and can only be found in Evans' account, where he was highly critical after the event. Like many Abbey documents, the original appears to have disappeared from the archives, and therefore its provenance is unproven. It lacked any objectivity, was based upon opinion with little recourse to facts. It was virtually a 'tabloid newspaper' article rather than a useful intelligence report. How, if genuine, did this report ever manage to be issued? It should be compared with an opinion about the same building from an officer who commanded many of those '2,000 American boys', Walker of the 36th Division:

> This was a valuable historical monument, which should have been preserved. The Germans were not using it and I can see no advantage in destroying it. No tactical advantage will result since the Germans can make as much use of the rubble for observation and gun positions as of the building itself.[16]

The morning of the 15 February was clear and bright with sunrise just after 7:00am, on what Romans would call *una giornata da B-17*.[17] Attacking early in the morning usually resulted in fewer clouds as the sun had not yet warmed the ground sufficiently to allow water to condense. The medium bombers, attacking around lunchtime had much more cloud to deal with. Evans taxied his lead aircraft at 7:00am Greenwich Mean Time, 8:00am local time, just as dawn was breaking, leading his squadron of twelve B-17s. Two aircraft from the 2nd Bombardment Group failed to take off that morning and another turned back, leaving 37 aircraft to complete the mission. It was a short hop, a 'milk run' with no opposition expected or encountered.[18] At precisely 8:10am, he set the engines at 2,500rpm, released the brakes on *Miss Laid* and as the aircraft reached 110-miles per hour he pulled back on the yolk and the B-17 lifted into the air, climbing away from Amendola at 135-miles per hour. The gunners in the aircraft congregated in the nose during take-off to ensure the weight was distributed forward. Each aircraft would take-off at 30-second intervals, making formation on their predecessor until all aircraft were organised.

The formation reached its rendezvous point at 10,000-feet at around 8:30am after sorting itself out into the planned combat formation. The other bombardment groups in the wing followed the same procedures, forming what was known as a *Combat Wave*. These were 35-aircraft from the 97th Bombardment Group, 38 from the 99th Bombardment Group and 32 from the 301st Bombardment Group making a grand total of 142-B-17s over the target, 136 of which dropped their bombs or incendiaries.[19]

The entire formation then set a course for their first course mark, the city of Benevento to the southwest. No enemy air opposition was expected on this mission and the gunners did not carry out their usual 50-calibre machine gun test firing. Reaching Benevento, the aircrews could see Naples directly in front of them with Mount Vesuvius, quietly smouldering before erupting violently a month later. Many Neapolitans believed this to be God's revenge for the attack.[20]

16   Walker diary entry, 16 February 1944 in Blumenson, *Salerno to Cassino*, p.413.
17   Katz, p.219.
18   Evans, p.16-17.
19   AFHRA Reel A6377, Frame 1542. HQ MASAF INTOPS Summary 208 dated 15 February 1944.
20   Gervasi, p.569.

Evans, and all the aircraft behind him conducted a climbing right turn, heading at an altitude of 16,000-feet towards the initial point (IP) at Vairano to the northwest, which it was wing procedure to approach on a heading of 270-degrees magnetic.[21] Before this the 500lb bombs would have been armed and the safety pins presented to the bombardier to confirm arming. The bombs became fully armed about 1,000-feet after leaving the aircraft when a small propeller fitted to the nose of the bomb had turned the requisite number of times. The IP could be clearly identified by the two highways and railroad meeting in the town. Each bombardment group was around six to seven miles long and separated by two minutes. The entire formation was around 25-30-miles long.[22] The IP was that position where the formation is on the heading and at the altitude where the bombs will be delivered and where there is sufficient distance from the target for it to have levelled out and be heading in the right direction, usually between 15 and 20-miles from the target. Manoeuvring after the IP would be minimal unless heavy defences were expected. It was the critical point on any mass bombing attack because if the lead aircraft is out, the remainder would also be off-target. Evans reached the IP at 17,000 feet, the altitude that the bombardier considered optimal for the operation. This altitude was somewhat lower than the wing procedure, which suggested the leader's group should be at 25,000 feet. This is probably due to the proximity of the target and the assessed lack of anti-aircraft defences. The aircraft of the other formations were spread out in altitude between 15,000 and 20,200-feet. At the IP, 'Miss Laid' turned slightly right onto its final attack heading 305-degrees magnetic, with the morning sun behind them. Never fly into the sun, that's where the fighters hide! The formation, now with only six feet separation between wing tips was only 18-miles or eight minutes flying time from its target.

Everything now depended upon Harbin in *Miss Laid*. He had an extremely good 'circular error' record, which made him the best bombardier in the group. He was on his 48th mission, and would complete 51, the last three with Evans, before returning home. Not all were as good as Harbin. The training system for bombardiers had barely half the number of Norden bombsights it required and many of these were older than the M-7 variant in operational use.[23] The training schools were unable to replicate operational conditions and even the best bombardiers would have struggled to hit a target as small as the Abbey. Human error when using the Norden bombsight also contributed to inaccuracy of bombing, as did poor maintenance and variable production quality of the precision instrument.

It was a clear winter's day over Cassino at 9:28am on 15 February 1944 as Evans led his formation in the final stages of the morning's mission. He flew *Miss Laid* at 155-miles per hour and remained straight and level. The B-17 could fly at speeds of up to 250-miles per hour, but the slower speed was generally flown to allow damaged aircraft to remain in formation.[24] Even so, Evans flew his formation even slower than the usual 180-miles per hour. Falling out was often deadly, but not today. Harbin used the Norden M-7 bombsight to calculate the exact moment the bombs should be released, after obtaining the wind speed and drift from the aircraft navigator. He would have prepared his bombsight prior to reaching the IP. This could

21   AFHRA Reel A1592, Headquarters Fifth Bombardment Wing (H), Operations Memorandum dated 11 February 1943.
22   AFHRA Reel A6377, History of Fifteenth Air Force, pp.267-8; Mahoney, p.412.
23   McFarland, p.158.
24   Parris, Kindle Loc 45.

382 Plumes of Smoke

take 35-40-minutes 'chasing the bubble' to level the gyroscopes. Because this was such a short flight, Harbin would have been extremely busy. At the IP he would have followed a standard checklist. His first action would have been to allow the bombs to drop by switching on the bomb racks; he would then have opened the bomb-bay doors. Once *Miss Laid* was flying straight and level at the required bombing altitude, he would have uncaged the gyroscopes. Using the bombsight's knobs, and telescopic sight, he would have found the target and placed the vertical and then the horizontal cross-hairs on the Abbey, having calculated the aircraft's drift and rate. Minute course alterations were relayed to Evans by Harbin through the pilot's directional indicator dial. This was an instrument that many bombardiers found annoying as there was always a time lag between the request for a course alteration and the pilot changing course. Many crews favoured slaving the aircraft automatic pilot, a far more sensitive instrument, to the bombsight.[25] Muirhead used both instruments to refine his attack heading but Evans does not expand upon his preferences. Once the Abbey was static in the cross-hairs he locked the telescope onto the target, slaving the autopilot to the bombsight, and when the telescope sector indicator and the rate sector indicator coincided and when the aircraft reached the correct dropping angle in relation to the Abbey, the Norden released the weapons automatically. Harbin then told Evans 'Bombs away'.[26] His aircraft released its twelve 500lb bombs and as the bombs are released the aircraft lurched slightly at the sudden loss of weight. Evans donned a portable oxygen mask as Nabers took the controls, and rushed from the pilot's seat to the bomb-bay to see the first bombs strike the target area 17,000-feet below. Evans observed *Miss Laid's* bombs strike the ground below about 35-seconds after release. A fraction of a second later he saw the second aircraft's bombs strike the ground. Standard procedure was then for the aircraft to conduct a left-turn from the target to escape and rally.

These were the first of around 1,200 such bombs and 66.5-tons of incendiary bombs. They were followed later by 283 – M65A1- 1,000lb bombs dropped by 89-medium bombers.[27] The attack on the Abbey was not a single coordinated strike, but three separate disconnected actions by the bombardment wings. In fewer than three hours after taking-off, Evans' aircraft and the remainder of the heavy bombers were back on the ground in Foggia, suffering no losses.[28] Later the mediums had similar results. In total that day, 534.5 short tons of bombs and incendiaries were dropped on a single building.[29] The use of 100-pound (they weighed only 65lbs) incendiaries was a rare event, with less than 20-missions in total employing this weapon throughout its period in Italy.[30] The M47A-1 incendiary was filled with white phosphorous. The Abbey was not an obvious target for this weapon, being mainly constructed of stone, which is not flam-

25 Muirhead, pp.117-118.
26 McFarland, p.232.
27 Molony, p.713. Only 89 Medium bombers from 112 reached the target. See Report to the British Official Historian by G.R.M. Hartcup. According to the latter, 23 returned to base without expending ordnance.
28 96th Bombardment Squadron was based at Amendola Airfield, part of the Foggia airfield complex.
29 If 101 B-17 dropped 12 x 500lbs GP bombs this is a total of 1212 weapons dropped or 606,000lbs. That is either 271 long/imperial tons (2240lb), or 303 short tons (2000lb) or 275 metric tonnes (2204lb). 6 x B-17 didn't drop and 35 ac from 97th Bombardment Group dropped 66.6 short tons of incendiaries. 89 x Mediums (47 x B-25 & 42 x B-26) dropped 162 x 1000lb and around 168 x 1000lb weapons respectively or 330,000lbs or 165 short tons. The grand total of tonnage dropped on the Abbey was therefore 534.5 short tons.
30 Mahoney, p.414.

mable. This adds to the likelihood that the aircraft were loaded for another target in Germany or Austria rather than for the Abbey.

When they delivered their ordnance through the morning and early afternoon the watching troops had never witnessed anything like it. The soldiers saw the bombs fall 'like little black stones...the ground all around us shook with gigantic shocks as they exploded.'[31] Buckley, present on the day commented for the *Daily Telegraph*, 'They flew in perfect formation with that arrogant dignity which distinguishes bomber aircraft as they set out upon a sortie. As they passed over the crest of the Monastery Hill small jets of flame and spatters of black earth leaped into the air from the summit.'[32]

Lardner described the atmosphere as people gathered to watch the destruction of the venerable old building:

> A holiday atmosphere prevailed among the soldiers. For almost all the men in Fifth Army, this Tuesday was a rare day off from the war. Soldiers all over the Liri Valley scrambled for positions from which they could watch. Some stood on stone walls, others climbed trees for better views. Observers – soldiers, generals, reporters – were scattered over the slopes of Monte Trocchio, the hill that faced Monte Cassino, three miles away across the valley. A group of doctors and nurses had driven up in jeeps from the hospital in Naples. They settled themselves on Monte Trocchio with a picnic of K-rations, prepared to enjoy the show.[33]

The operational security of the attack was not a consideration as every journalist and medical officer in Naples seemed to know that it was going to happen beforehand. Buckley recalled that the bombing of the Abbey was widely publicized for days before the attack, which is strange as the record shows that only the bad weather in the north allowed the attack to go ahead. The need for the attack and all its potential consequences were, according to Buckley, widely discussed. He offered a tantalising remark that the attack was briefed off the record as 'a political issue,' but expanded no further.[34] Journalist Martha Gellhorn, who watched from Monte Trocchio alongside many in this party atmosphere summed up her feelings as the building was destroyed, 'I watched it sitting on a stone wall and saw the monastery turning into a muddle of dust and heard the big bangs and was absolutely delighted and cheered like all the other fools.'[35]

In between the heavy and medium bombers, came the heavy artillery. Starting at 10:30am, over 300-rounds of 240mm, 155mm, 8-inch and 4.5-inch artillery continued the destruction. The subsequent attack by the medium bombers was also unusual as it was the only time in the weeks before the attack that medium bombers had been used in the Liri Valley. The attack by medium bombers followed those of the heavy bombers in two waves, at around 11:00am and around 1:30pm. Eaker was impressed by the general performance of the medium bombers, especially the 42nd Bombardment Wing. In a report to Arnold in March 1944, he commented favourably concerning his medium bomber wings:

31   Bond, p.116.
32   Christopher Buckley, *The Road To Rome* (London: Hodder and Stoughton, 1945), p.296.
33   Schultz, *Crossing The Rapido*, p.227.
34   Buckley, p.294.
35   Atkinson, p.437.

Cannon has several excellent subordinate Commanders – Webster who commands the 42nd Wing has one of the best organisations I have seen. He is absolutely outstanding. Knapp, who commands the B-25s is rapidly getting his organisation into shape. It is not nearly up to the standard of the 42nd Wing, but Knapp's assumption of command is going to take care of that in time.[36]

Although the weather was often too poor for medium bomber operations in early 1944, the TBF's efforts had mostly been aimed at relieving the German pressure at Anzio. Of the 53 medium bomber missions between 5 February and 24 February 1944, 24 of them were in direct support of the troops at Anzio and another 22 conducted indirect interdiction missions in support of the Anzio force. In the days following the German attack at Anzio on 16 February the entire effort of the TBF was thrown at repulsing the attack. This involved the commitment of 813-bombers and fighter-bombers dropping nearly 1,000-tons of bombs.[37]

Following the attack on the Abbey at around noon on 15 February, Senger sent the following message to his immediate superior, *Generaloberst* von Vietinghoff:

> The 90th Panzer Grenadier Division reports that the Abbey Montecassino was bombed on 15 February at 0930 by 31, at 0940 by 34, and at 1000 by 18 four-motor bombers. Damage still to be determined.
>
> There are numerous civilian refugees in the monastery.
>
> Notice of the attack was given by dropping leaflets with the justification that German machine guns were in the Abbey.
>
> Commander Cassino, Colonel Schultz, Commanding Officer 1st Parachute Regiment, reports in this regard that the troops had not installed arms in the monastery. The divisional order, that in case of extreme danger the severely wounded were to be brought into the monastery, has not been used up to now. Field police have maintained steady watch that no German soldier entered the building. The enemy measures therefore lack any legal basis.[38]

One of Senger's staff officers shouted, 'What the hell is going on?' when explosions rattled the windows of XIV *Panzerkorps'* headquarters at Castelmassimo.[39]

36   AFHRA Reel A6030, History of MAAF, December 1943 – September 1944, Volume 1, Chapter II, p.47.
37   Matthew St Clair, *The Twelfth US Air Force: Tactical and Operational Innovations in the Mediterranean Theater of Operations, 1943-1944* (Maxwell AFB, AL: USAF Air University Press, 2007), p.58.
38   Blumenson, *Salerno to Cassino*, p.413.
39   Trulli, Location 608.

22

The Results

For the bomber crews, the people on the ground are entirely abstract; they are targets. By contrast, the experience of their victims is of the most terrible concrete reality. The sharp juxtaposition of abstract and concrete is a phenomenon unique to aerial bombing.

Yuki Tanaka
Hiroshima Peace Institute[1]

Each day, Norstad prepared a report on the previous day's operations for the signature of General Eaker. This report was dispatched to Spaatz, Portal and Arnold. It was often signed-off by Devers, the senior American, although not on 16 February. We also know that Eaker was in Benghazi, Libya on the morning of 16 February, returning to Italy later that day. There is no dispatch time on the report, so it is unclear whether it was approved by Eaker or whether it was sent by one of his subordinates without him seeing it. It read:

> Report ending 1800 hours 15 February. Strategic attacked communications targets in central Italy and hammered the Monastery at Cassino. Tactical's medium bombers hit the Cassino Monastery, fighters patrolled the Anzio beachhead area, and carried out offensive sweeps. Coastal hit docks and shipping on Northwest Italian coast, carried out offensive recons in central Italy and attacked Radar station on Yugoslav coast in addition to normal patrols. Photo Wing covered targets in Northern and Central Italy.
>
> Strategic details: On the night 14.15 February, 64 Wellingtons dropped 129 tons on Albano/Cecchina/Campoleone roads. No claims or losses. During day 15 February, 142 B-17s dropped 353 tons on Monastery at Cassino with excellent results. No encounters or losses.
>
> Tactical details: During the day, 15 Feb, 70 B-25s and 42 B-26s pounded the Cassino Monastery and Abbey Hill with excellent results. [2]

---

1   Yuki Tanaka, Introduction in Yuki Tanaka and Marilyn B Young (eds.), *Bombing Civilians: A Twentieth Century History* (New York: The New Press, 2009), p.1.

2   AFHRA Iris No 2000902, Daily Operations Report Reference Number AI-333, dated 16 February 1944.

These reports are usually matter-of-fact statements. The use of words such as 'hammered' and 'pounded' is uncommon. Why these verbs were used only on this occasion is unknown but raises the question as to the motive of highlighting the attacks in journalistic terms. Most other reports used fewer pejorative terms such as 'attacked', 'bombed', 'hit' or 'dropped'. The report covering the XII ASC's attack on the Abbey on the 17 February using fighter-bombers reverted to the more usual terminology.[3]

As soon as they landed, bomber crews were expected to immediately complete a thorough debriefing by their respective intelligence staff. The briefing was in the form of the mission report. Evans said that he saw 'Miss Laid's' bombs strike the southwestern portion of the Abbey. For most of the bombers, the crew either did not see the bombs strike the ground or the explosions were either too distant or obscured by dust or debris to see what they hit. According to the B-17 bomb strike photographs, of the maximum of 1,212 bombs that were dropped only around 35 were seen to strike the Abbey.[4] The last heavy bombardment group to drop its bombs was the 97th. The group started with 36-aircraft, but one failed to reach the target, leaving 35 dropping their incendiaries. The 340th Bomb Squadron contributed nine B-17s to the attack, led by the squadron operations officer. The following entry was made in their squadron diary:

> 15 February – Monastery at Cassino Italy, 100-pound (inced) Mission No.238. Our bombs started several fires in the buildings of the Monastery principally in the Large East block. No bursts fell closer than halfway between the town of Cassino and the Monastery. A few fell within about 200 yards of the road to the southeast of the Monastery. The Squadron took off with nine aircraft led by Lt Prather, all of them went over the target.[5]

Their sister squadron, the 341st, commented that the 'Effect of bombing was devastating', but added little further detail. This squadron also contributed nine aircraft.

The following summary report was made after the attack by Fifteenth Air Force:

> 37 B-17s of the 2nd Bomb Group, 35 of the 97th Bomb Group, 38 of the 99th Bomb Group and 32 of the 301st Bomb Group dropped 287 tons of 500lb GP and 66.5 tons of 100lb incendiary bombs between 0925/1003 hours from 15,000/20,200 feet. One A/C returned early, and 6 A/C were over the target but returned bombs to base due to mechanical difficulties. No E/A were seen; all B-17s returned to base. Slight to moderate heavy flak with increasing accuracy was encountered at the target. Bomb strike photos show at least 35 direct hits with 500-pound bombs on Monastery buildings and inner court yards. Damage to the eastern half was particularly extensive due in part to a severe explosion in that area. There were many hits in the outer courtyard and on the small buildings bordering it. The entrance road was cratered in several places and damaging near misses surrounded the building especially on the North side. There were 40/50 direct hits by incendiaries covering the principal buildings and courtyard. The Monastery appears completely demolished.[6]

3   AFHRA Iris No 2000902, Daily Operations Report Reference Number AI-351, dated 18 February 1944.
4   AFHRA Reel A6377, Frame 1542; HQ MASAF INTOPS Summary 208 dated 15 February 1944.
5   AFHRA Reel A0583, Frame 0332; 340th Bombardment Squadron Diary dated February 1944.
6   AFHRA Reel A6377, Frame 1542. HQ MASAF INTOPS Summary 208 dated 15 February 1944.

Post-attack image of the Abbey. Cursory analysis of the building shows damage, but not destruction. The black line shows the frontline on 15 February 1944. (NARA RG342-FH-000155)

The large explosion reported in the eastern part of the building was almost certainly the result of a bomb striking the cave used for ammunition storage. This cave had been occupied since December 1943 and its presence, although not in the Abbey itself, had been a constant source of friction between the Abbot and the Germans. Viewing the newsreels of the attack, a large explosion is evident in the first few air strikes. This explosion is far too large for a single 500lb bomb. It is not clear whether the Germans re-occupied the cave after its occupants were captured or whether the ammunition had been abandoned.

The 89-medium bombers that reached the target came from three bombardment groups, two flying B-25s from the 321st and 340th Bombardment Groups of the 57th Bombardment Wing and one flying B-26s from the 319th Bombardment Group of the 42nd Bombardment Wing. The third bombardment group of the 57th Bombardment Wing, the 17th Bombardment Group did not attack the Abbey because it was obscured by clouds.

B-25 Mitchell from 57th Bombardment Wing of the Mediterranean Allied Tactical Air Force pictured bombing in the vicinity of Cassino on 15 March 1944. (NARA RG342-FH-000166)

The review of medium bomber operations reported that the 340th Bombardment Group, then commanded by Colonel Charles Jones, narrowly missed the Abbey, but that the other two groups scored direct hits.[7] The TBF also received a Consolidated Photographic Interpretation Report of the XII Bomber Command's results.[8] These photographs were from the cameras carried aboard the bombers, rather than images taken from the photo-reconnaissance aircraft of MAPRW. The photography showed the initial attacks of 340th Bombardment Group narrowly missed the Abbey, but the smoke and dust produced by the attack obscured any further analysis. The photo-report did not include any reports on the success of the 321st Bombardment Group. The diaries of the 340th's squadrons make different claims, a common problem.

The 486th Bomb Squadron attacked the Abbey with 12-aircraft. Their diary reported that the attack did not involve the squadron commander, Major Robert Hackney.[9] The aircraft took

7   Medium bomber operations, 1 January--28 August 1944. – World War II Operational Documents – Ike Skelton Combined Arms Research Library (CARL) Digital Library (oclc.org) <https://cgsc. contentdm.oclc.org/digital/collection/p4013coll8/id/1386/rec/1> (accessed 13 October 2023).
8   AFHRA Reel B0999, Frame 0813, HQ TBF PI Report 180 dated 15 February 1944.
9   486th Squadron, War Diary, February 1944.

off from Pompeii airfield at 10:06am and dropped 36 x 1,000lb bombs at 10:59am. The war diary compiled by Lieutenant Clifford Swearingen, claimed most of the bombs landed 'in or near the buildings, causing fires and explosions.' It also made the point that the photographs they took did not reveal much as the Abbey was obscured by smoke.

The 487th Squadron commanded by Major Lewis Parsons, claimed that at least some bombs from their 6-aircraft that took part hit their target.[10] Parsons did not fly with his squadron on the Abbey mission.

> The Abbey on Monte Cassino, which the Germans were shrewdly using as a Fortress was the target for six of our ships today. The formation was over the target at 1059 hours, forming a good pattern and dropped their 23 x 1000 bombs with excellent results, although several bombs fell short of the target and landed on the slopes of the monastery. Several explosions and large fires were observed emitting from the building.[11]

The 488th Bomb Squadron, commanded by Major Randall Cassada, attacked the Abbey with 11-aircraft, dropping 32 x 1,000lb bombs.[12] The formation from this squadron was led by Lieutenant Robert Dean, killed the next day over the Anzio beachhead. In the post-mission report, the squadron assistant S-2, Lieutenant John Murphey, reported that the aircraft released their weapons from an altitude of 10,300-feet, on a heading of 260°, reporting that the 'bomb pattern laid directly through Abbey buildings.' They reported the weather as being 'slightly hazy.' Murphey also stated in the sortie report, written immediately after the aircraft returned that there was an 'explosion in the center of the Monastery as the formation turned off.'[13]

The 489th Bombardment Squadron attacked with six aircraft personally led by its Commanding Officer, Major Alexander Parrish. The intelligence section (S-2) of the squadron wrote a separate special account of the attack, prepared by Lieutenant Jack Casper the assistant S-2.[14] In his report, Casper called the bombing an 'unfortunate necessity of war that has made worldwide headlines.' He then stated the standard reason that the Germans had turned the Abbey into an 'impregnable stronghold.' He quoted a message from XII Bomber Command that reported the medium bombers did most of the damage to the Abbey. The message read: 'Ground observers witnessing attack on Monte Cassino today unanimously agree that of all attacks, including four (4) B-17 Groups, the mediums stole the show. Congratulations to all concerned.'[15]

The diary described in detail the squadron's participation. The six aircraft took off in the first flight of the group at 10:05am, delivered their bombs at 11:00am and landed back at Pompeii airfield at 11:30am. Although the weather was generally fine, the final bomb run encountered some cloud that permitted only a four-second window where the Abbey was visible. Of the 23 x 1,000lb bombs delivered, 21 had very short delays to allow them to get inside the building

10   487th Squadron, War Diary, February 1944; AFHRA Reel A6019 Frame 1044.
11   *487th Bombardment Squadron History* <http://www.reddog1944.com/487thHistoryNARAdocuments. htm#FEB151944> (accessed 17 November 2022).
12   488th Squadron War Diary, February 1944.
13   488th Squadron War Diary, February 1944.
14   Special Account, 489th Bombardment Squadron (M), 340th Bombardment Group (M), Abbey Attack in War Diary 489th Bombardment Squadron, February 1944.
15   489th Squadron War Diary, February 1944.

before detonation. One weapon had a 6-hour delay, and a further weapon had a 12-hour delay. These final two weapons could only have been used to counter any German troops occupying the ruins of the building. They may also have killed civilian rescue parties looking for survivors. This is possibly further evidence that the Allies expected the Abbey to be turned into a defensive strongpoint.

The attack by these medium bombers was also carried out at a much lower altitude than for the heavies, dropping from 10,700 feet. They also flew much faster at 240-knots indicated airspeed. The medium bombers attacked the Abbey from an almost easterly direction on a heading of 255°. The 489th Bomb Squadron report claimed that their bomb pattern fell to the east of the Abbey, although they reported some direct hits along the south edge of the building. They confirmed that their sister squadron, the 488th Bomb Squadron laid a 'perfect pattern on the structure.'[16] Finally, Casper reported that the Squadron encountered no enemy aircraft and only light and distant flak in the vicinity of the small town of Atina.

The second B-25 equipped bombardment group was the 321st Bombardment Group, comprising four bombardment squadrons and commanded by Lieutenant Colonel Charles Olmsted. This bombardment group launched 35-aircraft from their base in the Foggia complex, involving all four squadrons. The aircraft departed between 10:10am and 10:36am, but only 12-aircraft reached the target due to severe icing above their home base. Some aircraft also got lost in the clouds, losing formation and returning to base. No aircraft from the 448th Bombardment Squadron reached the target at all. The successful 12-aircraft delivered their 48 x 1,000lb bombs from between 11-12,500 feet at 11:20am, again from an easterly direction. Five weapons were delivered with a 2-hour fuse delay. The mission report, compiled by Captain Malcolm Haven, the Group Intelligence Officer, reported that the target was partially obscured by cloud and that the aircraft encountered light flak over the target area. One element reported a direct hit, although some bombs were observed striking the surrounding area.

The other medium bomber involved in the mission was the B-26 of the 319th Bombardment Group. A second B-26 group was tasked to attack the Abbey but was forced to a secondary target.[17] This Group had been assigned to XII Bomber Command since 1 January 1944 and was commanded by Colonel Joseph Holzapple.[18] He was absent on temporary duty at the time, and Major Charles Robinson commanded the group in his absence.[19] At the time of the attack this group was based at Decimommanu airfield in Sardinia, where it had been since November 1943 after its move from Tunisia. The 319th flew two waves to the target, at 1:21pm and 1:32pm, claiming hits on the Abbey for both. Poor quality imagery of the results of these strikes shows that possibly half of their 1,000lb bombs struck the building, with the remainder falling nearby. Again, the buildings were obscured by dust and smoke. In their account the group laud the performance of medium bombers and accuse the heavies of ploughing up the countryside. One officer, possibly the acting group commander, when asked to comment about the attack in the pre-mission briefing was reported as saying, 'Gentlemen, let's run those monks out of there.'[20] One gets the feeling from the account of a showcase target, giving the infantry a 'grandstand

---

16   Sortie Report, dated 1145hrs, 15 Feb 1944 in 489th Squadron, War Diary, February 1944.
17   AFHRA Reel B0949, History of 42nd Bombardment Wing (Medium), pp.22-23.
18   Operational Summary, 319th Bombardment Group (M), 42nd Bombardment Wing, Twelfth Air Force, Nov 42 – Dec 44, 10 Jan 45.
19   War Diary, 319th Bombardment Group, Jan-Feb 1944.
20   War Diary, 319th Bombardment Group, Jan-Feb 1944.

view of our bombing'. Cannon sent a message of congratulation to the unit claiming that he and other high-ranking officers said that 'the B-26 job was the best they had ever seen.'[21] Not all agreed. One Engineer from the 36th Infantry Division commented, 'The air jockeys would possibly like to forget that some of their bombs fell ten miles behind us; they also owe me the price of a good bulldozer.'[22]

Despite this supreme quality, the attack was not mentioned in the recommendation for a Presidential Unit Citation for the 42nd Bombardment Wing for 'outstanding performance of duty in action against the enemy from 1 January to 3 May 1944.'[23] The citation, signed by Cannon on 11 May, three months after the attack, lauded the wing's performance at Anzio, bridge-busting, airfield attack and attacks against marshalling yards, but the Abbey bombing was conspicuous by its absence. This is despite the unit history calling the bombing the 'high-spot of the month' and the receipt of personal congratulations from three general officers, Saville, D'Albiac and Cannon himself. Surely, this performance warranted a front and centre mention in the citation? It was not completely expunged, but it was tucked away in the Anzio annex to the citation – the bit no-one reads, signed by the operations officer, not the general. Was this an oversight or a deliberate omission of an act that in the intervening months had become an embarrassment? A couple of months before this, AAF HQ on 31 March had raised concerns about some poor press coverage where the Cassino operations had placed the AAF in an 'embarrassing position of which sensationalists are quite willing to take full advantage.'[24]

The attack on the Abbey and on the town a month later by the medium bombers were the only times that these aircraft were used in the support of ground forces in the Cassino battle. There were no attacks against other German positions around Cassino or the Liri Valley, many of which stubbornly held up the Allied advance in late January and early February 1944. As well as for the heavies, 15 February was a one-off, an event that looked more like a show of force or a publicity stunt than a serious attempt to dislodge the intricate German defensive positions. If this were not the case, why were these positions not attacked again and again until they achieved success? As opposed to one mission against Cassino, medium bombers supported the Anzio beachhead with 24-close support missions from 5-24 February 1944.[25] These were either CAS or battlefield interdiction missions. The multitude of peaks and strongpoints on the massif that held up Allied progress for the next 3-months were not touched again by anything but fighter-bombers. Why?

21   War Diary, 319th Bombardment Group, Jan-Feb 1944.
22   Canciani, p.159.
23   AFHRA Reel B0949, Recommendation for Citation by the President of the United States for the 42nd Bombardment Wing (M) for Outstanding Performance of Duty In Action Against The Enemy, dated 11 May 1944.
24   AFHRA Reel A1372, Memorandum for Colonel Loutzenheiser, Public Relations of the Army Air Forces, dated 31 March 1944.
25   *Medium Bomber Operations 1 Jan–28 Aug 1944* <https://cgsc.contentdm.oclc.org/digital/collection/p4013coll8/id/1386/rec/1> (accessed 11 May 2017).

The mediums. Four x 1000lb bombs head towards the Abbey. The shadow suggests that this is mid-afternoon, so probably the attack of the 42nd Bombardment Wing's B-26s (NARA RG342-FH-000145)

23

What did the Spooks Say?

I think that we had probably better keep quiet about Monte Cassino and let it be forgotten. The evidence on which the order to bomb was given is not satisfactory.

Victor Cavendish-Bentinck
Chairman
Joint Intelligence Sub-Committee
British Cabinet War Office
2 March 1944[1]

If Lewin was correct about Alexander's pre-eminent position regarding the quantity and quality of intelligence, determining who occupied a single building, isolated on a hill in full view should not be a difficult task. Looking at Montecassino today, the Abbey is surrounded by woodland and the hill is verdant. It was not so in 1944. There were no trees, bushes or shrubs to hide behind. The hill had been cleared of everything but a few thorny thickets to allow maximum observation. There was literally nowhere to hide. There was no difference between the intelligence received by Alexander and Clark. Why then was there such a disagreement over the proof of Military Necessity? From numerous sources of information listed in the chapter on proving Military Necessity it would be remarkable if the Germans could occupy the building without Allied intelligence knowing it. Clark stated in a post war interview, 'I knew everyone who went in that abbey.'[2]

What evidence existed that could have influenced the decision that the destruction of the building was a Military Necessity? As has already been stated, ULTRA gave no indication of German occupation.[3] Only two ULTRA messages, decrypted from the *Luftwaffe* RED key mentioned the Abbey. Both were intercepted after the bombing on 19 February, and could therefore have played no part in the decision to attack it.[4] There was no evidence from high-level human intelligence sources from SIS or OSS that the Abbey was being used for military purposes.

1   TNA FO371/43817: Folio 3019, Minute 2 dated 2 March 1944.
2   Hapgood and Richardson, p.169
3   Hinsley et al, p.193fn
4   TNA DEFE 3/140: VLs 6650 and 6655.

General Alexander receives a briefing on photographic reconnaissance from an RAF Flight Lieutenant of MAPRW. (NARA RG342-FH-000090)

There was also no evidence from PR that the Germans were using the Abbey.[5] There were several reports in the days leading up to and following the bombing that included photography of the Abbey. In none of these was any German activity reported by the FAPIC. There were a couple of reports that placed German military activity close to the Abbey. On 27 January 1944, a reconnaissance mission flown by Lt Elliot of the USAAF's 12th Reconnaissance Squadron identified four *Nebelwerfers* on the Via Serpentina, only a few hundred yards from the Abbey. The *Nebelwerfer* was a type of multiple launch rocket system.[6] The monks called it *la raganella*, the noisemaker.[7] Reconnaissance reports from the 3 February, however, noted that the *Nebelwerfers* were no longer there.[8] A tank or self-propelled gun was identified in the same general area on the 28 January and a gun-emplacement was occupied on 10 February. Both

5   Staerck, 72. 4th Indian Division Intelligence Summary No.20 Annex B, 12 February 1944, lists all German defences identified by PR. No position that corresponds with the Abbey is amongst these positions. 4th Indian Division War Diary.
6   TNA AIR 34/407- FAPIC interpretation Reports, General Interpretation Report No. 106 dated 27 January 1944, Frame 12SC.25.4154.
7   Grossetti and Matronola, p.91.
8   TNA AIR 34/40: FAPIC interpretation Reports, dated 3 February 1944, Frame 55B.379.4064.

sightings were several hundred yards from the Abbey.[9] The Abbey was covered on 10 February by a vertical photograph taken by a 12th Reconnaissance Squadron aircraft from 22,500 feet. There was no PR coverage of the Abbey on 13 February due to poor weather.[10] The next sortie in FAPIC's records was General Interpretation Report 120 which occurred on 15 February following the bombing. This sortie was flown late in the afternoon by Lieutenant Carl Dolk of the 12th Reconnaissance Squadron at an altitude of 3,900 feet, indicating that his photography was probably oblique.[11] This was a 'dicing' mission and used cameras of 6- and 12-inch focal lengths. The 12th RS generally carried out PR tasking on behalf of Fifth Army, but Dolk was not the first pilot to photograph the destroyed Abbey. Records show that sometime after 2:30pm, an hour after the last bomb had fallen, Lieutenant Hersey was tasked by the 15th Army Group with taking photographs of the Abbey. He flew at a higher altitude than Dolk, probably 20-30000 feet, and used a 24-inch focal length camera to retrieve three photo frames of the destroyed Abbey. Hersey flew the standard vertical photography mission.[12]

The high-level intelligence sources had not provided evidence that the Abbey was being used for military purposes. Lower-level SIGINT provided nothing more plausible. There were only two instances of 'Y'-Service intercepts that could have pointed towards occupation. One of these was intercepted during the bombing when the message 'bombed out, am clearing out' was sent in the clear.[13] This was far from conclusive evidence of German occupation. As it was concurrent with the actual attack, it did not contribute towards the decision. US strategic bombing, despite claiming precision, was often wildly inaccurate. Around 80 per cent or more of the bombs dropped by the heavy bombers, fell outside the Abbey perimeter and there was no argument that German units were on Monte Cassino. More than half the bombs dropped should have been more than 1,000 feet from the building. Images of the attack vividly illustrated the imprecision and the lack of vegetation on Monte Cassino.

This 'bombed out' message, besides being received during the bombing and therefore irrelevant in the decision to undertake it, could have come from any number of adjacent positions. Photographs of the attack illustrated bombs striking a long way from the Abbey and proved that this communication could have been hundreds of yards away. This message could have come from anywhere. The second message originated on the 3rd *Fallschirmjager* Regiment net. It was initially translated as 'Is the battalion HQ still in the monastery?' This appeared to be crucial evidence until it turned out that Abt, which had been translated as *Abteilung* or battalion referred to Father Diamare. The message actually read 'Is the Abbot in the Monastery?'[14] An article in the *Guardian* newspaper in April 2000 suggested that this was the piece of evidence convincing Allied generals to attack:

9   TNA AIR 34/407: FAPIC interpretation Reports, dated 28 January and 10 February 1944. Frames 55B.365.3116 and 12SC.29.3006.
10   TNA AIR 34/407: FAPIC interpretation Reports, General Interpretation Report No. 119 dated 13 February 1944.
11   TNA AIR 34/407: FAPIC interpretation Reports, General Interpretation Report No 120 dated 15 February 1944, Frame 12PR.412.5008.
12   TNA AIR 34/400: Photo Interpretation Report G51 dated 15 February 1944. Frames 15SG.279.3008, 3009 & 3010.
13   RAF Narrative – The Italian Campaign 1943-1945 – Volume 1, p.287.
14   Hunt, pp.246-7.

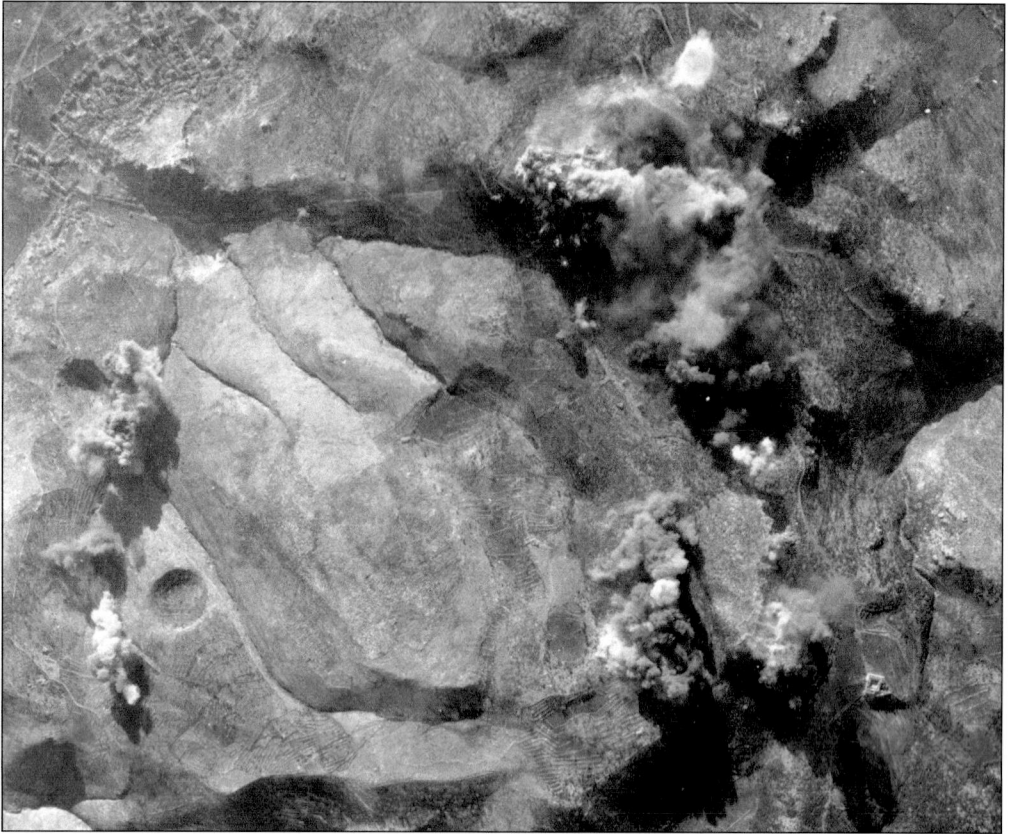

Inaccurate bombing. An image taken by an aircraft from the 2nd Bombardment Group shows that the Abbey has taken several direct hits, but also shows several explosions a great distance from the building. (NARA RG342-FH-000130)

The world's most glorious monastery, at Monte Cassino in Italy, was destroyed during the second world war because of a mistake by a British junior officer, according to new evidence in a book due out this week.

The officer – translating an intercepted radio message – mistook the German word for abbot for a similar word meaning battalion. His version convinced his superiors this meant a German military unit was using the monastery as its command post, in breach of a Vatican agreement which treated it as neutral.

Allied generals ordered a huge bombing attack. Only when the planes were in the air did a British intelligence officer, Colonel David Hunt, recheck the full radio intercept. He found that what it actually said was: 'The abbot is with the monks in the monastery'.

'Tragically, this was discovered too late,' the book says. 'The bombers were already approaching.'[15]

---

15   John Ezard, Error led to Bombing of Monte Cassino, *The Guardian*. <https://www.theguardian.com/world/2000/apr/04/johnezard> (accessed 18 April 2020).

There is a remote possibility that a single piece of intercepted conversation could have mistak-enly led to the attack, however this seems too simplistic. It was rightly dismissed by Italy veteran and military historian John Strawson.[16] The original intercept does not appear to have survived, but it could only be a credible reason if it had arrived prior to the decision being taken; that was probably the afternoon on 13 February 1944 if the timeline concerning the production of propaganda leaflets is a valid guide. If Hunt investigated the intercept as the bombers were in the air, it had probably been received at Alexander's Headquarters in Caserta only a few hours before. Why would Hunt look at something older? What would have made him think to do so? Most importantly, although this incident was detailed in Hunt's book, it is not included in the Supreme Commander's list of 'irrefutable' evidence. The reason for its absence can only be speculative but can be boiled down to two things. It was either not identified or deemed unim-portant at the time or it was left out of the report because it did not support the conclusions that Wilson wished to draw.

This was the total number of relevant 'Y'-intercepts. If the Abbey was a German observation position, its occupants were ineffective at directing German gunners. It would have been diffi-cult to provide forward observation communication via landline alone, due to Allied counter-battery fire that forced units to relocate regularly. Despite reports that German artillery used landline exclusively, connecting and reconnecting a wire every time a gun relocated would be an onerous and hazardous task. Captured German soldiers from a communications section suggested that landline telephone was the preferred means of communication with artillery batteries.[17] The terrain surrounding the Abbey was very difficult and under constant fire. It is a fair assumption that landlines would have been regularly damaged, either requiring constant repair or use of reversionary radio communications. Bond described field telephone lines being severed by German artillery on the massif. The Allied artillery was of greater intensity than that of the Germans and the telephone lines would have been constantly broken. The History of SIGINT in the Second World War states that German artillery units were active on the airwaves and that they were generally the least secure. Medium-frequency radio broadcasts from the artillery regiments of the 15th *Panzer-Grenadier* and 90th *Panzer-Grenadier* Divisions were regularly intercepted.[18] Any communication via radio from inside the Abbey would have been intercepted and geo-located by the extensive Allied Direction Finding or 'goniometry' equipment that provided such excellent service in the counter-battery role. The Germans were aware of this and evidence from a II US Corps prisoner interrogation on 8 February suggested that *Nebelwerfer* units used radio only in emergencies and that they were forbidden to do so unless absolutely necessary.[19] Radio units supporting artillery units were constantly on the move to avoid being hit. Even if the second intercept did give an indication of German occupa-tion, it does seem unusual that it was the only communication from a battalion headquarters, commanding around 600-officers and men, that was intercepted? Why did the Germans use their radios to send this message if they were under orders for radio silence? Landlines cannot be intercepted, and their use would provide no evidence for Allied intelligence.

16   Strawson, p.151.
17   NARA RG338, NND 903618, II Corps Records, Intelligence Summary No 84, dated 9 February 1944, Para 3f (1).
18   HW 41/125, p.104.
19   NARA RG338, NND 903618, II Corps Records, Intelligence Summary No 84, dated 9 February 1944, Para 3f (1).

With the 'Y'-Service drawing a blank, the evidence supporting Military Necessity had to come from captured prisoners, refugees and reports from patrolling near the Abbey. There were 12-pieces of evidence, entitled 'irrefutable' in the AFHQ signal presented by Wilson on 9 March when he was required to report to the British CoS, who acted as executive on behalf of the CCS.[20] The majority of this evidence was extracted from hand-written reports received by signallers from observation points and the POW cage. Jones did not have access to these reports when he compiled his 1949 report for the Cabinet Office.[21] A number of them are relevant to activity around the Abbey (author italics):

041500 Feb 44 – Report No12: A German message *(radio?)* was intercepted by 3 DIA *(FEC)* at 1125hrs. '400m SW of Abbey of M CASSINO, MGs and guns near KANIG *(?)*. Will you be ready to fire?'

042300 Feb 44 – Report No39: Reports a Bn Sgt Major from the 132nd Inf Regt *(44th Inf Div)* walked into the Command Post. Stated that the 3rd Para Bn CP was at Hill 468 *(Albaneta Farm)*, 211th Regt *(90th PG Div)* Bn Command Post 1500m West of Abbey (G830206). Two Bns of the 211th Regt garrisoned in Cassino. 1 bn of Paras arrived at G835207 *(1km W of Abbey)*, 3 tanks behind Abbey. 15th PG Div to S of Cassino. He also reported 'neutral zone' signs around the Abbey.

051450 Feb 44 – Report No18: Report from Wigwag2 *(OP)*: At 1335 Battle reported 10 vehicles seen going West on Highway 6 – 3 pulling guns. Strike reported at 1335 – 7 enemy planes bombed Cairo (G845250). At 1335 Wildwood *(OP)* reported someone is shooting around Monastery, shells landing by walls. At 1415 Wildwood reported direct hit on West side of Monastery, some smoke, looks like its burning. Fire coming from N and NW.

051820 Feb 44 – Report No34: Report to II Corps: Progress very slow – same type of opposition – gave latest positions – Counterbattery quite active in vicinity of CERVARO late afternoon G9219 square – gave details of bombings of CASSINO and CAIRO. Gave details of PW reports 4th Mtn Bn and Bn Sgt Major – Nebelwerfer flashes at G863191 *(West bank of R Gari, S of Cassino)* – 10 vehicles moving West on Highway 6 in vicinity of AQUINO 1335hrs, 3 pulling guns. 2 reports of German arty on Monastery.

051855 Feb 44 – Report No37: Report to 135RCT: One platoon of 10 men reached cave which had been occupied by SP Gun, just below Monastery – came back with 17 PWs. Red *(?)* was unable to go in direction of Abbey since 133RCT's pressure on Hill 193 *(Castle Hill)* pushed Germans West towards Abbey, thus bringing any behind Red's left flank – Red had to change direction to meet attack – Wizard Blue swept around 593 and 569 on West side due to attack toward Abbey. Met heavy small arms fire from Hill 447 would not dos [sic] – Blue has now pulled back and is going to establish physical contact with Red. Red is along Hills 450, 445 and 303. *(c400m N of Abbey)*. Blue has received considerable mortar from West (S LUCIA). White *(?)* quiet in same position.

052135 Feb 44 – Report No47: Report to 135RCT: 13 Prisoners of War taken from cave in the vicinity of Monastery. 11 from 71 Werfer Regt- 8 Battery, 1 from 3rd Bn 361st Inf Regt *(90th PG Div)*, 1 from 8th Bn 132nd Inf Regt *(44th Inf Div)*. Captured at G846209

20   Message from General Wilson to British Chiefs of Staff, MEDCOS 64, 9 March 1944.
21   TNA CAB 106/699, p.22.

(Near road on N Wall of Abbey). Were half asleep in bunkers when surprised. Moved into position last night possibly to set up OP but orders were vague on this point.

060900 Feb 44 – Report No77: Report to 135RCT: Wizard Blue *(?)* received MG fire from bunkers at base of Abbey between road and Abbey – small arms fire coming from Hill 193.

061830 Feb 44 – Report No19: Report to 135RCT: Blue down in platoon receiving fire from bunkers West of Abbey. Bunkers are on West side of Monastery Hill and just South of where it says Abbey de Monte Cassino. White is on Hill 593 *(1.2km NW of Abbey)* and fired into Hill 468 *(Albaneta Farm, 1.3km NW of Abbey)*. Blue is quiet – little mortar and arty fire. Nothing in the Abbey but enemy is on slope just short of Abbey.

061925 Feb 44 – Report No22: Report from Lt Klapper at PW Cage: 2 PWs say they were building an OP on East slope of road, 100yds away from Abbey which they didn't know was neutral. 3 Para Regt is generally NW of Abbey at Monte Cassino to another small Abbey *(Albaneta Farm?)* which is Bn CP. SE of Bn CP is 12 Company, 9 Company then 10 Company. 11 Company is unlocated. 9 Company counterattack night of 4th Feb in direction of Hill 569 *(1km NW of Abbey)*.

061945 Feb 44 – Report No23: Report from Lt Heid at PW Cage: PW from 9th Co Para Regt arrived night before last. Strength 30-40 men, 10 Light MG. Position: Small Abbey at G833217 *(Albaneta Farm)*. Behind this Abbey in draw are mortars of 12 Company. At this Abbey is one squad of 12 Company with Heavy MG. On their right is 9 Company, then 11 Company (in line last night) and then 10 Company in line 1st Feb. Some arty along Highway 6 at G822203 *(Close to Church of Santa Scolastica)* and further along is trail they use to go into line. Abbey is used as aid station.

080540 Feb 44 – Report No40: From 168RCT: Red flares went up just South of Abbey. *(II Corps Intel Summary suggests Red Flares indicate 'enemy is attacking'.)*

081516 Feb 44 – Report No6: From MP Cage: Total PWs from 30 Jan – 8 Feb – 680.

081835 Feb 44 – Report No20: From Winnies(?): PW from 9 Company 361st Infantry Regt *(90th PG Division)*. Claim Bn aid station on Massa Albanetta and Bn CP between there and Hill 569.

082350 Feb 44 – Report No39: From Lt Klapper PW Cage: PW from 9 Company 361st Infantry Regt *(90th PG Division)*. Stated that Bn aid station was in Abbey *(Albaneta Farm? See Report 23 above)*.

091045 Feb 44 – Report No63: From Wisecrack *(OP)*: 6rds of Nebelwerfer at 1030 fell on Abbey. 250 yds from OP#2. 10rds of red smoke launched 400yds East of Abbey.

091250 Feb 44 – Report No2: OP reported small arms fire coming from inside Abbey during our air raid this morning. Not confirmed.

091705 Feb 44 – Report No13: From Speedy (34th Div): At 1300hrs 2 Bn 135 Inf received counterattack from the vicinity of Hill 468 *(Albaneta Farm)* 135 is getting continuous pressure along Hill 593 which started last night. Counterattack consisted of fire and movement, mortar and automatic weapons fire. 133RCT gained 1 building or so and 1 or 2 PWs. They are not being pushed back and are not being counterattacked. Situation the same. 168 Inf – situation same. Receiving considerable Nebelwerfer, mortar and arty fire. We are not any closer to Abbey and have nothing new as whether Germans are using Abbey.

100130 Feb 44 – Report No26: From 168RCT: 4 Green flares from vicinity of the Abbey.

100315 Feb 44 – Report No28: From Wigwag OP: Liberty observed 1 x White Flare at 0306hrs and 1 green flare 1 minute later over Abbey.

101555 Feb 44 – Report No8: From Wigwag: 4 white flares went up just behind the Monastery, 2 at a time at 1552hrs.

102050 Feb 44 – Report No16: From Wisecrack: OP reports 1 Amber flare on Monastery Hill.

121030 Feb 44 – Report No49: From Widespread 2: Our position near barracks got hell of shelling early this morning, coming from back of Cairo…Made holes as big as 500lb bombs and fragments 2½ feet long were dug out. Also a lot of 88mm coming from behind Abbey.

121412 Feb 44 – Report No7: From Speedy (34th Div) Status quo, arty now let up. Pressure is still on along our front. Believe we took a few PWs around Cassino. 36 Div took PWs from 1,2,4 Companies of 1 Flieger (Para) Regt in general vicinity of Hill 593 *(1200m NW of Abbey)*. They were brought in 2-4 days ago … to reinforce weak spots.

122300 Feb 44 – Report No47: From Wigwag 2: Windy B OP at G88851827) just observed 3 green flares go up from near the Abbey. *(OP on NW of Monte Trocchio, 5km from Abbey)*.

122305 Feb 44 – Report No48: From Wisdom 2: OP at G890184 reports 9 green flares just went up in vicinity of Abbey. *(OP on NW of Monte Trocchio, 5km from Abbey)*.

131455 Feb 44 – Report No8: From Wizard 6: 16 airbursts were seen over dome of Abbey 12 feet up. Airbursts also over Cairo and Castellone.

131945 Feb 44 – Report No25: Willow and Wisdom at 1925 reported that their OPs saw a white flare go up from behind Abbey.

132250 Feb 44 – Report No26: From Wigwag 2: OPs report 2 white, and 1 amber flare just went up from rear of Abbey.

142120 Feb 44 – Report No21: From Wisecrack: 5 amber, 1 red flare 300yds N of Abbey. No evidence of any reaction.

150410 Feb 44 – Report No31: From 34th Div Arty: Willow OP reports a yellow flare just now over Abbey.

151025 Feb 44 – Report No39: From Wigwag: 1020hrs Bn OP *(Wisdom)* reports 50 to 100 enemy coming out of South end of Monastery – taking them under fire.

151040 Feb 44 – Report No42: From Wigwag: 1025hrs – Windy OP – another flare behind Hill 593. 1030hrs – Wisdom 6 – at least 200 Germans have come out of Monastery – firing on them.

151200 Feb 44 – Report No47: From Wigwag: All activity also after 2nd group of planes dropped bombs, saw 9 Germans coming out of center down at South end of Monastery – 1 was carrying a rifle – 4 carried packs and 4 carried nothing. They stopped at small building to South. Haven't come out yet.[22]

These reports and the corps intelligence summaries provided a vivid first-hand record of the observed activity around the Abbey in the days leading up to its destruction. It is strange, however, that despite the momentous events happening on the morning of 15 February 1944,

---

22　NARA RG407, NND 735017, Box 8151 – WWII Operations Reports, 1940-48 34th Infantry Division, 334-2.4 Jan 1944 to 334-2.4 Feb 1944.

there are no reports in the US archives between just after 4:00am and 10:20am or between 11:00am and 1:30pm when the medium bombers attacked. It is incredible that the Monte Trocchio OPs reported nothing during these periods. The defences around the Abbey on 6 February were reported as being heavy and a tank may have been placed on the approaches to the Abbey on the Via Serpentina.[23] On 7 February, US II Corps reported pillboxes constructed close to the Abbey.[24] In its summary for 8 February, US II Corps intelligence mentioned strong defensive positions circling the Abbey and stubborn resistance.[25] An advance towards the Abbey by American troops received heavy mortar fire, although the source of the fire was not specified. The next day they recorded sniper and machine-gun activity on the slopes of Monastery Hill alongside flares directly over the Abbey.[26]

The 135th Regiment's official account was typical. On 3 February its 2nd Battalion observed large numbers of enemy gathering for a counter-attack and that 'Cannon Company observers expose themselves to great peril to direct fire upon the enemy.'[27] On 4 February, a patrol was despatched to ask the monks whether there were any Germans inside. They returned having failed to reach their objective.[28] In the 135th Regiment at least, there was uncertainty of who occupied the building. Otherwise, why would they send a patrol on such a hazardous mission to discover information already known? The next day a patrol comprising a sergeant and 14-riflemen reached a cave directly below the walls. This patrol captured between 14 and 17-German soldiers in the cave dug below the kitchen on the east side of the Abbey.[29] These were the same captured Germans reported in Reports 37 and 47 that were received in the early evening of 5 February, although the number varies. In addition to the infantry, artillery observation positions surrounded Monte Cassino and spotter aircraft were used regularly to observe the battlefield.

23   NARA RG338, NND 903618, II Corps Records, Intelligence Summary No 81, dated 6 February 1944, Para 2a (1).
24   NARA RG338, NND 903618, II Corps Records, Intelligence Summary No 83, dated 8 February 1944, Para 2a (1).
25   NARA RG338, NND 903618, II Corps Records, Intelligence Summary No 84, dated 9 February 1944, Para 2a (1).
26   NARA RG338, NND 903618, II Corps Records, Intelligence Summary No 85, dated 10 February 1944, Para 2b (6) a.
27   Breit, 'Phase VIII 135th Infantry Regiment History' pp.20-21.
28   Breit, 'Phase VIII 135th Infantry Regiment History' p.23.
29   Breit, 'Phase VIII 135th Infantry Regiment History' p.24.

24

Irrefutable Evidence

I'd listen to various intelligence guys, and I'd say: 'Tell me exactly where you got your information.'
And after I'd ask this question about six times, I never got a satisfactory answer.
Brigadier-General Gordon P. Saville
Acting Commanding General XII Air Support Command, February 1944
On the occupancy of Monte Cassino[1]

As the weeks passed, evidence that the Germans had made military use of the Abbey remained absent. It was not certain that no Germans were in the Abbey, but as Fifth Army Chief Intelligence Officer, Colonel Howard, pointed out, any occupation could only be by a small number of Germans, perhaps conducting observation. There was no evidence of the Abbey being strongly held by a formation capable of defending it against a brigade-sized attack. An observation position would have been a handful of men at most, with personal weapons, perhaps a few grenades, a pair of binoculars and a field telephone or possibly a VHF radio. They would not have had any crew-served weapons such as the MG-42 machine gun. There was certainty that several hundred Italian civilians took refuge within the building alongside a small number of monks. The weight of firepower from German positions within the Abbey would have been very light, far less than what it became afterwards. A few men with rifles do not constitute a 'fortress', a description often used. Their presence would have been insignificant. It was interlocking and mutually supporting German positions on the heights around the Abbey, all of which were ignored by the air planners, that prevented the Americans, the Indians and lastly the Poles from breaching the *Gustav* Line.

Key individuals held the view, supported by analysis of intelligence and diplomatic reporting, that the Abbey was not being used by the Germans at all. Howard stated, 'I had sufficient information to indicate that the Abbey was not being used by the Germans for defensive purposes. I told them there was no reason whatsoever to bomb it.'[2] This emphatic statement was supported by all senior US Army commanders, as well as the intelligence chief of US II Corps, Colonel Mercer Walter, the Deputy Commander of 34th Division, Brigadier General Frederick Butler

---

1   AFHRA Iris NO 1103217, Interview with Major General Gordon Saville, San Antonio, Texas, dated
      9 February 1970, p.46.
2   Hapgood and Richardson, p.168.

and the commander of 168th Infantry, Colonel Mark Boatner. Saville, the commander of the USAAF's XII ASC, thought that 'I think we did it wrong at Monte Cassino,'[3] yet all this testimony, available in archives, remained unused by British authors or by the British Supreme Commander in his report. The views of American officers, who had been immersed in the battle for weeks, can be summed up by Clark, 'I say that the bombing of the Abbey which sat high on the hill southwest of Cassino, was a mistake – and I say it with the full knowledge of the controversy that has raged around this episode.'[4] He also observed:

> I say now that there is irrefutable evidence that no German soldier, except emissaries, was ever inside the Monastery for purposes other than to take care of the sick or to sightsee – and after the battle started, they didn't have a chance for any sightseeing. Not only was the bombing of the Abbey an unnecessary psychological mistake in the propaganda field, but it was a tactical military mistake of the first magnitude. It only made our job more difficult, more costly in terms of men, machines and time.[5]

Many of these officers were beholden to Clark for their careers. Howard, for example, had been a family friend of the Clarks since before the war, but their views cannot be brushed aside.[6]

Despite all this, the building was destroyed. Shortly afterwards, questions began to be asked of the military authorities in Italy as to why? Not surprisingly, this started with German propaganda, accusing the Allies of cultural vandalism. The Vatican authorities soon started to ask some very awkward questions of the British and American diplomatic representatives. As these questions seeped back to their respective capitals, British Foreign Office officials embarked on a damage limitation project. They demanded answers from their military colleagues in the War Office and Cabinet Office, and to see the evidence that justified the attack. After significant delays the following was provided by Wilson's staff nearly three weeks later. The day before this was despatched a note from Major General Lowell Rooks, the US Deputy Chief of Staff to Wilson wrote to AFHQ senior staff, saying, 'The message is to be so drafted that there is no indication of doubt as to the Germans occupying the Abbey.'[7] Not surprisingly, those that compiled the evidence obliged:

THIS IS MEDCOS 64 In reply to COSMED 51 OZ1218 March 4.

1.   Prior to bombing CASSINO ABBEY following information received concerning GERMAN occupation. Reports emanate from II Corps except where otherwise stated.

A.   6 February. Reported that tank had been dug in to cover approaches to ABBEY. Enemy defences extremely well prepared and bunkers dug in also to cover ABBEY approaches.

---

3   AFHRA Iris NO 1103217, Interview with Major General Gordon Saville, San Antonio, Texas, dated 9 February 1970, p.46.
4   Clark, p.249.
5   Clark, p.249.
6   Maurine Clark, pp.74-5.
7   TNA CAB 106/699: AFHQ Office of the Chief of Staff, Minutes of the Commander-in-Chief's Meeting, dated 8 March 1944.

B.   8 February. Enemy resistance to our attack in CASSINO ABBEY area extremely severe. Small arms and machine gun fire received from carefully sited emplacements in town and very close to ABBEY.

C.   8 February. Pillboxes reported built very close to ABBEY.

D.   9 February. Italian civilian stated he left ABBEY area on 7 February and had frequently been in ABBEY during last month. Reported there were 30 machine guns and approximately 80 soldiers in the building.

E.   9 February. PW staff Sergeant from 3rd Bn 132nd Inf Regt states its HQ and OP Para Bn and Bn Aid Station were all together in the ABBEY.

F.   9 February. Enemy resistance particularly in area surrounding ABBEY stubborn. Strong positions encircling ABBEY were reported.

G.   10 February. Battalion Commander 133rd US Inf Regt reported telescope in middle row of windows on east face ABBEY. Enemy moving around base of building on north side.

H.   10 February. Heavy enemy MG mortar fire had been received on slightest movement of our troops in vicinity of ABBEY.

I.   At 0730A on 16 Feb considerable small arms fire on MONASTERY HILL reported. At 2200A intense MG fire reported coming from ABBEY.

J.   February 16. Destruction of foliage by bombing revealed many trenches, weapon pits and entrances to dugouts in the area of the ABBEY.

K.   On 17 February civilian who left ABBEY on 15 February reported that about 100 metres northeast of mule trail which runs from ABBEY to G.8362133 [sic] were MG emplacements in zigzag formation at 50 metres intervals from G842209 to 838213.

L.   On 18 February MG fire out of north wall of ABBEY.

2.   There is no doubt that the CASSINO ABBEY was part of the GERMAN main defensive position with a commanding position controlling the LIRI VALLEY GAP. If our attacks were to succeed it was necessary to neutralise this area. In these circumstances and with the information available concerning GERMAN dispositions in the ABBEY locality the air attack was fully justified.

3.   Consider that the information in paragraph 1 should not be given to the VATICAN since the GERMANS might well try to produce faked evidence controverting it.

4.   As similar instances may arise in the future suggest that we should confine our statement to the fact that the military authorities on the spot have irrefutable evidence that the CASSINO ABBEY was part of the main GERMAN defensive line.

All this evidence, authorised by AFHQ's Deputy G-2, Colonel Charles Sloane Jr, originated with US II Corps. In his letter Wilson claimed that these provided 'irrefutable evidence that the Cassino Abbey was part of the main German Defensive line.'[8] Sloan's immediate superior,

8   TNA CAB 106/699: MEDCOS 64, dated 9 March 1944.

Brigadier Strong, who had remained in charge of intelligence after Eisenhower's departure, added no confidence to the supposed irrefutable when he stated in his 1969 memoirs:

> The monastery was the subject of a major controversy concerning whether it was occupied by German troops and therefore a target for air attack. Whatever the truth about this matter, the building dominated the whole countryside, and I could understand the reasons why some Allied commanders were demanding its destruction.[9]

The responsibility for producing the evidence from intelligence was Strong's. Why did he therefore say, 'whatever the truth?' Surely, his irrefutable evidence is the truth? From the above, although written much later, the evidence did not hold much water inside Wilson's headquarters either.

It may add to clarity by looking closely at the 'irrefutable'. Each piece of evidence shall be covered in turn:

> *6 February. Reported that tank had been dug in to cover approaches to ABBEY. Enemy defences extremely well prepared and bunkers dug in also to cover ABBEY approaches.*
> A.   The evidence of German tanks covering the approach to the Abbey did not prove that the building was being used. The attack on 15 February was not against the tanks.

> *8 February. Enemy resistance to our attack in CASSINO ABBEY area extremely severe. Small arms and machine gun fire received from carefully sited emplacements in town and very close to ABBEY.*
> B.   The resistance to the attack came from emplacements close to the Abbey and from Cassino town. There was no proof that defenders were sited inside the Abbey.

> *8 February. Pillboxes reported built very close to ABBEY.*
> C.   Pillboxes close to the Abbey are not inside the Abbey.

> *9 February. Italian civilian stated he left ABBEY area on 7 February and had frequently been in ABBEY during last month. Reported there were 30-machine guns and approximately 80-soldiers in the building.*
> D.   This appears as credible evidence of Germans using the Abbey. It came from an Italian civilian who, on 9 February, told interrogators that he left the Abbey on 7 February having been in the building frequently.[10] This is possibly the person whom the Abbot called 'an American spy' in a conversation with an AFHQ liaison officer.[11] In a report to the Director Military Intelligence at the British War Office, AFHQ dismissed civilian statements as 'conflicting and unreliable.'[12] This evaluation of the reliability of civilian reporting matches conflicting reporting in 4th Indian Division

9   Strong, p.166.
10   NARA RG338, NND 903618, II Corps Records, Intelligence Summary No. 84, dated 9 February 1944, Para 3k.
11   TNA WO 204/5735: Advanced Allied Force Headquarters Liaison Section, MONTE CASSINO dated 7 January 1946.
12   MI14/11/38/44 German Troops at MONTE CASSINO Abbey, 25 February 1944

Intelligence Summaries.[13] This report did not appear in 4th Indian Division's intelligence Summary until late on 14 February, three days after the initial bombing request. It was first reported by II US Corps on 9 February.[14] It could therefore have played no part in the decision for the attack, regardless of whether commanders chose to believe single-source unverified intelligence because II Corps did not make the request. Before Wilson's report was sent to London, Howard received another report on 28 February concerning four Italian women who were in the Abbey when it was bombed. Part of the testimony read:

We did not see any guns within the Abbey or any German soldiers except two German officers who came up now and again to treat wounded civilians. However, on our way up to the Abbey, we saw two light tanks on the road that leads to the top of the mountain about 300 metres from the Abbey, and a mortar was set up behind a funicular station at the foot.[15]

These women had been around the Abbey, either inside or outside, since 29 January and were detained by Indian soldiers early on 16 February. Their account directly contradicted Evidence D, yet it was not used by Wilson in his list of 'Irrefutable Evidence.' This evidence was no more valid, but it appears some evidence was more irrefutable than other evidence. The ladies' evidence was also backed up by the Abbot and monks, whereas the Italian civilian evidence was not. Interviews made by French journalist Pierre Ichac in mid-March 1944 confirmed their story.[16] His article, based on these interviews, was suppressed by the Fifth Army Chief of Staff, Alfred Gruenther, he claims.[17]

9 February. PW staff Sergeant from 3rd Bn 132nd Inf Regt states its HQ and OP Para Bn and Bn Aid Station were all together in the ABBEY.

E.   Again, superficially, this offers highly substantive evidence that first appeared in the 9 February New Zealand Corps Intelligence Summary. They issued the following text:

PW, a S/Sgt, HQ Coy III/132 states that HQ III/132 and OP Para Bn and RAP are all together in the Abbey on Point 468(G8321) marked with a Red Cross flag. He states that from 15-30 Jan, the HQ III Bn (Bn UREIG) and one platoon 13 Coy with 2 x 75mm inf how in position were in the same house with the RAP at G.845238.[18]

13   See 4th Indian Division Intelligence Summaries 25, 26 and 27, 15, 16 and 18 February 1944.
14   4th Indian Division Intelligence Summary No.25, 14 February 1944.
15   TNA CAB 106/699: 70. MAAF Microfilm, Held by Air Historical Branch – 28 February 1944 Memo for Colonel Howard.
16   I BOMBARDAMENTI DI MONTECASSINO E CASSINO IN UNA TESTIMONIANZA DEL MARZO 1944 <http://www.dalvolturnoacassino.it/asp/doc.asp?id=226> (accessed 20 April 2022).
17   Ichac, 161.
18   Prisoner of War, Staff Sergeant, Headquarters Company 3rd Battalion/132nd Regiment states that Headquarters 3rd Battalion/132nd Regiment and Observation Position, *Fallschirmjager* Battalion and Regimental Aid Post are all together in the Abbey on Point 468 (G8321) marked with a Red Cross flag. He states that from 15-30 January, the Headquarters 3rd Battalion (Battalion UREIG) and one platoon 13 Company with 2 x 75mm infantry howitzers in position were in the same house with the Regimental Aid Post at G.845238.

Occupation of this building at Albaneta (Point 468), about a mile from the Abbey was cited by Wilson's staff as 'irrefutable evidence' that the Abbey was occupied by Germans. (Author)

Although it appears to contain some compelling evidence, referring specifically to the Abbey, this report cannot stand basic analytical scrutiny. This incident was reported by 34th Division POW cage on 4 February but the II US Corps intelligence summary that initially reported this incident was issued on 9 February. No Red Cross flag had ever been observed flying from the Abbey. It was labelled as a 'violation of the GENEVA Convention.'[19] The 'irrefutable evidence' message did not include this part of the original report. According to the tasking order issued to Evans, the location of the Abbey is G.843209 and not G.8321 which is two-thirds of a mile to the north-west. The 5th Bombardment Wing position is supported by the original AFHQ message dated 4 November that placed the Abbey on the list of protected locations. The 4th Indian Division Proposed Plan for Air Bombardment, Monte Cassino dated 14 February gave the location of the Abbey as G.84472063, about 1000-feet south-east of the USAAF Fifteenth Air Force location and even further away from the prisoner of war's position. This location also tallied with that being used by the New Zealand Corps which an AHB history quoted as G.844208 and the USAAF Twelfth Air Force position, G.844210.[20] All these positions were close to the Abbey buildings whose centre position from a 1944 map is G.845207. The prisoner was from the 132nd Regiment, which was part of 44th Infantry Division.[21] This division had handed over responsibility for the Abbey to paratroopers from *Kampfgruppe* Schultz two days previously.

19   NARA RG338, NND 903618, II Corps Records, Intelligence Summary No 84, dated 9 February 1944, Para 3f (3).
20   TNA AIR 23/6598 Air Historical Branch History of NZ Corps Operations, 1949 <http://57thbombwing.com/340th_History/487th_History/transcripts/340th_Missions.pdf> (accessed 24 September 2021).
21   Fifth Army History Part IV, p.227.

The Abbey was on Point 516 and not Point 468. The prisoner's description matched another stubborn battlefield feature, known to the Allies as Albaneta Farm (G.832217) situated north-west of the Abbey. An additional source could be traced back to the evening of 6 February when messages were received from the POW cage that called Albaneta Farm 'a small Abbey' that was fortified and occupied by 30-40-men from 1st *Fallschirmjager* Division and was a battalion command post.[22] On 12 February, US II Corps intelligence stated the following about the building on Point 468:

It is reported that the building on Hill 468 (G832217) has been heavily fortified and that the enemy is employing automatic weapons and mortars from within the building. Last night hand-grenades and automatic weapons were reported used in close-in fighting.[23]

US II Corps intelligence summaries in the days prior to the bombing often associated Point 468 with the 'Monastery' or 'Abbey'.[24] This mistake appeared to have been carried through to Wilson's report. Was it possible that, as incredulous as it seems, the occupation of the Abbey and Albaneta Farm were mixed-up due to the exhausted division getting its hill heights wrong. During the handover between the tired Americans and new Indian divisions, the Indians could have assumed that the Americans were talking about Montecassino Abbey when in fact they were discussing 'the small Abbey' on Point 468? This was a possibility, but it will be never certainly known what was discussed by tired, cold men over their bird tables in divisional and regimental command posts as they handed over their duties to men fresh into the battle and uncertain of the ground and the situation. Did the Indians interpret the fortifications on Albaneta Farm, reported as 'the Abbey' by US observation posts as being the actual Abbey? The request for the bombing of the Abbey was initiated on 11 February, shortly after the senior Indian officers returned from their reconnaissance. This information was not reported until its Intelligence Summary No.22 on 12 February, after the initial Indian request to bomb the Abbey, so it may not have played a part in the decision-making process, although it was available before the decision was taken. It was not placed as a prominent feature in the Indian Intelligence report and was tucked away in Part 2.[25] It should be noted that in the same summary, and with greater prominence, they reported that enemy dispositions in the Abbey area are 'not altogether clear'.[26] Which Abbey they were referring to was also not clear.

9 February. Enemy resistance particularly in area surrounding ABBEY stubborn. Strong positions encircling ABBEY were reported.
F.   Positions surrounding or encircling the Abbey were not inside the Abbey.

22   NARA RG407, NND 735017, Box 8151 – WWII Operations Reports, 1940-48 34th Infantry Division, 334-2.4 Jan 1944 to 334-2.4 Feb 1944. Message 22 from Lt Klapper at PW cage, 061925 February 1944 and Message 23 from Lt Heid at PW Cage, 061945 February 1944.
23   NARA RG338, NND 903618, II Corps Records, Intelligence Summary No 87, dated 12 February 1944, Para 2a (1).
24   For Example: NARA RG338, NND 903618, II Corps Records, Intelligence Summary No 88, dated 13 February 1944, Para 6.
25   4th Indian Division Intelligence Summary No.22, 12 February 1944.
26   4th Indian Division Intelligence Summary No.22, 12 February 1944.

10 February. Battalion Commander 133rd US Inf Regt reported telescope in middle row of windows on east face ABBEY. Enemy moving around base of building on north side.

G.   This was the only evidence that involved direct observation. On 10 February an American battalion commander was reported to have observed a telescope in a window on the eastern face of the Abbey. The actual observation, according to the US II Corps Intelligence Summary of 10 February was on 7 February:

> Battalion CO, 133 Inf reports seeing a scope in middle row of windows on E face of ABBEY DI MONTE CASSINO at 070800A. This window had no pane and was covered by a blanket. On the same date, this officer observed a scope in upper right window on E face of Abbey. Enemy have been observed moving around the base of the building on the N side.[27]

This commander was from the 133rd RCT, probably either the CO of 1st or 3rd Battalion. The third battalion in the division, the 100th *'Nisei'* had been moved into reserve on 6 February and was located between the barracks and Caira village, not returning to regimental duty until after the report. Unlike the other regiments, the 133rd was not deployed on the Cassino massif, but to the north of the town below the Abbey on the road to the village of Caira. Its task was to capture Cassino town. Despite supporting the theory that the Germans used the Abbey for observation, the officer offered no evidence that a German was on the other end of the telescope. He was also the only observer of this event, and he had already seen another scope in another window! Although the exact location of the officer was not specified, if he were in the northern part of Cassino along the Via Caira he could not have been closer to the Abbey walls than 1500-yards on 7 February. By early 8 February the 1st Battalion was approaching the northern slope of Point 193 (Castle Hill), about 1300-yards from the Abbey. They remained in that same rough location as of 11 February. The 3rd Battalion, was on the left flank of the regimental advance, reaching the northern edge of the town early on 8 February, around a mile from the eastern wall of the Abbey. Spotting a small telescope from that distance was improbable, and why was only one of the two observations used? Standing at a spot along Via Caira roughly where this observation was said to have been made, it is difficult to see, even with binoculars, and it would have been impossible to positively identify a telescope in the Abbey windows.

10 February. Heavy enemy MG mortar fire had been received on slightest movement of our troops in vicinity of ABBEY.

H.   The heavy MG fire against US troops, were not from German troops inside the Abbey.

At 0730A on 16 Feb considerable small arms fire on MONASTERY HILL reported. At 2200A intense MG fire reported coming from ABBEY.

I.   This is irrefutable evidence. The Germans were using the Abbey as a defensive position, possibly by late on 16 February. It was after the bombing. It could not be used as evidence to prove occupation prior to the bombing.

27   NARA RG338, NND 903618, II Corps Records, Intelligence Summary No 85, dated 10 February 1944, Para 3d.

This is roughly the position from where a battalion commander from the 133rd Infantry claims to have seen a telescope in a window on the Abbey's eastern face. Even with powerful binoculars, this seems highly unlikely. (Author)

February 16. Destruction of foliage by bombing revealed many trenches, weapon pits and entrances to dugouts in the area of the ABBEY.

J.   German defences had been revealed on Monastery Hill, not in the Abbey itself. These were observed on 16 February so could not justify the bombing decision as the information was only revealed after the bombing had occurred.

On 17 February civilian who left ABBEY on 15 February reported that about 100 metres north-east of mule trail which runs from ABBEY to G.8362133 [sic] were MG emplacements in zigzag formation at 50-metres intervals from G842209 to 838213.

K.   The civilian reported MG positions 100-metres from the Abbey, but not inside the Abbey. Should single-source unverified reporting justify the decision? As with the last piece of evidence, it was only revealed after the bombing and therefore is irrelevant.

On 18 February MG fire out of north wall of ABBEY.

L.   The Germans had deployed into the ruins by 18 February. This piece of evidence, although again irrefutable, was irrelevant.

Of the twelve pieces of 'irrefutable evidence', four occurred after the bombing, when the Germans had occupied the ruins, even though MEDCOS 64 claimed that the information was judged *prior* to the bombing. Another five described heavy resistance to Allied attacks in the Abbey's vicinity, or of German positions close to the building. Wilson's report relied on three pieces of

Message from
Observation Posts on
Monte Trocchio following
the attack on the Abbey. –
'50 to 100 enemy coming
out of S end of Monastery
– taking them under fire'
(NARA RG407)

evidence (D, E and G)
to support his claim of
'irrefutable evidence'.[28]
Of these three pieces,
one can be dismissed as
mistaken identity and
the two others are of extremely doubtful provenance, relying on single-source unverified civilian
reporting which was contradicted by separate, but unused, reporting and a single visual sighting
that seemed at best unprovable.

Another piece of evidence that could have been used and was employed by *The Times* in its
16 February edition, was that 'German soldiers were seen to run from the buildings.'[29] This was
based on an observation post report from Wisdom 6 located on Monte Trocchio, three miles
from the Abbey.[30] It stated the following: 'Several groups of German soldiers, totalling about
200, were observed leaving the Monastery and going S(outh) after the initial bombings this
morning. These were taken under fire.'[31]

In *The Times* report a 'white cloth or sheet' was reported at 2:00pm hanging from a window on
the east side of the building. At that distance it is unlikely that the observers could have determined whether the 200-individuals were soldiers or civilians. This report was quoted in Jones'
1949 report as having come from an Indian OP. He stated that he could find no evidence of it in
the British archives. The reason for this is that the report was actually from a US OP.[32] A report
from the Fifth Army Psychological Warfare Branch on 5 March supported the hypothesis that
these 200-individuals were Italian civilians. The author of this report, written prior to the release
of Wilson's evidence, Lieutenant Alfred De Grazia, said that after the bombing the civilians
'started to run from the Abbey in panic, the Allied artillery observers mistook them for Germans
and ordered them fired upon.'[33] This is supported by Father Matronola, the Abbot's secretary and
present in the Abbey. He stated in a letter to Herbert Bloch in 1972 that, 'The people fleeing

28   TNA CAB 106/699: MEDCOS 64, 9 March 1944, Items D, E and G.
29   *The Times*, 16th February 1944, Issue 49781, p.4.
30   NARA RG407 NND 735017, Box 8151 – WWII Operations Reports, 1940-48 34th Infantry
     Division, 334-2.4 Jan 1944 to 334-2.4 Feb 1944. Message 42, 151040 February 1944.
31   NARA RG338, NND 903618, II Corps Records, Intelligence Summary No. 90 dated 15 February
     1944, Para 2a.
32   TNA CAB 106/699, p.30.
33   TNA CAB 106/699, p.143.

This is the view of the Abbey from the top of Monte Trocchio, some three miles distant. Observation Post Wisdom reported soldiers fleeing after the attack, but from the distance it would be impossible to distinguish soldiers from civilians (Author)

in haste from the inside were refugees. Many of these died during the flight.'[34] French journalist Pierre Ichac wrote that, 'It is useless to add that, fifteen days later, the article where I had reported the statements that were too revealing was still kept in secret at the Allied General Staff of Caserta, on the desk of General Gruenther. He would never go back.'[35] He is referring to his interviews with Italians who survived the bombing, none of whom saw Germans in the Abbey.

The Times also reported that the attack was made 'only after careful consideration of the facts and after reference to London and Washington'.[36] The piece described the civilians known to be in the Abbey and the Allied leafleting efforts to warn them. It stated, 'It is to be hoped that they took their chance and went.'[37] Why was this seemingly strong evidence not used by Wilson? All newspaper copy was censored so this must have been approved. It certainly wasn't the war correspondent that saw the Germans leaving; he stated that he was driving down the Via Casalina near Mignano when the bombing started. It was something he picked up later. There was no documentary evidence that the attack on the Abbey was referred to either London or Washington, hence the clamour to the British Minister in the Vatican for information. If they had been consulted beforehand, and all the facts considered, why would Wilson have had to provide 'irrefutable evidence'? These 'facts' would already have been known and considered by the Allied chiefs. As we now know, and they knew then, the 'soldiers' running out of the Abbey during the bombing were in fact civilians taking their chance!

34 Bloch, p.28.
35 *Dal Volturno a Cassino* <http://www.dalvolturnoacassino.it/asp/doc.asp?id=226> (accessed 10 October 2022).
36 *The Times* Issue 49781, p.4.
37 *The Times* Issue 49781, p.4.

25

Mandarins

I handed His Eminence a summary (accuracy not guaranteed).
Sir Francis D'Arcy Osborne
His Majesty's Minister to the Holy See
21st February 1944[1]

On the day of the bombing, Osborne transmitted a message to the British Foreign Office. The message referenced Baron Weisäcker's actions the day before and was in reaction to the warning leaflet dropped on the Abbey:

> On February 14th German Ambassador to Holy See transmitted to Abbot Primate of the Benedictines the following statement: 'German military authorities assert that the news of German defence works at Abbey of Monte Cassino are false. It is absolutely untrue that there are artillery, mortars or machine guns there. There are no large (Grossere) troop concentrations there (in the neighbourhood of the Monastery). Everything possible has been done to prevent Monte Cassino from becoming a traffic point (durchgangsplatz).'
>
> Today German Ambassador handed to the Abbot and to the Under Secretary at the Vatican a further statement specifying as follows: according to information from competent German authorities there are neither artillery, mortars nor machine guns posted in monastery of Monte Cassino, or its immediate surroundings nor are there any German troops there.[2]

This message was registered in the Foreign Office on 16 February and was actioned by Rumbold.[3] The same information was also passed to Rumbold's superior, Cadogan, in a letter from Godfrey who had received a telegram from the Papal Secretary of State.[4] Maglione was also in touch with Cicognani in Washington DC, messaging at 2:15pm, barely an hour after the last bomb fell:

1   Minister to Holy See to Foreign Office, Telegram No. 107, 21 February 1944.
2   TNA FO 371/43817: Folio R2516 Minister to Holy See to Foreign Office, Telegram No. 92, 15 February 1944. Jones, p.58.
3   TNA FO 371/43817: Folio R2516 dated 16 February 1944.
4   TNA FO 371/4381: Folio R2649 dated 19 February 1944.

On the bombardment of the Abbey of Monte Cassino. American press puts forward the need to bomb Montecassino Abbey because it has become (so they say) not only an observatory, but also a fortress of the enemy. Please inform me (?) in this regard in order not to leave any stone unturned and take new steps with the United States Government.[5]

One mouthpiece of the Salo Italian Republic, *Il Regime Fascista*, was to respond on 17 February:

The attack carried out by 'allied' air formations unleashed their vandalistic fury on one of the most important monuments of European Catholic civilization despite the fact that the Vatican, according to news from reliable sources has made some moves on the two belligerent sides in recent days in order to obtain that the Abbey of Monte Cassino was spared from the war offense.[6]

It was down to the Supreme Allied Commander to defend the action when the German propaganda machine swung into action and when diplomatic missions received inevitable complaints from the Vatican. London expected to have Wilson's evidence by 24 February, but was still waiting the next day. Meanwhile, the Germans broadcasted further statements by Diamare and Kesselring. Kesselring issued a denial that the Germans had been using the Monastery. His explanation of the previous months was truthful according to the evidence now available and there was no intelligence to refute it. His final paragraph, although written for propaganda purposes would have struck a resonance with the Vatican and neutrals:

As the responsible commander-in-chief in Italy, I therefore declare: United States soldiery, devoid of all culture, have in powerless rage, senselessly destroyed one of Italy's most treasured edifices and have murdered Italian civilian refugees and children – with their bombs and artillery fire. Thus it has once again been proven that Anglo-Saxon and Bolshevik warfare has only one aim: to destroy the venerable proofs of European culture. I feel deep contempt for the cynical mendacity and the hypocritical statements by which the Anglo-Saxon command tried to shift the responsibility onto my shoulders and onto my soldiers.[7]

Following up on Kesselring's statement was a much more vitriolic and political statement by the Wilhelmstrasse.[8] The Germans reported that Diamare observed:

Though during the last few weeks, the main fighting line moved nearer and nearer to Monte Cassino it was firmly believed, on account of assurances given and repeatedly broadcast that at least the area of the sacred Monastery would be spared from direct attacks. Until 5th February this sacred area was inhabited only by a small group of monks who had stayed behind for its protection and about 15 people (only three men among them) who had been excepted from the last evacuation because they were ill or wounded and the state

---

5   Canciani, p.139.
6   Canciani, pp.144-5.
7   TNA FO 371/43817: Folio R2678, Text Of Statement On The Bombing Of Monte Cassino And Castel Gandolfo, 17 February 1944.
8   TNA FO 371/43817: Folio R2679 dated 17 February 1944.

of their health did not permit their transport. But since the rumour of the safety of Monte Cassino persisted, more and more people arrived who, even against my wish sought refuge on the surrounding farms. On 5th February after the Americans had carried out a strong artillery bombardment during which one of the farm buildings was hit, some of these poor frightened women implored us in tears to be allowed shelter in the Monastery itself.

For humanity's sake I had the gates opened to them. Unfortunately, together with these some 50 persons, a crowd pushed their way in who, up to that moment, had been dispersed in the surrounding district.

Now they penetrated into all the rooms of the Monastery.

When on the afternoon of 14th February, the Anglo-Americans dropped leaflets asking all civilians to evacuate Monte Cassino, it was impossible for most of them to venture outside because of the continuous heavy bombardment. For this reason, at the time of the air attack on 15th February, a large number of people were in the Monastery. A considerable number, though it cannot be ascertained how many – are probably buried underneath the ruins.

ONCE AGAIN I CAN GIVE THE SOLEMN AND FIRM DECLARATION THAT UP TO THE MOMENT IN WHICH THE SMALL GROUP OF MONKS SUCCEEDED TOGETHER WITH THE WOUNDED AND INVALIDS IN MAKING THEIR WAY THROUGH THE RUINS TO SAFETY – THAT IS TO 17TH FEBRUARY AT 1730 IN THE AFTERNOON – NOT THE SMALLEST GERMAN TROOP FORMATION NOR WEAPONS OF ANY KIND HAD BEEN IN THE SACRED AREA OF MONTE CASSINO.

Gregario, Diamare, Bishop and Abbot of
Monte Cassino

Initially dismissed as propaganda, Diamare's statements quickly gained traction.[9] The next day the Vatican unofficially stated its views in the *L'Osservatore Romano*, calling the attack 'a repudiation of the very laws of humanity', extracts of which were sent to Washington by Tittmann.[10] Another occupant of the Abbey, Father Oderiso Graziosi also made a statement saying, 'In the inside of the Abbey, and throughout its whole perimeter there were no German troops or warlike preparations of any kind'.[11] This was broadcast by the German Telegraph Service on 21 February. He denied that German soldiers ran from the Abbey following the bombing and said that the Allied aircraft were able to bomb the Abbey unobstructed because there were no anti-aircraft guns in the vicinity. In an attempt to deflect the quickly evident number of civilian casualties inflicted by the attack, the *New York Times* claimed in its 20 February edition that the Germans forced the civilians to stay after the leaflets were dropped. The British press agency *Reuters* followed a similar line, falsely claiming that the Germans had locked the civilians in the Abbey.[12]

9   Hapgood and Richardson, pp.221-225.
10   Tasciotti, p.169.
11   TNA CAB 106/699, p.118.
12   Tasciotti, p.173.

It was the constant bombardment that caused the civilians to remain rather than any German attempt to create a propaganda coup using them as human shields. Some senior Nazis such as Goebbels and Ribbentrop were sensitive to publicity and world opinion regarding damage to Vatican and religious property. Despite occasional rantings by Hitler over occupying Vatican City, its continuance as neutral territory gave Germany an advantage in the Abbey narrative.[13] In July 1943, Hitler had reassured Pius that the Vatican would be respected in the event the Germans occupied Rome.[14] In London, following several telegrams from Osborne and an increasing propaganda campaign from the enemy, the British Foreign Office began its quest to find out what happened. This investigation involved high-level officials, all reporting to Sargent, the Deputy Permanent Under-Secretary, his boss Cadogan and ultimately Eden, all of whom became involved in the correspondence. Also involved outside the Foreign Office were senior officials from the War Cabinet Office, JIC and the Political Warfare Executive. As February 1944 ended, the justification failed to materialise. The Vatican's complaints and the German propaganda machine gained credibility. By 23 February Osborne reported that the 'streets of Rome and Vienna plastered posters of destruction of Abbey of Monte Cassino.'[15] The Allies had not produced proof that Germans used the Abbey, and the pressure was rising. As March progressed it became obvious to the mandarins in London that, despite Wilson's evidence, they never would and that the best course of action was to bury the matter.

The investigation started with Rumbold, and in his handwritten note of 16 February he believed the Germans were using the Abbey, but that evidence was required. His note asked for a 'definite statement' on the German use of the Abbey.[16] The request for information was sent by Dew, Head of the Southern Department to Lieutenant Colonel J L Carver of the War Cabinet Offices Secretariat on 17 February asking him to 'describe as precisely as possible the military use which the Germans have in fact been making use of the Abbey.'[17] He also asked, 'If there has not been a report from AFHQ, perhaps you could ask for one.'[18] This request was forwarded to AFHQ after Carver consulted his boss, Hollis, the Senior Military Assistant Secretary of the War Cabinet.[19]

As well as Osborne, Tittmann also began to receive complaints from the Vatican authorities. Following the bombing of Castelgandolfo the Church had been annoyed at some of the propaganda suggesting that the Papal property was 'saturated with Germans' but had been somewhat acceptant that such things would happen in war. The bombing of the Abbey was met with anger. On 19 February Tittmann wrote to the US State Department:

> Re Bombing of Monte Cassino by Allies. Vatican is outwardly assuming a noncommittal attitude...It is evident, however, high Vatican officials are holding Allies responsible. Cardinal Maglione spoke to me about the matter this morning with some heat. He said

13   Adleman and Walton, p.83.
14   Kertzer, p.350.
15   Minister to Holy See to Foreign Office, Telegram No. 116, 23 February 1944.
16   TNA FO 371/43817: Folio R2516 dated 16 February 1944.
17   TNA FO 371/43817: Folio R2516, Note from A R Dew of Foreign Office to Colonel Carver of War Cabinet Office, R2516/32/22: 17 February 1944.
18   TNA FO 371/43817: Folio R2516 Note from A R Dew of Foreign Office to Colonel Carver of War Cabinet Office, R2516/32/22: 17 February 1944.
19   Note from Colonel Carver to General Hollis, 18 February 1944, in TNA CAB 106/699, p.60.

that he was convinced from evidence at hand that there were no German soldiers, gun emplacements, etc, in Monastery…He added he thought the bombing entirely unnecessary from a military point of view, was a 'colossal blunder' and a 'piece of gross stupidity' on the part of the Allies. It will unfavourably distort pro-Allied opinion everywhere.[20]

Like the good diplomat, Tittmann defended the actions of his government, offering the usual Military Necessity argument, but he was not persuasive. Maglione, the Pope's chief political and diplomatic aide, claimed to have sources not open to Tittmann that supported his criticism, whereas the American was forced to admit that he had only the BBC upon which to draw. Maglione's source was probably the Abbot, who was received by the Pope and interviewed at length by Tardini, one of Pius' principal aides.[21] Abbot Diamare reiterated, this time with no Germans present, that the Germans had not used the Abbey for any military purposes. He also told the monsignor of the ammunition cave and his complaints to the German authorities and fact that they did not respect the 300-metre 'neutral zone.'[22] Tardini was no fan of the Nazis, likening Hitler to Attila the Hun, so he had no reason to favour their denials.[23]

Osborne added further pressure on 21 February by reporting that according to the 'studiously moderate' Vatican that 'unbiased opinion…unanimously convinced that there were no Germans in the Abbey.'[24] Maglione received a report around 21 February that concluded:

In reality, the German soldiers in the immediate vicinity of Montecassino as far as we have been able to ascertain, were very few, a few dozen, and the Anglo-American, if they had not been right about them was only because of inexperience or inability. In spite of everything, the Anglo-Americans could well have saved the monastery building by attacking the German positions directly at low altitude, as they sometimes did.[25]

The Germans pressed the Vatican to issue a statement that the Allies had destroyed the Abbey and that the Germans were not using it. The Cardinal Secretary of State refused to do this but stated that he would probably have to do so eventually. Osborne was very keen to establish the truth of the BBC reports of Germans escaping from the Abbey. The next day his telegram suggested that the Germans may have been spreading 'information to the effect that certain churches ecclesiastical property or cultural monuments are being used by the Germans for military purposes. Thereby it is hoped that Allied bombings of such edifices will provide propaganda material for asserting Allied vandalism, or at least incompetence.'[26]

By 26 February AFHQ had still not provided material to satisfy the Foreign Office's request.[27] The day before, McDermott was told by Carver that the 'Army had bungled the question of

20   Tittmann, p.201.
21   Chadwick, p.282.
22   Tasciotti, p.179.
23   Cornwell, p.221.
24   Telegram No.108, Holy See to Foreign Office, 21 February 1944.
25   Tasciotti, p.188.
26   Minister to Holy See to Foreign Office, Telegram No. 116, 23 February 1944
27   TNA CAB 106/699: Note from Colonel Carver to General Hollis, Monte Cassino Abbey as a Military Objective, 26 February 1944.

enquiries about Monte Cassino.'[28] The reply to the War Office had not contained sufficient information so they sent it to the War Cabinet Office who now took up the case. The issue was then referred to the British CoS who, on 4 March, demanded that Wilson provide 'detailed information…at the earliest possible moment'. In addition to Wilson, the message was also copied to Brigadier Ian Jacob, the Military Assistant Secretary to the War Cabinet, the Foreign Secretary and the First Sea Lord. The message read thus:

> COSMED 51.
> 1. GERMAN authorities at the Vatican and GERMAN propaganda are making great play of alleged vandalism by Allied Forces in destroying Monte Cassino Abbey which they state contained no artillery, mortars, machine guns or defence works. They state that there were no large concentrations of troops in the neighbourhood of the Monastery.
> 2. The Foreign Office are anxious to obtain material which can be passed to the Vatican describing as precisely as possible the military use which the GERMANS have in fact been making of the Abbey and which led to your decision to attack it.
> 3. In the absence of any reliable information OSBORNE reports that he is informed on what seems to be good authority that GERMAN agents are instructed from time to time to spread in circles believed to have Allied connections, information to the effect that certain churches, ecclesiastical property or cultural monuments are being used by the GERMANS for military purposes whereby it is hoped that Allied bombings of such edifices will provide propaganda material. It is all the more important, therefore, that we should be provided with detailed information regarding GERMAN use of Monte Cassino Abbey at the earliest possible moment.
> Has been RELAYED TO HQS MAAF.[29]

The tone of the request from London still favoured the theory that the German claims of not using the Abbey were false or that there was some skulduggery at play, using the occupation of the Abbey to gain a propaganda coup. Gould in his history continued this theme of trying to pin the blame on trickery saying that 'there is plenty of evidence pointing to a deliberate trick.'[30] Yet the evidence was weak and circumstantial and has not improved with time as he suggested it would. He offered no concrete facts or smoking gun, of any conspiracy. It was almost inconceivable that Senger, the German commander in the area, would have stooped to doing this with his connections to the Benedictine Order. Kesselring too was an Italophile and a Roman Catholic and the source of the order not to occupy the Abbey. He was also therefore unlikely to be responsible for such an act. That was not to say that others less scrupulous and more committed to the Nazi cause would not have done so. If they did, how did any false information get into the decision-making process? This information would not have come from tactical sources and only the report by the Italian civilian attracts suspicion. It was more likely that deception would have flowed into Allied commands through strategic sources such as SIS or OSS after being planted on their agents. It was unlikely that the Germans would have fed deception through wireless

---

28   TNA FO 371/43817: Folio R2894, Minute to file dated 25 February 1944.
29   COSMED 51, 4 March 1944.
30   Gould, p.289.

messages unless they suspected that the Allies could read them. It is well documented that they had no idea that their *Enigma* machines were compromised. There was no evidence from any of these organisations that contributed to the decision. The attack was a bottom-up request from 4th Indian Division and not a top-down order. There is no evidence in the intelligence that supported the claim that the Germans tricked the Allies.

At the end of February, no proof of occupation had been received. On 29 February, Scarlett, a senior British diplomat, wrote a somewhat exasperated minute:

> As regards Monte Cassino we can carry the Allied case no further until incontrovertible reports of military eyewitnesses specifying with precision what use German Armed forces were actually seen to make of the Monastery are available. What we want is the evidence on which the order to bomb was given.[31]

In response, the Chairman of the Cabinet Office's JIC gave his view on the bombing. The JIC was the principal intelligence authority for the British Government upon whose intelligence policy decisions were made. By the beginning of March, no evidence of German occupation of the Abbey had been unearthed. It is this paragraph from Cavendish-Bentinck the Chairman of the JIC, that proved beyond doubt that the bombing of the Abbey of Montecassino was not justified by Military Necessity:

> I think that we had probably better keep quiet about Monte Cassino and let it be forgotten. The evidence on which the order to bomb was given is not satisfactory. There is no proof that the Germans were in fact using the monastery, but they were firing from sites very close to it.[32]

By early March, the British Foreign Office was becoming concerned about the Allied reputation in the light of the bombing and the likelihood that other works of artistic importance would be destroyed as the Allies moved northwards. On 1 March, Scarlett wrote a minute covering the issue:

> There is no doubt that from the Political Warfare point of view, the destruction of Monte Cassino without an immediate compensating military advantage, is a 'bear' point. An indefinite repetition of such incidents might cause our shares to depreciate dangerously.
>
> Once Rome is reached and passed, not a day will go by in which some work of major artistic and cultural importance is not jeopardised. It is certain that the military authorities will be unable to save many of them even if they want to. It is equally certain that enemy propaganda will exploit the destruction of each building in turn and will thereby succeed to a certain extent in creating anti-allied feeling in Northern Italy. If PWE is to do anything to counteract this, it must be provided with a definite statement of policy on which to work. Sir James Grigg's recent assurances in the House of Commons are not enough …
>
> It must however be clearly understood that if the Germans, as they have done in the past and are likely to do in the future, make use of these monuments for the purposes of their

31   TNA FO 371/43817: Folio 3019, Minute 5 dated 29 February 1944.
32   TNA FO 371/43817: Folio 3019, Minute 2 dated 2 March 1944.

General Eisenhower in conversation with British Foreign Secretary Sir Anthony Eden. Eisenhower placed the Abbey on a protected list. Eden and his civil servants hushed up the lack of evidence for its destruction. (NARA)

military operations against the Allied forces, there is no alternative but to take appropriate military countermeasures which may inevitably result in the damage or destruction we are concerned to avoid.'[33]

Scarlett's minute resulted in some debate. It was clear from his words that the use or occupation of historic and artistic monuments was the deciding factor in whether military action would be taken. This point echoed Osborne and came at a time when Wilson had still not provided any tangible evidence. Sargent suggested that the occupation by the Germans question in the future should not simply be decided by troops' 'visual reconnaissance, but by multiple sources of intelligence such as air reconnaissance and agents' reports. Sargent, like others such as Osborne and Cavendish-Bentinck, assumed that the Germans would use suspicious activity to lure the Allies into committing more damage to important sites. He wrote that this is what Cavendish-Bentinck thought the Germans did at Montecassino, although as we have seen there is no proof from the intelligence that Cavendish-Bentinck possessed to support this. Sargent finally accused the Germans of 'playing up the destruction of Monte Cassino' as if the British would not have done the same![34] In response, Eden wrote the following remarkable statement, 'I was relieved

33 TNA FO 371/43817: Folio 2998, Minute 2 dated 1 March 1944.
34 TNA FO 371/43817: Folio 2998, Minute 4 dated 4 March 1944.

to hear that Monte Cassino was of little architectural importance. Even so I don't know why we should show dramatic pictures of its destruction in our cinemas! We are a strange people.'[35]

Those in power did not want a debate in Parliament, but the members of the House of Commons were not easily controlled and the attack on the Abbey became a political issue on 7 March when the Labour Member of Parliament, Ivor Thomas, asked the Secretary of State for War, 'Can the honourable gentleman say what military advantage derived from the bombing and shelling of this ancient sanctuary?'[36] Thomas, before his election to Parliament in 1943, had been involved in intelligence and propaganda work against the Italian Fascist State. There was no response from the Secretary of State, because he had no idea. The next minute came from Cavendish-Bentinck on 10 March. This came the day after Wilson despatched his evidence, although Cavendish-Bentinck had yet to see it. He was aware that AFHQ was gathering more evidence but did not yet know what it was. He suggested that when he received the telegram that 'it should be interesting.'[37] Again, he asserted, without the slightest evidence, German skulduggery in order to draw Allied fire onto historic buildings. Considering the decision to bomb, if not the method of bombing, was British, he had the temerity to say that, 'the most we can do is to impress on our own commanders, and more especially the Americans, the necessity for care.'[38]

The pressure on the Allies increased further on the afternoon of 12 March when Pope Pius XII took to his balcony high above St Peter's Square. Preventing the bombing of Rome by the Allies had become somewhat of an obsession. He was criticised for putting its safety above everything else. Speaking to a crowd of several hundred thousand he roundly criticised the Allies' air war:

> If each one of the world's cities struck by an air war that respects no limits or laws is in itself a tremendous accusation against the cruelty of such methods of fighting, how can We believe that anyone would dare to transform Rome – this nurturing City that belongs to all people for all time and on which the eyes of the Christian and civilised world are now focused, watching in trepidation – to transform her, We say, into a battlefield, a theatre of war, thus perpetrating an act as militarily inglorious as it would be an abomination in the eyes of God and to humanity conscious of its highest and most intangible spiritual and moral values?[39]

That there was no similar sentiment concerning the bombing of other cities, or any public criticism of German atrocities does not detract from the validity of his remarks. A few days later, on 14 March 1944, and while the flurry of messages was at its height, Eaker wrote a pre-emptory letter to Arnold explaining the care they were taking:

> Dear General,
> It is already quite evident as a result of the Cassino Abbey bombing that there will be much discussion as to whether Air Forces in this theatre are needlessly and carelessly destroying antiquities or ancient church landmarks.

---

35   TNA FO 371/43817: Folio 2998, Minute 5 dated 5 March 1944.
36   Tasciotti, p.205.
37   TNA FO 371/43817: Folio 2998, Minute 6 dated 10 March 1944.
38   TNA FO 371/43817: Folio 2998, Minute 6 dated 10 March 1944.
39   Katz, p.194.

We have been at great pains here to brief our combat leaders and crews to ensure that such is not the case. I thought it might be of interest to you and help you in combatting some of the press and public discussion on this subject if I sent you our volume of instructions and photographs on the antiquities and monuments of culture in the Italian theatre. This is enclosed.

Please be assured that we do everything possible to prevent wanton or careless destruction of these relics and that we shall, at the same time, acquaint the press representatives here of our efforts in that direction. Thereby, we shall hope to cause you as little annoyance and trouble as possible on this score.

Sincerely,
IRA C EAKER
Lt General, USA
Commanding[40]

On first reading this somewhat weakens the theory that the heavy bombers were used as a demonstration of daylight precision bombing, but it actually reassures Arnold that his force takes precautions to prevent accidental damage to historic buildings. The attack on the Abbey was not accidental. Its failure was an embarrassment, especially as Eaker may not have had anything to do with it. The list included with the letter was issued by 15th Army Group on 17 February 1944. The Abbey was still on the list.

At his daily staff meeting on 8 March, Wilson ordered his intelligence staff to:

prepare and despatch a message to the British Chiefs of Staff on the facts...The message is to be so drafted that there is to be no indication of doubt as to the Germans occupying the Abbey. The British Chiefs of Staff are to be informed further that, in the Commander-in-Chief's opinion, the Vatican should not be given any information which may provide a loop-hole for use as propaganda.[41]

With regard to the last sentence, the horse had bolted. Why did Wilson stress the issue of doubt and why did he think that the Vatican would be a source of adverse propaganda – they were not the enemy? If there was no doubt that the Germans were using the Abbey, as he claimed, he would not have needed to instruct his staff to that effect? He was therefore implying that there was doubt, but that this must not be publicly exposed. This instruction resulted in the detailed message, MEDCOS 64 of 9 March which listed the 12-pieces of 'irrefutable evidence.' Although never expressed, the weakness of the evidence would have been identified by AFHQ, hence the ambivalence of Wilson's intelligence chief, General Strong. Wilson asked again on 15 March that the evidence not be disclosed and that no detailed justification be revealed, in a message that reinforced his view about passing evidence to the Vatican.[42] This message read: 'Wish to re-emphasise that detailed reasons for bombing of Cassino Abbey should not be passed to the Vatican as it is impossible to

---

40   AFHRA Reel A6030, MAAF History, C–in–C Correspondence, Eaker to Arnold dated 14 March 1944.
41   AFHQ Minutes of the Commander-in-Chief's Meeting, 8 March 1944.
42   AFHQ Minutes of the Commander-in-Chief's Meeting, 15 March 1944 and MEDCOS 69 dated 15 March 1944.

obtain definite proof on all points.'[43] Wilson had now admitted that he could not prove the Germans used the Abbey. It was not surprising that he was keen not to reveal this to the Vatican. In a minute raised in the British Foreign Office on 11 March, Scarlett observed that 'there is not a great deal of information that the Abbey itself was used by the Germans.'[44] Scarlett also thought that the claim that the Allies had 'irrefutable evidence' without actually offering any, would not be satisfactory. He added that Wilson's evidence did 'not make a very impressive case' and that 'we had better leave matters alone.'[45] The British Political Warfare Executive, responsible for strategic propaganda agreed that the evidence did 'not, in their view, constitute an irrefutable propaganda case.'[46] Scarlett suggested two courses of action, anodyne guidance to Osborne in the Vatican or silence on the subject. His superior, Sir Orme Sargent, chose silence.[47]

Wilson's demand that evidence should not be provided to the Vatican because of its propaganda potential was spurious. If his evidence was 'irrefutable', then its value was in the public domain, as definite proof that the Abbey was destroyed within the Laws of War and the fault lay squarely with the occupying Germans. Considering the poor reputation of German forces for respecting the Laws of War, this would have been an open door to a propaganda victory. It would also have acted as a powerful counter-message to that of the Germans, who had made use of Diamare to press their innocence. As it was, the evidence was hardly irrefutable. In fact, there was no evidence! Why did Wilson feel it necessary to follow-up MEDCOS 64? The answer potentially lay in the fact that, by his own admission, he had no proof that the Germans occupied the Abbey and could not justify the destruction with facts. This would have been obvious had the evidence been passed to the Vatican. The British authorities were not convinced either and did not think it would hold up in any propaganda exchange with the Germans, who were largely telling the truth, although with elaboration. It was not clear whether the Foreign Office communicated their decision to keep silent on the subject to Wilson. There were, however, no further records of direct discussions concerning the Abbey from the British Foreign Office after 16 March.

Osborne wrote to the Foreign Office that day to complain that he had seen no proof of German occupation, or that the Abbey's destruction has aided the Allied advance:

> It is quite clear, and the Vatican do not question it, that military necessities and security precautions must override other considerations, and there is the further fact that German engagements are quite unreliable. Hence it is clearly very difficult for us to give undertakings to spare particular religious institutions (Monte Cassino etc) or particular towns (Florence, Orvieto etc). But the example of Monte Cassino has been unfortunate; we said we must bomb the Abbey because it was being used by the Germans, and because their use of it was holding up our advance but, as far as I am aware, no proof is forthcoming that the Abbey (as distinct from its territory) was being used by the Germans, and its destruction has not facilitated our advance; on the other hand the Germans have been provided

43   TNA CAB 106/699: MEDCOS 69, Wilson message to COS and JCS 15 March 1944.
44   TNA FO 371/43817: Folio R3891, Minute 1 dated 11 March 1944.
45   TNA FO 371/43817: Folio R3891, Minute 1 dated 11 March 1944.
46   TNA FO 371/43817: Folio R3891, Minute 2 dated 15 March 1944.
47   TNA FO 371/43817: Folio R3891, Minute 3 dated 16 March 1944.

with invaluable propaganda and with the use of the ruins as an observation and artillery post. British Broadcasting Corporation stated that the Germans were seen escaping from the Abbey, but I have never received confirmation, requested in my Telegram No.108, nor have I received authorisation to express regret for the death of several hundred refugees and damage to the Papal property at Castel Gandolfo. [48]

The silence desired by the Foreign Office was, however, broken by a communication between the Cardinal Secretary of State, Maglione and Archbishop Godfrey, which the latter passed on to the Foreign Office on 22 March. Godfrey relayed the 'sorrow that the bombing of Monte Cassino has caused.' The desire of the Foreign Office to stick their fingers in their ears is clear from the resultant minute written by Scarlett to Cavendish-Bentinck on 24 March:

> The Vatican have already made all these points to Sir D Osborne and have taken sorrowful pleasure in pointing out that the destruction of the Abbey has apparently served no visible military use. There is no doubt that the Military made a blunder in bombing the Abbey to bits, that the evidence of its use by the Germans is of the slenderest description (see R3891) and that its destruction has provided German propaganda with a bull point. It will be seen from minutes on R3891 that our best policy is really to preserve silence about Monte Cassino.[49]

In the final word from the Foreign Office, an internal minute responding to a letter by Conservative MP Pierse Loftus on 24 March, conceded that:

> We certainly made a mistake in bombing the Abbey of Monte Cassino, of which German propaganda has made full use, both with the Vatican and elsewhere, since it has not served any visible military purpose and the evidence that the Abbey was being used by the Germans is extremely slender – so slender that we cannot offer any excuses to the Vatican.[50]

Publicly, there was no doubt about Wilson's evidence in Washington and the British decision to remain silent was not reciprocated. Roosevelt had promised the Vatican that the Abbey would be protected in July 1943, but had changed his tune when, on the day after the bombing he said, 'I read in the afternoon papers about the bombing of the abbey of Montecassino by our forces. In the reports it was clearly explained that the reason why it was bombed is that the Germans were using it to bombard us. It was a German stronghold, with artillery and everything necessary.'

Despite the unlikely story that he read it first in the newspaper, this was the story as wired by *United Press* Cassino correspondent James A. Roper on the day of the bombing:

> More than 200 American bombers and dozens of artillery pieces this morning pounded the Abbey of Montecassino, forcing the Germans to emerge like ants from the ancient Benedictine buildings, which the enemy had fortified in violation of every convention...

48   COS (44) 82nd Meeting, Bombing of Vatican Property, 10 March 1944. British Minister to Holy See to Foreign Office Telegram No 163, 16 March 44
49   TNA FO 371/43870: Folio R4552, Minute 1, dated 23 March 1944.
50   TNA FO 371/43870: Folio R4982, Minute 1, dated 24 March 1944.

it was a decisive step in saving American lives ending the battle of Cassino as soon as possible. And it was accomplished only after using every means to force the Germans to respect the religious neutrality of the monastery, the oldest in the world. When the Germans continued to hold observation posts and machine gun nests in the buildings, 24-hours' notice was given in leaflets to the 2000 monks and civilians believed to be in the monastery. But it is not known whether they have wandered off or are hiding in the deep basement of the abbey.[51]

Had Roper considered at all whether the monks and civilians that had been blown to smithereens in the attack or whether 'wandering off' was even an option? The notice from the leaflet was much less than 24-hours. The *New York Times* ran Roosevelt's comments on 16 February, also gathering the views of senior American Catholic clerics. The attack of a Catholic Abbey by air forces from a country with over 20-million Roman Catholics was more problematic than for the largely Anglican British. The Archbishops of Baltimore, New Orleans and Atlanta all fell into line. All blamed the Germans for using the Abbey. Whether their Most Reverends' support would have been so forthcoming if they had known the true strength of the evidence will never be known. The Archbishop of Milan, Cardinal Schuster, who had a reputation for supporting the previous Fascist government, did not share his American Colleagues' views, 'History will establish the responsibilities and issue the judgement against those false Christians who are the worst of the barbarians, the Lombards and the Saracens who in centuries past destroyed that oasis of civilisation that was Monte Cassino.'[52]

On 13 March, Maglione wrote to Cicognani to deliver a message to Roosevelt. It was delivered to his official envoy, Myron C Taylor, 'The destruction of the Abbey of Monte Cassino falsely described as a German fortress was a sad lesson for the Holy See in the dangers of such erroneous assertions.'[53] In response to the Papal address, the US Department of State and then the President issued a press release regarding damage to antiquities that maintained the erroneous assertion that the Germans were using these sites:

> In answer to inquiries at the press conference today concerning the remarks of His Holiness Pope Pius XII reported in this morning's press, Secretary of State Cordell Hull said:
> I think we all understand that the Allied military authorities in Italy are dealing with considerations of military necessity forced on them by the activities and attitude of the German military forces. Naturally, we are as much interested as any government or any individual in the preservation of religious shrines, historic structures and human lives. I am sure that our military people have that same view. It is my understanding that the Allied military authorities are pursuing a policy of avoiding damage to such shrines and monuments to the extent humanly possible in modern warfare and in the circumstances which face them. If the Germans were not entrenched in these places or were they as interested as we are in protecting religious shrines and monuments and in preserving the lives of innocent civilians and refugees, no question would arise.[54]

---

51   Canciani, p.137.
52   Tasciotti, p.174.
53   Tasciotti, p.210.
54   US Department of State, Press Release No 82, 13 March 1944.

MARCH 14, 1944
STATEMENT BY THE PRESIDENT
Everyone knows the Nazi record on religion. Both at home and abroad, Hitler and his followers have waged a ruthless war against the churches of all faiths.

Now the German Army has used the Holy City of Rome as a military center. No one could have been surprised by this – it is only the latest of Hitler's many affronts to religion. It is a logical step in the Nazi policy of total war – a policy which treats nothing as sacred.

We on our side have made freedom of religion one of the principles for which we are fighting this war. We have tried scrupulously – often at considerable sacrifice – to spare religious and cultural monuments, and we shall continue to do so.[55]

One senses that Pius may have hit a raw nerve. On 17 March 1944, the Secretary of War, Stimson, said that he had received a report on the bombing that gave 'positive and unequivocal evidence' of German use.[56] This was presumably Wilson's report, and in the absence of other evidence, it can be assumed that Roosevelt's views had been moulded by this 'irrefutable evidence.' That was confirmed on 21 March when the President sent the following message to Taylor:

General Wilson reported in great detail the reasons for the military action against the abbey. His report seems convincing to me and I suggest that you reply to the Delegate on my behalf that the Allied military commanders in the field have irrefutable evidence that the abbey formed a part of the German defensive line in that area. I think it best not to go into further details.[57]

Taylor passed on this message the next day.

In late March, General Arnold was possibly unaware of the controversies concerning the differences of opinion over the attack. Eaker, although often in direct communication with Arnold, tended not to go around the chain of command. In a fascinating letter dated 21 March and entitled FOR GENERAL ARNOLD'S EYES ONLY, he asked him whether he would wish information via the back door? He wrote the following in guarded terms, as if he were describing a fictional occurrence:

Let us suppose that General Clark, as the Army Commander, did not want a single bomb on Cassino Abbey, but that General Freyberg, one of his subordinate Corps Commanders went over his head or around him and asked the Army Group Commander to have it bombed. We bomb it and it causes an uproar from the Churchmen. You ask us then why we bombed it; we make an investigation and discover a difference of view between the Ground Commanders. This situation, if known to you, would account for some of the things that might seem inexplicable. On the other hand, if you reported this to the CCS a course of action might well be taken which would be offensive to General Wilson and might be injurious to senior subordinates.

55   Presidential Statement, 14 March 1944.
56   Conduct of Campaign Defended, *The Times*, 17 March 1944, Issue 49807, p.4.
57   Tasciotti, p.221.

It must be clear to you, therefore, that much of the information which in my opinion would be of great value to you cannot be transmitted to you in normal intelligence reports or other official reports.[58]

This letter has several potential inferences. Eaker does not trust his British chain of command to pass on the inconvenient truths to the CCS. The letter suggests that he considered that Arnold lacked awareness of controversies and disagreements over the bombing. Any report supplied through official channels would have to tow the party line, rather than being a true reflection of his views. Eaker suggests that the air forces were unaware of the differences between ground force commanders and Slessor claimed no early involvement of air planners. More speculatively, it indicates a difficult relationship between the British and Americans. That three British generals bully Clark would not have improved this fractious relationship. This letter also supports the argument that the flight over the Abbey by Eaker could not have taken place as previously suggested and that Eaker himself was not at Caserta during the decisive period. After all, had they flown over the Abbey, he would have known the purpose of the flight?

Despite having no further 'definite proof', Wilson publicly argued in his published despatch that the Abbey was 'occupied and fortified…and formed the pivot on which the German defensive system was based.'[59] These words were not the originals, as he had changed and made stronger the argument of an earlier draft and a later revised draft which said, 'The Cassino Monastery dominated all approaches to the town and to Highway 6 and we <u>believed it to be</u> [emphasis added] a key point in the German defensive system.'[60] The wording regarding the Abbey is much stronger in the published final account and suggested clear military use. This was an attempt by Wilson to strengthen his justification from early drafts to the final published despatch, but with no further evidence. Was Wilson asked to revise his account as part of Cavendish-Bentinck's burial process or did he make the decision himself? It seems unlikely we will ever know. The only evidence discovered after 15 February weakened the Allied case, and no intelligence pointed to other conclusions which could account for Wilson's change of wording. Wilson was not the only senior officer to wordsmith more compelling reasoning in final pieces from their first drafts. Eaker in his 1974 piece on the bombing recounting the views of subordinate commanders started with the statement that: 'All the involved subordinate commanders were permitted to express their views.' This didn't portray the right message, as we know for a fact that some subordinate air commanders were against the attack, not least Saville, his own subordinate and officer responsible for tactical air support. Eaker's final published piece, which strengthened the collective responsibility, but which isn't true, read: 'All the involved subordinate commanders were in general agreement.'[61] It has often been claimed that Eaker was not supportive of bombing the Abbey so why did he go out of his way 30-years later to alter a true statement to a false one? The diaries and biographies of individuals such as Clark and Walker had been long published and gave a diametrically opposed view. Most obviously, Eaker wasn't there.

---

58   AFHRA Reel A6030, MAAF History, C-in-C Correspondence, Eaker to Arnold dated 21 March 1944.
59   Wilson 'Report to CCS', 30-1
60   TNA WO 204/456: Draft Despatch to Combined Chiefs of Staff. CAB 106/668 Wilson's Revised Draft.
61   AFHRA Reel 23197, Eaker, Why We Bombed Monte Cassino, 1974, Draft.

That April, the Vatican communicated to the US that the Abbey had been 'falsely described as a German fortress'. The final word in the US came from Cordell Hull on 4 May to Tittmann. He said the following:

> In agreement with the War Department you can at your discretion reply to the Vatican memorandum of April 12th repeating that the Allied Commander in the field have irrefutable proof that the Abbey of Monte Cassino was part of the German defensive system. At the moment we have no further comments to make.[62]

Tittmann informed the Vatican that the Allies had 'unquestionable evidence' that the Abbey formed part of the German defensive system. This again was almost certainly Wilson's discredited 'irrefutable evidence'. Tittmann passed this to Maglione on 23 May 1944. The irony is that the Americans, none of whose field commanders thought that the Abbey should be bombed are by this time rigidly sticking by the 'irrefutable evidence.' The evidence they didn't want the Vatican to see. The British, whose commanders pressed for the attack, have now at the governmental level completely discounted Wilson's evidence and chosen to keep quiet. Both nations have the same evidence, yet they have decided to deal with it in opposite ways. The evidence is very weak, so it is difficult to see how the Americans would have been convinced by it, if the British were not.

Quiet until this point, the Vatican went public with its criticism of the Allied action and issued a Memorandum from the Vatican Secretary of State over the bombing. By May 1944 even Eisenhower, who had ensured the Abbey was on a protected list and had warned of using Military Necessity as military convenience, had apparently bought into the strengthening myth that the Germans had used the Abbey. In his statement, Eisenhower appeared to be completely unconcerned that hundreds of Italian civilians had been needlessly killed. Journalist Thomas Allen of the *Washington Times,* when writing about the 'Monuments Men' in 2009, stated that Eisenhower made his statement to avoid a repetition of the Abbey bombing after D-Day.[63] When in command in the Mediterranean, he tried, albeit under pressure from his superiors in the War Department, to protect buildings. No similar effort was made to protect Italian civilians.

It was obvious from the Foreign Office correspondence, and as Rome became increasingly threatened, that bombing policy in Italy was concerning officials. Although not specifically referring to the bombing of the Abbey, Sir Orme Sargent, wrote to the British CoS Committee on 3 April 1944 regarding the bombing of Rome and Vatican property. This was in response to German propaganda and pleas from the Roman Catholic world to prevent Rome's destruction. The letter urged the CoS to examine potential courses of action as the Allied armies approached. Eden believed that the case for allowing Rome to become an open city was stronger than in 1943 when the Italians signed their armistice. Sargent was critical of Allied bombing policy stating that there was 'considerable resentment' from Italians; that Italy was becoming more sympathetic to the Germans; and that Russian prestige was gaining in Italy:

62   Tasciotti, p.224.
63   Thomas B. Allen, Dying for Art and Country, *Washington Times*, 29 November 2009.

Perhaps the Chiefs of Staff could weigh the military importance and value of the present bombing of <u>so-called military targets</u> [emphasis added by author] throughout Italy as against the political and moral effects which this bombing is undoubtedly producing on the Italian population and on world public opinion, in addition to the actual damage it is doing to buildings and works of art. May the remedy not lie in a more careful choice of military targets and in a greater use of expert precision bombing? [64]

After Rome's liberation, Churchill visited in August 1944. On 17 August he met with Alexander on Monte Trocchio where he could see the ruined Abbey for the first time. He then flew over the building in Alex's Dakota aircraft. A few days later, he had an audience with Pope Pius XII. They discussed the war and the dangers of communism. The destruction of the Abbey was not mentioned.

The extraordinary controversy over the destruction of the Abbey continued after the fighting was over. In October 1945 the Vatican produced a booklet regarding the Abbey. This booklet was distributed to visitors to the ruins and was based upon a Vatican report entitled '*The Monastery of Monte Cassino – Final Phase – July 1944*.' A copy of the booklet and report came into the possession of Tittmann, still US Charge d'Affaires to the Holy See. He complained to Monsignor Tardini, the head of Vatican Secretary of State's Foreign Section, that the booklet was wrong about the use that the Germans made of the Abbey. He continued to base this complaint on Wilson's 'irrefutable evidence' and wanted the booklet's wording changed. Tittmann loyally offered evidence of German use of the territory surrounding the Abbey, but none for inside it. The justification had therefore shifted to using the territory around the Abbey. Tittmann now said that German occupation was not the decisive factor in the decision. The facts were, however, that it remained the decisive factor in law, and Tittmann's explanation was not persuasive. The advice of Victor Cavendish-Bentinck to keep quiet because of the lack of evidence of occupation testified to this fact.

Tittmann was given permission to share the Vatican report with Osborne. Osborne, who knew that Wilson's evidence was weak, wrote a letter to the new Labour Party Foreign Secretary, Ernest Bevin, calling the Vatican's report 'tendentious and misleading.' He had also stopped saying that the Germans were using the Abbey or that they had tricked the Allies into bombing it. Instead, like Tittmann, he made the new claim that the Germans were using the territory around the Abbey. This was true, but the bombers didn't attack the territory around the Abbey. The one thing that all sides agreed upon was that the no further controversy should be courted.[65] Nobody wanted to revive the argument. Following the publication of the booklet by the Vatican, AFHQ continued to look for evidence that would support the assertion that there were Germans using the Abbey on 15 February 1944. In early 1946, in a letter to AFHQ, an officer suggested that the 2nd Polish Corps who had captured the Abbey in May 1944 had found a notebook used by a German artillery observer, *Hauptmann* Bauer, on 15 February.[66] This notebook has not resurfaced since and has never been used to justify the attack. The pres-

64   TNA CAB 80/82: COS (44) 316(O), 4 April 1944.
65   TNA FO 371/60797, British Legation To The Holy See to Foreign Secretary dated 20 December 1945.
66   TNA WO 204/5735, Advanced Allied Force Headquarters Liaison Section, MONTE CASSINO dated 7 January 1946.

ence of an observation officer in the Abbey in May does not prove that he was there in February and without the notebook it is unlikely that any proof would be forthcoming. This does show, however, that AFHQ and perhaps the Allies more generally, continued to grasp at straws for evidence to support their decision.

Sometime after the war the fate of the Abbey once again reared its head in the corridors of power. This time it was about offering money to help restore the Abbey. On 28 June 1949, Mr A G Blake wrote to the Private Secretary to the Chancellor of the Exchequer, Sir Richard Stafford-Cripps. Blake had heard Stafford-Cripps talk to a United Christian front at the Albert Hall. His suggestion was that as a 'gesture of goodwill a presentation in kind should be made towards the restoration of Monte Cassino Abbey.'[67] He added that 'the nation and not Church of England was responsible for its destruction.' Blake suggested that the British may wish to donate works of art to replace those destroyed. Beyond his Catholicism, Blake appears to have no other connection to the Abbey. In response, Stafford-Cripps sought Foreign Office advice on 1 July 1949 on what his response should be. His secretary wrote to an official working for Bevin on 4 July.[68] He asked the Foreign Office's Western Department for a response. The ingrained attitudes of some British civil servants were then exposed. One official thought that although it would be a 'generous act', he feared that 'the cry of 'Popery' would surely be heard.'[69] A more practical and less sectarian opinion came from another official who wrote, 'My own ears are deaf to cries of 'Popery!' To help restore the Abbey would obviously be a Christian, humane and civilised gesture. But in these hard times I fear that the cry of 'No cash!' was to rule it out.'[70] The response on 12 July was non-committal. They agreed that help would be 'a Christian and civilised action for HM Government', but also threw the issue back to HM Treasury. A month later, and probably not by coincidence, Major Jones was asked to write his report.

67   TNA FO 371/79530: Folio Z4757, A.G. Blake letter to E.H. Appleyard dated 28 June 1949.
68   TNA FO 371/79530: Folio Z4757, E H Appleyard letter to P F Kinna dated 4 July 1949.
69   TNA FO 371/79530: Folio Z4757, Minute by MB Jacomb dated 6 July 1949.
70   TNA FO 371/79530: Folio Z4757, Minute by John Russell, Western Dept, 7 July 1949.

26

Aftermath

History is a set of lies agreed upon.
     Napoleon Bonaparte

Arguments over whether the attack on the Abbey was justified have perpetuated over the decades and each side has shifted ground as more information has become available. The first arguments, mostly claiming that the Abbey was being used by the Germans for military purposes began before war's end. After it ended, it soon became clear that no such use had been made of the building, although this was known well enough before the bombing. Once it had been publicly established that the Germans were not using the Abbey, the bombing apologists shifted to positions either that they would have used it or that it didn't matter whether it was used. Its position, close to the German lines, was justification enough. The final common reason was that the building itself was a psychological enemy that drained the morale of the soldiers fighting in its shadow. They offered an impassioned and empathetic perspective on what it must have been like to fight below the Abbey, but passion disturbs their objectivity. The law is not written with emotion in mind and whilst one may have sympathy, the fact remains that to justify Military Necessity the Abbey had to be occupied by the enemy. The late historian, Danilo Veneruso, writing in *L'Osservatore Romano*, on the fiftieth anniversary of the Abbey's destruction wrote of the excuses given by the chroniclers of the battles:

> So improbable were the military motivations put forward that some even went so far as to present the destruction of the Abbey as a punishment inflicted by the Allies on the Church, which was hit in one of its most sacred places, for not having given complete support to the cause that they were fighting for.[1]

Although there were despatches from the principal formations and commanding officers, the first substantive published account came in 1945 when Fred Majdalany published his short book – *The Monastery*. This book set the tone for future works. What seems to be misunderstood is that although Majdalany was at Cassino, he was an officer of the British 78th Infantry Division.

---

1   Canciani, p.105.

This division was transferred to Freyberg's New Zealand Corps in March 1944.[2] Majdalany was not at Cassino when the Abbey was intact. He claimed that the Abbey was being used by the Germans and nobody should dispute his claim, because it was when he was there. To Majdalany, it was the building that was 'watching you', rather than the German soldiers. This was a common theme amongst many writers – the building itself was animate and malevolent. It was the Abbey's use before its destruction that was at issue, not after. Majdalany presented his views on the broken building, conflating the two, painting it in almost dystopian terms. Even the dust sheet of his book was forbidding and haunting with a dark gloomy Abbey perched menacingly – a view of the building that he never personally witnessed. For Majdalany, the Abbey was the enemy. He claimed that the Germans had turned the 'Monastery into a fortress.'[3] This view came from personal experience which emerged after the building's destruction. Its occupation and fortification were not in doubt, but had no relevance to the bombing. He used vivid rhetoric to animate the Abbey, making it a force to be reckoned with. 'It dominated and overshadowed their bodies and minds', he said. Without offering evidence he continued that 'the Monastery had become the bogey of every operation' as if the building had a life and mind of its own. Even the damage caused by the bombers was used to support the narrative by creating 'evil-looking prongs of masonry', calling it a 'sleeping monster.'[4] His argument was colourful and compelling for the uninitiated and for many who should have known better. It offered a first-hand perspective of a brave man who was there, with statements such as:

> It was the Monastery itself that was now the enemy. The very word ran through every conversation with the tireless rhythm of the wheels of a train. The Monastery…The Monastery … The Monastery … You couldn't get away from it. It possessed the imagination, it infected every mood, it tugged at the senses with the constancy of gravity.[5]

Majdalany may have been quoted more than any other author on the battles. This was despite the emotional and irrational tone of an account that often bordered on fiction. His accounts were given greater credibility through positive reviews by eminent historians such as John Terraine.[6] Undoubtedly, his battalion suffered greatly at the hands of soldiers lodged inside the Abbey and that experience dimmed his objectivity. His account, and his subsequent book *Portrait of a Battle* written in 1957 conflated his personal experience with the facts beforehand. This made his account of little value as a historical testimony. The second book was longer, but followed the same general theme as the first.

In his account he rightly identified that 'observation was the overriding issue at Cassino.'[7] He was also correct that the Abbey offered a panoramic view of the valley below. The flaw in his argument was that there were a hundred other places that offered a similar or better view. Nowhere in his book did Majdalany suggest that any of these warranted the air armada unleashed. He accused those who did not agree with him as expressing the 'naïve foolishness

2   TNA WO 214/29: Italian Campaign January – February 1944, Leese to Alexander letter, 6 February 1944.
3   Majdalany, *Monastery*, p.8.
4   Majdalany, *Monastery*, p.17, p.35.
5   Majdalany, *Monastery*, p.66.
6   John Terraine, Book Reviews, *The New Republic*, October 1957.
7   Majdalany, *Portrait,* p.120.

of the uninformed.'[8] He was the first, but by no means the last author to confuse rudeness with argument. Published seven years after Clark's memoir, the second Majdalany book was highly critical of the 'uninformed' army general and his view that the bombing was a mistake. He arrogantly dismissed Clark's opinion as an 'angry apologia.'[9]

A year before *The Monastery* was published, the truth was available. On 26 August 1949, Major Francis Jones of the Cabinet Office Historical Section was asked to produce an account of the bombing by his boss Brigadier Latham. Who originated the request was unclear, as was the eventual use that was made of the report, but it would not have been asked for on a whim. Someone fairly high-up asked for it, and the timing fits the enquiry to the British Chancellor of the Exchequer, and this is the most likely reason for the Jones report. As referenced in the last chapter, discussions were being had around this time about costs of reconstruction. The report may have been an assessment of liability by the British. If so, Jones' conclusions were probably not well-received. Just after Jones' report, the Committee for the Control of Official Histories suggested that the British government should commission a series of books on the war. Included in this was a commission by Eric Linklater, *The Campaign in Italy*, published in 1951. The book was first sponsored by the Military Adviser to the Ministry of Information, Lord Burnham, in early 1944 and was supported by Eisenhower.[10] Linklater's few lines concerning the destruction of the Abbey were almost entirely semi-fictional as well as being semi-official, claiming that the Abbey had been made into a fortress and that its 'spiritual purpose also served a secular intention.'[11] He also falsely claimed that 'only a dozen missiles went astray.'[12] The Abbey had no secular purpose other than as a civilian refuge and the bombing was wildly inaccurate. Linklater's book, published after Major Jones' report is notable that the conclusions were poles apart and the report was not cited. Why had the available evidence, which had been examined previously through Foreign Office files and the completely different conclusions made by Jones been completely ignored in Linklater's semi-official account which was officially published by the British?

Jones' conclusions were clear, and the report was buried under the 30-year rule. Specifically, he was asked to review the following:

a) To enquire into the circumstances leading to the initial bombing of the Cassino Abbey;
b) to discover who ordered this bombing; and
c) to establish whether the Germans had used the building for military purposes prior to the initial bombing.[13]

He submitted his report on 20 October 1949. The distribution of the report beyond Latham was limited, but at least six copies were produced, the sixth of which was sent to W M Gould at the RAF's AHB, who assisted in the report's compilation. It could, therefore have been a source for Guy Hartcup in his report for the Official Historian 16-years later, but was not referenced in

8   Majdalany, *Portrait,* p.117.
9   Majdalany, *Portrait,* p.118.
10   Chandler et al, *Eisenhower Papers, Vol III*, p.1780.
11   Eric, Linklater, *The Campaign in Italy* (London: HMSO, 1977), p.173.
12   Linklater, p.174.
13   TNA CAB 106/699, p.4.

the resulting Official History. The genesis and use of Jones' work remain an intriguing mystery today. Official reports, however, are neither commissioned nor written for no purpose.

Jones examined all the records that were available to him at the time. These were mostly British and AFHQ military records, but he did not use many of the USAAF records as these were not available to him. Nor did he use any German records beyond a piece from von Vietinghoff. Jones concluded:

> It is clear that General Wilson was not in possession of conclusive evidence prior to the bombing, and it is equally clear that he was not in a position to produce it subsequent to the bombing when asked to do so from London. The only direct evidence from the Allied side is an American statement that on 10th February 'a telescope' was seen in a window but does not say whether there were Germans in attendance. Statements of German prisoners and Italians must be open to suspicion, particularly as there is also conflicting evidence from such sources...There is no evidence in the documents that I have seen, which proves to my personal satisfaction that the enemy used the Abbey prior to 15th February 1944.[14]

It was known at an early stage, just over five-years after the event, from the Jones report that the evidence failed to support any of the conclusions of British authors on the battles, Majdalany, Jackson, Strawson and others. The myth of Military Necessity continued to be perpetuated even as Francis Jones was writing his report.

Jones' report, not visible to the public for many years, was available to organizations such as the Official Historians or the AHB. In the 1949 report, after examining all available intelligence summaries, Jones concluded above that there was no substantive evidence of the Germans occupying the Abbey.[15] The information available to Jones from the Foreign Office was incomplete. Although he had transcripts of many diplomatic telegrams sent from Osborne from the Holy See, he did not gain access to the Foreign Office files themselves. He probably only had access to copies of these messages that were sent to the War Cabinet Office. Consequently, he did not see the hand-written minutes placed on the files by officials before and after the bombing. He also did not use the report gained by Osborne in late 1945 produced by the Vatican. Having relooked at the evidence available to Jones, and other evidence and reports, such as those above that were not available to him, it remains the case that although some reporting supported a German occupation, the evidence was unreliable and should not have formed the basis of a predictably controversial decision. This was fully recognised by the senior British intelligence authority at the time, the Chairman of the Cabinet Office's JIC. Jones reached the same conclusion independently of the intelligence community.

In the same year as Jones' report, another report on the attack was produced as part of an account of New Zealand Corps operations. This report, which can be found in AHB files was written by Major Russell and regurgitated all the discounted reasoning for the bombing. The report suggested that the Abbey was the 'keep' of the German fortress and that it had been put into a 'strong state of defence', calling it the 'hub of the defensive system'.[16] This report made serious errors in detail. The weather was fine from 12 February it said, when in fact the

---

14   TNA CAB 106/699, p.39.
15   TNA CAB 106/699, pp.19-20.
16   TNA AIR 23/6598: Air Historical Branch History of NZ Corps, Major Russell, 1949.

weather was poor until the 14 February. Whilst unimportant in itself it opened the inference that German occupation was observed by air reconnaissance, which it was not. In the face of all the evidence the author claimed that the 'bombing was so accurate, few casualties were incurred' and 'a dozen bombs dropped astray.'[17] I doubt the soldiers from 4th Indian Division would agree, but they were not consulted. Probably more than a thousand bombs missed the target. The errors in this 'historical' account were so large that the only conclusions that can be drawn are that it was either a remarkably shoddy piece of work or that the facts had been obscured deliberately or through cognitive dissonance.

Gould wrote the AHB's own Italian Campaign narrative; he used Jones' report in his account and most of the primary evidence. Yet Gould's conclusion is different from Jones', although he had started to begrudgingly retreat from the 'Germans used it' position to the second line of defence that 'it didn't matter whether they used it' or 'they might have used it'. In defiance of all the evidence from British sources, he claimed the unimportance of German occupation and repeated the baseless claims of German trickery. His conclusion is worth quoting at length:

> In the foregoing pages an endeavour has been made to present the facts as a military jurist would view them, for it is of great importance that, in such a case, fundamental definitions be agreed on …while it is being pointed out that Cassino Abbey and its territory formed part of the main German defensive position and, therefore, had to be reduced. Even if, (and this cannot at this stage be proved), not a solitary German put foot in Cassino Abbey or in its territory before 15 February 1944, those few acres of ground provided a potential enemy refuge. They were part of a complex; they were a military unit, a position to be treated as a whole. Without possession of it, military control of the mountain was impossible. In the sweep of operations up Italy towards victory in some problematical future, to the Allied forces the entire country was potential enemy territory. They had Hitler's own word for it, for had he not directed the Germans to fight for every inch of ground? While it is likely that von Senger and other Germans were no less appreciative than the Allies of the spiritual value of Monte Cassino Abbey, it is improbable knowing what we do of the philosophy of the Nazis and observing how quickly after the event they occupied the Abbey and the Propaganda Ministry's alacrity in embroidering the theme, that German exploitation of the situation was anything but cold-blooded and calculating. [18]

Gould had no access to additional information yet made a few sweeping statements that hopefully no 'military jurist' would make. The claim that the entire mountain was a 'military unit' was nonsense; the Abbey was not part of any military unit, hence the strenuous efforts to prove German occupation. They did use all the territory up to the walls of the Abbey. Hitler had demanded that every inch be fought over, but Senger was well known for a liberal interpretation of the Fuhrer's orders. Gould's claim that the Allies were as appreciative as the Germans of the Abbey is unsustainable. The Germans, for whatever reasons, evacuated as much of the art as they could, and then made sure that the Abbey was not used as a defensive position when battle was joined. The Allies did not even have the cultural value of the Abbey as a factor when

17   TNA AIR 23/6598: Air Historical Branch History of NZ Corps, Major Russell, 1949.
18   Gould, p.291.

deciding to destroy it. As far as can be ascertained by records the 'Monuments Men', experts in cultural property, were not consulted.

Germany exploited its destruction, but no less than the Allies would have had the positions been reversed. The statement that the Germans had a poor reputation was insufficient cause; as Jones quite correctly stated in his conclusion, and which Gould ignored was that the Allies had no proof that their promises were meaningless. The assertion that they were 'cold-blooded and calculating' did not trump actual evidence. The actions of the enemy are never a moral justification for criminal behaviour. As Schaffer observed, 'How often was something done in the name of Military Necessity that could have been avoided through more careful reflection?'[19]

The first, and perhaps most influential, senior leader memoir from the US was that of Mark Clark, *Calculated Risk*, published in 1950. Clark's account was published close enough to events to allow a clear memory of events, undimmed by time and others' works. He was strenuous in his opposition to the bombing. His blow-by-blow recollection offered the reader a detailed account of how the decision was reached within Army command chains, but not how that decision was executed by the Air Forces. Many of the following accounts, especially from Americans, use Clark's memoir as the basis for a perspective that Clark was bullied into approving the act by the British. Perhaps with some justification, he tried to shift the blame to others, but did not fully explain why, if he was so sure that the bombing would be 'a tactical military mistake of the first magnitude,' did he not offer more strenuous opposition?[20] What three-star general knowingly commits such a grievous error? It does have a 'protest too much' whiff, and this assertion is supported by the diary of Freyberg, an account written at the time without the benefits of reflection. In Freyberg's diary, while clearly against the attack, Clark offers less resistance than *Calculated Risk* suggests. Clark's argument why there was no Military Necessity was based upon several factors, the most important of which was that the Germans were not using the Abbey for military purposes. His other arguments were that there were observation posts aplenty and that the military advantage was negligible. He suggested that a ruined Abbey would offer greater defensive potential to the Germans. Clark concluded that there was neither Military Necessity nor advantage in destroying the building. His view, he says, was supported by all his US subordinate commanders.

Another eyewitness account that is often quoted in relation to the bombing of the Abbey, but from the other end of the trench, is that of Lieutenant Harold Bond from the 141st Infantry Regiment. Despite being written 20-years after the event, *Return To Cassino* was a vivid reminder of the trials faced by the infantryman. Arriving from a replacement depot on the day of the 20 January 1944 attack, he was not part of the action on the Rapido. Despite not being involved, Bond described how his new battalion CO and all but one company commander had been killed or wounded.[21] He was assigned to be in charge of a mortar platoon. It was at this time that Bond first saw the Abbey. Like Majdalany, he brought the building to life with his narrative when he wrote, 'Like a lion it crouched, dominating all approaches, watching every move made by the armies down below.'[22]

19   Schaffer, p. xiv.
20   Clark, p.249.
21   Bond, pp.36-37.
22   Bond, p.39.

Bond used the visualisation of the crouching hunter to add danger and malice. He believed the more experienced soldiers about the Abbey's occupation, but he regretted its destruction as it 'symbolized what we were fighting for.'[23] Whilst the soldiers may well have thought the Abbey was being used as an OP, they had no solid evidence. The reason German artillery was so accurate was that Clark had chosen the most obvious attack locations. The Germans had been given preparation time to zero their guns. They needed no-one in the Abbey. Bond and his platoon were deployed onto the massif around 7 February to join Ryder's 34th Infantry Division and their own 142nd Infantry. He recounted how the companies of the regiment were around half-strength, painting a picture of an understrength division, full of new recruits with poor morale; incapable of conducting offensive operations in the harshest of conditions.[24] When he described the deployment of his platoon, he used his experience as Head of the English Department of the Ivy League Dartmouth College, taking the reader on a journey that could have been to Mordor rather than Cassino: 'There was a good deal of firing up on the great black mass which towered above and in front of us, and from the flashes of exploding shells we could occasionally see the abbey, which was otherwise buried in an impenetrable gloom.'[25] Throughout, both Bond and his men expressed no doubts that the Abbey was being used by the Germans, although at no point did he see the enemy. His account has been used as justification because of the effect it had on morale. This was an irrational, but understandable, reason. The destruction of the Abbey, and its subsequent occupation would only make the task of the assaulting Allied troops worse. The next to try, the Poles, would find this out in May 1944.

Another book at the centre of the argument for those who claim the attack on the Abbey was either a justifiable error or a tragic mistake was first published in 1966 and republished, with more material, in 1990.[26] This was Sir David Hunt's *A Don at War*. Hunt was a senior member of Alexander's intelligence staff and was also partly responsible for the authorship of his Official Despatch and a contributor to Molony's Official History. The evidence in question concerned an intercept that mistakenly reported a German battalion (*Abteilung*) in the Monastery whereas the message really asked whether the Abbot remained. This was used by John Ezard in 2000 when he claimed that it was new evidence included in a new book by Alexander's aide, Sir Rupert Clarke, that solved the mystery.[27] Actually, Hunt himself had used the incident ten years earlier.[28] Clarke claimed that he only realised the mistake as the bombers approached, but Hunt made no such claim. Clarke and Hunt were paid-up members of the British establishment. Neither were dissenting voices in a wartime controversy, and both remained fiercely loyal to Alexander. Clarke added an appendix on what others thought of Alexander; he only chose complimentary comments.[29] Hunt's illuminating evidence, whilst a possible explanation is itself full of mysteries. The incriminating piece of intelligence that gave Hunt his road to Damascus moment could not be found in the archives of the 15th Army Group. This is not that surprising, as many records

23   Bond, p.113.
24   Bond, p.66.
25   Bond, p.69.
26   The majority of Hunt's additional material was related to the use of ULTRA. This remained closed to the public in 1966.
27   Clarke, p.137 and John Ezard, 'Error led to Bombing of Monte Cassino', *The Guardian*. <https://www.theguardian.com/world/2000/apr/04/johnezard> (accessed 18 April 2020).
28   Hunt, pp.246-7.
29   Clarke, pp.228-30.

concerning this time have not survived. That it was not used in Wilson's evidence was also not surprising. Evidence that the attack resulted from a mistake did not fit the 'irrefutable' narrative, which was determined to prove occupation. It was surprising that this evidence was not in Alexander's Official Despatch from June 1950. It is more surprising that the evidence did not appear in the Official History, either in its first draft, which Hunt had a hand in writing, or in the final version which explored the decision to bomb the Abbey in depth. No other memoir or account made any reference to it. If it happened, he kept it to himself for at least 35-years.

The first American Official History, the first official word of any of the Allies, was Craven and Cate's history of the USAAF and it did not agree with Clark's view. The authors had also not seen Jones' work, and Crane pointed out that they did not always gain access to 'controversial issues.'[30] They continued to justify the attack based upon Wilson's discredited 'irrefutable evidence.'[31] As usual with accounts from the US, the Official History inferred, based upon Clark's memoir, that it was all the fault of perfidious Albion. The blame for the attack was placed squarely on Freyberg. They also used another favourite tactic to explain the attack, they diminished its importance. In this case they stated that the controversy is 'somewhat academic.'[32] This conclusion could be accepted if it were not for the following statement:

> The question of whether or not the Allies were justified in bombing the abbey may be solved by asking and answering one very simple question: on 15 February 1944 did the Allied leaders, after careful investigation, believe that the abbey was being used for military purposes? The answer is: they did.[33]

The evidence showed that at the time of the bombing this statement was not true. When the request was delivered by Freyberg, the evidence used by Wilson in his cable to the CoS to justify it was either not available or tucked away in obscure reports. None of the intelligence was collated beforehand justifying the attack. This evidence was soundly dismissed by the British Foreign Office when it appeared several weeks later. It was not credible to use in an Official History. The Allies did not carry out a 'careful investigation' and most of the generals closely associated with ground operations at Cassino, Americans at that. did not agree with this Official History's conclusion. Craven and Cate also justified the bombing by citing Eaker's flight over the Abbey, which did not happen. In their foreword, the authors summed up the Official Historian's view of the bombing:

> On 15 February US bombers destroyed the Benedictine Abbey at Monte Cassino... The reluctance of AAF leaders to bomb cultural or historical monuments is sufficiently documented in this history – witness the extreme care exercised in hitting military targets at Rome; the tragedy in the case on Monte Cassino is made more bitter by its futility as a military act.[34]

Whether the Allies took 'extreme care' is very much open to debate.

30   Crane, p.145.
31   Craven and Cate, p.363.
32   Craven and Cate, p.363.
33   Craven and Cate, p.363.
34   Craven and Cate, p. vii.

Majdalany and the USAAF historians were not the only ones who took issue with Clark's account. In 1950, , in a rebuttal to Clark in *The Times*, Kippenberger wrote that the US 34th Division had been fired upon from the Abbey walls from 6 February.[35] His claims are weak. No such report exists in the division's historical account or in the relevant regimental war histories. He also said that the Abbey was an 'ideal observation post', thereby justifying its destruction because of the possibility of a few soldiers and a pair of binoculars.[36] He also showed a poor grasp of German army procedures because as we have seen the German commander thought that it was such an obvious place that it was the least likely place he would have positioned his observers.

The official voice of New Zealand was first heard in 1957 when N C Phillips completed the Official History of the Italian Campaign. Phillips' account began with the familiar emotive tone, referring to the Abbey as a 'hateful tapestry.'[37] Phillips recognised its importance by devoting an entire chapter to its destruction.[38] Not surprisingly, and probably rightly, he did not place the responsibility on Freyberg. He understandably shifted the responsibility for the decision to Alexander.[39] He made the valid point that Clark was a victim of 'British encirclement' in the making of the decision. At no point did Phillips state whether the decision to destroy the Abbey was justified, but made the point that Freyberg requested it and Alexander approved it. Although still a closed report until the early 1980s, Jones' Abbey bombing report was always available to researchers and was uniquely used by Phillips, who gives Jones credit in his preface.[40] Why was it not used by other Official Historians such as C J C Moloney?

It took a while, until the late 1960s and early 1970s for the Official Historians of the British and Americans to deliver their verdicts. The first to appear was the Green Book, *Salerno to Cassino*, completed in 1967, published in 1969 and written by Martin Blumenson. Although the British Official History of the war in the Mediterranean began publication in 1954, the fifth volume that covered Italy in 1943 and early 1944 was not published until 1973. Its principal author, C J C Moloney, benefited from Blumenson's work. Blumenson appears sympathetic towards Clark; indeed, he penned his biography. He also dedicated an entire chapter to events surrounding the attack on the Abbey. This chapter was perhaps the most detailed examination of the chain of events that concluded with the bombing of the Abbey from the ground forces' perspective. Despite his exhaustive analysis as to why Clark did not think there was Military Necessity to bomb the Abbey, Blumenson then justified the attack based upon the proximity of German positions. He also unquestionably accepted Wilson's 'irrefutable evidence', despite again knowing that Clark's view did not support them. He even quoted the II Corps Chief Intelligence Officer, Colonel Walter, whose organisation accumulated all the 'irrefutable evidence'. Walter stated that there had been no reports of firing from the building and that there were up to 2,000 civilians inside. Blumenson also accepts the Eaker flight as contributing evidence. He offered no explanation for why Freyberg's 36-fighter bombers became a strategic armada, but he speculated that he thought that Eaker and Devers pressed for the heavies as 'air force planners seized on the

---

35   *The Times*, 19 October 1950, Issue 51826, p.3.
36   *The Times*, 19 October 1950, Issue 51826, p.3.
37   Phillips, p.196.
38   Phillips, pp.201-224.
39   Phillips, p.208.
40   Phillips, pp.vi-vii.

opportunity to demonstrate the power of the bomber.'[41] What Blumenson called an 'experiment' is circumstantial but highly credible.

The British account differed little from Blumenson's. Molony used Eisenhower's 29 December 1943 statement to justify the Military Necessity to attack the Abbey. This said, 'If we have to choose between destroying a famous building and sacrificing our own men , then our men's lives count infinitely more and the buildings must go.'[42] Few would argue with this sentiment, but a few pages earlier, Molony stated that: 'There is abundant and convincing evidence that the Germans made no use whatever of the Abbey's buildings until after the Allies had wrecked them by bombing.'[43] How then can it be reconciled that a building that had no soldiers in it threatens the lives of 'our own men'? This is not mere hindsight. Clark in his contemporary account discounted this argument for Military Necessity. Molony, however, may have unwittingly hit upon, although he didn't quote, another part of Eisenhower's statement that concerned 'personal convenience' when he made the point regarding the pressure that Alexander and Wilson were under from Churchill.[44] The views of the American commanders, who disagreed with the decision were relegated to the footnotes, whereas the British views remained in the main text.[45] Molony then goes on to say that both Tuker and Alexander deplored the decision they were forced to take. There was no evidence at the time that this was the case. The British history claimed that the leaflets dropped in the vicinity of the Abbey on 14 February stated that the building would be bombed the next day.[46] This statement is wrong; the leaflet did not state that the building was to bombed, nor did it give a date. Molony appeared to have made limited use of Hartcup's work and no use at all of the Jones report. The facts were stretched just enough to create doubt.

The first publicly published argument from the German perspective was printed in German in 1950 by Kesselring's Chief of Staff, *Generalleutnant* Siegfried Westphal. Published a year later in English, *The German Army in the West*, was a broad account of his duties. Westphal explained the destruction of the Abbey as Allied ignorance rather than wilfulness.[47] His boss, in his 1953 memoir simply stated that the Abbey was unoccupied by German troops.[48] The first substantive front-line account by the Germans was published in 1956, and in English in 1964. *The Times* reviewed this account of the battle from a German battalion commander from the 1st *Fallschirmjäger* Division, *Major* Rudolf Böhmler, who occupied the ruins of the Abbey following its destruction. Whilst the reviewer praised the quality of the message, the messenger's conclusions are damned by faint praise.[49] Böhmler was against the bombing of the Abbey, although he was not there on the actual day of the attack. He made it clear that only a few Germans entered the building, none for military purposes.[50] Böhmler devoted an entire chapter to the Abbey and its tone occasionally verged on protesting too much. He was generous to Clark

41   Blumenson, *Salerno to Cassino*, p.409.
42   Molony, p.709.
43   Molony, p.695.
44   Molony, p.705.
45   Molony, p.709, fn.1.
46   Molony, p.713.
47   Westphal, p.155-6.
48   Kesselring, p.195.
49   *The Times*, Issue 55940, 20 February 1964, p.17.
50   Böhmler, p.176.

for his resistance to the attack, but made no other comments on blame, stating that: 'Monte Cassino fell victim to human inefficiency, political considerations and the brutalizing influences of war.'[51] He argued persuasively that the head-on attack against the strongest element of the German defences made no military sense. Böhmler died in 1968. Nearly a half century later his book was re-published in 2015. The foreword for this new edition was penned by Professor Peter Caddick-Adams, a supporter for the bombing, with whom Böhmler would have strongly disagreed. Although Caddick-Adams resisted detailed argument he couldn't resist casting doubt on the German occupation. [52] Caddick-Adams knew full well what the Germans did, as his own account published in 2013 testifies. Despite it being the pivot of their defences, as Kesselring admitted, they strictly observed its neutrality throughout. Böhmler's book was perhaps the first published account that offered substantial evidence that this was the case in the face of an accepted wisdom that the Germans were the villains. Jones' report of course was gathering dust in the Cabinet Office archives.

The next nail in the coffin of the Allied account was also from a German. In 1960, Senger published his memoir, translated into English in 1963, entitled *Neither Fear Nor Hope*. He was universally accepted as an anti-Nazi soldier who dutifully carried out the orders he was given and was one of the best defensive corps commanders. Senger could see no military reason why the Abbey was attacked, although it cannot have been a surprise as he would never have used it as an observation position because it was likely to be attacked.[53] Senger also largely exonerated Clark, but he bases this on Clark's memoir. Senger's major criticism was not that they bombed the Abbey, but that after the failure of US II Corps' attack on 11 February, that they showed so little imagination, trying to do the same thing in the face of heightened defences, and yet expecting a different result.[54]

Following Majdalany, over the next decades, there were several accounts by British soldiers, many of whom fought in the campaign in some capacity. In 1967, General Sir William Jackson, a veteran of the later Cassino battles wrote *The Battle For Italy*. Whilst a detailed and credible account, with a foreword by Alexander, Jackson only looked at the battles from a soldier's perspective. Air forces are hardly mentioned and only when they offered support to the army. Jackson's view of the destruction of the Abbey continued the usual theme of British officers. He discussed the possibilities of Tuker avoiding the Abbey, but then in contradiction justified its destruction.[55] As with many others he belittled the debate of Military Necessity, despite it being a fundamental element of the Law of War.[56] Jackson made many points that other British soldiers have made. Later he admitted that another way was found, thereby making any attack on the Abbey militarily unnecessary. The British stuck to the adage 'absence of evidence does not equal evidence of absence'. He also justified the attack on the basis that German positions around the Abbey sealed its fate. General Jackson showed little understanding of the command and control of forces in the attack on the Abbey. He looked at the decision-making process only through an army lens and assumed that only Alexander and Wilson had a say. He omitted the fact that the strategic air forces primarily operated under

51   Böhmler, p.182.
52   Böhmler, p. ix.
53   Senger, *Neither Fear Nor Hope*, p.202.
54   Senger, *Neither Fear Nor Hope*, p.206.
55   Jackson, pp.193-4.
56   Jackson, pp.193-4.

Spaatz and Eaker. He added that the decision was 'endorsed by the Chiefs of Staff.'[57] There was no evidence that it was.

Another veteran, E D 'Birdie' Smith of the Gurkha Regiment wrote his account of the battles in 1975. The conclusions followed the British trend of argument as he cast a balanced and critical eye over the decisions. He concluded that its destruction was pointless and a military blunder, but still justified it because of its impact on morale and through its use as an observation post.[58] He stated that the Germans used wireless and telephones to direct their artillery, but there was no intelligence whatsoever that they did this from the Abbey, and there would have been. There was evidence that they did not, and this was well known to Fifth Army. In the paperback publication of his book in 1989, following more controversy over Herbert Bloch's highly critical pamphlet on the attack, Smith strongly defended Tuker's role. Yet another Italian veteran, Rayleigh Trevelyan, wrote *Rome 44* in 1981. Whilst exploring the battles, he examined in depth the situation in the Italian capital prior to its capture. He described the situation in Rome as far as the Vatican and the Abbey were concerned making the point that the Allies did not believe any German promises. Whilst this may have been true of diplomats such as Osborne, it was certainly not true in the intelligence centres at American formations close to Cassino. Trevelyan called the attack on the Abbey 'a windfall' for German propaganda.[59] Like many others, he pointed out that Allied soldiers all thought the Abbey was being used as an observation post, implying that this had a psychological and morale impact. He avoided making a judgement on whether the attack was justified. Trevelyan was one of the few authors who speculated that sectarian issues may be behind the decision, but the evidence for any malicious religious machinations is lacking.[60] Alexander, an Ulster Protestant, had shown no bias beyond obvious class differences to the Roman Catholic faith. Trevelyan accepted much of Wilson's evidence, and he also used Eaker's now mythical overflight to suggest it provided evidence to his American colleagues. It didn't, because it never happened. Trevelyan finished with the observation that the Germans could not be trusted. Whilst understandable, it was not only the Germans that stated that the Abbey was not used for military activity. He went to some length to exonerate Tuker, commenting that he did not want a head-on attack against the Abbey. Trevelyan's account made use of the Foreign Office files regarding the attack, but no use of the Jones report.

In 1986, *Tug of War,* was written by former soldiers, Dominic Graham and Shelford Bidwell. Their account was superbly knowledgeable about the strategy and tactics employed. They were critical of both Alexander and Clark throughout the key period of the Cassino and Anzio battles. Regarding the Abbey, the authors identified that it would 'hypnotise' all the commanders in the battles, identifying a root cause of the attack on the Abbey.[61] Clark, had he released his formations to assist on the flanks and earlier in the mountains could have succeeded without destroying the Abbey. He was swayed by national pride, verging on paranoia against his principal ally and he exploited the weakness of his British commander. Alexander, they concluded, failed to order the reinforcement which resulted in the Indians then taking over from exhausted formations, broken in futile attacks. Timely reinforcement may have given the attack that impetus it needed

---

57   Jackson, p.194.
58   Smith, p.205.
59   Trevelyan, p.119.
60   Trevelyan, p.124.
61   Graham and Bidwell, p.151.

to overcome weakening defences. By the time the Indians were ready, they were almost back to square one. In talking about who gave the order for the Abbey to be bombed, they concluded that it was Alexander at the insistence of Clark. As previously discussed, neither Clark nor Alexander could <u>order</u> air support.[62] They could only <u>request</u> it. The authors suggested that the procedures for requesting air support were not fully developed in Fifth Army. In fact, the procedures between Fifth Army and the Strategic Air Force were non-existent because army support was never their role.[63] They correctly pointed out that had there been a threat of excessive casualties, Freyberg could appeal to Wellington. The New Zealand government had no pull on the bombers either nor were its soldiers threatened as it was Indian troops attacking Monastery Hill. The assertion that it was Clark who insisted on the use of heavy bombers, rather than the fighter-bombers of Freyberg's request is possible, but little evidence supports it. The authors claimed that Eaker agreed to use his heavy bombers for political reasons to appease Arnold.[64] This is plausible, but Eaker's absence in the crucial days prior to the bombing makes it likely that it was one of his principal subordinates that took this decision.

They use the occupation was a 'red herring' argument as the hill was a 'legitimate objective'. The first judgement was wrong, although the second is correct. The hill was legitimate, as were dozens of others that were not soaked by bombs. These others did not have a large Abbey at their summit; most did have German positions. What is a red herring was the 330-yard zone around the Abbey that they pointed out was abandoned by the German defenders. It held no power in the international treaties in force at the time, whereas the Abbey itself was protected by law unless it was used for military purposes. Nevertheless, these authors concluded correctly that Clark was fighting two battles; one military, one political. He lost both when the Abbey was destroyed. He failed tactically when the Indians failed to successfully take the hill and he failed politically when the Germans used the attack as an open goal for their propaganda narrative.[65]

In 1987, another Italian campaign veteran and experienced officer, Major General John Strawson wrote his views in his book *The Italian Campaign*. Strawson drew widely upon previous authors. He sat on the fence as to whether the Germans occupied the Abbey, although the evidence was overwhelming that they did not. One senses wishful thinking in Strawson's conclusions. Strawson's main justification for the destruction of the Abbey, however, followed that of Kippenberger that 'If not occupied on one day, it could be on the next.'[66] Strawson failed to challenge the entire tactical sense in attacking this position, although he acknowledged that value of the attack was 'questionable.'[67] An attack that had questionable tactical value clearly lacked Military Necessity.

Accounts of the destruction of the Abbey from the American perspective are often sympathetic to Clark's dilemma with Freyberg and Alexander. There are fewer accounts by old soldiers. Most tended to heap the blame on the British. Typical of this was Adleman and Walton who wrote *Rome Fell Today* in 1968. Using many first-hand accounts, mostly American and including Clark interviews, they concluded that the 'wiping out of the Abbey was an act of historic vandalism which transcended military protocol … one of the most serious mistakes of

---

62   Graham and Bidwell, p.180.
63   Graham and Bidwell, p.194.
64   Graham and Bidwell, p.200.
65   Graham and Bidwell, p.182.
66   Strawson, p.150.
67   Strawson, p.151.

the campaign.'[68] Despite being highly critical of the decision to bomb the Abbey, these authors did not criticise Clark for his unwillingness to stand on his principals. A similar conclusion was reached by Edwin Hoyt in his 2002 book *Backwater War*. Hoyt suggested that all the American officers were united in their belief that there was no necessity to destroy the Abbey and that the rubble would be used by the Germans afterwards and that there would be worldwide damage to the Allied cause in Roman Catholic countries. Again, blame was almost removed from Clark completely. Clark had no problems disagreeing with Alexander at Anzio and again at Valmontone, but not for the bombing of the Abbey.[69]

US military historian Carlo D'Este, adopted another line in *Fatal Decision* in 1991. Unlike most US authors D'Este does not exonerate Clark. He suggested that his inaction 'was a major factor' in the attack.[70] This view may be unfair as most sources suggested that Clark argued vigorously against attacking. D'Este joins the commentators in the 'it didn't matter' corner when he stated that the Abbey was 'an essential component of the German defences.'[71] Like some of his British colleagues, he makes the observation that had the 34th Division offensive in the mountains been halted before the division was exhausted and had the Indians taken up the offensive sooner, the equally exhausted Germans may have succumbed. D'Este accurately described the inaccuracy of Allied bombers, the propaganda victory handed to the Germans and the futility of an attack where the ground follow-up force was unready. He concluded with the comment, 'The bombing of the Abbey of Monte Cassino was the crowning example of the failure of Allied strategy in Italy in 1944. The Allies had not reaped a single military benefit from it and had instead committed a major blunder.'[72] D'Este's view of Allied strategy proposes that the battles in Italy were designed to lead to decisive victory. Whilst the generals may have desired this, it was not the strategic intent, whose entire design was to be nothing more than to contain German combat divisions, a task in which it was entirely successful.

Another balanced and non-judgemental account came from Rick Atkinson in his *The Day of Battle* (2007). In this account, he vividly described the conditions faced by the common soldier. His harrowing narrative whilst not an excuse for the attack on the Abbey acted at least as a reason. Atkinson accepted the Eaker flight as being an important plank in the Allied evidence, but rightly dismissed Wilson's evidence. He avoided pointing the finger of blame at any party to the attack instead he blamed the war, 'once again something had been lost in this dark epoch of loss.'[73]

As the soldier-historians in Britain began to disappear in the 1980s, the baton of controversy was taken up by professional historians. One of the most critical, and most detailed, accounts is *The Hollow Victory* by John Ellis published in 1984. Despite being highly critical of many decisions taken by allied generals, Ellis fell into line as far as the bombing of the Abbey was concerned. He clearly had great sympathy with the views of Tuker and Juin that a wide envelopment of Cassino was a more effective way of breaching the *Gustav* Line. He fell into the same traps as some other authors on the subject regarding the Abbey. He used the 'on the main line of

68   Adleman and Walton, p.179.
69   Edwin P. Hoyt, *Backwater War: The Allied Campaign In Italy, 1943-1945* (Westport CT: Praeger Publishing, 2002), pp.136-139.
70   Carlo D'Este, *Fatal Decision* (London: Fontana Books, 1991), p.259.
71   D'Este, p.259.
72   D'Este, p.261.
73   Atkinson, p.441.

defence' argument that its fate was sealed when it became entangled with the German defensive line. Ellis also argued that the destruction was justified because 'Alexander had his finger accurately on the pulse of his troops.'[74] Both these arguments are entirely true, but excuse rather than justify the attack. Neither its location nor its morale effect carried any weight in the Military Necessity argument. This is a legal judgement based upon evidence, not emotive opinion.

Also published in 1984 and updated in 2002, was the account of David Hapgood and David Richardson. This account was one of the first revisionist accounts that made widespread use of the diaries of Matronola and Grossetti and the history of Leccisotti. This book correctly identifies the problems with the 'irrefutable evidence,' especially the error with misidentifying the prisoner from Albaneta Farm. It also offers the suggestion that the attack with heavy bombers was a demonstration by a failing USAAF. Unfortunately, as in previous and future accounts, this analysis is circumstantial as the documentary evidence to prove it has not surfaced. Unlike many historians, Hapgood and Richardson provide a holistic account of the Abbey's destruction and not the narrow military viewpoint that had been almost universally provided by historians. Equally good in this respect, although never published in English, is the 2013 account by Italian journalist Nando Tasciotti. These three authors have researched more widely than almost everyone else, sourcing many of the diplomatic messages and those of the Vatican. Both make widespread use of the Jones report, something that the majority of military historians have not done. They are balanced assessments of the destruction of the Abbey that quite rightly judge that the building's destruction was a colossal mistake. The same year, one of the surviving monks, Agostino Saccomanno, was asked to give his account of whether the Germans occupied the Abbey:

> No, they weren't there, any statement to the contrary is false and the efforts of English historians above all to question whether they were there are entirely specious. Lord Alexander, who returned to Montecassino three times after the war asked us quite tendentious questions as if to find a justification for what was decided by Allied commands. We also replied to Lord Alexander that the Germans were not there.[75]

The argument that the attack on the Abbey was a grave and unlawful mistake, was invigorated by Catholic scholar and historian of Montecassino, Herbert Bloch, who in 1973 wrote a piece for the periodical *Benedictina*. In 1976, this was turned into a short book that was published and sold by the Abbey. Bloch was perhaps the first author since the Papal pamphlet to be entirely critical of the bombing, using many available texts and interviews to reach his conclusions. He also relied on interviews with Matronola, the secretary to the Abbot, who was himself Abbot in 1973. Matronola was present during the bombing, assisted in the evacuation and accompanied Diamare during the period of his interviews with the Germans. Bloch's account has biases but is mostly an accurate account. He has, however, been pilloried, mostly in Britain. In 1983, he was forced to defend his article in *The Times* following letters from publisher John Canning and author Rayleigh Trevelyan. Canning, author and publisher with the UK's Century Books, but with no apparent connection to the battle, is worth quoting in full so that the reader can judge the extent of the controversy nearly four decades later:

74   Ellis, *Hollow Victory*, p.172.
75   Canciano, p.189.

Sir, I have recently returned from a short stay near Salerno during which I visited the Abbey at Monte Cassino. I was deeply impressed by the magnificent work of reconstruction still in progress and moved by the recollection of the many lives lost in the fighting of 1943-44.

The experience, however, was marred for me by the fact that the only account of the abbey's destruction in 1944 available there is a booklet with an overwhelmingly pro-German bias. Further, it carried the abbey's imprint, thus imparting to it the hallmark of authority.

The author, a one-time German citizen launches a bitter and unfair attack on the Allied C-in-C at the time, General Sir Harold Alexander, and also on two of his subordinate generals who called for the bombing of February 15 1944 – Major General Francis Tuker, commander of the 4th Indian Division and Lieutenant General Sir Bernard Freyberg, commander of the New Zealand Corps.

On the other hand, General Frido von Senger und Etterlin, who commanded the 14th Panzer Corps is held up as a shining example of scrupulous consideration for the integrity of the abbey. The fact that the German Command hinged the Gustav Line on Monastery Hill, and the abbey is conceded only grudgingly, as though this was an incidental and peripheral factor.

The author assumes that the Allies should have known or could easily have found out that the abbey was not occupied by the Germans at the time of the bombing, though not disputing that the latter's defences were dug into the hill right up to the monastery walls. It is an assumption all too easy to make in hindsight and quite unjustifiable. Even such an eagle-eyed airman as Ira C Eaker, flying a Piper Cub 500-feet above Monte Cassino, attested to seeing German troops entering and leaving the abbey.

Moreover, in the mind of every Allied soldier at Cassino, enemy occupation of the monastery was a fact; its monumental and all-pervading presence became a symbol of German dominance of the battlefield. Lord Alexander was later to write: 'When soldiers are fighting for a just cause and are prepared to suffer death and mutilation in the process, bricks and mortar, no matter how venerable, cannot be allowed to weigh against human lives.'

That the bombing of the abbey was a tragedy no one disputes. But to impute blame to one side only is both dishonest and unfair. It blights the memory of the Commonwealth and Polish soldiers whose graves at the foot of Monastery Hill so movingly attest to their sacrifice.

The fact that thousands of people from all over the world are gaining their only knowledge of the battle from this publication must surely be a matter of concern to us. The present abbot is a good man with a high reputation. Peace and reconciliation are the watchwords of his great Order; 'Pax' is engraved on the abbey's portals. Would he not be enhancing these precepts if, in the interests of justice and understanding, he were to permit another publication into the monastery bookstall which expressed the Allied dilemma and anguish of 1944?

The recent visit to this country of Pope John Paul II marked the adulthood of the Roman Catholic community in this country. Could not perhaps one or more of its distinguished lay figures take up this matter in an appropriate way?[76]

76   John Canning, 'Destruction of Monte Cassino' in *The Times*, Letters to the Editor dated Monday 23 August 1982.

Canning, whose expertise in the history of the abbey or the war more broadly is uncertain, throws the entire armoury of apologia at Bloch. Firstly, he tries *ad hominem* attacks by creating a bias through Bloch's German nationality. He is clearly unaware, or perhaps ignores, that he is a Jew who was forced to leave both Nazi Germany and Fascist Italy prior to the outbreak of war, as pointed out in the *Times* a few days later by the art historian, wartime OSS member, and fellow Jew, Professor Ernst Kitzinger.[77] His brother was murdered by the Nazis. He holds no flame for the Nazi regime and to suggest that he does is ridiculous. His pamphlet was not pro-German, but it did not concur with the Allied narrative. These are not the same thing. He then proceeds to complain that the Abbey bookshop does not sell an account more favourable to the Allies. The Benedictine Order was entirely certain of its position with regards to blame. It blamed the Allies in all respects. Why would the monks sell a book they fundamentally disagreed with? Perhaps Mr Canning also expected to see works on paganism in the bookshop? He then commits a number of factual errors, all designed to enhance his spurious position. Alexander, as we have already described, was not the Allied C-in-C; Eaker did not fly over the Abbey prior to the attack; those with the closest association with the Abbey during the fighting did not think the Germans were using it. Finally, and perhaps most unforgivably, Canning used the sacrifice of those who fought there as an emotive device. It should be remembered that prior to the attack on the Abbey no Commonwealth or Polish soldier had fought near the building. Those that died, all died after the attack. It was the Americans that suffered prior to its destruction. Their commanders did not feel the decision to be justified, yet Mr Canning completely omits this fact or even their sacrifice. Canning would doubtlessly be disappointed by other accounts to be found in the Abbey bookshop. The account of Leccisotti and the monks' diary by Eusebio Grossetti and Matronola both provide contemporary perspectives of the events surrounding the bombing; both deny German use of the Abbey. What motivated Canning to write this letter over the seemingly trivial lack of books in a bookshop? This appears to be Canning's only Letter to the Editor. Trevelyan wrote in support of Canning a few days later.[78] His aim was clearly to have Bloch's pamphlet, that was at this time several years into print with a very limited distribution, removed from circulation. Fortunately, others, including a retired Royal Artillery Chaplain disagreed.[79] Bloch's pamphlet was imperfect, as was Trevelyan's *Rome 44*, published in 1981, as is this account. That does not warrant a campaign that amounts to censorship. He was rightly indignant at the attempt to suppress his account of the attack.[80]

In a similar vein and published in Cassino by my old acquaintance Federico Lamberti in 1989, is the battlefield tour guide of Colonel John Green. As well as a guide to the battlefield, Green provides the reader, most likely a visitor to the town and Abbey with a short history. He loyally followed the British viewpoint, agreeing wholeheartedly that there was a Military Necessity to destroy the Abbey. He bases this viewpoint on the 'irrefutable evidence' of Wilson, which does not bear even light scrutiny. Even Green recognises that one of the key pieces

77 Ernst Kitzinger, 'Destruction of Monte Cassino' in *The Times*, Letters to the Editor dated Friday 27 August.
78 Rayleigh Trevelyan, 'Destruction of Monte Cassino' in *The Times*, Letters to the Editor dated Thursday 26 August 1982.
79 David Stevens, 'Destruction of Monte Cassino' in *The Times*, Letters to the Editor dated Friday 27 August 1982.
80 Herbert Bloch, 'Destruction of Monte Cassino' in *The Times*, Letters to the Editor dated Friday 7 January 1983.

of evidence, the prisoner from Point 468, does not refer to the Abbey, yet this fails to shift his position. He suggests that this provided 'strong suspicions but not 'proof'' of German use. This is clearly insufficient to warrant the destruction of a religious building and the deaths of hundreds of innocent civilians. Unable to demonstrate adequate necessity, he then goes on to criticise those who do not agree with him. He calls them 'naïve' if they viewed occupation as the only reason. In the Law of War and in the eyes of the British Foreign Office, this was the only reason. Green uses all the other reasons, all of which have been dismissed, to justify the attack. He then accuses the critics as being mainly 'non-military' and in an 'armchair making lofty pronouncements.' Many of these armchair 'critics' were very experienced military officers, many of them far more familiar with the battlefield than the Colonel. The argument that they were bombing the feature holds no credibility. If that were the case other features such as Point 593, Point 575 and the Albaneta Farm would have received equal treatment. These features were undoubtedly German positions that caused the Allies difficulties. None received the same aerial bombardment. The Colonel was right about the difficulties of making decisions when in command, but Generals Clark, Walker, Keyes, Ryder and Juin who were there at the time, and who all criticised the decision had not seen an armchair for some while! Green appeared to believe that decisions made rashly in the heat of battle are better than those made calmly and deliberately. What is naïve is an officer who believes that the laws of war do not apply to us as they apply to the enemy. We have no moral right to criticise behaviour if we do not uphold the highest standards ourselves. The worst thing about this pamphlet, however, is that it was aimed at tourists and veterans visiting Cassino and was on sale in several shops in the town. At least Mr Canning would be pleased with this literary diversity.

There are multiple accounts from New Zealand historians in addition to Phillips. Whilst they were diligent in their use of evidence, most clearly wished to exonerate their national hero. This was not an unreasonable thing to do, and he was a tactical commander who wanted the best for his troops. Matthew Wright's 2003 book offered compelling evidence that Freyberg did not ask for heavy bombers, and this is supported by US air doctrine which instructed ground commanders to ask for an effect, leaving the method to the airmen. There were several statements that contradicted Wright's argument. It did not matter what Freyberg asked for, there remained no Military Necessity to attack the Abbey. Psychological reasons do not equate to Military Necessity. A more recent account of the battles was published by New Zealanders Jeffrey Plowman and Perry Rowe in 2011. Their book was highly detailed but concentrated very heavily on the activities of ground forces. There was very little attention paid to air support. They did, however, take a view on the bombing of the Abbey. Whilst they accepted that the Germans did not use the Abbey for military purposes, they defended the argument of Military Necessity by claiming that because the Germans used every inch of territory up to the walls of the Abbey, this allowed them to fire upon Allied positions from a position of impunity. This is not a new argument, nor is it correct.

There have been a few recent British contributions to the debate. One was in 2003 when Matthew Parker devoted a chapter to its destruction in his book *Monte Cassino*. Parker concentrated very much on the land battle, drawing on many personal recollections of those who fought there. In this it was a tactical account that viewed the decisions made from the perspective of the frontline soldier. Whilst this offered a richness to the narrative, it lacked the objectivity that the making of these decisions required. It was also highly selective and ignored many of the adverse voices, mostly American, that were against the attack. Parker had little understanding of the air battle, and he made a few basic factual errors that affected the power of his argument.[81] The sloppy use of nomenclature showed a disinterest of the role of airpower and its relationship with ground forces in Italy. Regarding the Abbey, Parker decided to justify the attack using the whole armoury of reasoning previously discussed. He did not reference the Foreign Office files where the occupation of the Abbey was the principal requirement to justify its destruction. Parker discussed the high morale of the New Zealand Corps up to the end of its furlough in the first week of February, but then used Alexander's justification of the psychological threat of the building. Perhaps most unsatisfactory is that Parker claimed that Wilson used his 'irrefutable evidence' at the time of the bombing to justify the attack. This evidence was not used on 15 February and was only compiled nearly a month later. Even then it was rejected by London. He falsely gave an impression that the attack was at least made upon some evidential basis taken from intelligence. This was not the case and almost half of Wilson's evidence was gathered after the attack.

A more neutral position was taken by British historian Ian Gooderson in 2003 and again in 2008. He was one of the few authors to refer to Jones' 1949 report.[82] Despite the conclusions of Jones that the Abbey was not being used by the Germans as an observation position or anything else, Gooderson can't resist dipping his toe into the psychological reasoning, using the term 'watchful eyes.'[83] Much of this again concentrated on witness testimony from soldiers at Cassino after the destruction of the Abbey such as Majdalany and not therefore a valid justification in the first place. In general, he avoided passing judgement on the correctness of the decision, rather sticking to its difficulties. In a very detailed book on the battles, renowned British historian and experienced guide to the Cassino battlefield, Peter Caddick-Adams published his *Ten Armies in Hell* in 2013. This book is excellent in its coverage of the four battles, but again it focuses on the travails of the common soldier. Whilst this is creditable, it is also naturally in sympathy with the extreme difficulties encountered, and therefore often views the battle in narrow focus. Caddick-Adams is clearly an expert on land warfare of the period, but he shows a less sure touch when recounting the air battle. His major error was in assuming that just because three British generals decided that there was Military Necessity, that this was in fact the case. Military Necessity was a legal term, defined in internationally agreed treaties. It was not based around the opinions of three men, or it should not have been. He then described the usual stack of evidence that had been taken after the fact, discredited, unused in the actual decision or in the case of Eaker's flight, imaginary.

Not all accounts of the battles came from an Anglo-American or German perspective. In 1980, Polish veteran and author, Janusz Piekalkiewicz wrote his account, which not surprisingly devotes considerable time to the Polish action, as the II Polish Corps struggled to conquer the Abbey and the surrounding heights. Nevertheless, in his perspective on the battles leading up to the Polish action, he offers the view that the bombing of the Abbey was an unnecessary act that gained no military advantage and that a wide flanking movement as advocated by Juin and Tuker would have been more fruitful. Juin himself in his memoir calls the attack a 'rash experiment.' One of the latest books, written in 2017 by Greek historian Angelos Mansolas followed

---

81   Parker, pp.174-5.
82   Gooderson, *A Hard Way to Fight a War*, p.338.
83   Gooderson, *A Hard Way to Fight a War*, p.274.

some of the usual paths and offered reasons, mostly psychological and morale-based without giving a judgement on their validity.

This review of the opposing sides in what is an ongoing Fifth Battle of Cassino, that has been raging since 15 February 1944 is by no means comprehensive. I have not included in this chapter the memoirs of Kesselring, Alexander or Wilson, nor the biographies of the airmen involved. Their positions are either laid out in their relevant chapters and do not need repeating or have not been expressed definitively. This chapter demonstrates that there has been a constant flow of work since the end of the Second World War and that the argument has continued well into the 21st Century. Without the full operational record, I see no reason for it to stop here.

Conclusions

For want of me the world's course will not fail:
When all its work is done, the lie shall rot;
The truth is great, and shall prevail,
When none cares whether it prevail or not
'Magna est Veritas'
Coventry Patmore

The Italian Campaign has been heavily criticized as a secondary theatre that was not worth the effort. It was a British obsession making no contribution to ultimate victory. At the strategic level, at least before June 1944, it achieved what it set out to achieve. Historians judged its success against the ways and means rather than against the ends. The peril faced by the infantrymen struggling in the cold winter and in almost unbearable circumstances is emotive and emotion sells books. The dry, even dull operational and strategic levels required cold calculation, a much less lucrative subject. Generals and air marshals rarely attract the excitement and derring-do of the ground soldier or valiant pilot. It is their decisions, rather than any individual heroism that decides the fates of nations. The mud, the weather, the arguably better German infantryman, the slow progress; these are what the effectiveness of the campaign is judged against. For all of these to be relevant, there had to be a significant number of Germans present to defend. If these were in Italy, they were not in France or Russia, where the end would be decided. The mere slowness of the Allied campaign in Italy, frustrating to all, fixed more than 20-German divisions. A rapid victory – in Rome by October – would have allowed the Germans to withdraw, employing them elsewhere.

The Abbey's destruction was a culmination of events and circumstances, of short-sightedness and perceived opportunities. Its importance to western cultural heritage is inarguable:

The Abbey of Monte Cassino was more than just bricks and mortar. It was a reminder of past civilisations, cultures and peoples; a physical embodiment or specimen of continuous tradition. Its material presence housed a memory of the past, one kept alive in spirit through its art and architectural treasures. In this way, the Abbey represented a shared identity, whose resilience across numerous centuries contributed to the preservation and idealisation of Western civilisation.[1]

---

1   Rennie, p.171.

As Liddell-Hart questions, is it right to 'preserve European civilisation through practising the most uncivilised means of warfare that the world has known since the Mongol devastations?'[2] In a war of this magnitude, it would be wrong to suggest that the destruction of this one building changed how the Law of Armed Conflict was applied. There were many examples of destruction that contributed to the development of International Humanitarian Law. Yet its notoriety has endured, and it was specifically referenced by an ICRC lawyer in 2004 as having contributed to the development of the 1954 Hague Convention for the protection of cultural property.[3] Even by 1955, and despite the enormous damage caused, there remained no specific rules for aerial bombing. British legal theorist, Professor Julius Stone gave the opinion that, 'in no sense but a rhetorical one, can there still be said to have emerged a body of intelligible rules of air warfare comparable to the traditional rules of land and sea warfare.' More recently, the targeting of civilians and civilian objects has been outlawed in the First Additional Protocol to the 1949 Geneva Conventions of 1977.[4] This Protocol is now the key benchmark for rules on targeting, by which signatory states are held accountable. Its articles are mostly considered as customary law and under it the Abbey, a civilian structure of religious and cultural significance, would not be legally targeted unless being used for military purposes and when there was no other way to gain military advantage. The mere dropping of warning leaflets to helpless civilians would now be entirely inappropriate and unsatisfactory. Eisenhower's order that 'nothing can stand against the argument of Military Necessity' is no longer completely true, if it ever was. Military Necessity no longer stands alone as the arbiter of destruction. To be lawful a potential target must also be a valid Military Objective. In addition, Military Necessity has been joined by three other core principles of Humanity, Proportionality and Distinction. These have been adopted as the measures upon which targeting decisions are made, and all principles must be met.[5] Despite this, all the rules since 1945 continue to have Military Necessity in some form as a caveat or escape clause.

The Laws of War and the quality of intelligence, however, were of small consequence as commanders tried to retrieve both the situation and their tarnished reputations. Freyberg was concerned about national casualties, and Tuker wanted to give his men a chance.[6] Clark, architect of the scheme of battle and with thoughts of Anzio uppermost, disagreed, but was not prepared to risk his reputation by altering his tactical approach. Nor was he willing to take the blame for failure when it was simpler to accuse British bullies. Throughout this incident, his leadership showed a marked lack of moral courage. Had he not been prepared to attack

2   Liddell-Hart, Revolutions in Warfare, p.75.
3   Francois Bugnion, *The origins and development of the legal protection of cultural property in the event of armed conflict. International Committee of the Red Cross*, 14 November 2004 <http://www.icrc.org/web/eng/siteeng0.nsf/htmlall/65SHTJ?OpenDocument&style=cu> (accessed 7 April 2010).
4   Article 52 (3) to Protocol Additional to the Geneva Conventions of 12 August 1949 and relating to the Protection of Victims of International Armed Conflicts (Protocol I), 8 June 1977. This Article specifically refers to doubts over whether a civilian object such as a place of worship is being used for military purposes and in such cases forbids attacks. Article 53 specifically prohibits attacks against cultural and religious sites. <http://www.icrc.org/ihl.nsf/FULL/470?OpenDocument> (accessed 15 July 2010).
5   These are laid down by the US in Joint Chiefs of Staff Publication JP3-60 – Joint Targeting dated 13 April 2007. A similar document exists for the UK Ministry of Defence, Joint Service Publication 900, but retains a classification.
6   Danchev and Todman, p.536.

the Abbey he should have sought an alternative plan. Alexander considered several levels, and he could see the tactical benefits of improved morale if the Abbey was destroyed, but was also aware of his position with the Prime Minister and the wider risk to Britain's influence. He needed to assert himself as a decisive and authoritative commander, show firmness with the Americans and get the stalled campaign moving. The Abbey offered an ideal opportunity, a highly visible example of his resolution. He could not do it himself and Wilson was the ultimate authority.[7] His exact role in authorizing the attack remains unclear, but was probably small, and he almost certainly acted through an informal arrangement, using bombers not required over Germany. He was left to pick up the pieces afterwards and was responsible for 'sexing-up' evidence, thereby generating the subsequent controversy. Eaker, absent from his headquarters in the critical days, had no part to play in the decision.

Whatever the circumstances, intelligence never proved that the Abbey was a defended place, occupied by the Germans. Even without modern legal safeguards, the attack failed to satisfy the Allies' own definitions of Military Necessity. The attack could not be justified in law at the time. To justify it morally is not relevant,[8] as the moral or ethical dimension does not alter the legal position.[9] The three moral justifications suggested; Military Necessity; no reasonable alternative; and that the military advantage outweighed the death of several hundred civilians and the destruction of an irreplaceable historic monument, are all based upon the perceived essential nature of seizing the Abbey. As success was finally achieved without seizing it, this contention of necessity must be false. The safeguards introduced since have in theory strengthened the protection given to cultural and religious sites, although practise has often been very different. Perhaps this protection was partly bought through the controversy surrounding its sacrifice. If so, it was bought dearly.

In his memoirs, Clark wrote, 'British intelligence was excellent, but their estimates did not always reflect their true opinions. Sometimes they were overly optimistic about a difficult job to be done.'[10] This was an attack whose final decisions were based upon assumptions, wishful thinking and opinion. As was often the case, senior intelligence officers sometimes acted as echo chambers for their commanders' views rather than as impartial advisers. It was assumed, but not proven, that German promises were worthless. Ellis made this point, but he failed to grasp that the messages stating that no Germans were in the Abbey did not come from Goebbels' propaganda machine, but from an anti-Nazi Vatican mission in Rome who had no desire or requirement to blame the Allies.[11] The Allies' opinions of German intentions were simplistic and always based upon the worst case. Not all Germans were Nazis or barbarians who cared nothing for the Laws of War. Senger was an honourable man; an old-fashioned German soldier who kept his word. He was also an anglophile, a Roman Catholic and a lay member of the Benedictine Order. He had already risked not only his career, but his life and liberty, by refusing to shoot Italian prisoners in defiance of a direct order. There is little evidence from intelligence reports that the Allies took any of this culturally important information into account. They did not know their enemy, the first duty of intelligence. In the aftermath, the British were a bit

7   Danchev and Todman, pp.526-529.
8   Reuben E Brigety II, 'Moral Ambiguities in the Bombing of Monte Cassino', *Journal of Military Ethics* 4:2, (2005), pp.139-141.
9   Steinhoff, p.143.
10   Clark, *Calculated Risk*, p.228-9.
11   Ellis, *Hollow Victory*, p.170.

sniffy about the Germans taking advantage of their cock-up with the Abbey. Yet they would have made use of this powerful location had the positions been reversed. The Allies had a record of using religious sites for military purposes, as did the Germans.[12] During her time in Italy Margaret Bourke-White was at one point accommodated in a monk's cell and the monastery was used as an Officers' Mess.[13] Truscott used a monastery as an observation point during the Volturno crossings.[14] It was partly this 'mirror-imaging', and partly past experiences more than any substantive evidence that sealed the Abbey's fate. Afterwards there was then a stubborn reluctance to face the fact that the Germans had behaved properly, at least on this occasion, whereas the Allies had not. This sustained the myth in many post-war histories and the mainly British historiography of the battle.[15]

Despite a general US disapproval of the bombing at the time, they all closed ranks afterwards. In the USAAF classified magazine *Impact* the attack was justified through the same flawed evidence.[16] Even today, some historians and military lawyers cling to the argument that Military Necessity justified the destruction, even if they grudgingly accept that the building was not occupied by the Germans.[17] Some will not even admit this.[18] Despite Clark's view, and that of his US general officers and intelligence officers, the Fifth Army Official History stated: 'observers used it constantly to direct fire; snipers had fired from it...The hallowed Benedictine monastery, thus far spared by Fifth Army, was a definite military objective.' None of this was true. Why did Clark, whose signature it carried approve it if he was so against the attack, as his later memoir and interviews claim? Perhaps he didn't read it, or perhaps he was less opposed to the attack than he would later claim? Clark and Howard knew there were no Germans in the Abbey. It is incredible that Alexander and Freyberg claim that they did not. Fifth Army knew that hundreds of refugees were in the building, delivering a misleading warning leaflet that was impossible to heed.[19] The claim that it 'was not clear whether the presence of civilians was known to the allies' is simply not true.[20] The delivery of a warning, via leaflet in Italian which began 'Italian Friends', proves beyond doubt that this is the case. Geoffrey Best argued that to leave out of the account that civilians would die and that 'defensive positions would be weakened through a soaking in bombs,' was 'deluded'.[21] As Bloch suggested in his account of the bombing this 'infamous leaflet, then, instead of serving as a warning, became a death warrant for the band of innocent men, women and children.'[22] The civilians inside the Abbey were under no illusions about their safety. They knew that leaving the Abbey would have resulted in them coming under fire from one side or the other.[23] Considering the level of detail known about German formations and dispositions, it is inconceivable that had it been occupied, definite

---

12   Clayton, p.339. This is not the Camadoli Monastery in Arezzo province to the East of Florence which acted as a repository for Florentine art.
13   Bourke-White, p.108.
14   Truscott, p.271.
15   Fifth Army History, Part IV, p.98.
16   Crane, p.60.
17   Rogers, pp.93-94.
18   National Library of New Zealand.
19   Clark, p.252.
20   Rogers, p.94.
21   Best, p.62.
22   Bloch, p.27.
23   Leccisotti, p.122.

evidence would not have been gained.[24] Rogers considered that the civilian deaths 'may not have been disproportionate.'[25] By inference he also must have believed that the opposite was also possible, yet he defended the faulty assertion that the flimsy intelligence justified the Abbey as a military objective.

If the available sources could not detect evidence of occupation, two conclusions should have been drawn. That the building was not occupied or, that any occupation had little effect on the battle. The use of the buildings for firing positions would have been easily detected, and its use as an observation post should have resulted in emissions from observers directing their artillery or commanding their infantry companies via radio. Neither ever was. The so-called machine-guns reported by the civilian refugee were never reported as firing at anyone. The constant movement of German artillery to avoid counter-battery fire negated continuous use of landline for fire direction purposes. VHF transmissions from the German paratroopers were readily intercepted and there was no evidence that they came from the Abbey. Consequently, the claim that the destruction met the requirements of Military Necessity cannot be supported by intelligence.

Having established that the Germans were not using the Abbey for military purposes, does this absolve them from responsibility? The answer to this question is no. The Germans were aware that civilians and monks were located within the Abbey. The Abbot and the monks, according to the post-war Vatican report, had continuously remonstrated with the Germans regarding their construction of defensive works and storage facilities within close proximity to the Abbey walls.[26] They had made previous efforts to evacuate monks and civilians from the building as the intensity of fighting increased, but perhaps a further 800-civilians had sought refuge. The monks had been offered opportunities to leave but had always refused. It is likely therefore that the Germans had met their responsibilities with regards to the protection of Abbey inmates. They had deliberately constructed the *Gustav* Line at Cassino. This was militarily sensible, but it resulted in the Abbey becoming part of the defensive line by its mere presence, regardless of whether it was occupied. The great bulk of the building and the definite location of German forces around it and on adjacent hills could be seen to render the Abbey as a shield. The US 34th Infantry Division in its history certainly thought this. [27] The Abbot was clear that there had been considerable damage inflicted on the building by artillery from both sides before it was destroyed. The Abbey was being *de facto* used as a shield, but there is no evidence that the Germans placed their defences near it specifically for that purpose. The defences would have been in those positions regardless of the fortuitous position of the Abbey.

At least one German POW, an *Oberstleutnant* in the 1st *Fallschirmjager* Division recognised his part in the destruction:

The very thought of my responsibilities at Cassino is enough to turn my hair grey ... Sooner or later I shall appear before an American court martial to answer for my share

24   See 4th Indian Division Intelligence Summary No. 20 dated 12 February 1944 for example. War Diary of 4th Indian Division

25   Rogers, p.94.

26   TNA FO371/60797, Vatican Secretariat of State, Monte Cassino The Last Days, p.4.

27   *The Story of the 34th Infantry Division: Louisiana to Pisa* <http://cgsc.cdmhost.com/cdm/singleitem/collection/p4013coll8/id/3983/rec/8> (accessed 11 May 2017).

456 Plumes of Smoke

in the business, on account of what happened to the Monastery alone … I was ordered by Heilmann to hold the Monastery. I shouldn't like to stand together with him in the dock.[28]

Those senior Allied officers who could have made the decision to bomb the Abbey need to be examined. The records are opaque over which of them made the final decision to use an armada of medium and heavy bombers. The list is quite short, but there is no final signature. Because of the lack of records, it is impossible to definitively pass judgement, but some are more likely than others. Tuker is widely recorded as having demanded the bombing to prevent excessive casualties in 4th Indian Division. He cannot be legally responsible because he was not in command of the division when the request was made on 11 February 1944; this was Dimoline. Tuker was influential, but not responsible for the destruction. Likewise, Dimoline made a request for air support but did not ask for heavy bombers. He also had no command-and-control powers to task air forces; he too cannot be held legally responsible. Above them in the chain of command was Freyberg. He could have turned down Dimoline's request, but he did not. He honestly believed that the Germans occupied the Abbey and judged that the 4th Indian Division's request was valid. He made little effort to positively prove that the Abbey was defended, and this makes him culpable. Once Freyberg realised that the attack would be in daylight and could not be followed-up by ground assault, he should have cancelled it, as there was no longer military advantage. He stubbornly refused to meet his division commanders to discuss it and applied pressure to Dimoline not to forego air support. He did not have the command-and-control powers to order the attack and Freyberg did not ask for heavy bombers, asking instead for fighter-bombers from Saville's XII ASC. He did not refuse them when they were offered, however. Freyberg's error was one of omission rather than commission – he omitted to consult intelligence and he omitted to cancel the attack when it was no longer advantageous.

Clark has always been associated with bombing the Abbey, although he claimed that he was strongly against it. This claim is supported by other officers, and he made futile efforts to prevent the attack. Clark maintained that he knew there were no Germans in the Abbey and that there were civilians present. He could have made greater efforts, up to and including resignation, but he did not. There are claims that the use of heavy bombers was his idea, but this evidence is thin. As with Freyberg, his responsibility was one of omission as once the decision was made, he had no powers to stop it after it had passed up the chain of command. When assessing the role of Clark in the events surrounding the bombing, it is crucial that his character and his decisions are not conflated. It would be easy to suggest that in his immediate American superior's words, he was 'cold…conceited…selfish' and draw the conclusions that he was a poor leader. Whilst this may be the opinion of some, other words from Jacob Devers' efficiency report, 'resourceful officer … secures excellent results…superior performance', told another tale. Clark has become the bogeyman of Cassino more because of his personality than his decisions. One area where his character adversely affected his judgement was in his antipathy for the British. He was never universally popular, even with his own colleagues. Many officers were jealous of his rapid promotion; others he annoyed with his careerism. Even his wife was an active part of the Clark campaign, keeping positive stories running in the press at home.

---

28 *COC* <http://cgsc.cdmhost.com/cdm/compoundobject/collection/p4013coll8/id/1422/rec/6 P72> Colonel Ludwig Heilmann commanded III *Fallschirmjager* Regt in Cassino. It is unclear whether the officer is talking about the Monastery before or after its destruction.

He had some incredibly tough calls to make. Admittedly, some were of his own making, but mostly they were thrust upon him. Some of his choices he made well, some badly; on occasion he abdicated responsibility when he should have grasped it. Napoleon once famously said, 'You can ask me for anything, except time.' Despite the secondary nature of his command, and its starvation of resources, Clark's biggest shortfall, in his own mind, was time. He had little time to allow his shattered formations to recuperate; he could not spare the time to take a broader outflanking of the Cassino position or to wait for better weather. This forced him into sending understrength and tired divisions into unwinnable situations. He did not show great tactical flair or imagination and he was willing to pay a heavy butcher's bill to get Rome. Although he was urged on by Churchill, who was equally committed to getting to the Italian capital before it became irrelevant, this time constraint was entirely of his own making in his desire, some may say obsession, with reaching Rome before OVERLORD. Clark was opposed to the bombing of the Abbey, not just after but at the time. He did not even watch the event. Nevertheless, his vigour in pursuing a goal that was never asked of him added significantly to the inevitability of the Abbey's destruction. For this alone, he must take some part of the blame.

This is because Clark, although he did not want the Abbey bombed, had become fixated by the head-on approach to Cassino. He would not countenance Tuker's and Juin's manoeuvrist approach. Why? There could be several reasons, the most obvious of which is the imminence of the German attack on Anzio that had been revealed to him from ULTRA and spies in Rome did not allow the luxury of a longer sweep through the mountains. Tuker, Juin and probably Freyberg would not have been aware of this intelligence. Even Lucas, the commander at Anzio, may not have been informed. Clark was also concerned about logistics issues, particularly the availability of mules and skinners for mountain resupply. Had he waited, the strategic bombers would not have been available for another 10-days because of their higher priority strategic task on the famed Big Week of February 1944. Whether he was aware of this is not known, but MAAF certainly would have known that this operation would go ahead as soon as the weather allowed. There are other more human reasons for continuing the direct approach. American boys had suffered high casualties trying to take the Abbey; was this to be all for nothing? Today we would call this the sunken cost fallacy. The direct approach, attacking and destroying the enemy's main strength was the US Army's favoured form of fighting. Clark was a proud, some would say an arrogant, man. Being unable to succeed, would have been a considerable dent to his ego and he was not a reflective man who would change his mind easily. Whatever the reason, his unwillingness to adapt his tactics consigned the Abbey to oblivion whether he desired that outcome or not.

Next in the chain of command was the Army Group commander, Alexander. He was supportive of the attack, despite later admitting that he didn't know whether the building was occupied by the enemy. He therefore did not know whether it was a military objective. He justified it for the morale effect of destroying a building that had become a dark shadow. Improving troops' morale is not a valid justification of Military Necessity. Alexander was the final arbiter of the land force's request and had he applied the legal principles he would have turned it down. That he did not makes him legally responsible for the attack. Even so, Alexander did not possess the powers to order the bombers and it is uncertain whether he knew beforehand that they would be used. Why was Alexander, a general with a reputation for lacking grip and for bonhomie and consensual command, so insistent that Freyberg got his way? Many authors have suggested that this was due to the special position he held as the representative of New

Zealand, but there were no New Zealand troops involved in assaulting the Abbey. The risk of New Zealand casualties was the same regardless of what happened to the Abbey. Freyberg had no valid reason to withdraw them if the attack failed. Was Freyberg's friendship with Churchill a more compelling reason? It may be that Alexander, who was Churchill's 'favourite general' of whom, according to Churchill's biographer, the Prime Minister said 'had a grand capacity for war,' feared losing his sparkle and favoured position.[29]

The Americans were now in the ascendant and were beginning to dominate events. Britain was running out of manpower and could not compete with American military growth, thus losing influence at the Big Three meetings. Mediterranean operations formed part of Britain's strategy but held no interest to the Americans beyond supporting OVERLORD. Italy had not succeeded as Churchill had hoped; Alexander was the general in command. It is unfair to blame Alexander entirely for the lack of rapid success. He had not, in his order on 2nd January 1944, asked his generals to capture Rome. He was also not helped by grand strategic decision-making, the weather, limited amphibious capacity, a polyglot force and by poor performances by some of his subordinates, such as Lucas, who was accused of timidity at Anzio. Continued failure, even to reach the objectives he had ordered, would see further diminution of British influence. Brooke's diary entry for 8 February and Churchill's reminder of Alexander's responsibilities a few days later indicate that his shortcomings were becoming apparent. It is feasible that Alexander used Freyberg's national position and the argument of maintaining morale to impose British power on reluctant Americans and to relieve pressure on his leadership.

In the air forces, the XII ASC commander, Saville, had nothing to do with the decision to attack the Abbey. He controlled only fighter-bombers and he claimed in post-war interviews that he did not agree with the attack. Above him were the Air Force commanders, Twining and Cannon. These officers are judged separately as they ultimately worked through different chains of command. Cannon, in command of all Allied tactical aircraft had full control over the medium bombers. He had the ability to order or cancel the attack based upon his relationship with Alexander, with whom he was collocated. Twining had less operational freedom as his heavy bombers were under the command of Spaatz. Operational control was generally delegated to Eaker, but Twining could not have ordered the attack on his own authority. As the attack was a joint tactical/strategic venture, it is almost certain that it was coordinated through MAAF rather than between these two generals. The final orders are missing to confirm this, although orders from Norstad suggest that Cannon would be the coordinating authority. The commission of such a strike should have included a rigorous legal check on the target's validity. As with Freyberg, Twining and Cannon are guilty of incompetence in their responsibilities, rather than the wilful destruction of the building and the murder of civilians. They took the land forces request at face value rather than conducting their own due diligence. Above the air forces was MAAF, commanded by Eaker. He had the ability to switch heavy bombers to tactical targets if the weather for the primary task was poor. He had access to all the intelligence and was usually collocated with Alexander and Cannon. He should have been able to make a judgement on the legal validity of the target based upon the Laws of War. He is the first officer we have examined who could have made the decision. The question is, did he? All evidence proves that Eaker was not in Italy throughout the crucial period and no communications between him and his staff have emerged. He continues to exercise command responsibility for the decisions of his staff if

29   Gilbert, p.726.

they commit an unlawful act for which he has not provided sufficient direction and guidance. His deputy may have made the decision, or it may have been Norstad, his Director of Operations. Regardless, it is most likely that the decision to bomb the Abbey in the manner it occurred came from MAAF and therefore occurred on Eaker's authority. Whilst circumstantial, with little supporting hard archival evidence, it is entirely feasible, that the USAAF's 'bomber mafia' of which Spaatz, Eaker and several of his senior staff were fully paid-up members, used the attack as a demonstration of the bomber's power. This was at a time when the doctrine's prospects seemed bleak and when failure loomed large, with dire consequences for the future air force. If this was the intention, then the attack was not a Military Necessity against a military objective for military advantage; it had more to do with saving a failing vision and averting the continuance of the air force being shackled to the army. The deaths of several hundred innocents cannot be judged as proportionate by any reasonable military commander and unnecessary suffering was the result. Whilst Eaker may bear ultimate Command Responsibility for the attack, was MAAF ordered or pressured to carry it out from above?

There were only two officers who could have properly applied this pressure; Wilson and Devers. Devers, as Commanding General of North African Theatre United States Army (NATOUSA) was Eaker's direct US superior, but even he could not order him to use the heavy bombers as they belonged to Spaatz. Neither could Wilson, Eaker's operational superior, because according to CCS directives only in an emergency could the order to use heavy bombers for tactical purposes be issued. Only Wilson and Devers could issue this order formally, not Alexander. What was this emergency? No emergency was declared, and records confirm that Eaker desired an informal relationship in this regard. Wilson could have been pressured to approve the attack by Alexander, but there is no archival evidence. Phillips in the New Zealand Official History stated that Wilson was not even consulted and that the attack was authorised by Alexander, but records for this are equally absent. How then was it authorised? No official records of the decision to have been found. There is no surviving direction from AFHQ or a request from 15th Army Group for these assets, nor an operation order from either MAAF or Fifteenth Air Force authorising their use. Consequently, the officer who provided the final order remains unknown. The 5th Bombardment Wing issued orders to conduct the attack, but the origin of these is also absent. Did Alexander and MAAF simply not bother to ask, or was it an informal agreement with Wilson or Devers, carrying out what was in effect an off the books mission? Did one of Eaker's senior officers use his initiative as Spaatz and Arnold encouraged them to do? In theory, Arnold could be ignored, but in practice he held great influence over all the USAAF commanders, and he held absolute authority over the futures of his airmen. He often challenged Eaker about the use of his force and had already removed him from his cherished command in England. Or, as is likely by Eaker's absence, was it a more junior officer in MAAF, such as Norstad, that decided on the heavies? It was the prerogative, under FM 100-20, of the air force to decide how to meet the ground force's requests. If Arnold had any say in it, this privilege would be jealously guarded as it had been hard won over many years of battle within the US War Department stretching back to the days of Mitchell. Devers could, however, probably have stopped the bombing of the Abbey as it was not a USSTAF priority target, but a theatre-level tactical target for which Devers bore US command responsibility. Arnold's correspondence with Eaker certainly encouraged him to make better use of his entire force. Despite only victor's justice being applied at the Nuremburg tribunal where only the vanquished were in the dock, it is clear from the Charter of the Tribunal that both Wilson and Devers were responsible for the actions of their subordinates: 'Leaders, organisers, instigators and accomplices participating in the formulation or execution of a common plan or conspiracy to commit any of the crimes listed in the Charter are responsible for all acts performed by any persons in execution of such plans.'[30]

The attack could have been prevented at the political level, but there is no archive material that suggests it was ever referred to either London or Washington and that the politicians didn't know about the attack until after the event.

The advocates of American daylight precision bombing, and these included most key USAAF officers from Arnold downwards, desperately needed visible confirmation of the effectiveness of their heavy bomber force. The fate of the United States Air Force, still in the womb of the Army, depended upon it. The independence that all these senior officers craved rested upon proof in battle, against fierce rivalry from the ground forces and especially the navy that a third service was unnecessary. Arnold had come a long way in three years. He had a seat on the Allied command top table; he had achieved parity with ground forces; he had successfully broken the ground support doctrine of his predecessors; and his force numbered over two million men. His force, however, still contained the word 'Army'. Yet operational success eluded him. Insufficient bombers, a lack of long-range fighter escort, little evidence that Germany was succumbing to the pressure and heavy losses had dented confidence in the project by the end of 1943. A low-risk yet high visibility target was an ideal opportunity to show the world what they could do – a repeat of *Ostfriesland, Barling Bomber, Question Mark* or *Rex*. No supporting evidence has been unearthed, beyond commentary from some of those around at the time, but Arnold's intent was clear and those in the positions to decide were all kindred spirits who would not let an opportunity slip. A number of officers have suggested that this was the intention of the attack.

The competency to make the decision was questionable as many of the experienced staff officers had been poached by Eisenhower, including Brigadier General George McDonald, the senior USAAF intelligence officer, and soon to follow was promoted Major General Strong, the overall AFHQ intelligence chief.[31] Many senior officers including Wilson, Eaker and Twining had been in their posts barely a month.[32] For MAAF, it was in the process of shifting its units from North Africa to Italy. Eaker, despite personal reservations, was under pressure to use his enormous air force more effectively, even though he had only limited influence on heavy bomber operations. There is no direct evidence that Eaker deliberately lied about his flight before the attack, he probably just got muddled in the heat of frenetic battle, but the silence of Devers, who must have known, is suspicious. The flight was another Monte Cassino myth that was pounced upon by post-war commentators who were keen to find justifying evidence. As his appointment diary confirms, Eaker was elsewhere. If it was off the books, the subsequent controversy should have resulted in disciplinary action, but there was none. It is likely that the final decision

30   C.H.B. Garroway, 'Command Responsibility: victors' justice or just desserts?' in Richard Burchill, Nigel D. White and Justin Morris (eds.), *International Conflict and Security Law: Essays in Memory of Hilaire McCoubrey* (Cambridge: Cambridge University Press, 2005), pp.71-72.
31   Eisenhower took his Chief of Staff, Lieutenant-General Walter Beddell-Smith; his Deputy Chief of Staff, Major-General J F Whiteley; his Air Force commander, Lieutenant-General Carl Spaatz (replaced by Eaker); his Tactical Air Force commander, Air Marshal Sir Arthur Coningham (replaced as MATAF commander by Cannon); and his Strategic Air Force commander, Lieutenant-General James Doolittle (replaced as MASAF commander by Twining).
32   Eaker arrived in the Mediterranean Theatre on 15 January. His deputy, Slessor, arrived the day before. Parton, pp.3-10.

was Wilson's, but his approval was more rubber stamp than active involvement. Eisenhower's Military Necessity order of December had not been rescinded. Wilson had too little direct input in a decision that was not supported by any of his American battlefield commanders, and which would have political consequences with the Vatican, and which offered a huge propaganda opportunity to the Germans. The Supreme Commander should have had greater influence upon the decision than he appears to have had.

From all those who could have had responsibility, who was responsible? For the order to attack the Abbey in a general sense, the responsibility ultimately lies at the feet of the land force commander, Alexander. Any air attack request could have been vetoed by responsible air commanders if it was considered unnecessary or disproportionate. The decision to use heavy bombers was a decision that lay entirely with the air forces, and therefore even though not present, Eaker bears command authority. Why did the air forces feel they could use these bombers against this clearly controversial target? This is a question complicated by the change in command in January 1944. Eisenhower issued his direction on 29 December 1943 when he was both Allied Commander-in-Chief and Commanding General of NATOUSA. The Monuments Men were in theory a brake upon decisions of this kind, but they were not employed and there were no other checks and balances to ensure that Eisenhower's direction was followed. Wilson did not rescind Eisenhower's directive, but neither did he emplace the measures to ensure its compliance. Following the change in command, Eisenhower's command roles were divided between Wilson and Devers. It was Devers who exercised full command of all US Army forces in Italy, including Eaker's bombers. Wilson exercised this level of command over British forces, but only operational command over US forces. He could have approved the attack as Commander-in-Chief, but the final decision may have been a national rather than allied authority for which Devers was ultimately responsible. The exercise of full command includes the national interpretation of the Law of War, a consideration in all uses of force, and the implementation of discipline. Wilson did not have these powers over Americans, but Devers did. Finally, the politicians even though oblivious to the attack are not unblameworthy. Direction to the military over what was acceptable and what was not was their responsibility, one which they failed to fulfil in their pursuit of victory.

In the final judgement however, we must separate responsibility from authority. A few senior officers had the authority to act, but only one, in my opinion, and with the full knowledge that the entire record has been lost, bears responsibility. This officer gave no orders to bomb the Abbey and probably had no idea that it would happen. Those that ordered the use of heavy bombers exercised authority based upon the intent of the responsible officer. Understanding your commander's intent was, and remains, the most important skill that a subordinate commander or staff officer can possess. This officer's interests lay beyond a secondary theatre in the Mediterranean. His vision, which those that probably arranged for the destruction of the Abbey were enthusiastic fellow travellers, was to create a new revolution in military affairs in the United States. He wished to supplant the earthbound and outdated army and navy as the country's principal protector. These men were very much in the mind of their commander. Many of them had at one point done his thinking for him. The crucible of battle in the end-days of 1943 was tarnishing this vision despite the vast resources devoted to it, and an event was needed to show the world what they could do. An opportunity came about on 15 February 1944, and it was taken. This was not an opportunity that they created, but one they ruthlessly exploited. As far as the record can tell, no land commander asked for the heavy bombers that day. Following the new air doctrine, the decision to use these weapons lies entirely with the air forces. Whilst the authority for the attack dwells elsewhere, the responsibility for the doom of the Abbey of Montecassino lies squarely with the Commanding General of the USAAF, General Henry Harley 'Hap' Arnold.

My final point, goes back to the Preface of this book, in that whatever rebuilding and restoration is applied to this and other buildings, the decisions made, and the damage inflicted is permanent, both to the buildings and to those within them. Politicians, commanders and military staff need to be reminded, and the Abbey of Montecassino is an excellent reminder, that the consequences of using military firepower are irreversible and profound, both on buildings and people. Before it is used, those that wield this immense force should understand the damage they will cause and thoroughly analyse whether this is worth it. To paraphrase General Eisenhower, military or personal convenience does not equal Military Necessity. As Ruskin observed in 1849:

> Do not let us deceive ourselves in this important matter, it is impossible, as impossible as to raise the dead, to restore anything that has ever been great or beautiful in architecture.[33]

33   John Ruskin, *The Seven Lamps of Architecture* cited by Rennie, p.184.

Bibliography

Primary Sources

Hansard
House of Lords Debate: Preservation of Art and Historical Treasures, Hansard dated 16 February 1944

United States National Archives and Records Administration
US NARA RG338, NND 903618: II Corps Records intelligence Summary No 81, dated 6 February 1944, Para 2a (1)

US NARA RG338, NND 903618: II Corps Records intelligence Summary No 83, dated 8 February 1944, Para 2a (1)

US NARA, RG338, NND 903618: II Corps Records intelligence Summary No 84, dated 9 February 1944

US NARA RG338, NND 903618: II Corps Records intelligence Summary No 85, dated 10 February 1944, Para 2b (6) a

US NARA RG338, NND 903618: II Corps Records intelligence Summary No 87, dated 12 February 1944, Para 2a (1)

US NARA RG338, NND 903618: II Corps Records intelligence Summary No 88, dated 13 February 1944, Para 6

US NARA RG338, NND 903618: II Corps Records intelligence Summary No 89, dated 14 February 1944, Para 5b

US NARA RG338, NND 903618: II Corps Records intelligence Summary No 89, dated 14 February 1944, Annex – German Soldiers' Morale

US NARA RG338, NND 903618: II Corps Records intelligence Summary No 90, dated 15 February 1944, Para 2a

US NARA RG407, NND 735017: Box 8151 – WWII Operations Reports, 1940-48 34th Infantry Division, 334-2.4 Jan 1944 to 334-2.4 Feb 1944

The National Archives of the UK
AIR 23/884: JCS 625 Personal For Eaker From Slessor, dated 18 April 1944

AIR 23/6598: Air Historical Branch History of NZ Corps Operations, 1949

AIR 34/400: Photo Interpretation Report G51. Frames 15SG.279.3008, 3009 & 3010, dated 15 February 1944

AIR 34/407: FAPIC interpretation Reports, General Interpretation Report No 106 dated 27 January 1944. Frame 12SC.25.4154

AIR 34/407: FAPIC interpretation Reports, dated 3 February 1944. Frame 55B.379.4064

AIR 34/407: FAPIC interpretation Reports, dated 28 January and 10 February 1944. Frames 55B.365.3116 and 12SC.29.3006

AIR 34/407: FAPIC interpretation Reports, General Interpretation Report No 119 dated 13 February 1944

AIR 34/407: FAPIC interpretation Reports, General Interpretation Report No 120 dated 15 February 1944. Frame 12PR.412.5008

AIR 51/81: Loose Minute AVM D'Albiac TAF/7/Air dated 9 February 1944

AIR 51/81: MATAF message DTG 131425A Feb 44, dated 13 February 1944

AIR 51/81: MAAF Operations Instruction No 11 dated 4 March 1944

AIR 51/81/184: Redline Message Cannon/Norstad dated 14 January 1944

AIR 51/81/184: Redline Message Norstad/Cannon dated 15 January 1944

AIR 51/81/184: Message from Norstad to MASAF and MATAF dated 25 January 1944

AIR 75/38: Papers of Sir John Slessor, Draft Official History of the Mediterranean and Middle East Campaign, Chapter XVIII

AIR 75/69: Papers of Sir John Slessor, The Italian Campaign, AOC/101/Air, Letter from Slessor to Portal dated 27 January 1944

AIR 75/69: Papers of Sir John Slessor, The Italian Campaign, JCS 183 Personal Letter from Slessor to Portal, February 1944

AIR 75/69: Papers of Sir John Slessor, The Italian Campaign, Letter to AM Linnell and AVM Robb dated 22 February 1944

AIR 75/69: Papers of Sir John Slessor, The Italian Campaign, Report to General Arnold – The Effect Of Air Power In A Land Offensive dated 18 June 1944

AIR 75/69: Papers of Sir John Slessor, The Italian Campaign, Letter to H A St G Saunders Esq dated 19 July 1948

AIR 75/69: Papers of Sir John Slessor, The Italian Campaign, Letter from H A St G Saunders Esq dated 20 July 1948

AIR 75/138: Allied Force Headquarters. *Supreme Allied Commander's Despatch – Italian Campaign 10 May 1944 – 12 August 1944*. Caserta IT (1944)

CAB 24/48: The Legal Aspect of Bombardment From The Air, General Staff, War Office, dated 12 April 1918

CAB 44/138: Italy Operations Winter 1943/4, Part IV – Operations in the Cassino Sector – 20 January – 31 March 1944

CAB 44/39: New Zealand War Narrative

CAB 65/41/23: War Cabinet Minutes 23 (44) dated 21 February 1944

CAB 69/2: Meeting at 10 Downing Street dated 18 April 1941

CAB 69/2: DO (41) 45th Meeting of the War Cabinet Defence Committee (Operations) dated 3 July 1941

CAB 69/2: DO (41) 52nd Meeting War Cabinet Defence Committee (Operations), dated 21 July 1941

CAB 79/71/12: dated 1 March 1944

CAB 80/74/513: COS (43) 513 Part A, QUADRANT Record of Plenary Meetings and the Proceedings of the Combined Chiefs of Staff, Quebec, August 1943, dated 11 September 1943

CAB 80/75/615: COS (43) 615 (0), Plan JAEL Deception Policy for the Against Germany

CAB 80/75/639: COS (43) 639 (0), RELATION OF OVERLORD TO MEDITERRANEAN
Minute by the Prime Minister (D178/3), dated 19 October 1943

CAB 80/76/680: COS (43) 680 (0), Plan FOYNES, dated 9 November 1943

CAB 80/76/708: COS (43) 708 (0), OVERLORD AND THE MEDITERRANEAN –
Draft Aide Memoire dated 11 November 1943

CAB 80/76/708: COS (43) 708 (0), OVERLORD AND THE MEDITERRANEAN –
ANNEX II – Memorandum for the President and Prime Minister from General Smuts

CAB 80/80: COS (44) 147 (O), OPERATION SHINGLE – PROPORTION OF VEHICLES
– Minute By Prime Minister dated 9 February 1944

CAB 80/82: COS (44) 316(O) dated 4 April 1944

CAB 101/229: The Bombing of Cassino Abbey, 15th February 1944. Report to the Official
Historian, dated 2 April 1965

CAB 106/361: US Army Lessons from Italy, 1 Feb – 30 Sep 1944

CAB 106/699: Report on the Bombing of MONTE CASSINO ABBEY – 15 February 1944.
London: Cabinet Office Historical section, 1949

CAB 106/699: Folio No.02003, ORIG No. 6285, Protected Sites, General Eisenhower to 15th
Army Group, dated 4 November 1943

CAB 106/699: JCH/DW/jw, MGS 619.3, Monuments and Fine Arts – Monastery of Monte
Cassino. Allied Force Headquarters Military Government Section to 15th Army Group,
dated 5 November 1943

CAB 106/699: ORIG No. 0-1478, Copy of AFHQ ORIG No. 6285, 15th Army Group to
Fifth and Eighth Armies, 5 November 1943

CAB 106/699: Folio No.02542, ORIG No. 4426-7034, Response to War Department Message
concerning cultural property, General Eisenhower to US War Department, dated 5
November 1943

CAB 106/699: Minister to Holy See to Foreign Office, Telegram No. 410, 7 November 1943

CAB 106/699: Folio No. 05697, ORIG No. 1207, 15AG Informed Abbey would not be occupied by Germans, General Eisenhower to 15th Army Group, 15 November 1943

CAB 106/699: AG.000.4-1, Allied Force Headquarters, Office of the Commander-in-Chief,
Historical Monuments, dated 29 December 1943

CAB 106/699: R-8408/7777 FAN 322, Vatican Property, From CCS to General Wilson, dated
22 January 1944

CAB 106/699: MEDCOS 27, Copy of Eaker message concerning sanctuary from bombing,
General Wilson to British Chiefs of Staff, dated 2 February 1944

CAB 106/699: 4 Ind Div Intelligence Summary No.19, dated 4 February 1944

CAB 106/699: 4 Ind Div Intelligence Summary No.20, dated 9 February 1944

CAB 106/699: NZ Corps Operation Instruction No.4, dated 9 February 1944

CAB 106/699: 4 Ind Div Intelligence Summary No.21, dated 10 February 1944

CAB 106/699: 4 Ind Div Intelligence Summary No.22, dated 11 February 1944

CAB 106/699: Minister to Holy See to Foreign Office, Telegram No. 87, 11 February 1944

CAB 106/699: Headquarters 15th Army Group, Operations Instruction No.42, dated 11
February 1944

CAB 106/699: 4 Ind Div Operation Instruction No.3, dated 11 February 1944

CAB 106/699: Memorandum 433/G from Commander 4th Indian Division to NZ Corps, Operations, dated 12 February 1944

CAB 106/699: Memorandum 433/1/G from Commander 4th Indian Division to NZ Corps, Operations, dated 12 February 1944

CAB 106/699: 4 Ind Div Intelligence Summary No.23, dated 13 February 1944

CAB 106/699: 4 Ind Div Intelligence Summary No.25, dated 15 February 1944

CAB 106/699: Memorandum 410/G from Commander 4th Indian Division to NZ Corps, Direct Air Support, dated 18 February 1944

CAB 106/699: Minister to Holy See to Foreign Office, Telegram No. 107, 21 February 1944

CAB 106/699: Minister to Holy See to Foreign Office, Telegram No. 108, 21 February 1944

CAB 106/699: Minister to Holy See to Foreign Office, Telegram No. 116, 23 February 1944

CAB 106/699: MI14/11/238/44, German Troops at MONTE CASSINO Abbey, Letter from Directorate of Military Intelligence to Colonel Carver, Offices of the War Cabinet, dated 25 February 1944

CAB 106/699: Minister to Holy See to Foreign Office, Telegram No. 120, 25 February 1944

CAB 106/699: Memorandum for Colonel Howard, H.Q. Fifth Army, Office of the A C of S G-2, Monte Cassino Abbey, dated 28 February 1944

CAB 106/699: COSMED 51, OZ1218, Request for Information on German Use of Abbey, British Chiefs of Staff to General Wilson, dated 4 March 1944

CAB106/699: Minister to Holy See to Foreign Office, Telegram No. 138, 6 March 1944

CAB106/699: Minister to Holy See to Foreign Office, Telegram No. 146, 8 March 1944

CAB 106/699: AFHQ Office of the Chief of Staff, Minutes of the Commander-in-Chief's Meeting, 8 March 1944

CAB 106/699: MEDCOS 64, Ref No. 62136. Response to British Chiefs of Staff Request for Information, General Wilson to British Chiefs of Staff, dated 9 March 1944

CAB 106/699: MEDCOS 69, Admission of impossibility of obtaining definite proof, General Wilson to British Chiefs of Staff, dated 15 March 1944

CAB 106/699: Minister to Holy See to Foreign Office, Telegram No. 163, 16 March 1944

DEFE 3/140: VLs 6650 and 6655

FO 371/37330: Folio R12578, Note Verbale No 70279/S dated 25 October 1943.

FO 371/37330: Folio R10941, Letter from Archbishop Willian Godfrey to Sir Alexander Cadogan dated 28 October 1943

FO 371/37330: Folio R10960, Foreign Office To Resident Minister's Office Algiers No 2483 dated 2 November 1943

FO 371/37330: Folio R12785, Note Verbale No 72939/S dated 7 November 1943

FO 371/37330: Folio R11534, Message tp. AFHQ Algiers, Minute 1 dated 10 November 1943

FO 371/37330: Folio R12393, Letter to Sir Leonard Woolley

FO 371/37330: Folio R12950. Holy See To Foreign Office Telegram 461 dated 7 December 1943

FO 371/37330: Folio R12785, Foreign Office To Resident Minister in Algiers Telegram 2950, dated 9 December 1943

FO 371/37330: Folio R13678, Holy See To Foreign Office Telegram 484 dated 21 December 1943

FO 371/43817:Orme Sargent on Artistic Buildings, dated 28 December 1943

FO 371/43817: Folio R627, Letter from Roger Makins to Sir Anthony Rumbold dated 5 January 1944

FO 371/43817: Folio R423, Letter from Archbishop Willian Godfrey to Sir Alexander Cadogan dated 6 January 1944

FO 371/43817: Folio R1991, Preservation of the Abbey of Monte Cassino, Note 74804S of 8 January – Secretary of State to British Legation to the Holy See

FO 371/43817: Draft Reply to Godfrey letter- dated 8 January 1944

FO 371/37330: Folio R13678, Foreign Office To Resident Minister Algiers Telegram 63, dated 9 January 1944

FO 371/43817: R509, Telegram 12 from Holy See to Foreign Office dated 10 January 1944

FO 371/43817: Folio R1197, Italy – Air Attack on Tiber Dams – Reference COS (44) 12 Meeting (O) Minute 1 dated 20 January 1944

FO 371/43817: Folio R1991 Minute 1, McDermott to War Office dated 8 February 1944

FO 371/43817: Folio R2320, Rumbold to Hollis, dated 13 February 1944

FO 371/43817: Folio R2516 Minister to Holy See to Foreign Office, Telegram No. 92, 15 February 1944

FO 371/43817: Folio R2678, Text Of Statement On The Bombing Of Monte Cassino And Castel Gandolfo, 17 February 1944

FO 371/43817: Folio R2516, Note from A R Dew of Foreign Office to Colonel Carver of War Cabinet Office, R2516/32/22, 17 February 1944

FO 371/43817: Folio R2679, German Foreign Ministry Statement, dated 17 February 1944

FO 371/43817: Folio R2649, Letter Godfrey to Cadogan, dated 19 February 1944

FO 371/43817: Folio R2998, Holy See To Foreign Office Telegram No. 115 dated 23 February 1944

FO 371/43817: Folio R2894, Minute to file, Carver to McDermott, dated 25 February 1944

FO 371/43817: Folio R3019, Minute 5, Scarlett Note, dated 29 February 1944

FO 371/43817: Folio R2998, Minute 2, Scarlett Note. dated 1 March 1944

FO 371/43817: Folio R3019, Minute 2, Cavendish-Bentinck Admission, dated 2 March 1944

FO 371/43817: Folio R2998, Minute 4, Sargent Note, dated 4 March 1944

FO 371/43817: Folio R2998, Minute 5, Eden Comment, dated 5 March 1944

FO 371/43817: Folio R2998, Minute 6, Cavendish-Bentinck Note, dated 10 March 1944

FO 371/43817: Folio R3891, Minute 1, Scarlett Note, dated 11 March 1944

FO 371/43870: Folio R4252, Telegram 159, Holy See To Foreign Office, dated 12 March 1944

FO 371/43817: Folio R3891, Minute 2, PWE Viewpoint, dated 15 March 1944

FO 371/43817: Folio R3891, Minute 3, Sargent Direction, dated 16 March 1944

FO 371/43870: Folio R4294, Telegram 167, Holy See To Foreign Office, dated 16 March 1944

FO 371/43870: Folio R4558, Message from Mr De Valera, dated 17 March 1944

FO 371/43870: Folio R4294, Minute 1, McDermott Note, dated 18 March 1944

FO 371/43870: Folio R4709, Telegram 174, Holy See To Foreign Office, dated 18 March 1944

FO 371/43870: Folio R4763, Telegram 183, Holy See To Foreign Office, dated 21 March 1944. Minute by PM to CAS dated 28 March 1944

FO 371/43870: Folio R4733, Letter Spanish Embassy to PUS Foreign Office, dated 23 March 1944

FO 371/43870: Folio R4552, Scarlett Note, Minute 1, dated 23 March 1944

FO 371/43870: Folio R4982, Minute 1, Scarlett to Loftus, dated 24 March 1944

FO 371/43870: Folio R4552, Minute 2, Allen Note, dated 26 March 1944

FO 371/43870: Folio R4944, Australian High Commission To Dominions Office, dated 27 March 1944

FO 371/43870: Telegram 103, Foreign Office To Holy See, dated 29 March 1944

FO 371/43870: Folio R4944, Australian High Commission To Dominions Office, dated 30 March 1944

FO 371/43817: Folio R6902, Telegram No 290 Holy See To Foreign Office dated 28 April 1944

FO 371/43817: Folio R8268, Holy See To Foreign Office No 362 dated 24 May 1944

FO 371/43817: Folio R8268, Minute 1, McDermott on Subiaco Bombing, dated 26 May 1944

FO 371/43817: Folio R8268, Foreign Office To Holy See Telegram 188 dated 27 May 1944

FO 371/43817: Folio R8417, Holy See To Foreign Office Telegram 377 dated 28 May 1944

FO 371/43817: Folio R8417, Minute 1, McDermott Note. dated 30 May 1944

FO 371/43817: Folio R8487, Holy See To Foreign Office Telegram 378 dated 30 May 1944

FO 371/43817: Folio R8487, Minute 1, McDermott Note, dated 31 May 1944

FO 371/43817: Folio R8800, Resident Minister's Office Algiers To Foreign Office Telegram 731 dated 4 June 1944

FO 371/60797: Vatican Secretariat of State, Monte Cassino The Last Days

FO 371/60797: British Legation To The Holy See to Foreign Secretary dated 20 December 1945

FO 371/79530: Folio Z4757, A G Blake letter to E H Appleyard dated 28 June 1949

FO 371/79530: Folio Z4757, E H Appleyard letter to P F Kinna dated 4 July 1949

FO 371/79530: Folio Z4757, Minute by MB Jacomb dated 6 July 1949

FO 371/79530: Folio Z4757, Minute by John Russell, Western Dept, 7 July 1949

HW 41/125: History of Signal Intelligence in the Field (Europe and Africa – 1939-1945

HW 49/1: The History of the Special Liaison Units – Mediterranean and Western Europe

WO 70/55: Appreciation of the Situation in Italy on 7 February 1944, Allied Forces Headquarters, dated 7 February 1944

WO 170/118: MAIU (West) War Diary

WO 193/751: AFHQ G-2 Report – German Morale In Italy dated 24 February 1944

WO 204/456: Draft Report by The Supreme Allied Commander Mediterranean to the Combined Chiefs of Staff on The Italian Campaign – 8th January 1944 to 10th May 1944

WO 204/ 968: Allied Force Headquarters, Office of Assistant Chief of Staff, G-2, Weekly Intelligence Summary No. 77, dated 12 February 1944

WO 204/980: Allied Force Headquarters, G-2 Report No.462, dated 12 February 1944

WO 204/1066: Msg ref A-277, MAAF to AFHQ and 15th Air Force, dated 11 January 1944

WO 204/1066: Msg to Colonel Archibald, AFHQ G-3 (Ops) from Director of Plans MAAF, dated 12 January 1944

WO 204/1077: MAAF, Historic Monuments dated 23 February 1944

WO 204/3692: Msg AGWAR to Fifteenth Army Group, Ref 22236 dated 1 January 1944

WO 204/3692: Folio No.02112, ORIG No. 8464instructions Issued to Commanders concerning Abbey, Fifth Army to 15th Army Group, dated 6 January 1944

WO 204/3692: Msg ref MA1001, Alexander to Wilson, dated 14 January 1944

WO 204/3692: Msg ref 26928 Wilson to Alexander,dated 15 January 1944

WO 204/3692: Msg ref W309 Wilson to Marshall dated 16 January 1944

WO 204/3692: Alexander Letter dated 17 February 1944, Property of Historical and
    Educational Importance in Italy – Preservation of
WO 204/3692: Msg ref MA1123, Alexander to Wilson, dated 29 February 1944
WO 204/3692: Msg ref 59209, Wilson to Alexander dated 2 March 1944
WO 204/4354: Lessons Applicable To The Air Operations
WO 204/5735: Advanced Allied Force Headquarters Liaison Section, MONTE CASSINO
    dated 7 January 1946
WO 204/6420: AFHQ Psychological Warfare Branch: Combat Propaganda – Leaflet
    Distribution To Date, dated 1 February 1944
WO 204/6734: Report of Board of Officers Appointed By Letter Headquarters Allied Control
    Commission dated 24 July 1944
WO 204/12836: OSS Special detachment G-2, Headquarters Fifth Army, Clandestine
    Transportation, 12 January 1944
WO 214/14: Churchill Undated Special Unnumbered Message to Alexander in Alexander's
    Papers, Undated
WO 214/14: ORIG No. MA 1091, Personal Memorandum from Alexander to Churchill,
    Alexander's Papers, dated 11 February 1944
WO 214/14: 141210/1248/1305. Special Unnumbered Signal from Churchill to Alexander.
    Alexander's Papers, dated 14 February 1944
WO 214/29: Italian Campaign January – February 1944. Letter Eaker to Alexander, dated 4
    February 1944
WO 214/29: Italian Campaign January – Letter Leese to Alexander, dated February 1944
WO 214/30: Minutes of Commander-in-Chief's Conference on ANVIL dated 18 February
    1944
WO 214/38: FOLIO 07519, AFHQ to ACMF and Fifth Army, dated 10 February 1944

Combined Chiefs of Staff Messages
Combined Chiefs of Staff: CCS 387 (Sextant), dated 3 November 1943
Combined Chiefs of Staff: CCS 300/3 (Sextant), dated 18 November 1943
Combined Chiefs of Staff: CCS 400 (Sextant), dated 18 November 1943
Combined Chiefs of Staff: CCS 403 (Sextant), dated 21 November 1943
Combined Chiefs of Staff: CCS 400/1 (Sextant), dated 26 November 1943
Combined Chiefs of Staff: CCS 379/7 (Sextant), dated 27 November 1943
Combined Chiefs of Staff: CCS 400/2 (Sextant), dated 4 December 1943
Combined Chiefs of Staff: CCS 387/3 (Sextant), dated 5 December 1943
Minutes, 134th CCS Meeting, Mena House Cairo, dated 4 December 1943
Minutes, 138th CCS Meeting, Mena House Cairo, dated 7 December 1943

Allied Forces Headquarters (AFHQ) Mediterranean Messages
HQAMG Monuments Fine Arts & Archives Sub-Commission, First Monthly Report for
    November 1943 dated 4 December 1943
Folio No.08804intentions 15 Air Force for February 15, dated 15 February 1944
Minutes of the Commander-in Chief's Meeting, dated 8 March 1944, Paragraph 4. –
    BOMBING OF CASSINO ABBEY
Office of Strategic Services, Memorandum to Colonel Ordway, dated 11 March 1944

Minutes of the Commander-in Chief's Meeting, dated 15 March 1944, Paragraph 2. –
    BOMBING OF CASSINO ABBEY

15th Army Group Messages

Headquarters 15th Army Group, Operations Instruction No.32, dated 2 January 1944
Headquarters 15th Army Group, Operations Instruction No.34, dated 12 January 1944
Message 699, AFSC: X 228/08, COSINTREP 14, Fifth Army Situation Report, 15 Army
    Group to AFHQ G3, dated 8 February 1944
Message 718, AFSC:X 282/9, Relief of II US Corps by NZ Corps, Lieutenant-General
    Gammell to General Wilson, dated 9 February 1944
Message 724, AFSC:X 151/10, FIFTH ARMY Situation 100930, 15th Army Group to
    AFHQ G3, dated 10 February 1944
Message 775, AFSC:X 101/15, FIFTH ARMY Situation at 150900, 15th Army Group to
    AFHQ G3, dated 15 February 1944
Message 782, AFSC:X 170/15, Fifth Army situation 151700, 15th Army Group to AFHQ G3,
    dated 15 February 1944
HQ AAI Admin Instruction 10 – Preservation of Property of Historical or Educational
    Importance In Italy, dated 30 March 1944

Fifth Army Messages

HQ Fifth Army, Outline Plan Operation SHINGLE dated 19 October 1943
HQ Fifth Army. Outline Plan Operation SHINGLE – Appendix 2 to Annex I dated 7 January
    1944
HQ Fifth Army, Outline Plan Operation SHINGLE – Annex 2 dated 12 January 1944
HQ Fifth Army, SHINGLE intelligence Summary No.9 dated 16 January 1944
HQ Fifth Army, Outline Plan Operation SHINGLE – Intelligence Annex dated 18 January
    1944
HQ II Corps 353/91 CG Lesson Learned, dated 16 June 1944

New Zealand Corps Messages

Sheet 763, 2 New Zealand Expeditionary Forces, Monthly Narrative, dated February 1944

MAAF Archival Material

Operational Summary, 319th Bombardment Group (M), 42nd Bombardment Wing, Twelfth
    Air Force, Nov 42 – 44, dated 10 January 45
MAAF 410, AFHQ 9413, AFSC:N 1144/10, Request for Comments on MAAF, General
    Arnold to Lieutenant-General Eaker, dated 10 February 1944
War Diary, 319th Bombardment Group, Jan-Feb 1944
War Diary, 486th Bombardment Squadron, Feb 1944
War Diary, 488th Bombardment Squadron, Feb 1944
War Diary, 489th Bombardment Squadron, Jan-Feb 1944
Operational Summary, 319th Bombardment Group (M), 42nd Bombardment Wing,
    Twelfth Air Force, Nov 42 – Dec 44, dated 10 January 45
Air Power in the Mediterranean November 1942 – February 1945, HQ MAAF, dated 27
    February 1945

Air Surrender Documents, HQ MAAF Intelligence Section, Army Air Forces Statistical Charts, 1940-45, dated July 1945

United States Air Force Historical Research Agency Files

AFHRA Reel A1372: Memorandum for General Marshall, Bombing Units for United Kingdom, dated 5 February 1943

AFHRA Reel A1372: Memorandum from Chief of Air Staff to Colonel Cabell dated 5 February 1943

AFHRA Reel A1592: Headquarters Fifth Bombardment Wing (H), Operations Memorandum dated 11 February 1943

AFHRA Reel A1592: The Air Force in a Task Force, Chapter V: The Bomber Command dated March 1943

AFHRA Reel A1372: Memorandum for General Giles, Allocation of Heavy and Medium Bombers, dated 6 May 1943

AFHRA Reel A1592: Transcript of Press Conference of Maj Gen I C Eaker dated 10 June 1943

AFHRA Reel A1372: Memorandum for Colonel Maxwell incendiary Bomb Tests at Dugway, dated 22 June 1943

AFHRA Reel A1592: Eaker Letter, 8th Air Force Attack on 25 June, dated 26 June 1943

AFHRA Reel A1372: Employment of Air Forces In Support of Land Operations – 15AG/2055/ G(Trg), dated 21 July 1943

AFHRA Reel A6338: Message, Northwest African Strategic Air Force ACOS A-3 to 5th, 42nd and 57th BWs dated 11 September 1943

AFHRA Reel A6111: Group Captain Cross, Lessons Learned Report of No 242 Group RAF, Report to AOC DAF, 10 in Frame 0197, 18 September 1943

AFHRA Reel A1372: HQ AAF, Office of Management Control, Combined Allied Serviceable Air Strength, dated 16 October 1943

AFHRA Iris No 2000469: Note On The Deployment Of Tactical Bomber Force, dated 23 October 1943

AFHRA Reel 23111: Diary of Leland D Baldwin dated 23 October 1943

AFHRA Reel A6030: History of MAAF, December 1943 – September 1944, Volume 2, FAN 254 CCS to Eisenhower, 23 October 1943

AFHRA Reel A1372: Letter Portal to Arnold dated 24 October 1943

AFHRA Reel A0583: 340th Bombardment Squadron History, dated December 1943

AFHRA Reel A0583: 341st Bombardment Squadron History, dated December 1943

AFHRA Reel A6377: Frame 1420. USSAFE Operational Directive to CG 15th Air Force, dated 11 January 1944

AFHRA Reel A1376: Memorandum For The Commanding General, Army Air Forces, Diversion from Mission of Strategic Air Forces, dated 28 January 1944

AFHRA Reel A6377: Frame 1430, HQ MAAF Strategic Bombing Directive to 15th Air Force, dated 3 February 1944

AFHRA Reel A1376: Letter Spaatz to Arnold dated 5 February 1944

AFHRA Reel A6060: Figures from MAAF aircraft (US, UK, Fr), Frame 044, dated 6 February 1944

AFHRA Iris No 2000469: Letter A106, Letter MATAF to 12th Air Force dated 13 February 1944

AFHRA Reel A1376: FACS8, CCS for General Eisenhower dated 13 February 1944

AFHRA Reel A5548: REDLINE IE187NT, CS95NT dated 13 February 1944, REDLINE CS99NT dated 14 February 1944, REDLINE CS100NT dated 14 February 1944 and REDLINE CS99IE dated 14 February 1944

AFHRA Iris No 2000472: HQ 12 ASC Memorandum to CG MATAF dated 15 February 1944

AFHRA Reel A6030: C-IN-C MAAF Diary Entries and Daily Staff Meeting minutes – 8-15 February 1944

AFHRA Reel A6377: Frame 1542. HQ MASAF INTOPS Summary 208, dated 15 February 1944

AFHRA Reel B0897: Frame 0992, 5th Bombardment Wing War Diary, – Entry for 15 February 1944

AFHRA Reel B0999: Frame 0813, HQ TBF PI Report 180, dated 15 February 1944

AFHRA Iris No 2000902: Daily Operations Report, Reference Number AI-333, dated 16 February 1944

AFHRA Iris No 2000469: HQ ACMF to CG MATAF, ACMF/9018/G(Air), Air Liaison Officers, dated 18 February 1944

AFHRA Iris No 2000902: Daily Operations Report Reference Number AI-351, dated 18 February 1944

AFHRA Reel A6377: Frame 1434. HQ MAAF Bombing Directive, dated 18 February 1944

AFHRA Iris No 2000472: HQ MATAF Memorandum to HQ MAAF, dated 21 February 1944

AFHRA Reel A6030: MAAF C-in-C Diary entry – dated 22 February 1944

AFHRA Reel A0583: Frame 0332. 340th Bombardment Squadron Diary, dated February 1944

AFHRA Reel A6019: Frame 1044, 487th Squadron, War Diary, dated February 1944

AFHRA Reel A6030: MAAF C-in-C Correspondence, Letter Arnold to Eaker undated letter (Feb/Mar 44)

AFHRA Reel A6030: MAAF C-in-C Correspondence, Letter Eaker to Arnold dated 6 March 1944

AFHRA Reel A6030: MAAF History, C-in-C Correspondence, Eaker to Arnold dated 14 March 1944

AFHRA Reel A6030: C-IN-C MAAF Diary Entries and Daily Staff Meeting minutes – dated 13-15 March 1944

AFHRA Reel A6030: History of MAAF, C-in-C Correspondence, Eaker to Twining dated 17 March 1944

AFHRA Reel A6030: MAAF C-in-C Correspondence, Eaker to Arnold 21 March 1944

AFHRA Reel A1372: Memorandum for Colonel Loutzenheiser, Public Relations of the Army Air Forces, dated 31 March 1944

AFHRA Iris No 1040018: HQ 12 ASC, Air Estimate and Plan for Support of 5th Army in the Present Situation, dated March 1944

AFHRA Reel A6445: SUPPLEMENT C TO MEMO 45-2 – Mission Report, dated 1 April 1944

AFHRA Reel A6030: MAAF C-in-C Correspondence, Eaker to Devers dated 6 April 1944

AFHRA Reel A1372: Letter Norstad to Kuter dated 9 April 1944

AFHRA Reel A6030: MAAF C-in-C Correspondence, Eaker to Wilson dated 12 April 1944

AFHRA Reel A1376: Letter Arnold to Clark dated 19 April 1944

AFHRA Reel A6030: MAAF C-in-C Correspondence, Giles to Eaker dated 25 April 1944

AFHRA Reel A1372: Letter Clark to Arnold dated 26 April 1944

AFHRA Reel A6024: General Eaker to General Arnold – The Employment of Bombers and Fighter-Bombers in Co-operation with the Army. Para 11c, Frame 0654, dated April 1944

AFHRA Reel A6024: Cassino Operations letter to AFHQ, HQ AAI 48/1/G(Ops) dated 4 May 1944. Frame 0662

AFHRA Reel A6111: Frames 1114-1115. AFHQ Operation Memorandum No 54 – The Employment of Bombers and Fighter-Bombers in Co-Operation with the Army, dated 6 May 1944

AFHRA Reel A6030: MAAF C-in-C Correspondence, Eaker to Arnold dated 7 May 1944

AFHRA Reel B0949: Recommendation for Citation by the President of the United States for the 42nd Bombardment Wing (M) for Outstanding Performance of Duty In Action Against The Enemy, dated 11 May 1944

AFHRA Reel A6030: MAAF C-in-C Correspondence, Eaker to Arnold dated 22 May 1944

AFHRA Reel A6111: Frames 1215-1216. Scope, Responsibility and Function of the G-2 TARGET Section, HQ Fifth Army, dated 27 May 1944

AFHRA Reel B0949: War Diary of 42nd Bombardment Wing. Entry for 5 June 1944

AFHRA Reel B0949: War Diary of 42nd Bombardment Wing. Entry for 6 June 1944

AFHRA Reel C0043: Frame 0340, Operational Statistics for MAPRW 1 January 1944 thru 31 May 1944, dated 15 June 1944

AFHRA Reel C0043: Frame 0070. HQ 90th PRW A-2 (Historical Section), 90th PRW Monthly Historical Report for May 1944, dated 30 June 1944

AFHRA Reel A6030: History of MAAF, December 1943 – September 1944, Volume 2, AFSC N1187/9 dated 9 February 1945

AFHRA Reel A1372: Frames 377-8, AAF Policy Book, dated February 1945

AFHRA Reel A6112: Frame 0064, The Relative Effectiveness of Various Types of Bombs and Fuses, AAF Evaluation Board in ETO, dated 1 June 1945

AFHRA Reel 23324: Ira C Eaker, Letter to Mr Brian Burke, dated 29 March 1965

AFHRA Reel 23268: Eaker letter to Vincent Flaherty in Eaker Correspondence, Frame 1400, dated 9 January 1975

AFHRA Reel 25169: Formations in the Fifteenth

AFHRA Reel 23324: Ira C Eaker Comment on Monte Cassino and the Bombs by Martin Blumenson

AFHRA Reel 23268: Ira C Eaker, Personal Letters

AFHRA Reel A1372: Memorandum for Colonel Cabell informal Comments on Incendiary Bomb Status

AFHRA Reel A1592: AFDIS-ID/3B Selection of Circular Probable Error (CEP) Applicable to Combat Bombing at 25000ft Altitude by Heavy Bombardment Units of the VIII Bomber Command

AFHRA Reel A6030: History of MAAF, December 1943 – September 1944, Volume 1, Chapter II

AFHRA Reel A6111: Tactical Air Command's Close Support of the Fifth Army, HQ MAAF, Frame 1104-5

AFHRA Reel A6377: Frame 1408, Fifteenth Air Force Operations – 1st November 1943 – 1st
    March 1944
AFHRA Reel A6377: History of Fifteenth Air Force
AFHRA Reel B0948: Frame 1435, A Short History of the 42nd Bomb Wing
AFHRA Reel B0949: History of 42nd Bombardment Wing (Medium), Appendix J – Chart
    Of Bombing Accuracy
AFHRA Reel B0949: History of the 42nd Bombardment Wing (medium)
AFHRA Reel B0996: A History of the 57th Bomb Wing to November 1944
AFHRA Reel C0043: Frame 0063, 90th PRW Wing History Apr-Jun 1944
AFHRA Reel C0043: Frame 0247, Types Of Photographic Interpretation Done By MAPRW
    Interpretation Sections, Headquarters 1944, 90th PRW A-2 Historical Section
AFHRA Iris NO 1103217: United States Air Force Oral History Program. Interview with
    Major General Gordon Saville. San Antonio, Texas, dated 9 February 1970
AFHRA Iris No 1036066: United States Air Force Oral History Program. Interview of Lt Gen
    Ira C Eaker by Hugh N Ahmann, dated 10-11 February 1975
AFHRA Iris No 1077003: USAF Oral History Program interview with Gen Norstad, 1979

Memoirs

Alexander, Harold, *The Memoirs of Field-Marshal Earl Alexander of Tunis 1940-1945*. London:
    Cassell, 1962
Arnold, Henry H, *Global Mission*. Blue Ridge Summit PA: TAB Books, 1989
Bond, Harold, *Return to Cassino*. London: J.M. Dent & Sons, 1964
Churchill, Winston, *The Second World War, Volume 5, Closing The Ring*. London: The Reprint
    Society, 1954
Clark, Mark, *Calculated Risk*. New York: Enigma Books, 2007
Clark, Maurine, *Captain's Bride, General's Lady*. New York: McGraw-Hill Book Company, 1956
Clarke, Rupert, *With Alex At War: From the Irrawaddy to the Po, 1941-1945*. Barnsley UK: Leo
    Cooper, 2000
Clayton, Aileen, *The Enemy is Listening*. New York: Ballantine Books, 1980
Corvo, Max, *OSS Italy 1942-1945*. New York: Enigma Books, 2005
Cunningham, Andrew, *A Sailor's Odyssey*. Hutchinson & Co (Publishers) Ltd, 1952
Doughty, Roswell K, *Invading Hitler's Europe: From Salerno to the Capture of Göring – The Memoir
    of a US Intelligence Officer*. Barnsley UK: Pen & Sword Books, 2020
Evans, Bradford, *The Bombing of Monte Cassino*. Cassino: Pubblicazioni Cassinesi, 1988
Gervasi, Frank, *The Violent Decade: A Foreign Correspondent in Europe and the Middle East 1935-
    1945*. New York: W W Norton, 1989
Harris, Arthur, *Bomber Offensive*. London: Greenhill Books, 1998
Hunt, David, *A Don At War*. London: Frank Cass, 1990
Juin, Alphonse, *La Campagne d'Italie*. Paris: Editions Guy Victor, 1962
Kesselring, Albert, *The Memoirs of Field-Marshal Kesselring*. London: Greenhill Books, 2007
Kippenberger, Howard, *Infantry Brigadier*. London: Oxford University Press, 1949
Leasor, James and Hollis, Leslie, *War At The Top*. London: The Companion Book Club, 1959

LeMay, Curtis with Kantor, MacKinley, *Mission With LeMay*. Garden City NY: Doubleday and Company, 1965

Lee Harvey, J M, *D-Day Dodger*. London: William Kimber, 1979

Macmillan, Harold, *Blast of War*. London: Macmillan, 1967

Millington, Edward Geoffrey Lyall, *The Unseen Eye*. London, Panther Books, 1965

Muirhead, John, *Those Who Fall*. London: Bantam Press, 1986

Murphy, Audie, *To Hell and Back*. New York: Perma Books, 1955

Sevareid, Eric, *Not So Wild A Dream*. New York: Diversion Books, 2017 (1976 Kindle Edition)

Slessor, John, *The Central Blue*. London: Cassel, 1956

Strong, Kenneth, *Intelligence At The Top*. London: Doubleday, 1969

Tedder, Arthur, *With Prejudice*. London: Cassell, 1966

Tittmann, Harold, *Inside The Vatican Of Pius XII*. New York: Doubleday, 2004

Tompkins, Peter, *Spion in Rome*. Utrecht NL: Prisma Boeken, 1966

Truscott, Lucian, *Command Missions*. New Orleans LA: Quid Pro Books, 2012

Von Senger und Etterlin, Frido, *Neither Fear Nor Hope*. Novato CA: Presidio Press, 1989

Von Weizsäcker, Ernst, *The Memoirs of Ernst von Weizsäcker, Head of the German Foreign Office 1938-1943 (Translated by John Andrews)*. London: Victor Gollancz Ltd, 1951

Walters, Vernon, *Silent Missions*. Garden City, NY: Doubleday and Company Inc, 1978

Wedemeyer, Albert, *Wedemeyer Reports!* New York: Henry Holt and Company, 1959+

Wells, Lloyd M, *From Anzio to the Alps: An American Soldier's Story*. Columbia MS: University of Missouri, 2004

Westphal, Siegfried, *The German Army in the West*. London: Cassell, 1951

Wilson, Henry, *Field-Marshal Lord Wilson of Libya: Eight Years Overseas 1939-1947*. London: Hutchinson & Co. Publishers), 1951

Zuckerman, Solly, *From Apes to Warlords*. London: Collins, 1988

Interviews

Speer, Albert. Interview with the US Strategic Bomber Surveyin MAAF Air Surrender Documents, dated 17 May 1945

Fries, Walter. Commitment of the 29th Panzer Grenadier Division during the German Counterattack for the Elimination of the ANZIO–NETTUNO Beachhead in February 1944. HQ European Command – Office of the Chief Historian, dated 1 May 1947

Luttrell, James. 'The Operations of the 168th Infantry (34th Infantry Division) in the Rapido River Crossing, 28 January –10 February 1944', Academic Department, US Army Infantry School, Fort Benning, 1949

Air Historical Branch Translation No VII/97. The Campaign in Italy Chapter VII – General von Vietinghoff, December 1947. Translated by Air Ministry, AHB6, June 1950

Interview with General Jacob L. Devers for Eisenhower Library with Dr Maclyn Burg, 19 August 1974.

Putney, Diane. ULTRA and the Army Air Forces in World War II: An Interview with Associate Justice of the Supreme Court Lewis F Powell Jr. Washington DC: Office of Air Force History, 1987

Diaries and Personal Papers

Arnold, Henry H, *American Airpower Comes of Age: General Henry H 'Hap' Arnold's World War II Diaries, Volume 1.* USA: Progressive Management Publications, 2002

Arnold, Henry H, *American Airpower Comes of Age: General Henry H 'Hap' Arnold's World War II Diaries, Volume 2.* USA: Progressive Management Publications, 2002

Butcher, Harry. *My Three Years with Eisenhower.* New York: Simon and Schuster, 1946

Chandler, Alfred D, Ambrose, Stephen E; Hobbs, Joseph P, Thompson, Edwin A; and Smith, Elizabeth F. *The Papers of Dwight David Eisenhower – The War Years, Volume II.* Baltimore, MD: The Johns Hopkins Press, 1971

Danchev, Alex and Todman, Daniel. *War Diaries 1939-1945: Field Marshal Lord Alanbrooke.* London: Wiedenfeld and Nicolson, 2001

Ferrell, Robert. *The Eisenhower Diaries.* New York: W.W. Norton, 1981

Freyberg, Bernard. *NZEF General Officer Commanding's Diary – Part IV, September 1943 to October 1944.* New Zealand National Archives, R16700590

Frido von Senger und Etterlin. *MS C095b: War Diary of the Italian Campaign.* Foreign Military Studies, Historical Division, US Army HQ in Europe, 1953

Grossetti, Eusebio and Matronola, Martino (edited by Faustino Avagliano), *Monte Cassino Under Fire: War Diaries From The Abbey.* Cassino: Abbazia Di Montecassino, 2017

Kennedy, Paul A. *Battlefield Surgeon: Life and Death on the Front Lines in World War II.* Lexington KY: The University Press of Kentucky, 2016

Macmillan, Harold. *War Diaries:The Mediterranean 1943-1945.* London: Papermac, 1984

Sulzberger, Cyrus L. *A Long Row of Candles.* Toronto: The Macmillan Company, 1969

Walker, Fred L. *From Texas To Rome.* El Dorado Hills, CA: Savas Publishing, 2014

Biographies

Adams, John A, *General Jacob Devers: World War II's Forgotten Four Star.* Bloomington IN: Indiana University Press, 2015

Ambrose, Stephen, *The Supreme Commander: The War Years of Dwight D Eisenhower.* Jackson MS, University Press of Mississippi, 1999

Barber, Laurie and Tonkin-Covell, John, *Freyberg: Churchill's Salamander.* London: Century Hutchinson, 1990

Battistelli, Pier Paolo, *Albert Kesselring.* Oxford: Osprey Publishing, 2012

Carver, Michael, *Harding of Petherton.* London: Weidenfeld and Nicolson, 1978

Blumenson, Martin, *Mark Clark.* New York NY: Congdon & Weed Inc, 1984

Bryant, Arthur, *The Turn of the Tide 1939-1943.* London: Grafton Books, 1986

Bryant, Arthur, *Triumph in the West 1943-1946.* London: Fontana Books, 1965

Cave-Brown, Anthony, *Wild Bill Donovan: The Last Hero.* New York NY: Times Books, 1982

Daso, Dik Alan, *Hap Arnold and the Evolution of American Air Power.* Washington DC: Smithsonian Institute Press, 2000

Davies, Richard G, *Carl A Spaatz and the Air War in Europe.* Washington DC: Smithsonian Institution Press, 1992

Fraser, David, *Alanbrooke.* London: Harper Collins, 1997

Gilbert, Martin, *Churchill: A Life.* London: Heinemann, 1991

Jordan, Robert S, *Norstad: Cold War NATO Supreme Commander.* New York: St Martin's Press, 2000

Laslie, Brian D, *Architect of Air Power: General Laurence Kuter and the Birth of the US Air Force.* Lexington KY: The University Press of Kentucky, 2017

Libbey, James K, *Alexander P. de Seversky and the Quest for Air Power.* Washington DC: Potomac Books, 2013

L. James Binder, *Lemnitzer: A Soldier for His Time.* Washington DC: Brassey's Inc, 1997

Macksey, Kenneth, *Kesselring: The Making of the Luftwaffe.* London: Batsford Books, 1978

Mead, Richard, *The Last Great Cavalryman: The Life of General Sir Richard McCreery.* Barnsley: Pen & Sword, 2012

Mets, David R, *Master of Airpower: General Carl A Spaatz.* Novato CA: Presidio Press, 1997

Mikolashek, Jon B, *General Mark Clark Commander of America's Fifth Army in World War II and Liberator of Rome.* Havertown PA: Casemate Publishers, 2013

Nicolson Nigel, *Alex: The Life of Field Marshal Earl Alexander of Tunis.* London: Widenfield and Nicolson, 1973

Orange, Vincent, *Coningham,* London: Methuen, 1990

Orange, Vincent, *Slessor: Bomber Champion.* London: Grub Street, 2006

Parton, James, *Air Force Spoken Here: General Ira Eaker and the Command of the Air.* Maxwell AFB AL: Air University Press, 2000

Payson O'Brien, Philips, *The Second Most Powerful Man In The World: The Life of Admiral William D Leahy, Roosevelt's Chief of Staff.* New York: Dutton, 2019

Singleton-Gates, Peter, *General Lord Freyberg VC.* London: Michael Joseph, 1963

Trulli, Guiseppe, *Von Senger: un uomo, un generale.* Italia Storica E-Book

Wheeler, James Scott, *Jacob L Devers: A General's Life.* Lexington KY: The University Press of Kentucky, 2015

Secondary Sources

Adleman, Robert H and Walton, George, *Rome Fell Today.* London: Leslie Frewin Publishers, 1969

Aldrich, Richard J, *The Hidden Hand: Britain, America and Cold War Secret Intelligence.* Woodstock New York: Overlook Press, 2002

Atkinson, Rick, *The Day of Battle: The War in Sicily and Italy, 1943-1944.* New York NY: Henry Holt and Company, 2007

Armstrong, Anne, *Unconditional Surrender: The Impact of the Casablanca Policy upon World War II.* Westport CT: Greenwood Press, 1961

Baedeker, Karl, *Baedeker's Southern Italy and Sicily.* Leipzig, Baedeker's, 1880

Belote, Howard D, *Once in a Blue Moon: Airmen in Theater Command.* Maxwell AFB AL: Air University College of Aerospace Doctrine Research and Education, Air University Press, 2000

Bennett, Ralph, *ULTRA and Mediterranean Strategy – 1941-1945.* London: Hamish Hamilton, 1989

Best, Geoffrey, *War & Law Since 1945.* Oxford: Oxford University Press, 1997

Blackwell, Ian, *Cassino.* Barnsley: Pen and Sword Military, 2005

Blackwell, Ian, *Fifth Army in Italy 1943-1945: A Coalition At War*. Barnsley: Pen and Sword Military, 2012

Blaxland, Gregory, *Alexander's Generals: The Italian Campaign 1944-45*. London: William Kimber, 1979

Bloch, Herbert, *The Bombardment of Monte Cassino*. Cassino: Montecassino, 1979

Blumenson, Martin, *Bloody River: The Real Tragedy of the Rapido*. College Station TX: Texas A&M University Press, 1998

Blumenson, Martin, *Salerno to Cassino*. Washington DC: Center of Military History, United States Army, 1993

Blumenson, Martin and Stokesbury, James, *Masters of The Art of Command*. Boston MA: Houghton Mifflin Company, 1975

Böhmler, Rudolf, *Monte Cassino: A German View*. Barnsley: Pen & Sword Books, 2015

Boothby, William, *The Law of Targeting*. Oxford: Oxford University Press, 2012

Bourke-White, Margaret, *Purple Heart Valley: A Combat Chronicle of the War in Italy*. Pickle Publishing, 2015

Brett-Smith, Richard, *Hitler's Generals*. London: Osprey Publishing, 1976

Brooks-Tomblin, Barbara. *GI Nightingales: The Army Nurse Corps of World War II*. Lexington KY: Kentucky University Press, 1996

Buckley, Christopher, *The Road To Rome*. London: Hodder and Stoughton, 1945

Caddick-Adams, Peter, *Monte Cassino: Ten Armies in Hell*. London: Preface Publishing, 2011

Canciani, Mario. *Il Fronte di Cassino*. Formia: Stabalimento Graficart, 2003

Carter, Kit and Mueller, Robert, *US Army Air Forces in World War II – Combat Chronology 1941-1945*. Washington DC: Center for Air Force History, 1991

Carver, Michael. *The Imperial War Museum Book of the War in Italy 1943-1945*. London: Pan Books, 2002

Casey, Steven, *The War Beat, Europe: The American Media at War Against Nazi Germany*. Oxford: Oxford Scholarship Online, 2017

Chadwick, Owen, *Britain and the Vatican During the Second World War*. Cambridge: Cambridge University Press, 1986

Citino, Robert M, *The Wehrmacht's Last Stand: The German Campaigns of 1944-1945*. Lawrence KS: University Press of Kansas, 2017

Clark, Lloyd, *Anzio: The Friction of War*. London: Headline Publishing Group, 2006

Clayton, Anthony, *Three Marshals of France*. London: Brassey's, 1992

Cornell, Charles, *Monte Cassino: The Historic Battle*. London: Elek Books Ltd, 1963

Cornwell, John, *Hitler's Pope: The Secret History of Pius XII*. London: Penguin Books, 2000

Crane, Conrad, *Bombs, Cities and Civilians*. Wichita KS: University Press of Kansas, 1993

Craven, Wesley Frank and Cate, James Lea, *The Army Air Forces In World War II, Volume Three: Europe: ARGUMENT To VE Day – January 1944 To May 1945*. Washington DC: Office of Air Force History, 1983

D'Este, Carlo, *Fatal Decision*. London: Fontana Books, 1991

Dagnini Brey, Ilaria, *The Venus Fixers*. New York NY: Picador Books, 2009

Dengler, David, *Seeing The Enemy: Army Air Force Aerial Reconnaissance Support to US Army Operations in the Mediterranean in World War II*. Fort Leavenworth KT: US Army Command and General Staff College, 1998

De Seversky, Alexander, *Victory Through Air Power*. New York: Simon and Schuster, 1942

Dinstein, Yoram, *The Conduct of Hostilities under the Law of International Armed Conflict.* Cambridge: Cambridge University Press, 2004

Edsel, Robert M, *Saving Italy – The Race To Rescue A Nation's Treasures From The Nazis.* New York: W.W. Norton & Co, 2013

Ehlers, Robert S, *The Mediterranean Air War: Airpower and Allied Victory in World War II.* Wichita, KS: University Press of Kansas, 2015

Ehrman, John, *Grand Strategy Volume V, August 1943 – September 1944.* London: His Majesty's Stationery Office, 1956

Ellis, John, *Cassino: The Hollow Victory.* London: Andre Deutsch, 1984

Ellis, John, *The Sharp End: The Fighting Man in World War II.* London: Pimlico Books

Forty, George, *Battle for Monte Cassino.* Hersham: Ian Allan Publishing, 2004

Fuller, J F C, *The Second World War 1939-1945.* London: Eyre & Spottiswoode, 1962

Fraser, David, *And We Shall Shock Them: The British Army in the Second World War.* London: Hodder & Stoughton, 1993

Gaston, James, *Planning the American Air War: Four Men and Nine Days in 1941.* Washington DC: National Defense University Press, 1982

Gentile, Benedetta & Bianchini, Francesco, *I Misteri dell'Abbazia.* Firenze: Casa Editrice Le Lettere, 2014

Gooderson, Ian, *Cassino 1944.* London: Brasseys, 2003

Gooderson, Ian, *A Hard Way to Fight a War: The Allied Campaign in Italy in the Second World War.* London: Conway Books, 2008

Gooderson, Ian, *Power at the Battlefront – Allied Close Air Support in Europe – 1943-45.* London: Frank Cass, 1998

Graham, Dominick and Bidwell, Shelford, *Tug of War: The Battle for Italy 1943-45.* Barnsley: Pen & Sword Military Classics, 2004

Gray, Peter, *The Leadership, Direction and Legitimacy of the RAF Bomber Offensive from Inception to 1945.* London: Continuum International Publishing, 2012

Green J H, *Cassino 1944.* Cassino, Lamberti Editore, 1989

Greer, Thomas. *The Development of Air Doctrine in the Army Air Arm 1917-1941.* Washington DC: Office of Air Force History, 1985

Grif, Henry, *The Mules of Monte Cassino.* Brown Fedora Books, 2010

Hall, David. *Learning How to Fight Together: The British Experience with Joint Air-Land Warfare.* Maxwell AFB AL: Air University, Air Force Research Institute, 2009

Hallion, Richard P, *Strike From The Sky: The History of Battlefield Air Attack, 1911-1945.* Shrewsbury: Airlife Publishing Ltd, 1989

Halsey Ross, Stewart, *Strategic Bombing by the United States in World War II – The Myths and the Facts.* Jefferson NC: Mc Farland & Company, 2003

Hansell, Haywood S, *The Air Plan That Defeated Hitler.* New York NY: Arno Press, 1980

Hapgood, David and Richardson, David, *Monte Cassino – The Story of the Most Controversial Battle of World War II.* Cambridge MA: Da Capo Press, 2002

Hastings, Max, *Bomber Command.* London: Michael Joseph, 1979

Haun, Phil, *Lectures of the Air Corps Tactical School and American Strategic Bombing in World War II.* Lexington KY: The University Press of Kentucky, 2019

Hess, William, *B-17 Flying Fortress Units of the MTO.* London, Osprey Publishing, 2003

Higgins, Trumbell, *Soft Underbelly: The Anglo-American Controversy over the Italian Campaign 1938-1945*. New York: Macmillan, 1968

Hinsley, F H, Thomas, E.E. Ranson, C F G and Knight R C, *British Intelligence in the Second World War, Volume 3, Part 1*. London: HMSO, 1984

Hobbs, Joseph P, *Dear General: Eisenhower's Wartime Letters to Marshall*. Baltimore MD: Johns Hopkins University Press, 1999

Howard, Michael, *The Mediterranean Strategy in the Second World War*. London: Weidenfeld and Nicolson, 1968

Howe, George F, *United States Cryptologic History: Sources in Cryptologic History Series IV Volume 1: American Signal Intelligence in Northwest Africa and Western Europe*. Fort Meade; Maryland: National Security Agency, 1980 (published in 2010)

Hoyt, Edwin P, *Backwater War: The Allied Campaign in Italy, 1943-1945*. Westport CT: Praeger Publishing, 2002

Ichac, Pierre, *Nous Marchions Vers La France*. Paris: Amiot Dumont, 1954

Jablonski, Edward, *Flying Fortress*. Garden City NY: Doubleday Publishing, 1965

Jackson, W G F, *The Battle for Italy*. London: B.T Batsford Ltd, 1967

Jeffrey, Keith, *MI-6: The History of The Secret Intelligence Service 1909-1949*. London: Bloomsbury Publishing, 2010

Johnson, David E, *Fast Tanks and Heavy Bombers: Innovation in the US Army 1917-1945*. Ithaca NY: Cornell University Press, 1998

Judge Advocate General's School, *Law of Land Warfare*. Ann Arbor MI: United States War Department, 1943

Katz, Robert, *The Battle for Rome: The Germans, The Allies, The Partisans and The Pope*. New York NY: Simon and Schuster, 2003

Kertzer, David, *The Pope At War*. New York NY: Random House, 2022

King, Glenn L, *From Salerno To Rome: General Mark Clark And The Challenges Of Coalition Warfare*. Pickle Partners Publishing, 2014

Kreger, William G, *A Condensed History of the 135thh Infantry – From Gettysburg To The Po*. Minnesota Military Museum

Kreis, John F, *Piercing The Fog*. Washington DC: Air Force History and Museum Program, 1996

Kurowski, Franz, *Battleground Italy 1943-1945: The German Armed Forces in the Battle for the 'Boot'*. Winnipeg: J.J. Fedorowicz Publishing Inc, 2003

Kurowski, Franz, *Jump Into Hell: German Paratroopers in World War II*. Lanham MD: Stackpole Publishing, 2022.

Lamb, Richard. *War In Italy: 1943-1945 A Brutal Story*. Abingdon: John Murray Publishers, 1993 (2019 Kindle Edition)

Leccisotti, Tommaso, *Monte Cassino*. Cassino: Abbey of Monte Cassino, 1987

Lewin, Ronald, *ULTRA Goes To War: The Secret Story*. London: Book Club Associates, 1978

Liddell-Hart, Basil, *The Revolution in Warfare*. London: Faber & Faber Ltd, 1946.

Liddell Hart, Basil, *History of The Second World War*. London: Papermac, 1997

Liddell-Hart, Basil, *Strategy*. London: Faber & Faber Ltd, 1991

Linklater, Eric, *The Campaign in Italy*. London: HMSO, 1977

MacBean, John and Hogben, Arthur, *Bombs Gone: The Development and Use of British Air-dropped Weapons from 1912 to the Present Day*. Wellingborough: Patrick Stephens Ltd, 1990

Mahoney, Kevin, *Fifteenth Air Force Against the Axis*. Plymouth: Scarecrow Press, 2013

Majdalany, Fred, *The Monastery*. London: John Lane The Bodley Head, 1945

Majdalany, Fred, *Cassino: Portrait of a Battle*. London: Longmans, Green and Co, 1957

Mansolas, Angelos, *Monte Cassino January–May 1944 The Legend of the Green Devils*. Fonthill Media, 2017

Mark, Eduard, *Aerial Interdiction: Air Power and the Land Battle in Three American Wars*. Washington DC: Center for Air Force History, 1994

Matloff, Maurice, *Strategic Planning for Coalition Warfare, 1943-1944*. Washington DC: Center of Military History, United States Army, 1994

Maurer Maurer, *Air Force Combat Units of World War II*. Washington DC: Office of Air Force History, 1983

McCoubrey, Hilaire, *International Humanitarian Law*. Aldershot: Dartmouth Publishing Co, 1990

McCoy-Smith, Perry, *The Air Force Plans for Peace*. Baltimore MD, Johns Hopkins Press, 1970

McCrary, John and Shermann, David, *First of the Many*. London: Robson Books, 1981

McDonald, Charles B, *The Mighty Endeavour: American Armed Forces in the European Theatre in World War II*. Oxford: Oxford University Press, 1969

McFarland, Stephen L, *America's Pursuit of Precision Bombing, 1910 -1945*. Washington DC: Smithsonian Institution Press, 1995

Merchant, Major Jason M, *The 34th Infantry Division at Cassino and Anzio: The Role of Operational Art in the Italian Campaign*. Fort Leavenworth, KS: US Army School of Advanced Military Studies, 2017

Miller, Donald, *Masters of the Air*. New York NY: Simon and Schuster, 2007

Molony C J C, *The Mediterranean and Middle East Volume V, Part II: The Campaign in Sicily 1943 and The Campaign in Italy 3rd September 1943 to 31st March 1944*. Uckfield: The Naval & Military Press Ltd, 2004

Morris, Eric, *Circles of Hell*. London: Hutchinson Publishing, 1993

Morrison, Wilbur, *Fortress Without A Roof,* London, W H Allen, 1982

Moy, Timothy, *War Machines: Transforming Technologies in the US Military, 1920-1940*. College Station TX: Texas A&M University Press, 2001

Murray, Williamson, *Luftwaffe: Strategy for Defeat 1933-45*. London: Grafton Books, 1988

Nalty, Bernard C, Shiner, John F and Watson, George M. *With Courage: The US Army Air Forces in World War II*. Washington DC: Air Force History and Museums Program, 1994

Orange, Vincent, *Churchill and his Airmen*. London, Grub Street, 2013

Orend, Brian, *The Morality of War*. Plymouth: Broadview Press, 2006

Overy, Richard, *The Bombing War*. London: Penguin Books, 2013

Pardini, Albert L, *The Legendary Norden Bombsight*. Atglen PA: Schiffer Military History, 1999

Parker, Matthew, *Monte Cassino*. London: Headline Book Publishing, 2004

Parris, George, *Memoirs of Foggia Book III 1943-1944,* Kindle Edition

Perret, Geoffrey, *Winged Victory The Army Air Forces in World War II*. New York NY: Random House, 1993

Phillips N C, *Official History of New Zealand in the Second World War – Italy Volume 1 – The Sangro to Cassino*. Wellington: War History Branch Department of Internal Affairs, 1957

Piekalkiewicz, Janusz, *Cassino: Anatomy of the battle*. London: Book Club Associates, 1980

Plowman Jeffrey and Rowe Perry, *The Battles of Monte Cassino: Then and Now*. Old Harlow: Battle of Britain Publishing, 2011

Porch, Douglas, *The Path To Victory: The Mediterranean Theater in World War II*. New York NY: Farah, Straus and Giroux, 2003

Pyle, Ernie, *Brave Men*. New York: Henry Holt & Co, 1945

Quarrie, Bruce, *German Airborne Divisions: Mediterranean Theatre 1942-45*. Oxford: Osprey Publishing, 2005

Rennie, Kriston, *The Destruction and Recovery of Monte Cassino, 529-1964*. Amsterdam: Amsterdam University Press, 2021

Reynolds, David, *In Command of History*. London: Penguin Books, 2004

Richard, Charles W, *The Second Was First*. Bend, OR: Maverick Publications, 1999

Richards, Denis and St George Saunders, Hilary, *Royal Air Force 1939-45, Volume II – The Fight Avails*. London: HMSO, 1954

Rogers, A P V, *Law on the Battlefield*. Manchester: Manchester University Press, 2004

Ross, Stewart Halsey, *Strategic Bombing by the United States in World War II*. Jefferson NC: McFarland and Co Inc, 2003

Russell, Edward T and Johnson, Robert M, *Africa To The Alps: The Army Air Forces in the Mediterranean Theater*. Washington DC: Air Force History And Museums Program, 1999

Rust, Kenn C, *Fifteenth Air Force Story*. Temple City CA: Historical Aviation Album, 1976

Sandri, Leonardo, *La 90 Panzergrenadier Division Sul Fronte Italiano: Una Documentazione*. Milan: Edito in Proprio, 2021

Sandri Leonardo, *La 1 Fallschirmjager Division Sul Fronte Italiano 1943-1945: Una Documentazione*. Milan: Edito in Proprio, 2022

Sandri Leonardo, *La 29 Panzer Grenadier Division Sul Fronte Italiano 1943-1945: Una Documentazione*. Milan: Edito in Proprio, 2022

Schaffer, Ronald, *Wings of Judgement: American Bombing in World War II*. Oxford: Oxford University Press, 1985

Schultz, Duane, *Crossing The Rapido*. Yardley, PA: Westholme Publishing, 2011

Second Bombardment Association, *Defenders of Liberty – 2nd Bombardment Group/Wing 1918-1993*. Paducah KY: Turner Publishing Company, 1998

Shepperd, G A, *The Italian Campaign 1943-45*. London: Arthur Baker Ltd, 1968

Shores, Christopher, Massimello, Giovanni, Guest, Russell, Olynyk, Frank, Bock, Winfried, Thomas, Andy. *A History of the Mediterranean Air War 1940-1945. Volume Four – Sicily to Italy and the Fall of Rome, 14 May 1943- 5 June 1944*. London: Grub Street Publishing, 2018

Smith, E D, *The Battles For Cassino*. Newton Abbott, Devon: David and Charles Publishers, 1989

Solis, Gary, *The Law Of Armed Conflict*. Cambridge: Cambridge University Press, 2012

Spaight J M, *Air Power and War Rights*. Milton Keynes: Gale MOML Print Editions, 2010 (reprint of 1924 Edition)

Spaight J M, *Air Power and War Rights Third Edition*. London: Longmans, Green and Co, 1947

Staerck, Chris, *Allied Photo Reconnaissance of World War Two*. San Diego CA: Thunder Bay Press, 1998

St Clair, Matthew. *The Twelfth US Air Force – Tactical and Operational Innovations in the Mediterranean Theater of Operations, 1943-1944*. Maxwell AFB, AL: USAF Air University Press, 2007

Stevens G R, *Fourth Indian Division*. Uckfield: The Naval & Military Press Ltd, 2011 reprint of 1948 edition

Stevens G R, *The Tiger Triumphs*. London: HMSO, 1946

St George Saunders, Hilary, *Royal Air Force 1939-45, Volume III – The Fight Is Won*. London: HMSO, 1954

Strawson, John, *The Italian Campaign*. London: Secker & Warburg, 1987

Tasciotti, Nando, *Montecassino 1944: Errors, Lies and Provocations*. Rome: Castelvecchi RX, 2013

Thomas, Ward, *The Ethics of Destruction*. Ithaca NY: Cornell University Press, 2001

Tillman, Barrett, *Forgotten Fifteenth: The Daring Airmen Who Crippled Hitler's War Machine*. Washington DC: Regnery Publishing, 2014

Trevelyan, Raleigh, *Rome 44: The Battle for the Eternal City*. London: Secker & Warburg, 1981

Trevor-Roper, Hugh, *Hitler's War Directives 1939-1945*. London: Pan Books Ltd, 1966

Tuker, Francis, *The Pattern of War*. London: Cassell, 1948

Vaughan-Thomas, Wynford, *Anzio*. London: Longmans, 1961

Walzer, Michael, *Just and Unjust Wars: A Moral Argument with Historical Illustrations*. New York NY: Basic Books, 1992

Webster, Charles and Frankland, Noble, *The Strategic Air Offensive Against Germany, Volumes I-IV*. London: HMSO, 1961

Weigley, Russell F, *The American Way of War*. Bloomington IN: Indiana University Press, 1973

Williams, Tony, *Cassino: New Zealand Soldiers in the Battle for Italy*. Auckland: Penguin Books, 2002

Wright, Matthew, *Italian Odyssey – The Second New Zealand Division in Italy 1943-45*. Wellington: Intruder Books, 2003

Official Reports and Manuals

Bombardiers Information File. HQ USAAF, Washington DC, (1944)

Fifth Army History Part IV – 16th January 1944 – 31st March 1944, Cassino and Anzio

(G.260700/VFW/2/50) Royal Air Force Narrative – The Italian Campaign 1943-1945: Volume I – Planning and Invasion to the Fall of Rome. Air Historical Branch

German Version of the History of the Italian Campaign, United States Army in Europe Historical Division – 7th September 1949

History of AFHQ Part Three – December 1943 – July 1944 – Section 1 and 2

HQ MAAF. Air Power in the Mediterranean, November 1942-February 1945. Caserta IT, dated 27 February 1945. Air power in the Mediterranean, November 1942-February 1945. – World War II Operational Documents – Ike Skelton Combined Arms Research Library (CARL) Digital Library (oclc.org)

HQ USAAF Report. Defeat. Washington DC: Headquarters Army Air Forces, 1946

Joint Air-Ground Action Part 2, US Ground Liaison Officer School, dated July 1945

HQ Twelfth Air Force, Medium Bomber Operations – 1 January – 28 August 1944, dated 15 February 45

North Atlantic Treaty Organisation, Allied Administrative Publication AAP-06, Glossary of Terms, 2015

Notes from Theatres of War. No.20: Italy 1943/1944. London: The War Office, 1945

Parton, James. The History of the Mediterranean Allied Air Forces – 10 December 1943 to 1 September 1944. Caserta Italy: Headquarters Mediterranean Allied Air Forces, 1945

Pickert, Wolfgang. The Impact Of Allied Air Attacks On German Divisions And Other Army Forces In Zones Of Combat. Karlsruhe Germany: Luftkrieg, 1958 (AFHRA Reel K1026Y)

Roberts Commission. Report of The American Commission for The Protection and Salvage of Artistic and Historic Monuments in War Areas. Uncommon Valor Series Edition. Washington DC, 1946

Second World War 60th Anniversary. The Battles For Monte Cassino Central Italy 12 January – 5 June 1944. London: UK Ministry of Defence, 2005

Spaight, J M. International Law of the Air, 1939-1945 – Confidential Supplement To Air Power And War Rights. London: Air Ministry – Air Historical Branch, 1946

Terminal Ballistic Data Volume 1 – Bombing, Office of the Chief of Ordnance, Washington DC, dated August 1944

The Relative Effectiveness of Various Types of Bombs and Fuses, AAF Evaluation Board in ETO, dated 1 June 1945

UK Ministry of Defence. Manual of the Law of Armed Conflict. Oxford: Oxford University Press, 2005. (also known as Joint Service Publication 383)

US War Department. Field Manual FM 1-5 Army Air Forces Field Manual – Employment of Aviation of the Army. Washington DC, dated 18 January 1943

US War Department. Air Corps Field Manual FM 1-35, Aerial Photography. Washington DC, dated 1940

US War Department. Basic Field Manual FM 30-21, Military Intelligence – Role of Aerial Photography. Washington DC, dated 1940

US War Department. Field Manual FM 31-35. Aviation in Support of Ground Forces. Washington DC dated 9 April 1942

US War Department. Field Manual FM 100-20. Washington DC, dated July 1943

US Army Close Air Support Requirements Board. Close Air Support History. Command and General Staff College, Fort Leavenworth, dated 29 August 1963

VIII Bomber Command Operational Research Report, Analysis of VIII Bomber Command Operations From The Point Of View of Bombing Accuracy – 1 January 1943 to 15 October 1943, dated 1 November 1943

Wilson, Henry. Report by The Supreme Allied Commander Mediterranean to the Combined Chiefs of Staff on The Italian Campaign – 8 January 1944 to 10 May 1944. London: HMSO, 1946

W M Gould, The Italian Campaign Volume 1, Air Historical Branch, 1948

W.T. Beckmann, G. Church, W. Coombs, L.S. Hawthorn, R. Horstmann, Norton, HW 11/5, Air And Military History, Vol.5, Italy 1943-1945. Bletchley Park: Government Code and Cypher School

Newspapers and Periodicals

Magazine Extracts, Volume 7, Issues 16-18, United States Office of War Information, dated 21st April 1941

The Times, US Attack North of Cassino, Issue 49765, dated 1 February 1944

The Times, Monastery Used As Observation Post, Issue 49776, dated 10 February 1944

The Times, Monastery Used As Gun-Post, Issue 49777, dated 11 February 1944

The Times, Shelling Of Monte Cassino Abbey 'The Time Has Come'. London; UK, Issue 49780, dated 15 February 1944

The Times, Abbey Heavily Bombed – Germans Seen Fleeing From The Buildings. London UK, Issue 49781, dated 16 February 1944

The Times, Care for Historic Buildings: Mr Roosevelt Quotes Allied Order. London: UK, Issue 49781, dated 16 February 1944

The Times, War and Art, Issue 49782, 17 February 1944

The Spectator. Sir Harold Nicolson, Marginal Comments, dated 25 February 1944

US Department of State, Press Release No 82, dated 13 March 1944

The Times, Conduct of Campaign Defende, Issue 49807, dated 17 March 1944

The Times, Enemy Hidden In River Bed, Issue 49864, dated 24 May 1944

The Times, Issue 50406, dated 21 March 1946

Supplement to the London Gazette. Alexander, Harold, The Allied Armies in Italy from 3 September 1943 to 12 December 1944. London: HMSO, 1950,1 2879

The Times, 51826, dated 19 October 1950

The Times, Tuker, F.S. Bombing of Cassino. Letter to the Editor. London: UK, Issue 51832, dated 25 October 1950

The Times, Julius Schlegel, Monte Cassino Treasures, Issue 52153, dated 1951

The New Republic, Terraine, John, Book Reviews, dated October 1957

The Times, Issue 55940, dated 20 February 1964

National Security Affairs, Ira C Eaker, Why We Bombed Monte Cassino, dated 28 April 1974

The Times, John Canning, 'Destruction of Monte Cassino' in Letters to the Editor dated 23 August 1982

The Times, Rayleigh Trevelyan, 'Destruction of Monte Cassino' in Letters to the Editor, dated 26 August 1982

The Times, Ernst Kitzinger, 'Destruction of Monte Cassino in Letters to the Editor, dated 27 August 1982

The Times, David Stevens, 'Destruction of Monte Cassino' in Letters to the Editor, dated 27 August 1982

The Times, Herbert Bloch, 'Destruction of Monte Cassino' in Letters to the Editor, dated 7 January 1983

New York Times, Justice Bentley Kassal, 'Fog of War' Letter to the Editor, dated 7 October 2007

Washington Times, Allen, Thomas B. Dying for Art and Country, dated 29 November 2009

Journal Articles

Bellamy, Alex, 'The Ethics of Terror Bombing: Beyond Supreme Emergency', *Journal of Military Ethics*, 7:1 (2008), pp.41-65

Brigety II, Reuben E. 'Moral Ambiguities in the Bombing of Monte Cassino', *Journal of Military Ethics* 4:2, (2005), pp139-141

Brookes, Andrew. 'Air Power in the Italian Campaign', *RUSI Journal* 141:6, (1996), pp.55-62

Brookes, Andrew, 'How Precious is Culture?', *RUSI Journal*, 145:5, (2000), pp.53-58

Colvin, David and Hodges, Richard, 'Tempting Providence The Bombing of Monte Cassino', *History Today*, 44:2, (1994), pp.13-20

Correll, John T. 'Daylight Precision Bombing', *Air Force Magazine*, October, (2008), pp.60-64

Davis, Richard G. 'Take Down That Damned Sign – Doolittle as Combat Commander', *Air Power History*, Winter, (1993), pp.16-20

De Lee, Nigel. 'Moral Ambiguities in the Bombing of Monte Cassino', *Journal of Military Ethics* 4:2, (2005), pp.129-138

Desaussure, Hamilton. 'The Laws of Air Warfare – Are There Any?'*international Lawyer* 5:3, (1971), pp.527-548

Forest, Craig. 'The Doctrine of Military Necessity and the Protection of Cultural Property During Armed Conflicts', *The California Western International Law Journal)* 37:2 (2007), pp.43

Harmon, Christopher C. '"Are We Beasts?": Churchill and The Moral Question of World War 2 'Area Bombing''. *The Newport Papers: Center for Naval Warfare Studies*, Paper No. 1, (1991), pp.1-34

Higgins, Trumbull. 'The Anglo-Americans Historians' War in the Mediterranean, 1942-1945', *Military Affairs*, 34:3 (1970), pp.84-88

Holden-Reid, Brian. 'The Italian Campaign 1943-45: A reappraisal of allied generalship', *Journal of Strategic Studies* 13:1 (1990), pp.128-161

Keiler, Jonathan, 'The End of Proportionality', *Parameters*, Spring 2009, pp.53-64

Kingseed, Cole, Review Essay, The Anzio Campaign, *Parameters*, Winter 2008-9, pp.126-7

Levinson, Sanford. 'Responsibility for Crimes of War', *Philosophy and Public Affairs*, 2:3 (1973), pp.244-273

Luban, David. 'Military Necessity and the Culture of Military Law', *Leiden Journal of International Law*, 26, (2013), pp.315-339

McMahan, Jeff. 'The Sources and Status of Just War Principles', *Journal of Military Ethics* 6:2 (2007), pp.91-106

Nahlik, Stanislav. 'International Law and the Protection of Cultural Property in Armed Conflict', *Hastings Law Journal*, 27:5, (1976), pp.1066-1087

Nurick, Lester. 'The Distinction between Combatant and Noncombatant in the Law of War', *The American Journal of International Law* 39:4 (1945), pp.680-697

Olsthoorn, Peter, 'Intentions and Consequences in Military Ethics', *Journal of Military Ethics*, 10:2, (2011), pp.81-93

Rose, Patrick. 'Allies at War: British and US Army Command Culture in the Italian Campaign, 1943-1944', *Journal of Strategic Studies* 36:1 (2013), pp.42-75

Schwenkenbecher, Anne. 'Collateral Damage and the Principle of Due Care', *Journal of Military Ethics* 13:2, (2014), pp.94-105

Steinhoff, Uwe. 'Moral Ambiguities in the Bombing of Monte Cassino', *Journal of Military Ethics* 4:2, (2005), pp.142-143

Chapters in Edited Volumes

Blumenson, Martin. 'General Lucas at Anzio' in Kent Roberts Greenfield (ed.), *Command Decisions* (Washington DC: Center of Military History, Department of the Army, 2000), pp.323-350.

Böhmler, Rudolf. 'Stalemate at Cassino: The German View' in Barrie Pitt (ed.), *History of the Second World War Volume 4* (Bristol: Purnell Publishing, 1967), pp.1688-1696.

Coady, CAJ. 'Bombing and the Morality of War' in Yuki Tanaka and Marilyn B Young (ed.), *Bombing Civilians: A Twentieth Century History* (New York: The New Press, 2009), pp.191-214.

Cook, Martin L. 'Ethical Issues in Targeting' in Paul A.L. Ducheine, Michael N Schmitt and Frans P B Osinga (eds.), *Targeting: The Challenges of Modern Warfare* (The Hague: Asser Press, 2016), pp.147-158.

Davis-Biddle, Tami. 'Strategic Bombardment: Expectation, Theory and Practice in the Early Twentieth Century' in Matthew Evangelista and Henry Shue (eds.), *The American Way of Bombing* (London, Cornell University Press, 2014), pp.27-46.

Farrar-Hockley, Anthony. 'Stalemate at Cassino: The Allied View' in Barrie Pitt (ed.) *History of the Second World War Volume 4* (Bristol: Purnell Publishing, 1967), pp.1681-1687.

Garroway, C.H.B. 'Command Responsibility: Victors' justice or Just Desserts?' in Richard Burchill, Nigel D White and Justin Morris (eds.)*international Conflict and Security Law: Essays in Memory of Hilaire McCoubrey* (Cambridge: Cambridge University Press, 2005), pp.68-83.

Green, John. 'The Battles For Cassino' in Winston Ramsay (ed.) *After The Battle 13* (London: Battle of Britain Prints International, 1985), pp.1-22.

Gribaudi, Gabriella. 'The True Cause of the 'Moral Collapse': People, Fascists and Authorities under the Bombs. Naples and the Countryside, 1940-1944'in Claudia Baldoli, Andrew Knapp and Richard Overy (eds.), *Bombing, States and Peoples In Western Europe 1940-1945* (London: Continuum International Publishing, 2011), pp.219-238.

Jeffreys, Alan. 'Indian Army Training for the Italian Campaign and Lessons Learnt' in Andrew L Hargreaves, Patrick J Rose and Matthew C Ford (eds.), *Allied Fighting Effectiveness in North Africa and Italy, 1942-1945* (Leiden NL: Brill, 2014), pp.103-119.

Leighton, Richard M. 'OVERLORD Versus the Mediterranean at the Cairo-Teheran Conferences' in Kent Roberts Greenfield (ed.), *Command Decisions* (Washington DC: Center of Military History, Department of the Army, 2000), pp.255-286.

Le Roy, Francois and Perkins, Drew. Visionary Leadership: Henry H. 'Hap' Arnold in Harry S Laver and Jeffrey J Matthews (eds.), *The Art of Command: Military Leadership from George Washington to Colin Powell* (Lexington KY: The University Press of Kentucky, 2017), p157-179.

Mann, Christopher. 'Failures in Command and Control: The Experience of 4th Indian Division at the Second Battle of Cassino, February 1944' in Andrew L Hargreaves, Patrick J Rose and Matthew C Ford (eds.), *Allied Fighting Effectiveness in North Africa and Italy, 1942-1945* (Leiden NL: Brill, 2014), p189-205.

Mavrogordato, Ralph S. 'Hitler's Decision on the Defence of Italy', Kent Roberts Greenfield (ed.), *Command Decisions* (Washington DC: Center of Military History, Department of the Army, 2000), p303-322.

Meyer, Leo J. 'The Decision To Invade North Africa (TORCH)'in Kent Roberts Greenfield (ed.), *Command Decisions* (Washington DC: Center of Military History, Department of the Army, 2000), p173-198.

Mortensen, Daniel. 'The Legend of Laurence Kuter' in Daniel R Mortensen (ed.), *Airpower and Ground Armies – Essays on the Evolution of Anglo-American Air Doctrine 1940-1943* (Maxwell, AL: Air University Press, 1998), pp.93-146.

Nezzo, Marta. 'The Defence of Works of Art from Bombing in Italy during the Second World War' in Claudia Baldoli, Andrew Knapp and Richard Overy (eds.), *Bombing, States and Peoples In Western Europe 1940-1945* (London: Continuum International Publishing, 2011), pp.101-120.

Oderberg, David. 'Doctrine of Double Effect' in Timothy O'Connor and Constantine Sandis (eds.), *A Companion to the Philosophy of Action* (London: Blackwell Publishing, 2010), pp.324-330.

Orange, Vincent. 'Getting Together' in Daniel R Mortensen (ed.), *Airpower and Ground Armies – Essays on the Evolution of Anglo-American Air Doctrine, 1940-43*, (Maxwell AL: Air University Press, 1998), pp.1-44.

Overy, Richard. 'Introduction' in Claudia Baldoli, Andrew Knapp and Richard Overy (eds.), *Bombing, States and Peoples In Western Europe 1940-1945* (London: Continuum International Publishing, 2011), pp.1-20.

'Round 1: AAF Clips Enemy At Cassino' in *Impact: The Army Air Forces' Confidential Picture History of World War II Book* (Harrisburg PA: Historical Times Inc, 1982)

Selden, Mark. 'A Forgotten Holocaust: US Bombing Strategy, The Destruction Of Japanese Cities, and the American Way of War from the Pacific War to Iraq' in Yuki Tanaka and Marilyn B Young (eds.), *Bombing Civilians – A Twentieth Century History* (New York: The New Press, 2009), pp.77-96.

Tanaka, Yuki. 'Introduction' in Yuki Tanaka and Marilyn B Young (eds.), *Bombing Civilians :A Twentieth Century History* (New York: The New Press, 2009), pp.1-7.

Index

PEOPLE

Abrignani, Captain V., 259

Adams J., 323

Adleman R.H., 443

Ainsworth, Colonel, H.M., 166

Airey, Brigadier T.S., 242

Alexander, General Sir H.R.L.G., 34, 38, 40-42, 47, 55, 60, 64, 77-78, 80, 82-83, 87, 90, 103, 110, 117, 119-123, 144-145, 148, 151, 156-161, 164, 166-168, 171-173, 184, 190, 198-199, 221, 236, 239, 242, 262, 265-266, 268-274, 296, 302-303, 309, 318, 321, 323, 329, 331, 334, 339, 342, 346, 393, 397, 429, 437-447, 449-450, 453-454, 457-459, 461

Aligernus, Abbot, 107

Aligheri, D., 111

Aligheri, P., 111

Allen, Colonel F., 310

Allen R., 202

Anderson, Lieutenant General Sir K.A.N., 331-332

Andrews, Lieutenant General F.M., 154, 278, 289-290

Aquinas, Saint T., 111, 220

Arnold, General, H.H. xxi, 149, 195, 212, 260, 276-280, 283, 285, 288-295, 297, 299, 302, 306, 308, 311, 313-316, 318-321, 323, 331, 337, 345, 347-348, 355, 370-372, 383, 385, 421-422, 426-427, 443, 459, 460, 462

Ascalesi, Archbishop A., 179

Ashby, Lieutenant Colonel C.J.F., 253

Atkinson, Brigadier General J.H., 370

Atkinson R., 444

Auchinleck, General Sir C.J.E., 118, 150, 160, 263, 330

Augustine, Saint Archbishop of Canterbury, 116

Baade, Major General E-G., 67-69, 96, 113, 220, 245

Badoglio, Prime Minister, P., 25, 212

Baker, Secretary N.D., 275

Baldwin L.D., 248

Barnes, Bishop E.W., 233

Barratt, Air Marshal Sir A.S., 209, 210

Barth T., 358

Barthelmess, Lieutenant Colonel K.T., 310

Bartoli, Professor A., 177

Barton, Major, 357

Bauer, Hauptmann, 429

Beck, Generaloberst L.A.T., 191

Becker, Hauptmann M., 111, 176, 177

Beddell-Smith, Major General W., 164, 165

Bell, Lieutenant Colonel R., 137, 261

Benedict of Nursia, Saint., 105-106, 111, 113, 115, 185

Benedict XIII, Pope, 109

Benedict XVI, Pope, 115

Bennett, Staff Sergeant E., 377, 379

Bertharius, Abbot, 107

Bessel, Generalmajor H., 112

Best, Professor G., 203, 205, 454

Bevin E., 429-430

Bidwell, Brigadier R.G.S., 171, 442

Biggini, Minister C., 175-176

Bishop, Lieutenant H., 259

Blake A.G., 430

Bloch, Professor, H., xvi, 90, 105, 411, 442, 445, 447, 454

Blumenson, M., 72, 155, 266, 271, 325, 439, 440

Boatner, Colonel M.M., 403
Bohmler, Major R., 100, 142, 325, 440-441
Bond, Second Lieutenant H., 87-88, 436, 437
Bonomi, Prime Minister I., 114
Boothby, Air Commodore W., 218
Borin O., 258
Born, Brigadier General C., 181, 374
Bourke-White, M., 85, 454
Boyle, H., 72
Bradley, Lieutenant General O.N., 87-88, 152, 155, 161, 164-165, 170
Brann, Brigadier General D., 76, 271
Brooke, General, Sir A.F., 26, 29-33, 35, 37-38, 41, 55, 83, 158-161, 163, 173, 257, 272-274, 335, 346, 458
Brookes, A., 216
Bruce Lockhart J.B., 256
Buckley, C., 55, 197, 383
Bulmer-Thomas I., 421
Burke B., 320
Burnham, Lord E.F., 433
Butcher, Commander, H., 25
Butler, Brigadier General F.B., 402

Cabell, Colonel C.P., 290
Caddick-Adams, Professor P., 136, 214, 441, 449
Cadogan, Sir A.M.G., 193, 201, 413, 416
Canaris, Admiral W., 67, 191
Canning J., 445, 447-448
Cannon, Major General J.K., 139, 263, 272, 300-302, 305-306, 309, 321, 339, 340, 342-344, 347, 384, 391, 458
Caperton, Private First Class, 104
Carver, Colonel J.L., 416-417
Casper, Lieutenant J., 389-390
Cassada, Major R., 389
Cate J.L., 438
Cavallaro L., 324
Cavendish-Bentinck V.F.W, 202, 419-421, 424, 427, 429
Chamberlain, Prime Minister A.N., 204, 207, 210, 216
Championnet, General J-E., 109
Charlemagne, Emperor, 106-107
Chennault, Major General C.L., 288
Churchill, Prime Minister, W.S., xviii, xix, xx, 23-24, 27, 29, 31, 37, 41, 47, 58, 64, 77-78, 82-83, 117-118, 124, 146, 148, 155-156,

158-160, 162, 168, 172, 180, 183, 201, 211, 214, 228, 233, 263, 270, 273-274, 276, 280, 285, 287, 290, 296, 299, 329, 429, 440, 458
Cicognani, Archbishop A., 188-189, 197, 200, 413, 425
Clark, Lieutenant General, M.W., xiv, 34, 38, 48, 54, 56-57, 61, 63-66, 69-72, 75-78, 80-83, 86-88, 91, 93, 96, 98, 103-104, 117, 119-120, 122, 125, 128-130, 133-135, 137, 141, 148, 152-153, 155, 159, 161-162, 164-170, 172-173, 236, 241-243, 248, 250, 252, 262, 265-268, 270-272, 286, 300, 302-303, 320, 323, 327, 336, 340, 342-345, 393, 403, 426-427, 433, 436-440, 443-444, 448, 452-454, 456-457
Clark, Maurine., 167
Clarke, Captain R.W.J., 242, 437
Clements, Major J., 90, 92
Coady, C.A.J., 228
Coningham, Air Marshal Sir A., 120, 286, 300-301, 312, 331
Connell, C., 90
Conrath, Generalleutnant, P., 176
Corderman, Colonel W.P., 241
Coughlin, Father C., 181
Craig, General M., 278
Crane C., 438
Craven W.F., 438
Cross, Group Captain K.B.B., 330, 332
Crowell T., 374
Cummings, Lieutenant J., 79
Cunningham, Admiral Sir A.B.C, 145, 158, 171, 418
Cunningham, Lieutenant General Sir A.G., 330

D'Albiac, Air Vice Marshal J.H., 306, 391
D'Arcy-Osborne, Sir F.G., 181, 185-186, 188-190, 197-198, 200-201, 258, 328, 413, 416-418, 420, 423-424, 429, 434, 442
D'Este, C.W., 214, 444
D'Oyly-Hughes, Colonel R., 371
Daly J., 270
Dawley, Major General E., 168
Dean, Lieutenant R., 389
De Angelis F., 373
De Grazia, Lieutenant A., 411
De Jomini, Baron, A., 27, 28
Delbruck, H., 27

De Medici, Giovanni, 109
De Monsabert, General de Division, J de G.,
    57, 93, 96, 120
De Salis, Tenente Colonello Count, 114
De Sanctis, G, xvi
De Seversky A.N.P., 276, 279-280, 285, 288
Desiderius, Abbot, 107
Deusdedit, Abbot, 107
De Valera E., 201
Devers, Lieutenant General J, L., 86, 148-156,
    159, 164-165, 170, 259, 272, 299, 318,
    320-321, 323, 325, 327, 337-341, 363, 385,
    439, 456, 459-461
Dew A.R., 416
Diamare, Abbot Bishop G., 112-113, 176-179,
    185, 195, 197, 200, 387, 395-396, 405-406,
    413-415, 417, 423
Dickens, C., 109
Dill, Field Marshal, Sir J.G., 29, 151, 299
Dimoline, Brigadier H.K., 128-129, 133,
    136-138, 141, 143, 262, 346, 456
Dody, General de Division A-M., 57
Dolk, Lieutenant C., 395
Donovan, Brigadier General W.J., 191, 257-259
Doolittle, Major General J., 180
Douhet, G., 226, 288, 300
Dowing R., 197
Downes D., 258
Dulles A., 259

Eaker, Lieutenant General, I.C., xxi, 137,
    149, 154-156, 200, 202, 211-212, 214,
    221-222, 242, 263, 267-268, 272, 278, 281,
    283, 289-294, 296-299, 301-303, 307, 311,
    313-316, 318-321, 323-328, 338-348, 363,
    367, 370-371, 383, 385, 422, 427, 438-439,
    442-444, 446-447, 449, 453, 458-461
Eden, Sir R.A., 211, 416, 418, 420, 428
Eisenhower, General, D.D., xviii, 25, 34-38,
    42-43, 48, 50, 76-77, 84, 126, 148, 150-156,
    158, 161-166, 170, 188-189, 191-193, 195,
    212-213, 217, 222, 226, 230-231, 235, 243,
    257, 281, 283, 297, 301, 308-309, 313, 331-333,
    336-338, 405, 428, 433, 440, 460-462
Eisenhower J., 163, 166
Elliot, Lieutenant, 394
Ellis J., 444-445, 453
Evans, Major, B., xix, 236, 362-364, 366, 368,
    377-382, 386, 407

Everett, Lieutenant W., 87
Ezard J., 437

Fansaga, C., 109
Fechet, Major General J.E., 278
Ferdinand II, King of Aragon, 109
Ferebee, Major T.W., 356
Flaherty, Vincent, 318, 325
Forbes G., 269
Fosdick R.E., 183
Fournier A., 243
Fraser, Prime Minister P., 118, 151
Frederick of Lorraine, Cardinal Abbot, 107
Frederick II, Holy Roman Emperor, 108
Freyberg, Lieutenant General, Sir B.C.,
    xii, xix, 90, 104, 117-122, 125, 126-138,
    141-143, 150, 160-161, 172-173, 214-216,
    230, 240-241, 260-263, 265, 268, 270-274,
    321, 342, 344, 346, 351-352, 366, 373-374,
    426, 432, 436, 438-439, 443, 446, 448, 454,
    456-458
Frick H.C., 173
Friedrich, J., 226
Fries, Generalleutnant W., 178-179
Fuller, J.F.C., 27, 172

Gable, Captain W.C., 293
Gammell, Lieutenant General, Sir J.A.H., 321
Gander L.M., 235
Garibaldi, 113
Gelatius II, Pope, 108
Gellhorn M., 383
George, Lieutenant Colonel H.L., 212
George VI, King, 127, 148, 185
Gervasi, F, 23, 72, 324, 326, 344
Gibson, Wing Commander G.P., 352
Giglio, M. (Cervo), 81, 258
Giles, Lieutenant General B.M., 289, 291, 323
Giordano, L., 111, 114
Giraud, General d'Armee H., 64
Giscard, Duke of Apulia R., 108, 111
Gladstone, Prime Minister W., 109
Glavin, Colonel E., 259
Glennie, Lieutenant Colonel J., 138
Godfrey, Archbishop W., 188, 193, 202, 413,
    424
Goebbels P.J., 416, 453
Gooderson, I., 84, 333, 449
Goring, Riechsmarschal H., 111, 177, 314

Gorrell, Lieutenant Colonel E.S., 275
Gould, W.H., 74, 221, 328, 418, 433, 435-436
Graham D.S., 171, 442
Grayling, A.C., 226
Graziosi, Father O., 415
Green, Colonel J.H., 214, 447, 448
Gregory the Great, Pope Saint, 105, 111
Grey C., 276
Grigg, Minister Sir P.J., 183, 419
Grossetti, Dom, E, 54, 445, 447
Gruenther, Major General A., 70-71, 76, 125, 137, 142, 242, 263, 265, 266, 268, 271-272, 302, 373-374, 406, 412

Hackney, Major R., 388
Halder, Generaloberst F., 191
Hallion R., 335
Hamilton, General Sir I., 159
Hansborough, Lieutenant Colonel J., 372
Hapgood D., 445
Harbin, Lieutenant J., 377, 381-382
Harding, Lieutenant General, Sir A.F., 47, 121-122, 159, 242, 265-266, 268, 270, 272
Harmon, Major General E., 70
Harris, Air Chief Marshal, Sir A.T., 151, 211, 283, 307, 313
Hartcup G.R.M., 214, 220, 340, 376, 433, 440
Haven, Captain M., 390
Hawkesworth, Major General, J., 69-70
Heid, Lieutenant, 399
Henry, Major S.W., 377
Hersey, Lieutenant, 395
Hinsley, Sir F.H., 243
Hitler, A., xviii, 26-27, 29, 34, 36, 40-41, 43-44, 46-48, 50, 52, 64, 75, 83, 179, 186-188, 202-203, 243, 416, 426, 435
Hollis, Major General L., 173, 197-198, 416
Holzapple, Colonel J., 390
House, Major General E., 300, 302
Howard, Colonel E.B., 241-242, 247-248, 402-403, 406, 454
Howard, Sir M., 159
Hoyt E., 444
Hube, General der Panzertruppen H-V., 175-176
Hudleston, Air Commodore E.C., 303-304
Hull, Secretary C., 179, 182, 425, 428
Hull, Colonel H.B., 242, 292, 318
Hunt, Lieutenant Colonel, D., 33, 239, 257, 396-397, 437

Hunter, First Lieutenant, R., 86
Huntington, Colonel E., 258
Huston, J., 54

Ichac P., 406, 412
Inskip, Sir T.H.W, 207

Jackson, Justice, R., xx
Jackson, General Sir W.G.F., 434, 441
Jacob, Brigadier C.I.E., 418
Jodl, Generaloberst, A.J.F., 48, 50
John III, Abbot, 107
John XXII, Pope, 108
John Paul II, Pope, 115, 446
Jones, Colonel C., 388
Jones, Major F., 134, 215, 222, 373, 398, 430, 433-436, 438-442, 445, 449
Juin, General de Corps d'Armee, A.P., 57, 63-64, 70-71, 93, 95-97, 110, 120, 130, 133, 230, 267, 313, 444, 448-449, 457

Kassal, Justice B., 195
Kelly, Captain C.P., 292
Kesselring, Generalfeldmarschal, A., 36, 44-45, 47-48, 50, 52, 54, 56, 64-67, 69, 72, 78-81, 96, 101, 112, 175-176, 178-179, 202, 231, 243, 258, 261, 348, 414, 418, 440-441, 450
Keyes, Major General, G., 56-57, 70, 72, 83, 97, 120, 136, 166, 173, 266, 326, 448
King, Admiral, E.J., 30, 281
Kippenberger, Brigadier, H.K. xii, 88, 120, 171, 173, 215, 261, 342, 439, 443
Kitzinger, Professor E., 447
Klapper, Lieutenant, 399
Knapp, Brigadier General R.D., 306, 384
Koibe F., 259
Kratzert, Major R., 100, 103, 137, 139, 142
Kuter, Major General L.S., 286, 294, 296, 314-315, 331, 355-357, 367, 370

Lamberti, F., xii, xiii, 447
Lang, Archbishop Lord W., 233
Lardner, J., 372, 383
Latham, Lord C., 231
Latham, Brigadier H., 215, 433
Lauer, Colonel F.J., 310
Lauterpacht, Sir H., 214
La Vizzera G., 179

Lawrence, Colonel C.W., 376
Lazzari M., 177, 178
Leahy, Admiral, W.D., 24, 27-29, 34
Leccisotti, Dom T., 105, 185, 197, 373, 445, 447
Leese, Lieutenant General, Sir O.W.H., 370
Le May, Major General C.E., 149, 289, 298
Lemnitzer, Brigadier General L., 87, 242, 268-269, 316
Leo X, Pope, 109
Letters, Staff Sergeant K., 377, 379
Levinson S., 203
Lewin G.R., 236, 393
Liddell-Hart, B., 27, 80, 159, 172, 224, 452
Lieber, Professor F., 217-218
Lincoln, President A., 217-218
Lindemann, Sir F.A., 203, 211
Linklater E.R.S., 433
Linnarz, Generalleutnant V., 336
Linnell, Air Marshal Sir F.J., 234
Loftus P.C., 424
Lombardi, Monsignor, 200
Louis XII, King of France, 109
Lovett, Brigadier O., 136-138, 141-142
Lovett, Assistant Secretary R.A., 294
Luard, Group Captain J.C.E., 242
Lucas, Major General J.P., 60, 79, 81-83, 160, 168, 241, 457, 458
Ludlow-Hewitt, Air Chief Marshal, Sir E.R., 207

MacArthur, General D., 278
Macmillan M.H., 151, 158, 161, 170, 188-189, 191, 274
Maglione, Cardinal, L., xiv, 187, 189-190, 194, 197, 200, 413, 416-417, 424-425, 428
Mainwaring, Brigadier R.B., 242
Maitland-Wilson, General, Sir H., xxii, 58, 110, 145, 150-152, 158-159, 195, 198, 200, 222, 232, 236, 272-274, 287, 309, 320-321, 323, 337-338, 340-342, 345, 347, 370, 397, 403, 405-406, 408, 410-412, 414, 416, 418, 420-424, 426-429, 434, 438, 440-442, 444, 447, 449-450, 453, 459-461
Majdalany F., 87, 90, 92, 135, 213, 431-434, 436, 439, 441, 449
Malfatti F., 258
Malkin, Sir H.W., 207, 208
Malzer, Generalleutnant K., 258

Mansolas A., 449
Marshall, General, G.C., 24, 27-29, 31-32, 34-37, 76, 126, 153-155, 162-163, 165-166, 168, 171, 180, 189, 193, 257, 277-279, 281, 286, 290, 299, 323, 336
Mathieu, Brigadier General M., 109
Matronola, Dom M., 103, 113, 179, 411, 445, 447
Matloff M., 174
Mauldin, Sergeant W., 170
Mayer, Lieutenant S., 377, 379
McCloy, Assistant Secretary J.J., 192, 331
McCormack, Colonel A.T., 241
McCoubrey, H., 218
McCreery, Lieutenant General, Sir R.L., 64-65, 70-72, 258
McDermott G., 197, 201, 417
McDonald, Brigadier General G.C., 460
McMahan, J., 226
McNair, Lieutenant General, L., 162, 286
Merchant, Major J., 104
Meyer, Chaplain, 178
Miele A., 373
Mikolashek J., 169
Milch, Generaloberst, E, 45
Millington, Group Captain G., 252, 254
Mitchell, Brigadier General W.L., 275, 277-279, 292, 297, 459
Molony C.J.C., 437, 439-440
Momyer, Colonel W.W., 331
Montini, Monsignor G., 126, 185
Montgomery, General, Sir B.L., 40, 91, 118, 120, 152, 156-157, 159, 161, 168, 170-171, 173, 329, 331-332, 334-335
Moorehead, A.M., 54
Morra N., 373
Morrison W., 359
Mountbatten, Vice Admiral Lord L.F.A.V.N, 156
Muirhead J., 359, 370, 382
Murat, J., 113
Murphey, Lieutenant J., 389
Murphy, Ambassador R., 161, 163
Mussolini, B, 26, 37, 180, 186

Nabers, Second Lieutenant B., 377, 379, 382
Naylor, Colonel, W.K., 28
Newall Air Chief Marshal, Sir C.L.N., 206
Newton, Major N., 184

Nicolson, Sir H.G., 233-234
Nicolson N., 157, 243
Norden K.L., 289, 355
Norstad, Brigadier General L., 122, 198,
    294-295, 309, 315-316, 323, 339, 342, 347,
    352, 370, 385, 458-459

O'Flaherty, Monsignor, 186
O'Hare A., 196
O'Hare, Lieutenant Colonel, 372
Olds, Colonel R., 310, 357
Olivier, General J-P., 109
Olmsted, Lieutenant Colonel C., 390
Orange, Professor V., 92
Oster, Oberst H.P., 191

Pacatte, Captain A., 258
Pacelli E., 181, 186
Pancho Villa, 56, 151
Park, Air Chief Marshal, Sir K.R., 321
Parker M., 448, 449
Parkinson, Brigadier G., 90
Parrish, Major A., 389
Parton J., 347
Patrick, Major General M.M., 277-278, 297
Patton, Lieutenant General G.S., 56-57, 152,
    159, 164-166, 170, 331
Paul VI, Pope, 115, 126
Pavolini A., 177
Peter of Yugoslavia, King, 321
Peters, Staff Sergeant J., 377, 379
Petronax of Brescia, Abbot, 106
Pewitt, Major E., 360
Phillips N.C., 439, 448, 459
Piekalkiewicz J., 449
Pierse, Air Chief Marshal, Sir R.E.C., 276
Pignatelli, Princess, 259
Pius XI, Pope, 186
Pius XII, Pope, 179-181, 183, 185, 187,
    200-201, 416, 421, 426, 429
Polifka, Colonel K., 249
Pollack, Oberst F., 178
Pollio, Generale A., 112
Porch D., 151
Portal, Air Chief Marshal, Sir C.F.A., 31, 123,
    145, 169, 199, 211-212, 279, 283, 285, 292,
    298-299, 307, 331, 335, 338, 348, 385
Pound, Admiral of the Fleet, Sir D.P.R., 31
Powell, Major L.F., 241-242

Prather, Lieutenant, 386
Pyle, E., 85, 88, 256

Queree, Brigadier R., 129, 136, 142-143, 261

Rea, Abbot Dom I., 114
Reilly, Major, 138
Rice, Colonel H., 310
Richardson D., 445
Richardson, Staff Sergeant W., 377, 379
Robb, Air Vice Marshal J.M., 234
Roberts, Justice O.J., 182
Robinson, Major C., 390
Roger of Sicily, 111
Rogers, Major General A.P.V., 211, 218, 455
Rome, Staff Sergeant O., 377, 379
Rommel, Generalfeldmarschal, E, 39, 44, 46,
    47, 50, 119
Rooks, Major General L.W., 403
Roosevelt, Colonel E., 248-249
Roosevelt, President, F.D., 24, 27-29, 37, 146,
    158, 179-183, 193, 195, 201, 209, 212, 224,
    270, 278, 280, 285, 287, 295, 323, 424-426
Roper J.A., 424-425
Royce, Major General R., 321
Rudd H., 326-327, 357
Rumbold, Sir H.A.C., 193, 198, 222, 413
Ruskin J., 462
Russell, Major, 434
Ryan, Colonel, P, 183
Ryder, Major General C.W., 58, 93, 104, 120,
    266, 437, 448

Saccomanno, Dom A., 445
Salmond, Major General Sir J.M., 356
Samuel, Lord H.L., 233
Sargent, Sir H.O.G., 181, 188, 201, 416, 420,
    423, 428
Saville, Brigadier General, G.P., 34, 195, 263, 300,
    302, 315, 321, 342-345, 391, 403, 456, 458
Scarlett P., 202, 419-420, 423-424
Schaffer R., 436
Schlegel, Oberstleutnant J., 110-111, 176
Schmidt, Major W., 100
Schultz, Oberst K-L.,139, 384
Schuster, Archbishop of Milan, 114, 425
Scolastica, Saint, 399
Sevareid A.E., 168, 193, 227
Sheehy, Captain J., 101

Shimirz, Colonel, M., 48

Simon, Lord J.A., 231-233

Simpson, Doctor A., 328

Sinclair, Sir A.H.M., 298, 300

Sions H., 170

Slessor, Air Marshal, Sir J., 91, 122-124, 145, 160, 169, 199, 234, 267-268, 299, 305, 307, 321, 323, 330, 335, 342, 347-348, 427

Sloane, Colonel C., 404

Sluman, Lieutenant Colonel C.D., 370

Smith, E.D., 90, 442

Spaatz, General C.A., 137, 149-152, 212-213, 242, 248, 263, 272, 278, 283, 285, 287, 292, 294, 296-297, 299-300, 307, 309, 314, 320, 324, 331, 338-343, 347, 370, 375, 385, 442, 458-459

Spaight J.M., 205-206, 216

Spellman, Archbishop F.J., 179, 182-183

Stafford-Cripps, Sir R., 430

Stalin, President, J., 24, 33, 228

Steinbeck J.E., 293

Stenhouse, Lieutenant Colonel E., 129

Stephen IX, Pope, 107-108

Stettinius, Deputy Secretary E., 189

Stewart, Lieutenant Colonel J.M., 293

St George-Saunders H.A., 268, 321, 328

Stimson, Secretary, H.L., 34, 212, 426

Stone, Professor J., 452

Storey, Lieutenant Colonel R., 242

Stratemeyer, Major General G.E., 285, 290

Strawson, Major General J., 396, 434, 443

Strong, Brigadier K.W.D., 43, 405, 422, 460

Sturzo, Father Don L., 179

Sulzberger, C, 23, 72, 196

Summerall, General C.P., 278

Sussman, Technical Sergeant H., 377, 379

Swearingen, Lieutenant C., 389

Swinton, 1st Viscount, 206, 208

Tardini, Monsignor D., 200-201, 417

Tasciotti N., 445

Tate, Brigadier General R., 78

Taylor, M, 23, 425

Tedder, Air Chief Marshal, Sir A.W., 42, 158, 171, 193, 194, 299-300, 329-334, 348

Templer, Major General G.W.R., 159

Thomas, Senator E.D., 358

Thomas, Professor W., 228

Thompson E.K., 293

Tibbetts, Major P., 297

Timberlake, Colonel E., 365

Tittmann, Charge d'affaires H., 114, 179, 181, 190, 193, 195, 415-417, 428, 429

Tompkins P., 257-259

Travis, Commander E.W.H, 241

Trenchard, Marshal of the Royal Air Force, Lord H.M., 231, 295

Trevelyan W.R., 442, 445, 447

Truman, President H.S., 152

Truscott, Major General L., 71, 77, 155-156, 159, 166, 300-301, 332, 338, 454

Tuker, Major General, F.I.V., 91, 112, 120, 126-131, 133-136, 150, 230, 236, 260, 262-263, 267-268, 335, 352-353, 440-444, 446, 449, 452, 456-457

Twining, Major General N.F., 139, 263, 272, 308-310, 336, 370, 374, 376-377, 458, 460

Urban V, Pope, 109

Veneruso D., 431

Victor II, Pope, 107

Victor III, Pope, 108

Victor Emanuel III, King, 180-181, 212

Victoria, Queen, 157

Von Arnim, Generaloberst H-J.B.T., 127

Von Clausewitz, C.P.G., xvii, 28

Von Kessel, Baron A., 187-188, 191

Von Lieberich, General K.M., 109

Von Mackensen, Generaloberst E., 76, 82-83

Von Pohl, General der Flieger, Ritter M., 80

Von Ribbentrop, J., 416

Von Richthofen, General der Flieger, W., 46

Von Senger und Etterlin, General der Panzertruppen, F.,46-47, 50, 53-54, 58, 63-65, 67-68, 72, 74, 95-96, 99, 100-101, 113, 124, 175-176, 179, 258, 327, 384, 418, 441, 446, 453

Von Stauffenberg, Colonel, C., 53

Von Stotzingen, Baron F., 54, 198, 413

Von Vietinghoff Gennant Scheel, Generaloberst, H., 48, 50, 55-56, 58, 65, 72, 96, 101, 374, 384, 434

Von Weizsacker, Baron Freiherr E., 186, 187-191, 194, 413

Walker, Major General, F., 56, 70, 72, 88, 96, 120, 166, 168, 266, 380, 427

Walter, Colonel M.C., 402, 439
Walters, Captain, V., 161, 167
Walton G., 443
Walzer, M., 223-224, 230, 232
Wandrey, J., 85
Warlimont, General der Artillerie, W, 50
Wavell, Field Marshal, Sir A.P., 118
Weaver, Lieutenant Colonel B., 373, 374
Webster, Brigadier General R.M., 304, 384
Wedemeyer, Brigadier General, A.C., 26, 336
Weigley, R., 27-29
Weir, Brigadier C., 129
Wells, Colonel, 241, 242
Wells, Lieutenant L.M., 91
Welsh, Air Marshal, Sir W.L., 307
Wessel W., 178
Westover, Major General O.M., 278
Westphal, Generalleutnant, S., 47, 54, 66, 80, 236, 440

Wever, Generalleutnant, W., 45
Wilson, Lieutenant Colonel D., 288
Winterbotham, Group Captain F.W., 238, 241, 243
Woolley, Lieutenant Colonel, Sir C.L., 183, 192-193, 198
Woolley, Air Commodore F., 242
Wright M., 261, 448
Wyatt, Colonel A., 88, 171

Young, Colonel C., 374

Zaccaria, Brother, 179
Zachary, Pope, 106
Zotone of Benevento, Prince, 107
Zuckerman, Professor S., 193-194, 283, 305-306

PLACES

Abbey of Montecassino (Monastery/Point 516), xii-xiv, xix-xxii, 50, 54-58, 64, 67-68, 72, 74, 83, 84, 88-93, 97-116, 124, 126-139, 141-144, 146, 150-151, 156, 167, 170-171, 175-179, 181, 183-186, 188-191, 193-197, 199-206, 208, 211-212, 214, 216-217, 219-220, 223, 225-230, 232, 234-235, 243-245, 247-248, 255-256, 259-263, 265-273, 288-289, 294, 296-297, 300-301, 303-305, 308-310, 312-313, 315-316, 318, 320-321, 323-324, 327-328, 335-336, 341, 343-348, 352-353, 356-357, 359, 361-362, 364, 366-369, 371-377, 379-391, 393-404, 406-410, 412-425, 427-437, 441-444, 446-449, 451, 453-456, 458, 460-462
Abruzzi Mountains, 56, 58, 113, 115
Alban Hills, 61, 77-80, 82, 101
Albano, 221, 385
Algiers, 38, 163, 190, 321, 323, 340, 344-345, 347, 352
Alto Adige, 258
Amendola, 310, 377, 380
Antheor Viaduct, 352
Anzio (Operation SHINGLE), xix, 27, 36, 40, 41, 48, 52, 56, 58, 61, 64, 66, 69, 71, 76-84, 96, 104, 124, 135, 138, 144-145, 159-160,

166, 169, 171, 221, 241, 243, 250, 253, 258, 265-266, 270, 272, 274, 305-306, 314, 316, 338-339, 341-342, 347, 352, 384, 389, 391, 442, 444, 452, 457-458
Appenines, 253
Aquino, 220, 398
Ardeatine Cave, 47, 229
Argentina, 201
Athens, 210
Atina, 63-64, 93, 230, 390
Aurunci Mountains, 70
Ausente Valley, 65-66
Australia, 202
Avezzano, 56

Barbara Line, 52
Bari, 256-257, 310, 316, 372, 376
Battipaglia, 305, 336
Belmonte, 93, 96
Benevento, 376, 380
Benghazi, 323, 385
Berlin, 225, 239-240, 259
Bletchley Park, 160, 237-241
Blida Airfield, 352
Bremen, 290
Brenner Pass, 308

Brownwood, Texas, 167

Caesar Line, 101
Cairo, Egypt (SEXTANT), 29, 50, 77, 118,
    298, 308, 316, 321, 323, 327, 336
Cairo, Italy, 96-98, 102, 119-120, 137, 210,
    256, 267, 398, 400, 409
Caledon, 156
Camberley, 130, 157
Campoleone, 82, 385
Cannes, 352
Cape Bon, 132
Capua, 107
Cardito dei Collelungo, 53
Carthage, 77
Casablanca (SYMBOL), 23-24, 26, 191, 214,
    290, 296
Caserta, 130, 242, 258, 300, 302, 316, 319, 321,
    323, 339, 397, 412, 427
Cassino, xii, xix-xx, 40, 42, 48, 50, 52, 54,
    56, 58-59, 61, 63-64, 67, 69-70, 72, 74-75,
    80, 83-84, 86, 88, 90, 93, 95-98, 100-105,
    117-120, 122, 126, 128-129, 131, 143-145,
    156, 159, 167, 172, 193, 202, 219, 222-223,
    225, 235-237, 240, 244-245, 250, 259-260,
    263, 267, 269-270, 303, 313-315, 320,
    324-326, 328, 335, 340, 342-343, 345-346,
    352, 358, 363, 367, 370, 376, 381, 386,
    391, 398, 403, 409, 425, 431-432, 436-438,
    441-442, 444, 447-450, 455-457
Castelforte, 65-66, 69
Castelgandolfo, 36, 179, 198, 221-222, 343,
    416, 424
Castelmassimo, 113, 384
Castle Hill (Rocco Janula/Point 193), 190, 398,
    409
Cecchina, 385
Cerignola, 310-311
Cervaro, 58, 398
Charroux Abbey, 107
Civitavecchia, 66
Cluny Abbey, 107
Colle Belvedere, 64, 93, 95-96, 98
Colle d'Onofrio (Point 445), 98, 101, 138,
    143
Colle Majola, 98, 244
Colle Sant Angelo, 93, 99, 103, 229
Colmar Pocket, 153
Constantinople, 105

Corsica, 37-38, 53, 258
Crete, 118-119, 139, 151, 240, 321

Dartmouth College, 437
Death Valley, 98, 101, 138, 142-143
Decimommanu, 390
Denver, 377
Dieppe, 41
Doctor's House, 100, 138
Dresden, 203, 228

Eboli, xix, 305, 336
Ecuador, 201
El Alamein, 68, 119, 127
Enfidaville, 131
Eulogimenopolis, 105

Florence, 198-199, 234, 370, 423
Foggia, xx, 44, 48, 305-306, 310, 321, 376-377,
    382, 390
Fort Benning, 168
Fort Leavenworth, 278
Fort McKinley, 277
Fratocchie, 79
Frosinone, 61, 76, 77

Gaeta, 76
Garci, 131
Gari River, 48, 66-67, 398
Garigliano River, 48, 56, 64-67, 69-70, 96, 107,
    109, 159, 258
Genoa, 181
Gustav Line, xx, 42, 48, 50, 52-53, 55-56, 58,
    61, 63, 65-66, 69-72, 75-76, 78-80, 82-83,
    93, 95-96, 120, 195, 243, 250, 316, 402, 444,
    446, 455

Hamburg, 290
Hamm, 297
Harrow School, 156, 160
Hickam Field, 310
Hiroshima, 225, 297, 356
Hollywood, 278, 292

Ireland, 201

Kasserine Pass, 40, 165, 312, 331
Klagenfurt, 379
Kursk, xviii

L'Abbaye de Fleury, 106
L'Arena Hill, 63
La Manna Hill, 63
La Marsa, 248
La Propaia, 95
Leptis Magna, 183
Linz, 379
Liri Valley, xiv, 50, 63, 66, 72, 93, 98, 104-105,
    109, 119-120, 122, 263, 325, 342, 357, 377,
    383, 391, 404
Lorient, 363
Lucera, 310-311

Mainz, 56
Malta, 158, 206
Manna Farm, 96
Mareth, 132
Marrakech, 78
Masseria Albaneta (Farm)(Point 468), 93, 103,
    113, 136, 142-143, 229, 244, 398-399, 408,
    445, 448
Maxwell Field, Alabama, 275, 288, 308
Medjez el-Bab, 312
Messina, 25, 39
Mignano Gap, 53, 316, 412
Milan, 181
Minturno, 65, 67
Monte Abate, 64, 95, 96
Monte Bianco, 63
Monte Calvario (Point 593), xiii, 98-100,
    102-103, 133, 136-139, 141-142, 229, 237,
    245, 262-263, 398-400, 448
Monte Camino, 54, 55
Monte Carella, 63
Monte Castellone, 93, 96, 98, 103, 131, 136,
    374, 400
Monte Cifalco, 63, 93, 95, 97, 102, 267
Montecorvino Airfield, 38
Monte Lungo, 54
Monte Pantano, 97
Monte Porchia, 58
Monte Sammucro, 54
Monte Santa Croce, 93
Monte Sorrate, 52
Monte Trocchio, 58, 383, 400, 411, 429
Monte Vesuvio, 305, 380
Morocco, 165, 299

Nagasaki, 356

Naples, xx 38, 52, 67, 111, 132-133, 177, 184,
    192-193, 211, 216, 252, 257, 321, 373, 380,
    383
New York, 179, 182-183, 195, 305
Normandy (Operation OVERLORD),
    xviii-xix, 24, 26, 28-30, 33, 37-38, 40, 42,
    50, 55, 59, 64, 67, 77, 154-155, 159-160,
    164-165, 193, 203, 260, 270, 299, 301, 309,
    324, 341, 346-347, 457-458
Nuremburg, xix, 191, 204, 218, 459

Olivella, 93
Omaha Beach, 39
Orsogna, 127
Ortona, 75
Orvieto, 198, 423

Pantelleria, xix, 304
Parsons, Major L., 389
Pas de Calais, 40
Pearl Harbor, 238, 278, 280, 292, 310, 315
Peru, 201
Pescara, 48, 61
Phantom Ridge, 98, 142
Piedmonte san Germano, 93, 98
Pisa-Rimini Line, 43
Point 213, 97-98
Point 303, 398
Point 444, 142-143
Point 445, 138, 143, 398
Point 447, 398
Point 450, 398
Point 476, 143
Point 569, 99, 142-143, 398-399
Point 575, 142, 448
Point 706, 98
Poland, 209
Pompeii, 389
Ponte du Hoc, 39
Po River, 43, 48
Portella, 102
Portugal, 191
Position 'A', 52
Position 'B', 54
Position 'C', 55
Presenzano, 167, 241
Priverno, 67

Quebec (QUADRANT), 26, 30, 33, 44, 158, 308

Quetta, 157
Quirinal Palace, 181

Rapido River, 40, 48, 54, 56-57, 63, 66, 69-72,
    75, 88, 93, 95, 97, 104, 122, 141, 166-168,
    170, 173, 436
Regio di Calabria, 161
Rio Secco, 93, 95
Roccasecca, 113, 220
ROCHESTER, 237
Rome, xviii-xix, 18-19, 27, 34, 36, 42-44, 46-48,
    50, 52, 54, 58-61, 64, 66-67, 69, 75-82, 101,
    106-108, 122, 145, 159, 168, 176, 178, 180-181,
    186-187, 190, 198, 200-203, 210, 222, 227,
    258-259, 303, 319, 352, 373, 416, 421, 426,
    428-429, 438, 442, 451, 453, 457-458

Salerno (Operation AVALANCHE), xx, 38-39,
    41-44, 47, 53, 56, 61, 65, 81, 85, 148, 154,
    159, 161, 166, 168, 175, 250, 258, 305-306,
    336, 345, 446
Salo, 177, 414
San Ambrogio, 69
San Anselmo, 113
San Biagio, 63
San Germano, 105, 108-109
San Giovanni, 310
Sangro River, 56
San Lorenzo, 180-181
San Pietro Infine, 54, 316
San Severo, 250
Santa Lucia, 398
Sant Angelo in Theodice, 70, 72
Sant Elia, 63, 178
Sardinia, 25, 37, 38, 53, 257, 304-305, 390
Schweinfurt, 289, 366
Sicily (Operation HUSKY), xix, 25-27, 37-38,
    41, 46, 52-53, 56, 68-69, 75, 148, 154, 156,
    158-159, 161, 165, 171, 175, 250, 257, 301,
    304-305, 334
Snakeshead Ridge, 98, 137-138
Spain, 191, 201-202
Spoleto, 176
SS6 Via Casalina, 50, 102, 120, 122, 125,
    128-129, 131, 374, 412, 427
SS7 Via Appia, 79
Stalag Luft III, 379
Stalag Luft IV, 379
Stalingrad, 53, 61

Steyr, 379
St Nazaire, 359
Stoneville, 297
St Peter's Square, 186, 421
Subiaco, 105
Switzerland, 188, 202, 259

Takrouna, 131
Teano, 107
Tebaga Gap, 119-120
Teheran (EUREKA), 29-30, 33
Terracina, 65
Terrelle, 93, 96, 136, 230
The Pimple (Point 156), 97-98
Tokyo, 212
Torcello, 198
Tortorella, 310
Trieste, 61
Trigno, 250
Trigno River, 52
Tunisia, 40, 46, 61, 86, 120, 127, 131, 163, 165,
    242, 286, 300, 304, 310, 312, 316, 330-331,
    333, 352
Turin, 181, 352
Tyrhennian Sea, 52, 58

Uruguay, 201
US Military Academy, West Point, 28, 56, 151,
    162, 276, 308

Vairano, 376, 381
Valmontone, 79, 168, 444
Vatican, xxii, 111, 114-115, 178, 180, 185-188,
    191, 193, 195-198, 200-202, 210, 221-222, 229,
    232-233, 269, 395, 403-404, 412-418, 422-424,
    428-429, 434, 442, 445, 453, 455, 461
Velletri, 69, 78
Venafro, 54
Venice, 198
Via Serpentina, 394, 400
Vicenza, 352
Vienna, 416
Volturno River, 48, 52, 65, 253, 305, 377, 454

Washington DC (TRIDENT), 26-27, 29,
    37-38, 85, 182-183, 188-190, 290, 296, 299,
    323, 331, 345, 412-413, 415, 424, 460
Wellington, 443
Winterstellung (Bernhardt Line), 47-48, 54. 97

GENERAL INDEX

1st Fallschirmjager Division, 40, 80, 99, 244-245, 254, 408, 440, 455

1st Fallschirmjager Regiment, 139, 384, 400

1st Royal Sussex Regiment, 137-138, 141

1/9 Gurkha Rifles, 141-142

2nd Bombardment Group, USAAF, xix, 288, 310, 357, 362, 364, 376, 380, 386

2nd Division d'Infanterie Marocaine, 57, 63, 93

2nd New Zealand Division, 88, 91, 117-119, 215, 253

3rd Division d'Infanterie Algerienne, 57, 63, 93, 95-96, 398

3rd Fallschirmjager Regiment, 139, 395, 399

3rd Panzer-Grenadier Division, 40, 61, 63, 69, 71, 80

3rd Photographic Group, USAAF, 249, 252, 254

3rd Photographic Interpretation Detachment, USAAF, 253

3rd W/T Section, 243

4th Indian Infantry Division, 61, 88, 91, 103, 117, 120, 126-129, 131, 136-137, 141-144, 237, 321, 335, 346, 405-407, 419, 435, 446, 456

4e Regiment Tirailleurs Tunisiens (RTT), 96

4/6 Rajputana Rifles, 141

4/16 Punjab Regiment, 137-138

5th Bombardment Wing, USAAF, 288, 310, 327, 336, 361, 366, 370, 374-375, 379, 407, 459

5th Gebirgs Division, 58, 61, 63, 64, 96

5th Indian Infantry Brigade, 143

5th Panzer Division, 56

5th Photographic Group, USAAF, 250

5th Reconnaissance Squadron, USAAF, 252

6th Army Group, 155

6th New Zealand Infantry Brigade, 90

7th Army Air Support Control, 271, 300, 372

7th Gurkha Rifles, 90

7th Indian Infantry Brigade, 127, 129, 136-137, 143

8th Fighter Wing, USAAF, 305

8th Panzer Grenadier Regiment, 61

11th Indian Infantry Brigade, 127

12th Reconnaissance Squadron, USAAF, 394-395

15th Army Group, xxi, 34, 38, 47, 60, 76,

110, 119, 121, 149, 156, 170, 188, 241, 244, 256-257, 266, 300, 305, 309, 334, 395, 422, 437, 459

15th Panzer-Grenadier Division, 40, 53, 61, 63, 67, 70, 81, 397, 398

17th Bombardment Group, USAAF, 387

17th Panzer Division, 53

18th Army Group, 157

21st Army Group, 161

23rd Reconnaissance Squadron, USAAF, 252

26th Panzer Division, 40, 80, 336

29th Panzer-Grenadier Division, 40, 58, 67, 69, 83, 178, 179

33rd Fighter Group, USAAF, 331

36th Infantry Division Association, 166

42nd Bombardment Wing, USAAF, 288, 303-306, 369, 383-384, 387, 391

44th Hoch und Deutschmeister Infantry Division, 58, 61, 63, 65, 67, 98-99, 179, 195, 244, 254, 398, 407

57th Bombardment Wing, USAAF, 303, 305-306, 387

60 Squadron South African Air Force, 250

71st Infantry Division, 80

71st Werfer Regiment, 398

90th Panzer-Grenadier/Light Division, 40, 67-69, 96, 99-100, 103, 132, 245, 254, 374, 384, 397-399

90th Photographic Reconnaissance Wing, USAAF, 347

94th Infantry Division, 61, 64-65, 67

96th Bombardment Squadron, USAAF, xix, 377

97th Bombardment Group, USAAF, 297, 310, 364, 376, 380, 386

99th Bombardment Group, USAAF, 310, 364, 376, 380, 386

100th Nisei, Battalion, 97, 409

100 lb Incendiary bomb, 386

104th Grenadier Regiment, 70

105th Special W/T Section, 243

111th Tactical Reconnaissance Squadron, USAAF, 250

115th Grenadier Regiment, 68

123rd Radio Intercept Company, 244

128th British Infantry Brigade, 69

128th Signals Company, 243

129th Grenadier Regiment, 70

132nd Grenadier Regiment, 398, 404, 406-407

133rd Regimental Combat Team, 97-98, 398-399, 404, 409

135th Regimental Combat Team, 85-86, 97-99, 104, 143, 244, 398-399, 401

141st Regimental Combat Team, 72, 87, 102-103, 171, 436

142nd Regimental Combat Team, 72, 96, 98, 437

143rd Regimental Combat Team, 72, 167

168th Regimental Combat Team, 85, 97, 98, 100-102, 259, 399, 403

200th Panzer Grenadier Regiment, 67, 96, 100, 103

205 Group Royal Air Force, 307, 352

211th Grenadier Regiment, 61, 398

225 Squadron Royal Air Force, 252

242 Group Royal Air Force, 330

285 Wing Royal Air Force, 250, 252, 254

301st Bombardment Group, USAAF, 310-311, 364, 370, 376, 380, 386

305th Infantry Division, 63

319th Bombardment Group, USAAF, 242, 360, 387, 390

321st Bombardment Group, USAAF, 305, 387-388, 390

340th Bombardment Group, USAAF, 387-388

340th Bombardment Squadron, USAAF, 297, 386

341st Bombardment Squadron, USAAF, 310, 386

352nd Infantry Division, 39

361st Panzer Grenadier Regiment, 67, 96, 98, 100, 113, 398

448th Bombardment Squadron, USAAF, 390

486th Bombardment Squadron, USAAF, 388

487th Bombardment Squadron, USAAF, 389

488th Bombardment Squadron, USAAF 389-390

489th Bombardment Squadron, USAAF 389-390

500 lb General Purpose bomb, 265, 351, 353, 359, 364-367, 381-382, 386-387, 400

617 Squadron Royal Air Force, 352

682 Squadron Royal Air Force, 250

683 Squadron Royal Air Force, 250

709th Infantry Division, 39

716th Infantry Division, 39

849th Signal Intelligence Service, 243, 244

1000 Bomber Raid, 313

1000 lb General Purpose bomb, 132-133, 135, 263, 265, 271, 351, 353, 359, 365-367, 369, 382, 389-390

2000 lb General Purpose bomb, 352

2677th Headquarters Company, 257

12,000 lb Tallboy bomb, 353

Afrika Korps, 68

Air Corps Tactical School (ACTS), 212, 275, 283, 288, 304, 308, 357

Allied Force Headquarters (AFHQ), xxii, 27, 37-38, 110, 114, 148, 150, 190-191, 257, 263, 274, 296, 321, 327, 339, 361, 397, 404-405, 407, 416-417, 421-422, 429-430, 434, 459-460

Allied Force Headquarters Joint Intelligence Committee, 43, 48

Allied Force Headquarters Psychological Warfare Branch, 373, 411

Allied Military Government, 193

American Council of Learned Societies, 183

American Heritage, 202, 268, 325

Ampleforth Journal, 269

Avro Lancaster, 352, 365

B-17 Flying Fortress, 138, 149, 154, 276, 280, 289, 291-292, 296-297, 308, 310, 316, 321, 327, 352, 356, 359, 362, 364-368, 370, 375-377, 380-381, 386, 389

B-24 Liberator, 288, 310-311, 365

B-25 Mitchell, 288, 301, 303, 306, 323, 343, 369, 385, 387, 390

B-26 Marauder, 288, 301, 303, 305, 343, 369, 385, 390, 391

B-29 Superfortress, 308

Balkan Air Force (BAF), 300

Barling Bomber, 460

Benedictina, 445

Berlin International News Agency, 197

Blockbuster/High Capacity/Cookie Bombs, 132-135, 263, 280, 352-353, 365

British 1st Infantry Division, 60, 64

British 5th Infantry Division, 60, 65

British 46th (Midland) Infantry Division, 69

British 56th (London) Infantry Division, 65, 159

British 78th Infantry Division, 431

British Air Council, 207, 208
British Air Historical Branch, 74, 206, 214, 376, 433-435
British Air Ministry, 205, 209-211
British Broadcasting Corporation (BBC), 197, 232, 344, 417, 424
British Chiefs of Staff, 29, 38, 58, 77, 82, 148, 199, 210, 222, 273-274, 285, 318, 397, 418, 422, 428-429
British Civil Defence Committee, 231
British Committee for Imperial Defence, 208-209
British Defence Committee, 210-211
British Dominions Office, 201
British Eighth Army, 38, 48, 55-56, 60-61, 103, 117-118, 120, 156, 161, 189, 303, 319, 329, 331, 370
British First Army, 156, 331
British Foreign Office, xxii, 186, 191, 193, 197-198, 200-202, 207, 222, 274, 403, 413, 416-417, 419, 423-424, 428, 430, 434, 438, 442, 448-449
British Joint Staff Mission Washington DC, 151
British Ministry of Information, 193
British Political Warfare Executive (PWE), 193, 416, 419, 423
British (War) Cabinet Office, 198-199, 202, 215, 273, 398, 403, 416, 418-419, 433-434, 441
British War Office, 183, 197, 403, 405, 418
British X Corps, 43, 54, 56, 60, 64, 65-66, 69-70, 72, 170
Brussels Declaration 1874, 219

Circular Error Probable (CEP), 356-357, 363-365, 369-370
Collateral Damage, 219
Collier's, 72
Columbia Broadcasting System (CBS), 270
Combined Chiefs of Staff (CCS), 27, 32-33, 36-39, 76, 148, 150, 154, 171, 212, 272, 280-281, 298-299, 306-309, 337-338, 340, 397, 426, 427, 459
Commission for Protection and Salvage of Artistic Monuments, 183

Daily Mail, 196, 197
Daily Telegraph, 55, 235, 383

Desert Air Force (DAF), 300, 303, 329, 373
Deuxieme Bureau, 259
Doctrine of Double Effect, 206, 220, 227, 230

Fat Man, 356
Fifteenth Armeeoberkommando (AOK), 56
First Additional Protocol to the 1949 Geneva Convention 1977, 452
Fourteenth Armeeoberkommando (AOK), 76, 82, 101
Fourth Panzerarmee, 53
French Expeditionary Corps (FEC), 56-57, 63-64, 93, 96, 130, 244, 253
Frick Art Reference Library, 183

General Headquarters Air Force, 276, 289
General Purpose (GP) bomb, 349, 352, 365
Geneva Conventions, 217, 407
Government Code & Cypher School (GC&CS), 240-241

Hague Convention 1907, 204-206, 208-209, 216-217, 219
Hague Convention for the Protection of Cultural Property 1954, 452
Hague Draft Rules for Aerial Warfare 1923, 205-206
Handley Page Halifax, 352
Heersgruppencommando Centre, 46, 56
Heersgruppencommando C, 52, 240
Herman Goring Panzer Division, 61, 65, 67, 80, 110-111, 176-177

I Fallschirmjager Corps, 80-82
Il Regime Fascista, 414
Impact, 181, 454
Initial Point (IP), 357, 376-377, 381-382
International Committee of the Red Cross (ICRC), 452
International Court of Justice, 213
International Military Tribunal, 204, 218
Inter-Service Liaison Department, 257

Jane's All The World's Aircraft, 276
Joint Intelligence Sub-Committee (JIC), 27, 43, 202, 416, 419, 434
Joint Planning Staff, 202
Just War Theory, 223-224, 226

Kampfgruppe Baade, 67
Kampfgruppe Behr, 96
Kampfgruppe Corvin, 65
Kampfgruppe Schultz, 139, 407
Kriegsraison, 232-233

L'Osservatore Romano, 200, 233, 415, 431
Lateran Treaty 1929, 110, 186
Law of War/Armed Conflict/IHL, 203,
    209-210, 214-216, 218, 221-222, 423, 441,
    448, 452-453, 458, 461
Life Magazine, 293
LI Gebirgs Corps, 44
Little Boy, 356
Luftflotte 1, 45
Luftflotte 2, 240
Luftwaffe, xviii, 41, 44-45, 48, 61, 110, 112,
    206, 225, 231, 240-241, 280, 287, 306,
    309-310, 334, 341, 371, 393
LXXVI Panzer Corps, 44

MAGIC (Purple) Intelligence, 238
Mediterranean Air Command, 42, 333
Mediterranean Air Photographic
    Reconnaissance Wing (MAPRW), 248, 250,
    253, 388
Mediterranean Allied Air Forces (MAAF),
    122, 124, 149, 189, 198, 216, 221, 241, 242,
    244, 248-249, 252, 272, 281, 292, 296,
    299-300, 305-309, 314, 316, 321, 339, 341,
    347, 375, 418, 457-459
Mediterranean Allied Strategic Air Force
    (MASAF), 137, 139, 300, 303, 307-309, 312,
    336, 339, 345, 347, 371, 385, 443
Mediterranean Allied Tactical Air Force
    (MATAF), 139, 242, 250, 253, 300-301,
    303-306, 339, 342, 345, 347, 385
Mediterranean Army Interpretation Unit
    (MAIU), 252-253
Mediterranean Photographic Intelligence
    Centre (MPIC), 248, 252
Medium Capacity (MC) bomb, 353, 365
Military Objective, 198, 208, 452
Ministerial Limitations of Arms
    Sub-Committee, 207
Miss Laid, 377-382, 386
Monuments, Fine Arts and Archives (MFAA),
    184, 193

National Broadcasting Company (NBC), 270,
    325, 327, 344
National Security Affairs, 318, 340
Newsweek, 372
New York Times, 72, 195-196, 280, 344, 415,
    425
New Zealand Corps, xx, 90, 103-104, 117, 119,
    120-122, 126, 129-130, 133, 136-137, 141,
    244, 253, 260, 271, 273, 314, 321, 406-407,
    432, 434, 446, 449
Ninth Armeeoberkommando (AOK), 56
Norden M-Type Bombsight, 275-276, 283, 293,
    298, 355-358, 362, 364, 368, 381-382
North African Theatre of Operations, United
    States Army (NATOUSA), 86, 148-149,
    337-338, 459, 461
North West Africa Tactical Air Force, 301

Oberkommando des Heeres (OKH), 240
Oberkommando der Wehrmacht (OKW),
    46-47, 52
OB Suedwest, 52, 334
Office of Strategic Services (OSS), 81-83, 179,
    191, 257-259, 393, 418, 447
Operation ANVIL, 33, 59, 316
Operation ARGUMENT, 341
Operation AVENGER, 125, 143, 324
Operation BARBAROSSA, 56
Operation BAYTOWN, 35, 39, 161
Operation BOLERO, 154
Operation DICKENS, 143
Operation DRAGOON, 302
Operation FISCHFANG, 82-83, 258
Operation MARDER, 80
Operation MILLENIUM, 313
Operation PANTHER, 64-65
Operation POINTBLANK, 299, 307-308, 314,
    320, 336-337, 339, 341, 374, 375
Operation RANKIN, 30
Operation ROUNDUP, 24
Operation SLEDGEHAMMER, 24
Operation STRANGLE, 124, 305, 316
Operation TORCH, 24, 34-35, 46, 151,
    156-157, 162, 301, 316
Ostfriesland, 292, 460

P-38/F-5 Lightning, 249, 276
P-40 Kittybomber, 263, 265, 366
P-47 Thunderbolt, 326

P-51/A-36/F-6 Mustang, 250, 265, 271, 276, 283, 289

Photographic Reconnaissance Unit (PRU), 252

Polish Cypher Bureau, 239

Polish II Corps, 429, 449

Principle of Distinction, 452

Principle of Humanity, 452

Principle of Military Necessity, xxi-xxii, 90, 112, 114, 182, 188-189, 191-192, 198, 203-204, 213-214, 217-218, 221, 231, 267-268, 393, 397, 417, 419, 428, 431, 434, 436, 439-441, 443, 445, 447-449, 452-455, 457, 459, 461-462

Principle of Proportionality, 205-206, 227, 452

Question Mark, 292, 297, 460

Radio Vittoria, 81, 258

Redline Message System, 323, 336, 339, 345, 375

Reich Commissariat for Aviation, 44

Reichswehr Truppenamt, 44

Reuters, 415

Rex, 292, 460

Roberts Commission, 183-185

Rockefeller Foundation, 183

Royal Air Force Bomber Command, 207-208, 210-211, 276, 296, 299, 307, 313

Royal Air Force Coastal Command, 299

Royal Air Force Fighter Command, 283, 299

Royal United Services Institute (RUSI), 127, 216, 348

Secret Intelligence Service (SIS), 238, 256-257, 259, 393, 418

Single Shot Probability of Damage (SSPD), 356

Special Communications Unit (SCU), 238, 241

Special Liaison Units (SLU), 238, 241-242

Special Service Force, 227

Special Signals Unit No.1, 238

Stars and Stripes, 170

St Petersburg Treaty 1868, 218

Supreme Emergency, 230

Tactical Bomber Force (TBF), 81, 303-306, 384, 388

Tenth Armeeoberkommando (AOK), 34, 44, 47-48, 58, 75, 78, 80, 101, 112, 240

The Guardian, 395

The Spectator, 233

The Times, 154, 196, 232, 267, 373, 411-412, 439-440, 445, 447

Todt Organisation, 112

ULTRA Intelligence, 43-44, 47, 52, 72, 82-83, 118, 138, 238-243, 257, 324, 393, 457

Unconditional Surrender, 23, 224-225

United Nations Education Scientific and Cultural Organisation (UNESCO), 115

United Press, 424

United States 1st Armoured Division, 56, 70, 91

United States 2nd Armoured Division, 56

United States 3rd Armoured Division, 56

United States 3rd Infantry Division, 64, 69, 77, 155, 332

United States 9th Armoured Division, 56

United States 34th 'Red Bulls' Infantry Division, 56, 58, 64, 87-88, 93, 96-97, 103-104, 141, 143, 195, 215, 237, 266, 269, 314, 399-400, 402, 407, 437, 439, 444, 455

United States 36th 'Texans' Infantry Division, 54, 56, 69-72, 87-88, 97, 102, 103, 167-168, 266, 380, 391

United States 82nd Airborne Division, 60

United States Army Air Corps, 275-276, 278-279, 287, 357

United States Army Air Force, 287-290, 293, 295-297, 299, 303, 305, 310, 318, 331, 334-335, 340-342, 344, 349, 351, 352-353, 355-357, 362-363, 365-366, 377, 394, 403, 434, 438-439, 445, 454, 459-460, 462

United States Army Air Force Post-War Division, 294

United States Army Air Force Special Projects Office, 294

United States Army Forces in the Middle East (USAFIME), 321

United States Army Heritage and Education Centre, 272

United States Eighth Air Force, 154, 211, 281, 289, 292, 296, 298-299, 310, 319, 341, 359, 364, 367, 369, 371

United States Fifteenth Air Force, 81, 242, 250, 288, 300, 307-310, 314, 316, 320, 327, 336, 338-339, 341, 347, 358, 361, 363-364, 366-370, 372, 374, 386, 407, 459

United States Fifth Army, xviii, xx- xxi,
38, 43-44, 50, 52, 54-56, 58, 60-61, 64,
66, 70, 75-78, 82, 85, 93, 110, 119-121,
125-127, 129-130, 137, 141-142, 156, 159,
161, 163-166, 169, 189, 196, 221, 239, 241,
243-244, 250, 252-253, 256-259, 263, 265,
271, 300, 302-303, 305-306, 309, 316, 319,
321, 325, 332-333, 343, 372-373, 383, 402,
406, 442-443, 454

United States Fifth Army Photographic
Intelligence Centre (FAPIC), 250, 252-253,
393, 395

United States II Corps, 56, 70, 72, 93, 103,
104, 119, 122, 125, 128-129, 131, 156, 162,
164, 243-244, 253, 256, 261, 266, 314, 326,
327, 331, 397-398, 401-403, 406-409, 439,
441

United States Joint Chiefs of Staff, 28-29,
32, 34, 37-38, 148-149, 184, 281, 308, 314,
337-338

United States Military Intelligence Service
Special Branch, 241

United States Navy, 355

United States Navy Bureau of Ordnance, 355

United States Ninth Air Force, 305

United States Seventh Army, 57, 156

United States Signals Intelligence Service, 243

United States Signals Security Agency (SSA),
241

United States State Department, 183, 195

United States Strategic Air Forces in Europe
(USSTAF/USSAFE), 148, 151, 194,
287-288, 300, 306, 309, 314, 316, 337-338,
371, 459

United States Third Army, 57

United States Thirteenth Air Force, 308

United States Twelfth Air Force, 180, 288,
300-301, 304-305, 339, 347, 407

United States Twentieth Air Force, 308

United States VI Corps, 41, 43, 56, 60, 78, 80,
82, 168, 237, 332

United States War Department, 193, 277, 278,
289, 428, 459

Vickers Wellington, 352, 385

VIII Bomber Command, USAAF, 292,
367-368

Washington Times, 428

World Heritage Convention 1975, 115

XII Air Support Command USAAF, 34, 104,
195, 250, 252-253, 300-301, 303, 321, 332,
342-343, 372-373, 386, 403, 456, 458

XII Bomber Command, USAAF, 288, 301,
304-305, 310, 388-390

XIII Armeecorps, 56

XIV Panzer Corps, 44, 46, 52-53, 58, 60, 64,
66-67, 78, 81-82, 175, 384, 446

XXXXVI Armeecorps, 56

Yank Magazine, 170